School of American Research
Advanced Seminar Series

DOUGLAS W. SCHWARTZ, GENERAL EDITOR

SCHOOL OF AMERICAN RESEARCH
ADVANCED SEMINAR SERIES

Reconstructing Prehistoric Pueblo Societies
New Perspectives on the Pueblos
Structure and Process in Latin America
The Classic Maya Collapse
Methods and Theories of Anthropological Genetics
Sixteenth-Century Mexico
Ancient Civilization and Trade
Photography in Archaeological Research
Meaning in Anthropology
The Valley of Mexico
Demographic Anthropology
The Origins of Maya Civilization
Explanation of Prehistoric Change
Explorations in Ethnoarchaeology
Entrepreneurs in Cultural Context
The Dying Community
Southwestern Indian Ritual Drama
Lowland Maya Settlement Patterns
Simulations in Archaeology
Chan Chan
Shipwreck Anthropology
Elites

The Classic
Maya Collapse

The Classic
Maya Collapse

EDITED BY
T. PATRICK CULBERT

A SCHOOL OF AMERICAN RESEARCH BOOK

UNIVERSITY OF NEW MEXICO PRESS · Albuquerque

© 1973 by the School of American Research. All rights reserved.
Manufactured in the United States of America.
Library of Congress Catalog Card Number 72-94657.
International Standard Book Number 0-8263-0724-8.
Second paperbound printing with a new preface, 1983

To the memory of our colleagues in Maya Studies

E. WYLLYS ANDREWS IV WILLIAM R. BULLARD, JR.
(1916–1971)   (1926–1972)

Contents

Contents

Preface

The ninth in a series of advanced seminars, sponsored by the School of American Research, was held October 19–23, 1970, in Santa Fe, New Mexico. The topic of the seminar was the collapse of Classic Maya civilization.

Eleven scholars participated: Richard E. W. Adams (Department of Anthropology, University of Minnesota); E. Wyllys Andrews IV (Middle American Research Institute, Tulane University); William R. Bullard, Jr. (Florida State Museum, University of Florida); T. Patrick Culbert (Department of Anthropology, University of Arizona); John A. Graham (Department of Anthropology, University of California, Berkeley); Robert L. Rands (Department of Anthropology, Southern Illinois University); Jeremy A. Sabloff (Department of Anthropology, Harvard University); William T. Sanders (Department of Anthropology, Pennsylvania State University); Demitri B. Shimkin (Center for Advanced Study in the Behavioral Sciences); Malcolm C. Webb (Department of Anthropology and Geography, Louisiana State University in New Orleans); and Gordon R. Willey (Department of Anthropology, Harvard University).

Richard E. W. Adams, Jeremy A. Sabloff, Gordon R. Willey, and I had served as a planning committee and Gordon R. Willey was chairman of the seminar. Thirteen papers had been prepared and circulated before the seminar to communicate information and serve as a basis for the discussions. These papers were revised after the sessions and are presented in this volume. Additional papers were solicited from Frank P. Saul and William L. Rathje after the seminar since it had become apparent that their contributions were of critical importance to points raised during the sessions. Robert L. Rands agreed to summarize the chronological material and Gordon R. Willey and Demitri B. Shimkin accepted the responsibility of preparing a summary paper that would reflect the ideas and viewpoints that emerged during the seminar.

The collapse of Classic Maya civilization has been a problem of major interest to anthropologists for several generations. Yet despite years of debate, no single explanation for the phenomenon has won a consensus. The rationale behind the present reconsideration of the problem rests upon the fact that a series of major research projects have been undertaken in the Maya Lowlands in the last two decades that provide important masses of new data. To marshall this evidence and use it to retest the standard hypotheses about the Maya collapse was obviously the next step toward a solution. The format of a conference that included experts familiar with the data from recent research projects had already been used with great success at the Guatemala City Ceramic Conference (Willey, Culbert, and Adams 1967). We were delighted, then, when Douglas W. Schwartz, Director of the School of American Research, agreed to offer the facilities of his institution and sponsor a seminar on the Maya collapse.

At the seminar we did not, of course, solve the problem of the collapse. In fact, we are left with fairly major disagreements about the relative roles played by various factors. Yet I feel that we now understand far better the stresses that were inherent in Classic Maya society and that in this book we pose questions for research that will move us closer to a final solution.

Furthermore, I feel that a fundamentally new view of Maya society emerges in the following pages. All of the seminar participants had recognized that there were gaps and inconsistencies in the way we had been thinking about the Maya, and all of us had been experimenting with alternative formulations. I do not believe anyone anticipated, however, that a new model of Maya society would crystallize so rapidly or that we would agree so easily to ideas that a few years ago would have seemed untraditional, if not outrageous.

As anyone who has written about Mesoamerican archaeology realizes, the use of accents is the one question about which there may be even less agreement than there is about the Maya collapse. In this book, I have chosen to follow the style established by the Handbook of

xiv

Preface

Middle American Indians, which omits all accents except in direct quotations from Spanish and in the names of individuals.

We are all indebted to Douglas W. Schwartz, Director, to the members of the Board of Directors of the School of American Research, and to the community of Santa Fe. A special tradition going back to the days of Sylvanus Morley links both the School and Santa Fe with Maya studies. We were gratified to be able to continue that tradition, and the pleasure of our surroundings and the hospitality we received contributed to our endeavors. We are grateful to Mrs. Ella Schroeder and Mrs. Douglas Schwartz for their assistance and hospitality. We also appreciate the cooperation of the National Science Foundation in providing financial support for the seminar.

Our enthusiasm is tempered with sadness, however. Since the seminar, we have suffered a tragic loss in the untimely deaths of our colleagues E. Wyllys Andrews IV and William R. Bullard, Jr. They will be sorely missed—both as contributors to Maya archaeology and as friends. It is to them that we dedicate this volume.

T. Patrick Culbert

Preface to the
Third Printing,
1983

The early 1970s marked a turning point in archaeological thinking about the prehistory of the Maya Lowlands. The vast number of new data that had been generated by the large projects of the two preceding decades, the incompatibility of some of these data with the model of Maya society that had previously been accepted, and developments in the anthropological theory of early civilizations all dictated the necessity of reconsidering the nature and fate of Classic Maya civilization. In October 1970, the gathering of a group of scholars at the School of American Research for a seminar dealing with the Classic Maya collapse provided an ideal context for such a reconsideration. This volume, published in 1973 as a result of that seminar, has proven to be an influential one in more recent thinking about the Maya. A decade after its publication, it is appropriate to summarize recent trends and evaluate the ideas presented in this book.

Looking back, it seems to me that the most important of our accomplishments was to postulate a new structure for the Late Classic Maya society that immediately preceded the collapse. We started from a traditional model that made the Maya seem almost unique among early civilizations—a civilization of low population density constrained to only occasional aggregation at ceremonial centers by the limited productive capacity of slash-and-burn agriculture. The elite were confined to a role that was largely ritual and intellectual, for the simple subsistence and economic systems needed little management and the peaceful character of the Maya made military leadership unnecessary. The new data available to us soon made clear that this formulation could no longer be reconciled with archaeological facts. Instead, the Maya had

had much denser populations than previously imagined, had obviously needed more productive subsistence techniques than long-fallow swidden, and had lived in substantial numbers in the vicinities of their centers. These changed conditions presupposed considerably greater need for management, as did warfare, evidence for which had also become more visible. The Maya, in other words, had begun to seem much more akin to other early civilizations.

How have our knowledge and views of the Maya changed in the years since 1970? New field work has continued to add data, although increasing constraints upon funding have dictated a concentration upon smaller and more problem-oriented projects than those of the 1950s and 1960s.

Some of the most substantial increases in information have been in the realm of demography and subsistence. In 1970, site maps and mound counts were available only from Barton Ramie, Tikal, Altar de Sacrificios, and Seibal. Absolute population densities, even at these sites, were still hotly debated (Sanders, this volume: 328–32; Willey and Shimkin, this volume: 476–77). Since that time, the number of surveys has escalated, especially those dealing with more rural areas. Debates about Classic Maya population have not disappeared, but the estimates that prove debatable are now much higher than before.

The fact that the Maya must have used a subsistence system more productive than long-fallow slash-and-burn is no longer at issue and the techniques that could have been used to achieve greater productivity have been spelled out much more clearly than in 1970 (Harrison and Turner 1978; Flannery 1982). That the Maya used very extensive terrace systems in some parts of the lowlands has been archaeologically demonstrated (Turner 1978). Similarly, the existence of drainage systems to permit farming of low-lying areas seems to be generally accepted, and there is at least preliminary evidence (Adams, Brown, and Culbert 1981) that such systems may have been very extensive. Although archaeological data demonstrating shortened fallow or alternative, more productive, crops have not yet been forthcoming, theoretical models estimating the potential productivity and effects of such alterations in the milpa cycle have been discussed at length. In the process, a new debate about Maya subsistence and the collapse seems to be arising. Some researchers (Jones 1979; Freidel and Scarborough 1982) seem now convinced that the more intensive techniques used by the Maya were so productive that food supply should be ruled out as a factor in the collapse. Others (Sanders and Murdy 1982; Culbert n.d.) conclude that the systems now being proposed for Maya subsistence would have been exceedingly fragile, making the risk of subsistence failure even higher. The fact that both sides agree that management techniques and manpower supplies were critical factors, however, provides a common ground that may make the disagreement less crucial than it might seem.

The outstanding advance that contributes to an understanding of Classic Maya social organization has been the rapidly escalating interpretation of Maya inscriptions. That the inscriptions included historical information was already clear by 1970, but the careers of only a few monarchs had been deciphered. Since that time, the Maya have entered history. Relatively full dynastic sequences have now been established for most major sites providing information about the intricate network of upper-level elite interaction. The combination of this historical information (see especially Marcus 1976) and geographical techniques applied to site ranking (Adams and Jones 1981) provides a much clearer picture of regional political organization. Whereas Willey and Shimkin (this volume: 478) could speak only vaguely of regional capitals, we can now specify the size and interactions of the political units involved (Culbert n.d.).

Two new models for the structure of Classic Maya society have recently been proposed. Adams and Smith (1981) believe that the structure was feudal, while Sanders (1981) suggests a patron-client state model comparable to that of some African societies. Although the two models differ in several respects, they share the conviction that Maya political organization was loosely structured and did not correspond to the highly centralized bureaucratic structure seen in some other early states. Initial reaction to these models seems positive and it is likely that they will become influential among Mayanists, but the specific implications that they may hold for the collapse have not yet been explored in detail.

A new view of the transition between the Classic and Postclassic periods in the Maya Lowlands seems to be emerging—one that stresses greater continuity through the transition than is reflected in the articles in this volume. Jeremy A. Sabloff notes (personal communication) of a recent School of American Research seminar on the topic:

> Two major themes emerged at the seminar. The first is that
> there was a significant overlap among the Terminal Classic
> occupations in the southern lowlands, the Puuc region sites,
> and "Toltec" Chichen Itza. The traditional chronological view
> saw a direct succession from the collapse in the south to the
> heyday of the Puuc region sites to the Toltec takeover of
> Chichen Itza. The second concerns the time of the Classic-
> Postclassic transition in the Maya Lowlands. It is the accepted
> wisdom in the field, as expressed in virtually all the texts on
> the ancient Maya, that a major change in the development of
> Maya civilization comes with the Classic Maya collapse in the
> ninth century A.D. We would argue, however, that another
> significant implication of the overlap model is that the major
> change comes with the fall of Chichen Itza in the thirteenth
> century A.D., not with the fall of the classic centers in the
> South or with the rise of the Puuc sites in the north. In other
> words, we believe that there is greater continuity from the Late
> Preclassic phenomena that we now know at Mirador, Cerros,
> and other sites right on through the fall of Chichen Itza than
> there is between the decline of Chichen Itza and the rise of
> Mayapan. (Sabloff and Andrews V n.d.)

Willey and Shimkin's admirable summary article in this volume combines a series of stresses within Late Classic Maya society with a scenario of the collapse. The stresses they envision are divided into two sets, one of which is demographic and ecological in nature while the other focuses upon factors related to the structure of Maya society. Reconsiderations of the Maya collapse during the last ten years have been too numerous to consider here. Some of the more interesting have moved in the direction of quantitative approaches using computer simulation (Hosler, Sabloff, and Runge 1977; Lowe n.d.). The majority of the reconsiderations have focused upon social factors, especially trade and managerial capabilities, as critical factors in the collapse process. Those who favor an ecological base for the Maya collapse have certainly not been silent in recent years, but the necessity of digesting the rapidly accumulating demographic and subsistence data may have muted the tone of the arguments and may be leading to the disagreement suggested earlier.

Preface to the Third Printing

An interesting phenomenon is the paucity of recent explanations that relate the Maya collapse to military pressure from outside the Southern Lowlands. In this volume, a number of the articles make much of such a possibility and the majority of the participants at the seminar seem to favor an "invasion" component of the collapse. But Willey and Shimkin downplayed invasion in their summary article and the issue has received little further discussion. Evidence for hostility from external sources (including the Northern Lowlands) has, however, been accumulating in recent years and a reconsideration of the external relations of the Southern Lowlands is probably in order.

The publication of this volume has not been without impact in other archaeological areas, and civilizational collapse is a topic that has been drawing increased attention. Theoretical reasons for interest in the question have been pointed out by Yoffee (1979) and a recent Advanced Seminar at the School of American Research was devoted entirely to the general issue of the collapse of civilizations.

In the preface to the first printing of this volume, I pointed out that we had not solved the problem of the Maya collapse. Subsequent work has not led to a definitive solution, either, but our knowledge of the Maya has grown, at least partly as a result of some of the issues raised in the following pages.

May 1983   T. Patrick Culbert

ADAMS, RICHARD E. W., W. E. BROWN, JR., AND T. PATRICK CULBERT
1981 "Radar Mapping, Archaeology and Ancient Maya Land Use," *Science* 213:1457–63.
ADAMS, RICHARD E. W., AND RICHARD C. JONES
1981 "Spatial Patterns and Regional Growth Among Classic Maya Cities," *American Antiquity* 46:301–22.
ADAMS, RICHARD E. W., AND WOODRUFF D. SMITH
1981 "Feudal Models for Classic Maya Civilization," in *Lowland Maya Settlement Patterns*, ed. W. Ashmore (Albuquerque: University of New Mexico Press, School of American Research Advanced Seminar Series).
CULBERT, T. PATRICK
n.d. "The Collapse of Classic Maya Civilization," paper prepared for the School of American Research Seminar publication: *The Collapse of Ancient Civilizations*, ed. N. Yoffee and G. Cowgill.
FLANNERY, KENT V. (editor)
1982 *Maya Subsistence: Studies in Memory of Dennis E. Puleston* (New York: Academic Press).

FREIDEL, DAVID A., AND VERNON SCARBOROUGH
1982 "Subsistence, Trade, and Development of the Coastal Maya," in *Maya Subsistence: Studies in Memory of Dennis E. Puleston*, ed. K. V. Flannery (New York: Academic Press).
HARRISON, PETER D., AND B. L. TURNER II (editors)
1978 *Pre-Hispanic Maya Agriculture* (Albuquerque: University of New Mexico Press).
HOSLER, DOROTHY, JEREMY A. SABLOFF, AND DALE RUNGE
1977 "Model Development: A Case Study of the Maya Collapse," in *Social Process in Prehistory*, ed. N. Hammond (London: Academic Press).
JONES, CHRISTOPHER
1979 "Tikal as a Trading Center: Why it Rose and Fell," paper presented at the Forty Third International Congress of Americanists, Vancouver.
LOWE, JOHN W. G.
n.d. *The Dynamics of Apocalypse.* (Albuquerque: University of New Mexico Press).
MARCUS, JOYCE
1976 *Emblem and State in the Classic Maya Lowlands* (Washington, D.C.: Dumbarton Oaks).

SABLOFF, JEREMY A., AND E. W. ANDREWS V. (editors)
n.d. "Late Lowland Maya Civilization: Classic to Postclassic" (Manuscript, School of American Research, Santa Fe).
SANDERS, WILLIAM
1981 "Classic Maya Settlement Patterns and Ethnographic Analogy," in *Lowland Maya Settlement Patterns*, ed. W. Ashmore (Albuquerque: University of New Mexico Press, School of American Research Advanced Seminar Series).
SANDERS, WILLIAM T., AND CARSON N. MURDY
1982 "Cultural Evolution and Ecological Succession in the Valley of Guatemala: 1500 B.C.–A.D. 1524," in *Maya Subsistence: Studies in Memory of Dennis E. Puleston*, ed. K. V. Flannery (New York: Academic Press).
TURNER, B. L. II
1978 "Ancient Agricultural Land Use in the Central Maya Lowlands," in *Pre-Hispanic Maya Agriculture*, ed. P. D. Harrison and B. L. Turner II (Albuquerque: University of New Mexico Press).
YOFFEE, NORMAN
1979 "The Decline and Rise of Mesopotamian Civilization," *American Antiquity* 44:5–35.

PART I

Background

1
Introduction: A Prologue to Classic Maya Culture and the Problem of Its Collapse [1]

T. PATRICK CULBERT

Department of Anthropology
University of Arizona

The collapse of Lowland Maya Classic civilization is a very specific problem, narrowly delimited in time and space. We hope, however, that our consideration of the Maya collapse has a meaning in terms of cultural systematics that will be of interest to a wider audience than simply those concerned with Mesoamerican archaeology. It therefore behooves us to define the time and space parameters of our problem and to set the cultural and environmental background of the Maya Classic climax and decline.

The Maya Lowlands is the area of lowland hills and plains that extends from the Guatemalan-Chiapas Highlands northward to the Gulf of Mexico and the Caribbean Sea (see Figs. 1–4). The area is ecologically homogeneous, at least in comparison with the strikingly varied mountainous zones that border it. There was a fundamental base of prehistoric cultural similarity within the area and ties of trade and the sharing of patterns of elite culture, such as the calendric and hieroglyphic systems, united the area during the Classic Period, demonstrating continuing intercommunication.

Nevertheless, there is considerable variety within the Maya Lowlands. The major division, generally agreed by Mayanists to relate to significant cultural differences, is between the Northern Lowlands and the Southern Lowlands. In spite of the shared patterns and intercommunication mentioned above, the two sections show differences in architecture and ceramics, and there is enough gradation in ecological conditions to presuppose some variation in subsistence adaptation. The ties between the Northern and Southern Lowlands during the Classic Period are no more than a weak reflection of the intensive system of interaction that connected sites within the southern section at that time. The line between the two sectors in Figure 1 was drawn with no pretense of precision, since there is very little archaeological information from the area through which the suggested boundary passes. It is likely that as more information accumulates, the question of a precise "border" between the Northern Lowlands and Southern Lowlands will become trivial and the actual situation will be better reflected by a series of clines or intergrading zones.

There has been an information imbalance in Maya archaeology in favor of the Southern Lowlands. Most major investigations, both in recent years and in the past, have centered in the south with the result that the total archaeological framework for that sector is far more complete than that for the north. Of the participants at the Maya collapse conference, only E. Wyllys Andrews IV had extensive experience in the Northern Lowlands, and his paper represents the only Northern Lowlands–based viewpoint in this volume. The rest of the papers emphasize the Southern Lowlands and the conclusions are primarily applicable to that sector. Extension of the conclusions to the Northern Lowlands is difficult, both because so many fewer projects have been undertaken in the north and because the correlation of events in the two sectors remains a matter of debate.

Within each sector, still further divisions are necessary for dealing with the detailed problems treated in the rest of the book. All of the authors have operated in terms of a series of zones that both serve as a geographical convenience and relate to some degree of ecological and cultural differentiation within the Maya Lowlands. Because intensive work has been done in only a few sites within each zone and because

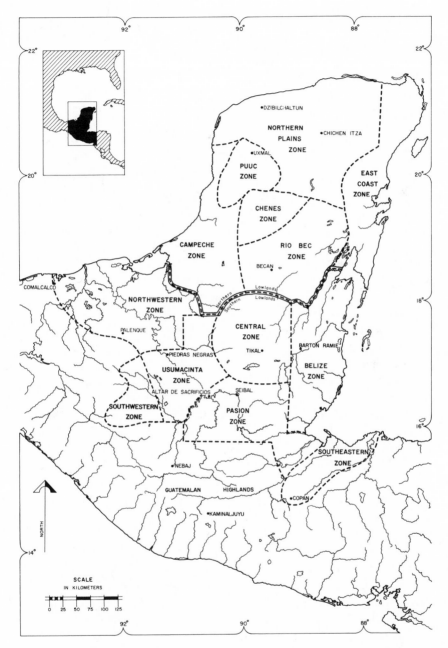

FIGURE 1. THE MAYA LOWLANDS: ARCHAEOLOGICAL ZONES

5

we lack broad regional surveys and ecological studies, the details of zonation remain unclear. The lines separating zones in Figure 1 and the textual comments that follow should, therefore, be considered suggestive rather than definitive.

At the heart of the Southern Lowlands is a Central Zone located in the north-central part of the Department of Peten in Guatemala. The zone can be delimited by a circle approximately 150 km. in diameter that would include Calakmul at its northern edge, Naranjo to the east, the area of Lake Peten Itza to the south, and a little-explored area with few reported sites to the west. The sites of Tikal (Carr and Hazard 1961; W. R. Coe 1962, 1963, 1965a, 1967) and Uaxactun (Kidder 1947; Ricketson and Ricketson 1937; R. E. Smith 1937, 1955; Wauchope 1934), near the center of the area, have been thoroughly investigated and serve as the basis for most of the conclusions about the character of the zone. The whole zone contains a series of large and very important sites and was characterized by a dense population and a leadership role in a number of kinds of cultural innovation. Topographic features include a series of flat-topped limestone ridges on which the sites are located and lower, seasonally swampy depressions (called *bajos*) which show almost no evidence of prehistoric occupation. Drainage is largely subterranean although there are a few lakes, the largest of which are Lake Peten Itza and Lake Yaxha. As Rathje (1971b) has emphasized, the Central Zone is deficient in natural resources and is the area of the Southern Lowlands farthest removed from access to external commodities.

At the eastern edge of the Southern Lowlands is the Belize Zone, roughly equivalent in extent to the modern political unit of Belize (British Honduras). Bullard (personal communication) feels that there was too much cultural diversity within this region to include within a single zone, but we retain a Belize Zone here as a unit of convenience for contrasting the eastern fringes of the Southern Lowlands with other areas. An unusually large number of sites have been investigated in the area. The most complete modern report is that of Willey, Bullard, et al. (1965) on the strip settlement along the Belize River at Barton Ramie. Pendergast's recent work at Altun Ha (1967a, 1969b), although not yet reported in full, adds important information. Earlier reported excavations include those at Benque Viejo (Thompson 1940); Baking Pot (Ricketson 1931); Caracol (Anderson 1958, 1959); San Jose

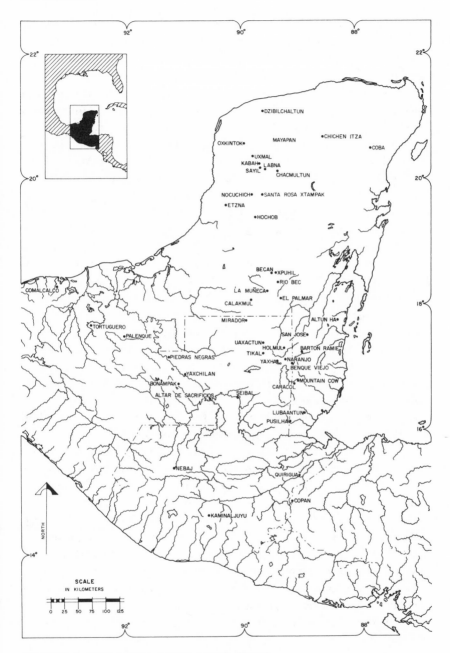

FIGURE 2. THE MAYA LOWLANDS: SITES

7

(Thompson 1939); Holmul (Merwin and Valliant 1932), just across the border in Guatemala but culturally similar to some Belize sites; and the sites of Lubaantun (Gann 1925; Joyce 1926) and Pusilha (Gann 1930; Gruning 1930), which lie south of the Maya Mountains.

The zone subsumes a relatively high degree of ecological diversity. Riverine environments, the coastal strip, and the Maya Mountains (a small range of volcanic origin) offer contrasting opportunities for exploitation. The area probably served as an important resource zone since both sea products and the volcanic stone from the Maya Mountains must have been in high demand in the interior parts of the lowlands.

The Southeastern Zone includes the extension of the Southern Lowlands necessary to take in the sites of Copan and Quirigua. Unfortunately, neither site has been investigated in recent times, although the Carnegie Institution conducted a large project at Copan in the 1930s and did sporadic work at Quirigua. (For Copan, see Gordon 1896; Morley 1911; Longyear 1952. For Quirigua, see Blackiston 1911; Hewett 1912; Morley 1913.) For both sites, the published information deals largely with the ceremonial precincts and provides little information about resident populations. Both Copan and Quirigua are at a slightly higher elevation than the Peten but still within the rain forest vegetational zone, and both occupy riverine environments. The position of the sites in areas of easy access to the full range of resources of the mountainous highlands and on rivers that provide natural thoroughfares makes them potential centers for commerce.

The Pasion Zone, which comprises the southernmost part of the Maya Lowlands, has been among the most thoroughly investigated areas of the Peten in recent years, thanks to the Harvard University projects at Altar de Sacrificios (Adams 1971; Willey and Smith 1969) and Seibal (Adams 1963a; Smith and Willey 1966a, 1966b, 1970; Sabloff 1970; Touretellot 1970; Willey 1970) and to Ian Graham's reconnaissance in more remote areas away from the river (Graham 1967). With the benefit of modern archaeological interests and techniques, the Harvard projects have provided a full range of data that include settlement pattern studies and housemound testing as well as the more traditional investigations of ceremonial precincts and artifact categories. Although much of the data is still unpublished, several participants at the Maya collapse seminar were thoroughly familiar with it. The Pa-

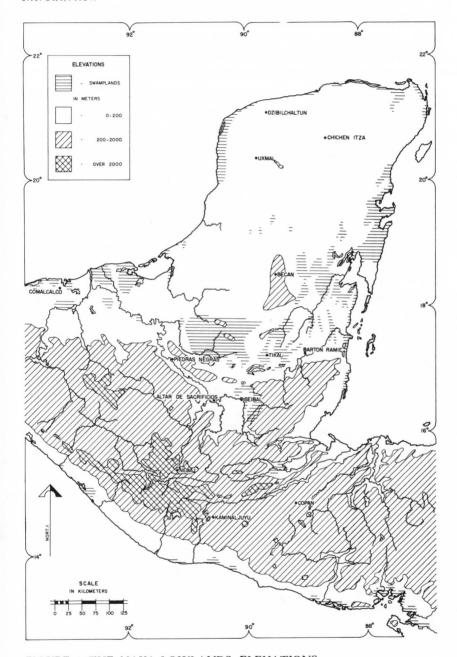

FIGURE 3. THE MAYA LOWLANDS: ELEVATIONS

sion Zone is fully within the lowlands in both climatological and ecological environment, but enjoys the benefits of river resources and the
channels of communication that the river offers to the Guatemalan
Highlands and Usumacinta Zone.

The Southwestern Zone takes in sites on the Chiapas Plateau in a
semiarid area at elevations in excess of 1,000 m. This zone, consequently, is outside of the lowlands environmentally, but it shares cultural features such as carved stone monuments and the corbeled arch
with the Southern Lowlands. Unfortunately, no more than exploratory
accounts of the Southwestern Zone are available, and the corner of the
lowlands that lies closest to it is terra incognita in the archaeological
sense.

The Usumacinta Zone includes a number of large and very important sites on or near the Usumacinta River on the western borders of
the Maya Lowlands. The zone is fully lowland in all senses, but is
within striking distance of the Central Chiapas Highlands. More important, the Usumacinta provides a channel of communication to the
Tabasco–Vera Cruz coastal plain and, hence, to non-Maya cultures
of considerable importance. Unfortunately, there has been surprisingly
little archaeological work in the Usumacinta Zone except for the University of Pennsylvania's project at Piedras Negras in the 1930s (Butler
1935; Satterthwaite 1936, 1943–54).

The Northwestern Zone lies to the northwest of the Maya Lowlands near the juncture of the Central Chiapas Highlands and the Tabasco coastal plain. Rands's (1967a, 1967b) recent investigation provides
excellent information on the region as a whole, and the ceremonial precincts of Palenque are well known and reported by Ruz (1952a, 1952b,
1952c, 1952d, 1952e, 1954, 1955, 1958a, 1958b, 1958c, 1958d). Although characterized by a vigorous development of Classic Maya art,
hieroglyphics, and architecture, the zone stands outside of the Southern Lowlands region of ceramic interconnections. The Northwestern
Zone is within the rain forest, but in an area of heavy rainfall where
double cropping is possible. Its location provides easy access to both
the Northern and Southern Maya Lowlands and to the Mexican
coastal plain as well as making the zone vulnerable to influences, both
peaceful and military, from outside the Maya Lowlands.

Although we know less about the Northern Maya Lowlands, there
are indications of an equally complex zonation in that sector as well.

Introduction

The Puuc Zone, named after a range of low hills that parallels the central western coast of the Yucatan Peninsula, includes a number of large and important sites (Uxmal, Labna, Sayil, Kabah) that share a characteristic architectual style. Andrews's work at the immense site of Dzibilchaltun (1960, 1962, 1965b, 1968) suggests a Northern Plains Zone. There might also be distinguished a Campeche Zone, an East Coast Zone, a Chenes Zone located in north-central Campeche and including the sites of Hochob and Santa Rosa Xtampak, and a Rio Bec Zone in southern Campeche known for such sites as Rio Bec, Xpuhil, and Becan. Ian Graham's recent report (1967) emphasizing the importance of the immense site of Mirador suggests the possibility of creating a North-Central Zone lying athwart the Guatemalan-Mexican border just to the north of the Central Zone of the Southern Lowlands. This area, badly neglected archaeologically but apparently containing dense remains of prehistoric population, may have served as an important bridge between the Northern and Southern Lowlands.

Throughout the Maya Lowlands, the climate is characterized by seasonal rains that begin in May and continue through November. The dry season offers only sporadic and undependable rains that are insufficient either for agriculture or to conserve drinking water supplies without reservoirs or other artificial means. The amount of annual rainfall varies on a north-south axis (see Fig. 4). At the northern tip of the Yucatan Peninsula only 20 to 30 inches of rain can be expected, but the total increases quite rapidly to the south to reach 40 to 60 inches in the Central Zone of the Southern Lowlands and as much as 120 inches annually in areas along the foothills of the Guatemalan Highlands at the southern border of the lowland region. Frost is unknown in the Maya Lowlands. Yearly temperatures average in excess of 25 degrees C. and show little variation between seasons. The seasonality of rainfall is a primary limiting factor for agriculture and most of the lowlands is a single crop zone, although a second, low-yield crop of fast-growing corn can be obtained in emergencies. In a few areas such as the slopes of the Guatemalan Highlands and the Palenque Zone at the foot of the Central Chiapas Highlands, rainfall patterns permit double cropping. Irrigation is unknown in both modern and Colonial times and is presumed to have been similarly absent prehistorically. Ridged-field systems have been reported along the Candelaria and Usumacinta rivers (Puleston and Puleston 1971), but there is as yet no

11

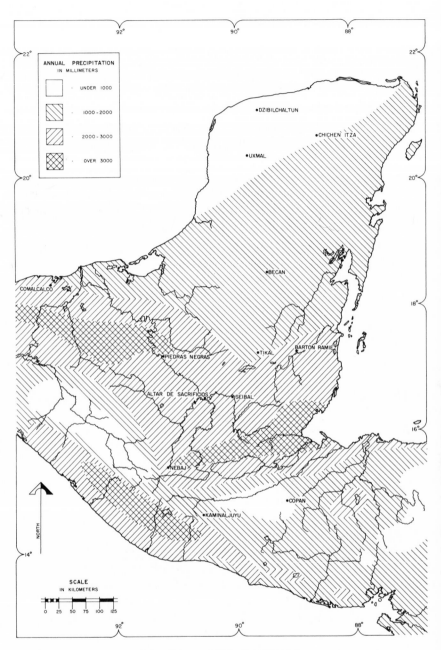

FIGURE 4. THE MAYA LOWLANDS: RAINFALL

indication that such systems were widespread. The natural vegetation of most of the Maya Lowlands is tropical rain forest. The exploitative potential for small populations is good since there are numerous edible fruits, roots, and nuts and some large and small game. This potential, however, declines rapidly with increasing population densities. It seems likely that by the peak population of Late Classic times very extensive parts of the rain forest had been destroyed by cultivation, decreasing wild plant and animal foods. The only native food material of high yield and nutritional quality is the nut of the *ramón* (breadnut) tree, a resource that was undoubtedly exploited and possibly cultivated by the ancient Maya (see Puleston 1968; Puleston and Puleston 1971).

A few natural resources are available in abundance in the Maya Lowlands. Limestone from underlying bedrock deposits is easily reached and quarried even without metal tools. Pockets of chert, some of excellent quality, occur within the limestone and provide raw material for tool manufacture. The rain forest supplies a variety of resources ranging from tropical hardwoods for construction or craft production to spices and *copal* incense. Native fauna provide commodities such as jaguar pelts and bird feathers that were prized for elite class costumes throughout Mesoamerica. On the other hand, some kinds of important raw materials are scarce or absent within the lowlands. Salt is available only from seacoast production along the Yucatecan coast or salt springs in the neighboring highlands zones. Volcanic stone for *manos* and *metates* occurs within the lowlands only in the Maya Mountains. Obsidian and semiprecious stones of volcanic origin must be brought in from highland areas.

The foregoing paragraphs outline the background within which the Maya worked out their destiny. This background was, of course, a part of a larger geographic-cultural scene, Mesoamerica. This Mesoamerican area, which comprises the southern two-thirds of Mexico and an adjoining portion of Central America, is a land of diverse topography and climate, ranging from high, temperate mountain valleys to tropical rain forests such as those described for the Maya Lowlands. The diversity of the area offers the possibility for symbiotic exchange of products between inhabitants of different zones, and the various Mesoamerican subareas, of which the Maya Lowlands is one, have had an interlinked cultural history since remote times.

Sedentary farming societies began to appear in southern Mesoamerica at about 2000 B.C., and the Mesoamerican cultural period from about this date to 1200 B.C. is generally referred to as the Early Preclassic Period. The remains of Early Preclassic communities are known from the Guatemalan Highlands and Pacific Coast, from Oaxaca, and from the Veracruz-Tabasco lowlands. To date, however, no evidences of human occupation dating this early have been found in the Maya Lowlands, and it would seem likely that the Maya Lowlands were first settled by village farmers coming from one or more ˙of these other Mesoamerican subareas. This first village settlement did not occur until about 1000 B.C. (in the Northern Lowlands) to 800 B.C. (in the Southern Lowlands). This was well into the Middle Preclassic Period, at which time some of the other Mesoamerican subareas were far along the way to more advanced levels of culture, as evidenced by large ceremonial center constructions, the beginnings of monumental art, and other traits of complex society. In the Maya Lowlands these more complex developments did not occur until somewhat later, in the Late Preclassic Period (c.400 B.C.–A.D. 250). Toward the end of the Late Preclassic, a number of traits appeared in the Southern Maya Lowlands that are considered to mark the inception of Maya Classic culture. Among these traits were the distinctively Lowland Maya corbeled arch, Maya polychrome pottery, distinctive Maya art motifs, and the first hieroglyphic stelae inscriptions that include dates in the Maya Long Count system of calendric notation. The origins of all of the traits which together define the beginnings of the Classic Period (A.D. 250–950) are not altogether clear. Some may have been of completely Maya origin, while others probably came from elsewhere in Mesoamerica or Central America. Whatever the origin of individual traits, the Lowland Maya transformed and embellished these earlier traditions in art, writing, and time-counting into highly distinctive forms and systems of their own. In sum, it is suggested that the Maya of the Southern Lowlands, after a relatively late start on the road to civilization as compared to some of their Mesoamerican neighbors, reached creative heights in the early centuries of the Christian era and in the span of a very few centuries evolved one of the most brilliant (from the standpoint of art, architecture, and intellectual attainments) of the pre-Columbian civilizations.

The dates for the Maya Lowland Preclassic occupations are based on radiocarbon determinations, but those for the Classic Period (Early

Classic, A.D. 250–600; Late Classic, A.D. 600–950) derive from the Maya stelae inscriptions of the Long Count calendar. The correlation of the Maya and Christian calendars is still a matter of debate. Throughout this volume, we use a correlation of the two calendars that is known as the Goodman-Martínez-Thompson (GMT) or 11.16.0.0.0 correlation. This correlation places the year A.D. 1539, which is attested by ethnohistoric sources to be at or near the end of a Maya 20-year period (*katun*), at 11.16.0.0.0 in the Maya calendar. A series of alternate correlations would place the Maya calendric count at 12.9.0.0.0 at this time. Using a 12.9.0.0.0 correlation would move all of our calendrically based dates back about 260 years. Thus, the date A.D. 250 that we suggest for the beginning of the Classic Period would be 10 B.C. with a 12.9.0.0.0 correlation. An 11.16.0.0.0 correlation is considered to be correct by almost all of the archaeologists who have worked in the Southern Maya Lowlands—hence its adoption here. It should be noted, however, that E. W. Andrews IV felt strongly that the correlation question remains unsolved and that the possibility of some earlier correlations, such as a 12.9.0.0.0 correlation, should be left open.

The Early Classic was a period of florescence in the Maya Lowlands. There is ample evidence for the existence of class distinctions and the accumulation of goods and labor in the creation of ceremonial complexes at a variety of centers. Whether the Lowland Maya reached the level of a state society during the Early Classic is a matter of debate, but a number of authorities feel that a chiefdom model is more appropriate (Sanders and Price 1968; Tourtellot and Sabloff 1972; Webb 1964). The Early Classic seems to have been a period of general cultural stability marked by a sphere of internal communication that fostered a high degree of uniformity within the Southern Lowlands and what were probably the closest ties that ever existed between the Southern and Northern Lowlands. The pace of change seems to have been relatively slow; although individual site sequences can usually be subdivided on the basis of minor changes in ceramics, there are no recognized subdivisions that crosscut the whole Lowland Region. Not all of the zones of the Southern Lowlands were equally populated in the Early Classic, since remains of that date have proved hard to locate in excavated sites in the Pasion and Palenque zones, and Early Classic monuments are uncommon in the Usumacinta Zone. During this period, the Lowland Maya had contacts with the vast zone controlled or influenced by the city of Teotihuacan in the Valley of Mexico. A few archaeologists feel that there was an actual conquest of all or part of the Maya Lowlands by Teotihuacan, but the majority opinion favors more amicable and less direct forms of economic and diplomatic interaction. There is certainly a strong possibility that contact, whatever its nature, with Teotihuacan stimulated important changes in Maya society.

The transition in the Maya Lowlands between Early Classic and Late Classic may have been marked by some sort of cultural disruption. The primary evidence for such a disruption is a decreased frequency of dated monuments from 9.5.0.0.0 to 9.9.0.0.0 in the Maya calendar (A.D. 504–613). Whether or not such a disruption actually took place, it had no long-range effect on cultural development, because by 9.10.0.0.0 (A.D. 633) the most vigorous interval in the history of Southern Lowland culture was under way.

During the Late Classic, an acceleration of the rate of change makes subdivision of the period both necessary and relatively easy. The subdivisions are based on ceramic sequences, since ceramics are the most common and most thoroughly studied remains of the Classic Maya. At a conference in Guatemala City in 1965 (Willey, Culbert, and Adams 1967), the first centuries of the Late Classic (A.D. 600–830) were designated the Tepeu 1–2 horizon, using the names from the prototype Peten ceramic sequence developed by Robert E. Smith (1955) at Uaxactun. In this volume, Tepeu 1 (A.D. 600–700) and Tepeu 2 (A.D. 700–830) are usually treated as separate intervals of time since the detailed problems discussed need a finer chronological scale. There is general agreement that the Late Classic Period represents the peak of cultural development in the Southern Lowlands. Population, construction, and evidences of sociocultural complexity add up to a cultural climax that is discussed more thoroughly in the following chapters.

The succeeding ceramic horizon, termed the Tepeu 3 horizon, is the period during which the processes of the downfall worked out their course. There are some difficulties in choosing a period term by which to designate the Tepeu 3 horizon. Traditionally, there has been a tendency to include the horizon as the last part of the Late Classic Period because of clear ceramic continuities with earlier horizons. On the other hand, most of the patterns that gave rise to the idea of Classicism had ceased by this time. We have, therefore, adopted the designation "Terminal Classic" in this volume with the hope that it will connote both the continuity and the destruction of previous patterns demonstrated in the archaeological record. Tepeu 3 is generally considered to have begun about A.D. 830 or 10.0.0.0 in the Maya Long Count calendar. Actually, a first sign of impending decline was a marked dropoff of monument and stela dedication after the *katun* ending of 9.18.0.0.0 (A.D. 790), late in the Tepeu 2 phase. By A.D. 830 this cultural arrest was well under way and evidences of it were reflected in nearly all of the Southern Lowlands centers, with the cessation of major architectural activities, the near disappearance of dated stelae, and the end of the elaborate polychrome pottery that had characterized Tepeu 2. The date A.D. 889 or 10.3.0.0.0 saw the last definitely dated monument in the south, although possibly some few stelae were set up as late as 10.4.0.0.0 (A.D. 909). After this, the major centers were largely abandoned. In some places the sustaining village and hamlet populations surrounding the centers disappeared at the same time; in others they seem to have continued in residence for a time, perhaps until about 10.6.0.0.0 (A.D. 948), when they, too, vanished.

The Classic Period is followed by the Postclassic, dated in round figures from A.D. 950 until the Spanish entry of 1520. As discussed by Bullard in this volume, Postclassic remains are but poorly represented in the Southern Lowlands, and the statement that the Maya failed to recover from the Classic collapse is amply justified. In parts of the Northern Lowlands, Maya culture continued to a vigorous Postclassic phase. This, however, leads us into the problems of the differences between the Southern and Northern Lowlands and of the correlation of their respective chronologies.

There is good agreement about the basic outlines of a Northern Lowlands sequence. After a Preclassic Period, there was an early development, represented in buried levels or early sections of a number of Yucatecan sites, that was clearly coeval with some part of the Southern Lowlands Classic. This was followed by a period of florescence during which the Puuc, Chenes, and Rio Bec sites and the architectural style that characterized them predominated. The style disappeared and many of the sites were abandoned at about the beginning of a period marked by a strong Mexican (Toltec) influence centered at the site of Chichen Itza. Finally, a post-Toltec era followed that lasted until the Spanish Conquest. These broad periods are given different names by different writers. Andrews (1965a), whose nomenclature we will use here, calls them Formative, Early, Pure Florescent, Modified Florescent, and Decadent, while Thompson (1966c) refers to them as Formative, Classic (which combines Andrews's Early and Pure Florescent periods), Mexican, and Mexican Absorption.

The primary problem lies in correlating the Northern Lowlands sequence with that of the Southern Lowlands. The traditional opinion (Thompson 1954, 1966c) has been that the Early Period corresponds with the southern Early Classic, while the Pure Florescent equates to the southern Late Classic. This would make the period of widespread cultural disintegration in the north essentially concurrent with the southern collapse, and E. W. Andrews IV has challenged this (Andrews 1960, this volume), arguing that the Northern Lowland Florescent Period cultures are largely post-Tepeu. The argument is an important one with reference to the problem of the Maya collapse, for if Andrews is correct there were two collapses, first one in the south and then one in the north, the latter being occasioned by the arrival of the Toltecs in northern Yucatan and Chichen Itza. Malcolm Webb (personal communication) offers still a third alternative: that the Pure Florescent in the north was intermediate in time between the possibilities already discussed. That is, he feels that the Pure Florescent began during the southern Late Classic but persisted for a significant time afterward. Unfortunately, the question cannot yet be settled,[2] but it presents alternatives which must be taken into account in any attempt to extend to Yucatan formulations concerning the collapse in the Southern Lowlands.

This brief introduction has attempted to set before the general reader some of the environmental and archaeological background of Maya Lowland culture. In turning more specifically to the Maya collapse, the presentation of more detailed background material is necessary. Chapters 2 and 3 undertake this task. Richard E. W. Adams reviews the historical background of the collapse problem and discusses the various theories that have previously been advanced toward its solution. Jeremy A. Sabloff then considers the themes that crosscut these explanatory theories. Let us move on, then, to these materials and the main topic of this volume.

Introduction

NOTES

1. A number of my colleagues from the Santa Fe seminar have contributed substantially to the preparation of this paper. I would like to note here my gratitude to Gordon R. Willey, Demitri B. Shimkin, Richard E. W. Adams, William R. Bullard, John A. Graham, and Jeremy A. Sabloff for their helpful suggestions.

2. The untimely death of E. W. Andrews IV on July 2, 1971, is a tragic loss to Maya archaeology. At the time of his death, Andrews was engaged in a study of the Rio Bec ruins of southern Campeche, a project which should throw light upon the problem of the alignment of the southern and northern chronologies. The analytical phases of the project are being carried on under the aegis of Tulane University.

2

The Collapse of Maya Civilization:
A Review of Previous Theories

RICHARD E. W. ADAMS

Department of Anthropology
University of Minnesota

INTRODUCTION

The purpose of this chapter is to define the problem of the Maya collapse, provide background material, review and analyze previous explanations, and to organize hypotheses and test expectations. The other, more specialized studies in this book, using points raised by this background, examine the implications of the new data available from recent work and test the older explanations against these data.

Paradoxically, in recent years it has seemed that an overall, comprehensive explanation might be beyond us at the moment when we were coming into possession of more detailed information about the collapse than ever before. Just as we recognized that Maya culture of the Classic Period was heavily regionalized, so it seemed that causes and specific circumstances of its collapse were at least regionalized, and perhaps even localized. And while our fund of information had grown on the culture area level, the data for any single region were often sparse or nonexistent. Obviously, however, to make any advance we had to control as many regions and the interrelations of their data as possible. For these reasons, we chose an organizational format for the collapse seminar that emphasized the individual region or site. Having established these patterns, we hoped to come to grips with the larger patterns and common denominators.

THE PROBLEM

The failure of Maya Classic culture has certain salient characteristics observable in the archaeological record. These can be restated in terms of what we think we know about the nature of Maya Classic society. We may thus make a series of tentative functional statements about the collapse. Summarized, these characteristics are as follows:

1. The failure of elite-class culture
   a. The abandonment of administrative and residential structures (palaces)
   b. Cessation of erection and refurbishment of funerary monuments and foci of ritual activities (temples)
   c. Cessation of manufacture of sculptured historical monuments and records (stelae)
   d. Cessation of the manufacture of luxury items such as the finest polychrome pottery, fine stonework, and jade carving for the use of an elite class
   e. Cessation of the use of calendrical and writing systems, at least in Classic Period forms
   f. Cessation of nearly all behavioral patterns associated with the above and other elite-class–directed activity, for example, the ball game played in formal courts. The processionals, rituals, visits, and conferences characteristic of Maya elite-class life lapsed
   g. From the above, it follows that the Classic Period elite class ceased to exist
2. The apparent rapid depopulation of the countryside and the ceremonial centers [1]
3. The relatively short period of occurrence—from 50 to 100 years [2]

REVIEW OF PREVIOUS EXPLANATIONS

The framework of discussion in this section is a classification of theories that strongly resembles others that have appeared before (Cowgill 1964; Willey 1964; Thompson 1954; Morley 1946). It is also similar to that of J. A. Sabloff (chapter 3), though not in all detail. I have used my own classification since it is tailored to the purposes of review while Sabloff's is more analytical and classificatory of individual elements extracted from the theories.

My classification follows, with principal exponents of the classes noted beside them.

1. Ecology (interrelations between man, his cultural systems, and natural systems)
   a. Soil exhaustion (O. F. Cook, W. T. Sanders)
   b. Water loss and erosion (C. W. Cooke and O. G. Ricketson)
   c. Savanna grass competition (O. F. Cook and S. G. Morley)
2. Catastrophism
   a. Earthquakes (E. MacKie)
   b. Hurricanes
3. Evolution (B. Meggers)
4. Disease (H. Spinden)
5. Demography (U. Cowgill and H. E. Hutchinson)
6. Social structure (J. E. S. Thompson, M. Altschuler, A. V. Kidder)
7. Invasion (R. E. W. Adams, G. Cowgill, J. A. Sabloff and G. R. Willey)

Individual theories are discussed in the above terms and discussed again as groups.

Ecology

Soil exhaustion. O. F. Cook advanced the hypothesis in 1921 that *milpa* agriculture is inherently destructive to the soil and encourages various deleterious effects including encroachment of grasses. His argument was that once a population dependent on a slash-and-burn system has grown enough to make necessary the reduction of the minimum rest period, then a rapid and disastrous decline in soil fertility will take place. Cook considered the *milpa* or swidden system primitive (note the title of his article). However, more recent studies have seemed to show that the system is indeed highly adaptive and efficient in specific tropical forest areas (Dumond 1961; Cowgill 1961, 1962). This modification, if correct (see Reina 1967; Sanders 1962, 1963 for partial counterarguments), has no effect on the basic premise. Cook and S. G. Morley (1920 : 452–547) believed that vast, agriculturally usable areas were abandoned only because of a basic flaw in or abuse of the cultivation system. Morley (1946 : 71–72) later modified his stand to favor the grass encroachment aspect after obtaining data from experimental studies done on the plot near Chichen Itza.

William T. Sanders, in his set of articles on the cultural ecology of the Maya Lowlands (1962, 1963), reviewed the problem with the aid of new data and the then-new theoretical tool of cultural ecology. Sanders added information from the Southern Lowlands and systematized and examined all pertinent information. He made population estimates based on archaeological work in eastern Quintana Roo, the Peten and the Belize Valley. He compared these settlement patterns with modern settlement patterns and concluded that they were essentially the same, and that, therefore, the agricultural systems must also have been the same. His consideration of the problem of the Maya collapse is more thorough and up to date than that of either Cook (1921) or Morley (1920), but he comes to about the same conclusion: Overuse of the swidden system leads to agricultural and, therefore, general cultural collapse.

Erosion and intensive agriculture. A variation of the soil exhaustion theory is that advanced by C. W. Cooke and O. G. Ricketson. Cooke (1931; and summarized in Ricketson and Ricketson 1937 : 10–11) argued that the present-day *bajos*, or logwood swamps, of the Southern Lowlands had once been a series of shallow lagoons or lakes. Swidden agriculture, heavy tropical rainfall, and consequent erosion were believed to have combined to take away available soil, and fill in the water basins, and to diminish the water available. *Bajos* in their present state then would be the direct result of *milpa* agriculture, and cultural decline would have followed agricultural decline.

Ricketson had modified this theory to the extent of insisting on the

24

presence of intensive agriculture. He based this assertion on the argument that the wasteful system of *milpa* cultivation "would never have supported the ancient Maya population at its peak" (Ricketson and Ricketson 1937 : 12). Ricketson's estimates of Maya population at Uaxactun have been the subject of some dispute recently, but the skepticism was aroused because most have believed he *underestimated* the ancient population (D. Puleston, personal communication; Adams 1965). Ricketson's argument gains force if his population estimates are revised upward. He also thought that there was evidence for soil denudation following intensive cultivation and cited the presence of agricultural terraces in terrain where they were needed. Finally, he noted that most of the Maya Lowlands did not need terracing, and that the lack of terracing was not conclusive evidence against intensive agriculture.

Savanna grass competition. Savanna grass competition was argued later by Morley to be the primary factor in the collapse of Maya agriculture. His latest statement about this was that "the repeated clearing and burning of ever-increasing areas of forest to serve as corn lands gradually converted the original forest into man-made grasslands, artificial savannas." When the process was nearly complete, he believed, agriculture as practiced by the ancient Maya came to an end, inasmuch as no implements were available for turning the soil; economic collapse then precipitated other factors such as social unrest, governmental disorganization, and religious disbelief (Morley 1946 : 71–72).

Discussion. All of the above theories, except for Ricketson's modification of Cooke, had certain assumptions in common. One was that maize was the primary food crop. All assumed that Maya agriculture and its subsistence base were the same in the Classic Period as in the sixteenth century. All, then, assumed that swidden cultivation was the system in use in Classic times. Another assumption held in common was that the major ecological features of the Maya Lowlands have not changed appreciably since the time of the Classic Period, except by man's agency. A final assumption was that settlement patterns in all zones are congruent with swidden agriculture.

All of these assumptions were rationally founded on at least fragmentary data available at the time the theories were formulated. Objections could be and have been made on the basis of limited data sample, but none save Ricketson, and recently Puleston, have questioned the basic assumptions. Such data included the observation made of modern Maya dependence on the swidden system and on maize as the primary crop. Further, it was noted that the sixteenth-century Spaniards repeatedly remarked on the mystical attachment of the Maya to maize as a life-sustaining crop. Controlled experiments and observations of nitrogen loss and grass competition as factors in crop declines reinforced these assumptions. This group of ecological theories has remained until recently one of the two strongest explanations of Maya Classic collapse. As will be seen, they still exert great influence, although not in the sense of prime-mover explanations as before. More often now, ecological factors are integrated into multifactor theories.

Ricketson's theory has been unique in its rejection, either implicit or explicit, of two major assumptions listed above. As noted, he believed that intensive agriculture was an imperative and that, therefore, swidden agriculture was not the only major cultivation system in Classic times. Angel Palerm has argued for intensive irrigation among the Lowland Maya (Wolf and Palerm 1961), but as Sanders (1962 : 89) has pointed out in a closely reasoned refutation, there is no evidence for it, and much against. Further, A. L. Smith's and U. Cowgill's (Cowgill and Hutchinson 1963a) examinations of *bajo* soil do not indicate heavy silting as causing these periodic swamps.

Ricketson also questioned the assumption that maize was the only major crop in the Classic Period food inventory (Ricketson and Ricketson 1937 : 12), suggesting that many other food resources could have been used. Recent work by Bronson (1966) indicates the probability that many root crops were used. More importantly, Puleston's studies (Haviland et al. 1968) at Tikal suggest strongly that *ramón* (breadnut) nuts were a staple crop among the Classic Maya. The implications include the raising of the potential population density, thus partially supporting Ricketson in a way he did not anticipate.

Catastrophism

Earthquakes. Euan MacKie proposed in 1961 that new evidence from the site of Xunantunich (Benque Viejo) on the Belize-Peten border demanded a reconsideration of the possibility that earthquakes had a major role in abandonment of the Southern Maya Lowlands. MacKie produced evidence that at least one major palace structure, and perhaps the whole ceremonial center, was damaged during Late Classic II times and the damage left unrepaired. He argues that the damage occurred prior to the abandonment and that it was caused by earthquakes. MacKie then extrapolated these events to the rest of the Lowlands and considered the possibility that these localized data and geological conditions may have validity for the entire Maya Lowlands.

A major objection to this theory has been that there is no evidence for major earthquakes in the Lowlands, although minor tremors do occur. However, it should also be noted that earthquakes do tend to occur in cycles. It is very difficult to detect the difference between earthquake damage, structural failure, and deterioration after abandonment.

Hurricanes. Hurricanes have seldom been mentioned as prime movers in the collapse, although they have been almost casually included in a number of discussions. Native chronicles of Yucatan do mention devastating hurricanes striking the peninsula in the fifteenth century, and such catastrophic storms have hit the area in historic times (cf. the Belize hurricane of 1961). United States Weather Bureau studies show that the hurricane pattern of the past 100 years has shifted somewhat. Whether this is a cyclical and self-adjusting phenomenon is unknown to me, although clarifying information may eventually be developed by the Hurricane Center in Miami.

Discussion. The effects of both storms and earthquakes are usually localized and sporadic. Further, no appreciable area has ever been permanently abandoned by reason of such occurrences. Thus no explanation of the collapse dependent on natural catastrophe has gained much currency or credibility.

Evolution

Betty Meggers (1954) theorized that the Maya had suffered a cultural collapse because of the inherently limited agricultural potential of their area. The collapse of Maya civilization, she proposed, was prima facie evidence of such limited potential. This also explained to her why the Maya were so unusual in establishing civilization in a tropical forest setting; the venture could not last and was foreordained to fail. Maya civilization, then, must have come from elsewhere.

The circular reasoning in this case has been attacked by the Hirshbergs (1957) and by W. R. Coe (1957). Coe also attacked the theory on the basis of simple misconstruction of the facts. Since Coe wrote, much more evidence for the in situ development of Maya culture has appeared, and other more convincing alternatives have been available. Finally, the newer studies of the swidden system, as well as the Tikal sustaining-area studies, have indicated a much higher potential for population support than was previously thought possible.

Disease

The disease theory of the collapse is represented primarily by a single line in Spinden's *The Ancient Civilizations of Mexico and Central America:* "There is good reason for believing that the sudden appearance of yellow fever may have had a part in the catastrophe" (1928 : 148). As in the case of hurricanes and earthquakes, numerous authors have casually included disease in a list of "straw-man" possibilities and have as casually discarded it. Spinden's specification of yellow fever is based on the assumption that this health scourge of historic times was also present in the pre-Columbian past. It is well known that yellow fever, malaria, syphilis, and smallpox were principal disease factors in the biological catastrophes that overtook the native New World populations between the sixteenth and eighteenth centuries. However, it was argued that all of these diseases are post-Conquest introductions from the Old World and, therefore, ineligible for serious consideration as elements in the collapse. However, it seems to me that there are some factors about disease which make it a more likely element in the collapse than previously believed. The post-Conquest depopulation is the only documented New World case of a demographic decline comparable in scope to that of the Maya collapse, and it was clearly disease related. Doubts have developed about the histories of diseases in the New World. It now seems likely that there was a New World reservoir of yellow fever (Shimkin, chapter 13), and there seem to be some pathological diagnostics of syphilis in prehistoric osteological material from the Maya Lowlands (Saul, chapter 14). Finally, it has been pointed out to me by Dr. G. B. Risse, Professor of History of Medicine, University of Minnesota, and is reemphasized by Shimkin, that introduced diseases are not necessary to set off a biological catastrophe. The reservoir of disease always present in any given population can act in an epidemic manner given the weakening of biochemical resistance in that population. The latter condition is usually due to malnutrition, according to Dr. Risse. Haviland's studies on the Tikal skeletal material seem to show poorer nutrition as the Classic Period approached its end (1967). Saul's Altar de Sacrificios studies show the same trends (personal communication). In sum, disease as at least one element in the collapse must be seriously reconsidered.

Demography

U. Cowgill and G. E. Hutchinson (1963c) noted a sex-ratio distinction in the births recorded in a small Peten town that emphasized female births. They found by statistical projection that if the trends had continued, the population would have been self-eliminating. A basic assumption was that the trend was a long-term one, and another was that the trend existed in Classic times. Further, the sample from the town was assumed to be representative. The authors concluded that such a situation might bring about a population decline and consequent collapse of Maya culture.

General skepticism has greeted this theory, owing to the assumptions involved, but then, neither is the theory well known.

Social Structure

Nearly as popular as the ecological group of theories, social-structural explanations have been advanced with some vigor by J. E. S. Thompson, A. V. Kidder, and Milton Altschuler.

Thompson's theory, as put forth in the two editions of his general book (1954 and 1966c), had three principal elements. The first was the presence of economic motivations for peasant revolt, with the increasingly onerous tribute burdens as a trigger. The second was the introduction of Central Mexican mercenaries for the purposes of social control, so that an atmosphere of militarism and secularism spread. Third was moral decay resulting from the associated and introduced ideological shifts. These three elements were seen as combining to produce a flash point at which the social system was destroyed by violent internal dissension. A basic assumption underlying Thompson's thesis was that the subsistence balance was the same in the Classic Period, the sixteenth century, and the ethnographic present. This meant that agricultural failure could be eliminated as a prime cause. Thompson, in his recent demographic paper (1967), seems to have added the possibility of malnutrition, disease, and loss of morale similar to that of the early sixteenth century as accountable for depopulation.

A. V. Kidder (in Smith 1950 : 1–12) thought the growth of the elite class and overdemands by this class on the rest of Maya society responsible for class estrangement and internal revolt.

Milton Altschuler (1958), in refuting Meggers's argument, approached the problem by arguing for social dissension as the most acceptable alternative to ecological-evolutionary collapse. He made the interesting point that kin-based Maya Classic aristocratic society would have been weak indeed if confronted with the need for putting down revolution. He has been joined in viewing Maya sociopolitical structures as fragile by M. D. Coe (1961), D. Kaplan (1963), and C. Erasmus (1965).

Discussion. Kidder and Altschuler offered social-structural reasons for a class-based, and essentially internal, breakdown of Maya society. Neither, however, offered a satisfactory explanation for depopulation.

Thompson's theory stands out from all the rest so far reviewed in being more "multifactored" than "prime mover" in category. However, his emphasis on the peasant-elite relationships *within* Maya society placed it more in the social-structural category than any other, in spite of the fact that he saw the ultimate causes as ideological and foreign. Finally, his theory was distinctive in dealing directly with the depopulation problem.

As regards archaeological confirmation of any of these theories, Sabloff and Willey (1967 : 317) noted that signs of internal social revolt are very hard to detect, and all evidence adduced to support such an interpretation could be alternatively construed.

Invasion

The possibility of explaining the Maya collapse in terms of invasion has existed since the detection of the Toltec intrusion into Yucatan. That is to say, this event, which is attested by archaeological evidence and native texts, provided a model of something that actually had happened. The logical possibility then existed that it had also happened earlier, albeit in another part of the Maya area. The possibility also existed that the Toltec intrusion was in some way connected with the Classic collapse. G. Cowgill (1964) reviewed and rejected all previously advanced theories and offered an alternative explanation that accounted for depopulation. He postulated a period of Mexican invasions with substantial population decline because of famine, death in warfare, and slavery, and, following this period, a consolidation of power by a small group of invaders with a capital at Chichen Itza. The new elite, he proposed, then forced resettlement of the remnants of Classic Period population from the Southern Lowlands to the zone around Chichen (Cowgill 1964 : 155–56).

Although I must admit to bias on this point, the strongest evidence for invasion of the Southern Maya Lowlands comes from the Altar de Sacrificios and Seibal projects carried on from 1958 to 1968. I have presented in detail one interpretation of the Pasion River material (1963a, 1963b, 1964, and 1971), and Sabloff and Willey have presented another (1967). These are summarized below and are also presented in elaborated versions in later chapters.

The ceramic sequence at Altar de Sacrificios is a long and essentially continuous one with trends and continuities established in the Preclassic and extending to the Late Classic Boca Complex. Boca is the next to last complex in the Altar sequence. It is also associated with a lapse in elite-class culture at Altar—stelae ceased to be erected, erection and refurbishment of monumental architecture ceased, and so on. Population continuities, however, are evidenced by continuities in the utilitarian ceramics. This simplification of ceremonial life at Altar suggests a crisis sufficiently grave to disrupt long-established, elite-class behavior patterns. At the same time, Boca Ceramic Sphere pottery (Willey, Culbert, and Adams 1967) is found at Seibal, associated with a florescence of ceremonial center life. At least thirteen monuments were erected in the space of about 80 years, and much monumental architecture of a distinctive nature was erected. E. W. Andrews has noted a building that would be characteristic of his Transition Period in Yucatan (personal communication; see Str. A-III on R. E. W. Adams's map 1963a). Sabloff and Willey (1967 : 322) note the presence of other Yucatecan architectural traits at Seibal. This architectural style is associated with Boca ceramics and also with the art style displaying Mexican traits. Boca ceramics end the site sequence at Seibal. At Altar de

Sacrificios, however, the sequence continues with the Jimba Complex. The latest pottery at the site shows no continuities with the immediately preceding Boca Complex except in the most elaborate types. These elaborate types are in small supply, and I regard them as trade items arriving at Altar during Boca times. The Jimba Fine Paste Complex, on the other hand, does show identities and great similarities to the fine paste complexes of lowland Tabasco, especially in the utilitarian types.

Sabloff and Willey have suggested that the Seibal florescence is based on an intrusion and takeover of Seibal by a group foreign to the Peten. I agree with this interpretation and, based on the Yucatecan similarities to be seen in Seibal architecture and sculpture, suggest that the intrusive group came from northern Yucatan or the intermediate lowlands. I further suggest that these persons formed an elite class and sparked the cultural florescence at Seibal. The Jimba Complex represents the invasion of the Maya Lowlands by a non-Maya group from the Gulf Coast lowlands who physically occupied the site of Altar de Sacrificios. Raiding from the Pasion River Zone further disrupted Maya Classic economic and social patterns and led to the collapse, including the collapse of the hybrid Maya culture at Seibal. Ecological factors and disease may have played a part in the disaster.

Obviously, the invasion is not the single cause of the Maya collapse, and the probable military takeover of Seibal preceding the collapse gives us a hint of what may have happened. Evidence of overpopulation and ecological stress comes from population estimates and physical anthropological studies. As noted before, the Altar de Sacrificios and Tikal skeletal material seems to indicate malnutrition as the Classic Period drew to an end. This may indicate a competitive situation for food resources, which may have contributed to a militarily competitive atmosphere.[3] This sort of military competition for resources would make the takeover at Seibal by a foreign group understandable. The Pasion is certainly more ecologically favorable than the Northern Lowlands and therefore would be attractive to groups from this zone.

Sabloff and Willey's (1967) interpretation of these Pasion data is somewhat different, although in general agreement with what has been presented above. The points of difference are that they regard the group intrusive to Seibal as the same as that which took over Altar de Sacrificios in the Jimba Phase. In other words, the Jimba and Boca complexes as distinguished at Altar de Sacrificios should be combined or Jimba should be regarded as derived from the Boca Complex. These invaders established themselves at Seibal and then raided other Maya sites, disrupting the *milpa* cycle and bringing about eventual economic and social collapse. The attempt by the invaders to maintain themselves in the Seibal center was unsuccessful, and Classic patterns ceased to exist.

Invasion, ecological pressures, and social disruption are all combined in the two variations presented above. The data are among the most complex yet to have been found, and the essential quarrel is over how to interpret them and how to extrapolate from them to other parts of the Maya Lowlands. It may be that excavations now under way at the fortress of Becan near the border between the Southern and Northern Lowlands will throw light on the military competition among Maya polities of the Classic Period.

SUMMARY

Reviewing the theories of the Maya Classic collapse, it seems that many are or were simply straw-man theories. That is to say, they were presented as background to be destroyed in favor of one of the ecological or social-structural theories. This is not to say that all such theoretical chaff has no merit. As shown above, at least disease should be taken seriously as one element. As I have noted in another article (Adams 1969 : 29), the explanations of the collapse have generally moved from the "prime mover" category to the multifactor approach. It should also be noted that most of the explanations are not mutually exclusive; recombinations and reformulations are plausible. This is demonstrated by Thompson's peasant revolt hypothesis, and by the invasion theories. Finally, I reiterate that which I have said elsewhere: the circumstances of the collapse were probably different, perhaps unique, from region to region and even from site to site.

NOTES

1. While ceremonial centers were abandoned, it is clear that at least in some regions populations lingered on. This seems to have been the case especially in the Belize Valley, the Central Peten Lakes District, and along the eastern coast of Yucatan in Quintana Roo. However, even these populations seemed to dwindle

rapidly or disappear. In areas such as Tikal, and in the Pasion Valley, there is little evidence of major population survivals. Most ceremonial centers show some evidence of postcollapse occupation, but it is fleeting. And the uses of the buildings are patently changed from highly specified and structured functions to casual domestic usage. The point is that, inside or outside the ceremonial centers, large districts seem to have been abandoned by former residents.

2. This is perhaps more an assumption than a proven fact, since it was initially based on the abrupt cessation of monument erection. However, we seem to have confirmation of the assumption from all major excavations carried on in the last 50 years. A major point of discussion might be the starting date of the disintegration of Classic patterns in any given region. Although this point is not discussed further below, it is an aspect that some participants dealt with in detail.

3. The fortress of Becan and the fortification ditch at Tikal are now known to be Tzakol 3 or terminal Early Classic. Late Classic fortifications are possible at Seibal.

3
Major Themes in the Past
Hypotheses of the Maya Collapse[1]

JEREMY A. SABLOFF

Department of Anthropology
Harvard University

Explanations of the collapse of Classic Maya civilization in the Southern Lowlands range from hypotheses that emphasize single catastrophic factors to ones that utilize concatenations of factors. Some hypotheses have been particularistic, others general. Some hypotheses have viewed the collapse in terms of environment and history in the Southern Lowlands itself, while others have looked at the collapse in terms of a wider *oikumene*.

Unfortunately for the archaeologist working as hypothesis-tester, it would appear that a multifaceted hypothesis is going to be of greatest utility (Adams 1969; Sabloff 1971a; Willey and Shimkin 1971a, and this volume). Because it is difficult to test complex hypotheses as whole entities, the best plan of attack would seem to be to isolate the various common themes in the hypotheses and look at their assumptions, their test expectations, and the relevant data that agree or disagree with the expectations. In chapter 2, Adams describes the specific hypotheses that have previously been proposed, while many of the following chapters discuss them in terms of data from specific sites. The intent of this chapter is to isolate the major themes present in the great range of collapse hypotheses and to comment briefly on the thematic combinations that have been suggested or that might be useful.

The principal criterion in choosing the classificatory scheme presented here has been the pragmatic one of testability. Several other frameworks might have been neater, but the one used here has the advantage of isolating testable elements. The framework is as follows:

A. Internal
  1. Natural
     a. Soil potential
     b. Demographic change (overpopulation)
     c. Earthquakes
     d. Hurricanes
     e. Climatic change
     f. Disease
     g. Insect pests
  2. Sociopolitical
     a. Peasant revolt
     b. Intersite warfare
B. External
  1. Economic
  2. Sociopolitical
     a. Invasion without resettlement
     b. Invasion with resettlement

The basic division in the framework is between those hypotheses that view the collapse of Classic Maya civilization in isolation from developments outside of the Southern Lowlands and those that view the collapse in terms of developments throughout the Mesoamerican culture area. The former is essentially traditional (including Spinden 1913, 1928; Huntington 1917; Cook 1921; Cooke 1931; Ricketson and Ricketson 1937; Morley 1946; Kidder in Smith 1950; Meggers 1954; Thompson 1954; Bartlett 1956; Altschuler 1958; MacKie 1961; Sanders 1962; Cowgill 1962; Cowgill and Hutchinson 1963c); the latter, which had some early popularity (e.g., Joyce 1914), has gained much new support in the past decade or so (Girard 1959; Adams 1964, 1971;

Cowgill 1964; Webb 1964; Jiménez Moreno 1966; Sabloff and Willey 1967). The lines between the two kinds of hypotheses are not rigid, however. J. E. S. Thompson's (1954) complex peasant-revolt hypothesis, essentially an "internal" formulation, includes the possibility of Mexican incursions, while Sabloff and Willey's invasion hypothesis, basically "external" in emphasis, talks about the "precarious man-nature balance in agriculture" in the Southern Lowlands and notes that one result of an invasion might have been a "tip[ping] of the balance" (1967 : 328).

The resurgence of "external" hypotheses may have been a reaction against the tendency of several Mayanists to look at the Classic Maya in isolation. Or, perhaps, the lack of data on neighboring areas or lack of coordination among the sequences in neighboring areas and the Maya Lowlands until recently has been the cause. Another possibility is that with the revival of evolutionary theory there has been a greater willingness to look at Mesoamerican civilization as an area-wide system.

The "internal" hypotheses can be grouped into three types: the natural/catastrophic, the natural/limited-ecological-potential, and the sociopolitical/noncoercive chiefdom. The former would include disease, insect pests, and climatic change. They are very difficult to prove because the hypothesized events leave little or no tangible archaeological remains. The contention of the limited-ecological-potential hypotheses is that the adaptation of the Classic Maya to their jungle environment was a tenuous one. The effects of the limited potential of the soil could have been direct (that is, soil exhaustion) or indirect (that is, increasing population led to attempts at intensive agriculture which in turn led to soil erosion). Another variant would hypothesize a catastrophic event causing the collapse of the vulnerable agricultural system. For example, a series of damaging hurricanes might have completely wrecked an overburdened *milpa* system and led to chaos and depopulation. Yet another possibility, which could be linked with the third type of "internal" hypothesis, is that a natural event such as a terrible earthquake might not only have affected the agricultural system but also have helped to destroy the Maya hierarchy as well.

The best known sociopolitical hypothesis is Thompson's (1954) peasant-revolt formulation. Essentially, what this hypothesis and variants such as the one described by Altschuler (1958) are saying is that the

37

Maya hierarchy, for whatever reasons, went too far in suppressing the peasantry without the institutional means of enforcing their policies (cf. Kaplan 1963; Erasmus 1965). These hypotheses are not necessarily distinct from the natural/limited-ecological-potential hypotheses, however, because, as has been pointed out by Tourtellot and Sabloff (1972), the nature of the lowland environment may not have permitted the development of more coercive polities in the Southern Maya Lowlands. This kind of link can also be seen in the hypothesis that the collapse was caused by intersite warfare ("civil war"). Intersite fighting could have led to the elimination of the ruling class, or it could have precipitated agricultural disruption through the burning of fields or the recruitment of farmers into standing armies.

The one hypothesis that really gets at the heart of the various themes just discussed was proposed by Betty J. Meggers (1954). Unfortunately, Meggers's hypothesis that Maya culture and the Southern Lowlands environment were seriously mismatched has been virtually discarded because it is based on the erroneous assumption that Classic Maya civilization was developed outside of the lowland environment and imported fully grown into the Peten (cf. Coe 1957). Nevertheless, it does appear that Meggers was not too far off the mark when she hypothesized that the Southern Lowland environment limited the growth of Maya civilization and provided an insufficient adaptive base for the flowering of a complex ranked or stratified society. Although the collapse may not have been as inexorable as Meggers would have us believe, her hypothesis does clearly focus our attention on the nature of the total environment in relation to the sociopolitical organization of the population it supported.

The importance of considering the total Mesoamerican ecosystem in any attempt to understand the causes of the collapse of Classic Maya civilization is recognized in the various "external" hypotheses. Many of these hypotheses compare the nature of the developmental trends in the Mesoamerican lowland and highland areas. Generally, it is felt that the ecological situation in the latter helped bring about the development of urban states in contrast to the development of fairly large but nonurban civilizations in the Southern Lowlands. These hypotheses see the collapse as a result of the expansion of the urban states in the ninth century A.D. The expansion is seen either as economic (Webb 1964) or political and military (Adams 1964; Cowgill 1964; Sabloff and Willey 1967). All the "external" hypotheses also depend to a certain extent on the "internal" ones. Economic collapse and the accompanying depopulation were possible, according to Webb's hypothesis, because the Maya did not (and could not) develop a significant mercantile class and trade in subsistence goods. Invasion might have led to a collapse because the Maya could not cope with the added element of having to battle a well-developed power over any extended period of time, or because the invaders toppled a fragile sociopolitical structure, or because the intruders could not effectively deal with a new agricultural situation, and so on. Depopulation might have occurred through resettlement or through the collapse of the agricultural system. Yet it is also possible that an invasion could have wiped out the Maya hierarchy and caused some population loss without causing widespread depopulation. As one can see, the many hypothetical variants, all the possible expectations, and the actual hard archaeological data will have to be sifted carefully if we are to clarify the nature of the collapse.

In order to succeed in explaining the causes of the collapse of Classic Maya civilization, we will have to take an intensive look at the various themes which are common to many of the hypotheses about the collapse. Moreover, it will be to our benefit to examine not only the individual themes and their test expectations in terms of the thematic combinations that have previously been proposed, but other thematic combinations that might be of some utility. In other words, if in testing the individual themes we find that a, b, c, d, and e are possible, while data relevant to f, g, and h contradict the expectations, then it may be worthwhile to look at *all* the possible combinations of a, b, c, d, and e. Furthermore, in these combinations and recombinations, both "internal" natural and sociopolitical hypotheses and "external" economic and sociopolitical hypotheses should be joined together in the hope that we will come to an understanding of the *total* adaptive picture in the Southern Maya Lowlands in the ninth century A.D. If we do succeed in this manner, then the complex causal hypothesis which we finally construct will be truly ecological in the sense that it will have comprehended "not only space and habitat but the sociocultural resources and groups beyond the society but within its experiential field" (Helm 1962 : 633).

NOTE

1. This chapter is a slightly revised version of a paper that was written in January 1970 and circulated to the participants prior to the seminar. The helpful comments and suggestions of R. E. W. Adams, T. P. Culbert, and G. R. Willey are gratefully acknowledged.

PART II

The Archaeological Record in Space and Time Perspective

4

The Classic Collapse in the Southern
Maya Lowlands: Chronology

ROBERT L. RANDS

Department of Anthropology
Southern Illinois University, Carbondale

Achievement of absolute dating is a fundamental goal in efforts to understand the collapse of Classic Maya civilization. A slight shift forward or backward in time can make a significant difference in how one visualizes the pattern of events. Such shifts might, for example, bear on "external" as opposed to "internal" explanations for the collapse. The possible role of alien intrusions, or of stress factors within Maya society that may have contributed to a crisis situation, cannot adequately be evaluated in the absence of a firmly anchored, minutely calibrated chronology that cuts across the area as a whole.

This chapter is concerned primarily with the dating of ceramic phases or complexes. It has not been intended to minimize the importance of other archaeological remains—sculptured monuments, burials and caches, elite and domestic architecture—in achieving temporal understanding of the collapse and its background. But at the present time, with the exception of dated monuments, our chronology is largely ceramically based. Needless to say, attempts at working out absolute dates for the ceramic complexes have leaned heavily on associations between pottery and the sculptured monuments. This has provided a measure of control in the effort to establish the duration and cross-dating of the various ceramic complexes. On the other hand, such "absolute" datings are subject to uncertainties inherent in alternative correlations of the Maya and Christian calendars. Following the consensus of the other authors in this book who are working in the Southern Maya Lowlands (although Andrews, working to the north, disagreed), the chronological charts presented herein are based on the 11.16.0.0.0 (Goodman-Martínez-Thompson) correlation.

Sites and regions in the Southen Maya Lowlands are arranged geographically in the chronological charts (Figs. 5–8). Viewed from left to right, as on a map, eight chronological columns form a section across the area, from the Trinidad–Lower Usumacinta Zone on the northwest to the Belize Valley on the east. Only the Late Classic and the Late Classic Transition–Early Postclassic periods are covered (for a broader chronological perspective see Willey, Culbert, and Adams 1967). Substantive data documenting most of the ceramic sequences are given in various background chapters in the present volume or in the references at the close of the chapter, though a number of comprehensive monographs are still in preparation.[1]

The eight sites or regions and the authors responsible for investigating or reporting on their ceramic chronologies are: Trinidad–Lower Usumacinta, Rands; Palenque, Rands; Piedras Negras, Rands; Altar de Sacrificios, Adams; Seibal, Sabloff; Tikal, Culbert; Uaxactun, Culbert and others; Belize Valley, Willey. In addition, Bullard provided information on the Central Peten Postclassic Tradition, which appears in the chronological charts for Tikal and the Belize Valley, respectively, as the Caban and New Town complexes.[2]

Synthesis of Ceramic Chronologies (Fig. 5)

Blackboard presentation of ceramic complexes, with accompanying discussion by seminar participants, formed the basis of the chronological synthesis given in Figure 5. Minor adjustments have subsequently been made. The chart is a conventional one, using horizontal lines to divide the chronological columns. This device inevitably obscures transitional phenomena as ceramic complexes interdigitate with one another. Moreover, degrees of uncertainty about dating felt by the ceramic analyst, as he compares one complex with another, are not indicated. Nevertheless, this standard mode of presentation has the merits of simplicity and readability, facilitating the comparison of regional sequences.

Aside from minor adjustments in chronology, Figure 5 differs in certain respects from published data on several of the ceramic complexes. At Palenque, Huipale is dropped as a separate complex, now being considered a late facet of Balunte. Nevertheless, the internal distinction in Balunte is a significant one, for the effective collapse of elite culture,

11.16.0.0.0 A.D.	CORRELATION	TRINIDAD-LOWER USUMACINTA	PALENQUE	PIEDRAS NEGRAS	ALTAR DE SACRIFICIOS	SEIBAL	TIKAL	UAXACTUN	BELIZE VALLEY
968	10.7.0.0.0	CHACBOLAY			POST JIMBA		(CENTRAL PETEN POSTCLASSIC TRADITION) CABAN		(CENTRAL PETEN POSTCLASSIC TRADITION) NEW TOWN
948	10.6.0.0.0						....		....
928	10.5.0.0.0		POST BALUNTE	POST TAMAY	JIMBA				
909	10.4.0.0.0						....		
889	10.3.0.0.0		....	....					....
869	10.2.0.0.0	JONUTA HORIZON			BOCA (LATE)	BAYAL	EZNAB		LATE SPANISH LOOKOUT-BENQUE VIEJO IV
849	10.1.0.0.0		....					TEPEU 3	
830	10.0.0.0.0		BALUNTE (LATE)	....					
810	9.19.0.0.0		....	TAMAY	BOCA (EARLY)	(TRANSITIONAL)			
790	9.18.0.0.0	NAAB (LATE) (?)	BALUNTE (EARLY)						EARLY SPANISH LOOKOUT-BENQUE VIEJO IIIB
771	9.17.0.0.0	-------		CHACALHAAZ		-------	IMIX	TEPEU 2	
751	9.16.0.0.0								
731	9.15.0.0.0	NAAB	MURCIELAGOS		PASION (LATE)				
711	9.14.0.0.0					TEPEJILOTE			
692	9.13.0.0.0				--------				
672	9.12.0.0.0			YAXCHE					TIGER RUN-BENQUE VIEJO IIIA
652	9.11.0.0.0	TAXINCHAN	OTOLUM		PASION (EARLY)		IK	TEPEU 1	
633	9.10.0.0.0								
613	9.9.0.0.0			BALCHE					
593	9.8.0.0.0								

FIGURE 5. CERAMIC COMPLEXES of the Late Classic and Late Classic Transition–Early Postclassic periods in the Southern Maya Lowlands, with estimated dates.

45

accompanied by severe population loss, appears to have taken place between the early and late facets of the complex. Continuity of basic ceramic patterns for a short interval of time following the collapse is indicated for Palenque. At Seibal, the Tepejilote Ceramic Complex is faceted to include a transition to the Bayal Complex, rather than being divided into "early" and "late" facets.

The Trinidad–Lower Usumacinta column is based primarily on Rands's work at Trinidad and on the Jonuta horizon of Berlin (1956), which has its major geographical locus farther downstream. The Jonuta horizon has been provisionally redefined in the combined sequence, Jonuta proper referring only to the time characterized by the strong occurrence of Fine Orange Ware of the Balancan Ceramic Group. Earlier portions of the Jonuta horizon, as originally described by Berlin, are for the most part temporal and, to a degree, cultural equivalents of the Naab Ceramic Complex. However, the late facet of Naab, which is unknown at Trinidad, is intended to have only provisional status. Further work in the vicinity of Trinidad may confirm the usefulness of the faceting of Naab or may require the recognition of a distinct ceramic complex. The suggested reordering of the Jonuta horizon and its relationship to Naab is explained in greater detail in chapter 9.

As shown in Figure 5, Late Classic ceramic complexes tend to begin slightly later on the western and eastern peripheries of the Southern Maya Lowlands than at more centrally located sites. The evidence for this is indirect. Early Classic developments in the northwest are spotty, generally meager. The beginning Late Classic Taxinchan Complex, as currently understood, represents a short but striking florescence at Trinidad. The change from the Early to Late Classic is long and gradual at Barton Ramie; indeed, the Tiger Run Ceramic Complex is described as essentially transitional to these periods (Willey, Bullard, Glass, and Gifford 1965 : 360). Ceramic developments in the Southern Maya Lowlands at about the beginning of the Late Classic Period may have been partially dependent on an innovative culture center located in the greater Peten. If so, the peripheries could well have been characterized by cultural lag, that is, retarded acquisition of ceramic attributes that are diagnostic in differentiating Early and Late Classic complexes in the area as a whole.

At the other end of the sequence, and more immediately germane to the present discussion, is a slight tendency for the Terminal Late Classic ceramic complexes to be of shorter duration than those earlier in the period. Several possible factors, singly or in combination, may account for this tendency. One factor is acceleration in the rate of cultural change caused by "internal" forces operative in Lowland Maya society. Another possible factor is the extinction of ceramic complexes, before they had run their course of expectable development, because of events connected with the collapse. At the time of the collapse, and for an uncertain interval thereafter, there may have occurred a disruption of sedentary life and of theocratic institutions which resulted in the dislocation of peoples, who maintained only short or sporadic occupation of the formerly great ceremonial centers.

Some tendency is also apparent in Figure 5 for Late Classic ceramic complexes on the west (Pasion, Usumacinta, and Palenque) to be of shorter duration than in the Peten heartland (Tikal and Uaxactun). If this is a valid observation, reflecting rate of ceramic change rather than some subjective factor such as a predeliction for splitting or lumping on the part of the various archaeologists as they define and facet their ceramic complexes, clues may be present about the dynamics of historical developments in the Southen Maya Lowlands. On the one hand, the greater conservatism of the Peten in portrayals of the human figure in monumental stone sculpture comes to mind; sites on the peripheries tended, if not to break with, at least significantly to modify the long-established Peten sculptural tradition. The reverse of this may be that over much of the Late Classic Period, marginal sites had greater exposure to cultural influences originating outside the "core" or "Classic" tradition. How sustained and ramified such influences may have been is a problem that requires solution before possible non-Classic intrusions at the time of the collapse can be put in proper perspective.

Toward Establishing an Absolute Chronology (Fig. 6)

One must guard against reading too much into the visually satisfying, neatly tiered appearance of the ceramic complexes as these are presented in Figure 5. The need to scrutinize the chronological columns carefully, insofar as possible making explicit our reasons for assigning absolute dates to the ceramic complexes, has led to the preparation of Figure 6. In this chart, estimated maximum and minimum datings for most of the ceramic complexes are indicated. The earliest dates which

(*Continued on p. 52*)

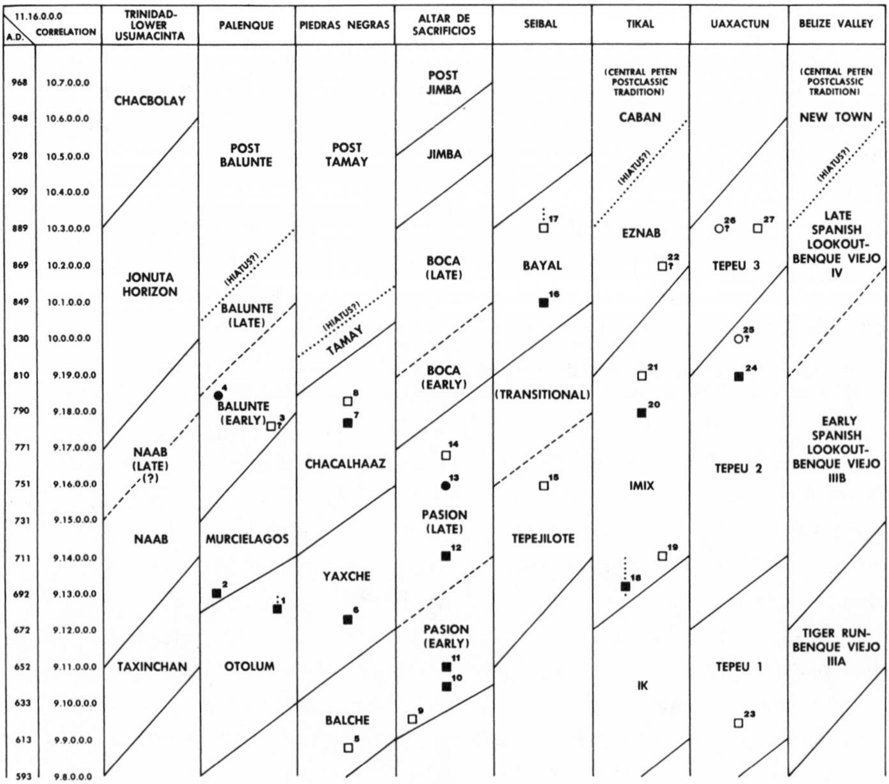

11.16.0.0.0 A.D. CORRELATION	TRINIDAD-LOWER USUMACINTA	PALENQUE	PIEDRAS NEGRAS	ALTAR DE SACRIFICIOS	SEIBAL	TIKAL	UAXACTUN	BELIZE VALLEY
968 — 10.7.0.0.0	CHACBOLAY			POST JIMBA		(CENTRAL PETEN POSTCLASSIC TRADITION)		(CENTRAL PETEN POSTCLASSIC TRADITION)
948 — 10.6.0.0.0						CABAN		NEW TOWN
928 — 10.5.0.0.0		POST BALUNTE	POST TAMAY	JIMBA		(HIATUS?)		(HIATUS?)
909 — 10.4.0.0.0								
889 — 10.3.0.0.0					□ 17	EZNAB	O? 26 □ 27	LATE SPANISH LOOKOUT-BENQUE VIEJO IV
869 — 10.2.0.0.0	JONUTA HORIZON	(HIATUS?)		BOCA (LATE)	BAYAL	□? 22	TEPEU 3	
849 — 10.1.0.0.0		BALUNTE (LATE)			■ 16			
830 — 10.0.0.0.0			TAMAY				O? 25	
810 — 9.19.0.0.0				BOCA (EARLY)		□ 21	■ 24	
790 — 9.18.0.0.0		● 4 BALUNTE (EARLY) □? 3	□ 8		(TRANSITIONAL)	■ 20		EARLY SPANISH LOOKOUT-BENQUE VIEJO IIIB
771 — 9.17.0.0.0	NAAB (LATE)		■ 7	CHACALHAAZ	□ 14		TEPEU 2	
751 — 9.16.0.0.0	-(?)				● 13	□ 15	IMIX	
731 — 9.15.0.0.0	NAAB	MURCIELAGOS		PASION (LATE)	TEPEJILOTE			
711 — 9.14.0.0.0					■ 12		□ 19	
692 — 9.13.0.0.0		■ 2	• 1	YAXCHE		■ 18		
672 — 9.12.0.0.0			■ 6	PASION (EARLY)				TIGER RUN-BENQUE VIEJO IIIA
652 — 9.11.0.0.0	TAXINCHAN	OTOLUM		■ 11		TEPEU 1		
633 — 9.10.0.0.0				■ 10	IK			
613 — 9.9.0.0.0		BALCHE	□ 9				□ 23	
593 — 9.8.0.0.0		□ 5						

■   Ceramic complex associated with dated monument
□   Ceramic complex inferentially associated with dated monument
●   Pottery vessel of known ceramic complex bears Maya date
O   Pottery vessel bears Maya date (date or ceramic complex in doubt)

FIGURE 6. CERAMIC COMPLEXES of the Late Classic and Late Classic Transition–Early Postclassic periods in the Southern Maya Lowlands, with estimated early and late beginning and terminal dates.

*   * .   *   *

Annotations to Figure 6

DD—Dedicatory date
SD—Style date (Proskouriakoff 1950; revised estimates by Proskouriakoff for Tikal in Coe, Shook, and Satterthwaite 1961)

Chronology

Palenque

1. Temple of the Inscriptions, tomb. DD: 9.13.0.0.0 (A.D. 692) (?). Sarcophagus 9.12.11.5.18 (A.D. 683). SD: 9.14.0.0.0 (A.D. 711)±2 *katuns*. Otolum Ceramic Complex (typologically late in complex). (Ruz Lhuillier 1955 : 83–90, 94, 103, pls. 8, 16, 17; Fuente 1965 : 41, 42, 124; Rands 1967a : Fig. 3*b, c*.)

2. Temple of the Foliated Cross, cache. DD: 9.13.0.0.0 (A.D. 692) (?). SD: 9.15.0.0.0 (A.D. 731)±2 *katuns*. Murcielagos Ceramic Complex. (Ruz Lhuillier 1958a : 88, pl. 23; Fuente 1965 : 41, 145; Rands 1967a, Fig. 3*d;* 1969 : Fig. 9*b*.)

3. Palace, Tablet of the 96 Glyphs. 9.17.13.0.7 (A.D. 783). Inferentially, Balunte Ceramic Complex (early facet) or possibly late in Murcielagos Complex. (Palacios 1937; Fuente 1965 : 42, 143.)

4. Vase bearing Initial Series inscription (Group III) (Fig. 9). 9.18.9.4.4 (A.D. 799). Balunte Ceramic Complex (early facet). (Ruz Lhuillier 1952d : 39–42, 45, Fig. 14; Fuente 1965 : 41.)

Piedras Negras

5. Stela 25 (Str. R-9). DD: 9.8.15.0.0 (A.D. 608) (?). The earliest stela at Piedras Negras, this monument inferentially equates with the Balche Ceramic Complex.

6. Stela 39. DD: 9.12.5.0.0 (A.D. 677). A Yaxche date is established for Stela 39, which is associated with Construction Period IV*c* of Str. K-5. R. E. Smith (1955 : 107) refers to the associated sherds as "the equivalent of Tepeu 1."

7. Throne 1 of Structure J-6. DD: 9.17.15.0.0 (A.D. 785). Chacalhaaz Ceramic Complex. This association is clearly established for Throne 1, which was set in a wall niche, the fill from the wall containing sherds of the Chacalhaaz Ceramic Complex.

8. Stela 12 (Str. O-13). DD: 9.18.5.0.0 (A.D. 795) (?). Apparently the latest dated monument at Piedras Negras, Stela 12, inferentially equates with the Chacalhaaz Ceramic Complex.

Altar de Sacrificios

9. Stela 9 (Str. A-I). DD: 9.9.15.0.0 (A.D. 628). Inferentially, Pasion Ceramic Complex (early facet). Stela 9, the latest sandstone monument, may relate to Pasion deposits in the latest sandstone construction within A-I. (Adams 1971 : 149–50.)

49

10. Stela 4 (Str. A-I). DD: 9.10.10.0.0 (A.D. 642). Pasion Ceramic Complex (early facet). Stela 4 is associated with limestone construction overlying Pasion deposits; hence early Pasion commences prior to 9.10.10.0.0 (A.D. 642). (Adams 1971 : 149–50.)

11. Stela 5 (Str. A-I). DD: 9.11.0.0.0 (A.D. 652). Pasion Ceramic Complex (early facet). See Note 10.

12. Stela 7 (Str. A-II). DD: 9.14.0.0.0 (A.D. 711). Pasion Ceramic Complex (late facet). Stela 7 is associated with fill of Str. A-II, the latest sherds of which are late Pasion. (Adams 1971 : 149–50.)

13. Altar Vase (Burial 96, Str. A-III). Probable Period Ending date of 9.16.0.0.0 (A.D. 751). Pasion Ceramic Complex (late facet), established by presence of other more diagnostic vessels in Burial 96 and the nearly contemporaneous Burial 128, as well as by fill covering both burials. (Adams 1971 : 69, 74–78, 149–50.)

14. Stela 15. 9.16.18.5.1 (A.D. 769). Inferentially, Pasion Ceramic Complex (late facet), on assumption that the latest monumental activity and large-scale construction dates from terminal Pasion. (Adams 1971 : 149–50.)

Seibal

15. Hieroglyphic Step (Str. A-1). DD: 9.16.0.0.0 (A.D. 751). Inferentially, Tepejilote Ceramic Complex. (Morley 1938, vol. 2 : 253–60; Graham 1971 : 152.)

16. Stelae 8, 9, 10, 11, 21 (Str. A-3). DD: 10.1.0.0.0 (A.D. 849). Bayal Ceramic Complex (latest pottery found in fill of A-3 belongs to Bayal). Calendar Round date on stucco frieze of Str. A-3, if a Period Ending date, reads 10.0.0.0.0 (A.D. 830). (Willey and Smith 1967a; Graham 1971 : 152.)

17. Stelae 20, 17, 18. Stela 20, DD: 10.3.0.0.0 (A.D. 889); Stelae 17 and 18, SD: ca. 10.3.5.0.0 (A.D. 894) or 10.3.10.0.0 (A.D. 899). Inferentially, Bayal Ceramic Complex, providing minimal dating for end of Bayal. (Adams 1971 : 151; Graham 1971 : 152.)

Tikal

18. Temple I, Burial 116. DD: (probable limits) 9.13.3.0.0–9.14.0.0.0 (A.D. 695–711). SD: (revised Proskouriakoff estimates) 9.17.10.0.0 (A.D. 780)±2 *katuns*, 9.16.0.0.0 (A.D. 751)±2 *katuns*. Radiocarbon dating (average of 5 beams): A.D. 684±37. Estimated closing

of tomb: between 9.13.0.0.0 (A.D. 692) and 9.14.0.0.0 (A.D. 711), probably by 9.13.15.0.0 (A.D. 707). Imix Ceramic Complex. (Coe, Shook, and Satterthwaite 1961 : 64, 70–71, 81; Satterthwaite and Ralph 1960 : 176–83; Satterthwaite 1964 : 207; W. Coe 1967 : 28–36.)

19. Stela 16, Stela P 49, Altar P 41 (Twin Pyramid Complex N). DD of Stela 16: 9.14.0.0.0 (A.D. 711). Inferentially, Imix Ceramic Complex, as cache pattern has been encountered only in Tepeu 2–related structures at Tikal (W. Coe 1963 : 55) and at Uaxactun (Smith 1950 : 34, 87, 103). The Stela 16 (Tikal) cache was of major importance in establishing a minimal dating for Tepeu 2 at Uaxactun (Smith 1955 : 107).

20. Stela 19 (Twin Pyramid Complex R). DD: 9.18.0.0.0 (A.D. 790). Imix Ceramic Complex (latest sherds in fill). (Satterthwaite 1958b : 99–102; Culbert, chapter 5 : 89.)

21. Temple III. SD of Lintel 2: 9.19.0.0.0 (A.D. 810) ± 2½ *katuns*. DD of Stela 24: 9.19.0.0.0 (A.D. 810) (?). Suspected to be latest of the Great Pyramids of Tikal. Inferentially, Imix Ceramic Complex—if so, provides the earliest possible dating for Eznab. (Coe, Shook, and Satterthwaite 1961 : 76–77; W. Coe 1965a : 44; Culbert, chapter 5 : 73.)

22. Stela and Altar 11 (Great Plaza). DD: 10.2.0.0.0 (A.D. 869). Typical cache pattern and other Classic features could indicate a date equivalent to late Imix (W. Coe 1962 : 487, 1965a : 53), although Culbert believes the Eznab Ceramic Complex to have already been extant (Culbert, chapter 5 : 89).

Uaxactun

23. Stela 6, associated with construction covering the Tepeu 1 burial, A23. Stela 6 possibly dated 9.9.6.2.3 (A.D. 619). SD: Early Classic? Inferentially, early Tepeu 1. (Smith 1950 : 26, 86–87, 96; Smith 1955 : 106–7.)

24. Stela 7 (Str. A-I). DD: 9.19.0.0.0 (A.D. 810). Tepeu 2, probably near close of the phase. (Smith 1955 : 107).

25. Vase, Burial A48 (Str. A-V). The stucco-painted cylindrical vase with ring-stand base is possibly dated 10.0.0.0.0 (A.D. 830). Burial also contains a Zacatel Cream–polychrome (Tepeu 2) vessel. (Smith 1950 : 40, 87, 99; Smith 1955 : 107, Figs. 1*h*, *i*, 11*a*, 43*b*, *13*.)

26. Fragmentary vessel (Str. A-V). Apparently bears a 10.3.0.0.0 (A.D. 889) date, although the sherd was found in a Tepeu 2 ceramic

level and is Zacatel Cream–polychrome type (Tepeu 2). (Smith 1955 : 107–8, Fig. 20.)

27. Stela 12 (Str. A-II). DD: 10.3.0.0.0 (A.D. 889). Latest dated monument at site, inferentially Tepeu 3. A. L. Smith (1950 : 48, 87) notes that Str. A-II appears to have been under construction after erection of Stela 12; R. E. Smith (1955 : 106) closes Tepeu 3 at 10.3.0.0.0 (A.D. 889).

* * * *

seem reasonable for the beginning and the end of a given complex appear on the left-hand side of the column; the latest plausible dates for commencing and terminating the complex are shown on the right. The extremely early and late dates given for the start of the complex are connected by a slanting line. A second diagonal line, more or less parallel to and above the first, connects the early and late terminal dates as suggested for the complex.

The early and late datings that have been indicated for beginning and ending the ceramic complexes are conditioned by a number of factors, some of which are discussed below. It would be a mistake, however, to ignore the arbitrary and subjective elements still present. In the absence of supporting data through more or less direct ceramic associations with the Maya Long Count, a span of three *katuns*—60 years —has generally been used to express the uncertainty as to both beginning and ending dates. Assignment of these ± 30-year datings is especially apparent in the Trinidad–Lower Usumacinta Valley and in the Belize Valley of British Honduras (extreme left and right columns in Fig. 6). Here, on the western and eastern peripheries of the Southern Maya Lowlands, dated monuments to which ceramic complexes might be linked are essentially absent. At the larger, more centrally located ceremonial centers, however, such ceramic linkages with dates in the Maya calendar have been achieved; and as a result the "play" between the termination of one ceramic complex and the beginning of the following complex has been reduced to as little as one and one-half *katun* (30 years). A two-*katun* (40-year) spread is more usual.

This may be looked at in another way. In addition to lack of direct associations between ceramic deposits and dated monuments, uncertainties shown by the slanting lines are expressions of a variety of problems familiar to the archaeologist. Among these problems are transitional interfingering between ceramic complexes, inadequate sampling, and difficulties in establishing firm cross-ties between sites, together with the possibility that sloping intersite horizons may occur. Also, although a consensus was reached by most contributors to the book in regard to general problems of chronology, uncertainties do remain in reconciling differing interpretations of the archaeological record. Some compromises had to be effected. In general, however, the ceramist who has published or is now preparing a particular site report bore the primary responsibility for dating the ceramic complexes at his site, as given in Figure 5. I prepared Figures 6–8 on the basis of discussions with other authors and published reports; the charts have been checked and amended by the other authors. Clearly, however, some hard choices occasionally had to be made in all the charts, and precisely where the lines were drawn is my responsibility.

As well as indicating upper and lower limits for the ceramic complexes, Figure 6 attempts to convey the rationale for dating the complexes in absolute terms. By means of one of the symbols explained in the legend to Figure 6, monumental constructions are indicated that are associated, on the one hand, with Maya sculptured dates and, on the other, with deposits of pottery that are identifiable as to ceramic complex. The pottery may occur as burial furnishings, caches, or as masonry fill. In the latter case, should more than a single ceramic complex be represented in the fill, the latest identifiable complex is considered to approximate the dedicatory date associated with the structure. In other words, an association has been at least provisionally established between a Maya Long Count date and a given ceramic complex, though the weight of the evidence varies somewhat according to the particular circumstances. Rarely, an even more direct association occurs between pottery and a Maya date, as exemplified by the carved Initial Series inscription on the vessel from Palenque shown in Figure 9. The general unreliability of dates painted on Maya pottery is notorious (J. E. S. Thompson 1962 : 14–18), although the evidence afforded by glyph-bearing pottery is occasionally significant, being indicated in Figure 6. Indirect associations between pottery and dated monuments are sometimes of value in deducing dates for a ceramic complex. A familiar argument runs as follows: inasmuch as pottery of the latest stratigraphically established Classic complex at a particular site has never been found to be associated with Postclassic activities, the latest dated stela associated with major architectural construction at the site must have been dedicated at a time when this Terminal Classic ceramic complex was still in existence. The earliest possible date for the Maya collapse and for Postclassic ceramics at the site is likewise provided.

Inspection of Figure 6 and its annotations provides a framework for several generalizations, as well as pointing to lacunae in our information.

To begin with, it should be noted that the Uaxactun sequence—which still serves as a basic reference point for Lowland Maya ceramic studies—provides only a single solid Late Classic association of a dated monument with a ceramic complex. Stela 7 bears the date 9.19.0.0.0 (A.D. 810) and is firmly fixed to Tepeu 2 ceramics (Note 24).[3] This is a strategic date for understanding what was happening close to the time of the Classic Maya collapse. However, it is a tribute to the perception of Robert E. Smith and A. Ledyard Smith that they were able to maximize available information, such as that provided by architectural sequences at Uaxactun and comparisons to datable ceramics at other sites. As a result they worked out an absolute chronology that remains viable today. To be sure, a number of problems are still unresolved at Uaxactun. Certain uncomfortably late dates appear on Tepeu 2 pottery or on pottery occurring in Tepeu 2 contexts (Notes 25, 26). R. E. Smith (1955) did not worry greatly about these, and probably rightly so; the frequent unreliability of glyphic texts painted on pottery has been alluded to above. Stela 12 (10.3.0.0.0, A.D. 889; Note 27), if indeed dedicated before work was completed on Structure A-II, marks a time prior to some sort of collapse in organized public architectural activities at the site (A. L. Smith 1950 : 48).

At Tikal, the beginnings of the Imix Ceramic Complex are well dated (Note 18), and this complex is shown to be present as late as 9.18.0.0.0 (A.D. 790; Stela 19, Note 20). Thereafter, judgment becomes deductive: how much "Classicism" need be expressed to be sure that Imix has not come to an end? The controversial nature of the evidence is apparent in the ways in which the latest dated monument at the site, Stela 11, has been regarded (10.2.0.0.0, A.D. 869; Note 22). The Classic formality of the monument, combined with the presence of a typically Classic cache pattern, suggests the continuation of hierarchical culture, although Culbert inclines to the belief that the Eznab Ceramic Complex was already in existence. The Imix-Eznab dividing line is shown in Figure 6 from as early as Temple III, with a possible 9.19.0.0.0 (A.D.

810) dating (Note 21), to as late as Stela 11. In Figure 5 the shift is indicated as taking place at 10.0.0.0.0 (A.D. 830).

Direct association of a ceramic complex with dated monuments does not occur until exceptionally late times at Seibal, but at 10.1.0.0.0 (A.D. 849) the Bayal Complex is firmly tied to the Maya calendar (Note 16). Four stelae bearing this dedicatory date were placed, one to a side, at the foot of Structure A-3; and a fifth stela, bearing the same date, was found in the central room of the temple. The stucco frieze of A-3 bears a Calendar Round date which may reach 10.0.0.0.0 (A.D. 830). The latest pottery found in the fill of the structure belongs to the Bayal Ceramic Complex. Certain of the stucco heads adorning the building resemble Fine Orange Ware figurines of the Bayal and, at Altar de Sacrificios, Jimba complexes. Numerous motifs which appear on Seibal stelae, including some of those associated with Structure A-3, also characterize the Pabellon Modeled-carved type of Fine Orange Ware (see Willey and Smith 1967a; Sabloff 1970). The evidence for placing the beginning of the Bayal Ceramic Complex at Seibal no later than 10.1.0.0.0 (A.D. 849) is incontrovertible. Stela 20, the latest securely dated monument at the site, and Stelae 17 and 18, which are placed slightly later on stylistic grounds, provide a minimal ending date for the complex from approximately 10.3.0.0.0 (A.D. 889) to 10.3.10.0.0 (A.D. 899; Note 17).

Altar de Sacrificios, during much of the Pasion Ceramic Complex, provides an exceptionally well documented series of associations between dated monuments and pottery (Notes 10–13). But as we move toward the critical closing *katuns* of Baktun 9, the monumental record comes to an end. Although Terminal Classic–transitional Postclassic ceramic developments are exceptionally well represented, it is necessary to turn to Seibal to obtain approximate Long Count datings. This is justified because of close correspondences between the Boca and Bayal ceramic complexes.

Two direct associations of dated monuments with ceramic complexes, Yaxche and Chacalhaaz, are available at Piedras Negras. The latter association, provided by Throne 1 at 9.17.15.0.0 (A.D. 785; Note 7), is germane to problems of dating the Classic collapse. Soon afterward, at 9.18.5.0.0 (A.D. 795), the latest surely dated monument at the site was dedicated (Note 8). Although direct ceramic associations are lacking, this superb sculpture, Stela 12, should equate with the

Chacalhaaz Ceramic Complex and may have been erected only a short time before the disruption of elite culture at the site. If so, Piedras Negras provides one of our best dated cases of abrupt and early decline from the heights of Classicism to virtual depopulation. Nevertheless, Proskouriakoff (1960 : 460) notes that six undated sculptures may serve to extend the record of monumental activity at the site to as late as 9.19.15.0.0 (A.D. 825). This possibility has been allowed for in Figure 6 by the slanting lines that separate the Chacalhaaz and Tamay ceramic complexes, although in Figure 5 Tamay is shown as commencing at 9.19.0.0.0 (A.D. 810).

At Palenque, despite the intricacies of the lengthy temple texts, one of the firmest dividing lines in the Maya area is established for terminal and beginning dates of sequent ceramic complexes. This line occurs at ca. 9.13.0.0.0 (A.D. 692), being provided by the Inscriptions tomb and Foliated Cross cache (Otolum and Murcielagos ceramic complexes, respectively; Notes 1, 2). The latest stone sculpture known at the site (9.17.13.0.7, A.D. 783; Note 3) is believed to equate in time with the Balunte Ceramic Complex. At least, some 15 years later the early facet of Balunte was in existence, as indicated by the Initial Series date of 9.18.9.4.4 (A.D. 799) carved on a fine paste blackware vessel (Fig. 9; Note 4).

The Classic Maya Polychrome and the Fine Paste Traditions (Figs. 7, 8)

Summary descriptions of the various ceramic complexes are beyond the scope of the present chapter. An overview of comparative chronological developments in two traditions should prove useful, however, and is attempted in Figures 7 and 8. One of these, the Classic Maya Polychrome tradition, has deep roots going back into the Early Classic and Protoclassic periods. In the Terminal Late Classic, however, polychrome pottery underwent a decline, qualitatively and quantitatively. At some sites the tradition continued for a time, though with greatly reduced vigor; at other sites it suffered a rapid extinction. The second tradition to be considered is that of Maya Fine Paste ceramics. In contradistinction to polychrome, fine paste pottery rarely occurred at most sites in the Southern Maya Lowlands until advanced Late Classic times. Its appearance generally seems intrusive; for, in addition to the absence of temper, fine paste pottery tends to be monochrome, to lack the characteristic slip of the Classic Gloss Wares, and often to have design and shape repertories that fall outside the norms of Classic Maya ceramics.

Considerable variation nevertheless exists within both the polychrome and fine paste traditions, as known in the Late Classic developments at sites discussed by conference participants. By means of distinct hachured symbols, Figure 7 shows those ceramic complexes in which polychrome pottery was of major or minor importance. The ab-

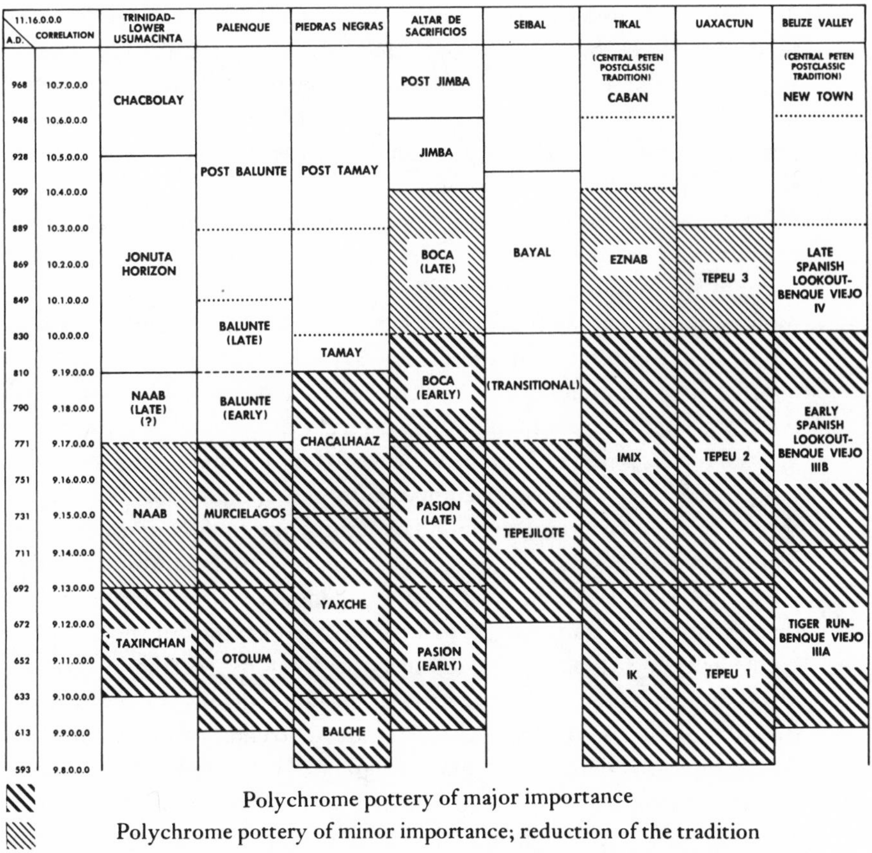

11.16.0.0.0 A.D. CORRELATION		TRINIDAD-LOWER USUMACINTA	PALENQUE	PIEDRAS NEGRAS	ALTAR DE SACRIFICIOS	SEIBAL	TIKAL	UAXACTUN	BELIZE VALLEY
968	10.7.0.0.0	CHACBOLAY			POST JIMBA		(CENTRAL PETEN POSTCLASSIC TRADITION) CABAN		(CENTRAL PETEN POSTCLASSIC TRADITION) NEW TOWN
948	10.6.0.0.0								
928	10.5.0.0.0	POST BALUNTE	POST TAMAY		JIMBA				
909	10.4.0.0.0								
889	10.3.0.0.0	JONUTA HORIZON			BOCA (LATE)	BAYAL	EZNAB		LATE SPANISH LOOKOUT-BENQUE VIEJO IV
869	10.2.0.0.0							TEPEU 3	
849	10.1.0.0.0								
830	10.0.0.0.0	BALUNTE (LATE)		TAMAY					
810	9.19.0.0.0				BOCA (EARLY)	(TRANSITIONAL)			EARLY SPANISH LOOKOUT-BENQUE VIEJO IIIB
790	9.18.0.0.0	NAAB (LATE)(?)	BALUNTE (EARLY)						
771	9.17.0.0.0			CHACALHAAZ			IMIX	TEPEU 2	
751	9.16.0.0.0								
731	9.15.0.0.0	NAAB	MURCIELAGOS		PASION (LATE)				
711	9.14.0.0.0					TEPEJILOTE			
692	9.13.0.0.0								
672	9.12.0.0.0	TAXINCHAN		YAXCHE					TIGER RUN-BENQUE VIEJO IIIA
652	9.11.0.0.0		OTOLUM		PASION (EARLY)		IK	TEPEU 1	
633	9.10.0.0.0								
613	9.9.0.0.0			BALCHE					
593	9.8.0.0.0								

⧅ Polychrome pottery of major importance

⧄ Polychrome pottery of minor importance; reduction of the tradition

FIGURE 7. THE CLASSIC MAYA POLYCHROME TRADITION in the Southern Maya Lowlands, with estimated dates for the Late Classic and Late Classic Transition–Early Postclassic periods.

sence or near absence of polychrome is also indicated. Inasmuch as the Late Classic ceramic complexes characterized by polychrome of "minor" importance succeeded complexes in which the tradition was more strongly entrenched, we are dealing, historically, with a process of reduction and decline. If the decline was on only a modest scale, for example in attention to aesthetic detail but without marked quantitative loss in the amount of polychrome pottery, the ceramic complex is considered still to have a strongly established polychrome tradition. Arbitrary judgments cannot be totally avoided. At Palenque, where Otolum Complex polychromes were locally produced but those of the Murcielagos Complex largely imported, a certain quantitative loss may be detected; yet, because technical and aesthetic standards seem not to have been lowered, no significant decline of the polychrome tradition is indicated. As one compares polychromes of Palenque with the Peten, however, it may be questioned whether at any time this tradition was actually of "major" importance at Palenque.[4]

Two levels in intensity of development within the fine paste tradition are indicated in Figure 8 by stippled symbols. These may be thought of, in approximate terms, as "rare to appreciable" and "common to abundant" within a given ceramic complex. Again, it has been impossible completely to avoid arbitrary assignments to one level or another. For example, if the Taman Paste Variant should prove to fall within the range of untempered pottery—or if, as Culbert (chapter 5) characterizes it, Taman may be "a local approximation to a fine paste ideal"—the Eznab Ceramic Complex might possibly be assigned to the "common to abundant" category of fine paste development. The emphasis accorded fine paste pottery by Sabloff in the Bayal Ceramic Complex of Seibal (chapter 7) indicates greater importance than Adams appears to suggest for fine paste materials in the generally equivalent Boca Complex (late facet) of Altar de Sacrificios (chapter 8). Many problems clearly remain to be worked out, but Figure 8 is thought to be useful as a general guide to trends through time and space. Horizontal bands of undulating lines also appear in Figure 8, serving to indicate within a 20-year period the time at which Fine Orange Ware of the Balancan (Z) or Altar (Y) ceramic groups is believed first to have appeared at the various sites. The most securely dated initial occurrence, by at least 10.1.0.0.0 (A.D. 849), is clearly in the Bayal Complex of Seibal, as discussed above (Note 16, Fig. 6). The

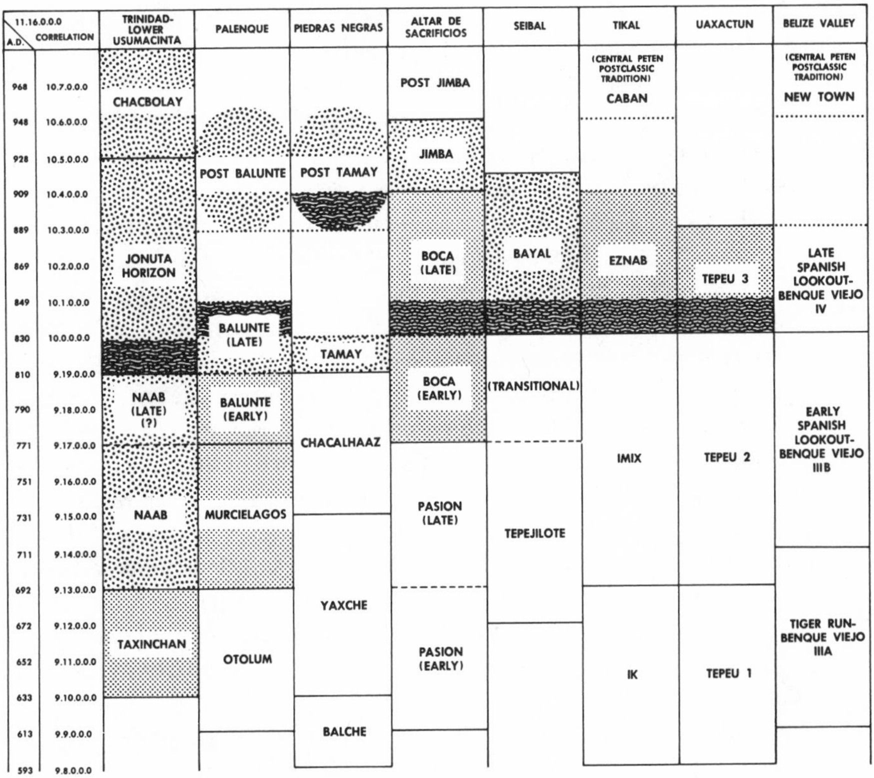

11.16.0.0.0 A.D. CORRELATION	TRINIDAD-LOWER USUMACINTA	PALENQUE	PIEDRAS NEGRAS	ALTAR DE SACRIFICIOS	SEIBAL	TIKAL	UAXACTUN	BELIZE VALLEY
968 — 10.7.0.0.0	CHACBOLAY			POST JIMBA		(CENTRAL PETEN POSTCLASSIC TRADITION) CABAN		(CENTRAL PETEN POSTCLASSIC TRADITION) NEW TOWN
948 — 10.6.0.0.0								
928 — 10.5.0.0.0		POST BALUNTE	POST TAMAY	JIMBA				
909 — 10.4.0.0.0								
889 — 10.3.0.0.0								
869 — 10.2.0.0.0	JONUTA HORIZON			BOCA (LATE)	BAYAL	EZNAB		LATE SPANISH LOOKOUT-BENQUE VIEJO IV
849 — 10.1.0.0.0							TEPEU 3	
830 — 10.0.0.0.0		BALUNTE (LATE)	TAMAY					
810 — 9.19.0.0.0	NAAB (LATE) (?)			BOCA (EARLY)	(TRANSITIONAL)			
790 — 9.18.0.0.0		BALUNTE (EARLY)						EARLY SPANISH LOOKOUT-BENQUE VIEJO IIIB
771 — 9.17.0.0.0			CHACALHAAZ			IMIX	TEPEU 2	
751 — 9.16.0.0.0								
731 — 9.15.0.0.0	NAAB	MURCIELAGOS		PASION (LATE)	TEPEJILOTE			
711 — 9.14.0.0.0								
692 — 9.13.0.0.0			YAXCHE					
672 — 9.12.0.0.0						IK	TEPEU 1	TIGER RUN-BENQUE VIEJO IIIA
652 — 9.11.0.0.0	TAXINCHAN	OTOLUM		PASION (EARLY)				
633 — 9.10.0.0.0								
613 — 9.9.0.0.0			BALCHE					
593 — 9.8.0.0.0								

Fine Paste ceramics common to abundant

Fine Paste ceramics rare to appreciable

Estimated initial appearance of Fine Orange Ware of the Altar and Balancan Ceramic Groups

FIGURE 8. THE FINE PASTE TRADITION in the Southern Maya Lowlands, with estimated dates for the Late Classic and Late Classic Transition–Early Postclassic periods.

general feeling that Fine Orange Ware has its homeland toward the Gulf Coast has led to placing the Balancan-Altar beginnings in the Jonuta horizon at a time slightly prior to the introduction at Seibal.

Polychrome pottery, epitomizing the Classic tradition in Lowland Maya ceramics, has its strongest development toward the eastern (right-hand) side of Figure 7, tending to die out somewhat sooner in the far west. Inspection of the chart also reveals a tendency for the tra-

59

dition to survive in attenuated form at certain of the more centrally located sites. Although the ceramic complexes are by no means of comparable content, Eznab, at Tikal (ca. 10.0.0.0.0–10.4.0.0.0, A.D. 830–909) seems to have experienced much of the same reduction in polychrome that occurred almost a century and a half earlier in the Naab Complex of Trinidad (ca. 9.13.0.0.0–9.17.0.0.0, A.D. 692–771). As the Central Peten Postclassic Tradition shows strong stylistic discontinuities with Classic ceramics, the existence of Ixpop or related polychromes in the New Town and Caban complexes is not indicated in Figure 7. These polychromes would, at best, appear to be of minor importance in times covered by the chart.

The pattern of developments in fine paste pottery is even more striking (Fig. 8). This tradition, foreign to the mainstream of Classic Maya ceramic history, has a long and sustained history in the far west but fingers into the Peten on successively later horizons, never really penetrating the Belize Valley on the east. The growing strength of the tradition is observed at various sites (Trinidad, Palenque, Altar de Sacrificios). At Trinidad and Palenque, early fine paste pottery is frequently polychrome (Taxinchan and Murcielagos ceramic complexes). Fine paste monochromes are established at Trinidad early in the Naab Complex (cream) and at Palenque in Balunte (cream, black, gray) and are known, although rarely, in the early facet of the Boca Complex (black-slipped fine gray). The Tamay Complex witnesses the sudden introduction of abundant fine paste pottery, stylistically affiliated with Fine Gray Ware of late Naab and the Jonuta horizon, apparently just after a sharp reduction occurred in the polychrome tradition at Piedras Negras. All of these developments take place before the significant appearance of Fine Orange Ware in the local sequences. At about the same time, the late facet of Balunte at Palenque is characterized by the growing importance of fine paste pottery, now largely Fine Gray Ware, and by the appearance, in small quantities, of Fine Orange Ware. On approximately the same temporal level, at the beginning of the relatively long Bayal Complex of Seibal, Fine Orange Ware, of the Altar Ceramic Group, makes a sudden appearance; and in a less dramatic way this appears to be true of nearly contemporaneous developments at Altar de Sacrificios, Tikal, and Uaxactun. Outside of the far west, the fine paste tradition climaxes in the Jimba Complex of Altar de Sacrificios.

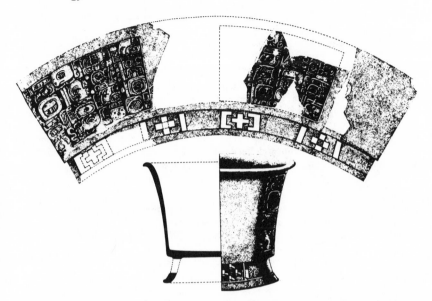

FIGURE 9. CARVED FINE PASTE BLACKWARE VESSEL, bearing 9.18.9.4.4 inscription (A.D. 799). Palenque, Balunte Ceramic Complex (early facet). Approximate scale 1:4 (see Fig. 6, Note 4).

Figures 7 and 8 should be viewed in juxtaposition. They make apparent the waxing of the Maya Fine Paste tradition, at the expense of Classic Maya Polychrome, as well as the importance of the former in the west from beginning Late Classic times. The stippled conventions in Figure 8 might be regarded as a textbook model of age-area theory. However, cutting sharply across the fine paste dispersal, on a remarkably synchronous horizon, is the introduction of the Altar and Balancan ceramic groups of Fine Orange Ware.[5] Over most of the region this ware clearly appears intrusive, as does the Fine Gray–affiliated pottery of Piedras Negras. Taken in conjunction with the more or less contemporaneous decline or displacement of the polychromes, some relationship between these intrusions and the Classic collapse, causal or otherwise, appears inescapable.

NOTES

1. Principal publications relating to the ceramic sequences discussed in the present chapter are: Trinidad–Lower Usumacinta: Berlin 1956; Rands 1969b. Pal-

enque: Rands and Rands 1957; Rands 1967a. Piedras Negras: Butler 1935. Altar de Sacrificios: Adams 1971. Seibal: Sabloff 1970. Tikal: Culbert 1963; W. Coe 1965a. Uaxactun: Smith 1955. Central Peten Postclassic Tradition: Bullard 1970b. Belize Valley: Thompson 1940; Willey, Bullard, Glass, and Gifford 1965.

2. It should be noted that R. E. Smith was not present at the Santa Fe conference, although Uaxactun has been included in the chronological charts and conference discussions because of its primary role in understanding Lowland Maya ceramic chronology. Also, J. C. Gifford, now preparing the final report on Barton Ramie pottery, did not attend the conference; Willey handled the Barton Ramie–Belize Valley material. Ceramic sequences from the Yucatan Peninsula, at the sites of Dzibilchaltun and Becan, were reported on by Andrews but have not been included in the present chapter (see chapter 12).

3. The "Notes" referred to herein are annotations following Figure 6, pp. 48 to 52.

4. Excessive weathering obfuscates evaluation of the polychrome tradition at Palenque. By standards of most of the Southern Maya Lowlands, however, it would be a strange tomb that, so richly stocked with jade, stucco work, and sculpture as was that of the Temple of the Inscriptions, contained, out of five vessels, only one polychrome vessel in its burial furniture.

5. Assignment of the introduction of the Balancan or Altar groups of Fine Orange Ware to the interval between 10.0.0.0.0 (A.D. 830) and 10.1.0.0.0 (A.D. 849) in five of the sequences may be a little too pat; we are straining at the boundaries of our knowledge when dealing with an interval as short as 20 years. Except at Palenque, the Fine Orange serves as a marker to commence a new ceramic complex, and we cannot be sure that certain diagnostics of the new complex had not already made an appearance. The problem is crucial in understanding the Classic collapse and clearly requires intensive investigation. Nevertheless, this shortcoming should not obscure the apparent rapidity of the spread of Fine Orange Altar and Fine Orange Balancan out of their presumed Gulf Coast homeland.

5
The Maya Downfall at Tikal[1]

T. PATRICK CULBERT

Department of Anthropology
University of Arizona

Tikal, both in location and in the size and vigor of its population and ceremonial development, typifies the Classic stage of Maya Lowland civilization. Located near the center of the Peten district of Guatemala, Tikal lies within a zone of tropical forest, and its populace must have been subject to all the problems posed by such an environment. The main ceremonial precincts of the site occupy a high ridge with small structures and outlying ceremonial groups distributed on neighboring lower eminences. The site is delimited by the large Bajo de Santa Fe on the east and a series of unnamed but extensive *bajos* to the west. There are no such natural barriers to residence on the north and south, but large earthworks provide convenient, and probably meaningful, boundaries (Puleston and Callendar 1967). So delimited, the Tikal Zone covers an area of 123 sq. km. of which a core area of 63 sq. km. demonstrates a considerably higher population density than the surrounding 60 sq. km. (Haviland 1970).

Occupation at Tikal began with the Eb Ceramic Complex, tentatively dated at 700–500 B.C. After the initial occupation, population steadily increased to a maximum reached during the Late Classic Period. Haviland (1965) has provided a conservative estimate of 10,000–11,000 as the peak population of the fully mapped 16 sq. km. area at the center of the site, and has more recently (1970) advanced an estimate of 39,000 inhabitants for the area of 63 sq. km. defined as a central zone. Ceramic distribution suggests both a spurt of population and an increasingly urban nature at the site in the early part of the Late Classic, followed by a drastic population decline at the time of collapse.

Tikal was established as a major ceremonial center by the time of the Late Preclassic Cauac Complex (150 B.C.–A.D. 200) and the archaeological data indicate continuity in religious patterns for more than a millennium thereafter (W. Coe 1962, 1965a). Whether or not Tikal was ever truly urban (Sanders and Price 1968; Haviland 1970), the site certainly fulfilled ceremonial functions for a large population, and immense sums of energy and resources were expended for religious structures and accouterments. The entire enterprise was directed by an elite class with important ceremonial roles whose existence is amply attested by iconography and burials.

As Tikal typifies the height of Maya Classic development, its pattern of decline fits the most dramatic reconstructions of the Maya downfall. The activities associated with elite ceremonialism came to a spectacular, and perhaps sudden, halt at the end of the Imix Ceramic Complex. The cessation of the stela cult and ceremonial construction, the drastic decline of population followed by eventual abandonment, the failure of systems of maintenance and sanitation, and the appearance of ceremonial activities that attempt, but fail miserably, to follow Classic practices, all give evidence of a cultural disintegration of major proportions.

The Tikal Project was fortunate in the early recognition and careful excavation of contexts bearing upon the downfall problem. The question of abnormal stelae settings arose during preliminary investigations at the site, and a series of examples of abnormal settings has been explored (Satterthwaite 1958a; Coe and Broman 1958; W. Coe 1962). The thorough study of room and surface debris and terminal activities in temples in the site center has already been published in part (Shook

1958; Adams and Trik 1961), and abundant additional data are available. More recently, Harrison's (1970) extensive excavations in the Central Acropolis have tapped what was probably the largest late settlement at the site. Outside of the 16 sq. km. area at the heart of the site to which most archaeological activity has been confined, the Sustaining Area Project under the direction of William Haviland and Dennis Puleston has provided information (Haviland et al. 1968; Fry 1969) to check the validity of inferences for outlying areas.

The lack of absolute dating control for the late time periods has necessitated a reliance on the ceramic chronology for the sequencing of events throughout much of the downfall period. The pertinent ceramic complexes are the Ik, Imix, Eznab, and Caban complexes. Ik, the earliest of the Late Classic complexes, terminated well before the start of the decline and is relevant only through its association with changes that led to the splendor that preceded the fall. The Imix Complex, associated with the Late Classic population and construction peak, probably persisted into the collapse period, but my inability to discover widely applicable criteria for temporal subdivision of the complex has handicapped our ability to deal with the temporal rate of decline processes. The succeeding Eznab Complex shows a clear continuity with Imix but fortunately includes a number of common and distinctive markers that make identification easy. Eznab is invariably associated with situations of cultural impoverishment. The final complex in the Tikal ceramic sequence, the Caban Complex, is poorly defined because of a paucity of collections. Nevertheless, it clearly represents a break with previous ceramic traditions and probably was associated with an intrusive population element that arrived after the end of Eznab.

An understanding of events at Tikal is critical for a general interpretation of the Classic Maya collapse. The sheer size of the site in terms of areal extent, monumental architecture, and estimated population must have placed it, together with a few other massive centers like Yaxchilan, Palenque, Copan, and Mirador, in a preeminent position in the Southern Maya Lowlands. Furthermore, Tikal lies in a part of the Peten that seems to have had an unusually dense population and a strong development of large ceremonial centers throughout the Classic Period.

Although the magnitude and importance of Tikal are undeniable, the degree to which the site dominated the regional organization of the

65

Maya Lowlands is still open to question. One possible viewpoint is that all the Classic Maya sites had the same level and kind of organization and that Tikal was no more than *primus inter pares*. A reconstruction of Maya political organization as consisting of semiautonomous city-states would be most compatible with this viewpoint.

An alternative viewpoint is that Tikal and the other very large Maya Lowland sites (we came during the seminar to refer to them as "super-sites") had reached a magnitude at which they had begun to demonstrate principles of organization different from those common throughout the rest of the region. In subsistence, these super-sites may have been partly dependent upon importation of foodstuffs from neighboring zones of less dense population. Economically, they could have been the organizing force behind large-scale trade networks, and, politically, they may even have been the centers of regional states.

When I arrived at the Santa Fe seminar, I distinctly favored the view that political units in the Maya Lowlands were relatively equivalent in terms of organizational principles. During the deliberations, however, I became more and more impressed by disjunctions between Tikal and the smaller sites discussed. The gap between an estimated population of 39,000 for Tikal and 10,000 for Seibal; the fact that obsidian abounds at Tikal and is scarce at Altar de Sacrificios, much closer to potential sources; my feeling that lower class standards of living continued to rise at Tikal until the period of collapse, compared to a feeling of several others that peasant living became increasingly impoverished in the Late Classic—all these things suggest that Tikal and/or the densely populated Central Peten Zone may have begun to differ fundamentally in character from other zones. Certainly, the question of the nature of regional organization in the period preceding the Maya collapse is fundamental to reconstruction of the disintegrative processes.

A second factor that makes the Tikal data critical to the general question of the collapse is the location of the site in the center of the Southern Lowlands. This location must have been disadvantageous in terms of access to external resources but would have provided considerable security in relation to military threats from outside the lowlands. The dense population and presumably delicate organization of the Central Zone would have made that area particularly vulnerable to internal disruption of either ecological or social origin. As long as the internal organization continued to function smoothly, however, this zone should have been the most difficult in the lowlands to disrupt by external force.

Finally, Tikal is interesting because of its proximity to the thoroughly investigated and much smaller site of Uaxactun (Wauchope 1934; Ricketson and Ricketson 1937; A. L. Smith 1937, 1950; R. E. Smith 1937, 1955; Kidder 1947). The juxtaposition of two sites of different size only 24 km. apart offers a possibility of testing a number of hypotheses about social processes.

DEMOGRAPHY

The change in size and distribution of population between the Imix and Eznab periods is perhaps the most striking feature of the downfall at Tikal. The site is literally covered with Imix pottery, almost everywhere in quantities large enough to indicate actual occupation. Haviland (1965 : 19) estimates that 95 percent of the 1,800 small structures on the site map (Carr and Hazard 1961) were used in Imix times and general excavation results suggest a comparable percentage of use for the 800 "ceremonial-elite" structures.

On the other hand, it has proved no problem to summarize in Table 1 all excavations that produced Eznab pottery in quantities sufficient to suggest occupation. In preparing the summary, I have used the term "location" to refer to a series of contiguous structures either spatially or architecturally separated from other such groupings. The Central Acropolis, for example, is considered to be a single location, as are the more isolated series of structures called "groups" in standard Tikal nomenclature. Large accumulations of Eznab pottery were encountered in only 14 locations. This compares to more than 200 locations that show comparable amounts of Imix pottery.

Inspection of Table 1 indicates that the heaviest concentration of Eznab population was in areas adjacent to the Great Plaza. Not only are three of the fourteen locations in these areas, but also the number of structures and number of rooms involved is greater than anywhere else at the site. The structures showing evidence of occupation are range structures either of the multiroom type frequently termed "palaces" or of a type with nine doorways and a single long chamber. Although probably of ceremonial function during Ik and Imix times,

TABLE 1

LOCATIONS OF LARGE EZNAB CERAMIC DEPOSITS
AT TIKAL

Location Number	Location on Tikal Site Map	Number of Structures Involved	Type of Structure(s) Involved
I	Central Acropolis	9–11	Range type, 9-doorway type
2	East Plaza	7–8	Range type, 9-doorway type
3	West Plaza	1	9-doorway type
4	Strs. 6E-142 to -152	4	Range type, pyramid
5	Strs. 7F-29, 7F-32	2	Range type
6	Str. 2C-15	1	Range type
7	Strs. 3C-60, 3C-62	2?	Range type
8	Str. 5C-15	1	9-doorway type (Twin Pyramid Complex)
9	Strs. 5G-10, 5G-12	3	Range type, pyramid
10	Str. 6F-51	1?	Pyramid (near range type)
11	Str. 5D-75	1	Isolated pyramid
12	In front of Str. 3D-41	1?	Pyramid
13	Str. 5E-22	1	Sweat bath
14	Chultun 4F-4		No associated structures

the nine-doorway buildings are quite unlike temples in general configuration and were almost certainly used for occupation in Eznab.

In six locations away from the Great Plaza, occupation also involved masonry, probably vaulted, range structures. In Location 4, in addition to the range-type structures, the large pyramidal structures, 6E-153 and 6E-146, show evidence of Eznab occupation. In Locations 9 and 10, small pyramidal mounds in the center of plazas are surrounded by Eznab debris, but in both these locations there are nearby "palaces" that may have been the actual loci of occupation.

Two locations in which heavy Eznab debris was found may have had ceremonial connotations. One is Structure 5D-75, a small isolated mound immediately south of Temple III. The ceramics in the location were associated with a deposit of Pach Complex *incensarios* that Ferree (1967 : 106) reports represent "presumably, but not certainly, censer activity." The second case of heavy Eznab debris in a likely ceremonial context was encountered by a test pit in front of Structure 3D-41, a small temple on the basal platform in front of the major temple in the

North Zone. Multiple uses would have been possible in this location, since both Structures 3D-41 and the platform on which it rests are large enough for occupation; but if the building was occupied, it is the only case of Eznab residence in a clearly identifiable temple structure.

Two further occurrences of Eznab midden deposits are unique situations. One of these is in Structure 5E-22, the only Tikal sweat bath. The drain of the structure was filled with burned debris of early Eznab date. Because of the burning in the deposit and the unlikely character of the structure for residence, continued use as a sweat bath seems indicated. The final Eznab deposit was found in Chultun 4F-4, near the Tikal Project camp and well away from visible structures.

In addition to these instances that produced enough material to suggest Eznab occupation, there are some ceramic samples that contain only a few Eznab sherds. The samples add another twenty-five locations, distributed randomly throughout the site, that have at least trace quantities of Eznab. The contexts, like those of midden deposits, are heavily weighted toward range-type structures with few smaller structures represented. The number of locations, however, is probably somewhat misleading. These samples include all of the dubious cases in which I scrupulously recorded one or two sherds that *might* be Eznab in large lots of earlier material. When one makes allowance for misidentifications, laboratory error, and cases in which an Eznab passerby may have dropped a pot in walking through a patch of unoccupied forest, these lots probably do not add much to an estimate of Eznab population and certainly add nothing to a knowledge of Eznab activities.

In summary, Eznab occupation in Central Tikal followed very characteristic patterns. The inhabitants lived mostly in vaulted structures and distributed their refuse in courtyards, down stairways, and even within rooms. The total avoidance of small structures for residence is surprising, even for a period with such light occupation.

An attempt to estimate the population of Central Tikal during the Eznab period can be little more than guesswork. The rooms occupied in the major community surrounding the Great Plaza might have provided living space for 400–500 people. Other known occupation areas would probably not add more than 100 to this figure, since most of the locations represent sites of a size suitable for only one or two families. The total figure might be doubled or tripled to account for untested areas of the site, giving a rough estimate of 1,000–2,000 total population in Central Tikal. It is undeniable that Eznab population is drastically reduced from the Imix population peak, probably by as much as 90 percent.

These results, however, apply to a zone close to the major ceremonial precincts of Tikal. It is a crucial question whether a similar population decline affected outlying areas. Caution in generalizing from results obtained in and near ceremonial precincts is particularly appropriate in a period of cultural crisis that had dire consequences for the elite segment of Maya society, and the suggestion has arisen repeatedly that the abandonment of the ceremonial centers at the end of the Classic Period represents a scattering of people into the bush rather than an actual depopulation.

The Tikal Sustaining Area Project (Haviland et al. 1968) was designed to investigate conditions in areas well away from the main ceremonial precincts. Results from the project do not support the hypothesis that the population of Tikal simply dispersed into rural areas following the collapse. Instead, everywhere within surveyed strips extending 12 km. north and south from the site center, the Eznab Complex is associated with the same demographic changes as occurred in Central Tikal. In a carefully designed sample, Fry (1969) tested 102 mound groups in the sustaining area and encountered Eznab sherds in only 16. Most of the occurrences were in trace amounts and may not have indicated actual occupation. Fry reaches the conclusion that "a substantial Eznab occupation for the peripheries of Tikal, regarded as a strong possibility by those who would like to see an internal social revolt as the explanation for the collapse of Classic Maya civilization, is precluded" (1969 : 167).

In terms of the contexts represented, Fry notes that "as in Central Tikal, Eznab deposits tend to be located in and around range-type structures and former ceremonial centers" (1969 : 166). The only definite occupation encountered was in a range structure at the small nucleated site of Chikin Tikal, about 3 km. west of Temple 4. Lesser concentrations of Eznab material occurred at the small sites of Bobal, 4.5 km. south of the site center; Navajuelal, 9.5 km. south; Uolantun, 5 km. southeast; and Jimbal, 14 km. northeast.

The Eznab period, therefore, is a period of decreased population in the entire site-zone of Tikal. By inference, signs of lessened activity in the ceremonial precincts of other Maya sites are not unlikely to be indicative of general population decline.

Evidence of the Postclassic Caban Complex is extremely scarce at Tikal. A concentration of sherds in Group 4F-1 near the Tikal Reservoir suggests the presence of a Caban house site. A lesser concentration of sherds in an area south of the Temple of the Inscriptions may be the remains of another house or camp. Some Caban sherds in the rooms and on the stairways of Temples 1 and 2 are probably the result of sporadic ceremonial visits or pilgrimages. In addition to these cases, there are about one dozen lots from scattered locations that contain one or two Caban sherds each. The Sustaining Area Project evidence suggests an equally sparse population. Fry (1969) reports one likely housemound location near Laguna Verde, a water source about 7 km. south of the site center. Two other lots in the surveyed strip south of Tikal produced a few Caban sherds and no material of the complex was recovered from tests pits to the north of the site. Clearly, Caban period occupation at Tikal can have consisted of no more than widely scattered individual houses that would have represented no greater population density than the near abandonment of recent times.

ECOLOGY

Few of the ecological studies conducted in connection with the Tikal Project have as yet produced conclusive results. Puleston's (1968) study of *ramón* tree distribution and production is a notable exception, and one that may bear upon the potential support capacity of the rain forest. The results of Olson's 1968 soil survey are not yet available, and the analysis of nonhuman bone has not begun.

The crucial question for Tikal subsistence adaptation remains the same as that for the entire Peten: could the land have supported the heavy population of Late Classic times? Although Tikal data do not contribute directly to the solution of the problem, population figures from the site have played a role in raising questions about the validity of the traditional *milpa* model of Maya subsistence.

Haviland (1965, 1969, 1970) has provided estimates for the peak population of Tikal. In the 16 sq. km. zone near the center of the site, he calculates a conservatively estimated figure of 10,000 population. Since this figure is based on complete mapping of the area and testing of a considerable number of small structures, it has a high degree of reliability—if one accepts the evidence for contemporaneous occupation of all mounds showing a single ceramic complex and an average family size of 5.6 (Haviland 1970 : 193).

The core 16 sq. km. zone, however, is an artificial creation of the mapping procedure, and strip surveys outward from the center of the site indicate that comparable population densities covered an area of about 63 sq. km. (Haviland 1970 : 190). Accepting the core zone density figure of 600–700 persons per square kilometer for this larger "Central Zone," Haviland reaches a peak population estimate of 39, 000 inhabitants for Central Tikal. Outside of the central zone is a peripheral zone that still lies within the earthworks (Puleston and Callendar 1967) that would seem to set boundaries to Tikal as a political unit. The peripheral zone adds 60 sq. km. to the site and Haviland suggests that this would include another 6,000 people. The total population of 45,000 distributed over 123 sq. km. would give a population density of 350–400 persons per square kilometer for the site.

Although objections can be raised to these population estimates on several grounds, it would take a major downward adjustment on all counts to bring prehistoric population figures within the range of densities—30–60 persons per square kilometer (Sanders 1962, 1963). —estimated as maximal for a slash-and-burn agricultural system in rain forest.

It seems likely, then, that the population of Tikal could not have been locally supported by a subsistence system comparable to that known from ethnographic accounts of the Maya Lowlands. Two possible explanations may be suggested. Either Tikal depended on large-scale importation of foodstuffs for a period of several centuries, or there are fundamental errors in the accepted reconstruction of the Lowland Maya Classic subsistence system. I have already espoused the latter alternative (Culbert 1969a, 1969b), and several possible mechanisms of increasing productivity beyond present figures have been suggested (Bronson 1966; Puleston 1968; Sanders, chapter 15).

CONSTRUCTION

Construction at Tikal declined from a peak period between 9.13.0.0.0 (A.D. 692) and 9.16.0.0.0 (A.D. 751) to minimal efforts during the time when Eznab ceramics were in vogue. Between 9.13.0.0.0 (A.D. 692) and 9.16.0.0.0 (A.D. 751), such massive projects as Temples 1, 2, and 4 (Satterthwaite and Coe 1968), four Twin Pyramid Complexes (Satterthwaite 1956), and probably many of the final structures in the Central Acropolis were completed. After this time, the only constructions securely dated to *katuns* 9.17.0.0.0 (A.D. 771) and 9.18.0.0.0 (A.D. 790) are additional Twin Pyramid Complexes (Satterthwaite 1956). By no means, of course, do these latter structures represent the total architectural activity of their time; there is evidence that Temple V was probably erected after 9.16.0.0.0 (A.D. 751), and 9.19.0.0.0 (A.D. 810) would seem to be the best guess for the dedicatory date associated with Temple III (Satterthwaite and Coe 1968 : 10–11). No suggestion has yet been made, however, that any major structure at the site dates as late as 10.0.0.0.0 (A.D. 830), though it should be remembered that there are dozens of impressive structures for which not even tentative dates have been advanced. Certainly, however, the pattern indicates that construction was on the wane by the beginning of Cycle 10.

Large construction projects associate firmly with the Imix Ceramic Complex, but never with the Eznab Complex, for all of the aforementioned structures from which fill samples have been obtained contain Imix sherds but no evidence of Eznab. In fact, no large structure at Tikal has ever produced Eznab sherds from the fill, and known Eznab constructions are tiny and usually show rudimentary techniques. One of the more ambitious projects of likely Eznab date is a small platform, 2 m. by 3 m. by 0.8 m. high, that was constructed in front of and overlapping the stairway of Structure 7F-30 (Coe and Broman 1958). Although sherds from the fill of the platform do not provide a conclusive date of building, the construction postdates Burial 1, which I believe to be Eznab (see pp. 75–76). In addition to this platform, a bench was secondarily added in Structure 7F-32, a range structure in the same group, in Eznab times. Although not associated with good ceramic samples, small platforms constructed on the top of the latest floor of the North Terrace of the Great Plaza seem likely to be of Eznab date. In other areas of Tikal, Eznab constructions include a crude retaining wall in the East Plaza ballcourt (W. Coe 1965a : 54) and floor patches in the Central Acropolis and in the North Acropolis. Excavators' descriptions specifically mention the poor quality of the workmanship in several of these structures. On the other hand, a persistence of some high-quality workmanship into Eznab times is demonstrated by the sealing of Burial 6 in the doorway between the inner rooms of Temple 1. I now believe that this burial is of Eznab date (see pp. 76–77), and Adams and Trik (1961 : 118) emphasize the skill used in concealing the patch in the original floor.

Mention should be made of what were once thought to be structures abandoned unfinished at the time of the Maya collapse. For many years, the massive platform at the east edge of the East Plaza was called the "Unfinished Acropolis." Test pits on the top of the platform, however, produced ceramic samples containing nothing later than Manik (Early Classic) sherds only slightly below the surface. It now appears likely that the construction is a dismantled Early Classic acropolis rather than one in the process of construction at the end of the Classic Period. A better candidate for late unfinished construction is a small platform, 5D-11, in the West Plaza. In excavating the structure in 1962, Peter Harrison discovered that the final structure, in spite of being associated with the tomb containing the impressive Burial 77, showed no trace of a stairway or of finishing masonry (reported in W. Coe 1963 : 49–50). There is nothing about the pottery in Burial 77, however, to suggest a date at the terminal end of Imix, and I think it more likely that the structure was completed and then robbed of stones than that it was left uncompleted.

The difference between Imix and Eznab times is as striking in architecture as it is demographically. Compared to the scale and virtuosity of Imix architectural activities, Eznab efforts are extremely impoverished. The rate of the architectural decline is difficult to judge, however, since we know neither the number of structures built in the last few *katuns* of Baktun 9 nor the exact date at which Eznab ceramics became established.

LATE ACTIVITIES
IN CEREMONIAL PRECINCTS

The excavations at Tikal, particularly those in ceremonial areas near the Great Plaza, have provided excellent information about activities that took place at some time after the cessation of major construction. The four activities involved are burials, the movement and resetting of stone monuments, the use of *copal* incense and *incensarios*, and the looting of tombs and caches. A consideration of these practices makes three points readily apparent. First, all of them have counterparts in full Classic times, although it is a matter of interpretation whether the late occurrences are the functional equivalents of their earlier counterparts. Second, some of the activities involve usages that are "abnormal" when viewed in the light of the rigidly standardized patterns of Classic times. Third, the activities are difficult to date and to sequence since they do not relate directly to carved dates or construction, and some of them are not associated with good ceramic samples. The aberrance of many of the patterns makes it likely that they postdate the time during which Classic standards prevailed, but how much later they were and how long they persevered has been a matter of continuing concern.

Although few burials at Tikal can be securely dated to Eznab times, the Eznab burials encountered demonstrate a preference for the locations (in or near temples) that were favored for elite burials in Classic times. The offerings that accompany the burials are impoverished when compared to the kinds of offerings that individuals buried in such locations commanded in earlier and better days, but it is clear that if temple locations continued to be valued for burials in Eznab times not all individuals had access to them.

Eznab burials play an important role in tying together ceramic, residential, and ceremonial patterns. Two burials of probable Eznab date are crucial in this respect. The first is Burial 1, encountered by Coe and Broman (1958) in their investigation of Stela 23. This burial, intruded through a plaza floor in front of Structure 7F-30, is associated with the construction of a small platform (Feature 1), the use of *incensarios*, and probably the resetting of Stela 23. The two vessels included among the burial offerings were thought by the excavators to represent different complexes (1958 : 40). They concluded that the large red bowl should be assigned a date equivalent to Tepeu 3 (Eznab) at Uaxactun, while the polychrome dish was considered to be a Tepeu 2 (Imix) type. Now that the Tikal sequence has been completed, however, it is possible to reconsider these temporal assignments. The large red bowl is, in fact, typologically indeterminate and could pertain to either the Imix Complex or the Eznab Complex. In favor of an Eznab date is the fact that this vessel shape was rarely encountered in a large sample of Imix burial offerings. The polychrome vessel (Fig. 10a) fea-

75

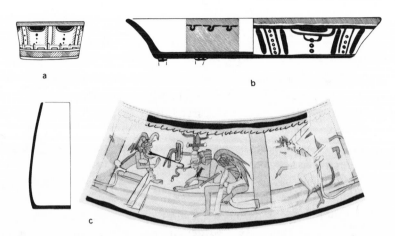

FIGURE 10. EZNAB COMPLEX POLYCHROME POTTERY. *a*, Vessel from Burial 1; *b*, vessel from Burial 6; *c*, figure-painted polychrome from Eznab midden. Approximate scale 1:6.

tures a "dress shirt" motif on the interior. Although this design occurs in both the Imix and Eznab complexes, it is, in terms of frequency of occurrence, particularly characteristic of Eznab. The fact that the large uppermost dot of the motif is outlined also suggests an Eznab date, since an outline is almost invariably present in Eznab examples and is rare in Imix. The combination of these typological features with the late stratigraphic position of the burial and the crude construction of the associated Feature 1 make an Eznab date close to a certainty.

Burial 6 provides a similar problem of dating a polychrome vessel (Fig. 10b) with a "dress shirt" design. In this case, the burial was placed in a cist intruded through the floor of Temple I (Adams and Trik 1961). The floor was carefully patched after the burial was placed, but was broken into at a later date. Most of the contents of Burial 6 were removed at this time, but a single piece of the "dress shirt" vessel remained in an undisturbed section, thus assuring the original context of other fragments of the vessel found in the scattered debris. The vessel is a Zacatel Cream Polychrome tripod plate with bevel lip. The "dress shirt" motif is repeated several times on the exterior, separated by panels containing vertical rows of dots within circles. Although all the elements of the design are common to both Imix and

Eznab, some of the details suggest that an Eznab date is preferable. The position of the "dress shirt" on the exterior of a plate, the outlined major dot in the "dress shirt," and the dot within circle motif in a vertical alignment are all common features of Eznab polychromes. The whole configuration is very similar to a plate from an Eznab midden context (Fig. 11e, p. 83). If the Eznab dating is correct, Burial 6 is an example of a late burial that is traditional in both location and style of construction.

Burial 201 is another example of an Eznab burial placed beneath the floor of a major temple, in this case, Structure 5D-22 in the North Acropolis (W. Coe 1965a : 55). The pit for Burial 201 broke into the Ik Complex tomb containing Burial 200, and the contents of the latter were looted. As the pit was being refilled, Burial 201 was placed near the top of the pit accompanied by a Sahcaba Modeled–carved vessel and an Achote Black dish. It is impossible to say whether the original excavation was undertaken to search for an early tomb or was primarily aimed at providing a spot for Burial 201. The seemingly offhand placement of the burial high in the fill, however, seems to suggest the former motive. In contrast to the situation in Burial 6, the pit containing Burial 201 was left unsealed.

An Eznab burial (Burial 168) was located during the excavation of the large pyramidal structure 6E-143. The burial was intruded through the final floor of an exterior stairblock platform and was then patched with plaster. The original function of the structure is unclear, as it combines features of both temples and palaces.

All of the Eznab burials discussed so far were in locations favored for elite burials in Classic times. This is not the case for the final Eznab burial, Burial 198, which was placed in a bench in palace 5D-46 in the Central Acropolis. Although the state of preservation of the bench prevents a firm conclusion, it seems likely that Burial 198 was intruded into a preexisting bench.

One of the basic activities of post-Imix ceremonialism was the transportation, modification, and reuse of stelae and altars of an earlier date. W. Coe (1965a : 54) estimates that 40 per cent of the monuments in the Plaza–Terrace–North Acropolis area represent cases of late movement and/or resetting, and there are numerous instances of the practice from other parts of Tikal and perhaps from as far away as the small neighboring site of Uolantun. Details of this complex of activities have been repeatedly documented in the literature (W. Coe 1965a : 54–56; Satterthwaite 1958; Coe and Broman 1958; Shook 1958; W. Coe 1962 : 484–86) and need not be discussed here.

The offering of *copal* incense in specially constructed *incensarios* is a time-honored Maya practice that is present throughout the Tikal sequence and, in fact, continues to the present day in many parts of the Maya area. This ceremonial complex, as indicated by broken censers, evidence of burning, and even balls of *copal,* is probably the best documented and most omnipresent of late ceremonial practices. Evidence of censer activity of Eznab times has been located in a bewildering variety of locations, including near small "shrine" platforms, near stelae, and even in domestic refuse.

A final pattern that can hesitantly be called "ceremonial" is the looting of burials and caches. Two examples of looted tombs have already been discussed (pp. 76–77) and other cases have been mentioned (W. Coe 1965a : 54). Large numbers of looted structure caches have been encountered (Adams and Trik 1961; W. Coe 1962 : 487), and the reuse of artifacts that must have come from stela caches shows that this type of cache suffered a similar fate. Although jade objects must frequently have been encountered by the looters, they are conspicuously absent from late debris and were not redeposited as offerings. This absence suggests the possibility that looting may have been done to obtain valuable objects for trade. At the same time, the purposeful redisposition of other objects as "substitute" offerings (W. Coe 1965a : 54, 56) suggests continuing ceremonial connotations. Once again, the preliminary evidence indicates that the patterns of activity were very complex, and only the final analysis and correlation of all the Tikal material will provide a complete understanding of the situation.

The carefully documented report of excavations around Stela 23 (Coe and Broman 1958) provides the best opportunity to view all of these activities as a single datable complex demonstrating both continuity and change in ceremonial patterns. The first "late" events near Stela 23 were the placing of the Eznab Burial 1 and the construction of the small platform (Feature 1) that partially overlies the stairway of Temple 7F-30. These activities may be interpreted as a logical and little changed continuation of a much earlier pattern. The first construction at the site of 7F-30 was initiated in late Manik times after the placing of the superb dedicatory Burial 160. A whole series of burials followed, several of the latest of Imix date. Many of the burials were associated with partial or complete reconstructions of the temple. Burial 1 may simply be the latest of the series, with the tiny platform the best the Eznab inhabitants could offer in the way of architectural refurbishing.

Ceremonies involving *incensarios* were related to the process, since censer fragments were found on the surface and within the fill of Feature 1 (Coe and Broman 1958 : 39). Fill material included four fragments of Pach Complex censers, and Tulix Complex censers occurred in surface lots near the temple structure.

Stela 23 was reset in front of Feature 1 and Structure 7F-30. Because of the relative positions of the stela and platform and the crudeness of the platform construction, Coe and Broman (1958 : 38) feel that the platform was in use at the time the stela was reset. Although no ceramics are directly associated with the resetting, it is very likely that the event occurred while Eznab ceramics were still in vogue. The reasons for this conclusion are the Eznab date for the construction of Feature 1 and the fact that there was Eznab residence in the nearby Structure 7F-32, while there were no sherds of later date in any collections from the group.

The cache located with the reset Stela 23 adds to the activities the practice of redepositing looted materials. The stela cache included sets of eccentric flints and of eccentric obsidians. At the time of the original report, Coe and Broman (1958 : 44–45) expressed doubt that the cache artifacts were manufactured at the time of deposition; and in a later publication, Coe states, "In Late Classic structure offerings, however, the common items were . . . eccentric obsidians (completely lacking in the current monument caches)" (1962 : 498). The cache of Stela 23, then, is aberrant and includes material that must have been obtained from an architectural offering.

The stela resetting and redeposited cache, of course, represent the "new ceremonialism" of late Tikal. Not only are the practices non-Classic, but the very choice of location is aberrant by Classic standards. Dating control is not good enough to indicate the exact date of these events. If the occupation of the group and use of Feature 1 continued for some time, the late ceremonialism might have occurred as much as a century after the more traditional Burial 1 and the construction of Feature 1.

The fact that the entire series of late ceremonial activities reviewed above is related with some certainty to the Eznab Complex does not mean some or all of the practices may not have continued into Caban times. In fact, there is evidence that some of them did. Burial 5, clearly dated to the Caban Complex by associated ceramics, was placed beneath the floor of Temple 1, directly above the Eznab Period Burial 6. The excavation of the pit for Burial 5 may have occasioned the disturbance and looting of the Burial 6 chamber, but Adams and Trik (1961 : 131) feel that both Burials 5 and 6 were disturbed at a still later date. Fragments of censers of the Postclassic Xnuk Censer Complex (Ferree 1967 : 115–16) were included in Burial 5 and the numerous *copal* fragments in Temple 1, including the cache (Cache 37) of *copal* balls, may well date to Caban times. Although there is no direct evidence to connect Caban people to other ceremonial activities, neither is there evidence to assure that all late activities were confined to Eznab times. The total picture of known Caban ceremonialism, however, suggests a far more sporadic kind of activity than that of Eznab times. Occasional visits from the Postclassic communities around Lake Peten Itza would seem to be indicated, rather than continuing activities of a resident population.

CERAMICS

Ceramic studies serve several functions in the analysis of the Maya collapse at Tikal. Perhaps most importantly, they provide a generally applicable tool for site chronology. Since nowhere within Tikal are late activities directly correlated with calendrical inscriptions or radiocarbon samples, assigning these activities to the Eznab and Caban periods depends upon ceramic associations. Similarly, the correlation of events at Tikal with those at other sites comes largely from information provided by ceramics. Finally, quantitative and qualitative comparisons of samples spanning the period of collapse facilitate inferences about continuity and change in the production and use of pottery.

Eznab Complex Types

Since preservation is good in Eznab samples, it was possible to obtain full type counts on almost all lots. A total of seventy-three samples, most of them from the Central Acropolis Eznab occupation, was quantified. Variability between lots in type frequencies was extremely high. For example, Cambio Unslipped, the predominant type, ranged between a low frequency of 2 percent and a high frequency of 74 percent. Consequently, median frequencies are the most meaningful measure of frequency of occurrence.

The two most common types from the Eznab Complex are Cambio Unslipped and Tinaja Red, with respective median frequencies of 34 percent and 26 percent of total sherds. Encanto Striated is the next most common type with a median of 15 percent. Maquina Brown and Achote Black are consistently present but usually in frequencies of less than 5 percent. Dichrome and polychrome types are totally absent from eleven of the seventy-three lots, and in most others occur with less than 5 percent frequency, although a few lots contain as much as 10–13 percent polychrome pottery. Several easily recognizable new types appear in the Eznab Complex, but none of them occurs in more than trace frequencies. One of the new types is Sahcaba Modeled-carved; another is Toh Brown, a new, undecorated type that frequently occurs in characteristic Sahcaba [2] shapes. Fine Orange Ware, usually of Altar Fine Orange types, shows scattered occurrences, and there are a few sherds of Fine Gray Ware. Saptan Impressed is another rare trade type.

Eznab monochrome and decorated types are technologically superior to those of the Imix Complex in paste and firing. Sherds of Tinaja Red, particularly, have a characteristic hardness that makes it possible to recognize unopened bags of Eznab pottery by their "ring." In dealing with paste composition, I have used named analytical units termed "paste variants," each of which is characterized by a distinctive combination of paste, texture, and inclusions. Paste variants are independent of types and consequently may be more inclusive (that is, crosscut several types) or less inclusive (that is, occur in only some examples of a single type). The Eznab Complex is marked by the appearance of the Taman Paste Variant, which has the finest texture and least temper of local Late Classic pastes. Taman Paste does not have the silty texture of Fine Orange Ware and it is buff-colored rather than orange, but it may be a local approximation to a fine-paste ideal. This suggestion would seem to be supported by the fact that Sahcaba Modeled-carved, the local imitation of Pabellon Modeled-carved, is made almost exclusively of Taman Paste. Taman Paste also occurs frequently in Tinaja

Red, though the Tinaja Paste Variant, a standard paste for monochrome pottery in all Late Classic complexes, still predominates in this type.

The typological characteristics of polychromes show interesting development in the Eznab Complex. The most characteristic examples of Eznab polychromes are a distinct degeneration from Imix standards. Colors are poorly controlled—the "cream" of Zacatel Cream Polychrome becomes a buff or tan; blacks shade off to brown, and so on. The execution of designs is sloppy, with uneven lines and rounded corners. Occurring in the same lots with such poorly executed polychromes, however, are some examples of superb polychrome craftmanship, fully up to the standards of earlier complexes. There is some possibility that the better sherds could have been derived from Imix contexts, but this seems unlikely because they are as well preserved as accompanying Eznab sherds. The most reasonable inference is that there was a time, at least during early Eznab, when a few craft specialists maintained high standards while others were producing second-rate work.

There were marked changes in the frequency of design motifs between Imix and Eznab polychromes (Figs. 10–12). The great variety of motifs characteristic of the former complex gave way to a drastically reduced repertoire consisting mostly of *kan* crosses (Fig. 11f, g), "dress shirts" (Fig. 11a-f), "rabbit-ear flowers" (Fig. 12a-c), and vertical rows of dots within circles (Fig. 11e). No new design motifs appeared in Eznab polychromes although there were modal changes in the manner of representing old motifs.

In addition to the problem of variation of quality in local pottery types, an interesting puzzle is posed by several nearly complete vessels of superb figure-painted polychrome that occur in Eznab middens (Fig. 10c). The painting style is quite unlike anything known locally, and although the vessel shape bears a general resemblance to Ik Complex barrel-shapes, it is widest at the base, a feature unparalleled in Ik shapes. William Coe believes that these vessels are early (probably Ik) pieces obtained as a result of tomb-robbing operations. In the absence of any specific evidence to support Coe's idea, I feel it to be a more conservative conclusion that the Eznab inhabitants of Tikal maintained trade contacts with some area in which a vigorous figure-painting style persisted.

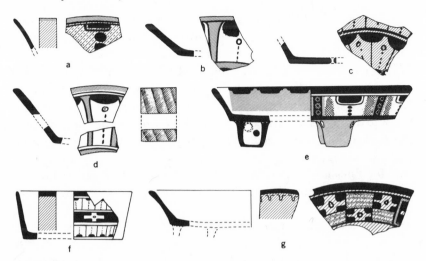

FIGURE 11. EZNAB COMPLEX POLYCHROME POTTERY from general midden deposits. Approximate scale 1:6.

The comparison of type frequency changes between the Imix and Eznab complexes is handicapped because the poor preservation of Imix collections prevented type counts for all but a few lots. Using a combined sample of well-preserved Ik and Imix lots provides about a dozen

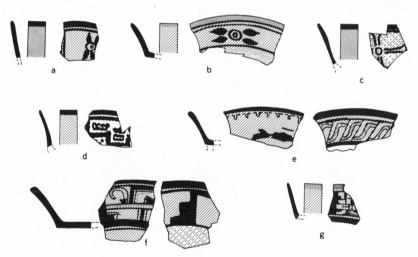

FIGURE 12. EZNAB COMPLEX POLYCHROME POTTERY from general midden deposits. Approximate scale 1:6.

83

lots for comparison with Eznab. The results do not suggest striking changes in type frequencies. The most consistent difference between earlier Late Classic complexes and the Eznab Complex is the decrease of decorated (polychrome and dichrome) sherds in Eznab. The median frequency of decorated sherds in Ik-Imix samples is 13 percent. In Eznab, the median frequency falls below 5 percent. The decrease in decorated types is associated with an increase in unslipped types in the Eznab Complex. The median frequency for Cambio Unslipped increases from 23 percent to 34 percent between the complexes, while that for Encanto Striated rises from 6 percent to 15 percent. The frequency distributions of red, brown, and black pottery change little between the two samples.

In spite of the fact that type frequencies do not show striking changes between the Imix and Eznab complexes, there are drastic changes in the surface treatment used for particular vessel shapes. Cylinders, small dishes and bowls, and tripod plates, which are almost invariably polychrome or dichrome in Imix, are usually monochrome red in Eznab. The use of a black slip on small flaring- or outcurving-side dishes in Eznab is another practice that does not have an Imix counterpart. Consideration of type-shape combinations, then, results in better qualitative distinctions between Imix and Eznab than the use of types alone.

Eznab Complex Shapes

There are marked differences between the Imix and Eznab complexes in vessel shapes. A series of new shapes appear in Eznab to provide easily recognized markers for the complex. Three of the new shapes, the incurved-rim tripod dish (Fig. 13a), the bulging-neck jar (Fig. 13b, c), and the tripod plate with notched sharp z-angle (Fig. 13f), are common enough that one or more are almost certain to appear in any lot containing a significant number of rim sherds. In addition, a number of rare vessel shapes are restricted to the Eznab Complex. These shapes include the bead-rim jar; the barrel with tall ring base (Fig. 13e); the everted-rim jar; and the everted-rim, composite silhouette vessel (Fig. 13d) (usually with *molcajete* interior).

There are also modal differences in shapes that distinguish Eznab from Imix. The tripod plate with beveled lip, a common Imix form, continues in small quantities in Eznab collections; but the tripod plate with rounded lip is the more common Eznab tripod. Many of the incurved-rim and restricted-orifice bowl shapes of the Imix Complex continue unchanged in Eznab, but a new variation in the position of grooved decoration appears. In this variation, the groove is located just below the lip (Fig. 13g-i), much higher on the vessel than on Imix grooved bowls.

In the quantitative analysis of vessel shapes, a set of four major shape classes was used. Three of the classes—wide-mouth jars, small-mouth jars, and large bowls—were internally homogeneous categories distinguished from each other by major differences in shape, size, and proportions. In addition, wide-mouth jars, which were always unslipped and heavily tempered, contrasted typologically with the red-slipped, less-tempered small-mouth jars and large bowls. The fourth category, designated "small vessels," contrasted clearly in basic shape with the first three categories but was internally heterogeneous since it included such divergent forms as cylinders, tripod plates, and various small bowls and dishes. In the Imix Complex, the small vessels contrasted typologically with other classes since these shapes were polychrome or dichrome. With the drastic decline of polychrome decora-

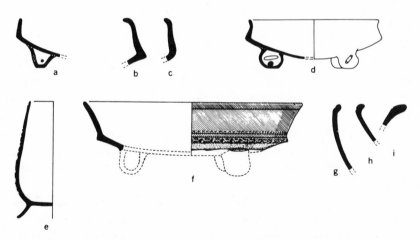

FIGURE 13. EZNAB COMPLEX VESSEL SHAPES. *a*, Incurved-rim tripod dish; *b, c*, bulging-neck jars; *d*, everted-rim, composite silhouette vessel; *e*, barrel with tall ring base; *f*, tripod plate with notched sharp Z-angle; *g, h*, incurved-rim bowls; *i*, restricted-orifice bowl. Approximate scale 1:6.

tion in Eznab, this strong typological contrast disappeared. The clear distinctions between classes in basic shape and size make it likely that the classes were used for different purposes in prehistoric Maya society.

Material was available for a thorough quantitative comparison of Imix and Eznab shape categories. Thirty-three Eznab samples were quantitatively analyzed, and a summary of the results is presented in Table 2. A series of seventeen quantified Imix samples was used for

TABLE 2

MAJOR SHAPE CATEGORIES IN THE
IMIX AND EZNAB COMPLEXES

	Small Vessels		Large Bowls		Small-mouth Jars		Wide-mouth Jars	
	Range (%)	Median (%)	Range (%)	Median (%)	Range (%)	Median (%)	Range (%)	Median (%)
Eznab Total	17–79	44	4–37	16	0–35	10	3–51	28
Imix	28–76	46	6–22	20	5–33	10	6–28	18
Imix Small Structures	28–49	36	6–22	22	5–21	12	10–28	21
Imix Large Structures	39–76	56	11–20	19	5–33	9	6–25	11

comparison. Since, however, the Imix samples come from contexts that display a range of architectural diversity not present in Eznab, a simple comparison may be misleading. Consequently, the Eznab samples were compared not only with the total Imix samples but also with two subsamples within the Imix set: the first, a subsample derived from small-structure contexts (and in theory closest to the presumed domestic contexts of Eznab) and the second, a subsample from large-structure, that is, ceremonial and/or elite residential contexts.

These data lead to some interesting inferences. The largest differences between samples occur in the small-vessel category in which there are much higher frequencies in Imix large-structure samples (median 56 percent) than in Imix samples from small structures (median 36 percent). The Eznab samples are very close in both range and median (17–79 percent, median 44 percent) to the Imix sample that combines both social contexts (28–76 percent, median 46 percent). This close-ness suggests that if the difference between the Imix sets was caused by different activity patterns in the two contexts, then *all* of the activities must have been represented in Eznab contexts.

The frequency of small-mouth jars is about the same in all the samples. Large-mouth jars, however, show a complex pattern. In Imix, the vessels seem to have had a differential use, appearing with greater frequency in small-structure samples (median 21 percent) than in ones from large structures (median 11 percent). Eznab frequencies (median 28 percent) exceed those from either Imix subsample. The increase in wide-mouth jars during Eznab may relate to a decrease in large bowls between Imix and Eznab. Both wide-mouth jars and large bowls are of a size and shape appropriate for storage functions, and ethnographic data (Thompson 1958) suggest the persistence of this function for similar shapes among the modern Maya. If the shapes are functionally equivalent, they may have been interchangeable. Comparing the Eznab and Imix small-structure frequency changes, there is a decrease in large-bowl median frequencies in Eznab (22 percent in Imix to 16 percent in Eznab) that matches the increase in wide-mouth jars (21 percent in Imix to 28 percent in Eznab). Consequently, the Eznab inhabitants of Tikal may have used wide-mouth jars for some of the purposes for which large bowls served in Imix times.

Since the small-vessel category included several different shapes, it was subdivided for a more detailed analysis. Counts of each shape were made and frequencies calculated on the basis of total small-vessel rim sherds. In the Eznab Complex, tripod plates are the most common small-vessel shape with a median frequency of 23 percent. The range of variability between lots is extremely high, from 8 percent to 90 percent. The next most common small-vessel shape in Eznab is the out-curving- to flaring-side bowl or dish, which has a median frequency of 21 percent and a range of 0 percent to 40 percent. Round-side bowls and dishes occur with a median frequency of 14 percent and a range of 0 percent to 40 percent. Cylinders and incurved-rim tripod dishes are present in most samples in low frequencies, and all other small-vessel shapes occur in fewer than one-half of the individual lots.

Again, the Eznab figures can be compared with the results for the Imix Complex. In the subdivision of the small-vessel category, it was unnecessary to distinguish between Imix samples from large and small structures because, in spite of the greater total frequency of small vessels in Imix large structures, the relative frequencies of individual small-vessel shapes did not vary much between the two contexts. Most small-vessel frequencies remained relatively stable between the Imix and Eznab complexes. The principal difference is a decreased frequency of cylinders and barrels and an increased frequency of round-side bowls and dishes in Eznab. A median frequency of 4 percent for cylinders and a general absence of barrels in Eznab compares with respective medians of 15 percent and 7 percent for the two shapes in Imix. Meanwhile, the Eznab median of 14 percent for round-side bowls and dishes is an increase over the 8 percent median in Imix. Although I have not tended to view barrels and cylinders as functionally equivalent to round-side bowls because of differences in basic proportions, vessels of both shapes might be used as drinking or serving vessels and may have a greater equivalence than I supposed.

Caban Ceramics

The Caban Ceramic Complex is too poorly known to allow more than a few brief comments. With the exception of a few decorated vessels in Burial 5 and in the surface debris around Temples I and II, all sherds are of monochrome red and unslipped types. Both types and shapes seem to be equivalents of ceramics of the New Town Complex from Barton Ramie (Willey et al. 1965).

My reasons for feeling that the Caban Complex represents a site-unit intrusion are basically typological. All of the types clearly identified as Caban are technologically quite unlike earlier types in such fundamental features as paste and inclusions. Caban shapes are either completely new or enough changed from earlier shapes to make it unlikely that they could be the direct outgrowth of local traditions. In view of the total lack of continuity, and the failure of Caban sherds to appear as exotics in Eznab samples, the most likely inference is that the users of Caban ceramics occupied or visited Tikal at some time after the end of Eznab ceramic production.

DATING PROBLEMS

The dating of events at Tikal is a critical problem for a general reconstruction of the history of the Maya decline and for testing hypotheses about the processes involved. Some of the most important issues center around the date at which the Eznab Ceramic Complex replaced the Imix Complex. That Imix ceramics were in production at 9.15.0.0.0 (A.D. 731) and 9.16.0.0.0 (A.D. 751) is clearly indicated by several burial offerings that can be related to Initial Series dates. The Twin Pyramid Complex constructed at 9.18.0.0.0 (A.D. 790) produced nothing later than Imix sherds from small fill samples, and there is no reason to think that the Imix Complex had terminated by that date. The only Initial Series date at Tikal later than 9.18.0.0.0 (A.D. 790) is 10.2.0.0.0 (A.D. 869), which appears on Stela 11. It is difficult to relate Stela 11, and its paired Altar 11, to ceramic complexes because the monuments are not associated with ceramic samples. W. Coe (1962 : 487) has cogently argued that Stela and Altar 11, which follow Classic standards in style, setting, and cache, can hardly have been contemporaneous with the "non-Classic" religious patterns discussed earlier. By extension, Coe and I (Willey, Culbert, and Adams 1967) inferred that the Imix Ceramic Complex must have continued until 10.2.0.0.0 (A.D. 869). As ceramic evidence increases for quite early dates for Eznab equivalent complexes at other sites, I like this conclusion far less, and now think it possible that Eznab ceramics came into use by 10.0.0.0.0 (A.D. 830). To accept this possibility involves the assumption that a Tikal Eznab population, already greatly diminished in numbers and economic strength, managed to resurrect (figuratively, one would hope) or import a craftsman skilled in traditional carving and ceremonial practices. This need not imply the contradiction of coexistent normal and abnormal monument settings, however, since there is no concrete evidence that abnormal settings need have begun at the beginning of Eznab.

If the Eznab Complex was present at 10.0.0.0.0 (A.D. 830), it means that most of the demographic decline at Tikal and the loss of ability to organize construction were accomplished facts by that time. This has two important implications. First, the decline was rapid and cannot have taken much more than a half-century. Second, Tikal must have been affected at the same time as, or even before, sites in the Usumacinta and Pasion zones, giving impetus to internal rather than external mechanisms as causative factors.

There are no real dating controls for the end of the Eznab Complex and for the Caban Complex. Largely on hunch, I tend to feel that Eznab may have lasted about 100 years. The Caban Complex is associated with both Tohil Plumbate and X-Fine Orange, so it may be tied to the dates for those trade wares, but there is no way even to guess at a total duration.

SUMMARY

In reviewing the Tikal data in the process of writing this paper, I was more impressed than ever before by the evidences of continuity of culture through the decline. The Eznab communities at Tikal are simply impoverished miniature copies of what Tikal was at its peak. Those communities that have been most fully investigated (the Great Plaza area and the Stela 23 group) contain the same fundamental parts as Classic communities—residential areas utilizing the most favored of early locations and ceremonial precincts that, by and large, continue to be the same structures used earlier. The ceremonial practices of which we have knowledge continue earlier forms, and I think that W. Coe's (1965a : 54–56) comments suggesting that the late Maya were attempting to carry on as well as possible are an apt summary of the situation.

The constellation of differences between Imix and Eznab times could all have been a direct result of a decreased population and a drastic decline of the general economic situation of Tikal. The loss of specialized knowledge and skills would be a logical outcome of the inability to support such luxuries. If we accept the hints that artisans capable of producing high-quality pottery, and perhaps even Stela and Altar 11, continued their work into early Eznab times, it would suggest that craft skills were dying out rather than being extinguished. The burial of some, but not all, individuals in favored locations suggests continuing differential access to these locations, even though without the wealth to accumulate luxurious burial offerings. One could construct a sequence of specific events that would show a gradual decline in the maintenance of traditional patterns and a growth of aberrant, that is, uninformed, practices. At the moment, however, such a reconstruction would be little more than an exercise in typological arrangement, and we must seek data to substantiate such a sequence before it can command respect as a reflection of a real rather than an imagined development.

To relate the changes at Tikal to demography and economy, however, says nothing about the reasons for demographic and economic collapse. In this regard, it is useful to apply, in the specific case of Tikal, the generalized arguments proposed by Willey and Shimkin in chapter 18. As the largest of the sites reviewed in detail at the seminar, Tikal would have been the strongest and most highly organized and yet the most vulnerable. At its peak, Tikal probably carried further than other sites the Late Classic trend to increased organization and complexity, and would consequently have been more subject to the stresses inherent in the organizational principles of the system.

In the realm of subsistence, the long-continued high population density at the site must have stretched local support capabilities to the ultimate. If the Maya developed a solution to the problem through importation of basic foodstuffs or protein-rich dietary supplements, additional stress would have been added to the organizational-administrative system, as well as vulnerability from hostile actions by people at the source of imported foods or along supply routes. The demand at Tikal for nonfood trade goods from the margins of or outside of the lowlands would have been unusually high because of both the high population and the size and scale of expenditures of the elite class. The central location of Tikal, far from the borders of the Maya area, would again have demanded greater organization and imposed a higher level of vulnerability (see Rathje, chapter 17).

Tikal was obviously successful in the competition for power and prestige posited in chapter 18. The economic benefits it reaped can be seen in the abundance of elite goods, and its political power and prestige are mirrored in the occurrence of the Tikal emblem-glyph at other sites. It may also have reaped jealousy and resistance from less favored sites or regions, and it is quite possible that a mechanism, perhaps the trigger, in the Tikal decline was pressure, either economic or military, from a coalition of other sites within the lowlands.

The position of Tikal, then, was a precarious one, representing both the pinnacle of Maya organizational accomplishments and the most extreme commitment to a system that may, in the long run, have been unworkable. Oversuccessful, overstrained, and probably overbearing, Tikal would have been at the mercy of any of a number of ecological, social, or political catastrophes capable of upsetting the delicate balance.

It does not seem to me that Tikal would have been similarly vulnerable to threats from outside the Maya Lowlands. Jungle warfare against a strong and well-organized opponent is no mean task, and the Central Peten should have been a last stronghold against external military pressure, resisting long after frontier sites had succumbed. Similarly, Tikal organizational strength would have protected it from a serious catastrophe as a result of non-Maya economic pressures. The size and far-flung nature of trade networks bringing goods to Tikal would have provided maximal alternatives for restructuring essential procurement systems should there have been troubles in a limited number of source or access areas. I must, then, take a stand as a strong proponent of an internal mechanism for the Maya collapse. Tikal succumbs too early and too rapidly for the trigger to have been external, and foreign incursions in parts of the Maya Lowlands seem to me to be the result rather than the cause of the Maya collapse.

NOTES

1. As in all Tikal enterprises, this work would have been impossible without the dedicated efforts of many people, to all of whom I wish to express my gratitude. Particularly helpful were revisions of the manuscript suggested by William R. Coe, Lisa Ferree, and William A. Haviland. At the same time, I must stress that the interpretations and errors are my own and that final views of the development and decline of Tikal may be quite different from the preliminary analysis presented here.

2. Variation in the type-variety naming system exists for certain possibly mold-made types. Some researchers use the term "modeled-carved" while others prefer "molded-carved." Rather than legislate type-variety nomenclature, I have retained whichever term was used by the authors in their original manuscripts. (Editor's note.)

6
Certain Aspects of the Late Classic to Postclassic Periods in the Belize Valley

GORDON R. WILLEY

Department of Anthropology
Harvard University

This chapter summarizes ceramic, settlement, architectural, and other changes in the archaeological record of the Late Classic to Postclassic Period transition in the Belize Valley of British Honduras. These data have been selected and presented in the context of the problem that is usually referred to as the Classic Maya cultural collapse. We are here concerned with how the event or events of the collapse are manifested in the archaeology of the Belize Valley and just when such events took place.

The data offered here have already been published, at least in greater part, in a monograph on the Belize Valley (Willey, Bullard, Glass, and Gifford 1965; hereinafter, WBGG 1965). In selecting and arranging the data from this monograph our attention will be focused primarily upon the span of time that could be bracketed by the Maya Long Count dates of 10.0.0.0.0 to 10.6.0.0.0 or from about A.D. 830 to 950 (11.16.0.0.0 correlation). This span is approximately the subperiod best known by the ceramic phase name Tepeu 3, although the chronological cutoff point for Tepeu 3 has varied with the different dating estimates assigned to it. For example, some authorities would prefer to see it terminated at nearer 10.3.0.0.0 or A.D. 889. In any event, our most immediate concern is with this century or so that saw the decline, collapse, or cessation of Maya hierarchic activity in the Southern Lowlands of the Maya area. We will, however, widen these chronological limits at times to take in the preceding century or more of the Tepeu 2 subperiod, going back to 9.14.0.0.0 or A.D. 710; and we will also move forward in time to consider the full chronological range of the Early Postclassic Period (up to about A.D. 1200 or 1300).

Our presentation begins with a very brief sketch of the archaeology of the Belize Valley. This sketch is followed with a more detailed examination of the data from the Barton Ramie site, our principal base of information and reference. However, in the course of this examination other sites in the valley, as well as some farther afield in the Southern Maya Lowlands, are also commented upon. A final section summarizes the discussion and offers observations and tentative interpretations.

BRIEF ARCHAEOLOGICAL SKETCH OF THE BELIZE VALLEY

The Belize Valley lies on the east-central edge of the Southern Maya Lowlands. The Belize River is formed by the conjunction of the Mopan and Macal rivers, streams that flow north along the Guatemalan–British Honduras border and unite near the town of El Cayo. The main course of the river then runs northeastward to the Caribbean. In the western one-half of British Honduras the Belize flows through limestone hill country covered with rain forest jungle. This is the country of the Maya ruins with which we are concerned. From Roaring Creek eastward to the sea the Belize cuts across savanna flatlands unsuited for agriculture. Here there are very few ruins.

In the valley and near the international line between Guatemala and Roaring Creek there is at least one major Maya ceremonial center ruin—,[1] Benque Viejo or Xunantunich (Thompson 1940). There are also a number of minor ceremonial centers; and thousands of small mounds or housemounds are located on the alluvial terraces of the Belize and can be found more or less continuously from Roaring Creek to

Benque Viejo. Quite probably these mounds continue beyond this point, along the Mopan and Macal tributaries, although these regions have not been systematically surveyed. Some of the minor ceremonial centers are also located on the alluvial terraces; however, others, and the major center of Benque Viejo, are located on high hills that border the course of the river at various points. Farther back from the valley, in the rolling hills of the hinterlands, the distribution of ruins is not known. It seems likely that the heaviest settlements existed along the river, given the benefits of water supply, ease of transportation, and fish resources; but it is only fair to say that we cannot be sure of this point, and we do know of both small housemound groups and mounds of minor ceremonial center size in these more distant hills. Perhaps significantly, the local people of the Belize Valley today do not consider the alluvial soils near the river as the best places for growing maize, though it will grow there; they prefer, instead, the flanks of the hills that lie at various distances from the river flats—up to two or three kilometers away.

The archaeology of the Belize Valley is similar to that of the Central Peten Zone, that is, to sites such as Holmul, Uaxactun, and Tikal. This observation refers primarily to ceramics. Hieroglyphics, monumental art, and architecture—as seen best at the major center of Benque Viejo—also have ties in this direction; but, of course, these hierarchic features relate more generally to the whole of the Southern Maya Lowlands.

The Belize Valley ceramic sequence begins with the Middle Preclassic horizon. This horizon, as well as the entire sequence, is best known from Barton Ramie where it is represented by the Jenney Creek Phase of the Mamom ceramic sphere (Willey, Culbert, and Adams 1967). A number of small house locations are associated with this phase at Barton Ramie. There is also a little house platform of this date at the very small ceremonial center of Nohoch Ek (Coe and Coe 1956); and although sherds relating to the Mamom sphere have been found at the major center of Benque Viejo (Thompson 1940), there are no indications at this center, or elsewhere in the valley, that Mamom-like ceramics are contemporaneous with any sizable ceremonial construction —a circumstance that accords, generally, with what we know of this horizon for the Southern Maya Lowlands as a whole.

Chicanel sphere ceramics follow those of the Mamom. At Barton

Ramie, the Barton Creek and Mount Hope phases (in that order) belong to the Chicanel or Late Preclassic horizon. As is true throughout the Peten, there are indications of population increase at this time; certainly there are more housemound constructions and more sites. The horizon is represented at Baking Pot (Bullard and Bullard 1965), Nohoch Ek, Benque Viejo, and a number of other places. Whether there was any big construction of this date at the larger sites of Baking Pot and Benque Viejo is unknown but, as substantial ceremonial building is associated with Chicanel at other Southern Lowlands sites, large-scale construction seems likely.

The Protoclassic horizon, with ceramics comparable to those of Holmul I, is heavily represented at Barton Ramie. The complex has an "intrusive" appearance, in that so many new forms, decoration techniques, and wares are introduced. This complex is called the Floral Park Phase. It is not clear just how many sites of this phase there are in the valley. Sherds of it appear, however, in the Baking Pot collections (WBGG 1965 : 304–9).

The succeeding Hermitage Phase at Barton Ramie is of Early Classic date and belongs to the Tzakol sphere. This horizon is also present at a number of minor ceremonial centers in the valley and at the major center of Benque Viejo. Again, reliable large-scale architectural digging information is lacking for these centers, although it is likely that most of them show some building for the period. However, probably less building occurred than in the succeeding Late Classic.

The Late Classic phases at Barton Ramie are the Tiger Run, which cross-dates with Tepeu 1, and the Spanish Lookout, which can be cross-dated with Tepeu 2 and 3. At Barton Ramie the housemound sampling excavations indicate a more or less steady population buildup from Preclassic through Classic times, but this buildup was especially pronounced for Spanish Lookout, where every mound tested showed an occupation for the phase. From all the data we were able to gather, this population expansion can be projected for the entire Belize Valley. A minor ceremonial center within the Barton Ramie group was certainly built upon—if not completely constructed—in Spanish Lookout times. The main ceremonial building at Baking Pot dates to both Tiger Run and Spanish Lookout (Bullard and Bullard 1965); the large minor center of Cahal Pech (Satterthwaite 1951) appears to be primarily a Late Classic construction. The larger buildings of the very minor center of Nohoch Ek are of this period (Coe and Coe 1956), and certainly the massive outer constructions of the Benque Viejo pyramids so date (Thompson 1940; MacKie 1961).

The terminal occupation of the Belize Valley appears to date to the early part of the Postclassic Period. This is known as the New Town Phase, so defined at Barton Ramie. New Town pottery has been found at Baking Pot (WBGG 1965 : 304–9), at the very small center of Warrie Head (WBGG 1965 : 311–12), and at a few other places in the valley; it seems to be missing, however, at Benque Viejo. It has wider relationships to the west, in the Peten, with the Caban Complex at Tikal (Willey, Culbert, and Adams 1967), and with pottery that Bullard (1970a) found at Macanche and that Cowgill (1963) encountered around Lake Peten. It should be noted that New Town pottery is quite distinct from, and obviously pertains to another tradition than, the Fine Orange wares of the Terminal Late Classic to Postclassic phases of the Pasion River (Adams 1971; Sabloff and Willey 1967; see also Willey, Culbert, and Adams 1967). At Barton Ramie, housemound occupance continued at a high level in the New Town Phase.

BARTON RAMIE: THE SPANISH LOOKOUT PHASE

With this background sketch, let us turn to particulars bearing directly on the latter part of the Late Classic and the Early Postclassic periods at Barton Ramie. In correlating the Barton Ramie sequence with that of Uaxactun, the Tiger Run Phase, as noted, can be matched with Tepeu 1 and is assigned dates of approximately A.D. 600 to 700. Tiger Run ceramics are very close to those of Uaxactun, Tikal, and other sites of the Central Zone, and they can be properly classed as being a part of the Tepeu ceramic sphere (Willey, Culbert, and Adams 1967). The Spanish Lookout Ceramic Complex, however, stands more apart from the Peten sites. Although there are obvious modal ties with the Tepeu 2 phase, Spanish Lookout is not considered a part of the Tepeu ceramic sphere. The pottery of early Spanish Lookout differs from that of the Peten in a number of features and especially in a partial changeover from a tradition of calcite temper to one of volcanic ash temper. This change is seen in the Belize Ceramic Group and in the ware known as Vinaceous Tawny. In fact, the Belize Valley seems to have been the manufacturing center for these ash-tempered wares, which were traded from the Belize Valley westward into the great sites of the Peten. In contrast, few Peten types are found in the Spanish Lookout Phase sites of the Belize Valley. This scarcity may reflect the marginal, somewhat provincial status of the Belize Valley region in relation to the more centrally located portions of the Southern Maya Lowlands at this peak of Maya Late Classic Period development in the eighth century A.D.

In the latter half of the Spanish Lookout Phase—let us say after about 10.0.0.0.0 or A.D. 830—there is another change in ceramic patterns. The ash-tempered pottery disappears; and calcite-tempered wares, which had never completely disappeared, are reasserted. There are other changes, too—polychrome painting is gone, and, in fact, there is very little decoration of any kind. This latter half of Spanish Lookout is believed to correlate with Tepeu 3 of Uaxactun and Tikal although it is not similar enough in content to be considered a part of the same ceramic sphere (the Eznab). The exact terminal date of Spanish Lookout is something of a problem, as, indeed, is the terminal date of Tepeu 3 and the other more or less contemporary phases throughout the Southern Lowlands. Gifford, in his Barton Ramie sequence chart (WBGG 1965 : 323), places this termination at A.D. 1000. I am inclined to think this a little late and prefer to set the date at somewhere between about A.D. 890 to 950, or from *katun* 10.3.0.0.0 to 10.6.0.0.0 (see, for example, the Tepeu 3 ending-date on the chart of Willey, Culbert, and Adams 1967 : Fig. 10). We are guessing, though, when it comes down to this fine shading of dates, and this is one of the problems that confronts us in an examination of the Maya collapse.

As to further archaeological cross-datings for Spanish Lookout, Gifford correlates the earlier part of the termination with Benque Viejo IIIB, the major later part with Benque Viejo IV, and a very terminal portion as post–Benque Viejo and coeval with San Jose V (for San Jose, see Thompson 1939). This dating is possible; but the Mount Maloney Black type, with its distinctive beveled-rim bowl, which Gifford uses for his terminal Spanish Lookout/post–Benque Viejo/San Jose V equation, is also abundantly present in Benque Viejo IV. I would prefer to terminate Spanish Lookout at the same point on the time chart as the termination of Benque Viejo IV—that is, at about A.D. 950. San Jose V may, or may not, have lasted longer than this.

Spanish Lookout ceramics, then, start with great vigor at about A.D. 700, although their makeup indicates the beginning of a regionalization and a divergence away from Peten styles and modes typical of Tepeu 2. At about A.D. 830 (10.0.0.0.0), or perhaps a little later, something of an aesthetic decline sets in; and at about A.D. 950 the phase comes to a close with a pottery complex considerably modified by the dropping out of the volcanic ash-tempered wares that were so typical of the earlier part of the phase. To repeat, this second half of the phase I would see as contemporaneous with Tepeu 3 and Benque Viejo IV.

As noted, population was at a maximum during the Spanish Lookout Phase at Barton Ramie—and probably over the entire Belize Valley. At Barton Ramie we know that a great many new house platforms were erected during this phase, and most of the earlier ones were built over or added to. Apparently, most of these Barton Ramie platforms had once been the bases for buildings of posts, thatch, and wattle and daub walls. In a few instances, particularly in the larger *plazuela* mounds, building walls were laid up in stone, at least in their basal portions; but most house construction must have been of perishable materials. The platforms were made of clay or earth, were surfaced with plaster and gravel floors, and frequently were faced with masonry retaining walls of dressed but uncoursed stones, though sometimes these retaining walls were plaster coated. Stairs leading from terraces to upper platforms and benches on platforms are frequent architectural features. In general, the Spanish Lookout Phase building materials and construction forms follow the patterns of the earlier periods at the site; however, the Spanish Lookout platforms tended to be somewhat more elaborate. Also: "the volume of Spanish Lookout Phase building is attested to not only by the number of mounds built or added to during the phase . . . but by the sizes of the actual increments of earth, stone, and plaster. Insofar as we could judge from our excavations most of the mounds studied had received half or more of their total bulk at this time" (WBGG 1965 : 291).

Also to be noted, the larger *plazuela* mound units were erected during the Tiger Run and Spanish Lookout phases in the Barton Ramie group. These units consisted of three or four structures, one of which was usually of considerable size, grouped around a raised plaza or court (WBGG 1965 : 293). In addition, the one substantial pyramid at Barton Ramie, BR-180-182, a mound rising 12 m. high and almost certainly of ceremonial import, was at least added to (if not fully constructed) during the Spanish Lookout Phase. It seems probable that these *plazuelas* and this minor ceremonial center pyramid reflect a growing aristocracy even within the outlying hamlets of the Belize Valley settlement.[2]

Some sixty burials were associated with the Spanish Lookout Phase at Barton Ramie. These burials were found in the dwelling mounds —below floors or in the flanks of the mounds. About one-half of them had some grave goods, including pottery and occasional ornaments and artifacts of bone, shell, or stone. No burials could be designated as very "rich," except within the modest relative spectrum of Barton Ramie. Those burials with the greatest amounts of goods were of early Spanish Lookout facet or belonged to the Tiger Run–Spanish Lookout transition (WBGG 1965 : 532–33). The skeletal material of the Barton Ramie burials was not well preserved, but from the measurements and observations that were taken on skeletons of all phases it was noticed that through time there was an increasing tendency toward a fragility and slenderness in bone structure. By Spanish Lookout times this condition was pronounced, and it may have been occasioned by growing nutritional problems (WBGG 1965 : 538).

BARTON RAMIE:
THE NEW TOWN PHASE

Our tests at Barton Ramie revealed sixty-five Spanish Lookout occupations out of the sixty-five mounds investigated. Of these same mounds, sixty-two also showed New Town Phase occupations superimposed over the Spanish Lookout levels. This continuity of occupation pattern is an argument for continuity of society or inhabitants. That is, one might reasonably suspect that the New Town people were the in situ descendants of the Spanish Lookout populations; however, the evidence for such a continuity is not conclusive. It is possible that a new group of people moved into the site after its abandonment by the Spanish Lookout Phase residents and established houses on the old mound platforms. Such house sites would have been selected to place living quarters above flood waters, for we have clear evidences of frequent seasonal floods during the Late Classic and Postclassic periods at Barton Ramie.

The ceramic evidence argues against continuity. As Gifford has pointed out (WBGG 1965 : 384–90), New Town pottery shows little in common with that of Spanish Lookout; it is in a quite different tradition. A good bit of the New Town pottery, especially that of the Augustine Ceramic Group, appears to have been made locally. By comparison to the Spanish Lookout pottery, it is relatively crude and slovenly. Much of the pottery of the phase is undecorated and even unslipped. The somewhat more frequently slipped and polychrome types of the Paxcaman Group are thought to be imports. Bullard (1970a, also this volume, chapter 11), in a general survey of Postclassic pottery of the Peten and the Belize Valley, considers New Town to be a part of what he has termed the "Central Peten Postclassic Tradition." According to Bullard, this tradition is distinguished by three principal ceramic groups: the Augustine, Paxcaman, and Topoxte. These groups are stylistically interrelated, and they overlap chronologically. In his view, which is supported by stratigraphy at the Peten site of Macanche, Augustine is the earliest of the three, Paxcaman comes next in time, and Topoxte is the latest. With this chronology in mind, Bullard interprets the Barton Ramie New Town Phase as having earlier and later facets. He notes that pottery of the Augustine Group is found on virtually all of the mounds at that site while Paxcaman types are more restricted in their distribution. Although the relative thinness of the deposition of New Town materials on most of the mounds precludes any sure stratigraphic separation of the two groups, it is Bullard's belief that there was a relatively large, earlier, Augustine–New Town occupation and that this was followed by a smaller Paxcaman–New Town occupation. Topoxte ceramics are not represented at Barton Ramie.

In Bullard's general scheme, these three ceramic divisions of the Postclassic correspond to Early, Middle, and Late Postclassic periods. The Early Postclassic he places at A.D. 950–1200; the Middle at A.D. 1200–1300; and the Late at A.D. 1300–1450. Assuming this to be the case, the Barton Ramie New Town Phase would thus span the Early and Middle Postclassic and would date from about A.D. 950 to 1300. Admittedly, this is a dating approximation. We lack radiocarbon dates; we also lack the kind of stratigraphy at Barton Ramie which would enable us to estimate whether or not there was a hiatus between the end of the Spanish Lookout Phase and the beginning of the New

Town Phase occupation. In fact, stratigraphic control on the New Town–like, or Central Peten Postclassic Tradition, phases from any part of the Peten or British Honduras is extremely weak, the only real exception being Macanche. We know that at Barton Ramie and around Lake Peten (Cowgill 1963) the ceramics of this tradition follow those of the Maya Late Classic, but that is about as far as the control goes. This situation is regrettable because it is just this kind of stratigraphy, bearing upon the nature and timing of the changeover between the Late Classic and the Early Postclassic, that we most desperately need to help us in clarifying what happened at the time of the collapse.

Bullard's Central Peten Postclassic Tradition is distributed around Lake Peten and the other lakes of the central part of the Peten Department, in the Belize Valley, and at Tikal. At the latter site, the central Peten Postclassic Tradition is represented in the Caban Phase, and there Culbert (Willey, Culbert, and Adams 1967) considers the discontinuity between it and the previous Late Classic ceramics so definite that he is inclined to postulate an occupation by a new people. Bullard notes that the broader archaeological associations of the Augustine and Paxcaman ceramic groups are with simple dwelling mound constructions; and these associations, plus the appearance of the pottery itself, suggest to Bullard a homogeneous peasantry lacking strong social distinctions. Gifford is of a similar opinion concerning the nature of New Town society. Significantly, New Town wares have not been reported from the Benque Viejo ceremonial center. A few sherds have turned up at Baking Pot, although there is nothing there to suggest possible correlation with any ceremonial construction activity. Their presence at Tikal and at Tayasal indicates that the people who made Augustine-Paxcaman pottery sometimes utilized earlier monumental works for burials or casual occupance, but this use is not related to significant construction work. All of this is in interesting contradistinction to the Late Postclassic Topoxte Ceramic Group associations. For at least at one site, Topoxte proper, the makers of this pottery also constructed a ceremonial center on a lake island.

At Barton Ramie there probably was no ceremonial building during the New Town Phase. In fact, the minor ceremonial center there, the Br-180-182 mounds, was one of the very few locations examined by us that yielded no New Town pottery. Among the dwelling mounds, some seventeen showed substantial building that can be dated as New Town (WBGG 1965 : 291, 293). At BR-35 there was a considerable depth of clay fill that contained mostly New Town sherds, and because these sherds did not appear to be intrusive the platform can be so dated. BR-123 displayed a superficial mantle of large stones and some alignments of stones that are attributed to New Town. These stone mantles were found at some of the other mounds. The mantles frequently covered not only the summit platforms but also the mound flanks, and possibly they were laid up as a protection against the erosive effects of flooding. However, most of the mantles were badly churned by tree growth and more recent agricultural activities, and often it was impossible to be certain of their New Town dating. But to conclude, by comparison with the massive amount of platform building that occurred at Barton Ramie in the Spanish Lookout Phase, New Town dwelling mound construction must be considered very minor. The New Town occupation was extensive, the construction minimal.

No burials could be dated definitely to New Town, although several were placed as either New Town or Spanish Lookout on the basis of their mound contexts. None had diagnostic grave goods with it or, in fact, grave goods of any consequence.

SUMMARY AND OBSERVATIONS

During the Middle and Late Preclassic, the Protoclassic, and the Early Classic periods, the populations of the Belize Valley appear to have been participants in the Northeast Peten regional developments of Maya culture. In the earlier part of the Late Classic Period—during Tepeu 1 times—this cultural alliance with sites immediately to the west and north continued. It is probable that through all of this Preclassic-to-Classic span the Belize Valley was somewhat marginal to the currents of culture change and development seen in places such as Tikal, Uaxactun, Holmul, and elsewhere; however, this marginality was reflected only in a thinning of the tangible expressions of Maya hierarchical culture.

In the later part of the Late Classic Period, the Belize Valley Spanish Lookout Phase is cross-dated with Tepeu 2 and Tepeu 3 of the Peten. There is, however, a notable divergence in ceramic trends and a suggestion that the flow of ceramic trade goods at this time was from the Belize Valley westward, rather than the reverse. This trend might be interpreted as reflecting a continuing, or increasing, economic and political marginality of the Belize Valley to the Central Peten Zone; but we need other supporting data to bolster this interpretation. In any event, the Spanish Lookout Phase saw a population maximum in the valley, with extensive domestic and ceremonial building. At about 10.0.0.0.0 or A.D. 830, there was something of a decline in Spanish Lookout ceramics, with the virtual disappearance of finer polychrome wares. This decline is seemingly correlated with a similar ceramic decline in Tepeu 3 in the Peten. We know, of course, that other aspects of Maya culture also declined during Tepeu 3 times in the Peten; and in the Belize Valley, the major ceremonial center of Benque Viejo seems to have been partially abandoned in the period after 10.0.0.0.0 (A.D. 830), the Tepeu 3–Benque Viejo IV–Late Spanish Lookout horizon. At Barton Ramie, however, full housemound occupance continued during this horizon. Unfortunately, it is not certain from our data at hand whether there was a decline in dwelling mound construction activities during this Tepeu 3–Late Spanish Lookout period. The only change that we can record—as noted above—was the decline in ceramic decoration. The dating on this Tepeu 3–Late Spanish Lookout period remains very approximate and debatable. Minimally, it probably spanned 10.0.0.0.0 to 10.3.0.0.0 or A.D. 830 to 889; maximally, it may have gone on to 10.6.0.0.0 or about A.D. 950 or even a bit later.

The Postclassic occupation in the Belize Valley is known as the New Town Phase, and is best defined from Barton Ramie. The New Town Phase is characterized by ceramics that show a break in tradition with the Spanish Lookout wares and belong instead, to what has been designated as a Central Peten Postclassic Ceramic Tradition, and to the earlier ceramic groups of that tradition—the Augustine and the Paxcaman. These ceramic groups have been dated by Bullard to the Early and Middle Postclassic periods, or to a time range estimated to have been from about A.D. 950 to 1300. If this dating is correct, then pottery of the earlier of these groups, the Augustine, should overlie that of the Late Spanish Lookout Phase at Barton Ramie, with little or no time gap between. The nature of the house platform occupance at Barton Ramie also suggests a continuity of settlement at that site from

Late Spanish Lookout into New Town. On the other hand, the differences between the Spanish Lookout and New Town pottery complexes could be interpreted as reflecting a population replacement. The question is not easily resolved with the information we now have.

Insofar as we know, no significant ceremonial or large-scale construction occurred in the Belize Valley during the New Town Phase or in Postclassic times. The major ceremonial center of Benque Viejo appears to have been deserted during this time.

A general overview of the data suggests the following as the most likely course of events in the Late Classic to Postclassic periods in the Belize Valley.

1. The Early Spanish Lookout Phase was the time of maximum population and cultural activity in the Belize Valley. This time correlates with the Tepeu 2 Phase of the Peten and with the widespread florescence of Late Classic Maya civilization in other parts of the Southern Lowlands.

2. At about 10.0.0.0.0 or A.D. 830, which coincides with the end of Tepeu 2 and the beginning of Tepeu 3, cultural activity declined relatively suddenly in the major ceremonial center of the Belize Valley, Benque Viejo. This decline can be correlated with the same decline noted elsewhere in Maya Lowlands ceremonial centers. In the Belize Valley the decline marks the beginning of the Late Spanish Lookout Phase. In the residential mounds at Barton Ramie polychrome pottery disappears at this time, but, otherwise, no definite evidence of population decline nor of housemound construction decline can be found.

3. At somewhere between 10.3.0.0.0 and 10.6.0.0.0, or between about A.D. 890 and 950, the Late Spanish Lookout Phase came to an end at Barton Ramie and appears to have been succeeded almost immediately by the New Town Phase. Most of the dwelling mounds occupied during the Spanish Lookout Phase continued to be occupied during the New Town Phase, and possibly the New Town peoples were the direct descendants of the Spanish Lookout peoples. If so, however, they had made radical changes in their ceramic tradition. Possibly the Spanish Lookout peoples had abandoned the site, and it was almost immediately reoccupied by New Town groups. The nature of New Town society is suggested as nonhierarchical and somewhat reduced. This inference is drawn from the absence of ceremonial constructions, the

absence of fine craft goods, the general humble quality of the material remains of the phase as contrasted with earlier Maya phases, and the lack of substantial domestic building.

4. Other occurrences of New Town–like ceramics in the Central Peten suggest that the New Town occupation lasted through the Early and Middle Postclassic periods, or from about A.D. 950 to 1300. After that, Barton Ramie was abandoned. We know that there were some few Maya settlements in the Belize Valley in early historic times, but the degree to which these settlements continued in a New Town tradition, or were derived from some other tradition, is not known. Available evidence indicates that the Belize Valley was very thinly populated—if populated at all—during the Late Postclassic Period.

5. The Maya Classic collapse in the Belize Valley is, thus, seen as a relatively swift breakdown of hierarchical culture in the mid-ninth century A.D. Major ceremonial centers, and ceremonial building and activity in general, never revived after this breakdown. Populations of the sustaining areas—as at Barton Ramie—continued in residence for another 100 years or so, maintaining the same ceramic traditions they possessed before the hierarchical breakdown. After this time, they either changed these ceramic traditions or were replaced by peoples bringing a new ceramic tradition. This terminal phase, the New Town, continued in the valley until the middle of the Postclassic Period, or for another 200 to 300 years. The level of culture during this time was simple, nonhierarchical.

NOTES

1. See Bullard (1960) for a definition of "major" and "minor" ceremonial centers.

2. William Rathje (1970b) has argued, on the basis of burials, their associated grave goods, and the nature and location of their interment, that Maya society of the Late Classic grew increasingly aristocratic—in contrast to earlier periods —with leadership in politico-religious matters falling more and more to hereditary groups or lineages. He infers this, particularly, from the numbers of Late Classic burials (of both sexes and all ages) found in the major ceremonial centers. The Barton Ramie evidence cited here tends partly to confirm this; however, the evidence also suggests that class differences and prerogatives were also being expressed in the more "rural" communities.

Continuity and Disruption during Terminal Late Classic Times at Seibal: Ceramic and Other Evidence

JEREMY A. SABLOFF

Department of Anthropology
Harvard University

INTRODUCTION

Seibal is a large lowland Maya center on the Rio Pasion in Guatemala.[1] The site was first discovered around 1890 (Arthes 1893) and later explored by T. Maler (1908) and S. G. Morley (1938). In the early 1960s, members of the Peabody Museum's Altar de Sacrificios expedition visited Seibal, and a new map of the site was made by R. E. W. Adams. The first excavations at Seibal, a series of test pits, were also made by Adams (1963a) at this time. In 1964, the Peabody Museum, with support from the National Science Foundation and private sources, initiated a major archaeological project at Seibal with G. R. Willey as project director and A. L. Smith as field director. Excavations were begun in the 1965 season and continued in the 1966 through 1968 seasons. Laboratory analysis was run concurrently with the excavations and proceeded through June 1969, when the project officially came to a close. A number of monographs describing the archaeological results of the Seibal Project are now being prepared.[2]

Seibal was chosen for excavation and survey for several reasons. Principally, it was noted that many of its monuments were dated to the Tenth Cycle in the Maya calendar and were among the latest in the Southern Maya Lowlands. In addition, a number of non–Classic Maya traits were depicted on these late stelae. It was thought that data uncovered at Seibal in conjunction with the information about the newly discovered Jimba Phase at Altar de Sacrificios would help to clarify the problem of the collapse of Classic Maya civilization; moreover, it was hoped that certain of the hypotheses about an invasion of the Rio Pasion area by foreigners, first formulated on the basis of the Altar work, would receive additional testing and amplification or correction at Seibal (Smith and Willey 1966a). In essence, the ceremonial center excavations and extensive peripheral survey and excavation at Seibal were a continuation of the Rio Pasion project begun at Altar de Sacrificios by Willey and Smith in 1958 (Willey and Smith 1969).

As new data were uncovered and continuing plans for new excavations at Seibal were made, various hypotheses about the nature of the site's Terminal Classic occupation were formulated and examined. The Altar de Sacrificios hypotheses were also examined in light of the larger body of data then available. We began to believe that the invasion hypothesis proposed by Adams, based on his studies at Altar de Sacrificios (Adams 1971), was applicable with some modifications (see Sabloff and Willey 1967) to the Seibal data. Similar general hypotheses about invasions of the Southern Lowlands had been proposed in recent years by Ruz (1953), Girard (1959), Cowgill (1964), Vogt (1946b), and Jiménez Moreno (1966), among others, and as far back as 1914 by Joyce (1914). But Adams was the first to use a quantity of excavated archaeological data to formulate and support his contentions.

Elsewhere, I have discussed my hypothesis that the invasion was successful in causing the collapse of Classic Maya civilization in the Southern Lowlands because it acted as an active triggering mechanism for a number of internal processes which had reached critical points prior to the invasion (Sabloff 1971a). These processes, including climax population or overpopulation and maximal use or overuse of the soil, as well as disruptions in trade and transportation, cumulatively brought about the disintegration of Classic Maya civilization once the precarious man-nature balance of the Southern Lowlands had been tipped by the invaders. In the following pages, however, I will focus attention on the specific archaeological data, especially the ceramic, which are relevant to the Bayal (or Terminal Late Classic) Phase at Seibal. These data will be presented and discussed in the context of the whole Classic sequence at the site.

THE PRE-BAYAL SEQUENCE

Seibal is located on the west bank of the Rio Pasion in the south-central part of the Department of Peten, Guatemala. The site is about one hundred kilometers south of Tikal and approximately the same distance upriver from Altar de Sacrificios. Located on several steep hills, the site consists of three principal ceremonial groups, Groups A, C, and D, and a large number of house units, as well as a limited number of outlying temples.

The site was first settled around 800 B.C., in the early Middle Preclassic Real Xe Phase. It grew during Escoba Mamom times and, by the Cantutse Chicanel Phase, had already become a sizable ceremonial center. At the end of the latter phase, that is, about A.D. 300, Seibal was virtually abandoned. The occupation of the site during the Early Classic Period (the Junco Phase) was sparse and population reached a very low ebb. Much of the decorated pottery of this period, obviously restricted in quantity, was almost certainly traded into Seibal, perhaps from the Uaxactun-Tikal area. There was no building or carving of monuments during the Junco Phase.

Ceramic evidence suggests an increasing population and an expanding occupation of the site in Tepejilote times (early Late Classic). Many of the small structure units were occupied at this time. Among the significant Tepejilote ceramic data are: the close similarities between the Seibal and Uaxactun polychromes; the identity in form between several locally made (?) vessels and Vinaceous Tawny Ware vessels, which are found only in the east-central Peten and British Honduras; the trading connections with southern British Honduras and perhaps the Alta Verapaz and the lower Usumacinta; and the somewhat restricted distribution of Tepejilote pottery within the ceremonial center. At the very end of the phase, there was a simultaneous cessation of the polychrome trade and an emphasis on certain censer types, plus a few architectural peculiarities (including both a brief building spurt and the possible noncompletion of a court complex in Group D).

The ceramic evidence has led us to hypothesize that the polychrome pottery was traded in from the east-central Peten and that some of the people who were responsible for the population buildup at Seibal in the seventh century A.D. may have come from sites immediately to the north. Moreover, we suspect that Group D, a compact, defensible group, was the ceremonial center of the site during Tepejilote times. Finally, some kind of disruption of the ceremonial area (and its inhabitants) in Group D occurred, more or less coincident (within 60 years) with the ending of trade with the east-central Peten and the beginning of the introduction of "foreign" traits.

THE BAYAL PHASE
AND ITS CERAMIC COMPLEX

The Bayal Phase (A.D. 830–930) was the final phase at Seibal, and it was the time of the most brilliant architectural and sculptural achievements at the site. Population reached a maximum during this period. Bayal ceramics were found in large quantities in most sections of the site, with the possible exception of parts of Group D.

Bayal ceramic diagnostics include: Fine Orange Ware; Fine Gray Ware; vases with pedestal bases; hollow handle ("ladle") form; hollow bulbous feet; solid conical feet; bowls with slightly to markedly incurved sides and circumferential grooves immediately below the lips on the exterior; tripod plates with heavy, incised designs on the interior floors; distinctive non–Classic Maya design motifs; modeled-carving; gadrooning; appliquéd spikes.

In addition, ceramic traits common to both the Tepejilote and Bayal complexes include: jars with outcurved necks and thickened (folded) or everted rims; bowls with slightly to markedly incurved sides, exterior thickened rims, and circumferential ridges or appliquéd fillets below rims on exteriors; impressed designs; unit stamping; regular striation with medium to heavy depth and width; red slip with much fire clouding and color variation; and easily erodable, thin red slip.

Group A appears to have been the preeminent group during the Bayal Phase. Thirteen carved stelae, as well as many plain monuments, were erected in Group A at this time. In addition, such structures as A-3, A-13, A-14, A-19, A-24, and A-54, and probably many other structures, were built during this phase. Although the basic form of the group had been established before the Bayal Phase, some new buildings were added at this time, and many new superstructures were added to existing structures. Much of the Bayal material in Group A was found in surface collections; however, a fair quantity was also found in architectural fill deposits.

Group C was also the scene of much Bayal activity. The platform at the juncture of the causeways, Structure C-4, and probably Structures C-9, 79 (the round structure), and the whole causeway system linking this group with the other groups, date to the Bayal Phase. Stela 14, at the juncture of the causeways, also dates to this time. Again, the Bayal material came mainly from surface collections or architectural fill deposits.

Group D revealed the most limited distribution of Bayal pottery of any part of the site. Although much general Late Classic material was found, definite Bayal sherds were limited to scattered sherds on several structures and in surface collections except for Court A (and especially the area around D-26), the East Plaza, and the plaza in front of Structure D-41. It should be noted that the three last-named locations, which had quantities of Bayal material, are all clustered in the northeast corner of Group D and that they are all near the end of Causeway III.

Heavy concentrations of Bayal pottery were discovered in the small-structure units. In fact, there are almost no units that do not have some evidence of Bayal occupation. It is also of interest to note that a much greater percentage of fine paste sherds was found in the small-structure units than in all other contexts in the site combined.

A large quantity of the Bayal sherds was discovered in surface collections and in architectural fill deposits underneath patios and platform benches. But more significantly, a fair quantity of sherds was found in occupational refuse deposits. These deposits usually had the form of thin sheetlike coverings around the various platforms in a unit.[3]

THE BAYAL COMPLEX
IN THE LATE CLASSIC SEQUENCE

Stratigraphy: Court A, Group D

The best Classic ceramic and architectural stratigraphy at Seibal was uncovered in the intensive excavations undertaken by Kent C. Day in Court A of Group D. The excavations revealed a five-part architectural sequence which began in Late Preclassic times and ended in Terminal Late Classic times.[4]

During the Cantutse Phase, a structure was built in the center of what was later to become the court. This structure is directly overlain by an early Tepejilote court with structures on all but the west side. In Court A, as well as in much of the site, the Early Classic is clearly missing. The early court is in turn overlain by another Tepejilote court with structures on all four sides of the court. It was at this time that an important Tepejilote refuse midden off the south side of the west "house" platform structure (D-26) was formed.

The only apparent major ceramic change between the two Tepejilote courts is a change in red monochrome types (from only Nanzal Red: Light Color Variety to a much smaller percentage of Nanzal Red that co-occurs with Tinaja Red: Variety Unspecified). The change involves a color difference and possibly some small form variations. In addition, there was a slight trend towards more cream polychromes (Tepeu 2 rather than 1 at Uaxactun) in the upper level, and there was a plate with a notched ridge (a Uaxactun Tepeu 2 trait) in the upper level and none in the lower.

Near the end of the Tepejilote Phase, the structures on the north, east, and south sides of the court were rebuilt—these are the surface structures today: D-27, D-28, and D-29—and the platform on the west side was covered with rubble. It is possible that a new superstructure was planned for the west side and that construction never passed the stage of building up a rubble fill. Another possibility is that it was planned to keep this side of the court open.

In the final construction stage, during the Bayal Phase, a house platform was built on top of the rubble on the west side of the court. Evidence of a fireplace on the platform and deep refuse deposits behind the structure were uncovered. In addition, a new room was probably added to the "palace" structure (D-29) at this time, as well as a new bench in another room. Some Bayal debris (occupational?) was found above the floor in this structure.

It should also be noted that deep, at least 60.0 cm., Bayal deposits, possibly refuse, were discovered in the East Plaza, which lies at the base of the back side of Structure D-27. Possibly this Bayal material was also refuse of the inhabitants of Court A.

Thus, the excavations in Court A uncovered two refuse deposits—one from the Tepejilote Phase and one from the Bayal Phase—with abundant pottery in both deposits. They also revealed the whole Classic sequence with the exception of the Junco Phase—the lack of which agrees with the evidence of the weakness of this phase in the rest of the site. Thirdly, the excavations add weight to the hypothesis that there was a distinct Tepejilote-Bayal transition facet [5] of the Tepejilote Phase. If proven, this hypothesis would further substantiate our theory that there was a non–Classic Maya takeover of Seibal in Bayal times. Finally, the Court A sequence shows the basic continuity of one-half dozen major Late Classic types from the Tepejilote Phase through the Bayal Phase. This continuity has had important consequences in dating various lots at Seibal and also has implications for the nature of the cultural change at Seibal during Terminal Late Classic times. With these considerations in mind, we now turn to a discussion of the continuity of certain Late Classic types.

Continuity of Late Classic Types

One of the major difficulties encountered in dating various lots at Seibal was the apparent continuity of some of the major Cambio, Encanto, and Tinaja Group types from Tepejilote through Bayal times (see Sabloff 1969 : Fig. 5, Table 1). When definite Bayal material (such as the many fine paste types, Cameron Incised, or Cubeta Incised) or definite Tepejilote material (such as the Saxche and Palmar Group polychromes or Nanzal Red) were present, it was often possible to accurately date a structure, level, or deposit. On other occasions, however, it was only possible to state that a lot had a Late Classic date.

It might be pointed out that there could be significant percentage differences in the quantities of the types between the two phases.

However, this possibility is difficult to test. Only one pure Tepejilote refuse deposit has been found. The type percentages in this deposit could be used to compare with the percentages in the many Bayal refuse deposits, but all the Bayal deposits were on or near the surface and readily subject to earlier admixture. Thus, it is virtually impossible to point to a definitely pure Bayal deposit at Seibal. Nevertheless, in cases where percentage comparisons have been made, no significant trends have appeared.

The preceding discussion raises a second point: if it is not possible to isolate a pure Bayal deposit, is it not a possibility that all the examples of the so-called continuous Late Classic types are really examples of Tepejilote admixture in the Bayal deposits? The argument against this point is reasonably strong. First of all, within Bayal refuse deposits of any depth, such as in the small-structure unit 24, there are no definite trends in type percentages from the top to the bottom of the deposits. If types such as Tinaja Red were really Tepejilote, one could expect a significant percentage reduction in the upper levels of the deposit. In addition, on the basis of the type percentages from the Court A Tepejilote midden, it can be seen that the half dozen types in question were present at that time in some quantity. Yet, at Altar de Sacrificios, some of these types, such as Encanto Striated (with heavy striation) and Pantano Impressed, are exclusively Boca (Terminal Late Classic) types, while others are present both in Boca times and earlier. Thus, the apparently unusual aspect of the Seibal situation in comparison to Altar is not the continuity of Tepejilote types into the Bayal Phase, but the presence of several "late" types in an earlier phase. Hence the lack of definitely pure Bayal deposits does not really weaken the case for continuity of certain Late Classic types at Seibal.

It should be stressed, moreover, that the continuity of certain Late Classic types is not a phenomenon restricted to Seibal only. A similar continuity is also present in some types at Uaxactun and Altar de Sacrificios. (Culbert [personal communication] reports equally strong continuities at Tikal.) At Uaxactun, for example, the differences between much of the Tepeu 1, 2, and 3 Peten Gloss monochrome pottery are not great.[6]

In addition, the manner in which the Tepeu 3 Complex was defined at Uaxactun may have helped to obliterate some of the typological continuities. R. E. Smith has stated: "Tepeu 3 was determined by subtracting all recognized earlier types from the vast surface accumulations" (Smith 1955 : 13). This determination was then apparently checked by "further excavation and comparison" (Smith 1955 : 13). In A-V, for example, Vault II*f*, *g*, and *h* constructions were considered to be Tepeu 3 and contained a combined total of 486 sherds. Yet there were also considerable quantities of Tepeu 1 and 2 sherds in these levels. Moreover, there were some Tepeu 3 sherds in Tepeu 1 and 2 levels in A-V. In explaining this occurrence, Smith (1955 : 201) states: "The percentages of these occurrences rise gradually from 3.4 in Vault II*a* to 12.4 in Vault II*h*, finally reaching 50.1 on the surface. The early appearance of late types is natural and to be expected. They may have been acquired from an area already manufacturing many of the Tepeu 3 types, or they may have been precursors, early attempts at something different." By his very technique of defining the Tepeu 3 Complex, Smith has tended to exclude the possibility that a given type could have maintained its quantitative peak throughout the Tepeu 2 and 3 complexes.

It should also be emphasized that in relation to the Cambio and Encanto Group types, Smith and Gifford (1966 : 173) state that these types are found, apparently with no significant percentage trend, in all three Tepeu complexes. But if an unslipped or striated type could have a three-complex peak, is there any valid cultural reason why a monochrome type could not have a two-complex peak? As Culbert (1968 : 4) has said, "Single-complex types are not very common in the ceramic sequences with which I have worked."

At Altar de Sacrificios, types such as Tinaja Red, Encanto Striated, Subin Red, and Chaquiste Impressed appear throughout the Late Classic, with different varieties in the various complexes (Adams 1971). However, I have not been able to see any consistent differences between the Subin and Bocul varieties of Subin Red and the Sekantutz and Macaw varieties of Chaquiste Impressed; and, given Adams's descriptions and illustrations, I would not be able to consistently sort sherds of these varieties from one another.

Thus, with the exception of some minor form changes at Uaxactun and Altar de Sacrificios, there is a great deal of typological continuity in unslipped and plain and simply decorated monochrome red (plus brown and orange) types at Seibal, Uaxactun, and Altar de Sacrificios, especially between the Tepeu 2– and Tepeu 3–like complexes. This continuity is in contrast to the many changes in the special wares, polychrome groups, and highly decorated types.

Finally, the continuity of important unslipped and monochrome jar and bowl types from the Tepejilote Phase to the Bayal Phase is significant in understanding the nature of the cultural changes that occurred at Seibal during Terminal Late Classic times. Despite the major changes in the ceremonial center attributable to the influence of non–Classic Maya peoples and the virtually complete change in decorated or "fancy" pottery, the local Seibal pottery-making industry continued producing pottery, and there was no change in the form or nature of the manufacture of basic cooking and storage pots.

In relation to the highly decorated types, however, it would appear that during Tepejilote times Seibal obtained most of its serving pottery from outside its sustaining area. The bulk of the polychrome pottery may have come from the east-central Peten, while a few pieces may have been obtained from the Alta Verapaz. Also some kind of contact, perhaps trading, existed with areas both upriver (Poptun, southern British Honduras) and downriver (Altar de Sacrificios, the lower Usumacinta); and Seibal participated in the general Tepeu ceramic sphere as defined by the Conference on the Prehistoric Ceramics of the Maya Lowlands (Willey, Culbert, and Adams 1967 : 310, Fig. 8). As we shall soon see, these trading relationships were radically changed in the following Bayal Phase.

The Tepejilote-Bayal Transition

The whole question of the continuity and discontinuity of Late Classic types at Seibal is relevant to the recognition of a late facet of the Tepejilote Complex which occupied an important transitional time period in Seibal's culture history. As will be discussed below, I was able to isolate an *incensario* subcomplex of the Tepejilote Complex. Much of this censer material (Cambio Unslipped: White Wash Variety and Pedregal Modeled: Appliquéd Head Variety) was found on and under the staircases of Structure D-32. It was associated with general Late Classic types and some eroded polychromes. In other words, there was no definite Bayal material, and the Tepejilote material was in an eroded state—more eroded than the Tepejilote pottery in the fill of Court A. In addition, the fourth architectural stage of Court A, the one in which the west side was left as a rubble heap, followed two stages of Tepejilote construction and preceded a stage of Bayal construction. It, too, is by and large associated with generalized Late Classic pottery. In Group A, the substructure of A-14, which probably dates to around 9.17.0.0.0 (A.D. 771), has similar ceramic association. Therefore, there would appear to have been a small time gap between the end of Tepejilote pottery use—much of it "fancy" polychrome plates, bowls, and vases—and the beginning of Bayal pottery use—including the fine paste plates, bowls, and vases. During this apparent gap, the Late Classic unslipped and monochrome jars and bowls continued to be made and used, and the number of modeled censers increased.

The evidence for the transition is definitely stronger in Group D. We know that at about this time the ceremonial locus of the site shifted from Group D to Group A. In addition, there was a change in the *incensario* ritual and in architectural and stylistic patterns, caused by the influences of non–Classic Maya peoples. In other words, a good case can be made for a change of elite at Seibal at the beginning of the Bayal Phase. Possibly trade with the central Peten for "fancy" serving and table pottery (polychromes) was cut off and this whole class of pottery was replaced by the importation of fine paste pottery by the new elite, who established their ceremonial headquarters in Group A. If so, one might expect to find evidence of mixed cultural patterns or some variation of an established pattern—or a "transitional period," in archaeological parlance—in Group D, the locus of the old ceremonialism. There could have been a brief emphasis on the old censer cult and a last gasp of ceremonial building.

Thus, there is some evidence for a Tepejilote-Bayal transitional facet at the end of the Tepejilote Phase. However, because of the lack of better, concrete data, this facet is only suggested and not established as part of the Seibal sequence. The seat of the old ceremonialism witnessed a greater transitional wrench than the rest of the site at the time of the incursion of non–Classic Maya influences, for a transitional facet is only present in Group D and not in the rest of the ceremonial center or in any of the small-structure units.

Further Evidence of Transition:
The Distribution of Incensarios

The locations and associations of the various *incensario* types—Cambio Unslipped: White Wash Variety; Pedregal Modeled: Appliquéd Head Variety; Miseria Appliquéd: Variety Unspecified; Miseria Appliquéd: Hollow Handle Variety—are suggestive enough to warrant a separate discussion. Much of the Cambio Unslipped: White Wash Variety material was found in Group D in Tepejilote, or Tepejilote-Bayal Transition, contexts, while much of the Miseria Appliquéd: Variety Unspecified and Miseria Appliquéd: Hollow Handle Variety material was discovered in Group A in Bayal contexts. In addition, a small quantity of these types was discovered in small-structure units and outlying structures. Unfortunately, the distribution of the censer types was not quite as clear-cut as the statement above would indicate. Nevertheless, the distributions and datings of the censer types are reasonably distinct.

The spiked (Miseria Appliquéd: Variety Unspecified) and ladle (Miseria Appliquéd: Hollow Handle Variety) censers' dating and locations are fairly secure. These types were found mostly in Group A with some examples in small structure units and outlying "temples"; the contexts were almost always Bayal. Only four Miseria Appliquéd: Variety Unspecified sherds were discovered in Group D, and two of these had Bayal associations. On the other hand, the bulk of the Cambio Unslipped: White Wash Variety and Pedregal Modeled: Appliquéd Head Variety material was found in Group D (especially D-32) in Tepejilote deposits.

However, a few examples of Pedregal Modeled: Appliquéd Head Variety were found in Group A and at the altar at the end of Causeway IV. In addition, in outlying "temple" 7527 (in Cache 17, a "votive" cache within the temple fill), some fragmentary examples of this type were associated with Miseria Appliquéd: Variety Unspecified and Miseria Appliquéd: Hollow Handle Variety sherds. But, as is true of most late phases, it is difficult to find deposits that do not have earlier admixtures. It is also possible that a few of the Tepejilote pieces were either used on into the later Bayal Phase or were saved and preserved because of their ceremonial significance.

Thus, what we have at Seibal in terms of the definitions proposed by the Conference on the Prehistoric Ceramics of the Maya Lowlands are two *incensario* subcomplexes.[7] That is to say, the Seibal censer types with their distinct functions and datings form subcomplexes of the Tepejilote and the Bayal complexes. In addition, as we have seen (pages 116–17), the existence of the Tepejilote *Incensario* Subcomplex suggested that it might be possible for us to define a temporally significant late facet of the Tepejilote Phase. But, as pointed out, the data are somewhat equivocal.

Obviously, the recognition of the two subcomplexes has potentially significant implications for understanding the processes of change at Seibal from Tepejilote to Bayal times. It would appear that as the ceremonial locus of the site shifted from Group D to Group A, there also was a shift in religious practices or in the nature of the *incensario* ritual. In other words, the older elaborate flanged cylinders with the sun god heads (Pedregal Modeled: Appliquéd Head Variety) and the separate bowls for burning the incense (Cambio Unslipped: White Wash Variety) were replaced by much simpler looking spiked (Miseria Appliquéd: Variety Unspecified) and ladle (Miseria Appliquéd: Hollow Handle Variety) *incensarios*. These later censers were associated with Tenth Cycle monuments and fine paste ceramics, and a few of them have forms that resemble Postclassic censers from Tikal and northern Yucatan.

THE BAYAL COMPLEX COMPARED WITH OTHER ''TEPEU 3'' COMPLEXES

Altar de Sacrificios and Uaxactun

The Boca Complex at Altar de Sacrificios displays close similarities to the Bayal Complex. Although the ceramic content of these two complexes is not identical, there is a high type-variety correlation, and the two complexes belong to their own Terminal Late Classic ceramic sphere—the Boca sphere (Willey, Culbert, and Adams 1967: 310–11). However, the Bayal Complex contains some types—such as Altar Orange, Trapiche Incised, Cedro Gadrooned, Tres

Naciones Gray—that are found in the succeeding Jimba Complex at Altar and are not present in the Boca Complex.

The Bayal Complex also shares some types with the Tepeu 3 Complex at Uaxactun but not to the same extent as with the Boca Complex. Tepeu 3 generally lacks such types as Subin Red, Chaquiste Impressed (both varieties), and Pantano Impressed (especially the stamped variety), which are important in the Rio Pasion area. Both spiked (Miseria Appliquéd) and modeled (Pedregal Modeled) censers are present in Tepeu 3. Interestingly enough, the Tepeu 3 Complex, like the Bayal, does have some forms that closely resemble fine paste forms (tripod plate with interior incision and bowl with incurved sides and "bead orifice"). The forms in non–fine paste wares were not generally found at Altar de Sacrificios, although R. E. Smith does illustrate a Cubeta Incised tripod plate from Altar (Smith 1955 : Fig. 31f1). There is a small quantity of fine paste pottery at Uaxactun including Pabellon Modeled-carved (mostly), Trapiche Incised, Cedro Gadrooned, and Tumba Black-on-orange from the Altar Group; Yalton Black-on-orange and Kilikan Composite from the Silho Group; and a Fine Gray tripod plate. In contrast to Seibal, only one whole Pabellon Modeled-carved vessel and one Pabellon Modeled-carved sherd definitely predate the end of major construction at Uaxactun.

In discussing the Bayal Complex of Seibal, Adams has stated: "As noted in the preliminary report on that site (Adams 1963a), there is no essential difference between the Tepeu 3 (Bayal Boca) Complex there and the ceramics which make up Boca Complex at Altar" (1971 : 149). And further:

> There is no evidence for the presence of a purely fine paste complex at Seibal equivalent to Jimba Complex at Altar. Neither is there evidence for the temporal extension and consequent qualitative development of the Seibal Bayal ceramics beyond the lifetime of the Altar Boca phase. In other words, the complexes are not only qualitatively nearly identical, but they are probably wholly contemporaneous, ending at about the same time, which is approximately the date of the last monuments at Seibal, 1c.4.0.0.0 (Adams 1971 : 149–51).

Although I am in general agreement with Adams, it is my belief that he partially misjudged the fine paste content of the Bayal Complex.[8]

He noted that during the Boca Phase at Altar de Sacrificios, some Jimba pottery, "mainly Pabellon Modeled-carved, Tumba Black-on-orange, and Poite Incised" (Adams 1971 : 135), was traded into the site. Yet virtually all the Jimba types from the Altar and Tres Naciones groups found at Seibal are from the Bayal Phase. Moreover, sherds of the Balancan Group, which Adams said were exclusively Jimba Phase at Altar de Sacrificios, are found at Seibal during the Bayal Phase. In addition, although there are no definite Silho Group pieces at Seibal, there are several modes, such as bulbous feet on tripod plates, which are closer to Silho Group traits than to those of the Altar Group (R. E. Smith, personal communication).

Adams also has stated that "There is proof that at least some of the Jimba pottery was manufactured at Altar during the Jimba Phase" (1971 : 135). Adams was referring here to the heavy fine paste jars and bowls found at Altar de Sacrificios and rarely found at Seibal. However, data from the neutron activation analyses of the Brookhaven National Laboratory would indicate that all the Altar de Sacrificios fine paste pottery, including the so-called utilitarian fine paste vessels, were traded into the site. Furthermore, the source area was the same as for all the Seibal fine paste pottery (Sayre, Chan, and Sabloff 1971).

Finally, Adams has pointed out that he was never able to isolate a pure Jimba deposit, always a very difficult task when dealing with the final phase of the site's occupation: "Unfortunately, no single complex deposit of Jimba material has been found in the Altar area to give absolute confirmation of its separation from Boca material. However, on the basis of the large amounts of negative evidence given in regard to Boca, it seems certain that this arrangement is correct" (1971 : 106). A brief note on the way in which Adams isolated the Jimba Complex might be in order at this time. According to Adams:

The complex (Boca) is found within the ceremonial group of Altar mixed with Jimba Complex. For this reason, these complexes were at first lumped together. Later, on a reconnaissance trip to Seibal it was found that an identical complex corresponding to Boca occurred there, but with no sign of Fine Orange or Fine Gray types in it. This suggested that the types that now comprise Jimba and Boca complexes were from separate temporal phases. After this, Boca Complex was found in a single phase deposit at

Altar confirming the separation into two complexes. Finally, during the 1962 and 1963 seasons all housemounds dug yielded evidence of Jimba occupation. A new aspect added by these excavations, however, was the fact that certain of the more elaborately decorated Jimba types do occur as trade pieces in Boca phase (1971 : 104).

In other words, the first suggestion of a Boca-Jimba split was based on a sampling error of Adams's pits at Seibal, where fine paste sherds do occur in some abundance (especially in small-structure contexts). Even with the new data on fine paste ceramics from Seibal available to Adams, this early suggestion apparently did not lose its importance for him; hence, in discussing the separation of the Boca and Jimba complexes, he is still able to say that "confirmatory evidence is available from Seibal" (Adams 1971 :106).

Adams also looks upon the Jimba vessels found during the Boca Phase and presumably the Bayal Phase as examples of limited, selective trade. But, as noted earlier, I think the situation at Seibal represents more than just the interchange of isolated vessels. Rather, it would appear that there was a replacement of one group of pottery with a special function by another group with a similar function. That is to say, the Tepejilote polychromes had a "serving" function; and when trade was cut off with a center to the north, where polychromes were made at least until 10.2.0.0.0 (A.D. 869; W. R. Coe, personal communication), this functional class of pottery was replaced by the fine paste class which was traded in from the homeland of the intruders. A few local imitations of the new imported vessels were made at Seibal, such as Cubeta Incised and Cameron Incised tripod plates and Achote Black bowls; but by and large, the functions of plates, small bowls, and vases were served by fine paste pottery.

Thus, Adams concludes about the Terminal Late Classic:

> The distinctive regional cast of Boca Complex and its uniformity throughout the Pasion Valley suggests that at least from Seibal to Altar there was a closely knit grouping, both culturally and politically, during Boca Phase. There is little doubt but that we are dealing in Seibal and at Altar with another site unit intrusion such as we probably have already seen in Salinas period. Domination of the Pasion Valley by an intrusive, militaristic, and "Mexi-

canized" Maya group with headquarters at Seibal and possibly Aguateca (Sabloff and Willey 1967) would have been the central historical fact in Boca Times (1967 : 162).

Adams believes this Bayal-Boca intrusion lasted until 10.4.0.0.0 (A.D. 909), at which time there was a second invasion in the Pasion Valley by a more Mexicanized group that occupied Altar de Sacrificios during the Jimba Phase, overran Seibal, and also raided the more northern areas of the Peten, helping to bring Classic Maya civilization to a close there.

I propose an alternative hypothesis based on the ceramic data discussed above: although the Jimba occupation of Altar de Sacrificios is probably a reality and part of it is at least later than the Bayal Phase, the Jimba occupation did not involve a different group than the one that occupied Seibal. In other words, there was simply a brief, continued, late occupation of Altar de Sacrificios by the invaders of the Pasion Valley after the local population had been removed and local pottery manufacture had ceased. Thus, it is my belief that there was one major intrusion into the Rio Pasion area which lasted at least several decades, and the Jimba occupation of Altar was just a slightly later and ceramically purer manifestation of it. Nevertheless, there obviously are some significant differences between the Terminal Late Classic situations at Seibal and Altar de Sacrificios. These deserve future study because they may help to shed light on the processes of culture change in relation to size of ceremonial center and supporting population, geographic position, trading relations, and so on.

Additional Speculations

To conclude, a few comments in a more speculative vein might be worthwhile. In discussing changes in Boca ceramics as compared with the earlier Pasion pottery, Adams says: "These ceramic changes are correlated with the cessation of monument erection and of large-scale monumental construction. At the same time, there may have been a radical increase in population as evidenced by simultaneous occupation of all housemounds at Altar" (1971 : 161). The end of monumental construction at Altar de Sacrificios also coincides with a great reduction in the importance of polychromes. The changes at Altar appar-

ently begin by 9.17.0.0.0 (A.D. 771) and are in full effect by 10.0.0.0.0
(A.D. 830). This situation partially contrasts with Seibal where polychromes also generally disappear, perhaps as early as 9.17.0.0.0 (A.D.
771) and certainly by 10.0.0.0.0 (A.D. 830), and where there is a significant increase in population, but at Seibal there is a burst of monumental activity—both sculptural and architectural—beginning around
9.17.0.0.0 (A.D 771) and culminating in the period from 10.0.0.0.0 (A.D.
830) to 10.3.0.0.0 (A.D. 889). Most of the differences between the two
sites are probably attributable to the fact that the hill-located, defensive
site of Seibal was chosen as a center ("capital") by the intruders.

Once some of the hypotheses, discussed in my thesis (Sabloff
1969 : 341–48; see also Tourtellot and Sabloff 1972), about ceramic
trade in the early Late Classic Period can be further investigated and
tested, the situation may become even clearer. If men in certain centers
were involved in the manufacture of polychromes and the erection of
monuments and structures but were also participants in warfare, it
might be hypothesized that during a time of war in the Southern Maya
Lowlands, polychrome manufacture and monumental activity would
cease, at least temporarily. If the Gulf Coast intruders began entering
the Pasion Valley at the end of the Ninth Cycle, there might have
been a withdrawal of men into the immediate area of the ceremonial
center (resulting in an increase in population) and a general halt in polychrome manufacture (Altar may have been a regional center of manufacture or have been supplied from lower down the Usumacinta) and
monumental work. After the site was secured, the intruders could have
killed many local men, moved them, or otherwise restrained them.
Local domestic pottery making by women, however, could have continued.

Seibal, on the other hand, apparently had a different fate, since it
was chosen as a local capital. Although there may have been a little disorganization at the end of the Ninth Cycle, the local men were utilized in the ceremonial center by the intruders. Since polychromes
were not manufactured locally, trade with the east-central Peten was
simply cut off and replaced by trade with the invaders' homeland. It is
even possible that some artisans were brought in from Altar de Sacrificios. The first carved monuments at Seibal were not made until about
9.18.0.0.0 (A.D. 790). These first monuments (Stelae 5, 6, and 7) were
placed in Group A (the center of the "new" ceremonialism, in contrast

to Group D). Two monuments depicted ball players.[9] It is possible that during approximately the first 40 years of contact with the intruders there was not much evidence of foreign influence in the art, but as control of the Pasion Valley and of Seibal was solidified, the foreign influences, and foreign conception of monumental art, increased.

Furthermore, at Tikal, polychrome manufacture and monumental work ceased at about the same time, coincident with many "Postclassic" activities (W. Coe 1965a) and fine paste pottery on the surface of the central area of the site. Meanwhile, local manufacture of domestic vessels continued. The situation may be the same at Uaxactun, though it apparently is not as clear as at Tikal.[10]

CERAMIC AND MONUMENTAL SIMILARITIES DURING THE BAYAL PHASE

As discussed in my paper on the fine paste ceremics of Seibal (Sabloff 1970), it can be shown that there are definite stylistic links between the designs on the carved stelae of Seibal and the Fine Orange ceramic type, Pabellon Modeled-carved. The traits which link the two are generally non–Classic Maya in nature (Sabloff 1969 : Table 7; 1970 : Fig. 83). This stylistic linkage is of some importance because it shows that the source of the imported pottery was ultimately responsible for the foreign influences on the monuments. Moreover, the influences observable on the stelae do not simply represent minor stylistic changes through time, but instead reflect significant cultural changes in the realms of the glyphic system, physical features, clothing and accessories, and the whole conception of the monuments.

It is of much interest that many of the non–Classic Maya traits which appear on the Seibal stelae and on the Pabellon Modeled-carved vessels can also be found on stone sculpture in the Puuc region and at Chichen Itza. These data would strengthen earlier suggestions by Proskouriakoff (1950, 1951) that there were non–Classic Maya influences in Yucatan before the Toltecs and by Rands (1954) that there are closer artistic connections between the sculpture of the Late Classic Maya of the Southern Lowlands and Chichen Itza than most archaeologists have recognized. In light of the neutron activation data that the fine paste pottery of Seibal and the Fine Orange of Chichen

Itza probably came from a common source (Sayre, Chan, and Sabloff 1971), although perhaps at slightly different times, and Thompson's discussion of the Putun invasions of Seibal and Chichen Itza (1970 : chapter 1), it is certainly reasonable to suggest that there were fairly close cultural connections between the groups which made and imported Pabellon Modeled-carved and invaded Seibal and influenced the sculptural style there, and those groups which immigrated to the Puuc area and to Chichen Itza. Moreover, the time gap between the influx of non–Classic Maya in the Southern Lowlands and the arrival of the Toltecs at Chichen Itza may have been quite small indeed (see Sabloff and Willey 1967).

Some of the traits (many of which are non-Classic) linking the pottery and monumental sculpture of Seibal, the Puuc, and Chichen Itza include: straight, long hair; beard and/or mustache; helmet under jaw; helmet with sprouting feathers, masked face; open slit mouth; non–Classic Maya facial features and facial expression; eye surrounded by circle; "late" earplugs; nose bead; peculiar pectoral bar; bead armlets, anklets, and wristlets; loincloth as only clothing; *atlatl* or curved staff; and non–Classic Maya glyphs.

It should be emphasized that this list is merely preliminary in nature. It is meant to act as an indication of the possibilities of a future correlation between ninth and tenth century A.D. sculpture in both the Southern and Northern Lowlands and a pottery type which had a wide geographical range at this time.[11]

The traits listed above are not the only non–Classic Maya ones found on the Seibal, Puuc, and Chichen Itza sculpture and Pabellon Modeled-carved vessels, but are merely the ones found on all of them. For example, the Seibal and Chichen Itza monuments share the snake motif and the speech-scroll motif, but no examples have been found on the pottery. Or, Pabellon Modeled-carved and the Puuc sculpture share a wide-brimmed hat, but this trait is missing from the Seibal stelae, and so on. Therefore, these traits were not mentioned above. In addition, some non–Classic Maya traits on the Seibal stelae would appear to be peculiar to the medium of stone and to monumental size and so cannot be used as a basis for comparison.

ADDITIONAL CERAMIC DATA

About a dozen partially complete vessels or sherds, of types which are often dated as Early Postclassic, were also found at Seibal (Sabloff 1969 : 301–11). These include a tripod plate type with bell-shaped feet, which is very similar to Ixpop Polychrome in design and form (see Willey et al. 1965 : 388, Figs. 252–53) and a monochrome red type, both of which have snail-shell temper and appear to be identical to Early Postclassic finds from the central Peten (Bullard, personal communication; see also Cowgill 1963). Another type is a red-on-cream armadillo effigy bowl that was found in two locations and is identical to Early Postclassic finds at Copan. Finally, an unusual gadrooned type and a Plumbate sherd found at Seibal also have a similar comparative date. All of these pieces, with the exception of the Plumbate sherd, were found in peripheral areas. Analysis of the proveniences by Gair Tourtellot has led him to hypothesize that the pieces were not vessels left by occasional pilgrims after the abandonment of the site but belong to the very end of the Bayal Phase (Tourtellot: in preparation). That is to say, they might date to somewhere in the tenth century A.D.

RELEVANT NONCERAMIC DATA OF THE BAYAL PHASE

In the final Seibal report, G. R. Willey will discuss the various lines of evidence which indicate that Seibal was invaded during the Terminal Late Classic Period by a group of non–Classic Maya peoples. Suffice it to say here that even without the ceramic evidence, the architectural, monumental, and artifactual data would all confirm the reality of the invasion of Seibal. I have previously mentioned some of the non–Classic or foreign traits on the Seibal monumental sculpture. J. E. S. Thompson, in his recent book *Maya History and Religion*, has concluded:

At Seibal, as it is well known, late stelae dated around A.D. 850 display striking non-Classic elements, notably non-Classic Maya features of the ruler(s) portrayed on Stelae 1, 8, 10, 11, and 14, which can hardly be distinguished from those of Putun-Itza notables at Chichen Itza. . . . There is one detail which, in my opinion is overwhelming evidence that this new dynasty was Putun. At the top of Stela 3 two masked individuals are seated facing each other; above their heads stand two similar glyphs of the Nahuatl day Cipactli (locally Cipacti). . . . The most reasonable conclusion is that these Cipactli glyphs inform us that the ruling family which established itself at Seibal at the close of the Classic period was named Cipactli . . . was of Putun speech, and was quite likely a branch of the Cipacti dynasty at Potonchan (1970 : 41–42).

Thompson further states that these people took over Ucanal on the headwater of the Belize River, and that the Putun were the invaders of Chichen Itza ("first invasion") of A.D. 918. Moreover, according to Thompson, they controlled much of the east coast of Yucatan and northern Tabasco–southern Campeche. He still believes, however, that the Classic Maya collapse was caused by a peasant revolt and that the new lords were swept away by the revolutionary tide just like the old Classic Maya elite (Thompson 1970 : Chapter 1; cf. Sabloff 1971b).

In relation to the architecture of Seibal, the presence of a round structure (Str. 79 on the second highest point of the site), a temple in the center of a plaza with four stairways (Str. A-13), three-member moldings, engaged drumlike columns, and house group burial platforms (shrines) all point to a foreign take-over. As Sanders and Price have said: "The introduction of large scale ceremonial architecture of a foreign style in a local sequence . . . is evidence that the foreign power in some manner has secured control over the surplus labor of a local population" (1968 : 166).

Other relevant finds include a jaguar-head altar supported by two dwarflike figures (possibly phallic) in front of the round structure; raw jade boulder caches; stucco heads with non–Classic Maya features on the frieze of Structure A-3; a reset, upside-down stela fragment with an altar (Stela 22); a few Altar-type figurines, a Tula-style jaguar carved on an altar in front of Stela 17 (dated to after 10.3.0.0.0 [A.D. 889]; see Graham, chapter 10), and an *hacha* stone.

Finally, the peripheral surveys of Gair Tourtellot indicate that the large outlying temples were abandoned by the beginning of the Bayal Phase. Apparently, there was a concentration of religious activities in the ceremonial center in Bayal times (Tourtellot: in preparation).

SUMMARY

The data derived from the study of the Late Classic pottery definitely support the hypothesis that Seibal was taken over by a non–Classic Maya group in the ninth century A.D. (and certainly by A.D. 830). The hypothesis is further confirmed by the Bayal monumental and architectural data. The significant ceramic data, which have been discussed above, can be summarized briefly as follows. First of all, pottery distributions indicate that there was a shift of the locus of ceremonial activity from Group D to Group A. Second, there probably was a change in the censer form—and presumably ritual—from modeled censers featuring a representation of the sun god to spike and ladle censers. Third, there was a virtual end to the trade of polychrome vessels and the "substitution" of fine paste vessels with similar forms (and, perhaps, functions). Fourth, the Altar, Balancan, and Tres Naciones Group fine paste pottery at Seibal, as well as Altar de Sacrificios and several other Peten sites, was all manufactured at the same center, which also supplied the Silho Group Fine Orange to Chichen Itza. Fifth, one of the Fine Orange types (Pabellon Modeled-carved) which was traded into Seibal, and many other sites, has stylistic links to the Seibal Tenth Cycle monuments. Many of these specific stylistic traits are non–Classic Maya in nature and are found on the sculpture of the Puuc and of Chichen Itza, too. Finally, there was a strong continuity in the domestic pottery from Tepejilote through Bayal times.

This ceramic evidence, combined with the preliminary peripheral structure survey data, which indicate that there was an increase in population from the Tepejilote to the Bayal Phase but no observable settlement pattern changes and, further, points to a central concentration of religious activities, supports the hypothesis that there was an elite intrusion at Seibal with major changes in the ceremonial center and its rituals and activities but little change in the supporting population. In other words, there was at least a partial, if not complete, changeover in the ruling elite at Seibal by the beginning of the Tenth Cycle in the Maya calendar.

NOTES

1. Much of this paper is adapted from my thesis (Sabloff 1969). Many people have given me aid and advice on the analysis of the Classic pottery from Seibal, including G. R. Willey, A. L. Smith, G. Tourtellot, R. E. Smith, R. E. W. Adams, and P. L. W. Sabloff; their help is gratefully acknowledged. Conversations with D. Shimkin have also helped to clarify my thinking about the collapse.

2. These monographs, written by G. R. Willey, A. L. Smith, G. Tourtellot, J. Graham, F. Saul, and myself, among others, will be published as *Memoirs of the Peabody Museum* in the near future (see Willey et al. [1968 : 42–43] for a discussion of the Seibal publishing plans). A number of published articles on the Seibal excavations are now available, including: Sabloff (1970); Sabloff and Willey (1967); Smith (1968); Smith and Willey (1966a, 1966b, 1970); Tourtellot (1970); Willey (1970); Willey and Smith (1967a, 1968).

3. The nature of these deposits and the predictability of their location is discussed in Tourtellot (in preparation).

4. This sequence is discussed in detail in A. L. Smith (in preparation).

5. The Conference on the Prehistoric Ceramics of the Maya Lowlands defined "facet" as follows:

A *facet* is a minor temporal subdivision of a ceramic complex; it is useful in cases where changes occur within a ceramic complex that are not sufficiently "convenient and easily distinguished" to warrant the separation of two independent complexes. Such subtleties as frequency-shifts between types, stylistic change, the appearance of new modes in a few types, or the introduction of new minor types might signal a facet change. The changes are generally of such a nature that a large sample is needed to detect them (Willey, Culbert, and Adams 1967 : 304).

6. Cf. Tasital Red, Ximil Incised, Gloria Impressed, Botifela Orange, Pasos Impressed, Tinaja Red, Pantano Impressed, Cameron Incised, and so on, excluding the Tinaja forms that are clearly late; see Smith and Gifford (1966) for references to the illustrations of these types in Smith (1955).

7. "A *subcomplex* is a subdivision of a complex that has significance in cultural interpretation other than that of chronological differentiation. Since inferences about culture are involved in recognizing subcomplexes, culturally significant designations may be used for subcomplexes" (Willey, Culbert, and Adams 1967 : 304).

8. The nature and significance of these ceramics are fully discussed and illustrated in Sabloff (1970).

9. It is important to note that the ball game may have been of much significance to the intruders as evidenced by the two late ball courts at Seibal, the *hacha* found there, and the heavy fine paste concentrations found on the surface of the Altar de Sacrificios ball court and, to a lesser extent, on the Piedras Negras ball court (Butler 1935).

10. After discussion among the authors in this volume and in light of the new data on the Seibal stelae presented by John A. Graham (chapter 10), R. E. W. Adams and I believe there is another hypothesis that satisfactorily explains most of the differences between our interpretations of the Seibal and Altar de Sacrifi-

cios data and that definitely deserves further thought and testing. In brief, it is now hypothesized that there were two intrusions in the Pasion Valley. These two intrusions, however, were probably closely related, and the cultural affinities of the intruders must not have been too diverse. The first and earlier intrusion involved peoples with Yucatecan affinities, while the second involved peoples with Gulf Coast–Tabascan affinities. The earlier intrusion, whose perpetrators may have been noticed and recorded as early as 9.17.0.0.0 (A.D. 771) on the hieroglyphic steps of Structure A-14 at Seibal and who may have been responsible for changes in the dating systems at Yaxchilan and one or more Petexbatun sites, is reflected on the early Tenth Cycle monuments at Seibal and was probably responsible for most of the changes at that site and in the Boca Phase at Altar de Sacrificios. The Tabascan intrusion was not post-Bayal. It was responsible for the late (10.2.0.0.0 [A.D. 869]–10.4.0.0.0 [A.D. 909]) monuments at Seibal and, sometime soon after, the abandonment of that site. It also led to the rise of the Jimba Phase at Altar. Thus, there was some overlap between the Bayal Phase and the Jimba Phase, but the Jimba Phase continued longer, presumably because of the strategic crossroads location of Altar.

In other words, we may be able to have our cake and eat it too. The earlier intrusions may have initiated the shock waves that helped trigger the internal processes that led to the collapse of Classic Maya civilization (see Willey and Shimkin, chapter 18; Sabloff 1971a), while the later intrusion may represent Thompson's Macedonians (Thompson 1970 : 5, 47) who swoop in for the spoils in the midst of a dying civilization. The later intruders would then have moved into better pickings in richer, more viable areas after several decades of occupation in the Pasion Valley.

Completion of the fine paste neutron activations studies by E. V. Sayre, G. Harbottle, R. Abascal, and their associates at the Brookhaven National Laboratory and the studies of John A. Graham and Gair Tourtellot on the Seibal stelae and settlement patterns, respectively, should also help to clarify the picture in the near future.

11. Certainly, John A. Graham's study of the stelae of Seibal, now in progress, will also throw much light on this question, especially in regard to Yucatecan and Tabascan influences.

8

Maya Collapse: Transformation and Termination in the Ceramic Sequence at Altar de Sacrificios

RICHARD E. W. ADAMS

Department of Anthropology
University of Minnesota

The ruins of Altar de Sacrificios, located on the Pasion River near its junction with the Chixoy, were excavated by Harvard University from 1958 to 1963. A preliminary volume (Willey and Smith 1969) and the ceramic report (Adams 1971) have already been published, and other reports are in preparation. This chapter aims at presenting the data from Altar de Sacrificios pertinent to the termination of Maya Classic civilization. The ceramic sequence is emphasized, but other kinds of information are considered. The concept of usage complementarity is presented and is followed by a summary of the Altar sequence. Alternative interpretations of the sequence are offered and discussed, and a consideration of other factors and a reconstruction of events concludes the chapter.[1]

CERAMIC COMPLEXES AND USAGE COMPLEMENTARITY

"A ceramic complex is the sum total of associated ceramics which has a convenient and easily distinguished geographical and temporal meaning" (Willey, Culbert, and Adams 1967 : 304). Implicit in this analyst-oriented definition is the culture-oriented concept of usage complementarity. Given a good enough sample, one that is large and representative, and given tight enough control over stratigraphy or seriation, ceramic complexes represent the total number of functional needs for pottery in a specific time and place. These uses may be derived from ethnographic studies, ethnohistoric information, archaeological context, and experimentation. Judging by pottery-using, pre-metal-using, or non-metal-using ethnographically reported cultures, the major functions of pottery are as containers for food and liquids and as cooking containers. Further specified, domestic needs of water carrying and storage, food preparation and storage containers, and serving vessels for prepared foods are satisfied by the quantitatively major types of any ethnographic ceramic complex. I believe that these same functions apply to the highest frequency types in each archaeological ceramic complex, and to those types whose shapes most closely approximate pottery used for a particular domestic function in ethnographic communities. Thus, restricted-necked jars are most suitable for water carriers in both ethnographic and archaeological complexes. Striation or handles for these jars seem alternative solutions to the problem of slipperiness. It also follows that the unslipped, striated, and monochrome archaeological types were mostly used for domestic purposes. In the Maya Classic Period, there are many more than just these type-classes, and presumably many elaborate types also served domestic functions. Judging by the frequencies and archaeological contexts of the renowned Maya polychromes, which occur in nearly every residential structure whether it be palace or humble housemound, they fulfilled the function of "best" pottery, much as did the familiar "Blue Willow" pattern of our own grandmothers' generation. Experimentation lends weight to the usage interpretations for many of the features of Maya pottery. Medial flanges, for example, seem to be the answer to the problem of how to handle hot serving dishes without burning one's fingers. Mortuary vessels, drums, incense burners, cult effigies, and trade exotics (connoisseur pieces) make up the nondomestic use groups of types for the Classic. Thus any well-sampled complex in the Altar sequence can reasonably be expected to represent types that were functionally complementary for the ancient users. Two other expectations follow. First, given the continuity of the most common types from one complex to another, one can infer that the mass of the population manufacturing and using those types also had continuity. Second, the test of the integrity of a ceramic tradition is in these very kinds of continuities. Likewise, a test of the integrity of a ceramic complex as representing culturally "real" types is in the usage complementarity of the types attributed to it. Thus, a handful of types that do not include pottery satisfactory for the majority of domestic functions is not a true complex, or is an incomplete sample of one. Conversely, a grouping of types in which the major functions are overfilled would lead one to suspect that more than one complex is involved.

THE ALTAR DE SACRIFICIOS SEQUENCE

To provide a context for the following discussion, I can do no better than to give a somewhat modified version of previous summaries of the sequence (Adams 1964, 1971).

The Altar sequence begins with a Middle Preclassic complex (Xe) that is one of the earliest (900 B.C.?) lowland complexes discovered to date. *Xe Complex* is very diverse in shape range and in the number of decorative techniques used. Favored shapes are low pans, neckless jars, and low-necked jars. White is favored as a slipped color. The only outside ties would seem to be modal linkages with Preclassic complexes of the Mexican Gulf Coast area and the Grijalva trench area of Chiapas and a type linkage to El Salvador. One other site, Seibal, 75 miles distant, has yielded another sample of this complex and is the only other member of the Xe ceramic sphere. Only the Seibal early facet of Xe Complex surely antedates the Altar material in the Maya Lowlands. The larger cultural association seems to be with a simple village farming situation. There is clear typological continuity into the early facet of San Felix Mamom that follows.

The well-known Mamom style ceramics of Middle Preclassic times are locally represented by the *San Felix Mamom Complex*. This, like Xe, is predominantly a complex of monochrome and unslipped pottery types, but Mamom shows greater standardization of color, form, and decorative techniques. Emphasis on red as a favored color, and on plates and striated, medium-necked jars, begins and continues into the following complex. Association with both simple ceremonial architecture and village residential structures begins.

The *Plancha Chicanel Complex* is very much a continuation of the San Felix Complex and continues the trend of standardization of shapes and decorative techniques through the Late Preclassic. Dichrome types become somewhat more popular, and in the late facet of Plancha there is experimentation in new and exotic forms, such as spouted jars with golden brown slips, and an appearance of multiplex-lined, painted dichrome types. The dichromes seem to be modally related to the positive-painted Usulutan types of El Salvador rather than to the resist-painted materials of the southern Guatemala Highlands. Large-scale ritual architecture is now grouped into a center at Altar, and some sort of social stratification is indicated for the period.

Salinas Floral Park belongs to the Protoclassic grouping of complexes that immediately precede the Classic Period. At Altar, this represents a rupturing of the long Preclassic tradition at about A.D. 150 by the introduction of many new ceramic ideas of a dramatic nature. The polychrome tradition begins with this complex, as well as a tradition of iconographically elaborate incense burners. Some carry-over from the Preclassic is indicated in the continuation of the striated unslipped domestic types. This broad dichotomy of new and very elaborate types combined with continuity of older and simpler domestic types is suggestive. Combined with the contemporary appearance of the stela cult and with much larger ceremonial architecture, this dichotomy implies cultural elements from an area at least outside the Pasion Valley and probably from farther away than that, perhaps from El Salvador. Possibly an intrusive elite class established itself at Altar during this period. It is noteworthy that the new elements are those associated with the elite segment of Classic culture. At the end of Salinas, full-scale Maya Classic culture in all its complexity is in operation.

The Early Classic complexes at Altar (Ayn and Veremos) belong to the Tzakol sphere and show strong continuity in the trends established in the preceding phase. Polychrome types are developed and proliferated as are other kinds of elaborately decorated pottery, such as gouged-incised and carved. Formality of art style seems to intensify. At the same time there is a continuity of monochrome and striated, unslipped types for domestic use. The *absence* of the strong Teotihuacan influence found at other Lowland Maya sites is notable at Altar. Only in a few burial situations are the distinctive Mexican Highland–derived forms found. In terms of quantity, the latest Early Classic complex (Veremos) is the weakest at the site.

Late Classic begins with the short-lived Chixoy Tepeu. The polychrome and other less elaborate types show essentially slow and gradual change in shape and decorative techniques as well as in physical characteristics. In terms of careful and masterful execution of elaborate ceramics, Chixoy is one of the high points of the Altar sequence, and there is a strong continuity between Chixoy and the early facet of the following Pasion Complex. At this point I shall narrow the focus to include more detail about the matter at hand.

Pasion Complex is dated from 9.9.0.0.0 (A.D. 613) to 9.17.0.0.0 (A.D. 771). The climax of most of the ceramic trends and traditions of the Classic Period, there is at this time a proliferation of polychrome-decorated bowl forms, footed forms, and modulations of the rims or upper walls of round-sided bowls. Cream polychromes are introduced, and tripod plates with notched and terraced basal ridges are typical. Large red-slipped caldrons continue and are decorated with impressions. Red monochrome jars appear. Heavier striation and greater eversion of the folded rims of large jars is noteworthy. Wide-flange censers with appliquéd and modeled decoration and ladle censers appear. The late facet shows no change in the striated and already-present monochromes. However, the appearance of resist technique combined with polychrome, of a thin-walled and almost fine paste monochrome red jar type, and of low beaker shapes in polychromes all are distinctive. Generally, there is the same high degree of artistic and technical proficiency that also characterized Chixoy. On the other hand, there is evidence of carelessness and loss of vigor of expression in many examples of Pasion pottery, with conventionalization of polychrome design exemplary of this trend. Continuities of ideas in the domestic types are strong and these types change the least rapidly. The same type and variety of striated water jar makes up about 20 percent of Chixoy samples and about 30 percent of Pasion samples.

Altar reached its apogee in this period in terms of size and extent of formal architecture, numbers of stelae, and amounts of elaborate pottery produced. Near-maximal population is indicated by occupation of nearly all housemounds. In terms of the elite-class segment of culture and the behavioral norms associated with them, this is the peak. Judging from evidence of residential occupation on range-type structures, the memorialization of the distinguished dead by funerary monuments, the erection of historical monuments with reference to members of the elite class, and the amounts of luxury pottery produced and associated with the elite-class residences, Maya society at Altar de Sacrificios conformed well to the model I have recently suggested (Adams 1971). This model is one with an essentially castelike upper class, intermediate classes of bureaucrats and craft specialists such as sculptors, and gradations of specialists and part-time specialists down to persons who mainly farmed and contributed only unskilled labor to communal and elite-class centers.

Two elite-class burials from this phase (97 and 128) give evidence of rather elaborate funerary customs involving the visiting of relatives from other centers upon the death of a member of the local upper class. Important persons from Tikal and Yaxchilan are thought to have visited Altar de Sacrificios in A.D. 754 and to have participated in a ritual memorializing the dead person (Burial 128). This ceremony was depicted on a polychrome pot that was buried with a sacrificial victim (Burial 97). This and other evidence indicate that Maya centers were probably tied together at the topmost elite level by kinship and marriage. We can infer from this that a level of political organization larger than city-state existed, which would be delicate and fragile, dependent on shifting marriage alliances and kinship relations.

It is in the apparent change in the function of Altar de Sacrificios as a ceremonial center or dispersed urban center, and in changes in the behavioral patterns of the directing elite, the Boca Phase differs from Pasion inferentially as well as materially.

Boca (Figs. 14, 15, and 16) as a complex shows modal similarities to what is going on elsewhere in the Peten but is distinctive enough to warrant establishment of a new ceramic sphere based on it and the Bayal Complex at Seibal. In addition, the complex, dating between 9.17.0.0.0 (A.D. 771) to about 10.4.0.0.0 (A.D. 909), occurs in unmodified form at all nine sites surveyed between Seibal and Altar de Sacrificios, an airline distance of about 75 miles.

Strong continuities persist between late Pasion and early Boca in the striated and monochrome types, although changes strong enough to warrant varietal distinctions do occur. Heavily folded rims and herringbone-pattern striation occur on the unslipped utility type. R. E. Smith has pointed out the similarity of this striation patterning to that

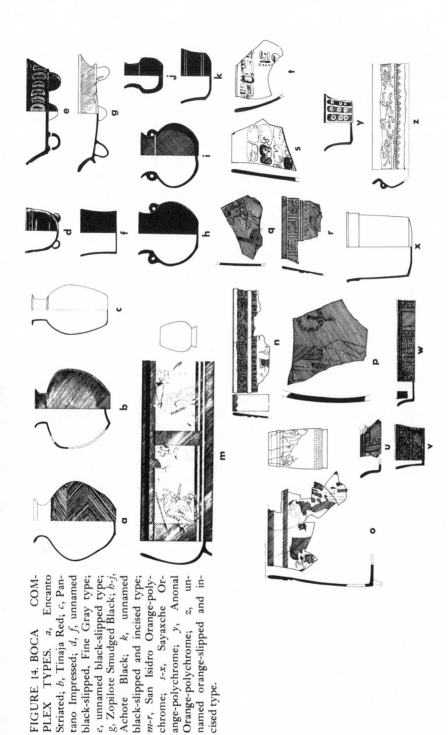

FIGURE 14. BOCA COMPLEX TYPES. *a*, Encanto Striated; *b*, Tinaja Red; *c*, Pantano Impressed; *d*, *f*, unnamed black-slipped, Fine Gray type; *e*, unnamed black-slipped type; *g*, Zopilote Smudged Black; *h-j*, Achote Black; *k*, unnamed black-slipped and incised type; *m-r*, San Isidro Orange-polychrome; *s-x*, Sayaxche Orange-polychrome; *y*, Anonal Orange-polychrome; *z*, unnamed orange-slipped and incised type.

found in the Cehpech Complex of northern Yucatan of approximately the same date. Subin Red caldrons are either shallower and more open or have a restricted orifice. Polychrome decoration is reduced to abstract design, or, in the case of the late facet types, naturalistic motifs are quite cursive. Interestingly, both war and ceremonial occasions are subjects for treatment. Polychrome as a whole is greatly diminished in its importance, the typical percentage in a Boca sample being about 5 percent compared to 12–18 percent for polychromes in an early Pasion sample and 7 percent in a late Pasion sample. The later Pasion sample is unsatisfactory, however; neither is it large nor is the deposition situation firmly that of refuse discard. Whereas Pasion Complex, especially in the late facet, showed a qualitative mixture of the excellent with the merely adequate in the elaborate types, Boca shows a marked decline in both quality and quantity. The execution of complex designs, when compared to the analogous work of preceding phases, is markedly inferior. Impressing appears as an important decorative technique.

Very wide flanged censers appear with primary decoration by modeling and painting. Animal and human effigy censers and a specific type of hourglass censer are diagnostic. These burners show a trend away from more abstract religious symbolism and toward anthropomorphism and zoomorphism.

Late in the phase, late facet, elaborately decorated Fine Orange and Fine Gray types show up as trade pieces. These are principally Pabellon Molded-carved: Pabellon Variety and the Poite Incised: Poite Variety grater bowls. A few rarer types, Xul Incised and Fine Slate, appear to be imports from the Yucatecan area, which includes the Rio Bec–Chenes Zone. Compared to the preceding complexes, Boca represents a drastic simplification in both decorative quality and range of modal variation. Maximal population is indicated for the Altar zone at this time based on the frequency of occurrence of Boca ceramics and especially their appearances in thirty-eight of the forty excavated housemounds or residential areas. Simplification in ceramics accompanies an apparent reorientation of local cultural norms. No stelae are erected during the Boca Phase, and only one altar; no major buildings are constructed or renovated. On the other hand, there is the appearance of figurines that include depictions of warriors in quilted cotton armor with rectangular shields. Some of these warriors have typical Maya

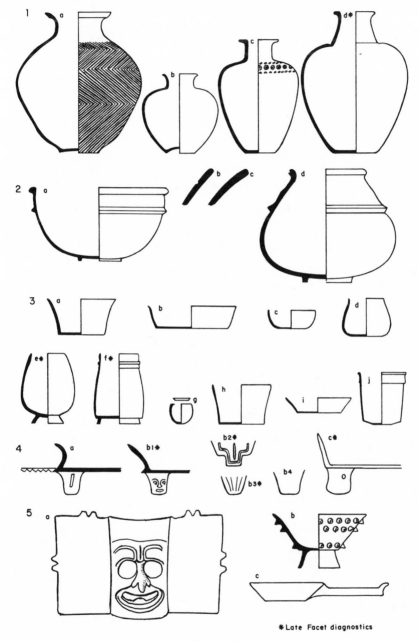

FIGURE 15. BOCA COMPLEX FORMS

*Late Facet diagnostics

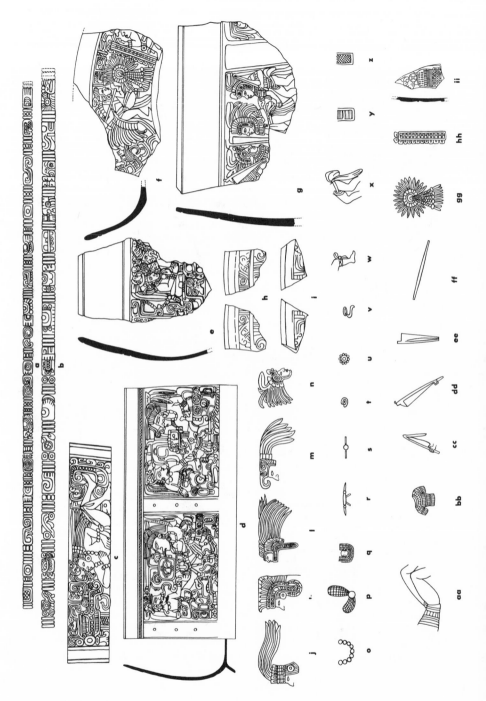

headdresses replete with plumes; a few depict deities usually thought foreign to the Maya area. At least one warrior holds a headdress with the goggle eyes of Tlaloc on it. The introduction of a specific type of *metate* at this time is noteworthy. This is Willey's fourth type from Altar de Sacrificios (1965 : 36), but it also occurs associated with late ceramics at Becan in the Rio Bec–Chenes Zone. These highly distinctive *metates* are also found at Seibal only in Boca Bayal Phase (Willey and Smith 1967b : 15). Stone phalli may be associated with the late Boca facet and may also be a linkage to the Northern Lowlands, where they occur more commonly.

Boca ceramics at Seibal, which Sabloff (chapter 7) discusses at length, are associated with a Tenth Cycle florescence that includes the erection of stelae with Mexican stylistic influence and the construction of buildings very similar to Puuc and Chenes styles of architecture (Willey and Smith 1966 : 19; and personal observation).

There is a hint that Boca Phase came to a violent end. One large test pit dug in an inner court at Altar de Sacrificios Structure A-I produced, in its upper levels, immense amounts of fired adobe from burned wattle and daub architecture. The palaces at Altar were perishable and were set on stone-faced platforms. Such platforms surrounded the court on three sides. Since underlying the burned adobe layer were Boca ceramics, a likely interpretation is that elite-class residential architecture burned at the end of the phase. We cannot be sure whether the firing was deliberate. If we accept the interpretation given below of a military intrusion by people of Jimba culture, then the fire may well have been deliberate.

Jimba Complex (Figs. 16 and 17) dates between 10.4.0.0.0 (A.D. 909) and 10.6.0.0.0 (A.D. 948), and is the final complex of the sequence. It represents a total disjunction of trend and tradition. No types carry over

FIGURE 16. PABELLON MOLDED-CARVED: PABELLON VARIETY; LATE BOCA AND JIMBA COMPLEXES. *a, b,* Glyph bands from complete bowls of 2d form; *c,* typical reclining figure scene from 2d bowl form, scene category 1; *d, e,* variations on scene category 2 from form 4a jars; *f,* scene category 3 from form 2d bowl (note square cartouche glyphs above the left human figure); *g,* scene category 3 from form 4a jar (note distinctive headdresses of the opposing human figures); *h, i,* mold fragments for 2d form bowls (drawings of the molds are to the right and of plasticene impressions to the left); *j–hh,* commonly occurring elements in scene categories 1–3; *ii,* fragment of a form 4d jar decorated with scene category 4.

from preceding complexes, with the exceptions of Pabellon Molded-carved and Poite Incised types, both regarded as trade imports into Altar during Boca Phase, when they occur only in burials and not as sherds. The occurrence of Jimba Complex only in Group A of the ceremonial center and in only fifteen of the forty housemound excavations argues for temporal separation from Boca, although the Group A samples are mixed with Boca. Disjunction of the complex with all others at the site argues independence for Jimba, as does the principle of usage complementarity. Jimba and Boca are independently complete and sufficient complexes; that is, there are sufficient types and variations within types to take care of all the functions required of pottery. This is so whether comparing the functions of pottery among ethnographic groups to the archaeological complexes, or in comparison of Jimba's implied functions to those implied for the other archaeological complexes. Furthermore, the combining of Jimba with Boca would result in "overfilled" functional categories, compared to any other complex in the sequence. The derivation of Jimba from Boca as suggested by Willey and Smith (1966 : 20) is unlikely because of the disjunction and the lack of continuities.

Tempering, or the lack of it, is the salient common denominator for the complex. Two major wares make up the complex, Fine Orange and Fine Gray. Within these wares, form, decorative techniques, and motifs define the types as belonging to two ceramic groups, the Altar Fine Orange Group and the Tres Naciones Fine Gray Group. The stylistic and shape differences between the groups are almost mutually exclusive. Certain informal tests indicate that the distinctive colors of the groups were deliberately achieved—refiring of Fine Gray pieces produces Fine Orange. Grater bowls, flaring-necked, big-bellied jars, open simple bowls, tripod-footed forms, and basins make up the majority of forms. Thin but hard slipping in either black or orange, black-on-orange dichrome, molded-carving, and incision are the dominant decorative techniques, although modeling does occur. No polychrome is known. Motifs are both naturalistic and abstract, predominantly the former. Glyphs occur decoratively and probably also functionally. Vessel walls of the smaller forms are typically thin, and sherds of all types give off a characteristic hard ring when tapped. In short, Jimba Complex represents an essentially monochrome tradition with decoration by surface manipulation rather than by contrast in color and/or

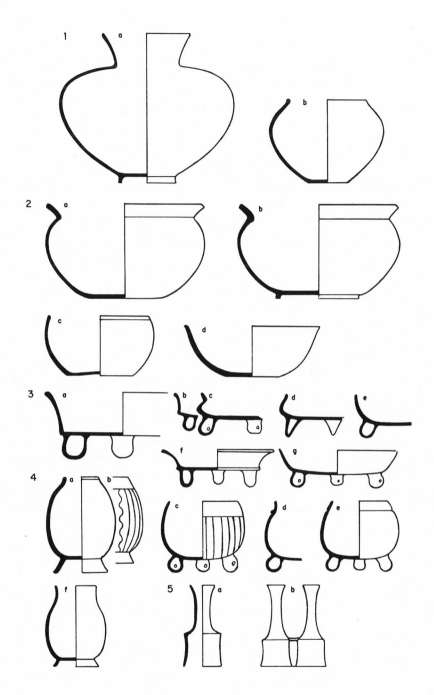

FIGURE 17. JIMBA COMPLEX FORMS

graphics. The two major monochrome types, which are also the two major domestic types, make up 84 percent of a sample of 2,644 sherds. This compares to the domestic functional types, striated and red-slipped monochromes, from an early Boca sample, which amount to 92 percent of a sample of 2,054 sherds but are associated with 5 percent polychromes.

The art style of the Pabellon Molded-carved type (see Fig. 16) is of particular interest because it is richly depictive. Four main categories of scenes are found:

1. Reclining human figures associated with a serpent whose body twines around and whose head the individual usually faces
2. Conference scenes in which two human figures, usually seated on serpent heads, seem to be engaged in discussion across a vegetation motif
3. Military scenes (rare but of great interest) in which warriors carry shields, attack other warriors, and in one case assault a wall
4. Mirror symmetry scenes in which two apparently aged persons wearing armadillo (?) shells or basketry and seated on animal heads face one another (serpent heads are again depicted)

The human physical type is closely related to that in the fine paste figurines and is distinct from depictions in the polychromes of preceding complexes. Most individuals of this dominant type have large jaws, straight noses, and vertical, apparently undeformed, foreheads. In one case, this dominant type seems in physical confrontation with a typical Maya type.

Costuming is mainly distinctive from that depicted on Classic Maya sculpture and on the polychromes.

Generic resemblences between Pabellon and the Toltec styles at Tula in Mexico and Chichen Itza are to be noted in the use of reclining figures as an important motif. General resemblance in costume motif is present. However, there are detailed differences; for example, the Pabellon human figures are always barefoot while Toltec depictions nearly always show sandals.

Pabellon, as well as other Altar Fine Orange Group types, seems to partake of both Classic Maya and Mexican styles, but forms a style distinctive from both.

Comparisons

Most of the Fine Orange types found at Altar belong, not surprisingly, to the Altar Fine Orange Group (the old Y group). However, detailed comparisons between Chorrito Plano-relief of Jimba Complex and Provincia Plano-relief of Balancan (Z) Fine Orange Group show close relationships in stylistic treatment and subject matter—principally the reclining figure. Further, the occurrence of Balancan Group types at Altar in Jimba Phase shows that they were probably contemporary with Altar Group and made by culturally related people. Some temporal overlap between Silho (X) Fine Orange Group and Altar Group is also indicated. However, Silho Group shows many more stylistic differences from Altar Group than does Balancan Group. The close correspondences between Altar and Balancan groups seem to indicate that the cultures producing the pottery at one time probably occupied contiguous areas. Berlin's work in lowland Tabasco has indicated that region as the probable manufacturing center for the Balancan Group. He specifies the Jonuta Zone (Berlin 1956 : 147).

At this point a few ethnographic details derived from the elaborate pieces of Jimba types are instructive. The mode of dress, or undress, of the humans depicted on Fine Orange vessels, and the fact that fish and peccaries are incised on the bottoms of the grater bowls, indicate that the people making this pottery probably came from an area with a hot climate, with jungle conditions, and with rivers—in short a region somewhat like Altar, lowland northern Chiapas, or the lowland Tabasco region. The first region is ruled out as the origin zone, having been occupied by persons of a distinct cultural tradition as partially represented by the Xe-Boca sequence. Lowland northern Chiapas was also occupied by people of Classic Maya Lowland tradition, exemplified by sites such as Palenque, Yaxchilan, Bonampak, and others. Taken with the evidence for physical proximity to the Balancan Zone, the Jonuta region in the Tabasco area seems most likely.

As noted in a stylistic analysis of Pabellon Molded-carved, there are certain stylistic affinities on a generic level with the Toltec style as represented at Tula. Sabloff (1970), however, has noted certain similarities with Tenth Cycle Mexicanized sculpture at Seibal. Further, there is a linkage to general ceramic developments in the Veracruz coast area in the importance of the tripod grater bowl form within the Jimba Complex. Grater bowls are a Gulf Coast tradition established in the Early Preclassic (MacNeish 1954). Further, Drucker (1943a) has shown that southern Veracruz is the home of a fine paste pottery tradition from Preclassic times on. Provincia Plano-relief of Jimba Complex seems to be part of a general Gulf Coast art style, on the basis of its close similarities to Las Flores Incised and Las Flores Relief from the Panuco region. Finally, the glyphic style of the Jimba pottery, particularly on the Pabellon Molded-carved, shows relations to both the Maya and Mexican writing systems (D. Kelley, personal communication). In short, the culture of the people producing Jimba Complex pottery was probably transitional between the polarities represented by the Tula Toltecs and the Late Classic Southern Lowland Maya. This possibility also argues for an intermediate geographic position roughly in the southern Veracruz and lowland Tabasco districts, a zone inhabited in the sixteenth century by Chontal-speaking Maya. It is noteworthy that the Itza who came into Postclassic northern Yucatan are thought by Roys and Thompson possibly to have been Chontal speakers.

Jimba Complex is accompanied by figurines made of fine pastes that often depict warriors of a style distinct from those of the Boca Phase.

A drastic decline in housemound occupations apparently indicates a decline in population. Behavioral norms of the Classic and even of the reoriented Boca Phase are abandoned. This is apparently the case at all of the ceremonial centers for 75 miles up to Seibal, which is itself abandoned at the end of the period of use of Boca pottery.

Post-Jimba Pottery

A small group of aberrant and insecurely placed types may represent a feeble ceramic development after the close of the Jimba Phase. These types include Tohil Plumbate and certain unslipped forms, including tripodal comal-like shapes. This group does not represent a complete ceramic complex in the sense of either secure association of types or usage complementarity. Tohil Plumbate was widely traded about 10.8.0.0.0 (A.D. 987). Following the apparently casual deposition of this material, there is a complete abandonment of the Altar region and disuse of the ceremonial center. Historical sources from the sixteenth century mention many canoes on the Ayn River (the old name for the Pasion) and a heavy population of Lacandon peoples, but these have left no trace in the archaeological record.

One crucial observation is that there are essential continuities in the sequence from the Preclassic through Classic complexes, extending through, but ending with, the Boca Complex. There are sudden changes and discontinuities, but not in the functional components of the complexes most intimately connected with daily life; that is, those usually classified as utilitarian or domestic pottery. I have argued (Adams 1971) that these types can be tied to the majority of the ancient population as serving the greatest needs met by pottery. The question of functional complementarity is further discussed elsewhere, but suffice to say that the only *total* disjunction in the Altar sequence is that between Boca and Jimba complexes. In every other case, for example between Preclassic Plancha and Protoclassic Salinas, the sudden and unpresaged changes are in the elaborate and often iconographically complex types. Thus the basic continuity of Xe to Boca periods argues the continuity of the culture bearers or basic population. I am not arguing for a basic continuity of the elite classes. Perhaps the elite class changed several times at Altar in personnel, quality, or both. This is pertinent to the situation at ninth-century Seibal. When we come to the Boca-Jimba disjunction, the complete lack of continuity between complexes argues for total population replacement. The fact of functional complementarity within each complex argues for their separation, even if we did not have stratigraphic and single-phase deposits demonstrating this separation.

DISCUSSION

Crucial points in the review and first-level interpretations given above are the reorientation of Maya elite-class culture at Altar during the Boca Phase and the subsequent appearance of a pottery complex of foreign tradition. Equally interesting are the questions of the reasons for the reorientation and the nature of the appearance of Jimba Complex.

The first question, that of cultural reorientation during Boca Phase, is interlocked with the cultural florescence at Seibal during the same period. While ceremonial-center or elite-class life during the Terminal

Classic is greatly diminished at Altar, major architectural construction is carried out and a large number of sculptured monuments are erected at Seibal. The resemblances between the architecture and sculptural style of Seibal and Mexicanized Maya Lowland culture north or west of the Peten has already been noted. Sabloff and Willey (1967) suggest, and I agree, that this florescence is probably a result of the intrusion into the Pasion Valley of an elite group from outside the Peten that took over Seibal. Domination of the Pasion Valley by Seibal may have followed; this is less certain. However, the reorientation of culture at Altar de Sacrificios during this time makes more sense if the reduction in importance of native elites at the Pasion ceremonial centers other than Seibal is accepted. An accentuated militaristic element seems to have been introduced into cultural patterns at Altar, judging by the figurines. In other words, I see some of the reorientation at Altar as a response to domination by an intrusive Mexicanized but still Maya elite at Seibal.

The second question, that of the nature of the appearance of Jimba Complex, depends for its solution on the first-level interpretations. It has been argued above that the weight of the evidence from Altar points to an origin zone along the bottom of the Mexican Gulf Coast. It is also argued that the appearance of Jimba is accompanied by a population decline and replacement. From these primary interpretations flow some implications based on geography and timing.

If the Jimba Complex is derived from an area on the frontier of the Maya Lowland area, then there is the problem of moving the culture bearers represented by the pottery across an intervening area between the origin zone and Altar de Sacrificios. To complicate the problem, this intervening area is known to have been occupied by variants of Maya Classic culture and to be littered with the remains of many ceremonial centers. At least two of these, Yaxchilan and Piedras Negras, had traditions of Late Classic warfare, of conquest, and of strong rulers. Proskouriakoff's studies (1960, 1963b, 1964) of the hieroglyphic texts and the depictive evidence in sculpture, as well as the associated and contemporary Bonampak murals, serve as evidence for this assertion. However, judging by the Maya records themselves, the stelae and lintels of these sites, the Usumacinta Zone ceremonial centers might already have been disorganized if not abandoned by the time

(10.4.0.0.0, A.D. 909) that Jimba Complex is carried to Altar de Sacrificios. The latest date at Bonampak is between 9.17.0.0.0 (A.D. 771) and 9.19.0.0.0 (A.D. 810), at Yaxchilan about 9.18.0.0.0 (A.D. 790), and at Piedras Negras about 9.19.0.0.0 (A.D. 810). The archaeology of this zone is still poorly known, but judging from the monumental record all sites in the Piedras Negras–Yaxchilan–Bonampak triangle ceased erecting stelae by about 9.19.0.0.0 (A.D. 810). The intimate association of these stelae with dynastic records, genealogies, and histories of the elite class would indicate a grave disturbance in Maya Classic society. In other words, by the time Jimba culture bearers intrude to Altar de Sacrificios, the states of the Usumacinta Zone may have been socially disorganized. It seems unlikely that these centers would passively allow the penetration of a culturally foreign and militaristic group through their area to occupy a strategically important zone. The implication is that Yaxchilan, Piedras Negras, and other important centers were overcome by either the Jimba culture bearers or by their cultural and military allies. Indeed, Proskouriakoff suggests that Yaxchilan may have been in the hands of an enemy by about 9.19.0.0.0 (A.D. 810; 1964 : 196–99).

The militaristic aspect of the Jimba figurines and the depictive data from Pabellon-type pottery imply that the penetration to the Altar Zone was not peaceful. The evidence for population decline in the period following Boca indicates the same. Finally, the other major element in a reorientation of the Boca Phase Maya culture may have been the pressures from just such groups as the Jimba.

Thus, perhaps the people who made Jimba pottery moved from lowland Chiapas–Tabasco, or ultimately from southern Veracruz, across the area east of Bonampak to the Usumacinta, upriver and southeast of Yaxchilan and Piedras Negras. This route provides easier access than does the route directly up the Usumacinta. From there, I suggest that the Jimba people moved down the Usumacinta against Yaxchilan and Piedras Negras, conquering these places or neutralizing them in some manner. During this initial penetration to the Usumacinta, about 9.19.0.0.0 (A.D. 810), and perhaps during the pause and regrouping there, the trade and conflict with the people of the late Boca Phase at Altar took place. Ultimately, based on the Seibal evidence, I believe that the Altar region was overrun and occupied by about 10.4.0.0.0

(A.D. 909). Seibal, with its astonishing Tenth Cycle florescence, came to an end shortly after this penetration, and, I postulate, at least as a partial result of it.

A small group of raiders in a hostile lowland zone could do a great deal with proper direction. Altar is located strategically with respect to both Maya highlands and lowlands. The Pasion and Salinas are easily navigable rivers; they make great regions of the lowlands accessible and ultimately lead to the highlands. The Usumacinta, formed by the junction of these rivers at Altar, leads down to the Gulf. The mouth of the Lacantun is not far off, and through that river and a network of other streams access can be had to the Gulf Coast plain. Raids could be made in a number of directions based on swift canoe travel along the rivers and strikes overland to more distant centers.

It is my suggestion that the collapse of the Usumacinta Zone had more than a local effect. Local conditions at sites far away from the Pasion may have determined the special nature of the collapse in any one region. However, there is evidence for military competition among the Maya polities of the Late Classic, perhaps because of problems of overpopulation. This competition would make more difficult any kind of viable coalition of Maya states. Indeed, the special mix of circumstances of the collapse from site to site seems to reflect political fragmentation. Reina (1967 : 15) has pointed out the fragility of the *milpa* cycle. Such an agricultural cycle could be badly upset with a little judicious raiding. Civil wars and local disasters, such as the locust plagues known historically from the Peten, may have combined with the morale-shaking news from the Pasion to induce abandonment or violent overthrow of the local leadership and their ceremonial centers.

Another interpretation of essentially the same evidence has been advanced by Sabloff and Willey (1967). They agree with the invasion theory, but wish to connect the invasion with non–Peten Maya pushing into the Pasion and taking over Seibal. They claim that the Seibal florescence (10.0.0.0.0, A.D. 830 to 10.3.0.0.0, A.D. 889) was a result of this takeover. The Seibal intruders, according to Sabloff and Willey, raided and wrecked the economy and social fabric of the more traditional Southern Lowlands centers:

A precarious man-nature balance in agriculture was upset, resulting in widespread starvation and population shiftings and displacement. Much of the old Maya aristocratic leadership was killed off. The invaders attempted to maintain several large Maya ceremonial centers, but this proved unsuccessful. Small bodies of Maya population did cluster around some of the Peten lakes and maintain themselves into the Postclassic Period; other Maya, and probably the military invaders, moved north to settle around those few large centers that remain in Yucatan (1967 : 329).

The principal evidence upon which this differing interpretation depends is stylistic linkage between the Tenth Cycle sculpture of Seibal and one of the Jimba types, Pabellon Molded-carved (Sabloff and Willey 1967 : 322). Twenty-two elements of stylistic affinity are listed by Sabloff (1970). However, examination of the evidence shows that:

1. There are at least 51 stylistic elements that can be isolated in Pabellon Molded-carved, and thus Sabloff's 22 represent a selected list.
2. Only 11 of these traits are distinct from Maya Classic sculptural tradition and common to Pabellon and the Seibal Tenth Cycle sculpture.
3. Twenty-three traits are common to Pabellon and Classic sculpture.
4. Sixteen traits are unique to Pabellon.
5. One trait is unaccounted for, as I am unable to find it in any of the material on Seibal or Altar at my disposal.
6. Seibal Tenth Cycle sculpture with all of its peculiarities is closer to Classic sculpture as defined by Proskouriakoff (1950) than it is to Pabellon.
7. At least some of the Seibal sculpture peculiarities are to be found in Chenes and Rio Bec style art. (See Appendixes A and B for documentation of these points.)

In any case, it seems clear that on the basis of disjunction of tradition, usage complementarity, known origin zones of fine paste tradition, and samples dealt with, the Altar evidence discussed in preceding sections lends much stronger support to the interpretation of Jimba Complex as an independent and disjunctive complex. Sabloff and Willey advocate combining the Boca and Jimba complexes, but I rejected this idea on the basis of usage complementarity and independent evidence for separation. The other alternative is derivation of Jimba from

Boca, here rejected on the grounds of disjunction of ceramic tradition.

An explanation must be advanced for the stylistic linkages between Seibal Tenth Cycle sculpture and Pabellon Molded-carved pottery. I suggest that both are the artifacts of cultures exposed to both Mexican and Maya influences. The Seibal intrusive elite were, I believe, Mexican-ized Maya in their adoption of certain Mexican deities—Tlaloc, Quetzalcoatl-Ehecatl, et al.—and their stylistic peculiarities. The Jimba culture bearers were probably people living along a cultural frontier, neither Classic Maya nor strictly Gulf Coast Mexican, but cer-tainly a mixture. In their case, however, the Mexican elements were derived from the same area as those in the Seibal sculpture, ultimately from cultures of the Mexican Gulf Coast.

Perhaps Altar's greater proximity to the Mexican lowlands rather than to the Northern Maya Lowlands is implicit in Sabloff and Wil-ley's preference for the coast to the Northern Lowlands as an origin zone for the Tenth Cycle invaders of Seibal. This can be explained if one considers both geography and the nature of redistribution centers in Mesoamerican prehistory.

Geographically, taking into account the transportation systems avail-able in pre-Hispanic times, it seems it was easier to go from the Gulf Coast of Mexico to northern Yucatan than from the coast overland and inland. The sixteenth-century trade routes seem to indicate this.

Apparently, the crucial factor in the distribution of certain trade items in Mesoamerica, whether or not a certain site received, say, quantities of obsidian, was that site's proximity to the redistribution center, not to the ultimate geographical source. For example, Altar de Sacrificios was nearer to the highland source of obsidian than was Tikal. Yet all of the obsidian represented by artifacts at Altar, and the little waste material, could fit into one not-very-large bag. Tikal is far-ther away, and off the rivers that give access to the highlands, and yet literally tons of obsidian were found there (W. R. Coe, personal com-munication). Thus Tikal may have been the redistribution center for obsidian for its area, and Altar's obsidian may conceivably have come from there or from some other redistribution point rather than directly from the highlands. One only need think of the Plumbate distribution patterns for another example.

As with artifacts, so with other traits and nonmaterial cultural elements. Thus, the Northern Maya Lowlands generally may have been more open to Mexican influence than the Southern Lowlands, have received such influences first, and then themselves have acted as redistributing agencies through such events as the Seibal elite-class intrusion.

Finally, the question of the Toltec intruders to Chichen Itza and their relationship, if any, to the Jimba culture group must be considered. H. E. D. Pollock has suggested that the Toltec invasion of Yucatan may be earlier than traditionally placed (1965 : 393, n. 27; 1952 : 238–39). Andrews's (1970 : 63) dates on the Balankanche Toltec censers as A.D. 860 ±130 conform to this suggestion. If, indeed, Toltec Chichen can be placed as beginning contemporarily with Terminal Classic in the Peten, then several alternative possibilities arise. First, the Jimba may have been a frontier semi–Classic Maya group shouldered aside or pushed ahead of the Toltecs on their way to Yucatan. Second, the Jimba may have been allies of the Toltecs, or they may also have been opportunists who rushed into the area, which was already shaken by the arrival of the Toltecs farther to the north. Finally, the Toltecs may have come later, themselves being the opportunists; and the initial penetration of the Maya Lowlands may have been made by groups including those that made Jimba pottery.

Similarities between Chenes and Rio Bec art and the Seibal Tenth Cycle sculpture may indicate an origin zone there. Based on my own and my students' 1970 work at the Becan site near the border between the Northern Lowlands and the Southern Lowlands, there is little doubt that the Chenes–Rio Bec style is contemporary with Late Classic Peten architecture. Further, there is little doubt but that the Rio Bec and Chenes styles are extinguished simultaneously with the collapse of the Peten Late Classic. This fact would tend to put this area in the same chronological lineup with the Southern Lowlands, and also subject to the same processual factors. There are differentiating features about the regional sequence at Becan, but close similarity to the south is clear as is related to the above points. J. W. Ball will document these conclusions in a forthcoming paper on the ceramics of the region. From wherever the non–Peten Maya are derived, I do think that they took over Seibal by at least 10.1.0.0.0 (A.D. 849) and ruled there along the lower Pasion until about 10.4.0.0.0 (A.D. 909), when a more Mexican and ultimately Gulf Coast–derived military group bested them and occupied Altar de Sacrificios. From that region the successful militarists raided deeper into Maya territory with consequent disastrous results.

Thompson has recently (1970) come out with an interpretation based largely on his detailed knowledge of the ethnohistorical sources and his much less detailed knowledge of Pasion River archaeology. The major points of his argument are (chap. 1, pp. 3–4):

1. The Putun or Chontal Maya group was peripheral to Classic civilization and located in the Usumacinta delta in the sixteenth century and, very likely, in the ninth century A.D.
2. The Putun were sea traders and penetrated inland to Chichen Itza and other places, conquering them.
3. Tula Toltecs penetrated to Yucatan later and the Putun at Chichen took in Quetzalcoatl-Kukulcan and his followers.
4. Earlier Putun groups, from around Potonchan, established a trading center at Altar de Sacrificios and, earlier still, had taken over Yaxchilan.
5. From Altar de Sacrificios, the Putun conquered Seibal.
6. "After the abandonment of the ceremonial centers and the overthrow of the Maya nobility, including the newly arrived Putun leaders, the remnant of the Putun established themselves south of the Pasion, naming their land Acala or Acalan (Land of the Canoe People) after their original homeland in the Grijalva-Usumacinta delta. There, under the loose designation Lacandon, they maintained their independence until 1695, with their largest town, renamed Dolores by the Spaniards, just north of the great bend of the upper Lacantun River."
7. Between A.D. 850 and 950, the Putun controlled, among other zones in the Maya Lowlands, the Pasion drainage.

Thompson's arguments regarding the Northern Lowlands and regions outside of the Pasion drainage do not concern us here, although they must be taken into consideration in any larger examination of the collapse. I do wish to meet Thompson's points in regard to the Pasion data.

Two preliminary observations are pertinent, however. First, Thompson has ignored archaeological data from Altar de Sacrificios and Seibal that directly contradict a crucial element of his theory, although these data were available to him. Second, Thompson takes the active fieldworkers in Maya archaeology to task for neglecting ethnohistory in their interpretations. There are at least two reasons for this alleged neglect. The first is that Thompson in this case has published an interpretation of the Pasion data before the excavators could appear in print with it in detailed and finished form. He may find more ethnohistory in the final reports than he expects. The second is that, although ethnohistory is important as an interpretative source, the main purpose of an archaeological monograph should be to present the data and the interpretations in a compartmentalized form. In the case of massive amounts of information resulting from long periods of fieldwork, the authors may prefer to present only the most conservative interpretations in the final report, reserving more speculative presentation for less fossilizing modes of publication—journals, for example.

Only points 4 and 5 on page 156 are directly relevant to the discussion in this chapter. Thompson's arguments hang on the following assumptions and equations.

1. The assumption that sixteenth-century ethnic and linguistic distributions accurately reflect the situation of the period of the Maya collapse, about 700 years before. He assumes that the Chontal were in the Grijalva-Usumacinta delta at the time of the Terminal Classic. *Comment:* This assumption is not necessarily so, though possible. Late Nahua intrusions to the Veracruz Gulf Coast may have been responsible for pushing the Chontal into their sixteenth-century position. Seven hundred undocumented years is a long time to take cultural and ethnic continuity on faith.

2. Identification of the Jimba Fine Orange and Fine Gray (archaically misspelled by Thompson as Ximba) complex at Altar de Sacrificios with the Chontal. This is based on the fact that Thompson accepts our argument of origin of the Y Group Fine Orange pottery tradition as around the bottom of the Gulf Coast area, perhaps even around Jonuta, upriver from Potonchan. *Comment:* Y Fine Orange and Jimba pottery may have been made by Chontal speakers, and, indeed, I argue for the origin zone that Thompson designates. However, I am loath to attach an ethnic tag to pottery. This smacks too much of the pioneering days of Mesoamerican archaeology when everything dug up had to be labeled with a known ethnic group name. Moreover, 700 years is too long to be sure. Potonchan has never been excavated, and its time

depth is unknown. The Jonuta site, where we do have evidence of Fine Orange wares being made in quantity, cannot yet be tied surely to any known ethnic group.

3. Identification of the Jimba Complex with the Seibal sculpture from the Tenth Cycle. *Comment:* This is unacceptable in the face of the evidence, cited earlier in this chapter, that Boca and Jimba are separate complexes in time and partly in space, and the association by Willey, Sabloff, and myself of Boca ceramics with the Tenth Cycle florescence at Seibal.

4. The identification of Cipactli glyphs on a ninth-century Seibal stela with the name, *Zipaque,* of a sixteenth-century ruling family at Potonchan. *Comment:* Seibal is 260 air miles from Potonchan. The glyphs and the rulers' name are 700 years apart. Thompson elsewhere argues for continuity of ruling dynasty names on the basis of a 110-year occurrence (1970 : 29–30), but a quantum jump is involved when one goes from one century to seven centuries in the affairs of families, dynasties, and men in general. This seems an unlikely interpretation, or at least highly speculative. The possibility for other interpretations exists. The Cipactli glyphs may indicate an actual date of importance to the Mexicanized Seibal rulers. After all, the Seibal glyphs do have numbers with them, seemingly indicating a calendrical value.

To summarize, Thompson's arguments are interesting and stimulating, but unconvincing in dealing with the archaeological data.

I would still maintain that it fits better with the evidence from the Pasion to derive the Mexicanized Maya elite at Seibal from a zone other than the fine paste zone of the Gulf Coast and to interpret the Jimba Complex as a separate and culturally distinct event. The latter would also, I argue, represent an intrusion, probably military, possibly, but not necessarily, of the Chontal, to the Altar de Sacrificios zone.

I will not quarrel here with the other points of Thompson's reconstruction of events, because they depend on the major elements dealt with above, are irrelevant to the Pasion data, or are highly ambiguous. This is an excellent example of the perils of an imbalanced consideration of a cultural-historical problem. The independently derived archaeological structure can be used to control the alternative interpretations.

NOTE

1. Most of the data contained in this chapter appear in my study of the Altar de Sacrificios ceramics (Adams 1971).

APPENDIX A

Comparisons of Samples of Fine Paste Types from Altar de Sacrificios and Seibal

Samples	A de S	Seibal
	(sherds/whole vessels)	

A. Jimba Complex as defined at Altar de Sacrificios

	A de S	Seibal
Tres Naciones Gray: Tres Naciones Variety	1081/2	100/0
Altar Orange: Altar Variety	926/8	150/0
Tumba Black-on-orange: Tumba Variety	65/6	30/5
Poite Incised: Poite Variety	263/6	75/3
Punctated Fine Orange	124/1	0/0
Trapiche Incised: Trapiche Variety	183/1	0/0
Trapiche Incised: Ixpayac Variety	59/2	0/0
Trapiche Incised: Variety Unspecified	0/0	75/1
Pabellon Molded-carved: Pabellon Variety	50/6	50/2
Provincia Plano-relief: Provincia Variety	21/0	15/1
Modeled Fine Orange (unnamed)	4/0	0/0
Cedro Gadrooned: Cedro Variety	25/0	35/0
Alta Gracia Gadrooned: Alta Gracia Variety	3/0	6/0
Chorrito Plano Relief: Chorrito Variety	20/0	0/0

B. Bayal-Boca fine paste types not at Altar de Sacrificios

	Seibal
Balancan Orange	14/0
Islas Gouged-incised: Islas Variety	35/1

C. Total fine paste type samples by site. Sample for Altar de Sacrificios is incomplete and based on only two collections. It is estimated that the incomplete sample for Altar is about 5 percent of the total. The sample for Seibal is also incomplete but represents about 66 percent of the total amount obtained at the site. Altar de Sacrificios:

Total analyzed sample from Op. 43X and 50A-C, A de S 2644 (38 percent) of total of 6,965 sherds. Totals of 43X and 50A-C were 129,000 and 10,290 sherds respectively. Thirty-two whole vessels from all collections.

Seibal:

Thirteen whole vessels and 590 sherds. Seibal has about 17 percent of the sherd sample at Altar based on these *incomplete* samples.

D. Comparison of frequencies of major domestic types at A de S and Seibal

	A de S (%)	Seibal (%)
Altar Orange	35	25
Tres Naciones Gray	41	17
Total of sample	76	42

E. The above suggests that either:

(1) the complex is functionally incomplete at Seibal, or

(2) sampling is incomplete at Seibal but a Jimba Complex is present based on the presence of 9 of its 10 diagnostic types as defined at Altar.

Comment: Number 2 is rejected on the grounds that the two domestic types at Seibal *lack* the shape repertoire (water jars, etc.) to make a functionally complementary and complete complex.

APPENDIX B

Stylistic Element Analysis
of Pabellon Molded-carved: Pabellon Variety

A. List of distinctive traits common to Seibal Tenth Cycle sculpture as in Sabloff 1970 : 403. An asterisk (*) denotes a trait also found in Classic Period sculpture, not Tenth Cycle. REWA denotes comments by R. E. W. Adams; TP denotes references to Tatiana Proskouriakoff 1950, *Maya Classic Sculpture.*

1. Hair style, brushed up. Comment, TP : fig. 76a (Ucanal St. 4)

2. Helmet. Comment, found in pre-Toltec Mexicanized sculpture TP : fig. 88a, b (Oxkintok)

*3. Plumes from headdress. Comment, TP : fig. 16

    *4. Beard. Comment, TP : figs. 19r, s, t; (Copan, Yaxchilan, Quiri-gua)

    *5. Round earplugs. Comment, TP : fig. 20 (Uaxactun, Xultun, Calakmul, Piedras Negras)

    *6. Bead necklaces. Comment, TP : fig. 21 (Itsimte, Naranjo)

    *7. Three element or bead bracelets. Comment, TP : fig. 27a–d (Naranjo, Tikal, Piedras Negras)

    8. Arm and leg bracelets

    *9. Nose bar. Comment, admittedly a rarity, but in Classic sculpture see TP : fig. 26d', e' (Yaxchilan)

    10. Distinctive staff. Comment, I am unable to find this in the literature available to me at this time

    11. Bar with three tassels across the chest

    *12. Chest disk (pectoral). Comment, this is a rarity in Pabellon Molded–carved. TP : fig. 22t, u

    13. Loincloths

    14. Bare feet

    *15. Faces with mouths slightly open. Comment, TP : fig. 9a (Xultun)

    16. Physical characteristics

    17. Maya and non-Maya glyph combinations. Comment, I would argue that there are no Maya glyphs recognizable in Pabellon Molded-carved pottery

    18. Square glyph

    19. Cipactli glyph

    *20. Mat for seating and characteristic sitting posture. Comment, TP : fig. 10

    *21. Thematic, confrontation. Comment, Copan Altar Q

    22. Outstretched hand, holding a glyph, Copan Altar Q (?)

B. Continued list of stylistic traits found in Pabellon Molded-carved: Pabellon Variety compiled by R. E. W. Adams. Reference to TP and RES, denoting R. E. Smith 1955, *Ceramic Sequence at Uaxactun, Guatemala*

    *23. Cotton-quilted armor. Comment, occurs in Boca Phase, Altar de Sacrificios figurines

    24. Eight Cozcacuauhtli glyphs

    25. Girdle

    26. Round shields with pendant streamers from the center

27. *Atlatls.* Comment, occur in Classic sculpture (Tikal St. 31) but are regarded in these cases as evidence of earlier Mexican influence from Teotihuacan

28. Earth monster seats for human figures in the "conference" scenes (category 2)

29. Ilhuitl-like glyph (REWA 1971 : fig. 67a)

*30. Beardless faces on recumbent figures, warriors, and "cocoon men" (scene categories 1, 3, and 4). Comment, reciprocal of item 4; Copan hieroglyphic stairway

31. Human trophy head headdresses

*32. Mask in front of the face. Comment, TP : fig. 19o, *p, q* (Yaxchilan, Copan)

*33. Nose "flower" (recumbent figure scenes only). Comment, Altar de Sacrificios Burial 128, Vessel catalog No. 58-135, regarded as an import from Alta Verapaz (REWA 1971 : figs. 77–80); Balancan-Morales, St. 4

34. Stylized wall or shield symbol

*35. Broad-brimmed hats. Comment, TP : fig. 18x (Tikal Altar V)

36. Cocoon body coverings

37. Mirror symmetry of scene

*38. Full-front death's head. Comment, RES : fig. 86n

*39. Vertical glyph panels. Comment, RES : fig. 86d, *e, f*

*40. Horizontal glyph bands (rims). Comment, quite common on Maya Classic pottery

41. Vertical zones undecorated except for three circle punctations

*42. Apron-style loin cloths. Comment, TP : fig. 24 (Tikal, Copan, Naranjo, etc.)

*43. Faces with mouths closed. Comment, reciprocal of item 15

44. Right angle face-framing headdress

45. Serpent-body platform (Scene category 2, REWA 1971 : fig. 67d, *e*)

*46. Dart. Comment, 1 instance (REWA 1971 : fig. 67ff)

*47. "Ladder" bracelets (REWA 1971 : fig. 67d, *e*, right panel, right figure)

48. Plumbed back-frame (REWA 1971 : fig. 67hh)

*49. Thematic: recumbent figure. Comment, Copan hieroglyphic stair, Aguateca or Dos Pilas sculpture

50. Thematic: war scenes (REWA 1971 : figs. 67a, *f*)

51. Thematic: mirror symmetry scene (Sabloff 1970 : fig. 43)

C. Comment

1. Summary of Sabloff list (items 1–22)

   Common to Pabellon, Seibal sculpture, and Classic
   sculpture   10

   Common to Pabellon, Seibal sculpture, and distinctive
   from Classic art   11

   Unaccounted for   <u>1</u>

            Total traits   22

2. Summary of combined trait list (items 1–51)

   Common to Pabellon, Siebal sculpture, and Classic
   sculpture and pottery   23

   Common to Pabellon and Seibal sculpture and not in
   Classic art   11

   Unique to Pabellon   16

   Unaccounted for   1

            Total traits   51

9
The Classic Maya Collapse:
Usumacinta Zone and
the Northwestern Periphery

ROBERT L. RANDS

Department of Anthropology
Southern Illinois University, Carbondale

Data bearing on the Classic Maya collapse vary from region to region within the Usumacinta Zone and the adjacent western lowlands. In some cases information that may be applicable is to be found in a wide range of materials including epigraphy, sculptural styles, and ceramics. In other regions, one or more of these elements is largely absent (for example, stone monuments are rare in the alluvial plain of the Lower Usumacinta). Again, the requisite archaeological investigations have yet to be made (note the rarity of settlement pattern studies over most of the area). My familiarity with some regions as opposed to others also results in uneven coverage. Not unexpectedly, this chapter is concerned primarily with the background of the collapse. Data pinpointing this event—or series of interrelated events—are difficult to isolate. Recognition that a collapse of Classic culture occurred may be based on disruptions of sociocultural patterns, with reintegration taking place on a significantly simpler cultural or demographic level, or, inferentially, by temporally significant lacunae in the archaeological record.

THEORETICAL OBSERVATIONS

The Usumacinta Zone and its western extension hold a place of special interest in hypotheses that explain the Classic Maya collapse in terms of external intrusions. This interest is, in part, caused by the sheer geographic marginality of the region. Beyond lies Mexico—and, as a matter of fact, at the time of the Spanish Conquest, Nahua-speaking towns were scattered among Maya speakers in part of this area. Also, certain hypotheses invoking intrusions accord special significance to the zone because the center for the supposedly invasion-linked dispersal of fine paste pottery in the Maya area is commonly believed to lie in Tabasco or adjacent regions (Smith 1958; Thompson 1970; Sayre, Chan, and Sabloff 1971). Stemming from this region, the intruders are thought by Sabloff and Willey (1967 : 329) to have "swept up the Usumacinta-Pasión drainage at the very end of the 9th Cycle," establishing themselves at Seibal and pushing into the southwestern and southern Peten. Adams, however, sees invaders reaching the Upper Usumacinta by another route—a network of streams, to the west of Bonampak, that leads to the supposed homeland of the Jimba Fine Paste Tradition in lowland Chiapas or Tabasco. From this southern point on the Usumacinta, the Jimba people are thought to have moved downstream against Yaxchilan and Piedras Negras (Adams, chapter 8, 1971 : 163–64).

As one turns to internal processes that may have contributed to the Classic Maya decline, the Usumacinta Zone and northwestern lowlands appear in some respects atypical. This is especially true in the north, where an alluvial riverine environment prevails. There, as well as to the south along the foothills of the Chiapas highlands, heavy rainfall coupled with a short dry season offers advantages for double cropping (Sanders 1962 : 87–88). The significance of this pattern for the Classic collapse over the Maya Lowlands as a whole is uncertain. Ecological stresses of the sort that frequently have been called on to explain the collapse would surely not have operated uniformly over the entire Maya Lowlands. An ecologically based crisis in one region, however, could have had economic and sociopolitical repercussions, stimulating additional crises, each of which was related to its particular environmental setting.

Well before the collapse, the peripheral position of the west in Maya culture history may have been a factor in the development of differences from the Maya heartland in the structuring of society. These differences could have come about as the result of: (1) more sustained exposure to non-Maya influences; (2) the modification of Classic traits as they spread outward and became incorporated in the local subcultures; or (3) a combination of these, plus accompanying ecological adjustments. An example, hypothetical but plausible, is that redistribution centers between the highlands and core cultures of the Maya Lowlands may have grown up on the borders of the Maya area, leading to the development of specialized institutions while serving as a focus for the flow of non–Lowland Maya ideas as well as goods. Given such a situation, the acceptance of culture traits diffusing out of the central parts of the lowlands could well have been selective. The point to be emphasized here is that sociocultural differences, whatever their causes, may have been intensified in a peripheral setting, and that such differences could have contributed to a varying set of responses to a terminal Classic crisis situation. One of our difficulties stems from not really knowing enough about the nature of Classic Maya society, as a whole or in its regional manifestations.

REGIONAL SUBDIVISIONS

The geographic scope of the present paper includes not only the Usumacinta proper but sites far enough away to fall into the drainage system of the lower Grijalva (for example, Palenque, Comalcalco). My fieldwork in Chiapas and Tabasco, extending outward from Palenque and focused on that site, has provided a perspective with a northwestern orientation, when the Southern Maya Lowlands are viewed as a whole. This westerly extension of the Usumacinta Zone provides an incomplete but useful cross section of a number of sites that occupy various gradations on a scale of Maya "Classicism."

As outlined here, the division of the Usumacinta Zone into Upper, Middle, and Lower sectors differs from designations that have become traditional in the archaeological literature (see Fig. 18). The *Upper Usumacinta sector*, corresponding in part to what Maler and others

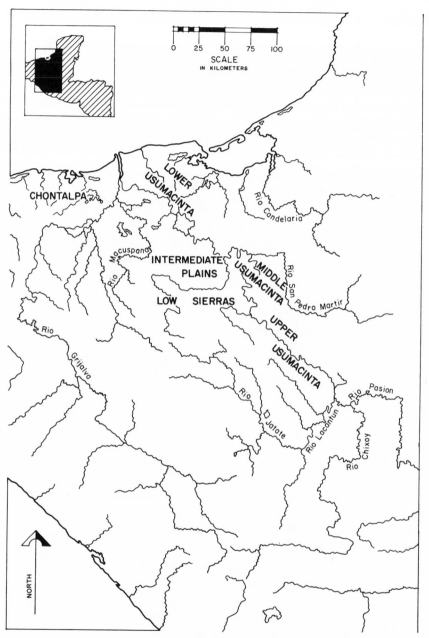

FIGURE 18. MAP OF USUMACINTA AND NORTHWESTERN ZONES

have termed the central portion of the Usumacinta Valley, ideally extends from the beginning of the Usumacinta proper, at the junction of the Pasion and Salinas (Chixoy) rivers, to Boca del Cerro—the gorge above Tenosique through which the river passes into the Tabasco plains. Within this sector lie the artistically vigorous Classic centers of Bonampak, Yaxchilan, and Piedras Negras. A series of rapids extending well to the north and south of Piedras Negras may have minimized the role of the river as an artery of contact (Satterthwaite 1943 : 8–9).

The *Middle Usumacinta sector,* as defined here, centers on that part of the river which meanders through a comparatively narrow flood plain, from Boca del Cerro to approximately the southern limits of Berlin's survey near Tecolpan (Berlin 1956). Limestone is unavailable locally, and stone masonry is absent. Occupations appear to have been most vigorous during the Preclassic and Late Classic periods. Postclassic remains occur in sufficient strength to suggest that the Middle Usumacinta did not undergo a demographic collapse comparable to, say, the Peten or Upper Usumacinta; on the other hand, indications are lacking of intensive Postclassic developments such as are found toward the Tabasco coast. Chontal speakers were evidently dominant in the Middle Usumacinta during the sixteenth and early seventeenth centuries (Scholes and Roys 1948 : 24–25).

In the *Lower Usumacinta sector,* the river branches into a series of distributaries. Even in the dry season, extensive lagoons exist behind natural levees. The best-known site is Jonuta, locus for Berlin's Jonuta horizon. The Postclassic Cintla horizon is also well represented (Berlin 1956). Apparently Xicalango and Jonuta were Mexican or partly Mexican towns in the sixteenth century, Xicalango sharing its commercial position as a redistribution center with the Chontal-speaking town of Potonchan (Scholes and Roys 1948 : 27–38).

Extending westward from the Middle Usumacinta are districts which I refer to as the Low Sierras and Intermediate Plains (Rands 1967a); to the north and west of these lies the Chontalpa. The *Low Sierras* consists of a rugged, heavily folded region that serves as the foothills of the Chiapas highlands. Elevations above sea level seldom exceed 600 m., and in its ecological potential the region is essentially "lowland." Geographical proximity to the highlands, to the fertile soils of the Chontalpa, and to the Usumacinta gives the region importance as the potential location of redistribution centers and the development of symbiotic relationships; for the most part, however, the ceramic patterns suggest marginality and cultural isolation. Situated on the frontal ridge overlooking the plains, Palenque, an outpost of elaborated Classic Maya patterns, is the best-known site in the Low Sierras. Strictly speaking not part of the region, but convenient to consider with it, are the sites of Pomona and Tortuguero, both having sculptural relationships to Palenque.[2] Tortuguero, in particular, appears to have occupied a strategic position on the shifting western frontier of Maya Classicism. Scattered Western and Lacandon Chol inhabited the Low Sierras in the latter part of the sixteenth century; Zoque towns lie to the west (Scholes and Roys 1948 : 38–45).

The *Intermediate Plains* (intermediate between the Low Sierras and the Middle Usumacinta) is marginal, for the most part characterized by relatively sparse populations. This is a region of dissected Pleistocene terraces with lateritic or glei soils. In the recent economic development of this part of Tabasco, forest has been converted rapidly into grasslands for cattle, little farming being practiced. Farmers in the vicinity of the Low Sierras have traditionally preferred clearing land for *milpas* in the sierras to farming the less productive flatlands. On the other hand, the *Chontalpa*, with recent alluvial soils, is highly fertile and supported an exceptionally heavy population at the time of Spanish contact. Sixteenth century settlements in the Chontalpa were mostly Chontal speaking, with Nahua towns, including the commerically dominant Cimatan, bordering on the most thickly populated district (Scholes and Roys 1948 : 24–27, 31). Sisson suggests that a sudden Late Classic increase in population and sociopolitical complexity may have been caused by the beginning of commercial production of cacao in the region (Sisson 1970 : 47). At this time Comalcalco, although substituting fired brick for stone masonry, as in the Lower Usumacinta, shows close relationship to the Classic Maya architectural style.

CLIMAX AND COLLAPSE: LATE CLASSIC OCCUPATIONS, CULTURAL DISCONTINUITIES, AND ABANDONMENT

Large-scale public works incorporating the corbeled vault, monuments bearing Initial Series inscriptions, and a distinctive sculptural style as defined by Proskouriakoff (1950) are among the diagnostics of Classic culture at elite centers over much of the Southern Maya Lowlands. Polychrome pottery belonging to the Tzakol-Tepeu stylistic tradition is an associated trait at most of these centers and also occurs at smaller contemporary sites where impressive architecture and sculpture are absent. Yet, in portions of the Usumacinta Zone and the northwestern periphery, not all of these traits may appear at a large site which is demonstrably Classic in chronological period and certain of its developmental characteristics. A striking example is Comalcalco, where surely dated inscriptions are unknown and polychrome pottery virtually absent. Even at Palenque, where the Classic tradition was refined and elaborated, there was severe reduction or complete loss of such important Classic traits as stelae, caches of eccentric flint or obsidian, and polychrome gloss wares.

Consideration of the Maya downfall must, therefore, be made in terms that are meaningful in a local or regional context, as well as on a pan-Maya or pan-Mesoamerican basis. The incidence and temporal position of dated monumental sculptures from the Upper Usumacinta and the Low Sierras are plotted in Figures 19 and 20. An ultimate objective, largely for future research, is to isolate phenomena associated with the collapse and to see how these relate to times of cultural or demographic climax. The existence of Classic and non-Classic styles is examined here, and developments in fine paste pottery are reviewed, at the time of and prior to the collapse.

Upper Usumacinta Sector

Cessation of elite activities appears to have coincided closely in time at the major Usumacinta sites, as is suggested by Figure 19, which utilizes accepted dates and Proskouriakoff's stylistic analysis to graph the number of dated monuments erected in a given *katun* at five sites in the sector.[3] Of these, Piedras Negras and Bonampak have the earliest terminal dates (9.18.5.0.0, A.D. 795 and ca. 9.18.10.0.0, A.D. 800, respectively), followed by La Mar (9.18.15.0.0, A.D. 805), El Cayo (9.19.0.0.0, A.D. 810± ?), and Yaxchilan (10.0.10.0.0, A.D. 840± 2 *katuns*). Actually, problems of dating are not this simple. Proskouriakoff (1960 : 460) suggests that six undated monuments at Piedras Negras may be assigned to the seventh series (or reign) at the site, extending the records of this se-

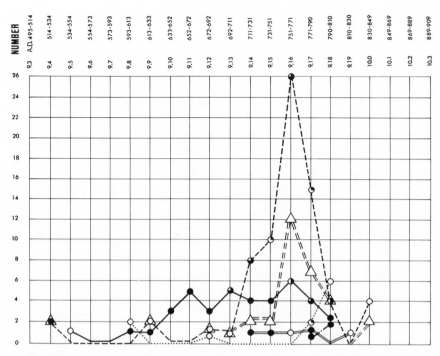

FIGURE 19. FREQUENCY OF INSCRIBED MONUMENTS, BY KATUN, AT UPPER USUMACINTA SITES. See legend to Fig. 20 for explanation of symbols.

ries to as late as 9.19.10.0.0 (A.D. 820) or 9.19.15.0.0 (A.D. 825). The possibility that a still later series may be represented by these monuments is also recognized. Again, although suggesting on stylistic grounds that Cycle 10 monuments occur at Yaxchilan, she has also held that the site may have fallen at about 9.19.0.0.0 (A.D. 810; Proskouriakoff 1950 : 198–99; Ruppert, Thompson, and Proskouriakoff 1955 : 32; Proskouriakoff 1964 : 197, 199). In general, it appears premature to argue that within the Upper Usumacinta sector the inscriptions support either upstream or downriver priority in the termination of monumental activities.

Additional trends are reflected in Figure 19. At the neighboring sites of Yaxchilan and Bonampak the greatest bursts of sculptural activity preceded the end of monument erection by a relatively brief time. To be sure, at the smaller center of Bonampak there is greater restriction in time than at Yaxchilan, and the florescence which took place dur-

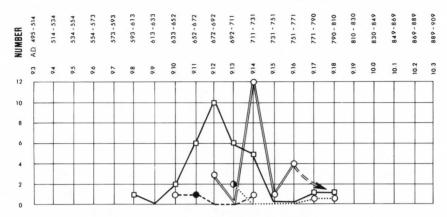

FIGURE 20. FREQUENCY OF MONUMENTS AND OTHER INSCRIBED OBJECTS, BY KATUN, AT SITES IN THE NORTHWESTERN LOWLANDS. Certain stylistically-dated objects without inscriptions are included. See Notes 3 and 6 for explanatory remarks. Symbols in Figs. 19, 20 have the following significance:

●   Accepted dates, mostly dedicatory

○   Style dates (after Proskouriakoff), questionable dates

◐ ◑ ◕   Totals include both accepted and stylistic or questionable dates (approximately 25%, 50%, and 75% of totals, respectively, are accepted dates)

△   Dates represent number of buildings and/or distinct monuments (e.g., stelae), rather than including all of the sculptures, such as lintels, that form part of a single structure (Yaxchilan only)

▲ △   Multiple lintels or other sculptures are unknown from a single structure; therefore dates reflect only distinct monuments and buildings. Symbols refer, respectively, to accepted dedicatory dates and to stylistic or questionable dates (Yaxchilan only)

□   As inscriptions may represent either dedicatory or nondedicatory dates, contemporaneity is often in doubt (Palenque only)

Symbols for sites (Fig. 19)	Symbols for sites (Fig. 20)
——— Piedras Negras	——— Palenque (inscriptions)
=== El Cayo	=== Palenque (style dates)
·········· Bonampak	==➤ Palenque (style date = Late Classic,
—·—·— La Mar	Dynamic Phase
	·········· Pomona
===➤ Yaxchilan	— — — Tortuguero

ing *Katuns* 15–18 was on a smaller scale at Bonampak. Nevertheless, the impression that maximum artistic creativity came only shortly before the collapse is strong at Bonampak, where the magnificent mural paintings of Structure 1, dated at approximately 9.18.10.0.0 (A.D. 800), are among the latest evidences of elite activities at the site.

173

For more than one and one-half centuries, monument erection at Piedras Negras was geared to *hotun* (5-year) intervals, and there was no comparable increase, toward the end of elite occupation, in the number of sculptures dedicated. Yet at Piedras Negras the latest monument that can be dated with reasonable assurance, Stela 12 (A.D. 795, GMT),[4] is one of the masterpieces of Maya sculpture. Showing the arraignment of prisoners, the scene is similar in subject matter and forcefulness of portrayal to one of the almost contemporary Bonampak murals. On the other hand, Proskouriakoff notes that "the standard Classic canons of art" were relaxed toward the close of the Yaxchilan occupation, during the reign of Shield-Jaguar's descendant, one of the late rulers of the site, "perhaps in consequence of his extreme preoccupation with war"; conflicting tendencies emerged "toward rigidity and simplification in sculpture" and "toward flamboyance and exaggeration of inessential detail" (Proskouriakoff 1964 : 195).

Whatever the relationships may have been between warfare and artistic developments in Terminal Classic Yaxchilan, motifs suggesting militarism and conquest were by no means confined to the very latest Classic Maya monuments. At Yaxchilan, the exceptional exploits of Shield-Jaguar appear to have taken place in *Katuns* 12 and 13 (Proskouriakoff 1963b, 1964), well prior to the peak of sculptural activity at the site (cf. Fig. 19). The warrior motif is among the earliest standardized thematic portrayals at Piedras Negras (Stela 26, A.D. 628). Moreover, one of the earliest wall panels at Piedras Negras ("Lintel" 2, A.D. 667) is among the more convincing representations of military organization in all of Classic Maya art (Fig. 21). Here, six armed, uniformly dressed subordinates are shown kneeling before a more elaborately costumed personage, behind whom a lieutenant stands. Shields and lances carried by all eight individuals appear to be almost identical. Present in the accompanying inscription is a glyph (T-678, J. E. S. Thompson 1962) showing a similarity of headdresses to those of the kneeling soldiers and, to judge by the visor, resembling that of the superior official, as well. The standardization of militaristic accouterments is striking. Although warfare may have intensified in the Late Classic Period, it appears unwarranted to consider this intensification as merely the diffusion of non-Maya practices or as a late, aberrant reaction to a Terminal Classic crisis situation.

Of the Upper Usumacinta sites, only Piedras Negras has been

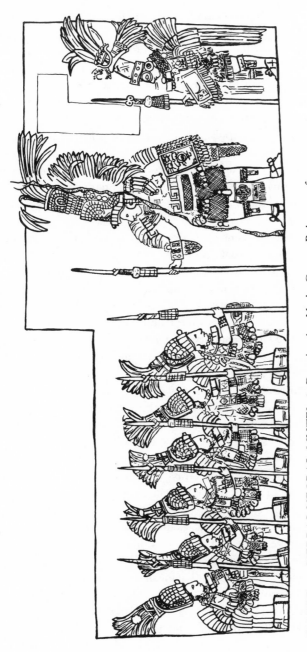

FIGURE 21. PIEDRAS NEGRAS, LINTEL 2. Drawing by Merle Greene Robertson from photograph; glyphs not shown.

investigated in sufficient detail to formulate a ceramic sequence, and the data are largely unpublished. In spite of a trend toward increasing differentiation from Peten norms, Piedras Negras is to be placed in the Tzakol and Tepeu ceramic spheres during most of the Classic Period (Naba through Chacalhaaz ceramic complexes). Polychrome pottery was produced in great quantities during the Chacalhaaz Complex but was highly standardized and aesthetically "sloppy" compared to that of the earlier Yaxche Complex. Abundant sherds of the Chacalhaaz Complex were embedded in the masonry of Structure J-6, providing a firm association with Throne 1. This throne, set into a special wall niche, bears inscriptions expressing the date 9.17.15.0.0 (A.D. 785); this dating agrees well with the Tepeu 2–like characteristics of Chacalhaaz pottery.

Effective abandonment of Piedras Negras apparently coincided with the end of the Chacalhaaz Ceramic Complex. At Structure J-12, however, surface deposits are characterized by fine paste monochrome pottery of the Tamay Ceramic Complex. Fine Gray Ware is present, as well as much larger quantities of stylistically related pottery that I am provisionally referring to as Fine Pale-orange Ware (Fig. 22b). In neither case do the significant stylistic affiliations lie with Fine Gray and Fine Orange wares of the Tres Naciones and Altar groups, as these are known in the Bayal, Boca, and Jimba complexes of Seibal and Altar de Sacrificios. Instead, affiliations exist to the north: to examples of Fine Gray Ware from Tabasco, Dzibilchaltun, and Yoxiha (Fig. 22a, c–e), to a few examples of Fine Gray from the Campeche coast (Ruz Lhuillier 1969), and to some Fine Gray of the Balunte Complex at Palenque (see Fig. 29 e; Rands and Rands 1957 : 147–48). Unlike the situation at Altar and Seibal, the Fine Gray Ware constituting this stylistically related ceramic group, Gray Chablekal, apparently predates the rise of Fine Orange Ware.

At Piedras Negras, the few examples of Fine Orange pottery that have been recovered belong mostly to the Altar Ceramic Group (especially Pabellon Modeled-carved, including gray-fired examples of this type). Provincia Plano-relief (Balancan Group) and Yalton Black-on-orange (Silho Group) are also known. The scattered examples of Fine Orange Ware from Piedras Negras seemingly do not belong to the Tamay Ceramic Complex but, on the basis of evidence from other sites, would appear to postdate Tamay. If this interpretation is correct, we are dealing with an initial incursion of fine paste pottery, having few if any antecedents in Chacalhaaz, coming either when the site was abandoned or at some indefinite but presumably short interval of time thereafter. Still later, there were apparently sporadic "driblets" of Fine Orange pottery to Piedras Negras, including materials that would be at

FIGURE 22. FINE GRAY WARE AND STYLISTICALLY AFFILIATED POTTERY. *a*, Yoxiha; *b*, Piedras Negras (Tamay Ceramic Complex); *c*, Tecolpan (Jonuta horizon: late Naab diagnostic); *d*, *e*, comparative examples from Yucatan. *a*, *c-e*, Fine Gray Ware (Gray Chablekal Group); *b*, Fine Pale-orange Ware. Incised monkey designs with dentate stamping (*a*, *d*), rocker dentate stamping (*c*), and punctuation (*e*). Incised design not shown in *b*. Approximate scale: *b*, 1:4; *c-e*, 1:6 (*a*, unavailable). *a*, after Blom and LaFarge (1926 : Fig. 189); *c*, after Berlin (1956 : Fig. 4*i*); *d*, *e*, after Brainerd (1958 : Fig. 36*d*, *b*).

home in the Jimba and Bayal-Boca complexes. The implications of this are twofold: (1) the Classic collapse at Piedras Negras preceded that at Altar and the "non-Classic" Seibal florescence; (2) if all of these sites did indeed fall as the result of military incursions (and if we can make one-to-one correlations between the invaders and the fine paste pottery they used), the same people were *not* responsible for the Classic downfall at Piedras Negras and in the Pasion Valley.

Fine paste sherds have been found at Yaxchilan in small surface collections (Sabloff and Willey 1967 : 324). The presence of Fine Orange Ware of the Silho Group is of considerable interest (Vaillant 1927 : Fig. 307).

Middle Usumacinta Sector

Except at the regionally transitional site of Pomona, dated monuments are unknown from the Middle Usumacinta. Ceramics provide a quite different picture of Late Classic developments than for the Upper Usumacinta. Corresponding changes are reflected, from polychrome to fine paste and from polychrome to monochrome; yet a significant amount of the fine paste ceramics on the Middle Usumacinta is not monochrome. My excavations at Trinidad and Calatrava, supplemented by surface collections from Tierra Blanca, form the basis for the following summary. (Calatrava might be considered as having a location transitional to the Lower Usumacinta or even in the latter sector, but it is convenient to discuss the site here.)

Following a long Preclassic sequence and a sparse Early Classic occupation, Trinidad can be placed in the Tepeu Ceramic Sphere during the Taxinchan Complex (Rands 1969b). Abundant volcanic-ash-tempered pottery shows resemblances to Saxche Orange–polychrome, suggesting a Tepeu 1 dating; certain shape modes are reminiscent of Tepeu 2. Coeval with the polychrome, and in some cases stylistically undifferentiated from it, are small quantities of untempered pottery (Fig. 23a; cf. Rands 1969b : Fig. 7a, c, e). Bichrome and resist painting are also present in the fine paste ceramics (Fig. 23c, e). Fine Cream (cream-buff paste) is most common among the fine-textured wares, and I suspect it may have been indigenous to the region. Pottery having a fine-textured orange paste is rare in the Taxinchan deposits and differs stylistically from recognized Fine Orange types, but some kind of ancestral relationship may exist (Fig. 23*f*).

The Naab Ceramic Complex follows at Trinidad and Tierra Blanca, equating roughly in time with Tepeu 2. After the Taxinchan interval, Trinidad once more is largely outside the Peten-oriented ceramic tradition. Developmentally, some of the trends of Tepeu 3 are foreshadowed. Tempered polychrome pottery almost disappears, being replaced by fine paste ceramics. The latter are usually monochrome (especially white slipped) (Fig. 24*b*), bichrome (red-on-white), resist (Fig. 24*a*), or smudged to a lustrous black (Rands 1969b : Fig. 8*d*). Fine paste polychrome also occurs, though rarely. Incising and other plastic techniques are moderately developed (Fig. 24*c*). Moldmade figurines, sometimes fine paste, occur. Fine Cream continues to be the most common of the untempered wares. Fine Gray is poorly represented at Trinidad but occurs more frequently in the collections from Tierra Blanca, suggesting that the Naab Ceramic Complex lasted somewhat later there as a provisional late facet. Fine Orange Ware has yet to appear in any strength. There is clear continuity from the preceding

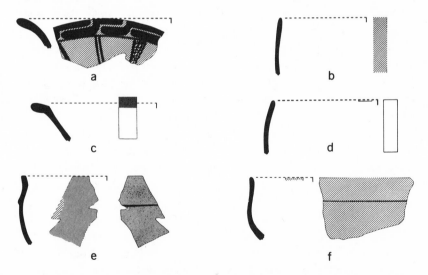

a

b

c

d

e

f

FIGURE 23. TRINIDAD, TAXINCHAN CERAMIC COMPLEX. *a-d*, Fine Cream Ware; *f*, Fine Orange Ware (type unspecified). *a*, Red-and-black-on-orange; *b, f*, orange; *c*, red-on-white; *d*, white; *e*, orange resist. Approximate scale 1:4.

Taxinchan Complex, but reduction in polychrome decoration, coupled with the rise of the previously extant white slip and untempered pastes, provides a reorientation of considerable importance.

The spectacular rise of Fine Orange Ware is documented stratigraphically at nearby Calatrava (Fig. 24d, e).[5] The Balancan Ceramic Group is best represented, although excessive weathering and occasional blurring of typological boundaries between members of the Balancan and Altar groups pose a number of unresolved problems. Terminal Classic Fine Orange Ware, of either the Balancan or Altar groups, is unknown from Trinidad and Tierra Blanca. However, Postclassic examples of the ware are present, the Silho Group being represented at Trinidad (Rands 1969b : Fig. 9c, d) and perhaps at Calatrava, and the Matillas Group at Calatrava.

The Middle Usumacinta appears to have been the locus for intensive developments in fine paste ceramics. If the innovating centers were not actually located in this region, they must have been close enough to permit sustained contacts, so that changes were mirrored, in detail, in the ceramic sequences of Trinidad, Tierra Blanca, and Calatrava. Fine Cream Ware rose to prominence out of a cultural base which included Tepeu style polychromes, and this development took place without rupturing the ceramic tradition in the manner of Upper Usumacinta–Pasion sites. The possible waning of Maya Classicism (as expressed in the disappearance of the Taxinchan polychromes) was accompanied by a more vigorous development of traits that were already present in the ceramic repertoire. The later intrusion of Fine Orange Ware may have constituted more of a cultural displacement. Even in this case, however, there is no indication of discontinuity on a scale such as that observed for Piedras Negras, especially in view of the sporadic earlier occurrences of untempered orange paste pottery (Fig. 23f).

Lower Usumacinta Sector

Dated monuments are again unknown, although Proskouriakoff (1950) places two low-relief sculptures from Jonuta in her Late Classic Dynamic Phase (9.16.0.0.0–9.19.0.0.0, A.D. 751–810). A prowling jaguar in Toltec style, modeled in stucco, is an interesting occurrence

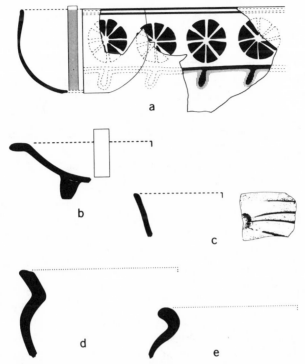

FIGURE 24. TRINIDAD (NAAB CERAMIC COMPLEX) AND CALA-
TRAVA (JONUTA HORIZON). *a-c*, Trinidad; *d, e*, Calatrava. *a-c*, Fine Cream
Ware; *d, e*, Fine Orange Ware. *a*, Resist (black, white, unslipped); *b*, white; *c*, in-
cised; *d, e*, Balancan Orange Type. Approximate scale: *a*, 1:6; *b-e*, 1:4.

at Atasta, but Berlin (1956) reports no pottery from the site earlier than
the Late Postclassic.

Berlin's excavations at Tecolpan and Jonuta indicate a succession of
Classic Maya polychrome, Black, and Fine Orange ceramics. The Fine
Orange is identified as Z (Balancan Group). Berlin notes that Fine
Gray Ware seems to have closer affiliations with the black pottery,
some of which is apparently fine textured, than with Fine Orange;
Fine Gray Ware, as well as the (Fine) Black, tends to have temporal
priority over Fine Orange. Ushered in by the fine paste monochromes,
the Jonuta horizon is considered to fall largely on a post–Tepeu 2
time level, with its beginnings perhaps contemporary with Tepeu 2.
The upper limit of the Jonuta horizon is the Early Postclassic, accord-

181

ing to Berlin, a few sherds of Tohil Plumbate and X (Silho Group) Fine Orange coming from the highest levels of his excavations at Tecolpan (Berlin 1956 : 114, 130–32).

For the most part, the trends noted by Berlin are consistent with data from the Middle Usumacinta sector. It should be noted, however, that Fine Cream may not be included among the wares described for Jonuta and Tecolpan (Berlin's "Red on buff" appears at least in part to be different). The Naab Ceramic Complex, which falls on a somewhat earlier time level than most of the Jonuta horizon materials, is poorly represented in collections from the Lower Usumacinta. To judge from Berlin's sherd counts, Fine Orange Ware—mostly of the Balancan Group—is somewhat better represented throughout his stratigraphic columns than at Calatrava, although it does not take over the upper level assemblages to quite the same degree. To emphasize these differences in the rise of Fine Orange Ware could easily prove misleading, however, tending to obscure the strongly similar pattern of development which is shown at Jonuta, Tecolpan, and Calatrava.

A redefinition of the Jonuta horizon, separating Terminal Classic from earlier, Tepeu-like developments, appears necessary. I have attempted this in chapter 4 (Figs. 5–8), from the perspective afforded by familiarity with the pottery of certain Middle Usumacinta sites, although in the absence of intimate knowledge of Lower Usumacinta ceramics. In the suggested subdivision of the Jonuta horizon, Jonuta proper is restricted to the period characterized by the strong occurrence of Fine Orange Ware of the Balancan Ceramic Group. Fine Gray Ware, largely if not entirely of the Gray Chablekal Group, is regarded as a diagnostic of the Lower Usumacinta equivalent of the late facet of the Naab Complex, extending into the early part of Jonuta. Fine paste, black-surfaced pottery is considered to be a characteristic feature of the Naab Complex (early facet) equivalent, continuing strongly into late Naab. Berlin's "Classic Maya" polychromes may fall partially in the early Naab equivalent or be still earlier in time; for the most part, this pottery appears to antedate Naab.

A number of difficulties, in addition to the cultural differences expectable between ceramics of the Lower and Middle Usumacinta sectors, are encountered in subdividing the Jonuta horizon. For example, the late facet of Naab is poorly represented in my work at Middle Usumacinta sites, and as a result developmental trends at Palenque have in part been relied on in formulating the characteristics of late Naab. Diagnostics of the Naab Complex (early facet), as known from Middle Usumacinta sites, are largely absent from Berlin's materials except for his "Black" ware, and only part of the Black pottery, undifferentiated in his sherd counts, appears to be untempered (Berlin 1956 : 121). Furthermore, stratigraphic evidence for the faceting of Naab is inconclusive, although such a division is suggested in certain of Berlin's excavations. The proposed reordering of the Jonuta horizon, admittedly provisional and subject to revised nomenclature as new ceramic complexes are defined, would lead to the following alignments within Berlin's stratigraphic test pits at Tecolpan and Jonuta (Berlin 1956 : Tables 1–4).

Tecolpan. Pit at south foot of main mound
Levels 1, 2	Jonuta
Level 3	Jonuta; Naab equivalent
Levels 4, 5	Jonuta; predominantly Naab equivalent

Tecolpan. Pit at south low construction
Level 1	Jonuta; Naab equivalent (late facet)
Levels 2, 3	Naab equivalent (early facet)
Level 4	Pre-Naab

Tecolpan. Pit east of main mound
Level 1	Jonuta
Level 2	Jonuta; Naab equivalent
Level 3	Naab equivalent; predominantly pre-Naab
Levels 4, 5	Predominantly pre-Naab

Jonuta. Pit near Usumacinta River
Level 1	Jonuta
Level 2	Jonuta; Naab equivalent (late facet)
Level 3	Jonuta; Naab equivalent

It should be noted that Berlin was keenly aware of the succession of polychrome, Black, Fine Gray, and Fine Orange wares, as reflected in the present subdivision of his Jonuta horizon (Berlin 1956 : 131–32). I will not attempt to relate the proposed formulation to the western part of Berlin's survey in the Huimango area.

Recently, Matheny (1970) has reported on the ceramics of Aguacatal, from the Xicalango Peninsula in western Campeche. Inspection of his Conchada and Mangle complexes may prove useful in future attempts to subdivide the Jonuta horizon.

The Low Sierras

A contrast to sites in the Upper Usumacinta sector (and most of the Southern Maya Lowlands) is evident in the pattern of dates on the monuments and in other inscriptions of Palenque. Whereas the climax of monument erection normally preceded the latest inscription from a given site by only a few *katuns*, if at all, at Palenque the peak of this practice falls considerably earlier (cf. graphs in Figs. 19, 20). Some thirty objects from Palenque with dated inscriptions—consisting mostly although not entirely of monumental sculpture—cover a longer span of time and reach a peak two *katuns* earlier than is indicated by Proskouriakoff's style analysis of eight major structures at the site.[6] The general pattern of dates is quite similar, however. The latest date known from Palenque, 9.18.9.4.4 (A.D. 799), is carved on a fine paste black vessel of the early Balunte Complex (Fig. 9, chapter 4). This handsome vessel is notable for its epigraphic sophistication (J. E. S. Thompson 1962 : 17–18). A single inscription is known from the preceding *katun*. Approximately 75 percent of the inscriptions fall in *Katuns* 11 through 14 (A.D. 652–731). This corresponds closely to the probable time span of the three dated monuments at the far-western site of Tortuguero (9.10.14.14.10–9.14.0.0.0, A.D. 647–711). To the east, inscriptions from Pomona conform only weakly to this pattern.

What is the significance of this atypical Palenque pattern? Had Palenque passed its Classic zenith at an unusually early time? Does the termination of monument erection at Tortuguero indicate abandonment of the site or a fading of the Classic tradition? Conclusive answers cannot be given to these questions, but certain observations are pertinent. The first concerns the complexity of the Palenque inscriptions, many of which cover past historical or mythological events; determination of a specific dedicatory date is often difficult. Secondly, inadequate archaeological exploration may make the pattern of dates appear more aberrant than is actually the case. Since the inauguration of intensive excavations at Palenque by Ruz in 1949, four of the five *Katun* 14 inscriptions and the single inscription from *Katun* 18 have come to light; yet dated sculptures earlier than those already known have not been found (Fuente 1965 : Table 2).

The Palenque practice of using wall tablets instead of stelae has resulted in the burying of many of these monuments in the rubble of collapsed buildings; large-scale architectural excavation has been required to unearth the sculptures. The most substantially built temples at Palenque, those still standing today, appear mostly to have been constructed during a short but brilliant burst of ceremonial activity. It is the inscriptions from these buildings, reaching dates late in the seventh century A.D., that have long been known from Palenque and that will almost certainly continue to make up the epigraphic climax of the site. It is probable, however, that the *Katun* 11 to *Katun* 14 dates will not loom quite so high on the graph quantifying Palenque's inscriptions as continuing investigations of smaller collapsed structures help to fill in the gap between this apogee and the abandonment of the site. Similar factors may apply to Tortuguero, or a complete abandonment of the Classic trait of dedicating stone sculptures may have taken place at that site. On the other hand, Tortuguero could have suffered depopulation—an exceptionally early case of Classic collapse on the Maya frontier.

Unusual variation is present in the sculptural styles of the Low Sierras. Several time-levels centering on the Late Classic may be represented, and it is possible that certain differences reflect cultural displacements at the time of the Classic collapse. Three traditions may be recognized, as well as the existence of miscellaneous atypical sculptures.

Maya Late Classic. Stylistic features and accouterments are widespread in the Southern Maya Lowlands, including the Upper Usumacinta sector. Fragmentary stelae from Pomona (Lizardi Ramos 1963 : Figs. 4, 8) conform to this tradition.

Classic Palenque. Wall tablets, bearing glyphic texts and/or representations of human figures, are the principal sculptured media for the Palenque style. Elsewhere, wall tablets apparently occur at Pomona, Chinikiha, Xupa, Miraflores, El Retiro, and Tortuguero.[7]

Tonina Style. Round-relief statuelike monuments date from the Late Classic Period but incorporate early mannerisms (Proskouriakoff 1950 : 121; 1968). Centered at Tonina, in the Chiapas highlands, the style is basically foreign to the Maya Lowlands. It occurs, however, on Stela 1 at Palenque [8] (9.13.0.0.0, A.D. 692), as well as at Tortuguero and Chuctiepa (Fig. 25c, d), and its influences were apparently felt in more ornate examples of Classic Maya art from Copan to Palenque (Rands 1969a).

Miscellaneous. Although certain inscriptions from Tortuguero are in fully Classic style, reflecting strong influences from Palenque (J. E. S. Thompson 1962 : Pl. 12), other inscribed monuments are atypical. Glyphs have an unusual arrangement on Stelae 1 and 2, being grouped within widely spaced cartouches. Human figures are lacking on both of these monuments, a probable jaguar with somewhat humanized features appearing in low relief in one case and the other stela being carved in the form of a serpent's body (Fig. 25a, b). These monuments apparently bear dates of A.D. 647 and A.D. 711 (9.10.15.0.0 and 9.14.0.0.0; Blom and LaFarge 1926 : 151–53). From Chinikiha comes another monument in essentially non-Classic style, a serpent head, carved in the round, having a plain or tenoned body. Generalized resemblances exist to a sculptured crocodile at Palenque.[9] Plain, pointed stelae occur at Palenque (La Picota) and Yoxiha.[10]

Of the sculptures considered above, only the serpent head from Chinikiha and perhaps the plain stelae can reasonably be thought to result from the introduction of a new style at the time of the general collapse in the Southern Maya Lowlands. Taken as a whole, however, the remarkable variation and apparent Late Classic dating of the various monuments suggest a situation in flux. More or less contemporary styles may have existed somewhere on the western flanks of the Maya area, in potential competition with one another and ready to assert themselves when the opportunity arose. Such an opportunity might occur either because of the movement of peoples or because of the waning of influences from hitherto more vigorous centers or ones that had been accorded higher prestige. The data from Tortuguero are especially fascinating in this connection. Present at the site, not necessarily in order of appearance, were the Tonina style, the Classic Palenque style, and an aberrant stela-and-glyph style which seemingly occurred at about the time of the Palenque-like monuments.

Ceramics in the Low Sierras show strong variation, both within the region as a whole and when compared with the pottery of other regions. Some aspects of this have been indicated previously (Rands

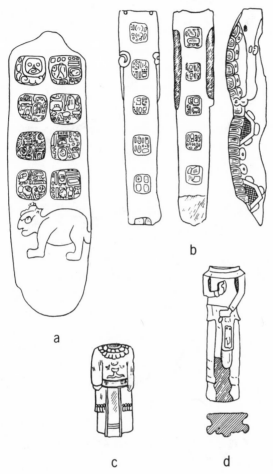

FIGURE 25. STONE SCULPTURES IN NON–CLASSIC MAYA STYLES. *a*, Tortuguero, Stela 1; *b*, Tortuguero, Stela 2; *c*, Tortuguero, Stela 3; *d*, Chuctiepa, Stela 1. After Blom and LaFarge (1926:Figs. 117–19, 174). Not to scale.

1967a); here, major attention will be given to fine paste pottery at Palenque.

Fine Brown Ware (Figs. 26*a–d*, 27, 28)

Following a weakly developed Preclassic occupation, the pottery of Palenque is dominated by sand-tempered Red-brown Ware, much of

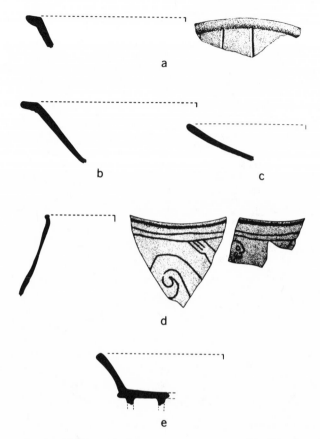

FIGURE 26. PALENQUE, PICOTA (*a-c*), AND BALUNTE (*d, e*) CERAMIC COMPLEXES. *a-d*, Fine Brown Ware; *e*, Fine Cream Ware (Black). *a*, Groove-incised; *d*, incised. Approximate scale 1:4.

which may be of local manufacture (Rands 1969b). In two of the ceramic complexes, however, a significant amount of buff-to-brown paste pottery is finely textured—in small quantities in the beginning Early Classic Picota Complex but with some frequency in the Balunte Complex, the temporal equivalent of late Tepeu 2. Fine Brown Ware appears more rarely in the Murcielagos Complex, equivalent to early Tepeu 2. Stylistic differences separate ceramics of the Picota and later complexes. The brown Picota pottery, fine paste as well as tempered, is characterized by red (nonwaxy) slip, vertical grooving that is often

188

widely spaced, everted rims, and heavy slab feet or ring-stand supports
(Fig. 26a–c; Rands 1967a : Fig. 2a–c). The survival of certain Preclassic modes is indicated. Elaborate resist painting occurs in Fine
Brown Ware of the Murcielagos Complex (Fig. 27). Usually monochrome, Fine Brown Ware of the Balunte Complex includes cylindrical
vases, low dishes, and flaring-wall beakers, among other vessel shapes.
Plastic decoration, especially incising, is characteristic (Figs. 26d, 28).
Techniques of decoration as well as vessel shapes are often shared with
the contemporaneous sand-tempered, Red-brown Ware. One need not
conclude that the Fine Brown Ware found at Palenque was locally
manufactured. Yet its abundance (unusually early in the Late Classic
Period when compared with most fine paste Maya pottery), its sustained importance, and the existence of basic stylistic affiliations with
pottery that is apparently indigenous to the site give every indication
that Fine Brown Ware was more closely linked to local ceramic traditions than is true of fine paste pottery at almost any other major ceremonial center in the Southern Maya Lowlands. One or more centers of
production not far from Palenque seem probable. The importation of
nonlocal clays, to be used by potters at Palenque, cannot be ruled out
as an alternative.

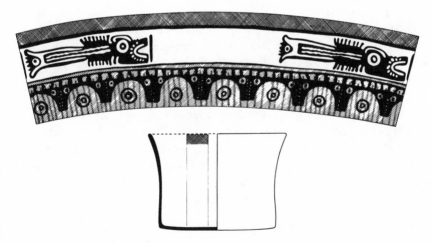

FIGURE 27. PALENQUE, MURCIELAGOS CERAMIC COMPLEX. Fine
Brown Ware. Resist (red, black, orange, cream). Approximate scale 1 :4.

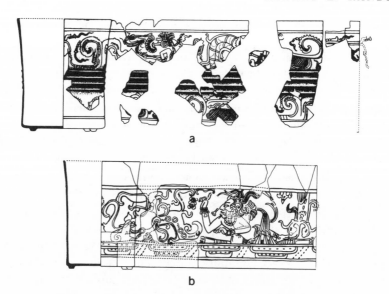

FIGURE 28. PALENQUE, BALUNTE CERAMIC COMPLEX. *a, b*(?), Early facet. Fine Brown Ware. *a,* Incised and fluted; *b,* incised cream. Approximate scale 1:12.

Fine Brown Ware and Fine Cream Ware (Fig. 26e)

Fine Brown Ware, with the color of paste and of unslipped or un-smudged surfaces normally ranging from brown to buff, and Fine Cream Ware, with an overlapping color range of buff to cream, have a number of technological and stylistic similarities. Among significant distinguishing features is the presence of abundant volcanic dust in Fine Cream Ware and its absence from Fine Brown. The dust is apparently a natural inclusion in the clay. Fine Cream Ware is effectively introduced to Palenque in the Murcielagos Complex, often as a polychrome, but is of lowered frequency in the Balunte Complex, when it is mostly black surfaced, coinciding with shifts in decoration and surface treatment in Fine Cream Ware at Trinidad during the Taxinchan and Naab complexes. Importation to Palenque from sources in the Middle Usumacinta sector appears plausible.

Fine Brown Ware and Fine Gray Ware (Fig. 29b–e)

For the most part, Fine Brown Ware is stylistically distinct from the better known fine paste wares of the Terminal Classic. Fine Gray becomes increasingly common in the Balunte Complex at Palenque, although it occurs in fully Classic contexts (for example, associated with the final major reconstruction of the north stairway of the Palace) as well as in surface deposits. Occasionally, features of shape and decoration are shared in Fine Brown and Fine Gray wares. The flat-base, flaring-wall beaker, a common vessel shape in Fine Brown (Fig. 27), is also present in Fine Gray Ware (Fig. 29c, d; Berlin 1956 : Fig. 4s). Cylindrical vases, though more characteristic of Fine Brown Ware (Fig. 28), are likewise known in finely textured, gray paste pottery (Fig. 29b). Monkeys, incised in the style commonly associated with Fine Gray Ware of the Chablekal Group (Fig. 22), occur, though very rarely, in Fine Brown Ware (Fig. 26d). Several fine paste specimens, including vessels with gray paste and the dentate-stamped decoration characteristic of the Gray Chablekal Group, have compositional properties—chemical and/or petrographic—which are diagnostic of Fine Brown Ware (Fig. 29a; Rands 1967a : Fig. 5a). To varying degrees, the examples which have been cited are atypical. Yet these specimens cannot be ignored when one considers questions of relationship among the untempered wares and the important problem of Palenque's contacts with as yet unknown centers for the production of fine paste pottery.

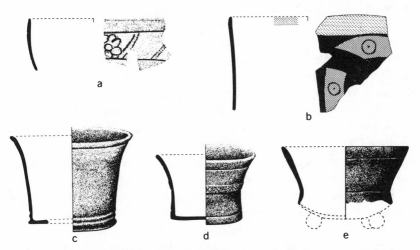

FIGURE 29. PALENQUE, BALUNTE CERAMIC COMPLEX. *a, b*(?), Early facet. *a*, Fine Brown Ware (Black); *b-e*, Fine Gray Ware. *a*, Incised and dentate-stamped; *b*, stuccoed (black, yellow, red, green) with incised nucleated circles; *d, e*, incised. Approximate scale 1:5.

Fine Brown Ware and Fine Orange Ware (Fig. 30)

Elements of design characteristic of Fine Orange Ware are anticipated in a number of Fine Brown specimens, some of which are clearly datable from the early facet of Balunte. Among these is an incised and fluted vase that depicts a reclining figure, apparently holding a shield (Fig. 28*a*). The recumbent figure is placed between elaborate scrolls. Margins of the scrolls are decorated with "cursive *m*s" in the style of Provincia Plano-relief as well as with tasseled circlet-and-"bone" embellishments in the tradition of Late Classic sculpture. Although the association of reclining human figures with scrolls is a recurrent feature of the Provincia Plano-relief type, execution of the scrollwork on the Fine Brown vase is closer to Classic norms. Unlike the compositions of either Classic sculpture or Fine Orange pottery, the reclining figure on the Palenque vase is accorded secondary importance to the scrollwork (contrast Provincia Plano-relief in Berlin 1956 : Fig. 3; Brainerd 1958 : Fig. 59). A semirecumbent figure on another incised, Fine Brown vase from Palenque (Fig. 28*b*) is reminiscent of the reclining figures in Fine Orange Ware, although correspondences are even closer to such Late Classic sculptures as Lintel 39, Yaxchilan (Maler 1903 : Pl. 65; ca. 9.17.10.0.0). Such Fine Brown Ware specimens, though few in number, may prove to be informative about certain aspects of the poorly known stylistic background of Fine Orange Ware. During early Balunte, while the Classic tradition was still vigorous at Palenque, adjacent regions, if not the site itself, appear to have participated in certain stylistic developments, derived mainly from Classic themes, which at a later time and place were to be reworked and incorporated in Fine Orange Ware of the Balancan and Altar groups. For the most part, however, the sources of the Fine Orange ceramic tradition were foreign to Palenque and its ceramic zone.

Fine Orange Ware is scarce at Palenque. The weathered condition of most sherds makes typing difficult—the Balancan Group seems to be best represented. Partial abandonment of the site, and certainly the effective rupturing of an elite Classic tradition, appears to have taken place at the close of the early facet of Balunte, before Fine Orange Ware had gained sufficient popularity to be imported in any quantity. The proximity of Palenque to sites on the Usumacinta such as Calatrava

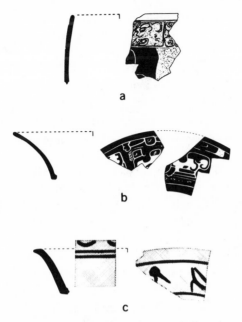

FIGURE 30. PALENQUE, BALUNTE CERAMIC COMPLEX (*a, b*) AND POST-BALUNTE (*c*). Fine Orange Ware. *a*, Gouged-incised, black and white paint; *b*, Provincia Plano-relief Type, black paint; *c*, Yalton Black-on-orange Type. Approximate scale 1:4.

and Tecolpan, where Fine Orange is very abundant, suggests that, had Palenque's late Balunte occupation been of long duration or had it involved a sizable population, Fine Orange Ware would have been much more plentiful. However, the rare occurrence of pottery belonging to the Silho Ceramic Group (Fig. 30*c*) indicates that a sporadic occupation of Palenque took place in post-Balunte times.

Although infrequent, certain examples of Fine Orange Ware at Palenque maintain exceptionally close affiliations with the Classic tradition. A gouged-incised sherd with sophisticated rendering of the glyph band (including Xul, T-758) is notable in this respect (Fig. 30*a*), contrasting with the sloppy workmanship that has been described for the Islas Gouged-incised type (Sabloff 1970 : 371). Late Classic stylistic features in Provincia Plano-relief are exemplified by comparing the Long-nosed God in Figure 30*b* with a Dynamic Phase sculpture from Jonuta (Proskouriakoff 1950 : Fig. 69*b*). In addition to the strongly

Classic iconography, tendrillike appendages of the scrollwork are seen in these examples and on several Baktun 10 stelae from Seibal, being a feature of Proskouriakoff's Dynamic and Decadent phases (Proskouriakoff 1950 : 35, Fig. 12*l*). Continuity with the essentials of the Classic style lends credence to the idea that the introduction of pottery of the Fine Orange Balancan and Altar groups did not represent a complete take-over of the region of Fine Orange production by non-Classic invaders. Rather, it appears that at least some potters, schooled in the ways of Classicism, stayed on, in one capacity or another, to leave their stamp on the rapidly evolving styles of Fine Orange pottery. It may also be that the Classic glyphic rendition in Figure 30*a* dates from an early Balunte horizon, when Classic modes of portrayal were still in vogue and when the stylistic and thematic characteristics of the Fine Orange Balancan and Altar groups had not yet emerged.

This brief consideration of fine paste wares at Palenque has focused on similarities between Fine Brown Ware, which has its strongest known occurrence at Palenque, and other wares, to the neglect of descriptive data that would emphasize differences. My purpose here was to point out that Fine Orange and Fine Gray pottery did not emerge *de novo*, entirely lacking technological or stylistic antecedents in Classic Maya culture. If, as appears probable, the fine paste tradition was carried primarily by non-Classic peoples, there must have been a fairly extended period of contact—acculturation that presumably resulted in the modification of both the Classic and non-Classic patterns in many aspects of culture other than ceramics. Palenque, as an outpost of Maya Classicism, apparently played an unusually significant role in this process, especially during the Murcielagos and early Balunte phases. Immediately prior to Murcielagos, one suspects that the forces promoting the Classic tradition were in ascendency in the Palenque region, whereas in late Balunte, Palenque's position as a center of Classicism had been shattered.

Tortuguero Fine Paste Wares (Fig. 31)

Excavations have not been carried out at Tortuguero, and ceramic sequences there are poorly understood. With the exception of occasional coarse unslipped sherds, almost all of the pottery collected from the site is finely textured. Monochrome wares are prevalent as are bichrome wares (red-on-orange, red-on-cream). The paste is exceptionally uniform, oxidized zones normally being orange-brown in color; a gray core is common. Wares are classifiable by color as Fine Gray and Fine Orange, in addition to the provisional designation of Fine Orange-brown Ware for the great bulk of the pottery. Yet on petrographic evidence there is a strong indication that all were manufactured at the same center, perhaps locally. Shape and decoration differ fundamentally from the Late Classic fine paste wares that have been discussed. On a presumably late level, affiliations are rather with the fine gray and black-surfaced pottery of Comalcalco. Cream-white slip

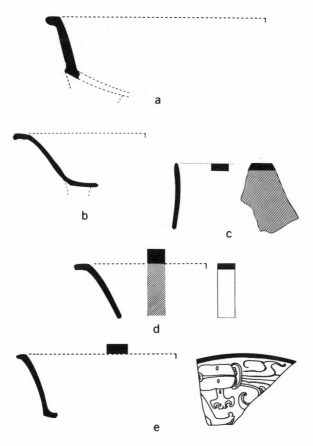

FIGURE 31. TORTUGUERO. Fine Orange-brown Ware. *a*, *b*, black; *c*, red-on-orange (cream exterior); *d*, incised, red-on-white. Approximate scale 1:4.

probably dates from the Late Classic Period. One design, incised in a cream slip, includes the foot of an apparently reclining human figure, suggesting decorative concepts of the Balancan Group (Fig. 31e); this sherd may be lightly tempered, however. Glossy slips and Early Classic shapes also occur on fine paste pottery at Tortuguero; cf. Figure 31a and Tzakol sharp-Z-angle Balanza Black tripod cylinders (Smith 1955 : Fig. 21a, 5–9). Everted-rim bowls have modal resemblances with fine paste and tempered pottery from the Early Classic Picota Complex of Palenque (Figs. 26a, b; 31a, b, d). Although rare, Dos Arroyos–style polychrome occurs at Tortuguero, including the Classic U-chain design (Rands 1967 : Fig. 12a). Taken as a whole, the pottery from Tortuguero shows what must be considered an extraordinary mixture of styles for such a homogeneous fine paste class. A significant time span is indicated.[11] Possible inferences to be drawn from this early concentration of fine paste pottery on the northwestern edge of the Maya Lowlands will be discussed in a later section.

It remains here to note miscellaneous data from Palenque that may pertain to the Classic collapse. In the Palace, crude walls were used to subdivide galleries into small rooms. Thin stone heads and fragments of plain yokes come from surface deposits in the same structure. Their presence and that of fragmentary onyx marble vases are considered by Ruz to indicate intrusions from the Veracruz Gulf Coast (Ruz Lhuillier 1953).

Intermediate Plains

Except in the east, these plains seem always to have been a barrier to the establishment of Usumacinta-like patterns. Sites are small and the sampling, though not satisfactory, suggests a population maximum toward the close of the Late Classic Period. At that time strongest ceramic affiliations are with the Low Sierras, and possibly population movements took place from that zone, perhaps in response to the pressures of an expanding population. The Intermediate Plains appears to have participated in the demographic collapse of Terminal Classic times. The absence of Fine Orange Ware in collections from the region forms a striking contrast to the abundance of this pottery at nearby Usumacinta sites.

Chontalpa

Comalcalco, with its well-known stucco reliefs [12] and Palenque-style architecture, is an imposing outpost of the Late Classic Maya tradition. Classic patterns do not extend to the pottery, although affiliations exist with the fine paste ceramics of Tortuguero (Fine Black, Fine Gray). Berlin places pottery from Huimango in the Jonuta horizon but notes differences, especially in Fine Orange Ware (Berlin 1956 : 128). Here, as at Tierra Nueva, specific stylistic relationships to the Classic Maya are noted only in moldmade figurines (Berlin 1956 : 133; Sanders 1963 : 216; Piña Chan and Navarette 1967 : 28).[13] Sisson's Chontalpa survey indicates a sudden Late Classic increase in size and number of sites, followed by smaller but even more numerous settlements in the Postclassic. Most of the later settlements belong to the early Cintla horizon (Sisson 1970 : 47–48). Slightly southeast of Sisson's survey, at Tierra Colorada on the Laguna Matillas, Fine Orange Ware of the Matillas (V) Group is also found abundantly. Clearly, the Chontalpa did not participate in the demographic collapse at the close of the Late Classic. An important question is whether Classic Maya influences had already begun to wane or whether these influences were cut off by the Maya downfall.

DISCUSSION

No attempt has been made in the present paper to develop either a specific hypothesis or a comprehensive theoretical orientation concerning the Classic Maya collapse. Rather, background information has been presented that might bear on the decline, as seen from the Usumacinta and the northwestern periphery. Implicit is the recognition that fine paste wares, especially Fine Orange, are in some way tied to events taking place at about the time of the downfall. Whether this is because of the prior association of these ceramics with non-Classic invaders or whether the collapse created a cultural vacuum into which new patterns moved rapidly is, I think, an open question. Perhaps these possibilities are not completely antithetical, and both, to some degree, hold true. For the collapse did not occur overnight; there was ample time and space for different responses to take place to a series of inter-related crisis situations.

A related point of view, sometimes implicit and at other times explicitly set forth, is that the peripheral position of the western lowlands resulted in a "spotty" development of Classic patterns for a considerable period prior to the collapse. Early Classic developments are extraordinarily difficult to isolate or to relate stylistically to contemporary developments in the greater Peten. There are indications that the Classic frontier may have been advancing or contracting at various points in time during the Late Classic Period. Perhaps it would be more correct to say that various Classic traits were diffusing outward or receding; rarely do we have sufficient information to deal with entire culture complexes or with the movements of people. In any case, it seems clear that there were relatively few centers west of the Usumacinta Valley where major expressions of Classic Maya culture took place, and even in those few—one thinks of Palenque and Comalcalco—there were significant variations on the Classic Maya themes. Enclaves that were non-Classic, or at best only minimally Classic, may have been in existence for a long time prior to the collapse. One of the more striking phenomena is that such a brilliant development of Maya culture as is evidenced at Palenque ever became established in the region, although Copan, in the far southeast, presents a somewhat analogous case.

Another point deserves further discussion, namely, the great degree of heterogeneity that exists within the Maya fine paste wares and in the ceramic contexts in which they are first known. In the present paper, data concerning variations in fine paste pottery have largely been confined to selected stylistic matters and the development of a temporal framework. Definition of wares and types, including detailed petrographic analyses, will be presented in forthcoming reports.

What is the possible significance of these fine paste variations to the Classic collapse? On one level, this question can be answered by cautioning that *identity* of "invaders" associated with a ware such as Fine Orange becomes a bit suspect (contrast the arguments in Sabloff and Willey [1967 : 325] and in the discussion of terminal developments at Piedras Negras in the present paper). The question of the significance of differences in fine paste ceramics also necessitates looking at the pottery from a broader temporal perspective. At the present time, considerable speculation is unavoidable in order to make a provisional reconstruction of the history of fine paste ceramics in the western lowlands.

Tortuguero is a key site with which to begin the discussion because of the apparently long time span of fine paste pottery at the site and because of its location on the northwestern Maya frontier. It seems reasonable that the untempered pottery of Tortuguero is one manifestation of a technological tradition that was ultimately derived from Preclassic fine paste wares of the Veracruz-Tabasco lowlands. The fine paste tradition may have had a long history on the northwestern border of the Maya Lowlands, exerting only a sporadic influence on the area during most of Classic times. Similarities of vessel form to pottery of the Picota Complex are strong enough to suggest relationships between the Tortuguero region and Palenque, resulting in the introduction of short-lived fine paste developments at the latter site. Something on the order of stimulus diffusion, passing from the northwestern frontier, could account for fine paste in the Taxinchan Complex of Trinidad. At least by times equivalent to Tepeu 2, there was an assimilation of Classic polychrome decorative concepts with fine paste technology (Taxinchan and the somewhat later Murcielagos Complex of Palenque). Fine Cream Ware was most common at Trinidad and Palenque, with Fine Brown Ware becoming increasingly important at the latter site and with sporadic pieces suggesting ancestral relationship to Fine Gray and Fine Orange. By the beginning of Naab at Trinidad (and somewhat later in the Balunte Complex of Palenque), monochromes had largely replaced polychrome pottery. The late facet of Naab and early Balunte saw Fine Gray Ware emerge as a popular fine paste alternative to cream. Palenque, it seems, lagged slightly behind Trinidad in the earlier fine paste developments; however, Palenque's adherence to the Classic ceramic tradition was probably not quite as fragile.

Meantime, untempered pottery at Tortuguero continued to show remarkable uniformity in paste, although stylistic changes had taken place from the Early Classic beginnings. Possibly, alternative methods of firing were coming into wider use, resulting in the production of reduced (Fine Gray) and more fully oxidized (Fine Orange) pottery, as distinct from the more generalized tradition of Fine Orange-brown ceramics at the site. But in the absence of stratigraphic excavations we can only speculate. In any event, paste characteristics of Fine Gray at

Tortuguero differ from much of the Fine Gray Ware that may have come into use at about the same time (or slightly later?) in Palenque and along the Middle Usumacinta. By at least this time, Tortuguero's affiliations with fine paste pottery from Comalcalco and the Chontalpa were probably considerably stronger than were its affiliations with the ceramics of the Usumacinta Valley.

By now—the temporal equivalent of terminal Tepeu 2—fine paste ceramics were well established along the Lower Usumacinta. Berlin's excavations at Jonuta and Tecolpan show the existence of Fine Orange Ware in most of the early levels, but it was not until upper levels, after the maximum occurrence of his finely textured Black and Fine Gray wares, that Z (Balancan Group) Fine Orange became dominant. These trends are approximated at Calatrava, although, as has been noted, Fine Cream developments of the Naab Complex seem largely absent from the lower Usumacinta River sites. Conversely, the full-fledged Jonuta horizon developments are unknown at Trinidad, probably because of the abandonment of the site, or at least that part of the site which has been investigated. Palenque also appears to have been largely abandoned by this time. The above-floor deposits of Fine Pale-orange Ware at Structure J-12, Piedras Negras, may date from this time, as is suggested by stylistic affiliations with Fine Gray Ware of the Jonuta horizon (late Naab equivalent, as redefined in the present paper). At Piedras Negras, this occupation may coincide with or be slightly later than the Terminal Classic collapse.

At least in the more diagnostic types, Fine Orange Ware of the Altar Group is weakly represented in materials known from the northwestern Maya Lowlands.[14] The Altar Group is better known at Piedras Negras than is Fine Orange Ware of the Balancan Group. It is tempting to look on Fine Pale-orange Ware at Piedras Negras as reflecting movements from the north and to regard the less abundant Altar Group as resulting from later sporadic movements that may have come down the Usumacinta. However, investigations in the many archaeologically unexplored parts of the northwestern lowlands or adjacent Campeche might reveal a northern homeland for Jimba-like ceramics.

This reconstruction brings into focus the partially conflicting versions of the invasion hypothesis as presented by Sabloff and Willey (1967) and by Adams (chapter 8). Adams has suggested that at about 9.19.0.0.0 (A.D. 810) "the people who made Jimba pottery moved from lowland Chiapas-Tabasco or ultimately from southern Veracruz, across the area east of Bonampak to the Usumacinta. . . . The mouth of the Lacanja is not far off from Altar and through it, and a network of other streams, access can be had to the Gulf Coast plain" (chapter 8). The rivers in question include the Lacuntun and Jatate, leading into the Chiapas highlands at the divide near Tonina, and the Tulija and Macuspana, flowing toward the north, ultimately to join and enter the Grijalva. As is clear from various passages in the present paper, I am intrigued by the frontier position of Tortuguero, near the Rio Macuspana, and by its possibly ancestral role in the development of Late Classic Maya fine paste wares. My survey in the upper Tulija (Encanto) Valley has shown the presence of "pure" Fine Orange sites. All of this might be taken as support for the Adams hypothesis. Nevertheless, because of the differences between Fine Orange-brown Ware, of Tortuguero, and Fine Orange Ware, Tortuguero could not have been the specific Jimba "homeland" of which Adams speaks.

Fine Orange Ware of the Silho Group occurs only lightly at a number of Usumacinta and northwestern lowland sites. At Palenque it is apparently better represented than are clearly diagnostic types of the Altar Group, although to judge from controlled excavations the quantity of Silho materials is still very small. (It is possible that the various Pocboc Gouged-incised vessels in museum collections, purportedly from Palenque, came from the Palenque district but not actually from the ruins. Or it may be that Palenque was reoccupied, perhaps for burial purposes, by people using Fine Orange Silho Group ceramics. In any case, unless the usual chronological placement of the Silho Ceramic Group vis-à-vis the Balancan Group and unless Late Classic developments in general are seriously awry, I cannot see how an occupation of Palenque by Silho Group people could have contributed significantly to the collapse at the site. Palenque should already have fallen.) [15]

Was the Classic Maya collapse caused by military incursions from without, by internal disruptions, or by some combination of the two? No attempt will be made to answer the question here, but certain data presented earlier merit further discussion. I refer to the tenuous hold of the Classic tradition in the northwestern lowlands. As an example, Classic polychromes were not strongly entrenched, and apparently it was relatively easy to slough them off without disrupting the principal ceramic patterns. Continuity of basic patterns would seem to indicate an ongoing population, seemingly the case at the close of the Taxinchan and Murcielagos complexes of Trinidad and Palenque. But "ease" in casting aside a tradition is at best only a partial answer. Why were not the contacts maintained that had brought Tepeu-like polychromes into the area in the first place? By times equivalent to Tepeu 2, was there a contraction or reduction taking place within the Maya Classic tradition itself—a loss of vigor, of economic stability, or of other characteristics that are expressed in the exertion of influence over a wide area? If, as seems probable, this was a time of expanding population, and if population growth resulted in the movement of peoples, why would this not have brought about continued dispersal of the Classic pattern? Why was the Late Classic Period characterized by increasing ceramic regionalism? What accounts for the aesthetic decline in polychrome pottery that at times appears to have taken place between Tepeu 1 and 2—or, as noted for Piedras Negras, between the Yaxche and Chacalhaaz ceramic complexes? I do not believe that "troubles on the frontier" for so long a period is a satisfactory answer for all of these questions.

As one turns from ceramics to the primary expressions of Maya elite culture—architecture and sculpture—a Tepeu 2 equivalent gives every indication of being the time of climax. Temple-pyramids were built higher; stela art was refined and elaborated. The climax appears to have been reached somewhat sooner in the far western center of Palenque (ca. 9.11.0.0.0–9.14.0.0.0; A.D. 652–731) than at many sites in the Southern Lowlands, where a dating around *Katuns* 15 to 18 comes to mind as the time of greatest brilliance in state and hierarchical activities. Yet, in terms of the ceramics, the latter dates fall at a time when regionalism had increased, aesthetic standards had often declined, and ceramic patterns had disappeared, as in the case of the northwestern lowland polychromes. Traditions in Classic Maya culture might be said to be undergoing simultaneous but noncongruent shifts. Society was, perhaps, moving in different directions at the same time.

NOTES

1. Ceramic investigations in the Middle Usumacinta sector, Low Sierras, and Intermediate Plains have been supported by the National Science Foundation (Grants GS-254, GS-1455X, GS-1455X1). Findings incorporated in the present

chapter also reflect support by the University Research Council of the University of North Carolina at Chapel Hill and, at Southern Illinois University at Carbondale, assistance from the Mesoamerican Cooperative Research Program and the Office of Research and Projects. The University Museum, University of Pennsylvania, has made possible an analysis of Piedras Negras pottery which, in part, is summarized in this chapter. My investigations in the Palenque region have benefited from the many-faceted aid provided by Professor Alberto Ruz Lhuillier and Heinrich Berlin. I am indebted to Dr. Linton Satterthwaite, Jr., for the opportunity of drawing on his unrivaled knowledge of ceramic and architectural associations at Piedras Negras.

2. Pomona is located not far from Boca del Cerro, near the common boundary of the Upper and Middle Usumacinta sectors and the Low Sierras. Tortuguero lies on the slope of the Cerro de Macuspana, an isolated eminence in the Tabasco plains. The Palenque "Wavy Bone" Emblem Glyph occurs at Tortuguero (J. E. S. Thompson 1962 : 196–97; 1965 : 355), lending weight to other connections that will be discussed between that site and Palenque.

3. Dates having a general acceptance are set off by distinct symbols in Figures 19 and 20 from less securely placed dates or stylistic datings. The former include some inscriptions which were accorded a single query (?) by Morley (1938) and others which reflect Proskouriakoff's reconsideration of certain inscriptions at Yaxchilan (Proskouriakoff 1963b, 1964). Nevertheless, a number of monuments, especially at Yaxchilan, are not included in the charts; these are mostly doubtful (??) and possible (???) dates of Morley for which there are no style dates. The stylistic datings in Figures 19 and 20 are based on peaks in Proskouriakoff's style graphs (Proskouriakoff 1950; Ruppert, Thompson, and Proskouriakoff 1955); the plus or minus range of her dates, usually ± 2 *katuns*, is not given. When it appears justified, monuments of uncertain provenience are totaled with the site to which they are most closely affiliated in style or epigraphic content. Accordingly, one might think in terms of the El Cayo region rather than the site of El Cayo, etc. The frequency at Yaxchilan of multiple sculptures such as lintels in a single structure leads to an extraordinarily high incidence of contemporaneous monuments, peaking sharply in *Katun* 16 (Fig. 19). For comparison, Figure 19 also graphs dates at Yaxchilan on the basis of distinct monuments (for example, stelae), in which the multiple sculptures which form part of a single building are accorded a combined frequency of one. On this basis, a similar pattern prevails in the dates, although the peak is lowered and the decline in *Katun* 18 appears somewhat less dramatic. In order to simplify an already complex chart, the lintels and murals of Structure 1, Bonampak, are not graphed by the alternative method just described for Yaxchilan, although this would reduce the frequency of *Katun* 18 monuments at Bonampak from six to one. Likewise at Palenque (Fig. 20), both the inscriptions and the stylistically dated sculptures and stuccoed panels are counted separately rather than on the basis of the number of buildings to which they pertain.

In addition to authors cited above (Morley 1938; Proskouriakoff 1950, 1963b, 1964; Ruppert, Thompson, and Proskouriakoff 1955), sources for monuments given in Figure 19 include Coe and Benson 1966 : Fig. 1 (El Cayo region); J. E. S. Thompson 1962 : Pl. 11 (La Mar); and von Winning 1968 : Pls. 467 (El Cayo region), 470, 471 (Yaxchilan region).

4. In the present paper, all dates in the Christian calendar follow the 11.16.0.0.0 (Goodman-Martínez-Thompson) correlation.

5. In a pit at Calatrava, 2 m. deep and excavated in 20-cm. levels, Fine Orange Ware was absent from the lowest deposits (late Naab Complex). Gaining steadily in importance, this ware came to comprise the entire ceramic assemblage near the surface, except for some coarse unslipped sherds. Utilitarian shapes also occur in Fine Orange Ware from Calatrava. Continuity in vessel shape is evident between Fine Orange basins and ash-tempered examples from the Naab Ceramic Complex (cf. Fig. 24e and Rands 1969b : Fig. 11).

6. Although generally comparable to Figure 19, the mode of presenting data in Figure 20 differs in certain important details (cf. Note 3). The complexity of Palenque inscriptions poses special problems, as many of the texts apparently deal with past rather than strictly contemporaneous subjects. Accordingly, dates at Palenque, taken largely from the compilation by Fuente (1965 : Table 2), are graphed with a separate set of conventions than are used for the Palenque style-datings by Proskouriakoff (1950). It should be noted, following Fuente, that a number of small, readily portable objects of pottery, jade, and limestone are included in the inscriptions plotted in Figure 20. The monumental sculptures and low relief stucco which Proskouriakoff has style dated form a partially different body of material. This difference may partly but does not fully explain the lag of up to several *katuns* that is apparent as the stylistic datings are compared with the inscriptions. In addition to the presumably noncontemporaneous nature of some of the Palenque texts, difficulties experienced in achieving satisfactory style datings at the site should be borne in mind (Proskouriakoff 1950 : 136–37, 149). In any case, comparison of Figures 19 and 20 indicates that the quantitative peak of monumental activities was significantly earlier at Palenque than at the Upper Usumacinta sites. Because of the complexities discussed here, as well as in Note 3, absolute frequencies within a particular *katun* cannot be taken too literally. Nevertheless, several basic patterns are suggested by the two charts. *Relatively early hierarchical climax:* Palenque. *Fairly extended hierarchical occupation with late climax:* Yaxchilan, Bonampak. *Extended hierarchical occupation without pronounced climax:* Piedras Negras. *Relatively early hierarchical occupation without pronounced climax:* Tortuguero. *Late hierarchical occupation without pronounced climax:* El Cayo, La Mar, Pomona.

In addition to authors cited above (Fuente 1965; Proskouriakoff 1950), sources for monuments included in Figure 20 are Acosta 1968 : Pl. 9 (Palenque); Blom and LaFarge 1926 : 151–53 (Tortuguero); Coe and Benson 1966 : Fig. 6 (Palenque region); Easby and Scott 1970 : Pl. 175 (Palenque region); Lizardi Ramos 1963 : 193, 200, Figs. 6, 7 (Pomona); and J. E. S. Thompson 1962 : Pl. 12 (Tortuguero).

7. Lizardi Ramos 1963 : Figs. 1, 6, 7; Greene Robertson n.d. : Fig. 15; Maler 1903 : Fig. 4; Berlin 1955b : Figs. 4, 5; Blom and LaFarge 1926 : 161–62, Fig. 116.

8. Maudslay 1889–1902, vol. 4 : Pl. 67c.

9. Berlin 1955b : Fig. 8; Blom and LaFarge 1926 : Fig. 132.

10. Blom and LaFarge 1926 : Figs. 149, 180.

11. Alternatively, ceramic traits originating on various time levels in more centrally located portions of the Maya area may have been retained, with some stylistic amalgamation, on the western periphery. Such a situation would be in accordance with classic age-area theory.

12. Proskouriakoff, although noting resemblances to the Palenque style in stucco reliefs from the Comalcalco tomb, also recognizes mannerisms, termed "Quality X," that are characteristic of a group of non-Classic sculptures in western Yucatan (Proskouriakoff 1950 : 149, 156; 1951 : 115, Fig. 5).

13. Even the Chontalpa figurines show a blend of Classic and non-Classic features, as pointed out by Thompson (1970 : 38).

14. Pabellon Modeled-carved is unknown from excavations at Palenque, although a barrel-shaped, ring-stand vase in the Trocadero bears this provenience (Lehmann 1935 : Fig. 9). Thompson argues that Y (Balancan Group) Fine Orange was manufactured by Putun (Chontal) Maya, presumably living in the Usumacinta Valley below Tenosique, "sufficiently far inland to be cut off from direct sea transport to Campeche and Yucatan, but not so far as to be well outside the alluvial delta" (1970 : 39).

15. A revision backward in time for the beginning of marked Mexican influences at Chichen Itza, to A.D. 918, is argued for by Thompson (1970 : 10–22). Precisely how this might affect the dating of Silho Group Fine Orange is still to be determined. Such a dating could lend support to ideas I have expressed previously about artistic relationships between the Chichen Itza "Toltec" and the Classic Maya, with special reference to Palenque (Rands 1954).

10
Aspects of Non-Classic Presences in the Inscriptions and Sculptural Art of Seibal

JOHN A. GRAHAM

Department of Anthropology
University of California, Berkeley

THE LATE CLASSIC BACKGROUND
TO THE NON-CLASSIC PRESENCES:
PUUC STYLE OF DATING
AND OTHER ASPECTS

Almost twenty-five years ago Proskouriakoff and Thompson (1947) presented a discussion of Classic Period Calendar Round dates such as 9 Ahau 17 Mol (where the month position is one less than is standard in Southern Lowland Classic epigraphy) and proposed for such notations the term "Puuc style of dating" because of their prevalence in northern Campeche and western Yucatan. They established that in that region the style occurred at least as early as 9.12.0.0.0 (A.D. 672). Proskouriakoff and Thompson further recognized the presence of such style notations at Yaxchilan on Stelae 18 and 20 (Proskouriakoff 1950, style dates, respectively, of 9.16.10.0.0 [A.D. 761] ± 2 *katuns* and 9.18.0.0.0 [A.D. 790] ± ?) which, along with other related monuments,

JOHN A. GRAHAM

present certain Puuc or Yucatecan sculptural features; and they sought to date this presence at between 9.15.0.0.0 (A.D. 731) and 10.0.0.0.0 (A.D. 830), the texts in question lacking unequivocal dedicatory dates.

In a subsequent study, Thompson (1952) sought to place the Puuc style 3 Eb 15 (16) Mol of Stela 18 at 9.14.17.15.12 (A.D. 729; transcribed as 9.14.16.15.12 in his paper) and the 6 Ix 16 (17) Kankin of Stela 20 at 9.16.2.9.14 (A.D. 753); he suggested that the dedicatory dates of the monuments might have been somewhat later. Proskouriakoff (1963b), on the other hand, now prefers to date Stela 20 earlier than her previous style date placement, because of references to "Shield-Jaguar" in the text; and she proposes 6 Ix 16 (17) Kankin at 9.13.9.14.14 (A.D. 701). The Yaxchilan accession of Shield-Jaguar is undated, but Proskouriakoff places his birth at about 9.10.15.0.0 (A.D. 647). Because of the Puuc style dates and other nonlocal sculptural details, Proskouriakoff conjectures that Shield-Jaguar may have been a foreigner who usurped Yaxchilan rule by a military or political coup.

At Bonampak, with so many ties to Yaxchilan, Lintel 3 of Structure 1 records a Puuc style-date of "3 or perhaps 1 Ix 1 Yax, or just possibly 1 Ceh" (Ruppert, Thompson, and Proskouriakoff 1955 : 37). In spite of the uncertainty of the exact reading of this Calendar Round, its Puuc style is unequivocal. The dedicatory dates of the three Structure 1 lintels are unknown, but Proskouriakoff's stylistic assessments suggest a dating around 9.18.0.0.0 (A.D. 790) or 9.19.0.0.0 (A.D. 810; Proskouriakoff 1950 : 185, gives a style date of 9.17.10.0.0 [A.D. 780] ± 2 katuns while the published graph in Ruppert, Thompson, and Proskouriakoff 1955 : 34, suggests perhaps 9.18.10.0.0 [A.D. 800] ± 2 katuns as a somewhat better placement). This divergence in time from the Puuc Calendar Rounds at Yaxchilan is puzzling, and it is unfortunate that the published illustrations of the Bonampak lintel texts are not more satisfactory for detailed study.

At Dos Pilas, I have studied a Puuc style date on the west hieroglyphic stairway of Structure 2 (Graham 1961). Here a Calendar Round of 3 Ix 16 (17) Muan can be placed securely at 9.12.5.9.15 (A.D. 678) while the dedicatory date of the stairway is probably the declared 9.12.7.0.0 8 Ahau 13 Tzec (A.D. 679), or possibly a position shortly after this (9.12.10.0.0?; A.D. 682), which might be recorded on a lower riser. It is interesting to note that there are no apparent references, at least under that appellation, to Shield-Jaguar in this text, which is concerned with a monotonously repeated phrase in which the individual referred to as "Captor of Macaw" and the tied-pouch emblem of Tikal figure as principal themes (as the Dos Pilas texts remain unpublished, it may be worth noting here in passing that the tied-pouch occurs with an astonishing frequency in the Dos Pilas texts, and this very significant linkage to Tikal is confirmed by other features).

Since Altar de Sacrificios occupies an intermediate and strategic position with respect to Yaxchilan, Bonampak, and Dos Pilas, it would be interesting to have a Puuc date from Altar, at present the most thoroughly investigated of the Lower Pasion sites. Although it has been possible to construct a good chronological framework for the ruin, its sculptures and texts are so fragmentary and so badly eroded that the apparent absence of an element is, as a rule, meaningless, and whether Puuc notation reached the site must remain unknown. Whatever political, religious, or other consequence these intriguing notations may presage, at Altar de Sacrificios the Classic pattern, so far as monuments are concerned, is broken after 9.17.0.0.0 (A.D. 771), when regular monument raising ceased. A smallish monument, Stela 2, was almost certainly raised at 10.1.0.0.0 (A.D. 859), but this may be understood to be under the aegis of the regime upstream at Seibal which celebrated this ending in such lavish manner.

With the martial theme of the Dos Pilas Structure 2 hieroglyphic stairway dating early in the Late Classic, there is no reason to think the Late Classic on the Lower Pasion was ever very peaceful for long. In the *katuns* preceding and following 9.17.0.0.0 (A.D. 771), there is ample indication of strife and of the successful campaigns of Dos Pilas and Aguateca, sites which continue to thrive past the eclipse (conquest?) of Altar de Sacrificios. The focus now upon sites with natural fortification possibilities (Seibal, Aguateca, Tamarindito–Dos Pilas) fits in neatly with the epigraphic picture and further underscores the bellicose aspects of the age. Eventually, however, it is Seibal that emerges by the end of the cycle as the paramount authority. The relationship of Seibal's ascendancy and of Aguateca's immediately preceding eminence is a fascinating matter for investigation, and abundant clues are present in the epigraphy of both sites where the emblem glyphs of each are prominent in the surviving texts.

JOHN A. GRAHAM

THE CHRONOLOGY
AND NON-CLASSIC FACIES
OF THE SEIBAL MONUMENTS

The chronological ordering of the epigraphy and monumental art of Seibal presents a series of problems not usually characteristic of Classic Southern Lowland sites. Only a single Initial Series record is known for Seibal. Most monuments were inscribed with Period Ending dates, with Calendar Round dates only, or with either no expressed dates or dates recorded in a non-Classic system that cannot as yet be related to other counts. While Period End dates are, of course, fully adequate for absolute chronological reckoning, the brevity of their statement endows them with a more precarious survival through the erosions of time and thus enhances potential chronological difficulties.

As a result of the epigraphic problems of chronological control, the dating of many important Seibal monuments must depend either partly or entirely upon assessment of stylistic aspects. Here, however, another complicating factor enters as a result of the strong infusions of non-Classic forces which have profoundly affected the natural development of the local traditions of the Maya Classic style. As the non-Classic infusions reintroduce features of Classic Maya stylistic development long since discarded in the Classic domain and hence highly anachronistic, style-dating becomes increasingly complicated and a challenging enterprise (Proskouriakoff 1950 : 153).

I have previously undertaken to style date the Seibal monuments discovered during my work at the site in 1961 (Graham 1963). The dates proposed then remain valid, and subsequent exploration of the site has added to this corpus only a single additional monument lacking a decipherable date. The 1963 dates, however, carried a ±2 *katun* time span, adequate for discussion in general terms of the infiltration of non-Classic elements, but not sufficiently precise for matters now at hand when it is desirable to identify specific aspects of the non-Classic intrusions. In this paper, therefore, I propose considerably more precise dating of the critical monuments.

In attempting to read the historical record of sculptures and their annotations in a largely undeciphered script, there are obviously many pitfalls, some of which are difficult to foresee and which have doubt-

less already ensnared me on more than one occasion. I will not cata-
logue all of these difficulties but merely emphasize the danger of dealing with exotics and the identification of their origins. Representational
sculpture and glyphic texts are not evenly distributed through the
Maya area; and the differential erosion of the various local stones as
well as the consequences of later local history have further aggravated
the unevenness of the record. Insufficient or no comparative material
exists from several potentially critical zones, and the ceramicist depends
on contrasts between the findings at individual sites and the broader
distribution of pottery in his work. One must be very aware of the
danger of stressing areas peripheral to actual origins when data from
the original area may be scarce or lacking and we perceive it only in
its paler marginal reflections. However, it is the absence of comparative
data from several zones that seem likely to have been crucial in late
Late Classic Times that causes me the greatest anxiety.

The term "non-Classic" was thoroughly characterized by Proskouriakoff (1951), and I have followed her in the explicit insistence that
non-Classic does not necessarily mean non-Maya (Graham 1963); the
non-Classic Maya must have outnumbered the Classic Maya, and
among some of them certain aspects of cultural achievement clearly ri-
valed, if not to say exceeded, the "Classic" Maya of the Southern Lowlands.

In the following adumbration of non-Classic groups at Seibal, I have
made no attempt to inventory all of the non-Classic elements which
occur in the art and epigraphy of that site. The traits which I cite
seem to me to be particularly useful in recognizing the groups at the
present stage of analysis; in themselves they are neither exclusive to the
group defined nor, in some respects, the most significant.

Seibal Non-Classic Facies A (Fig. 32)

The "A" group is constituted by figures such as are seen on Stelae 8,
10, 11, 14, 20, 21. Representatives of the group can be recognized on
other monuments as well, but erosion, dating, or other factors complicate the portrayal. These figures generally prefer Classic fashions of
dress accouterment but with significant exceptions and innovations;
their identification depends largely upon a physiognomy which suggests origins other than a purely local Classic context but is fortified by

the presence of other non-Classic (sometimes "archaistic" Classic) traits. The very striking and unmistakable quality of individual portraiture seen in the sculptures of this group was appreciated and singled out long ago by Spinden (1916).

Facies A is well dated at 10.1.0.0.0 (A.D. 859) through 10.3.0.0.0 (A.D. 899); their arrival, however, may well have been earlier as references appear to some of the Facies A lords in the hieroglyphic panels of Structure A-I, which on standard epigraphic grounds would be considered to date to 9.16.0.0.0 (A.D. 751). Furthermore, related exotic qualities are present from the very beginning of the Seibal sculptural rec-

FIGURE 32. NON-CLASSIC FIGURE OF FACIES A. Seibal Stela 14, probably carved during *Katun* 1 Ahau, ending at 10.3.0.0.0 (A.D. 869–889).

ord in Stelae 5 and 7. It is surely telling that the figures of these latter monuments are ball players, and that this was an era of significant new fashions in the art of the Lower Pasion, perhaps seen most dramatically in the ubiquitous recumbent-figure step panels. The general preference for Classic fashions of dress and the fact that all the monuments cited above, with the probable exception of Stela 14, celebrate Classic Maya *hotun* ends recorded in Classic terminology are doubtless excellent clues to the cultural aspirations of these lords.

The figures of Facies A show important ties to such monuments as Stela 4 of Ucanal, dated to 10.1.0.0.0 (A.D. 849), and Stelae 1 and 2 of Ixlu, dated at 10.1.10.0.0 (A.D. 859) and 10.2.10.0.0 (A.D. 879), respectively, as well as Comitan Stela 1,[1] dated to 10.2.5.0.0 (A.D. 874). Their derivation seems most likely to be found in the Northern Lowlands; certainly most of their exotic characteristics have greatest precedence there, whether they be "introduced" traits such as the "Toltec" slippers of the figure of Stela 14 (Fig. 32) (worn on only one foot at Chichen Itza, however) or "indigenous" traits such as the stela platform upon which Stelae 14, 15, and 16 stood.

Seibal Non-Classic Facies B (Fig. 33)

Figures of the group are especially to be recognized by their waistlength or longer hair, by absence, with minor exceptions, of elaborate Classic Maya attire and accouterment, and by a constellation of traits which seem significant in their combination but are not all exclusive to the group: squared cartouche glyphs, non-Classic dates or an absence of Classic *hotun* end dates, the large bead necklace, and other features. Figures of this facies are best seen on Stelae 3, 13, and 17.

The figures of Facies B appear to have Gulf Coast affinities—somewhere between western Yucatan and southern Veracruz. This area was one of several, Maya and non-Maya as well, where very long hair was fashionable at the arrival of the Spanish. *The Relación of Tlacotalpa (Papeles de Nueva Espana*, vol. 5) says of the men of Rio Alvarado, southern Veracruz, "cabellos largos como mujeres," and numerous references to the long hair of the men of Acalan are to be found in Scholes and Roys (1948).[2] Since the Spanish of the early sixteenth century did not wear their hair particularly short, these references are probably significant. The paneled design of Stela 3 (Fig. 33)

FIGURE 33. NON-CLASSIC FIGURE OF FACIES B. Seibal Stela 3, central register, with probable glyphic date of 10.2.5.3.10 1 Oc 8 Kankin (A.D. 874).

looks to Campeche and the Puuc for inspiration (Proskouriakoff 1950 : 160), and other features also point to the general Gulf Coast region.

Thompson (1970) echoes Morley (1938) in the interpretation of the squared cartouche glyphs of Stela 3 as names and adds the intriguing identification with the Acalan name, *Cipacti*. Although the glyph has frequently been referred to as "Mexican" by various commentators, I think it may have an old Maya background despite its obvious resemblance to the Mexican day sign, *Cipactli*. Stela 5 from Morales provides a glyph (at A9) in day sign cartouche, but with Affix T1, which almost surely is antecedent to the Seibal example. Morales Stela 5 is almost surely of early Late Classic age, probably about 9.10.0.0.0 (A.D. 633), and provides another pointer to the Tabasco and Gulf Coast area (Lizardi Ramos 1961).

Enough data are now available, or should shortly be available, for the solution of these squared cartouche notations. Depending upon the evidence of Seibal, I previously argued, though not insisting upon the interpretation, for their identification and use at Seibal as year-bearer notations (Graham 1963). Their initial position in Seibal texts, generally a lack of subsequent chronological statements, association with a world direction/count of the year phrase, and the probable interest in year-bearer statement and divination in another Seibal text of the period seems good evidence for the view, combined with the 1–13 coefficients and the no more than four different framed signs at Seibal. The Jimbal texts, however, follow the pattern of Ucanal 4 and now provide a total of more than four different framed elements, indicating at least additional usage for the squared cartouche notations. On the other hand, the recent publication of El Zapote Stela 5 with a squared cartouche glyph prefixed with a year sign would seem to look toward the Seibal interpretation (Easby and Scott 1970 : Fig. 170). This very important monument, at 9.0.0.0.0 (A.D. 435), establishes a very substantial antiquity for squared cartouche notation and beautifully fits Proskouriakoff's interpretation of the I : A5 pose as a Tenth Cycle reintroduction (Proskouriakoff 1950 : 153).

The chronology of Facies B and the relationship of Facies B to Facies A create various problems. In both cases, however, Stela 17 (Fig. 34) provides very significant clues since it portrays a representative of each group. On Stela 17, a figure on the right is attired in Classic costume, though some non-Classic elements are present; and in his left hand he holds the Manikin Scepter, evidently the supreme emblem of authority at Seibal since at least 10.1.0.0.0 (A.D. 849). The facial features of this figure are damaged, perhaps intentionally mutilated, but the figure is probably of Facies A. I have previously suggested that he makes the traditional gesture of submission or friendship with his right hand (Graham 1963). The figure on the left carries the "curved stick" weapon and is surely of Facies B. Stylistically, Stela 17 certainly dates

FIGURE 34. THE CONFRONTATION OF CULTURE TYPES. Seibal Stela 17, probably carved after 10.3.0.0.0. (A.D. 889).

very close in time to Stela 20, securely fixed at 10.3.0.0.0 (A.D. 889), but is clearly a bit later; I believe that a dating of about 10.3.10.0.0 (A.D. 889) ±5 *tuns* is strongly indicated, but I do not suggest a *hotun* dedication in view of the non-Classic nature of the stela.

Stelae 3 and 13, however, can hardly be considered so late. I believe the best reading of the Stela 3 Calendar Round is 1 Oc 8 Kankin, which I would place at 10.2.5.3.10 (A.D. 874). This rather tenuous epigraphic evidence confirms various stylistic considerations which lead me to place Stela 3, together with Stela 13, conceivably the work of

216

the same hand, within *Katun* 1 Ahau, ending at 10.3.0.0.0 (A.D. 889), a critical era to which Stelae 2, 14, and 15 as well almost surely belong.

If the precise dating of Facies B is not entirely satisfactory, the relationship to Facies A is even more intriguing. Does Facies B arrive with Facies A or, more likely, are the Facies B people a later addition? Are they originally allies of Facies A who eventually seize power for themselves? The relationship may have changed through time; the first depictions of Facies B do not emphasize weapons and suggest a quite special role.

THE SEIBAL NON-CLASSIC AND THE END OF CLASSIC MAYA CIVILIZATION

For the present I prefer not to commit myself to a broader reconstruction of events at Seibal and their specific relationship to the collapse of the Classic Maya tradition of the Southern Lowlands. Considering the data now available and the variety of at least possible, if not to say plausible, alternative interpretations that can be formulated, it appears wisest to concentrate in coming research upon defining the principal themes of the collapse and to avoid elaborate hypotheses of highly specific historical events, although tentatively offered hypotheses of a generalized nature should stimulate continued study. In any event it seems clear that in recent work one of the most tangible aspects of the Classic collapse, and one which is not simply of a parochial consequence, has been revealed at least in a general fashion.

A study of Southern Lowland Tenth Cycle sculptures clearly reveals the radical changes that the Classic world was undergoing, not only at Seibal but at most sites with preserved sculpture to testify. While there are many ties among these centers, only a few sites closely duplicate each other, and it is apparent that a highly complex series of events was transpiring. The situation doubtless reflects that different seats of Classic political authority existed, that all seats were not affected in the same manner simultaneously, that the seats showed varied responses and interacted differently among themselves, and, finally, that there were plural forces at work in the destruction of the Classic order. The absence of sky figures at Seibal, for example, is particularly noteworthy and together with other considerations places Seibal in a different theater from Ixlu, Ucanal, Tikal, Jimbal, and other sites where non-Classic features are also heralding the Classic breakup but in differing forms. It will be difficult to successfully unravel this history, which seems somewhat analogous to, though more complex than, the lengthy campaign of subjugation waged by the Spanish upon the Lowland Maya states some centuries later.

In the broadest sense the deaths or metamorphoses which civilizations suffer may be arranged into two groups. Cataclysmic destruction certainly has occurred throughout history, though perhaps not so commonly as popular writers portray. The Spanish assassination of Mesoamerican civilization is equivalent to the appearance of a new and insurmountable malignant virus from another planet or to the supposed cataclysmic destruction of Minoan civilization with the explosion of Santorin. Such episodes are reasonably attributed, enitrely or to all practical purposes, to single-factor explanations and should eventually be detected archaeologically and finally settled with a reasonable unanimity among the interested. With the data now in hand there is clearly no need to invoke such alien and cataclysmic explanations for the demise of Classic Maya civilization.

With respect to the second broad group of explanations, however, there are instances, such as Imperial Rome, where foreign warriors and dogma may indeed appear but who and which nevertheless derive from the larger sphere of established experience and interaction, and where an intricate interplay of external and internal factors often results. In a vein of somewhat cynical hyperbole, it might be suspected that in such instances as these we will long occupy ourselves with the stimulating pastime of searching out triggering mechanisms to internal stresses, and so on, and no doubt at times will come upon some correct aspects of the decline; but these will never solve the problem entirely, and we will probably never really and fully identify the relative significance of the various historical forces, their causes and consequences, to everyone's satisfaction. (These remarks of course assume a rejection of Marxian or other rigid theoretical schemes and dogma where answers are available before questions are asked.)

Since we are in fact frequently unable fully to resolve these questions with respect to literate civilizations of the recent past, archaeology cannot expect to succeed in endeavors fraught with even greater problems. Succeeding fashion will necessarily favor other causes and types of explanation, and the chief result will be to provide endless occupation for intellectuals so concerned. But continued exposure and definition of the associated events and forces, cultural processes, and ecological adjustments will allow us to better paint the portrait of collapsing civilization in the Southern Lowlands; and this is perhaps as much as we should expect.

NOTES

1. In noting this connection with Chiapas we should not overlook Proskouriakoff's suggestion of a non-Maya (probably in the sense of non-Classic) presence at Tonina (1950 : 138). It is also proper to note here that Proskouriakoff long ago and with far less data at hand perceptively read the sculptural record of such monuments as Comitan 1 to make "suspect the theory that the Maya civilization perished entirely from internal causes, and that its decline was unaccompanied by foreign infiltration" (Proskouriakoff 1950 : 153).

2. The long-haired Lacandon and Chol nearer to hand must not be overlooked (Thompson 1938 : 598).

11
Postclassic Culture in Central Peten and Adjacent British Honduras

WILLIAM R. BULLARD, JR.

Florida State Museum
University of Florida

The subject of this paper is the archaeological culture of the central part of Department of Peten, Guatemala, and adjacent British Honduras subsequent to the collapse of Classic Maya culture. At the outset it must be emphasized that Postclassic Peten culture is still poorly understood, with respect both to its internal development and its external connections. Nevertheless, it is apparent that throughout all or most of the Postclassic Period, central Peten was the seat of a cultural tradition distinct from the cultural traditions of other archaeologically known Maya regions of the period. Peten was not an empty land after the depopulation at the end of the Classic Period. It held an indigenous population of moderate size with its own culture history.

Was this population a holdover from the Classic Period peoples of the same area? What was the nature of their culture and society? What were their relationships with other Maya groups and their place in Postclassic Mesoamerica generally? We may not now be able to provide very complete answers, but these questions are pertinent to an understanding of the collapse of the Classic culture of the region.

THE CENTRAL PETEN
POSTCLASSIC TRADITION

The markers of the Peten Postclassic, as now known, are a series of pottery types which are classified into three ceramic groups (in type-variety terminology). The three are (1) the Augustine, (2) the Paxcaman, and (3) the Topoxte. These ceramic groups are closely related to each other by attributes of form and decoration. They reflect stylistic currents which were felt throughout the Maya area in the Postclassic Period, but together they form a conservative tradition which is distinctive. These ceramic groups form the basis of what I call "The Central Peten Postclassic Tradition."

Pottery of the Central Peten Postclassic Tradition has been found only rarely in Classic Period ceremonial ruins which have been excavated, and very little archaeological work has been directed specifically towards the Postclassic in Peten. George Cowgill made a surface survey and did limited testing at Lake Peten (Cowgill 1963). An intrusive grave was found in Temple 1 at Tikal (Adams and Trik 1961). Culbert (chapter 5) describes other finds at Tikal and vicinity which relate to the Central Peten Postclassic Tradition. In the Tikal sequence, this material makes up the Caban Complex. In western British Honduras, Postclassic Tradition pottery characterized the final occupation of the Barton Ramie site, known as the New Town Phase (Willey et al. 1965). My attention was drawn by Postclassic building remains at Topoxte at Lake Yaxha, and I made test excavations there (Bullard 1961, 1970b). More recently, I excavated a large domestic ruin on an island in Lake Macanche in an attempt to tie down the Postclassic sequence. In addition, I and others have made observations throughout the area, and casual finds have been made by lake divers and others principally around Lake Peten (for example, Berlin 1955a; Borhegyi 1963).

The maximum area of the tradition can be roughly delineated, although there appear to have been shifts within this area during the Postclassic Period (Fig. 35). Sites are found around Lake Peten and the other lakes of central Peten and on the upper Belize River system in British Honduras, and may follow that river as far as the coast near the

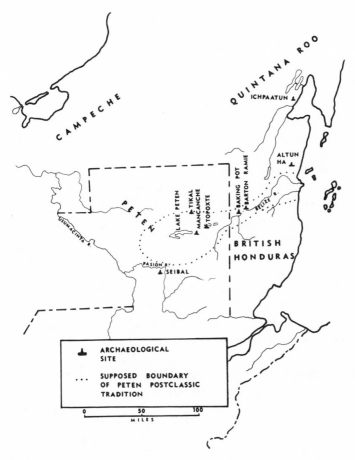

FIGURE 35. MAP SHOWING INFERRED LIMITS OF THE CENTRAL PETEN POSTCLASSIC TRADITION

city of Belize. However, Postclassic finds reported by Pendergast at Altun Ha suggest that the coastal area north of the Belize River belonged culturally with the Quintana Roo East Coast, at least in the Late Postclassic (Pendergast 1967b). Probably the Central Peten Postclassic Tradition spread down through the savannas of central Peten towards the Pasion River, but evidence is not conclusive so far. Two vessels belonging to the Paxcaman Ceramic Group were found at Seibal, apparently in Bayal Phase contexts (Sabloff, chapter 7). There is no evidence regarding the westward extent of the tradition.

THE TEPEU 3 HORIZON: TERMINAL CLASSIC

In defining the Peten Postclassic by the aforementioned ceramic tradition, it is not my intention to ignore the terminal populations who lingered on at several known Classic sites in Peten and British Honduras after the breakdown of Classic social patterns and the cessation of construction in the ceremonial centers. These populations made pottery which continued the Late Classic ceramic traditions: Tepeu 3 at Uaxactun, Eznab at Tikal, and such contemporary complexes in British Honduras as San Jose V and Late Spanish Lookout. Trade wares and stylistic evidence show that these populations lasted into what in area-wide terms is called the Early Postclassic. But these people did not last long, and the old Classic traditions in pottery making and other crafts faded with them. The traditions which replaced them in Peten were quite distinct.

I have chosen to regard these remnant populations around the Classic ceremonial centers as Terminal Classic—"Rump Classic" might be a better term—in order to distinguish them from the Central Peten Postclassic Tradition which is the main subject of this paper. An important problem is what the connection between the Terminal Classic and the Postclassic traditions may have been.

POTTERY OF THE CENTRAL PETEN POSTCLASSIC TRADITION

Since Peten Postclassic pottery is not well known through published sources, it is appropriate to make a few comments concerning it. The three major slipped ceramic groups are called Augustine, Paxcaman, and Topoxte. Of the first two, the Paxcaman Ceramic Group is much better known than the Augustine. Paxcaman was found in greater abundance around Lake Peten and at Macanche and is the only one of the two reported at Tikal. Augustine was found in greater quantity at Barton Ramie, but a complete description of the pottery at that site is not yet available. The third member of the trio is the Topoxte Ceramic Group, which has been found only at Lake Yaxha and as a late arrival at Macanche.

The ware of all three groups is a red ware. Augustine paste is often calcite tempered but appears to be more variable than the others. Paxcaman paste is fine textured with inclusions of small snail shells and is so uniform wherever found that a single manufacturing locale is indicated. Probably it was made at Lake Peten. Topoxte, also, has a distinctive paste and almost surely was manufactured at Lake Yaxha.

Augustine pottery is predominatly monochrome, but also includes a scarce polychrome type with designs similar to those on Ixpop Polychrome of the Paxcaman Group. There may also be rare incised types. Jar and deep bowl forms appear to be similar to those of the Paxcaman Group; indeed, only one really distinctive Augustine form has come to light so far, a small tripod dish with either plain scroll feet or effigy scroll feet of a unique sort, conceivably an abbreviated Tlaloc symbol (Fig. 36a, b). Because definition of the Augustine Ceramic Group rests

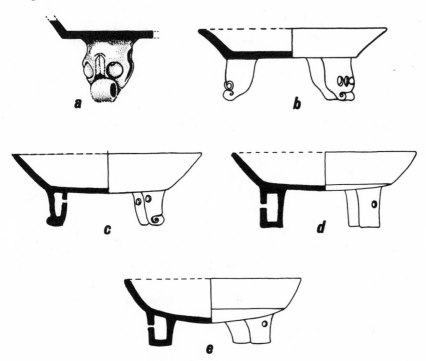

FIGURE 36. TRIPOD DISH FORMS OF THE PETEN POSTCLASSIC TRADITION. *a*, Augustine effigy foot; *b*, Augustine Red dish with effigy feet; *c*, Paxcaman Red; *d*, Ixpop Polychrome; *e*, Topoxte Cream Polychrome.

principally on only one or two recognizable modes of vessel form in addition to rather variable ware characteristics, I am suspicious about the validity of Augustine as a ceramic group and believe it should be a tentative designation until more is known.

The Paxcaman Group has three major types, all found in good stratigraphic association with each other. These are Paxcaman Red (monochrome), Ixpop Polychrome, and Picu Plano—relief. There is also another polychrome type, Saca Polychrome, which is closer in some attributes of form and decoration to the Topoxte Ceramic Group. As in the other ceramic groups of the Peten Postclassic Tradition, a common vessel form is a small tripod dish, monochrome dishes having scroll feet, polychrome dishes having cylindrical or slightly bell-shaped feet (Fig. 36c, d). There are also grater bowls, strap-handled jars, and a variety of other forms. This ceramic group is consistent and easily recognizable.

The Topoxte Ceramic Group is also consistent and easily recognizable. It lacks plano-relief or any incised type, but has a monochrome, Topoxte Red, and a polychrome, Topoxte Cream Polychrome. The latter has some design correspondences with Ixpop Polychrome of the Paxcaman Group, and there are other similarities in form and treatment which indicate a close connection with Paxcaman (Fig. 36e).

There are other ceramic groups in the Peten Postclassic besides these three, some of which will be mentioned in due course. But it is these three which predominate, and in which the Central Peten Postclassic Tradition is most clearly manifest.

In passing, it may be noted that in the New Town Phase at Barton Ramie, where the Augustine and Paxcaman groups both occur, the bulk of the complex has been described as "a rag-tag of crudely fashioned unslipped odds and ends very difficult to classify in any orderly way" (Gifford, in Willey et al. 1965 : 384). The same observations would not apply to the contemporary sites in Peten proper with which I am familiar. There, the unslipped accompanying types conform to consistent standards and are competently made.

CHRONOLOGICAL RELATIONSHIPS AMONG THE PRINCIPAL CERAMIC GROUPS

The evidence for the chronological relationships among the three principal Postclassic ceramic groups will be summarized below. The difficulties in assessing these relationships are several. There seems in general to have been remarkably little ceramic change throughout the Postclassic in Peten. Since paste differences between groups indicate different manufacturing centers, changing patterns of trade and contact may have affected the distribution of pottery to different subregions in varying ways. The component types within ceramic groups may have had somewhat different time spans. Moreover, I have already expressed suspicion about the validity of the Augustine Ceramic Group as a classificatory entity. Identifiable foreign trade pottery is scarce and almost absent from deposits so far excavated. Stylistic similarities to foreign pottery types are generally too diffuse to be of much help in pinpointing temporal relationships. Above all, there has been too little stratigraphic excavation.

Cowgill's Lake Peten survey did not turn up a definite stratigraphic relationship between the Augustine and Paxcaman ceramic groups, but on stylistic grounds he thought that Augustine was probably mainly Early Postclassic and Paxcaman mainly Middle to Late Postclassic. My tests at Macanche tended to confirm his inferences. The main occupation at the Macanche site was Paxcaman. Augustine sherds were very scarce, and the only two examples of the diagnostic Augustine effigy tripod supports were in clear association with a Tepeu 3 horizon complex called the Romero Phase, which stratigraphically preceded the Paxcaman pottery.

At Barton Ramie, Augustine and Paxcaman were found together in the uppermost levels, and both were treated as components of the New Town Phase. But I think the published sherd counts suggest a time difference between the two. Augustine pottery is more abundant than Paxcaman at Barton Ramie and is found in all New Town Phase mound occupations. Paxcaman pottery is a great deal more limited at the site; in fact, about one-half of the total number of Paxcaman sherds came from one mound. I think the situation is one of declining population, heaviest in an earlier period when Augustine pottery was current, and sparse during a later time when Paxcaman pottery was predominant.

Paxcaman Group pottery is at least one component of the Caban Complex at Tikal. Caban follows the Terminal Classic Eznab Complex, apparently discontinuously; it is also associated with Tohil Plumbate and X-Fine Orange, suggesting that the Caban Complex was at Tikal at a time contemporaneous with the Toltec Period at Chichen Itza (Culbert, chapter 5).

The Topoxte Ceramic Group at its home site at Lake Yaxha is associated with figurine censers related to those of Mayapan and Tulum, as well as with architectural traits consistent with a Late Postclassic placement. Topoxte pottery appears at the Macanche site at the end of the Paxcaman occupation there. But Topoxte pottery has a very limited geographical distribution and has not been found at Lake Peten. It is highly probable that Paxcaman pottery continued without major change into the Late Postclassic around Lake Peten. There are Paxcaman associations with figurine censers of the Topoxte type at Lake Peten, as well as resemblances between a minor Paxcaman type and the Topoxte Ceramic Group which indicate that this was so.

PERIODS OF THE
PETEN POSTCLASSIC

As a useful frame of reference, I have divided the Peten Postclassic into four periods as shown in Figure 37. They will be summarized below along with the evidence of gross settlement distribution. The periods are tentative. Period II is perhaps the weakest, and may need to be compressed or even split between Periods I and III.

Period I

In area-wide terms, Period I is Early Postclassic. Around such Classic centers as Tikal and Uaxactun, the surviving Terminal Classic populations were declining. All subsequent settlement of consequence was around the lakes and permanent rivers of Peten and British Honduras.

At Macanche, the Tepeu 3 horizon phase, the Romero Phase, belongs in the Terminal Classic category. It is worthy of note that the Romero Phase is ceramically closer to the Bayal Phase at Seibal than to Tepeu 3 proper at the closer site of Uaxactun. Specifically, the dominant types are Subin Red, Cameron Incised, Pantano Impressed, and

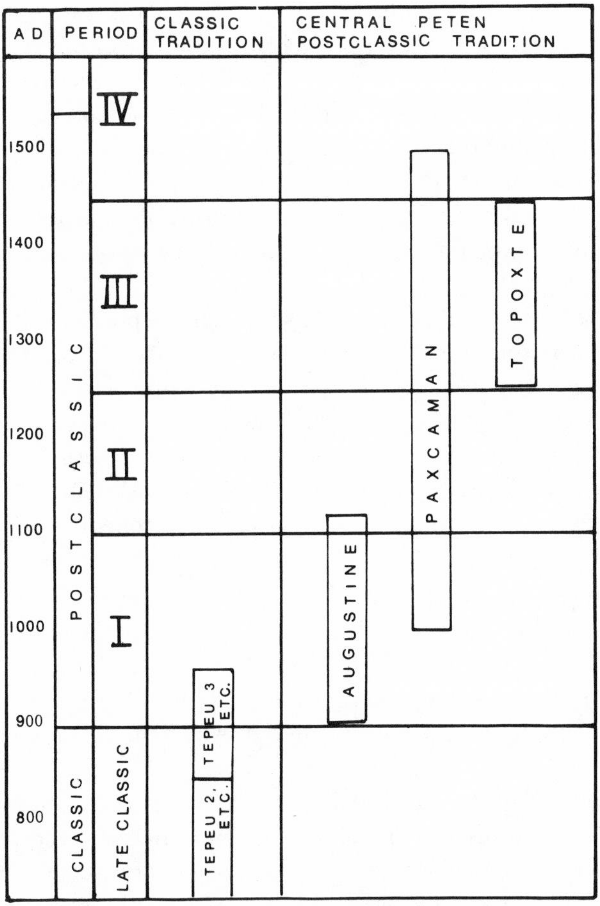

FIGURE 37. TENTATIVE SEQUENCE OF PETEN POSTCLASSIC PERIODS AND CERAMIC GROUPS

the jar component of Tinaja Red (Sabloff 1969). The Fine Orange component of the Bayal Phase, however, is absent.

Before the old Classic pottery traditions had completely faded, the Peten Postclassic Tradition was making its appearance in the form of the Augustine Ceramic Group. It appears in strength in two major areas: around Lake Peten and along the Belize River.

At least in the latter area, the new pottery tradition becomes established in the same places where there was a heavy Terminal Classic population, as the work of the Barton Ramie project has shown. Whether there was population continuity I regard as slightly problematical, and I will discuss this problem later. Perhaps the ragtag of difficult-to-classify odds and ends which Gifford describes in the New Town Phase represents the final gasp of Classic pottery tradition, and the Augustine pottery was traded in. But there is another mysterious pottery type of importance at Barton Ramie. This is Daylight Orange. Daylight Orange, which has an odd superficial resemblance to Chicanel pottery, is related neither to earlier Classic Period pottery nor to pottery of the Peten Postclassic Tradition. It has not been identified to date in Peten proper.

The distribution of Peten Postclassic Tradition pottery in Period I is apparently discontinuous. I found none at Lake Yaxha, the largest body of water between Lake Peten and the Belize River. I have mentioned that at Lake Macanche, which also is intermediary in location, diagnostic Augustine pottery modes were associated with the Terminal Classic Romero Phase. Possibly both Yaxha and Macanche were held during Period I by Terminal Classic groups antagonistic to the makers of the new pottery.

Period II

Period II is dominated ceramically by the Paxcaman Ceramic Group, although some elements of the Augustine Group probably continued.

The main occupation of the island site at Macanche occurred at this time. But at Barton Ramie and along the upper Belize River, the population was dropping. There was a small, seemingly isolated Period II site far to the east on the British Honduras coast between the Belize and Sibun rivers. It must have been a trading or fishing station, since the surroundings, a combination of savanna and mangrove swamp, are good for nothing else.

The process may not have been so much population reduction in the area of the Peten Postclassic Tradition as increasing fragmentation into smaller, more compact settlements, and probably greater concentration on Lake Peten and central Peten generally. Period II would correspond roughly with the time of the fall of Toltec Chichen Itza, and Roy's readings of the Yucatecan chronicles suggest that this was a time of considerable military and political activity throughout the peninsula (Roys 1962).

Period III

Period III is the time of Topoxte Ruin at Lake Yaxha. Topoxte is the only Peten site thus far found with significant surviving ceremonial construction. A small town, it was concentrated defensively on a group of islands in the lake, clearly the center of a small political state. The close links of the Topoxte Ceramic Group with the other pottery of the Peten Postclassic Tradition indicate that the populace of Topoxte was native to the area. But foreign stimulus or direction by a foreign elite probably accounted for its rise, as well as for the introduction of the widespread Late Postclassic ritual cult characterized by the use of figurine censers.

East of Lake Yaxha, the upper Belize River appears to have been virtually abandoned in Period III, with the probable exception of a few scattered villages whose existence has yet to be confirmed archaeologically. At Macanche, Topoxte pottery arrived at the close of the occupation. The Topoxte political state may have expanded to incorporate Macanche and the territory to the eastern end of Lake Peten. Around Lake Peten, it is highly probable that Paxcaman Group pottery continued to be made without major change.

Period IV

Period IV is the period of the historically known Peten Itza, who maintained their control over central Peten until the close of the seventeenth century. All sources agree that this group of Itza came from Yucatan, but their time of arrival is disputable. Some authorities favor a date around A.D. 1200, at the time of the Toltec Chichen Itza breakup, making them contemporary with Period III. Other authorities favor a date of about A.D. 1450, a date towards which I incline. In any event, the Peten-Itza have yet to be identified as an archaeological complex. No evidence exists from archaeological finds to date, including a large number of pottery vessels recovered from the lake bottom immediately adjacent to the Itza capital of Tayasal, indicating large-scale immigration into Peten from Yucatan during the Middle or Late Postclassic.

Cowgill found a few sherds around Lake Peten with paste characteristics similar to the Paxcaman Group, but these sherds differed sufficiently in forms and design motifs to be classified as a separate ceramic group which he named the Tachis. Cowgill believed Tachis belonged stylistically in the Late Postclassic and that it might have been a ritual ware. I did not find this pottery at Macanche or Topoxte and can add nothing more. Probably it belongs in Period IV or Periods III and IV. But it is so scarce that, by itself, it can hardly represent the Late Postclassic or Protohistoric occupation of Lake Peten; and one is forced to conclude either that there was a persistence of the Paxcaman types into Period IV or that only unslipped pottery was made during Period IV.

The most likely interpretation is that the Peten Itza movement into Peten was that of a relatively small cultural elite who asserted dominance over a local population who were making pottery in the old Peten Postclassic Tradition. As I indicated above, I think similar movement was responsible for the rise of Topoxte in Period III.

Topoxte apparently was abandoned early in Period IV, the Yaxha area remaining essentially uninhabited thereafter. From the accounts of Cortés and later missionaries, we know that the Period IV population was concentrated in the island town of Tayasal and in a number of other villages on Lake Peten, with a few outlying settlements elsewhere.

CERAMIC CONTINUITIES
AND RELATIONSHIPS

Having reviewed the outlines of the Postclassic history of central Peten, we will now turn to the ceramic evidence for Classic-Postclassic continuity and to the problem of the exterior relationships of the Peten Postclassic Tradition.

The Augustine Ceramic Group is not well known in its entirety and seems to be more variable than the other Postclassic slipped ceramic groups with respect to ware characteristics. Conceivably it represents a ceramic transition from the monochrome red wares of Tepeu. I mention this merely as a possibility. When one looks at the known forms classified as Augustine, and at the other Postclassic ceramics of Peten, continuity is not at all apparent.

To be sure, the common flat-bottomed tripod dish of the Augustine and Paxcaman groups has an overall resemblance to Tepeu tripod dishes, especially to those which have more or less cylindrical supports. But the Postclassic dishes are consistently smaller with distinctive and usually differently placed supports and a different placement of design, when design is present. The other pottery forms contrast quite strongly. Nor do I see a carry-over of Classic pottery design into the Postclassic. The design motifs and general style of the Postclassic polychrome and plano-relief types are quite distinctive.

The lack of continuity extends to unslipped types as well. The common large striated jars with outcurving necks of the Late Classic are replaced by smaller unstriated wide-mouthed jars with short vertical necks. There are even differences in container types. For example, the Postclassic form inventory seems to contain nothing comparable to the large incurved-rim bowls so common in the Late Classic.

If links with Tepeu pottery are difficult to see, it is equally difficult to see evidence that the pottery of the Peten Postclassic Tradition was influenced by the Fine Orange complex which entered southern Peten at the end of the Classic Period and was so well represented at Seibal and Altar de Sacrificios.

With regard to exterior relationships, the slipped ceramic groups of the Peten Postclassic have general resemblances to other Postclassic pottery in such features as strap-handled high-necked jars, grater bowls, a type of angled bulbous tripod support, and in the general character of designs. But close specific resemblances to other known complexes are elusive.

Some vessels of the Paxcaman Group found at Macanche have a grayish, rather soapy-looking slip which resembles Yucatecan Slate Ware in surface appearance to such an extent as to suggest that imitation was intended. But the resemblances are not otherwise close.

Both Gifford (Willey et al. 1965 : 388) and Cowgill (1963 : 81–83) have commented on the similarity between the flat-bottomed tripod dish form of the Augustine and Paxcaman groups and a tripod dish form of X Fine Orange. The resemblance really boils down to similarity between the "trumpet" supports which occur on the X Fine Orange form and on Ixpop Polychrome of the Paxcaman Group. There are also occasional individual design elements—guilloches, hooks, simple panel elements—which coincide with those of X Fine Orange and other Early Postclassic pottery types of Yucatan and Campeche. But the form inventories are really quite different, as are the majority of design elements and their treatment on the vessels.

It is unfortunate that on most of the polychrome sherds of the Pax-caman Ceramic Group which have been found, the lines of the designs have been so worn or eroded away that only traces remain. Clearly, most vessels, particularly the dishes, had rather simple standardized designs. But there are a number of polychrome and plano-relief vessels with more elaborate and sophisticated designs—scrolls, feathers, and other elements suggesting a stylistic relationship with Mixtec art and with the Late Postclassic mural art known at Santa Rita, British Honduras, and at Tulum: the style recently referred to by Robertson (1970) as the "Late Postclassic International Style" (Fig. 38). A common motif on the plano-relief found also on Ixpop Polychrome is a feathered serpent-monster, quite unlike the Toltec feathered serpents which appear at Chichen Itza (Fig. 38a). Probably none of these more elaborate vessels belong earlier than Period II and most may be Period III, the period of the introduction of figurine censers and of Topoxte.

A preliminary report on Topoxte referred to the resemblance between the tripod bowl form of Topoxte Cream Polychrome (Fig. 36e) and a common bowl form of Tulum Red (Bullard 1961 : 553). There are resemblances in form of tripod feet, but the Topoxte bowls in question are actually much more directly related in form and decoration to Ixpop Polychrome tripod dishes of the Paxcaman Group. I do not see the Topoxte Ceramic Group as particularly closely connected to Tulum Red, though they share certain widespread Postclassic attributes.

The cited examples are among the indications that the pottery of the Peten Postclassic Tradition was subject to a degree of foreign stylistic influence over the course of time. But the main point is that there does not now seem to be any Late Classic or Early Postclassic complex outside of Peten from which Peten Postclassic Tradition pottery can be said to be derived in its entirety. In a recent book, Eric Thompson (1970) has postulated a major expansion of Chontal or "Putun" Maya from southern Campeche and Tabasco at the close of the Classic into Quintana Roo, Yucatan, and southern Peten as far as Ucanal on a tributary of the Belize River. I cannot see that these people could have been directly responsible for the Postclassic culture of central Peten or

234

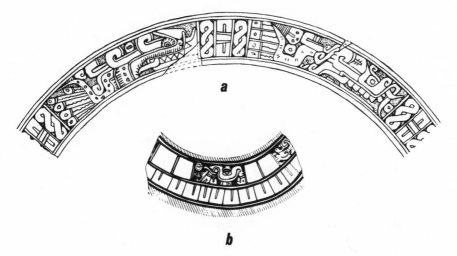

FIGURE 38. DESIGNS ON PAXCAMAN GROUP POTTERY FROM MA-
CANCHE. *a*, From Picu Plano-relief bowl with flaring collar; *b*, from Ixpop Polychrome restricted-orifice bowl.

that they could have influenced it significantly before about Period III,
the beginning of the Late Postclassic.

In sum, the ceramic evidence is inconclusive in indicating derivation
of central Peten Postclassic culture and population either from Classic
Period predecessors in the region or from any particular outside region.

RESIDENCE PATTERNS

Whereas the presence of permanent bodies of water seems to have
influenced Preclassic and Classic settlement of central Peten hardly at
all, all Postclassic settlement of consequence was focused on lakes and
the larger rivers. Augustine and Paxcaman pottery comes mostly from
domestic house ruins. The settlement pattern is not fully clear, but at
least during Periods I and II, settlements seem to have been small and
rather scattered, perhaps in strip patterns or in small villages. The Period III site, Topoxte, was a compact town, and historical sources suggest that Period IV settlement at Lake Peten was at least partly in
compact communities.

Sites with Postclassic pottery not infrequently also have Classic pottery, and the question arises whether there was continuity of residence by the same population at these sites from the Classic into the Postclassic. Excavation data comes only from Barton Ramie and Macanche. The single large house ruin on the island at Macanche I believe to have been reoccupied after abandonment by the Terminal Classic people.

At Barton Ramie, we believed that the New Town Phase represented continued occupation by the same populace who had been there at the end of the Classic. But the situation was not perfectly clear. Ordinarily, Classic Period house construction at this site, as elsewhere, included building platforms and terraces with stone retaining walls and plaster floors. Before the final occupation, these structures seem generally to have been buried beneath purposely deposited mantles of earth which converted them into earthen mounds. The houses of the New Town Phase people did not have well-made substructure platforms, but evidently stood on hillocks which had much the same appearance then as they do today. It is quite possible that the mounding over of the old platforms and terraces took place or began in the Late Spanish Lookout Phase, which was the Terminal Classic phase at Barton Ramie. But the data also permit the interpretation that the mounding was done by New Town Phase people who were reoccupying an abandoned settlement.

Continuity or not, there are indications of changes in domestic house architecture. Late Classic house ruins typically are in units composed of substructure platforms placed around little rectangular courts. From what I have seen, this pattern does not carry over in recognizable form into the Postclassic in Peten. The difference may be only that the Postclassic house builders put little effort into constructing neat stone-faced substructures, but it also could be that Postclassic house groups were fundamentally different in layout.

CEREMONIAL AND ELITE CENTERS

So far, there is no evidence that the makers of Augustine and Paxcaman pottery built elite centers or monumental ceremonial buildings. However, they did make some use of old Classic temples which were still intact, probably much in the same way that the Lacandon used to use standing buildings at Yaxchilan and Tzendales as shrines. The best examples are at Tikal. *Copal* had been burned in Temples I and II, and a burial put through the floor of Temple I, probably in period II to judge by the associated Paxcaman Group pottery and censers (Adams and Trik 1961).

A good deal of Postclassic pottery is to be found in the general vicinity of the ceremonial center of Ixlu, at the east end of Lake Peten. A test I made at the front of the principal mound at Ixlu produced Paxcaman pottery only in the topsoil; sherds associated with construction were all Classic. The same situation is probably to be found at the archaeological site called Tayasal, once erroneously thought to have been the ruins of the Peten-Itza capital of that name. The Guthe collection from Tayasal Ruin which is now in the Peabody Museum at Harvard contains mostly Preclassic and Classic sherds. Postclassic sherds are relatively few, although common in domestic sites in the immediate area.

On the Belize River, the single small temple mound at the Barton Ramie site proved to be among the few mounds tested which lacked evidence of use in the New Town Phase. The nearby Baking Pot ceremonial center also showed no trace of construction or ceremonial activity during the Postclassic Period.

In Period III, a substantial ceremonial and elite center was built at Topoxte, raising the possibility that similar buildings existed at other sites of the Peten Postclassic Tradition. If so, they have not been discovered. The Topoxte buildings included temples and low buildings comparable to the columned open halls at Late Postclassic sites elsewhere. Beam and mortar roofs were used instead of vaults. Doorways had columns, and stairways had balustrades with vertical upper zones. There were local peculiarities, but the architecture and layout conformed much more closely with that of such sites as Mayapan and Tulum than with the Classic architecture of Peten, and I see no derivation from the latter.

Temples and buildings perhaps similar to the open halls of Topoxte were seen at the Peten-Itza capital, Tayasal, in Period IV. Thompson quotes a revealing statement by a missionary that the Itza chiefs had private temples, but that "the common people worshipped in their *cavernas*, as they called them, in the woods and in caves, seldom or never going to the large temples" (1951 : 395). This picture is consistent with the notion that the Peten-Itza were a foreign elite group who never fully amalgamated with the native population they dominated. I suspect that a similar intrusion was responsible for the Topoxte ceremonial center, and that, left to their own devices, the native population of the Peten Postclassic Tradition did not construct specialized ceremonial buildings of a monumental nature.

TRADE

From what is known generally of the Postclassic archaeology of the Maya Lowlands, it could be supposed that a cross-peninsula trade may have passed from the Gulf of Mexico across central Peten and down the Belize River to the Caribbean coast. If this were so, we might expect that foreign items would be common in sites of the Peten Postclassic and that the trade would have fostered a relatively wealthy class of merchant elite.

So far, there is no good evidence that central Peten did participate to any great extent in foreign trade. Foreign potsherds are very scarce and not well associated with excavated deposits. This scarcity is true even at Topoxte, where architectural and censer traits suggest strong outside influence. When and if rich burial offerings or caches are found, the picture may change; but now there is no archaeological evidence of a market for foreign luxury goods or, with the possible exception of Topoxte and Tayasal, of a wealthy ruling class. The only articles of personal adornment found are simple shell and pottery beads.

Among utilitarian objects, obsidian flake blades are fairly common, as in the Classic Period, and must have come originally from the highlands. But use of volcanic stone and other imported raw materials other than obsidian seems to have been rare. *Metates* and *manos* are of limestone and presumably came from within the region.

That there was a lively internal trade, at least until Period III, is demonstrated particularly by the Paxcaman Ceramic Group. As mentioned earlier, this group has a very distinctive and uniform paste. The paste almost always has inclusions of tiny snail shells of genera which live in the silts of shallow fresh water lakes. There seems little doubt that Paxcaman pottery was made in one locale, and this was probably at Lake Peten where the pottery is very abundant. At Barton Ramie, the Augustine and other ceramic groups of the New Town Phase might have been produced locally, but the Paxcaman was surely brought by trade.

Topoxte pottery is also distinctive; but barring its late occurrence at Macanche and a sherd from uncertain context at Baking Pot, it has not been identified outside Lake Yaxha. I have seen none in the Cowgill and Guthe collections from Lake Peten, for example. Nor, it is interesting to note, did I find any Paxcaman sherds in my tests at Topoxte although there is stylistic and other evidence that the Paxcaman Ceramic Group persisted at the same time as Topoxte. Evidently, the people of lakes Yaxha and Peten were not exchanging pottery in Period III, and I suspect that their relations were not amicable.

NOTCHED SHERDS AND PESTLES

Two rather minor artifacts are worthy of mention because they are restricted to the Postclassic and may indicate outside contacts.

Small oval sherds notched at the end and especially made clay pellets with end notches are common in the New Town Phase at Barton Ramie and in association with Paxcaman and Topoxte pottery at Macanche. They have not been found in Classic Period deposits. Elsewhere, they are reported from Late Postclassic sites on the Quintana Roo coast (Sanders 1960 : 261) and in a contemporary Tulum-related complex at Altun Ha in coastal British Honduras (Pendergast 1967b : Fig. 3). The guess is that they were fishline weights.

The second item is a pestle of a size suitable for use with a grater bowl. The business end is expanded and roughened with little punctations; the other end terminates in an extraordinarily crudely modeled animal head. The objects have an oddly primitive look and are not common. One was found with Paxcaman pottery at Macanche; a few similar examples were found at Lake Peten. A fragment was found in the Tulum-related complex at Altun Ha (Pendergast 1967b : Fig. 4*f*). Brainerd illustrates specimens from Early Mexican Period contexts at Chichen Itza and refers to somewhat similar objects in the Tairona culture of Colombia (Brainerd 1958 : Fig. 72).

CONCLUSIONS

The present state of knowledge concerning the Peten Postclassic has only reached the point where specific problems have begun to emerge. There are many important gaps which must be filled before definitive conclusions can be reached. I am only too conscious of the extent to which my current conceptions are based on negative evidence.

However, it is significant that I have been unable to trace any obvious continuities of importance from the Classic into the Postclassic in pottery manufacture, residence patterns, or ceremonial and social patterns. One thing seems certain: the old Classic culture with its social controls was completely sundered and swept away. The Postclassic is a new chapter, if not, indeed, a new book.

Underscoring the change is the shift in settlement to the larger permanent lakes and rivers. Unless a new population immigrated into the area, the reasons for the shift can now only be speculated upon. The Classic people, and probably the Preclassic people before them, had in this region lived essentially dispersed, depending for the most part on a large number of very small sources of surface water. A change in rainfall pattern which led to seasonal drying of these small water sources could have forced shifts. But a climatic change of this sort has yet to be demonstrated. Morever, as is often pointed out, the magnitude of the collapse of the Classic civilization was such that a fluctuation in rainfall pattern could have played only a secondary role in the events of the time. Warfare or other social pressures which created a desire for settlement in large compact communities might have fostered a shift to the larger bodies of water, but the archaeology does not seem to indicate the growth of this kind of settlement in the Early Postclassic. The Postclassic population was certainly very much smaller than that of the Classic Period, and with the disappearance of the former political and territorial units, the surviving people may have merely gravitated to places where water supply was certain, the fishing was good, and communications were facilitated by waterways. But the distribution of Classic settlement shows that these advantages were not particularly valued in earlier times.

The distinctions between the Classic and Postclassic cultures are so sharp that it is necessary to question whether there was continuity in the basic population. But, if there was large-scale population replacement, it is equally difficult to pinpoint any one area from which it might have come.

The true picture was possibly that Classic Peten people survived in some places and that other Maya groups moved in from several areas to exploit the vacuum created by the Classic breakup. I would guess that at least some came from Quintana Roo and Campeche, perhaps as refugees from the Putun Maya invasions of which Thompson (1970) speaks. The cultural amalgamation of these groups is expressed archaeologically mainly by Augustine and Paxcaman pottery. The latter, at least, seems to have been manufactured in only one locale, and its distribution by trade may give an impression of unity which is deceptive.

My impression is that the Postclassic people of Peten existed mainly in peasant-level groups without strong social class differences or strong political controls. They seem to have been relatively isolated from the major cultural events which occurred elsewhere in the Yucatan Peninsula; there are no indications that they had appreciable influence on other Maya groups. In Thompson's (1967) characterization of Protohistoric Maya groups, they would rate as "static" rather than as "expansionist."

In the Late Postclassic, I think that they were subject to incursions by small expansionist "elite" groups, probably from the north. The historic Peten-Itza were one such group; the founders of Topoxte at Lake Yaxha were another. The latter were probably responsible for the introduction of the figurine censer cult and may themselves have been a branch of the Itza. The invaders brought political control and their own religious cults to central Peten but may not otherwise have strongly modified the indigenous Postclassic culture of the region.

12

The Development of Maya Civilization
after Abandonment of the Southern Cities

E. WYLLYS ANDREWS IV

Middle American Research Institute
Tulane University

INTRODUCTION

Much has been published in recent years about the collapse of Maya civilization and its causes. It might be wise to preface this chapter with a simple statement that in my belief no such thing happened. Rather, I think that at approximately the halfway point in the long course of Maya civilization, its magnificent southernmost cities went into sudden eclipse and the tropical forest in which they were built rid itself of at least a major portion of its population—a process which has not been reversed until recent times. The causes of this catastrophe, sociopolitical, military, or ecological (probably a combination of factors, as capably described by others elsewhere in this volume), are a matter of real importance to the study of the organics of human culture in the area and its independence from or dependence upon environmental control and whimsy. Work, however, has been so overconcentrated during recent decades in the southern quarter of the Maya Lowlands that an almost unconscious attitude has grown up that when its fire was extinguished, life was over for the Maya. Actually this was far from the case.

The Central and Northern Lowlands,[1] consisting of the Mexican states of Campeche and Yucatan and the Territory of Quintana Roo, have been from earliest to latest times very much in the mainstream of Maya culture. The first presently known pottery and the earliest domestic and ceremonial architecture are found in the Northern, not the Southern, Maya Lowlands. Middle Formative ceremonial centers in northwest Yucatan are by far the largest known, despite the relatively minimal extent of excavation in the north. From present (probably not final) evidence, the Formative civilizations developed earlier and more robustly in the Northern than in the Southern Lowlands. Architecture from the Mamom and pre-Mamom (Xe?) phases in the south is still unknown.

But thus far it is in the Southern Lowlands that we find the apparently earliest distinct traces of the complex and distinctive civilization we know as Maya. This new and unique syndrome of achievements seems to have been delayed in its northward spread for a century or more after the emergence of its components at what appears to have been the cultural epicenter. However, by the beginning of the Ninth Cycle in the Maya calendar (approximately A.D. 100–400),[2] Classic Maya culture appeared in full flower in the Northern Lowlands, and continued on a basis closely comparable to the south. Acanceh, Ake, Izamal, Coba, and Oxkintok were among the great northern cities of the first phase of the Early Period ("Early Classic" in the south [3]). All these continued into the second phase of the period ("Late Classic" in the south), and many others, notably Dzibilchaltun, grew to positions of great size and power. Proskouriakoff (1950) has noted very correctly that modal regionalisms in Maya art characterize much of the history of the northern three quarters of the Maya Lowlands.

During the Early Period, trade and communications within the Maya Lowlands and with external areas varied in intensity. In the first phase, relations with Teotihuacan and possibly other centers of the Mexican Highlands were clearly intensive. Some students have even interpreted this as a military invasion, a suggestion, as I see it, still based on very tenuous evidence. In the second half of the Early Period, either external trade routes were interrupted or Maya Classic civilization assumed a much more monolithic aloofness from the aesthetics of surrounding regions.

Maya Civilization after the Southern Cities

During most of the Early Period, the trend of culture within the lowlands seems to have been from south to north. Toward the end of the Early Period, the channels of cultural impact were suddenly reversed. In the declining decades in the south, beginning perhaps toward the close of the Ninth Cycle, the principal influences went from north to south. After a visit to Seibal in 1965, I wrote Gordon Willey at considerable length of my conviction and the final phases of both ceramics and architecture in the Pasion Valley were strongly and directly influenced by Yucatan culture in the north (Andrews, personal correspondence, 18 May 1965; Willey, Culbert, and Adams 1967 : 303). I believe that most experts in the region now concur with these views. Further relevant evidence will be presented below.

In terms of the Maya area as a whole, these terminal phenomena in the Peten, however, were still local manifestions which marked little more than halfway points in the progress of Maya civilization. The following section of this paper will be devoted to a brief analysis of the higher development of Maya culture in the remaining three-quarters of their habitat, which should in no way be regarded as the collapse of a civilization.

While "Classic" Maya civilization was withering on the stem in the far southern area, this was not the case in Campeche, Yucatan, and Quintana Roo. As its southern segments deteriorated, Maya civilization in the north substituted, for its extensive trade with the no-longer-productive Peten centers, more intensive relations with groups along the Bay of Campeche and cultural areas to the north and west. The resultant change in orientation led to a cultural upsurge in the north in no way less impressive than that which seems to have occurred in the far southern area more than half a millennium before. From the area just north of the Guatemala frontier to the northern tip of the peninsula, cities grew in this part of the world as they perhaps never had in the past. The myriad new architectural centers, probably more numerous than elsewhere in the entire Mesoamerican area, arose and spread in unparalleled fashion over a period of several centuries. To understand these developments properly, it will be necessary to review a number of investigational factors that many workers in the Southern Lowlands have tended to disregard.

As early as 1942, (Andrews 1942 : 262–63), I pointed out that what were then called the "Puuc" and "Toltec" cultures in Yucatan were

actually integral parts of a single cultural tradition and that they resembled each other much more closely than they resembled the abundance of Early Period ("Classic" in the southern terminology) remains,
which are liberally distributed in Yucatan. For this reason, I subsequently advocated that the term "Classic" be disallowed in the north,
as it excluded most of the later and perhaps optimal expressions of high
Maya civilizations (Andrews 1960 : 261–65, 1965a : 305 ff). These
suggestions were based on material, first uncovered in the late 1930s
and early 1940s, indicating that interrelated patterns of architecture,
ceramics, and sculpture on the northern peninsula, corresponding
closely with sister patterns in the Southern Lowlands, were not only
earlier than the cultures then known as "Puuc" but were separated by
a definite and demonstrable period of transition from the later cultures
to follow. This conclusion was at the time generally disregarded. Since
then, I believe, much more impressive evidence has been accumulated.
By the finish of excavations at Dzibilchaltun, it was abundantly clear
that the major post-Formative architectural remains fell into two quite
distinct structural traditions which were separated in time:

1. An early genre of building, characterized by simple profiles and
    elaborate facade ornamentation in carved stucco on a framework
    of block masonry, capped by true corbeled vaults. This was
    clearly affiliated with "Classic" architecture in the far south and
    with an increasing quantity of related material recently being dis-
    covered in the Central and Northern Lowlands. The cultural
    phase represented by these remains was designated the Early Pe-
    riod.

2. A totally distinctive genre characterized by monolithic concrete
    construction technics (and the disappearance of true wall masonry
    of functional corbeling as structural features). This tradition and
    the period it represents were named Florescent. The functional
    aesthetic characteristics of these complexes have previously been
    defined in much more detail (Andrews 1942, 1960, 1965a, 1965b)
    and will not be repeated here.

Not only were these styles aesthetically and technically distinct, but
they obviously represented different temporal horizons. As their geographic spreads were roughly coterminous, there were frequent physi-

cal superpositions in construction—the Florescent always over the Early Period.

More significantly, in a number of cases, there was solid evidence of gradual transition from one tradition to the other. This transition is seen at Dzibilchaltun, Yaxcopoil, Acancah, and Mulchic (Andrews 1942 : 257, 1965a : 296–310; Piña Chan 1963), at all of which sites Early Period construction gave way to the advanced technics of the Florescent during the multiple growth phases of individual buildings. This process involves two implications. First, such a transition would require an indeterminate but probably a considerable span of time which must be allotted its space in any scale of absolute time for the cultural events in the lowlands. Second, it implies that since this evolutionary process has not been observed elsewhere to date, it took place in the far Northern Lowlands, and it is probably here we should search for its dating criteria. It is not a process which one would expect to occur in different places at different times.

Probably the most important remaining question in establishing an overall appraisal of the development of Maya civilization is a coherent chronological alignment of the events which I have been discussing. A number of the most prominent Maya scholars have maintained for some time that the Florescent Period of the North and Central Lowlands (Puuc–Chenes–Rio Bec) is in considerable part coeval with the terminal stages of Classic culture in the south. As late as July 1970, Gordon Willey, agreeing with Lee Parsons (1969), favors an alignment "where the beginning of the Pure Florescent is made coeval with the beginning of Tepeu II at about A.D. 700" (1971 : 99). Such an alignment is an almost essential requirement for acceptance of the Goodman-Martínez-Hernández-Thompson correlation.

As remains attributable to the Florescent tradition are virtually non-existent in the Southern Lowlands, any judgment as to the alignments we are discussing, based on southern material, would tend to reflect the demands of proposed correlations of the Maya and Christian calendars, which I believe they do. For archaeological evidence, it is necessary to seek proper documentation in the Central and Northern Lowlands, where both of the cultural traditions are found side by side and in stratigraphic context.

THE NORTHERN AREA

In northern Yucatan, the only intensively excavated site with a long developmental history is Dzibilchaltun. The architectural sequence has been discussed above. In pottery, the Copo Complex prevailed in most of the northern area from the equivalent of the middle of Tzakol times through the entire Early Period and on through the Pure stage of the Florescent. Our ceramicists have not as yet definitively divided the Copo Complex into facets identifiable with Early Period and Pure Florescent architecture. Therefore, it has been necessary to rely heavily on trade wares from regions where pottery changed much more rapidly in the course of time. Our efforts fortunately were aided by an inordinately large proportion of trade pieces, enabling firm chronological inferences at a surprisingly early stage in the excavations.

During the first phase of the Early Period, northern ceramics consisted in significant part of polychrome basal-flanged vessels imported either from the Tzakol potters of the Peten or from some as yet undefined intermediate area. The second phase of the Early Period is characterized by a striking abundance of Peten trade material on the Tepeu 1–2 horizon, particularly of the later subphase. This important trade seems to have stopped by the beginning of the Florescent Period, presumably because of the collapse of the southern cities. None of the very numerous tombs and caches of the Florescent contained any of the Peten pottery which had earlier been so fashionable. Indeed trade with the Peten seems to have been replaced by increasing commercial contacts with the southern Gulf Coast and to have featured the importation of great quantities of Fine Orange and Fine Gray wares produced in that area. Both of these fine paste wares are horizon markers of Postclassic (post–Tepeu 2) times in the Peten and British Honduras (see chronological charts, pp. 45, 48).[4]

Much of the architectural stratigraphy at Dzibilchaltun (excepting tombs and caches) is that of redeposition, and the inferences must often be negative. Soil was so scarce and rock so expensive to quarry that virtually everything available was utilized in building construction. Thus later buildings reused the refuse of early inhabitants, and the fill of post-Florescent structures normally contains Formative Period and Early Period ceramic components. Structures could not be earlier than the latest sherd sealed within. And the absence of later wares in statistically significant samples would indicate the other side of the chronological bracket.

The ceramic-architectural column at Dzibilchaltun seems firm and unambiguous. At Uxmal, 55 miles to the south, the situation is much more simple and direct. Uxmal was a large city, one of the largest. To judge by the continuous building, burying, and rebuilding at such groups as the Adivino and the Casa del Gobernador, the construction sequence must be allowed a span of many years. Notably, there is no Early Period architecture at the site, nor is there anything later than the Pure Florescent. More significantly, of the several hundred thousand sherds excavated at the site by the Carnegie Institution and the Mexican Government, there was not a single fragment of Tepeu polychrome from the Peten—although there is a wealth of Fine Orange and Fine Gray trade pottery. The rise and fall of Uxmal thus seem to have occurred after the decline of the southern polychrome industries, namely, after the end of Tepeu 2 in the Peten and before the onset of the Modified Florescent. At several other Puuc sites, excavations have disclosed both Formative and Early Period pottery, but never in association with Florescent architecture. At Xkukican (Cottier 1967) there is a wealth of early pottery, which presumably accompanied the extensive Early Period architecture found there. Brainerd (1958) reported what he called "regional polychromes" from Labna, Kabah, and Sayil, which clearly had longer pedigrees than Uxmal, but these were all scant samples from the bottoms of trenches—quite unassociated with Florescent material.

In the northern area, in short, all evidence of intensive excavation points to a total lack of overlap (indeed a separation) between Early Period and Florescent cultural material. I know of no contradictory material from the far Southern Lowlands. Many specialists from the southlands, however, continue to be unreceptive to the cultural alignments suggested. If an agreement is to be reached, more data would clearly be helpful, preferably from the Central Lowland area, which is virtually unexplored. In this area, data should be obtainable to clarify the obvious differences in interpretation between northern and southern students.

THE CENTRAL AREA

There is little question that the distinctive architectural remains of the geographic regions called Puuc, Chenes, and Rio Bec of the Yucatan peninsula are intimately related. They are obviously segments of what I have defined as the Florescent tradition. Students have varied in their interpretations as to whether this complex forms a chronological horizon (I believe it does) or whether it consists of a series of geographic variants connecting "Puuc" culture of northern Yucatan with "Classic" culture of the Peten (cf. Pollock 1970; Willey 1971). Tulane University has devoted recent efforts to securing a stable architectural-ceramic stratigraphic column in this area. We chose the Rio Bec area, which forms the southern border of these obviously northern architectural traditions, as the optimal testing area for our questions.

After the first two seasons' work, architecture in this area in such proximity to the Peten seems to clearly define overlying and not overlapping traditions. In post-Formative times, these traditions are closely parallel to those of the Northern Lowlands. Earlier masonry, consisting essentially of block walls and vaults of enormous corbeled slabs presenting simple geometric profiles and elaborate facades of stucco decoration, is followed by buildings of concrete construction in wall and vault with a veneer of finely faced slabs. In the later structures, the facades consist, as in the north, of elaborate panels of carved stone mosaic covered by adornments in stucco and paint. The relationship between the earlier architectural tradition of far southern Campeche and the contemporaneous styles of "Classic" Peten in the south is unmistakable. The remarkable resemblance between the later elaborate concrete veneer architecture and that of Florescent structures in the north is equally so.

The ceramic associations of these differing architectural traditions are much more specific than in the north. Instead of the long-lived northern Copo Complex, parallel cultural events are associated in southern Campeche with two quite distinct complexes. The late Early Period remains are associated with what our project ceramicist has named the Bejuco Complex. Although very much an entity of its own, its dominant trade affinities are with Tepeu 2 in the south; and it is particularly rich in the characteristic polychromes of that phase. The overlying Florescent ("Rio Bec") architecture is accompanied by a radical change in ceramic affiliations.

The new complex, named Chintok, represents a phase of regional isolation in pottery development and consists in considerable part of local types. Although it seems to contain Tepeu-derived components, the distinctive polychromes are entirely absent—indicating that the nearby residents of the Peten had either ceased to manufacture or to export these diagnostic wares. Some traits characterizing Tepeu 3 (Terminal Classic) are present, but others are conspicuously absent. Copo trade sherds from the north are more frequent, but the Gulf Coast tradewares which accompany the complex in the north, Fine Gray or Orange, are noteworthily absent, although anomalously, later "Mexican" forms which postdate Copo (*and* Fine Gray) in Yucatan and first appear in the Modified Florescent Period (Zipche Complex) are present in Chintok. It is hoped that the inferentially contradictory trade patterns will be clarified in current excavations. Meantime, Chintok remains as a definitely post–Tepeu 2 complex as yet not strongly affiliated with the Terminal Classic or Postclassic ceramics of either the south or north.

Local architectural specializations also occur within the broader Florescent style and may properly be called subtraditions. The architecture of the Rio Bec area was distinguished by tall corner towers ornamented with small, steep staircases and miniature temples atop. These flanked long, low ranges of rooms often decorated with rectangular panels of curvilinear design. At Becan, these bordered steeply elevated plaza areas and were built as simple, formal temple structures with a single entrance and a monumental staircase facing the plaza; the rear consisted of four or five stories of palace-type rooms extending down to the flat areas below. In the high, hilly area known as "Los Chenes," facade decoration reached an elaboration unknown elsewhere, largely covered by conventionalized interwoven serpent motifs culminating in "serpent-mouth doorways" where entrance was made through the creature's gaping mouth, which bristled above and below with fangs.

In the Puuc Hills and on the flat northern plain of Yucatan, a third subtradition was characterized by emphasis on complex geometric facade decoration at the cost of curvilinear composition, a plethora of masks of the Long-nosed God (often superimposed in long vertical corner-panels), and a quite unparalleled perfection of veneer masonry with practically tenonless wall stones, perfectly squared and fitted and ground to a surface smoothness not found elsewhere. Other trends within the Florescent tradition were simply areal—without foci of concentration. For example, there was a marked trend from north to south to increase the extent of design detail executed in stucco. In the north, most of the finished design was carved in stone and often simply worked over with stucco, possibly as a base for elaboration in colored pigments. Farther south, the plaster workers' responsibility increased over the masons', until in the Rio Bec area only the basic layouts were carved in stone, most of the detail added in carved stucco.

The above brief words are an oversimplification, but they describe a clear process of geographic differentiation within a broad tradition on a single level in time. There is no evidence that an evolutionary process is represented, and considerable that it is not. First, diagnostics of all the subtraditions seem thoroughly mixed even within their foci of intensity. At Chicanna, near Xpuhil, for example, Florescent construction associated with Chintok pottery stratigraphically overlies Early Period architecture associated with Bejuco pottery. However, there is an indiscriminate mixture of "Rio Bec" and "Chenes" traits in the same Florescent structures, and at least one building combines "Puuc" style facade ornamentation of superimposed "Chac" corner masks and geometric decoration with "Chenes" serpent-doorways and rectangular curvilinear facade panels. There is no evidence that the minority of structures with towers in the Rio Bec area are earlier than those without.

Approximately midway between the Chenes and northern Yucatan, the city of Xkichmook shows a thorough blending of the two subtraditions, "Puuc" and "Chenes" traits occurring indiscriminately on the same structures—clearly a "frontier" mixture of regional styles. Farther to the north at Uxmal, attention frequently has been called to the unmistakable "Chenes" inspiration of the partially buried structure whose serpent-mouth doorway gives on the west stairway of the Casa del Adivino. When the structure was more thoroughly excavated in recent years, this was found to be the fourth of five structural superpositions. Phases I, II, III, and V were in conventional "Puuc" style, placing the "Chenes" structure late in the sequence. Interestingly, Phase I was associated with an abundance of Fine Gray and Fine Orange pottery (Sáenz 1969 : 21), both of which, as noted above, are Terminal Classic or Postclassic in the Peten.

Seven new radiocarbon dates in unquestionable association with "Rio Bec"–style structures at Becan and Chicanna double the number of determinations available for the Pure Florescent Period. The new total of fourteen median dates average A.D. 680, the seven Rio Bec readings average A.D. 662. If the single Uxmal date (GRO-613), lying one century outside of the span of the remaining northern dates, be disregarded, the average of all median dates would be A.D. 663, virtually identical. In either case, all seven of the Campeche dates (the first from the Central Lowlands) fall within the span bracketed by the 1-sigma variation of the northern dates. This agreement is so close as to speak strongly against suggested substantially earlier dating of the Rio Bec and Chenes subtraditions of the Florescent.

In summary, evidence from the central area indicates, as it does in the north, that the Florescent tradition postdates the termination of the southern Classic Period (that is, Tepeu 2). Architectural styles and technics as well as stratigraphy are closely parallel, although a transitional phase has not been identified, as it has in Yucatan. In the Rio Bec area, in contrast to the north, Florescent architecture and art are associated with a local ceramic complex (Chintok) quite distinct though possibly derived from the definitely Tepeu 2–equivalent pottery (Bejuco) identifying the late Early Period. The heavy frequency of Tepeu 2 polychromes as the prime index fossil of late Early Period architecture and pottery (Early Facet Copo and Bejuco) and its total absence from Florescent strata (Late Facet Copo and Chintok) rule out Willey's suggestion (1971 : 99) that the start of Tepeu 2 and that of the Florescent were approximately contemporaneous. Finally, available stratigraphic and radiocarbon evidence indicates general contemporaneity of the Rio Bec, Chenes, and Puuc subtraditions. Florescent styles seem to have evolved in the north and, spreading southward down the peninsula, to have made their influence felt as far south as the Pasion Valley in early Cycle 10.

LATER PERIODS

Spinden (1913), Tozzer (1957), Proskouriakoff (1950), and others have pointed out for some time that continental influences, probably from the Mexican Highlands, appeared early in the Pure Florescent. I would prefer to regard these as the same order of influence which all of us have long recognized in the first phase of the Early Period in the highlands of Guatemala and the Southern, Central, and Northern Lowlands. During the second phase of the Early Period, these strong external contacts were not noticeable. The sequence of events perhaps indicates a lack of viable trade channels or a course of local isolationism which might have been a factor in the collapse of the southern cities. The stagnation which occurred in the Southern Lowlands definitely did not appear in the north, where new and stimulating trade connections were apparently being made at this time.

For a while, cultural influences, as we have mentioned above, went from the Northern to the Southern Lowlands, apparently awakened by some new stimulus. This stimulus was strong in the north, so strong that, at least in the state of Yucatan after a short time, even Maya hieroglyphic writing seems to have disappeared. At Dzibilchaltun, inscriptions on hieroglyphic lintels were in Highland Mexican, not in Maya script, at the height of the Pure Florescent. These continental influences seem to have culminated in a fairly abrupt dominance in northern Yucatan of people who have been called Toltecs, though they never called themselves by any such name. Their ascendancy marked the end of the great cities of the Puuc area and, temporarily, of the Florescent cities on the low and well-watered plain to the north. Their capital was at Chichen Itza whence their military, religious, or political hegemony was so complete that no formal architectural construction is known, with minor exceptions at Xcopte on the northwestern coast and on the island of Cerritos (Andrews 1965b : 48) off the northeastern coast, both small and possible military garrisons.

Elsewhere on the northern flatlands, cities were apparently in a state of subjugation in which pottery was produced in abundance but no civil construction allowed. At Dzibilchaltun, which was an enormous site, Modified Florescent pottery is found in surprising quantity but no public works can be found. Underlying later construction, there are remains of Modified Florescent camp middens around the central plaza. Whoever the "Toltecs" were, they obviously dominated life in what is now the present state of Yucatan for a long time, and they dominated it in a very severe way. The monuments they left behind at Chichen Itza are monuments which no one could confuse with the collapse of a civilization. They are the largest at the site and include physical superposition of structures in different architectural styles (namely, sub-Castillo, Castillo, Chac Mool temple, Temple of the Warriors) that must represent a considerable span of time. I would very tentatively suggest 150–250 years.

The ceramic evidence, as it is gradually sorted out, indicates an equally long span. Various index fossils, such as X Fine Orange, Plumbate from highland Guatemala, and unmistakable imitations of censers from Tula, Hidalgo, all once considered as contemporary horizon markers, do not seem to occur in the same stratigraphic horizon. Tozzer (1957 : chap. 2) may well have been right, when he suggested that the so-called Toltec Period consisted of at least two quite distinct phases. Even further faceting may later be justified. There are indications from Becan that pottery wares and modes once considered contemporaneous mainland importations during the Modified Florescent may have to be separated in time. It seems very likely to me that this proposition will turn out to be correct. This phase in Maya history urgently needs intensive excavation and analysis.

The "Toltecs" appear to have stimulated the last upward surge of Maya civilization. Their origins are uncertain; their disappearance seems to represent their absorption by the Maya. Whoever they were, their impact on the Maya physical type and language was minimal.

The end of the Florescent Period in the Northern Lowlands appears to represent the removal of a great wedge of cultural tradition, at least strongly inspired from the southwestern portion of the peninsula and adjacent parts of continental Mexico. It does not look, from our present knowledge, like the withdrawal of any considerable population. The basic technics in ceramics, art, and architecture were fundamentally Maya. I have pointed out above that the Florescent tradition in architecture seems to have evolved in Yucatan. The Copo and Zipche ceramic complexes have no external equivalents, and art forms continued predominantly Maya. But marked foreign modalities became increasingly significant as the period progressed.

A vacuum left by the abrupt removal or demise of the Florescent tradition led to what George Vaillant rather aptly termed a "Maya renaissance" (Vaillant 1927) and Thompson a "resurgence" (1970 : 83). The first step in this return to pre-Florescent culture and technics is best seen at Dzibilchaltun, although this city never again became a major population center. Ceremonial construction began again in the area around the central plaza, which for so long had been only a camp site. At this time the Zipche Ceramic Complex was suddenly replaced by a complete panoply of pottery wares described as "Black-on-cream." This ware was defined as the Haaz Complex at Dzibilchaltun but is widely found elsewhere on the northern peninsula, always stratigraphically overlying Modified Florescent material. This complex underlies the principal deposits at Mayapan, but has not there been associated with architecture or found in pure samples. At least at Dzibilchaltun, this unique architecture and pottery form a clear chronological phase which must be allotted its span of absolute time in the cultural framework of the area.

The terminal phase of civilization in the Maya Lowlands, the Decadent Period, is that of the supposed hegemony of the Cocom dynasty at Mayapan. Most students agree that this began at approximately A.D. 1250. It was marked by a reversion to most of the technics of the Early Period. In architecture concrete-veneer construction vanished completely, to be replaced by the older block wall and corbeled vault. The elaborate carved-stone facades of the Florescent were replaced by decorations in carved stucco. Maya hieroglyphic writing, which had disappeared during the Florescent, returned to use. Finally, the slatewares characterizing both phases of the Florescent disappeared to be replaced by what Vaillant described as "lacquer" wares, more reminiscent of Early Period pottery. I suggested in 1961 (Andrews 1961 : 124) that this revival of pre-Florescent Maya culture probably drew on a reservoir of still existing early tradition on the Caribbean coast of Quintana Roo, which had not been disturbed by the Florescent intrusion into the western half of the peninsula. The heavily forested Caribbean coast from British Honduras to Cabo Catoche maintained an uninterrupted course of development from Formative times until at least shortly before the Conquest. The density of population must have been considerable, and the continuum of culture was notably unaffected by any of the factors discussed at such length at this symposium. There is reason to believe that the hallmarks of post-Florescent culture in Yucatan actually originated much earlier on the Caribbean littoral.

The thirteenth century "renaissance" in Yucatan was only partially successful. The glories of the Early and Florescent periods were never recreated. In all fields of endeavor, products of the artisan were vastly inferior to those of the past which he imitated. The word "decadent" is not an exaggeration. I would be most hesitant, however, to apply the word "collapse" or "post-collapse" to the culture phase. Mayapan was one of the larger cities built by the Maya, dotted with a surprising abundance of major monuments and ceremonial structures. Rulers of the city seem to have succeeded in maintaining tight political control over the northern part of the peninsula for a period of approximately two centuries, a feat perhaps unmatched in the peninsula's past. As happened in the Valley of Mexico and elsewhere, there was an aesthetic decline, accompanied by military and political expansion.

In 1441, a coalition of oppressed Mayas revolted against their masters and permanently destroyed the capital city of Mayapan. In the short period before the arrival of the Spanish, social anarchy seems to have been the rule, abetted by natural catastrophes and (soon after the first Spaniards were shipwrecked in the New World) by devastating epidemics of European disease. Any proper recovery from the 1441 revolution was effectively blocked by Spanish conquest. It should be noted in this context, however, that the first two Spanish expeditions to Mayaland were overwhelmingly defeated and many of their leaders killed or wounded. Hernández de Córdoba, leader of the first expedition, died of his wounds. Cortés conquered central Mexico in a few years with a handful of men. But the Mayas were not as effete as the Aztecs; it took three decades for the Spaniards to secure a permanent foothold on the peninsula. Three violent revolutions in the 1500s almost dislodged them in the early days. The entire peninsula rebelled under Jacinto Canek in 1761, slaughtering thousands. And in 1847–48, the irate Maya in the War of the Castes came within a hair's breadth of killing every Spaniard and *mestizo* in the Maya Lowlands. After this, despite repeated military efforts, the Maya maintained general control of the eastern portion of the peninsula until well into the 1920s.

SUMMARY

In the pages above, I have tried to demonstrate that when the great cities of the Southern Maya Lowlands collapsed at or about the start of Cycle 10 in the Maya calendar, no such thing happened to Maya civilization as a whole. It not only survived the southern disintegration but continued for at least several centuries before it reached its peak and entered into a process of aesthetic and intellectual decline. Probably more great Maya cities were built in the Central and Northern Lowlands after the collapse of the Peten area than had ever been built before, which bespeaks not only the survival and improvement of culture but a vastly greater and more effective utilization of the agricultural sustaining area on which they depended. The architecture of the Florescent cities, lacking perhaps a certain grandeur in aesthetic perspective, achieved a structural perfection previously unknown elsewhere in the New World.

After the demise of the Florescent tradition, which I would place in the eleventh century, a process of decline did begin. Aesthetics seem to have gradually become secondary to sociopolitical developments and suffered in the process. But as late as the middle of the fifteenth century, Maya civilization was still an extant entity. Any arbitrary date for its collapse after the fall of Mayapan would be relativistic and unwise.

Much of the reasoning above is postulated on the assumption that the Early and Florescent periods are valid chronological horizons. As far as I am aware, all existing archaeological evidence confirms this interpretation. In the far south, few data on this period exist. I think most students (very much including myself) have been influenced in our thinking by the fact that the chronological scheme forces a more than awkward plethora of cultural events into the relatively brief span of time allowed by an 11.16.0.0.0 correlation between the end of the Maya Initial Series and the foundation of Mayapan about A.D. 1250 in the Christian calendar.[5]

In introductory chapters 2 and 3, Adams and Sabloff have capably summarized and examined the quite numerous hypotheses that have been set forth to explain the abandonment of the far southern Maya cities and the heavy depopulation of the area around them. I agree that no solution acceptable to the majority of students has yet appeared. I also agree that probably more than one and perhaps several contributing factors will have to be combined in reaching a satisfactory explanation. I suggest that if Maya civilization continued to flower in the Central and Northern Lowlands, after it became virtually extinct in the south, these areas should form the ideal testing ground for hypotheses regarding collapse in the south. If any given set of conditions acted as determinant in one section of the lowlands, why did it fail to do so elsewhere? Reviewing Adams's careful list, I am impressed by the fact that very few of the ten principal theories were determinants in the north. I will briefly scan Adams's list. My remarks will seem haphazard, as I do not wish to undertake a formal review of the many factors which have been considered in much greater detail by others in this volume. I will limit myself to observations where evidence from the Central and Northern Maya areas may be pertinent.

Ecology

Much still remains to be learned about the archaeobotany and archaeometeorology of the Maya Lowlands. The situation is further complicated by the fact that the two are intimately related. In a porous limestone area such as the peninsula, major deforestation will usually result in the loss of surface soil and consequently a loss of the moisture retention ability of the zone. Where the critical rains are of cumulus origin, deforestation can and frequently does result in a marked decrease in rainfall. After deforestation for any considerable period, five hundred or more years are required to reestablish the soil and weather conditions necessary for a climax forest. The Southern Lowlands have been almost abandoned for that long, so that we cannot be sure that the high tropical forest of today is anything like the environment of Classic times. Conversely, the entire northern peninsula may have been covered by high forest until population density and consequent land usage reached a critical point. It is hoped that palynological studies, now well under way, may provide the answer to these problems of ecological differentiation. Pending this time, three observations seem pertinent:

1. The present Southern Lowlands, which were abandoned, now possess a depth and fertility of soil and abundance of rainfall vastly superior to the permanently and successfully occupied lands to the north. Farmers, who have been moving in increasing numbers from the semi-arid north to the fringes of the Peten in the south, have found that their crop yields, in terms of labor invested, have more than doubled. Apparently, some ecological factor other than land fertility and usability must be found to explain the abandonment of the southern area, unless soil exhaustion reached extremes far beyond that which the larger population of the Northern Lowlands easily survived. No such evidence exists to date.

2. Although the northern and southern extremes of the peninsula are now very separate ecological zones, the environment in the Rio Bec

area and that of the northern Peten (only 50 miles to the south) are virtually identical. While the southern cities were largely abandoned, the very dense populations of the Rio Bec continued successfully and productively for a number of centuries. Here again, some determinant other than simple ecology seems necessary.

3. When considering ecology as a possible factor in depopulation, we must remember that although civilization continued to evolve in the Central and Northern Lowlands after virtual abandonment of the south, parts of both the former areas were also depopulated at a much later date but well before the Spanish Conquest. The very numerous, large cities of the Puuc hills were abandoned as centers of civilization at the end of the Pure Florescent Period. In the central area, major monumental activity apparently ceased at about the same time at many of the larger sites like Becan. Ceramic evidence, however, indicates that a considerable population remained through the Modified Florescent. No Decadent Period pottery has yet been identified from Becan. However, at the site of El Chorro, approximately 10 miles southeast, a large broken stela was reerected on a rectangular platform clearly built in Decadent times. And a city centering around a ceremonial plaza ringed by vaulted or concrete roofed structures was built on the large island in the center of Lake Cilvituk in this period (Andrews 1943 : 36–44).

Catastrophism

I agree with Adams that earthquakes could hardly have been responsible for the depopulation of the entire arc stretching from Belize across the central Peten and then down the Pasion and Usumacinta drainages. Farther from the seismic epicenters, earthquakes do occur in Yucatan but have never been recorded of an intensity that could cause any damage. I think this possible factor can be dismissed.

I feel much the same about hurricanes, even though they did and do occur frequently in the lowlands. They might have caused sufficient damage to disorganize life at one or more ancient sites, but could not have had this effect on the area as a whole. Most (but not all) hurricanes that affect the peninsula originate in the Caribbean and move to the northwest across the land mass. They are usually weakened to insignificant tropical storms if they have not dissipated completely before passing over half the peninsula. They were obviously not a deterrent to continuing civilization in the Central and Northern Lowlands, and I doubt that they were in the south. It is noteworthy that the zone of the peninsula which is hardest hit by these storms, the East Coast, survived nicely from Formative times to the Spanish Conquest. Even after the great hurricanes which recently destroyed Belize and Chetumal, despite energetic government efforts to move these capitals to safer locations, the surviving populations in both cases immediately returned to rebuild their flimsy houses on the same spots.

Perhaps locust infestations and corn blights have been underestimated among the natural catastrophes confronting a dense population. Locust infestations are known to have had devastating effects in the northern area both before and after the Spanish Conquest. Leaf blight, such as that affecting the United States corn belt at present, will probably be remedied by modern laboratory techniques. It could have been, however, completely disastrous in an ancient agronomic society. Neither of these plagues would leave any archaeological evidence.

Disease

When I first worked in southern Campeche in the late thirties, the area was practically unpopulated because of disease, principally malaria. *Milperos* had entered the zone and, because of the exceptional fertility of the soil, could produce enough within three or four years to retire permanently in Ciudad Carmen or Campeche. Few did, because totally endemic malaria allowed no such life expectancy for these pioneers. The same area in 1970 is as healthy as an American country club, and the new pioneers are arriving in increasing quantity to enjoy the agronomic benefits which were so expensive a generation before. Disease is thus an obvious determinant of population and exploitation of these areas. But the very diseases which rendered these territories uninhabitable until a short time ago seem to have been brought in, as far as we know, by the Spanish conquerors. Smallpox, yellow fever, malaria, measles, and other lethal infections killed the majority of the population in the short time after the Conquest, notably in the heavily populated northeastern corner of Yucatan, which still remains completely abandoned. The demographic impact of these imported ailments to which the aboriginal population had achieved no immunity was catastrophic. However, every known aspect seems ascribable to

Old World origin, and there is no evidence of epidemic or plague in pre-Columbian times. Given the lack of any positive evidence, I would be most reluctant to accept postulations that a small part, but not all, of the Maya Lowlands collapsed through the introduction of communicable disease in a period when we know that cultural and economic relations between the north and the south were particularly intensive.

Evolution and Demography

It seems to me that these processes, if responsible factors, are closely linked. It is difficult to understand why they should cause the collapse of Tikal, Uaxactun, and neighboring cities and not affect the Rio Bec sites 60 miles to the north, where environment and rainfall are nearly identical. We have little reason to believe that the agronomic potential of the Peten was not superior to that of the Northern Lowlands, as it is today. Nevertheless, settlement pattern studies in the north, particularly at Dzibilchaltun in the late Early Period and Pure Florescent, and Mayapan in the Decadent, indicate population estimates much higher than any which have been postulated in the south.

There has been no indication that overpopulation beyond the sustaining potential of the surrounding country was a disintegrating factor in Maya culture. Helmuth Wagner (1969) has recently presented a thoughtful analysis of subsistence potential and its relation to the population density of the Maya. An interesting sidelight which he brought up is the possibility that in large parts of the lowlands swidden agriculture might not have been practicable until the introduction of the machete. In today's *milpas*, weed growth, which can be removed effectively only by hand, increases rapidly to the point where it becomes more feasible to clear new forested land with a machete. With pre-Columbian techniques of cutting and felling, however, the balance of effort was probably very different.

Sociopolitical Structures and Military Conquest

Evidence from the Northern Lowlands seems to negate all of the environmental factors discussed above, as determinants per se in the orderly development of Maya civilization. This civilization obviously waxed and waned during its long evolution, and geographic changes in focus are very clear. It therefore becomes necessary to search within the organics of the culture itself for the causes of the phenomena we are discussing. As civilization becomes more complex, it becomes more vulnerable—as we are discovering to our increasing horror in recent years. As solitary farming groups aggregate into larger interdependent units, the problems of maintenance and unity increase geometrically. Eric Thompson has long championed, as a determining factor of local collapse, disintegration of the ruling entities responsible for the guidance and control of individuals who in the formation of an increasingly complex society had largely lost the ability to act for themselves.

In contrast to environmental factors, which in the preceding discussions were demonstrated to have failed as determinants in cultural change in the Central and Northern Maya areas, sociopolitical change obviously was present and obviously played a decisive role in at least the second half of the development and the decline of Maya civilization. As we progress from simple archaeology into the realm of tradition and then into recorded history, the preeminence of these processes becomes increasingly apparent. Within this complex of disruptive factors, it will be some time before we can confidently discriminate between internal developments (religious change, dynastic failure, or more simple sociological adjustments to environmental stress) and the impact of external influence (intensive foreign cultural contact, military invasion, or actual ethnic shift). Thompson (1970) has thoughtfully and thoroughly evaluated these various alternatives.

The fact that the fabulous cities of the Puuc area were totally and finally abandoned at the very time of the emergence of the Toltec hegemony over the northwestern peninsula can hardly be considered coincidental. Water supply must have been extremely critical in their existence. The sparse present population depends entirely on very deep water caves (Andrews 1965c) and on water laboriously carried on human backs for twenty kilometers or more during the dry season. In ancient times the much greater population must have relied on the innumerable *chultuns*, which were the terminal storage points of water meticulously channeled from buildings and plaza areas in the ceremonial centers. A breakdown in maintenance and control of these water collection systems by elimination of the ruling groups could easily have led to abandonment of the centers themselves and major depopulation of the relatively rich sustaining areas surrounding them. Only modern well-digging and irrigation have enabled the reentry of considerable groups to the area. Thus a combination of sociopolitical and ecological factors, as Thompson carefully pointed out, can vitally affect human geography, even when neither in itself would have been a determinant.

Possibly but not demonstrably, ethnic shift may have played a major role in the subsequent history of Yucatan. Changes in the ruling classes certainly did. The Toltecs were either expelled or assimilated. And the final phase of Maya culture, radically different from that of the preceding era, clearly evolved under the overlordship of local dynasties, such as the Cocoms.

In summary, we find that in the Central and Northern Maya areas, purely environmental conditions seem to have played at best a secondary role to organic changes within the civilization itself. We also find that although collapse of the civilization as a whole never occurred, processes of gradual decline did make it more vulnerable to the calamities resulting from the arrival of the Spaniards in the New World.

NOTES

1. For the purposes of this chapter, Andrews uses a different subdivision of the Maya Lowlands than is used in other chapters. He uses the term "Southern Lowlands" in the same manner that it is used in chapter 1 and as do other authors, but subdivides what is elsewhere lumped as the Northern Lowlands into two regions, the "Central Lowlands" and "Northern Lowlands." Andrews's "Central Lowlands" includes the Rio Bec and Chenes zones mentioned in chapter 1 (see p. 11 and Fig. 1), and his "Northern Lowlands" includes all other zones north of the southern sector. A division such as this has important implications for architectural styles, a subject which only Andrews explores in detail. (Editor's note.)

2. Andrews allows here the possibility of either a 12.9.0.0.0 or an 11.16.0.0.0 correlation of the Maya and Christian calendars. See chapter 1, p. 15. (Editor's note.)

3. For a discussion of the correlation of periods in the Northern and Southern sectors of the Maya Lowlands, see chapter 1, p. 18. (Editor's note.)

4. At Dzibilchaltun, Fine Gray pottery first appears in two lots sealed under the primary floor of one structure (38) securely cross-dated with Tepeu 1. It appears in modest quantities in most lots of Tepeu 2–equivalent date. In the Pure Florescent, it is ever present in abundance—actually third in frequency of all slipped wares—and is extensively copied in wares of local manufacture. It disappears by the end of the Pure Florescent and is absent in the Modified Florescent ("Toltec") and following periods.

Z-type Fine Orange first appears sealed under the primary floor of Structure 4, Early Period, cross-dated as terminal Tepeu 1 or early Tepeu 2. It appears sporadically in late Early Period lots including one tomb (Str. 57), and more frequently in the Pure Florescent, disappearing at the end of the phase. In the Modified Florescent, it is replaced by X-type Fine Orange.

5. The chronological charts on pp. 45, 48, of necessity, present the symposium's views in terms of a single correlation of the Maya and European calendars, the Goodman-Martínez-Hernández-Thompson correlation, placing the Spanish Conquest at 11.16.0.0.0 in the Maya long count. A graphic presentation of the findings in so many subregions of the Maya Lowlands in terms of more than one correlation would be of such complex format as to be hardly usable. As this section aligns cultural events in the central and northern areas in a manner almost incompatible with the format chosen (too many events would lie above the top or below the bottom of the charts), I have suggested that these areas not be included. A simplified chart showing alternate cultural alignments of the northern and southern areas under 11.16.0.0.0 and 12.9.0.0.0 correlations has been published in a variety of journals (Andrews 1960, 1965a, 1965c, 1968) and should be readily available to most readers.

For obvious reasons the correlation problem, although germane to the topic of the present symposium, has been studiously avoided. I have pointed out that the cultural alignments suggested herein are difficult to accommodate within the framework of an 11.16.0.0.0 correlation, but fit comfortably within the exigencies of an earlier equation. And I believe they more than justify keeping the question an open one. However, no other day-by-day correlation currently exists complying as successfully as the 11.16.0.0.0 equation with the multiple requirements of epigraphic, astronomic, and ethnohistoric evidence.

Most ambiguously (and most unhappily for scientists in the many other fields where time is studied), this correlation has recently been labeled with the thoroughly preempted tag "GMT." It is hoped that this academic provincialism will not endure.

PART III

Approaches of Interpretation

13
Models for the Downfall: Some Ecological and Culture -Historical Considerations

DEMITRI B. SHIMKIN

*Center for Advanced Studies
in the Behavioral Sciences*

The deliberations and the research generated by the present study of the Maya downfall are important for the entire discipline of anthropology. If they are successful, levels of hypothesis formation, measurement, and proof may be developed which will establish correlated time-space sequences of patterns accounting for a large part of a defined set of changes in the size, distribution, and activities of a human population. This undertaking thus strives for basic advances in both concepts and techniques.

At the same time, this volume appears to be timely. Even a limited acquaintance with the relevant literature discloses the presence of much well-conceived and carefully executed research. And far more is clearly extant in other publications and in studies in manuscript and in progress. The contributions of a nonspecialist may perhaps act largely to stimulate the specialists to make explicit much of what is known informally, and to aid them in the translation of this knowledge into terms meaningful for anthropology as a whole. A human ecologist and Old World culture historian may also be useful in reminding specialists of the nature and requirements of ecological models, in reacting to data on possible system-perturbing variables ("causes"), and in suggesting and describing briefly a number of general and partial analogues to the Maya decline in Old World culture history.

NATURE, USES, AND DATA REQUIREMENTS OF ECOLOGICAL MODELS

It may be well to begin at a basic level; in this way, others can better evaluate the assumptions and logic on which my observations rest.

Following Carnap (1939 : esp. 56–69) I regard scientific propositions as specialized logical texts which link uniquely defined and observationally retrievable classes—operands (for example, male and female) and operators (coition) to yield transforms (in this case, children). These texts follow a rigorously defined sequential translation procedure—from statements in natural language, to those in symbolic language, and then in number language—gaining generality but losing precision (and its reciprocal, information) with each step. Number-language statements are then matched against models of anticipated relations to yield results retranslatable into natural languages. For instance, the deviation of observed linkages from a chosen random model is the test of "significance."

All scientific propositions, in common with all other logical models, necessarily encompass internally unprovable assumptions (Nagel and Newman 1958). Moreover, even the relations between the same statistics mapped on the same field may be transformed by the nature of the mathematical operation undertaken or by the absence or presence of added signification. For example, if the two series: 2, 4, 8, 16, 32, 64, . . . and 3, 9, 27, 81, 243, 729 . . . are related arithmetically, they are divergent; as logarithms, they are parallel; as powers, identical. Again, such a relationship as that between value added in manufacturing and the annual tonnage of freight transportation, by city in the United States, is at first sight purely random. However, if each city is labeled and if the relationship for each city is followed over time, the system is transformed into a rather stable lattice, which then becomes a set of coefficients once the city's mix of manufacturing output has been defined.

The multiplicity of solutions applies in another way. At one level, it is proper to speak of *Pasteurella pestis* as the cause of plague, or coition as the necessary precursor of children. At another, it may be critically important to expand the model, including, say, the concepts of reservoir, vector, and immunity, or those of oestrous cycle, sperm motility, pH, and artificial insemination. One type of solution defines limiting conditions without which a phenomenon cannot (or does not naturally) occur. The other specifies the set of relationships, the mechanics, of its generation (and potential manipulation or control).

Above all, it must be stressed that the acceptability of a model does not disprove the possibility of an indefinite series of other models, excepting only for its exact negative. The choice when more than one model fits may be one of elegance, level of analysis, or practicality.

The last is particularly crucial in the biosocial realm wherein needed observations are often numerous, costly, and imprecise. For example, the variety and number of actors, links, and transactions in any but the most trivial ecological, social, or economic networks is so great as to be testable only by successively more sophisticated sampling which progressively reduces discrepancies between independently measured control parameters and those derived from expanding sample results. For example, the energy structure of an ecosystem can be approximated from data on photosynthesis by the floral dominant, the conversion efficiencies of the major consumers at each trophic level, and the annual input of solar energy to the locality in question. However, high maturity, with much recycling by microbial transformers would raise expected values, while specific deficiencies or toxicities could lower them greatly (Odum 1969). In any case, the model used would be a vast simplification of reality.

The imprecision of biosocial data vastly favors linear or lattice models over higher order formulations. This may often require breaking processes into rather artificial segments and the introduction of dummy analytical sectors and coefficients. The last are particularly characteristic of econometric models, for example, "rest of the world" sectors.

With these cautions in mind, a review of the basic conceptual tools of the human ecologist—populations, physical systems (including ecosystems, cultural communities, and the epidemiological networks), and games—may now be undertaken.

Populations and, more specifically, sexually reproducing animal populations, have a number of characteristics associated with their behavioral and other self-perpetuating capacities (MacArthur and Connell 1966). They must be heterogeneous in sex; over time, in age; and, inevitably, in genotype. In consequence, they are characterized quantitatively and sometimes qualitatively by varying physiological requirements and capacities. Nutritional needs, physical mobility, and work and reproductive capacities vary with the specific, especially sex-and-age, composition of a population. Complementarities in capacity and, conversely, competitions for the same goals generate movements and transactions essential to the maintenance of the population. These are highly regulated in almost all animal species, with the end results both of limiting intrapopulation conflicts and of creating reserves of individuals available to replace losses, for example, in relation to breeding (Wynne-Edwards 1965). Variability, cooperation, and competition generate, in conjunction with variations in the habitat, differing patterns of time-space occupancy for the population. In general terms, this may be defined by Shelford's law, which analyzes habitat-occupancy patterns as the resultants of two opposing flows: movements out to the limit of tolerance by marginal indiviuals, and movements into the population preferendum by those dominant (Kendeigh 1961 : 10–12). For animals, the limits of tolerance are generally set by limits in food supply and in disease resistance.

All of these characteristics are rigorously applicable to man. They define, in great part, the needs and cultural capacities of particular populations. At the same time, man manipulates these characteristics extensively, through differential migration, sexual taboos and preferential matings, polygyny, and other mechanisms. These, in turn, have consequences which may be unperceived, let alone controlled, by man. The residence of women and children in small, poorly heated huts apart from the warmer, ever-smoky, and less insect-infested men's houses can result in differential exposures to disease with widespread effects on survival. Organized warfare can, as a by-product, break up polygyny, premarital segregation, and other devices limiting reproduction and hybridization. The out-migration of young men for war or work can, conversely, place heavy work burdens on women and consequent increases in abortions and infant mortality in the communities of origin.

In general, populations are specific types of a more general model which has been developed in operations research, the *physical system* (Wilson and Wilson 1965). This system is an organization of energy and materials which generates a specified output, say, people or monuments, plus an assortment of waste energy (heat) and materials (detritus). Its organizational features must include mechanisms of sensing, the control of flows, and the correction of system disbalances. Physical systems vary in their outputs and in a number of structural and operating characteristics. Among these are differing input/output ratios; for example, an open fire has a thermal efficiency, depending on the heat of the process, of 3 percent to 10 percent; at the same heats, the thermal efficiency of an oven, like the Chinese *k'ang*, runs from 30 percent to 50 percent of the energy input. The resource allocation systems may be automatic (for example, food distribution in many hunting bands), conditional (marketplaces) or randomized (gambling). Each system has corresponding properties: automatic allocations maximize the stability of operations under constant conditions; conditional allocations are the most efficient; and randomized operations are optimal under conditions of high uncertainty. Another characteristic is the degree of heat and waste recycling; the reusability of scrap copper and bronze, for example, presents possibilities of recovery and even new and different production hitherto absent with stone. Hence, while a given input of stone generates a constant stock with a growing inventory of detritus, metal use at equivalent inputs produces growing inventories of tools and ornaments and limited waste.[1] Finally, system controls tend toward one of two effective patterns—self-stabilization by way of feedbacks of information and of reserves of energy and materials, or self-stabilization through the discharge of the overload and the return to minimal functioning levels (as in the physiological defense of sleep).

Ecosystems are physical systems with a variety of specific properties (Odum 1969). Among these are characteristic bioenergetics, including fixed hierarchies of energy use and relative biomass, structural histories moving from less to greater diversity, and from greater to less bioproductivity, and so on. Many of these features apply also to the cultural communities of man, the total population-activity capacities of which are ultimately bounded by available energy. But human society, being within one species, has more interchangeability and, hence, more information than multispecies communities of the same complexity. It is far more effective as a handler of information, both through the special properties of the speech event and through the economical reinforcements gained by mechanical code storage, as by writing. With fire, cooking, and other devices, man has expanded his access to energy and materials; hence, the limitations of trophic levels are applicable to human societies only in modified form. Moreover, behavioral shifts in man, and their biological feedbacks (such as changes in reproduction rates), are far more extensive than in any other species (Center for Human Ecology 1969 : 56–77). Nevertheless, the characteristics of human populations and of man's relations with the habitat, for instance, via food and disease, are ubiquitous factors in all cultures.

Epidemiological networks and the closely allied *models of communications events* (Macdonald 1961; Shannon and Weaver 1949) present physical systems from the standpoint of pathways rather than aggregate outputs and organization. Both epidemiological and communications models are concerned with the movement and effects of a quantum (a disease vector or a message) transiting from one population to another. Essential components are the probability of conjunction of the two populations, the probability and effectiveness of the transmittal, and the susceptibility of the receiver, in each case. The elegance of the approach rests in its capacity for successively deeper analysis, since related conditions, for instance, the probability of particular behavior by a female mosquito, or dampening "noises," can be incorporated as they are determined.

Since epidemiology and communications events are bounded by real space-time, they can also be formulated as Markov chains. This formulation permits in turn the conduct of simulations to test the absolute limits of a system—when processes become extinct or when they become pandemic. Probabilistic simulations, so-called Monte Carlo techniques, are powerful means of testing the variabilities of systems and the consequences of perturbations upon them. They permit many operations not susceptible to determinate analysis, for example, the handling of dynamic equilibria and disequilibria such as those implicit in the Maya collapse.

Generalized game theory moves the analysis of events from the levels of structure and pathway to the levels of group and individual strategies. John Von Neumann's seminal insight (Von Neumann and Morgenstern 1947), that the maximization of return and the maximization of security are alternative solutions for virtually all systems, opened a new prospect for ethological and cultural theory (Shimkin 1966). Within a given inventory of resources, either accomplishment or the probability of survival can be maximized, but almost never both at once. Moreover, risks often threaten irretrievable disaster while accomplishments may have only remote, symbolic rewards. Thus the poor are prone to security maximizing while elites are more prone to seek maximum returns. Indeed, entire cultures, such as traditional India versus Imperial China, may be contrasted in this way. Cultural values may have truly profound ecological consequences.

In summary, the human ecologist has available today a considerable armament of theory. The pages below will indicate some applications of this armament to the problem of the Maya decline. They will consider potential elements for model building, based on internal and comparative data, and then formulate some suggestions for research design.

THE INFLUENCE OF SELECTED VARIABLES: A PRELIMINARY REVIEW

Inferences from general ecological models, comparative data, and a limited examination of the literature on Central America suggest six groups of variables likely to be the most significant in the temporal and regional growth, decline, and success or failure of recuperation of Maya Lowland culture. These are physical-resource balances (especially food, water, and fuel supplies) related to population; disease burdens; population dynamics and structure; labor supply and its allocation; systems and goals of social regulation; and resource accretions or losses from outside areas.

Physical-resource Balances

Despite several useful publications, the present level of study and analysis of the agricultural potential of the Maya Lowlands remains definitely inadequate. The need for better determinations of local variations and, probably, of varying patterns of secular changes must be stressed.

For example, the great variability in annual precipitation—114 inches in Pureto Barrios, Guatemala, and 35 inches at Campeche, on the Gulf of Mexico (Rumney 1968 : 511, 519)—reflects an even higher variability in the probability and duration of dry periods and in the intensity of annual evapo-transpiration. These factors in turn govern the possibility and consequences of slash-and-burn agriculture, which is most precarious wherever heavy, frequent precipitation inhibits burning, endangers the maturation of maize, and intensifies leaching and the probability of plant diseases. Cowgill and Hutchinson's pioneering study (1963a : esp.282) suggests a moderate reduction of rainfall and hence more favorable conditions for slash-and-burn cultivation relative to the present, in the vicinity of Tikal, in the "later Classic and Post Classic." Conversely, this reduction would have been deleterious to root agriculture and swampland harvesting. Validations of the Cowgill-Hutchinson finding and determinations of the spatial extent of this shift are much needed. A possibility exists that the changes at Tikal reflect shifts in hurricane tracks and are parts of much larger air-mass movements evident in the American Southwest where "diminishing alluviation toward the end of this period [A.D. 700–1200] probably reflects progressively drier conditions, higher temperatures and consequent privation" (Malde 1964 : 128; also Vivo Escoto 1964 : esp. 194–96).

Stevens (1964) has recently reviewed the soils of the area; the very different properties generated by different parent material—silaceous or limestone—and by secondary processes—alluvial or subaqueous—yield differing environments for maize, root crops, and tree crops and have different responses to slash-and-burn agriculture. These facts, the climatic variability alluded to earlier, and the degree of sophistication in agricultural practices revealed by Reina's (1967) study of the Lake Peten–Itza *milperos* give strong grounds for attributing to the Maya substantial variability and perhaps historic changes in agricultural practices. Bronson's (1966) suggestions that root crops, the sweet potato and manioc, especially, were formerly of basic importance for the meeting of caloric needs appear highly meritorious. Wagner advances, in addition, evidence of far more horticulture formerly than appears characteristic today (judging from Reina's data): "Some trees, particularly the useful breadnut (*Brosimum utile*, cluster on ancient Maya sites. The sapodilla (*Achras sapota*) of which some individuals are as much as 1,000 years old, was apparently dispersed with the help of man" (1964 : 230–32).

The Book of Chilam Balam contains, moreover, intriguing references to field measurement, which is certainly indicative of practices quite different from contemporary *milpa* agriculture: "It was Ah Ppizte who measured their land. But Lubte was the land where they rested, there were seven leagues of land. Ah May it was who fixed the corners of the land, he who set the corners in their places; the sweeper who swept the land was Mizcit Ahau" (Roys 1967 : 65, 74). Note also the position advanced by Palerm and Wolf: "We can find no solid reasons for the assumption that slash-and-burn agriculture was the only or even the major technique employed [by the Classic Lowland Maya] (1957 : esp. 28–29). They suggest also the possibility of an earlier system of cultivation of swamplands, like the highland *chinampas*.

Comparative data suggest, in addition, that changes in agricultural techniques may be critical factors in the replacement of civilizations, as in the case of the vast innovations in northern Europe between A.D. 550 and A.D. 900 (White 1963). These changes would not necessarily involve an increase in the total productivity of either the land or the worker; on the contrary, they might merely make more feasible the survival of small groups escaping from the oppressions of a slave society in sufficient numbers to change slow population growth into rapid decline.

Two other factors, shortages of household fuel and of sources of animal protein, might also have been significant in promoting the rise of today's highly dispersed pattern of resource use. At its peak, Maya civilization generated a significant demand for fuel for pottery and plaster (lime) manufacture. This demand would have been relatively high because of the apparent absence of thermally efficient furnaces or ovens. It probably preempted the best, most readily available timber and placed considerable burdens on household economies, both in gathering and transporting fuel and in fuel use by commoners. Fuel shortages could well have been factors in increasing the probabilities of both respiratory diseases (major scourges of the wet tropics, especially because of sharp nighttime drops in temperature) and gastrointestinal diseases (because of less adequate cooking). The search for easily available fuel, particularly in the wettest regions, would tend to eliminate stalks and brush, which in turn would reduce fodder for animals and shelter for birds.[2]

It is certain from comparative analysis and work on contemporary Maya (see "Disease Burdens" this chapter, pp. 279–84) that the supply of animal protein must be viewed as a critical factor historically. For this reason, both direct evidence from animal (including fish and bird) remains and data bearing on hydrographic history need much attention. I submit that Cowgill and Hutchinson's (1963a) conclusion that bog development at Tikal long preceded Maya culture requires much testing, especially in the hydrologically more active basins of the Rio San Pedro and Rio Usumacinta (Tamayo and West 1964). Moreover, changes profoundly affecting the bioproductivity of bogs may be associated with shifts from variable to constant water levels alone. As Odum states:

> It is strange that man does not readily recognize the importance of recurrent changes in water level in the natural situation such as the Everglades when similar pulses are the basis for some of his most enduring food culture systems. Alternate filling and draining of ponds has been a standard procedure in fish culture for centuries in Europe and the Orient. The flooding, draining, and soil-aeration procedure in rice culture is another example. The rice paddy is thus the cultivated analogue of the natural marsh or the intertidal ecosystem (1969 : 268).

In sum, it is my impression that much needs to be done, as yet, to develop plausible qualitative descriptions of Maya food production, including allied questions such as those of fuel procurement and water management. Quantitative measures of yield, by crop and per worker, need then to be estimated, with particular attention to variability. This is because the absence of efficient converters of root crops into animal protein, such as pigs, would limit effective carry-overs; at the same time, significant carry-over needs for seed would be an important factor limiting maize output, especially during periods of low yield; the centralized storage and distribution of maize seed would, in turn, be an important element of political power.[3] Thus a very considerable amount of research is needed to define primary industries and associated physical-resource balances in the ancient Maya economy. This information would, in turn, have important consequences for the more general models of Maya culture. Such research can be done by the study of modern conditions and practices, adjusted by representative information on the soils, hydrography, and botany of the past.

Disease Burdens

The importance of infectious diseases and malnutrition as potential factors in the Maya downfall has, in my opinion, been improperly minimized by archaeologists. Specifically, endemic infections of American trypanosomiasis (Chagas' disease), of the Ascaris worm, and of weanling diarrhea would be associated with increasing population densities and residential stabilities. They would intensify the effects of animal protein deficiencies and be intensified by them, with specially deleterious effects on infant and maternal survival and on adult work capacity. In addition, yellow fever, with permanent reservoirs in the monkey populations, cannot be dismissed as a possible periodic scourge which would be especially perilous to men penetrating or destroying the rain forest environment.

Chagas' disease is the consequence of infection by the protozoan, *Trypanosoma cruzi*, generally by way of feces deposited in the wake of anesthetized bites (chiefly on exposed regions of the body, especially the ocular conjunctiva, during the night) by assassin bugs (*Triatoma infestans* and others). The assassin bugs draw the infection from wild (swine, fox, bat, rodent, and monkey) and domestic (dog) reservoirs. Quiet, nocturnal arthropods whose bites are not immediately felt, assassin bugs are very difficult to exterminate in native houses with extensive thatching, cracks, and other hiding places. Abandonment or even burning of the structure may be essential.

González-Ángulo and Ryckman report:

Many species of Triatominae are host specific but T. dimidiata maculipennis on the Yucatan Peninsula is general in its feeding habits. This species has been collected in human habitations, chicken houses, caves, stables, and in debris near domestic animals. It occurs most commonly in chicken houses. More bugs were found in human habitations with palm thatched roofs than in houses with other roofing materials, and bug populations were higher in houses in which domestic animals were kept nearby (1967 : 44).

Xenodiagnoses were performed on man and animals in the town of Ticul, Yucatan because 33% of the bugs collected in this community were found to be infected with *Trypanosoma cruzi*. . . . (1967 : 45).

The infection [4] is generally acquired during the first years of life and usually is more severe in children than adults. It leads to a primary complex, of about a month's duration, generally marked by lymphatic inflammation. The chronic stage develops as the parasites move from the blood stream into tissue, especially muscle and glia, cells. The neurotoxic substances released by the parasites at this stage destroy ganglion cells, especially of the heart and all the hollow muscular organs. In experimentally infected rats, 80 percent of the ganglion cells of the heart may be destroyed during the acute phase. Denervation in turn produces generalized degeneration in the affected organs, especially the heart, colon, bronchus, and esophagus (Köberle 1968).

Mortality from Chagas' disease may result from secondary infections but is particularly associated with myocardia. A four-year study of a rural community in Venezuela (Belen) by Puigbó et al. (1968) disclosed a new infection rate of 16.3 percent of the population at risk, covering only those aged 5 and over. Forty-four percent of the population had serologically positive reactions on first examination. Over the four-year period, the study population, 812 persons aged 5 and over, with the median lying between only 17 and 18 years, suffered thirty-two deaths, twenty-two of which were caused by heart failure or were reported as "sudden deaths." In the 35 to 39 age group, seven out of ten deaths were from heart failure and "sudden death." [5]

Once thought to be a rare disease, American trypanosomiasis has been identified throughout the hemisphere from central Argentina to Texas, including specifically the Maya Lowlands. Its incidence has been determined with care in only a few countries. In Argentina, of 3.5 million people at risk in the endemic zones, it was believed that 700,-000 were infected in 1958. In Guatemala in 1959, 6,126 serological examinations disclosed 859 (14.0 percent) positives (National Research Council 1962 : 122–23). Overall, Köberle, the outstanding authority, believes that the World Health Organization's estimate of 7 million infected individuals in the Americas is absolutely minimal (1968 : 63–64).

The roundworm, *Ascaris*, for which the dog is a major host, is less devastating than *Trypanosoma cruzi*, yet of considerable importance in mortality and failures of development among children. It is particularly associated with heavy, wet soils, in which infestations cumulate with long human and dog residence. As Jeliffe reports:

. . . . the roundworm is often an important accessory in the ae-tiology of malnutrition in children, especially in the production of the kwashiorkor-nutritional oedema syndrome. . . . ascariasis is al-most inevitably present by the age of twelve months and it is dur-ing the subsequent few years that the nutritional ill-effects of the parasite are most likely to develop. The reasons for this are: (i) the likelihood of high degrees of infestation, as a result of direct hand-to-mouth infection from playing and crawling on soiled ground; (ii) this is the period of greatest food shortage, the child being between the stage of breast feeding and of sharing the slightly fuller adult diet; (iii) this is a period of very rapid growth, with high requirements of protein and vitamins; (iv) the relative hugeness of the parasite compared with the child; (v) the worms may possibly grow more easily with a low intestinal enzyme con-tent, as may occur at this age, as a result of the pancreatic damage of protein deficiency (1968 : 149).

Chronic parasitic infections and poor nutrition are periodically rein-forced by bacterial (*Shigella* and other) infections to produce acute diarrhea, especially among weanlings aged one to two. Scrimshaw's studies of four Guatemalan villages in 1959–62 (Scrimshaw, Taylor, and Gordon 1968 : 226–29, 240–53) show an attack rate averaging 18 percent for the entire population and a peak of 120 percent, an-nually, for the one-year-olds. For the entire population, diarrhea led to a mortality of 5.4 per 1,000, or 27 percent of the total deaths; for those aged one, the death rate was 35.6 per 1,000, or 41 percent of the total deaths. Among four-year-olds, the diarrheal death rate was substantially less, 9.6 per 1,000, but constituted 35 percent of all mortality. Although the unsanitary disposal of human feces (especially under unfavorable soil and water conditions) is clearly central to the transmission of weanling diarrhea, control measures by Scrimshaw's team, for example, privy construction, proved ineffectual. Seemingly, the distribution of pathogens and their transmission by water, food, rodents, and flies are too extensive for mitigation by partial measures.

Central America is a recognized area of high prevalence of the syndrome known as "protein-calorie malnutrition of early childhood," which includes the severe manifestations of kwashiorkor and nutritional marasmus. The first is an important cause of death; the second, so-called balanced starvation, results in growth retardation and severe wasting of muscle and of subcutaneous fat (Jeliffe 1968 : 114–43). In Guatemala, these deficiencies are associated with weaning which, in some regions, comes later for boys than girls.[6] By two to three years of age, in rural areas, infants subsist primarily on maize and starchy carbohydrates. Meat and eggs are commonly thought to produce digestive upsets in weanlings. Protein, vitamin A, and riboflavin are particularly lacking in the diet (Jeliffe 1968 : 71; Scrimshaw et al. 1969).

Just as the prevalence of serious, endemic diseases associated with sedentary residence suggests an important survival value to a shifting slash-and-burn economy, so the paucity of protein, especially animal protein, appears to have major socioeconomic consequences. Reina has stressed the significance attached by natives of the Lake Peten Itza region to the use of *milpas* as fodder by game: "The daily visits a milpero makes to his milpa are primarily for the purpose of watching for animals. . . . Climatic crises, such as drought, not only result in milpa failure, but also in the disappearance of game from the area. The shortage of food is then accentuated. 'Lack of corn means lack of meat'" (1967 : 16–17).

For all life, according to Liebig's rule, the limiting factor on development, distribution, and numbers is the least favorable one (Kendeigh 1961 : 12). There is perhaps some recognition of this in the pattern and low intensity of *milpa* production reported by Reina: if the meat supply is more constricting than the caloric (maize, manioc, breadnut), additions to the latter are irrational (that is, barring augmentation of protein resources through domestic animals or trade). Moreover, since hunting, forestry, and allied activities are men's work, women have a limited utility. Thus, Cowgill and Hutchinson's data (1963c : esp. 96) indicating recurrent deficits in the numbers of Indian girls, and, hence, at least indirect infanticide, made grim sense. Similar findings are widespread, for example, among Alaskan Athapaskans in 1949 (Shimkin 1955).

In general, the combined evidence on disease and nutrition thus far advanced suggests strong forces leading toward declining and dispersing populations among the Classic Period Maya. These could have been controlled by competent resource management to augment food supplies and to maintain reasonable levels of hygiene. These forces might, however, have been intensified by waves of yellow-fever mortality, especially among men of commoner class.

For many years, yellow fever was thought to be an import from the Old into the New World. However, discovery of an extensive reservoir of yellow fever among South and Central American monkeys (especially the howlers, *Alouatta*) and the transmission of the disease among them by indigenous vectors (the mosquito *Haemogogus spegazzinii* and the vampire bat) proved the contrary (Pavlovsky 1966).

At the same time, the disease in pre-Columbian days would normally have had a limited distribution, primarily among hunters and those clearing mature timber (National Research Council 1962 : 110–13). While some of these persons would die, many would acquire immunity to subsequent attacks. The transfer of the disease by a secondary vector (such as the mosquito, *Aëdes aegypti*) to a larger, nonimmune population would be essential for an epidemic. Two conditions would be needed: the movement of an infected host, say, a male war captive, into a concentration of susceptible townspeople and a cool period that would extend the infective duration of the secondary vector, which is four days at 37°C and eighteen days at 21°C (National Research Council 1962 : 30).

In order to estimate the impact of disease, particularly parasitoses or Chagas' disease synergic with malnutrition, the systematic study of skeletal material attributable to defined periods and areas of Maya archaeology and to different classes is indispensable. With such materials, both gross measurements and microscopic studies of long bones should provide critical data. Some inferences could also be developed from the relative abundance of animal bones.

The Book of Chilam Balam refers, in its traditional sections, to dysentery associated with bad water, and also to the excavation of deep wells (Roys 1967 : 70). It also states that, prior to the Spaniards: "There was then no sickness; they had then no aching bones; they had then no high fever; they had then no smallpox; they had then no abdominal pains; they had then no consumption; they had then no headache" (1967 : 83). This description suggests the late introduction of malaria, as well as smallpox (see also Roys 1967 : 138) and tuberculosis. The prophetic section refers to "such a pestilence that the vultures enter the houses, a time of great death among the wild animals" (1967 : 122). This description is characteristic of a major zoonotic disease, such as yellow fever, in a period of intense upsurge. Another reference is highly suggestive of Chagas' disease: "On this 20th day of January, 1782, there was an epidemic of inflammation here in the town of Chumayel. The swelling began at the neck and then descended. [It spread] from the little ones to the adults, until it swept the house, once it was introduced" (1967 : 143).

This source, the older Maya dictionaries, the inscriptions, and the iconography need careful review for epidemiological clues, in augmentation of the skeletal materials.

Population Dynamics and Structure (Table 3)

In human populations uninfluenced by major migrations and with essentially uncontrolled fertility, mortality rates and patterns are the structural determinants. Even at the same rates, mortality patterns differ substantially in various populations; they reflect specific exposures and practices, at childbirth, for example, which may produce important effects on one sex or a particular cohort. It is for this reason that attempts to develop representative series of sexed and age-estimated skeletal material need special encouragement.

As an interim measure, the population models developed from Arriaga's recent (1968) and careful life-table constructions for Guatemala in 1921 and 1940 may be advanced. These models are, unfortunately, heavily weighted toward the highland population. Given the period, they would also reflect the consequences of appreciable malarial mortality (National Research Council 1962 : 70). In other respects, they may be granted fair validity.

The two models also indicate the effects of general improvements in conditions of the type that might have occurred during the rise of the Classic Period. Nonetheless, they indicate very low life expectancies

TABLE 3
EFFECTS OF CHANGES IN LIFE EXPECTANCY
AT BIRTH UPON A STABLE POPULATION WITH
GUATEMALAN MORTALITY PATTERNS

I. Lower Life Expectancy (e_o, 25.67 years)

Item	Total	Male	Female	Sex Ratio (M/F)
Life expectancy in years at birth (e_o)	25.67	25.29	26.06	—
Age of population in years (%)				
All ages	100.0	100.0	100.0	103.8
0–4	13.0	13.0	13.1	102.9
5–14	20.9	20.9	20.9	103.5
15–44	47.5	48.1	46.8	106.7
15–29	27.1	27.3	26.9	105.4
30–44	20.4	20.7	19.9	108.3
45–59	12.6	12.6	12.7	102.8
60 and over	5.9	5.4	6.4	87.7
Annual birthrate required for replacement (per M)	39.8	—	—	105.7
Annual birthrate required per woman of reproductive age (15–44)				
Annual births (per M)	173	—	—	—
Lifetime births [a]	5.19	—	—	—
Pregnancies [b]	5.97	—	—	—

II. Higher Life Expectancy (e_o, 30.35 years)[c]

Item	Total	Male	Female	Sex Ratio (M/F)
Life expectancy in years at birth (e_o)	30.35	30.25	30.46	—
Age of population in years (%)				
All ages	100.0	100.0	100.0	105.0
0–4	11.8	11.7	11.9	103.1
5–14	19.8	19.7	19.9	104.0
15–44	46.8	47.4	46.2	107.8
15–29	26.2	26.4	26.0	106.4
30–44	20.6	21.0	20.2	109.5
45–59	14.0	14.0	13.9	105.8
60 and over	7.6	7.2	8.1	92.7
Annual birthrate required for replacement (per M)	33.7	—	—	105.7
Annual birthrate required per woman of reproductive age (15–44)				
Annual births (per M)	150	—	—	—
Lifetime births	4.49	—	—	—
Pregnancies	5.16	—	—	—

TABLE 3 (Continued)

III. Transition from Lower to Higher Life Expectancies Via
Natural Growth Rate of 1.10 percent for Fifteen Years

Item Population	Indices of Changes II/I × 100		
	Total	Male	Female
All ages	117.6	118.2	116.9
0–4	106.3	106.5	106.2
5–14	111.4	111.7	111.1
15–44	115.8	116.4	114.7
15–29	113.6	114.1	113.0
30–44	118.8	119.4	118.1
45–59	130.3	132.1	128.4
60 and over	151.2	155.7	147.2
Annual birthrate required for replacement (per M)	84.6	—	—
Annual birthrate required per woman of reproductive age (15–44) (per M)	86.7	—	—

Source: Arriaga (1968 : 131–44) for base data except sex ratio at birth (rural Indian), from Cowgill and Hutchinson (1963c : 93). The data apply to 1921.
ᵃ Annual rate times 30.
ᵇ Births plus 15 percent allowance for spontaneous abortion.
ᶜ Data are for 1940; see also source note, notes a and b.

(which were ubiquitous, outside the Costa Rica, in pre–World War II Latin America) and, consequently, the need for high fertilities to maintain population stability. The 1.10 percent rate of natural increase shown is probably the highest these populations could maintain biologically. Also, it should be noted that, even without institutions of female infanticide or quasi-infanticide through relative neglect,[7] the high mortalities associated with pregnancy, childbirth, and lactation in Guatemala in 1921 and 1940 produced small surpluses of males in the reproductive years, especially in the 30-to-44 age group. Moreover, the effects of population increase with the models used would be to reduce slightly the proportion of those younger than 15 and, hence, to reduce the burden of dependents upon those of working age; a population increase would also raise dramatically the numbers of older men—the leaders and carriers of culture.

Information is badly needed to assess the incidence of polygyny in the archaeological Maya population. The polygynous households of elite, older men would facilitate more widely spaced reproduction and longer nursing, and, hence, greatly reduced childhood mortality. The elite, furthermore, controlled food reserves. "There was only a portion [of what was needed] for them to eat together . . . but there was nowhere from which the quantity needed for existence could come. Compulsion and force were the tidings when he was seated (in authority) . . ." (Roys 1967 : 103). At the same time, the succession of a leader to authority was a period of testing of would-be chiefs, in the wake of which weaker claimants to power were killed (1967 : 88–93). Thompson (1966c : 73) refers also to the segregation of unmarried girls of noble blood as religious attendants. Clearly, the population dynamics of the elite classes were substantially different from those of the commoners who, in addition to shortages of women and food, were evidently subject to the corvée, enslavement, and sacrifice. It is likely, given the modest margins of survival developed in the population models used, that the commoner population had at best sporadic natural growth and was often recruited through slaving expeditions and trade. The concurrent growth of the elite population and increasing economic burdens upon the commoners are plausible hypotheses for the later phases of the Classic Period.[8] Thompson's well-known hypothesis (1966c : 305) of a peasant revolt could be somewhat extended to include prior shortages of labor and sacrificial victims, and perhaps appreciable levels of flight to the forests and peripheral areas. The small proportion of older men—2.5 percent to 3.5 percent of the population—would also mean that irreversible losses of skills could readily develop, especially under conditions of regional fragmentation.

In general, many alternatives of demographic decline can be postulated; the deficits need not have been great to generate cumulative cultural instabilities.

Labor Supplies and Their Allocation

The supply, productivity, and demand for human labor at the climax of Classic Maya civilization are parameters which need careful calculation. It is probable that labor demands substantially exceeded supplies at particular peak periods in the wake of chiefly accessions to power, or of epidemics, and that imbalances in labor demand and supply were important factors in precipitating conflicts that further intensified imbalances. As Erasmus (1968 : 187 ff.) suggests, the Maya did introduce labor-saving simplifications in the later stages of their monument-building history, when warfare and perhaps ideological changes were modifying priorities. Nevertheless, the labor-intensiveness of Maya culture is striking when compared to those of Old World cultures.

I am aware that many writers such as Erasmus (1965) have been optimistic about the availability of labor in the Maya population of society. I feel that there are substantial grounds for a much less sanguine assessment. First, it is important to include allowances for all the major Maya activities—land clearance; agriculture; house, road, and monument construction and maintenance; transportation; handicrafts, including pottery, tool, and cloth manufacturing; food preparation; ceremonial activities, including periods of fasting and passive isolation; education; and so on. Many of these, such as carrying notables in litters, or grinding grain with a quern, were undoubtedly extravagant consumers of labor. Moreover, while many writers minimize the complexity of Maya urbanism, I am impressed by the extensive specialization of structures and, hence, of activities enumerated by Thompson (1966c : 74–75). Sweathouses, reservoirs lined with stone or cement, underground aqueducts and bridges, as well as pyramids, ball courts, and other ceremonial edifices reflect occupational diversities which must be carefully accounted for a labor-force calculations. Backing up all of these, as well as the bureaucracy needed for record keeping and management, there had to be a substantial system of education.

Second, it is essential to consider labor requirements for auxiliary operations, such as carrying food and water for use by the porters or foresters, as well as direct inputs. Thus, harvesting, transporting, and storing maize may require more man-hours than field preparation, planting, and weeding combined (Congolese data, after Gourou 1958 : 71). Third, labor demands are often highly peaked, with intense work needed at a critical period. Reina's account of *milpa* agriculture in the Peten area (1967 : 4–6) stresses the limited duration—a few weeks—suitable each year for burning. Similarly, monument construction must have taken place in episodic bursts; Erasmus's model

(1965) of an essentially continuous effort for 250 years is implausible. Fourth, certain kinds of activities, particularly the maintenance of roads and structures, would be subject to deferral in times of stress. These would present hidden costs, such as those of increased triatomid infestation, or disproportionate efforts, at a later time. Finally, the burden of illness may sometimes have been intense, particularly among poorly nourished slaves. Gourou's example of the impact of severe malaria provides an excellent caution:

> In a period of six months a hundred workmen from a healthy district suffered the following casualties in unhealthy road work in French Indo-China—between 15 and 25 men were eliminated by death or evacuation; those remaining had, owing to temporary indisposition, lost 25 percent of their capacity for work; and the capacity for work of the group had fallen off by 50 percent (1958 : 71).

Systems and Goals of Social Regulation

It is my impression from reading rather variant descriptions of Classic Maya society, for example, Thompson (1966c : 91–100), Proskouriakoff (1960), Erasmus (1968), Willey (1956), and M. Coe (1965b), that the data are not contradictory factually, but indicate rather the different aspects and phases of a complex system with both substantial tensions and binding forces. According to Chinese accounts, supported by much archaeological evidence, the small Tocharian and Iranian states which flourished in A.D. 500–700 in Central Asia (Shimkin 1967) were basically similar. They rested on a pious peasantry which venerated hereditary leaders whose power was magnified through expert management skills and the enforcement of draconic laws, with collective liability, against offenders. Diversified manufacturers, high graphic artistry, and elaborate ceremonialism were maintained by specialists who, in part, circulated from statelet to statelet in search of commissions. Religious knowledge and literary skills were highly esteemed by the aristocracy, which limited internal conflicts by a balance of judicious assassinations, hostages, and marital alliances. These mechanisms and the limited power concentrated in small oases promoted a diffusion of culture within the aristocracy which assumed a cosmopolitan uniformity distinct from the variety of local peasant traditions. The loyalty of the peasants was maintained by religious feeling, ceremonial catharsis, access to kingly justice, and even measures of social security.

These small societies were insufficiently strong to resist great external powers—the Chinese, Uigurs, or Arabs. In part, they absorbed their conquerors; in part, they provided the bases of larger bureaucratized states; and, in part, they were dissipated into the surrounding mass of marginal villagers and nomads whose cultures they substantially enriched.

The importance of changes in values, a hypothesis particularly favored by Erasmus (1968), also finds much support in Old World culture history. The building of prestige structures—pyramids, triumphal arches, stadia, baths, and so on—and the shifts from ceremonial to ascetic expressions of piety have been in major degree the stylistic hallmarks of specific traditions. An excellent case study of such shifts is Bell's (1957) account of the transformations observable in Egypt through the first millenium B.C., from syncretic polytheisms served in varied temples by specialized priesthoods to mass religions of personal salvation with less investment in structures but with far-reaching social innovations, such as the manumission of slave converts. Thus, it is the absence of evidence for alternative resource allocations rather than the abandonment of particular institutions alone that would, in my judgment, indicate cultural decline.

Relations with Outside Areas

Sabloff and Willey (1967) stand on solid comparative ground in giving considerable weight to changes induced by external military intervention. The consequences of lost skills for the maintenance of fragile resource-management systems have been notably evident in the Old World deserts. Adams's (1962) study of the agricultural and population history of southwest Iran discloses, in particular, the shattering impact of the Mongol invasion.

At the same time, it is worth emphasizing that functional supersessions may have equivalent force. The loss of monopoly positions controlling specific prized commodities or the replacement of a general trading or administrative center often brings to a locality the loss of an entire system of associated central-place functions, specialists, and accumulated reserves of working and producing capital. The Roman conquest of Egypt flooded the Mediterranean with cheap grain, to the decisive detriment of such marginal suppliers as the Bosphorus kingdom of the Crimea (Gaydukevich 1949). The impact of transoceanic commerce on the overland caravan cities, of steam power on waterpower, and many other instances can be readily called to mind.

The rise of the Toltec cities and trading classes, and perhaps the replacement of overland by seaborne trade, of lowland by upland cacao, of flint by copper, might have been significant in perpetuating the collapse of Classic Maya civilization. It is not enough to ask why it fell; why it failed to revive is an integral part of the puzzle.

COMPARATIVE EVIDENCE: THE CASE OF ANGKOR

This chapter has cited a number of instances wherein data from other, especially Old World, cultures seemingly throw light upon the problem of Maya decline. In general, the comparative materials are most suggestive in indicating the destructive effects of epidemic and endemic diseases, the extensive consequences of technological and ideological changes, and the dependence of large-scale urbanization upon the central-place functions associated with political and commercial preeminence. They indicate also that critical weakenings in management capacity may, as in the case of Central Asia (Shimkin 1967), long antedate decisive declines in cultural complexity and in population. Capital consumption, living off the accumulations of past agricultural and other resource developments without adequate replacements, may yield enough to maintain an afterglow of culture, as in the case of Timur's Samarkand, long after the basic vitality of the society has vanished. This possibility needs to be examined in the case of Classic Maya culture.

At the same time, it should be submitted that at least one case, that of the civilization of Angkor (present-day Cambodia) between about A.D. 475 and A.D. 1431 (Wales 1965 : 1) exemplifies profound similarities in environment, developmental patterns, and apparent causes of collapse to Maya culture in the Southern Lowlands. A detailed study of this remarkable parallel may yield important clues to recurrent pro-

291

cesses; it would help also to isolate the truly distinctive features of each civilization.

Relevant data bearing on this comparison can be briefly sketched. Both areas are tropical rain forest lowlands drained by a major river system (Usumacinta, Mekong), but with some karst regions lacking surface systems. Both have an important central lake (Peten Itza, Tonle Sap). Both have variable soils, from laterites through rendzinas (calcimorphic) to hydromorphic soils. In both, forestry and slash-and-burn cultivation are important. Finally, both have major disease problems: Chagas' disease, Ascariasis, protein malnutrition, and yellow fever, in one; malaria, hookworm, multiple vitamin deficiencies, and tick- and louse-borne relapsing fevers, in the other (National Research Council 1962).

Yet, certain important differences must also be mentioned. Unlike Lake Peten Itza, which, at least today, is an isolated body, Tonle Sap is essentially a seasonal slough of the Mekong, which deposits great quantities of fish as well as fertilizing silt upon retreat (Wales 1965 : 8). Moreover, while the agricultural practices of the Classic Maya are still uncertain, the florescence at Angkor was definitely based on the storage of monsoon waters in reservoirs and their release to paddy-fields (Hall 1968 : 133–34). Domestic animals, particularly the water buffalo, augmented Angkor's energy resources; metals, apparently imported from other areas, provided reusable tool materials superior to Maya flint and obsidian. And the most devastating disease, malaria, developed to hyperendemic proportions only with the decline of large-scale water management rather than in association with more sedentary life, as is likely with Chagas' disease. The differences cited contributed to a greater intensity and duration of cultural florescence at Angkor than in the Maya Southern Lowlands.

Yet the climax patterns are remarkably alike. Reminiscent of Thompson's (1966c) sketches of the Maya is the description of Angkor Wat:

The central sanctuary, 130 feet high, stands on a square terrace 40 feet high and 750 feet square. At the corners rise four towers connected by galleries and communicating with the central shrine by covered passages. Around this immense central building is a lofty wall of galleries, with towers at its four corners. Beyond this there is a further enclosure measuring 850 by 1000 metres and surrounded by a wall of laterite and sandstone. The whole was surrounded by a moat 200 metres wide enclosing a total area of nearly a square mile (Hall 1968 : 115).

Yet, despite such immense monuments, the population remained dispersed.

The city itself, so far from being an urban agglomeration, was rather a collection of water works stretching far and wide beyond the palace and its immediate temples, with a considerable population densely settled along its causeways and canals, and much of its land cut up into cultivated holdings. In this connection, modern research has established the significant fact that each Khmer king, upon taking office, was expected to carry out works of public interest, particularly works of irrigation before starting upon his own temple-mountain (Hall 1968 : 134).

Esoteric knowledge, descent, and wealth were the foundations of authority and the justifications for lavish expenditures in Angkor, as among the Maya. Thus a noted inscription proclaimed:

Then a Brahman nomad Hiranyadāma, skilled in magic science, came from Janapada because His Majesty had invited him to make a ritual so that this country of Kambuja should be independent of Java and that there should be, in this country, one sole sovereign who should be *cakravartin* [world emperor] (Wales 1965 : 75–76).

In general, in Angkor society at its peak in the tenth century A.D..

The king as head of the state occupied so exalted a position in theory, and was committed to a life involving so much religious ceremonial, that he can have had little, if any, personal contact with his people. As the source of all authority, he was the guardian of law and order, the protector of religion, and the defender of his land against external foes. But he can have performed hardly any administrative functions. These were in the hands of a narrow oligarchy, with the chief offices held by members of the royal family and the great sacerdotal families. They intermarried and formed a class racially different from the rest of the population. But it is noteworthy that although they represented the Hindu tradition, they used Khmer names.

Like the king, only in a smaller way, the magnates erected shrines to their personal cults. The belief was that by erecting an image the "sacred ego" [*linga*] of the person to be worshipped became fixed in the stone, and the shrine would contain an inscription recommending to the founder's descendants the continuance of the cult. When he died it became his tomb. Thus the innumerable statues of Śiva, Vishnu, Harihara, Lakshmi, Parvati and of Bodhisattvas found on temple sites are portraits of kings, queens and magnates, while their names, carved on the statues, show a fusion of their personal titles with the names of gods and goddesses, with whom they are united (Hall 1968 : 108).

The rise and fall of Angkor are compatible with, say, Sabloff and Willey's (1967) reconstruction for the Maya. The culture developed locally, albeit with important influence from the Indo-Chinese state of Funan, on the lower Mekong. Far-flung trade played an important part in the rise of Angkor.

By the thirteenth century, Angkor's resources were being strained:

Thousands of villages were assigned for the upkeep of the great temples, while tens of thousands of officiants and hundreds of dancers were employed in their service, not to mention the army of labourers, masons, sculptors and decorators required for the construction work. Jayavarman VII may have been the greatest of all the Khmer monarchs, and it may be claimed that his reign represented the apogee of Cambodia, but he impoverished his people with heavy taxation and insatiable demands for forced labour and military service (Hall 1968 : 121).

Defeat by the T'ai led to a sudden collapse in both warfare and in monument building. Certain aspects of culture flourished after 1250:

Scholars occupied the first charges of the State; they were on terms of familiarity with kings. Their daughters were queens. They themselves were royal preceptors, grand judges, ministers. There was a "King of Professors" (Hall 1968 : 124).

But even this afterglow was soon undermined by the rise of ascetic Buddhism; in A.D. 1309, Jayavarman VIII abdicated to join a monastery (Hall 1968 : 125). The final abandonment of Angkor took place about

1444, after repeated captures and sackings by the T'ai, and a long, bloody civil war between rival factions of the Cambodian royalty (Hall 1968 : 132). Malarial infestation followed the ruin of the great water-management systems (Gourou 1958 : 8).

PRELIMINARY RECOMMENDATIONS FOR MODEL DESIGN

Let me now attempt to integrate the considerations of ecological theory and method, the review of substantive data on potentially significant factors in the Maya decline, and the comparative evidence into tentative suggestions on models to aid future research on this challenging problem. These suggestions embrace five broad steps: the design of a mechanical generating model for Classic Southern Lowland culture; then, the construction of a similar model for the period of decline; next, the reformulation and linkage of the two models by the use of Monte Carlo methods; fourth, the extension of mechanical model designs back to the Preclassic in the Southern Lowlands, and spatially across to Yucatan, and perhaps the Highland Maya; and fifth, the application of both mechanical and Monte Carlo models to comparative cases, especially the rise and fall of Angkor in Southeast Asia. Each phase of this effort would generate specific data needs for field testing; each new level of model building would both incorporate and refine all underlying models. The effort would constitute a considerable departure from today's anthropological methodology, but would, to the best of my knowledge, require no innovations in either computational hardware or in mathematical programs. It would, in essence, employ the methods of operations research first developed for military applications and now the daily tools of systems engineering in culture history.

The specific stages that are advanced for consideration may be described briefly.

The *mechanical generating model* of Classic Maya culture in the Southern Lowlands would seek to define the population-activity ("respiratory") capacity of the system, in its habitat, at a hypothetical climax equilibrium. The first task in building this model would be to estimate controlling parameters. What was the total area of occupancy and what types of productive resources did this embrace? It would be best to begin with the largest-scale modern soil maps and fullest contemporary crop data available, in order to get a consistent base. (Later, this base could be modified by using coefficients derived from ethnographic findings, or with adjustments for climatic changes, but with these changes always applied in a systematic and comparable way.)

The second task, utilizing settlement data, skeletal material, and modern censuses, would be to estimate the number and age-and-sex composition of the Classic Maya population. Derivative estimates would be those of the labor-force, of the potential leadership group, and of the minimum birth rate for replacement (my discussion of population dynamics and structure in this chapter is a first attempt in these directions).

The third task would be to specify the activities of the society, isolating major, noninterruptible tasks, periodic tasks, and episodic ones. Then these activities should be translated into man-year equivalents of labor. It would be worthwhile to develop at least approximate estimates not only for, say, monument building but also for indirect investments, such as the labor equivalent of the exotic jade treasures buried with high dignitaries (for example, Thompson 1966c : 79). Given reasonably comparable estimating procedures, it would be acceptable in a preliminary assessment to use coefficients from different areas and times for this model.

The mechanical generating model that could be devised at present, say, as a doctoral dissertation, would undoubtedly require the use of some flimsy data and would very likely reveal important gaps and inconsistencies in the body of extant information. These deficiencies, gaps, and inconsistencies would in turn become the objects of special studies out of which could come a second generation of culture-historical models.

The mechanical generating model of the period of decline would be constructed on the same basis as that for the Classic Period. It would seek to define the changes in population-activity capacity and in the pattern of activities, translated into estimates of labor-force allocation, that the Maya decline represented.

Connecting these two models would be a *Monte Carlo model*, which is a device for handling probabilistic phenomena, such as human behavior and history. Wiesenfeld's (1969) analysis of the interrelations between agricultural patterns, malaria, and human populations in sub-Saharan Africa illustrates an effective use of this important class of models. For the Maya case, four types of parameters would have to be estimated and superimposed upon the mechanical generating model of Classic Southern Lowland society to yield the basis of a suitable Monte Carlo model. The first would be estimates of variance in each important input/output coefficient, for example, between wet and dry years in the yields of crops. The second would be the definition of linkages in space (for example, the social integration of the Belize Valley [Willey 1956 : 778]) and in time through dynastic continuities (Proskouriakoff 1960), plus, correspondingly, of boundaries and discontinuities. Such data would be essential for the construction of diffusional ("epidemiological") chains and the breaks therein. The third component would be an evaluation of the nature and probable intensity of perturbing factors—the increment of mortality arising from an outburst of yellow fever, the labor taken up for monumental construction to memorialize a dead ruler, the losses in some invasion, and so on. In each case, such perturbations need to be grouped into one of two categories—those dispersing from a single origin and those, like the increasing likelihood of Chagas' infection, that probably have multiple origins. (These would involve different kinds of mathematical formulations.) Finally, evidence on periodicities, for instance, in climate, and on the synchronisms of events, say, sharp rises in intercommunity contacts, needs to be marshalled.

These data would, again, present only a crude and perhaps even an unworkable basis for a Monte Carlo model. But they would be valuable in providing clues: how large a loss of population, 5 percent or 50 percent, would constitute a local cultural disaster? Would interregional linkages be forces tending to dampen or intensify the effects of local disturbances? Over what period of time, ten years or one hundred, were continuous efforts of development maintained? And, more important, was Classic Maya society built on such a fragile base that unfortunate coincidences in climate and disease cycles, magnified by the presence of linkages to some critical level, would be enough to bring about irreversible disasters? Or, conversely, would some large, external forces be needed for plausible explanation?

Clearly the answers to be gained from a Monte Carlo model simulating possible courses in Maya history would be primarily valuable for further checks in the field. They would serve to eliminate some hypotheses and to stimulate research on others.

Given the attainment of satisfactory results for the limited space-time domain of the Classic-Postclassic sequence in the Southern Lowlands, it would be most useful to *extend model formulations* to a larger universe. If we assume that in a given domain, the transition $a \to b$ generated associated changes $c \to d$, we would improve the power of our findings by seeking reversibilities. For example, the *rise* of Maya culture in the Southern Lowlands should exemplify some pattern $b \to a$ which would generate the associated changes $d \to c$, all of which would be converses of the decline. Again, the absence of a renaissance after the decline should be associated with the absence of a generating element (say, relatively large scale trade) present in the period of Maya rise and disrupted in that of the decline. The pattern of extension to the Northern Lowlands and the highlands would involve similar hypothesis formulations and testings.

Such model extensions need not, by the way, await the development of Monte Carlo simulations. They can be tests of statistical contingency with added degrees of freedom, which can develop useful results even without attempts to reconstruct detailed processes or histories.

Finally, the utilization of the mechanical generating and Monte Carlo models of the Maya decline for the analysis of a parallel event, the decline of Angkor, could yield still another level of results. If successfully accomplished it would give new rigor to concepts of parallel evolution, and at the same time illuminate the unique cultural and historical features of each. Thus both the generalizing scientist and the humanist concerned with the unique and individual, the creative and personal, in human behavior could gain much.

In summary, I have sought to think out what might be done in the exploration of the problem of Maya decline utilizing today's capacities for model construction and use. Whether such an effort should be undertaken now is for the specialists in the field to answer. The effort needed would be substantial. I can only state that without such model building and testing even the limited concepts of "truth" and "validity" which modern mathematics permits cannot be attained, while their attainment in Maya studies would move cultural anthropology generally to a new methodological level.

NOTES

1. This topic is very well developed, theoretically and substantively, in Chernikov (1949).

2. Erasmus (1965 : 291) argues for an abundance of firewood, but his data seemingly reflect present rather than peak population densities at Tikal. His calculations embrace only organized wood cutting by men for lime production; aboriginally, it is most probable that fuel procurement for household needs was woman's work.

3. *The Book of Chilam Balam* refers to the breadnut, manioc, and xerophytic tree *Jatropha aconitifolia* as famine foods, presumably in Yucatan (Roys 1967 : 103–4).

4. Repeated reinfection appears to be characteristic. It is not clear from the literature whether this induces allergic sensitization, as in the case of streptococcus infections terminating in the rheumatic fever complex.

5. It must be noted that, calculated on the basis of the Venezuelan male life table for 1961, the mortality reported is not quite three-fourths the average for the nation. Evidently, the WHO team performed many sanitary and medical services unreported in the publication. In consequence, the significance of Chagas' disease as a factor in mortality under "normal" conditions is only generally indicated by this study. The population of 812 had the following age distribution: 5–14 years, 360; 15–24, 156; 25–44, 234; 45–64, 57; 65 and over, 5. The annual probabilities of death used were as follows: ages 5–14, .00755; 15–24, .01041; 25–44, .02189; 45–64, .08198; 65, .18566. See Arriaga (1968 : 275).

6. And thus would result in a higher mortality among infant girls.

7. These are not reflected in the national Guatemalan statistics.

8. See also Haviland (1967) who indicates a difference in stature between elite and commoner skeletons.

14
Disease in the Maya Area:
the Pre-Columbian Evidence[1]

F R A N K   P .   S A U L

Department of Anatomy
The Medical College of Ohio—Toledo

INTRODUCTION

Potential Clues from Skeletons

Human skeletons have the potential for providing direct evidence concerning population change including intrusions (in terms of genetically conditioned morphology) and disease burdens (in terms of pathologic lesions), to mention only two matters of interest to students of the ancient Maya (Fig. 39).

Unfortunately, Maya skeletal remains have been virtually ignored because they are often fragmentary, and furthermore, Maya skulls are often intentionally deformed. In spite of these deficiencies, properly restored and studied Maya skeletal materials can yield meaningful and pertinent information, as I hope will be shown in the following selective summary of my recent studies and those of a few others, past and present.

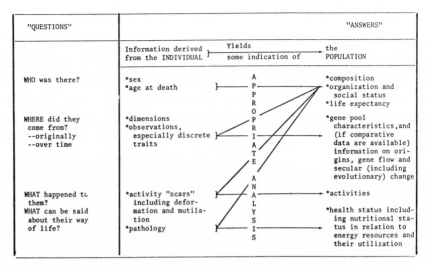

FIGURE 39. SOME POTENTIAL APPLICATIONS OF OSTEOBIO-
GRAPHIC ANALYSIS

Scope and Aims

I shall focus my attention on the health status of the ancient Maya
and discuss possible population change only in limited and peripheral
fashion. I do this for several reasons including: (1) the almost complete
lack of appropriate comparative morphological data for genetic analysis, and (2) the available data on stature decline (Table 4) that might
be advanced in support of population change are at least as susceptible
of explanation in terms of health status (Stewart 1953; Haviland 1968a;
Saul n.d.) and/or social class (Haviland, personal communication)
and their effects on growth patterns. For instance, the Altar males
do show a decline in stature over time (Table 4), but the possibility of
genetic continuity as originally suggested by continuity of cranial
keeling, convex nasal bridges, alveolar prognathism, and receding chins
(Saul 1968) is reinforced by Austin's recent study of the dental remains from Altar and Seibal (Austin 1970; Saul and Austin 1970). Using
dental traits selected for their previously reported value as genetic markers, Austin analyzed eleven discontinuous dental traits and the mesiodis-
tal and buccolingual crown diameters of 113 individuals from Altar
and Seibal, and concluded:

TABLE 4
MEAN MALE STATURE (BY CULTURE PERIOD)
AT ALTAR DE SACRIFICIOS, COMPARED WITH
OTHER ANCIENT AND MODERN MAYA (IN CM)

	Ancient Populations							
	Altar				Tikal (Haviland 1967)		Zaculeu (Stewart 1953)	
Culture Period	N	Genovés Mexican Formula (1967)	Trotter-Gleser Mexican Formula (1958)	N	Trotter-Gleser Mexican Formula (1958)	N	Pearson Formula	
I Preclassic	4	167.1	171.4	6	164.5	—	—	
II Early Classic	4	159.8	161.8	9	167.0	—	—	
III Late Classic	2	162.3	165.8	21	157.4	—	—	
(III or IV?)	1	160.5	163.4	—	—	—	—	
IV Postclassic	1	159.5	162.7	—	—	—	—	
All periods	12	162.7	165.9	36	161.0 [a]	40	159.1	
Range		(156.0–170.8)	(158.8–176.5)		(125.0–176.0) [b]		(Range not given)	

Note: Modern Populations—Mam: N61, Mean 155.97, Range 144.0–167.0 (Goff 1953a); Yucatan: N77, Mean 155.11, Range 145.0–165.0 (Steggerda 1932).
[a] My calculation from Haviland's data (1967).
[b] "Burial 24 is so abnormally small . . ." (Haviland 1967: 322).

Univariate analyses of all of the traits reveal that the populations show slightly more variation geographically than temporally. Multivariate analysis, in the form of a generalized distance function, of the discontinuous traits was also performed. The results indicate that, whether the individuals from the sites are considered as one population or as separate populations, there is greater genetic continuity through time than geographically. This does not support the postulate concerning large scale population intrusion into these two Maya communities during the Terminal Classic. Instead, the results suggest the persistence of local endogamy with relatively little change in the dental genes through time (Austin 1970 : 60–61).

In addition, I share D. B. Shimkin's opinion (chapter 13) that the importance of the disease burden as a potential factor in the Maya downfall has been improperly minimized, partially because data concerning Maya health status as recorded in the skeleton have been few and far between. Strangely, the same lack of physical evidence that may have discouraged prospective proponents of disease related theories concerning the Maya decline has encouraged an authority on modern Central American health to state (in an otherwise very useful article): "Accurate information on the nutritional conditions of pre-Columbian Mayan adults is also nonexistent, but all known facts indicate that although small, they were in general strong and healthy" (Behar 1968 : 116).

In order to discourage similar future confusion, I shall attempt to present what is known to date concerning the health status of the ancient Maya in terms of its applicability to the understanding of the collapse of the Classic Maya.

Sources of Information

My primary source of information has been the skeletal series from Altar de Sacrificios, Guatemala. Altar is located at the confluence of the Pasion and Salinas rivers in the southwestern part of the Department of Peten, Guatemala, and was excavated during the years 1959–63. The project, including concurrent and subsequent laboratory analyses, was conducted by the Peabody Museum of Harvard University, with G. R. Willey serving as Project Director and A. L. Smith as Field Director (Willey and Smith 1969).

The Altar population referred to in this chapter is, unless otherwise stated, composed of ninety individuals of known provenience, whose skeletal remains were actually available for study in the laboratory. (See Fig. 40 and Tables 5–8 for data on sex and age composition over time.) Approximately fifty-four other skeletons found during excavations were either unavailable for study (discarded in the field, and so on) or of unknown provenience. It had been hoped that field estimates of sex and age at death for unavailable individuals might be added to those available for laboratory evaluation, but inconsistencies

11.16.0.0.0 CORRELATION	TIME	MAJOR PERIODS	ALTAR DE SACRIFICIOS	UAXACTUN	TIKAL	BARTON RAMIE
11.10.0.0.0	1500	P O S T C L A S S I C				
	1400					
	1300					
11.0.0.0.0	1200					
	1100					
10.10.0.0.0	1000		POST JIMBA		CABAN	NEW TOWN
	900		JIMBA			
10.0.0.0.0	800	C Terminal	BOCA — Late Facet / Early Facet	TEPEU 3	EZNAB	SPANISH LOOKOUT
	700	L A Late	PASIÓN Late Facet	TEPEU 2	IMIX	
9.10.0.0.0	600	S	CHIXOY Early Facet / VEREMOS — Late Facet—	TEPEU I / 3	IK	TIGER RUN
	500	S	AYN Early Facet		Late Facet	HERMITAGE
9.0.0.0.0	400	I C Early		TZAKOL 2	MANIK Early Facet	
	300		SALINAS			
8.10.0.0.0	200	P		1	CAUAC-CIMI	FLORAL PARK
	100	R Proto- Classic	Late Facet		CAUAC	MOUNT HOPE
8.0.0.0.0	A.D. B.C.	E	PLANCHA	CHICANEL		
	100	C				
7.10.0.0.0	200	L Late	Early Facet		CHUEN	BARTON CREEK
	300	A				
7.0.0.0.0	400	S	SAN Late Facet		TZEC	JENNEY Late Facet
	500	S	FELIX	MAMOM Late Facet		CREEK
6.10.0.0.0	600	I Middle	Early Facet	Early Facet	EB	Early Facet
	700	C				
6.0.0.0.0	800		XE			
	900					
	1000					
	1500					

FIGURE 40. A CHRONOLOGICAL DIAGRAM FOR ALTAR DE SACRIFI-CIOS and other Lowland Maya sites. Drawn with reference to the 11.16.0.0.0. correlation and to the major periods of Mesoamerican archaeological chronology (prepared by R. E. W. Adams). Reproduced from Willey and Smith (1969).

TABLE 5

SUMMARY OF POPULATION COMPOSITION
AT ALTAR DE SACRIFICIOS

Culture Period	Subadult				Young Adult (20–34)			Middle Adult (35–54)			Old Adult (55+)			All Ages			Both Sexes
	B–4	5–9	10–14	15–19	M	F	?	M	F	?	M	F	?	M	F	?	
I Preclassic (1000BC–AD300)	6	1	1	—	4	1	2	3	1	1	1	—	—	8	2	11	21
II Early Classic (AD300–600)	2	—	—	—	3	—	2	1	—	1	1	1	—	5	1	5	11
III Late Classic (AD600–900)	5	2	—	1	4	3	2	3	3	2	—	—	—	7	6	12	25
(III or IV?) a	3	—	3	—	1	3	—	4	2	—	—	1	—	5	6	6	17
IV Postclassic (AD900–950)	—	1	1	1	2	2	1	2	3	—	2	1	—	6	6	4	16
All periods, subtotals	16	4	5	2	14	9	7	13	9	4	4	3	0	31	21	38	90
All periods, totals	27				30			26			7			90			90

Note: Most individuals shown are also assigned to cultural subperiods or phases, and many adults are also assigned to 4-year age subgroups. The population is represented by 90 studied individuals of known date (ca. 57 others were unavailable for study or of unknown date).

a These are individuals who are listed as belonging to either Boca Phase (Late Classic) or Jimba Phase (Postclassic) but could not be definitely assigned to one or the other.

TABLE 6
PERCENTAGES OF DEATHS OCCURRING DURING
ALL TIMES OF LIFE AT ALTAR DE SACRIFICIOS,
COMPARED WITH INDIAN KNOLL, PECOS,
AND RECENT GUATEMALA

Age at Death	Altar (N = 90)	Indian Knoll (Snow 1948) (N = 1,132)	Pecos (Hooton 1930) (N = 1,024)	Recent Guatemala [a] (Arriaga 1968) (N = 200,000)
−20	30.0	57.0	29.4	51.5
20–34	33.3	37.5	12.5	11.3
35–54	28.9	5.0	39.7	17.8
55+	7.8	0.4	18.4	19.5

[a] Obtained by combining the abridged 1921 male and female life tables.

between field and laboratory estimates for the laboratory sample led to the exclusion from consideration here of those for whom only field estimates were available.

In addition, several basic qualifications in regard to archaeologically derived materials must be kept in mind. As is true of most archaeological populations, the accuracy of the Altar sample in terms of its being a true microcosm of the actual population present at Altar is suspect in regard to the possibilities of differential burial practices and differential preser-

TABLE 7
PERCENTAGES OF DEATHS OCCURRING AFTER
15 YEARS OF AGE AT ALTAR DE SACRIFICIOS,
COMPARED WITH RECENT GUATEMALA

Age at Death	Altar (N = 65)	Recent Guatemala [a] (Arriaga 1968) (N = 102,595)
15–19	3.1	5.4
20–34	46.2	22.0
35–54	40.0	34.6
55+	10.8	37.9

[a] Obtained by combining the abridged 1921 male and female life tables.

vation relative to sex and age, as well as differential recovery by the excavator. Willey and Smith state:

> A total of 136 human burials was found in the Altar de Sacrificios excavations. These represented all periods of occupation and came from almost all parts of the site. A great many were found in and around Str. A-I, in Str. A-III, from the small mound Str. 2, and from other smaller mounds or "house mounds," which were located farther out to the west. Most were simple interments. Positions of skeletons varied: semi-flexed, flexed, seated, extended on back, and single skulls in cists all being recorded. . . . In general, grave goods were limited in quantity; there were, however, some richly furnished graves and tombs in Str. A-III. . . . In addition there were other burials, also of the Late Classic Period, which contained large numbers of grave items including pottery, jade beads, and carved shell ear ornaments. . . . As in most Maya lowland sites, the skeletal material from Altar de Sacrificios was in relatively poor condition, but all means were taken to preserve such bone material as we could (1969 : 29).

TABLE 8
MEAN AGE AT DEATH AT ALTAR DE SACRIFICIOS (BY CULTURE PERIOD), COMPARED WITH INDIAN KNOLL AND PECOS

Culture Period	Subadult (−20)		Adult (20+)					
			Male		Female		Both Sexes [a]	
	N	Years	N	Years	N	Years	N	Years
I Preclassic	8	3.1	8	38.6	2	33.0	13	36.7
II Early Classic	2	1.3	5	39.8	1	66.0	9	40.8
III Late Classic	8	4.3	7	33.9	6	36.0	17	35.4
(III or IV?)	6	5.8	5	40.4	6	40.8	11	40.6
IV Postclassic	3	12.3	6	45.5	6	44.2	13	43.5
All periods, by subgroups	27	4.8	31	39.4	21	40.9	63	39.0

Note: All periods, subadult and adult combined (N = 90), mean age = 28.8 yr. *Comparison:* Altar, mean age at death of adults (+20), N = 63, 39.0 yr.; Indian Knoll (Snow 1948), N = 485, 30.4 yr.; Pecos (Hooton 1930), N = 701, 47.8 yr.
[a] Includes adults of indeterminate sex.

I have reported on the Altar materials in preliminary fashion (Saul 1967a, 1967b, 1968), and the Altar monograph (Saul, n.d.) is in press.

Additional data have come from my still incomplete study of the skeletal remains from Seibal, Guatemala (Saul and Austin 1970), and my recently begun study of dental and other remains from Lubaantun, British Honduras. Seibal was also excavated by Harvard University expeditions under the supervision of G. R. Willey and A. L. Smith and is further discussed elsewhere in this volume, whereas Lubaantun was excavated by a University of Cambridge expedition directed by Norman Hammond. Supplementary data from other collections and the literature will be presented as available and appropriate.

Some Limitations of Palaeopathology

Before listing and discussing the signs of pathology found in Maya skeletons it is appropriate to note at least a few general limitations inherent in the data that follow. First of all, since we are dealing with archaeologically obtained materials, the derived data are subject to the usual archaeological sampling errors mentioned above. Additional complications may be present in palaeopathologic studies inasmuch as: (1) diagnoses must be based on information from fewer tissues of the body than in the living (aside from the fact that the patient cannot list his symptoms), and the tissues that are available are likely to have undergone important changes after death; (2) ordinarily, only those diseases that leave their "scars" on resistant tissues such as bone will come to our attention; (3) what "scars" are found may not be pathognomonic, or distinctive enough to permit pinpointing of the specific disease entity; and (4) in dealing with ancient materials it must be remembered that the disease itself may have undergone evolutionary changes from the past to the present. In the final report of the Altar skeletons (Saul n.d.), I have attempted to minimize some of these problems by providing more descriptive and other background material on the skeletal lesions themselves than can be presented here.

For the purposes of this chapter, I shall instead emphasize the potential implications of the lesions in terms of disease entities. I will, however, present tables showing the frequencies of specific lesions encountered in the Altar and Seibal series (Tables 9–19). In addition to listing presence (+) or absence (o) of the specific lesions, the number of individuals for whom a determination could not be made (?) is also shown. The percentage of affected individuals takes into account those for whom a determination could not be made, and is therefore a minimal percentage of occurrence. This inclusion is, in my opinion, less misleading than the all-too-frequent procedure of basing percentages on only the individuals in whom presence or absence could be determined.

SKELETAL INDICATIONS OF DISEASE AMONG THE ANCIENT MAYA

The following disease categories are not necessarily mutually exclusive. This is especially true in regard to the possible interrelationships between nutritional and infectious disease where one may set the scene for the other, and together they may act in synergistic fashion (Scrimshaw, Taylor, and Gordon 1968).

Trauma or Injury

A high frequency of lesions connected with trauma or injury would be suggestive of a rugged environment, where falls and similar accidents occur frequently, or of violence, perhaps related to warfare. Altar includes only two individuals with definite injuries in the form of healed fractures—a misaligned but well-healed clavicle and an ulna whose fracture callus configuration indicates that the injury occurred a few months prior to death (Fig. 41). This latter lesion is of the variety called a "parry" fracture wherein the mid-ulna, but usually not the radius, is fractured while protecting the head from a blow. Complicating the situation in this case is the fact that this 60-years-plus male possessed other pathological conditions including a fused sacroiliac joint (possibly ankylosing spondylitis or Marie-Strumpell's disease) that may have predisposed him to fracture by fall. However, falls are more likely to produce "Colles" fractures involving both the radius and the ulna near the wrist. Aside from these two instances of definite trauma there are several individuals with lesions that might involve trauma, but the relationship is too tenuous to describe them here.

More dramatic evidence of trauma comes to us from Chichen Itza:

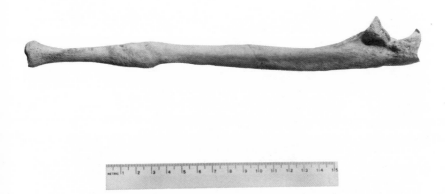

FIGURE 41. RIGHT ULNA OF ALTAR DE SACRIFICIOS BURIAL NO. 115, Ayn Phase, male, old adult, showing a healed, well-aligned fracture. The extent of the callus surrounding the break indicates that the injury was relatively recent prior to his death. Additional pathologic lesions noted for this individual include a fused sacroiliac joint and various ossified hemorrhages.

Three of the eight ladies who fell or were pushed into the Cenote had received, at some previous time, good bangs on various parts of the head, as evinced by old, healed and depressed circular lesions; and one female had suffered a fracture of the nose. One woman also had platybasia, a condition in which the skull base is pushed up into the cranial cavity. Two of the men had received head wounds which left depressed lesions. Altogether, it is suggested that the adult denizens of the Sacred Cenote may not have been generally beloved in their pre-sacrificial careers (Hooton 1940 : 277).

Nutritional and Related Diseases

Other than the previously mentioned instances of secular decline in stature (Table 4) that may relate to nutritional and/or other disease, if actual population replacement did not occur, there are several skeletal lesions present in the Maya area suggestive of nutritional problems. These lesions and their disease implications are as follows:

1. *Periodontal degeneration in conjunction with ossified subperiosteal hemorrhages* are suggestive of vitamin C deficiency, of which the most extreme form is scorbutus or "scurvy" (Figs. 42 and 43). It should

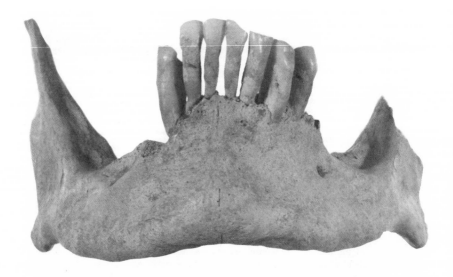

FIGURE 42. FRONT VIEW OF LOWER MANDIBLE OF ALTAR DE SACRIFICIOS BURIAL NO. 62, Jimba Phase, male, age 60+ years, showing severe periodontal degeneration. See Fig. 43 for associated massive ossified subperiosteal hemorrhage on tibia, that together with No. 62's severe periodontal degeneration is suggestive of extreme vitamin C deficiency or "scurvy."

FIGURE 43. MEDIAL VIEW OF THE LEFT TIBIA OF ALTAR DE SACRIFICIOS BURIAL NO. 62, Jimba Phase, male, age 60+ years, showing ossified remains of a massive subperiosteal hemorrhage. See Fig. 42 for associated lower mandible showing severe periodontal degeneration.

be noted that periodontal degeneration by itself could be caused by a variety of factors including loss of teeth and/or mechanical injury associated with calculus formation, both of which are found at Altar. Only when periodontal degeneration occurs in conjunction with ossified subperiosteal hemorrhages does the possibility arise of a common underlying factor of tissue (including especially capillary) fragility owing to a vitamin C deficiency.

These lesions occur separately and together in substantial frequencies throughout the history of Altar (Tables 9–11), and a preliminary study of the Seibal materials (Saul and Austin 1970) indicates their presence there as well. Tables 12 and 13 contain additional data on dental health at Altar and Seibal. Periodontal degeneration has been noted elsewhere in the Maya area on several occasions but ossified subperiosteal hemorrhages are rarely looked for or recognized in archaeo-

TABLE 9

PERIODONTAL DEGENERATION AT
ALTAR DE SACRIFICIOS (ADULTS ONLY)

Culture Period	?	o	+	N
Preclassic	4(31%)	1(8%)	8(62%)	13
Early Classic	3(33%)	0	6(67%)	9
Late Classic	5(29%)	0	12(71%)	17
Boca or Jimba	2(18%)	0	9(82%)	11
Postclassic	3(23%)	0	10(77%)	13
All periods	17(27%)	1(2%)	45(71%)	63

TABLE 10

OSSIFIED SUBPERIOSTEAL HEMORRHAGE AT
ALTAR DE SACRIFICIOS (ADULTS ONLY)

Culture Period	?	o	+	N
Preclassic	7(54%)	3(23%)	3(23%)	13
Early Classic	5(56%)	1(11%)	3(33%)	9
Late Classic	13(76%)	0	4(24%)	17
Boca or Jimba	6(55%)	1(9%)	4(36%)	11
Postclassic	9(69%)	1(8%)	3(23%)	13
All periods	40(63%)	6(10%)	17(27%)	63

TABLE 11

OSSIFIED SUBPERIOSTEAL HEMMORRHAGE AND
PERIODONTAL DEGENERATION AT ALTAR
DE SACRIFICIOS (ADULTS ONLY)

Culture Period	?	0	+	N
Preclassic	9(69%)	1(8%)	3(23%)	13
Early Classic	7(78%)	0	2(22%)	9
Late Classic	13(76%)	0	4(24%)	17
Boca or Jimba	7(64%)	0	4(36%)	11
Postclassic	11(85%)	0	2(15%)	13
All periods	47(75%)	1(2%)	15(24%)	63

TABLE 12

CARIES AND PREMORTEM TOOTH LOSS AT ALTAR
DE SACRIFICIOS (EVALUABLE YOUNG AND MIDDLE
ADULTS ONLY)

Culture Period	Number of Teeth per Person					N
	0	1–4	5–8	9–16	17–32	
Preclassic	2(20%)	3(30%)	3(30%)	2(20%)	0	10
Early Classic	1(20%)	1(20%)	1(20%)	2(40%)	0	5
Late Classic	0	5(50%)	1(10%)	3(30%)	1(10%)	10
Boca or Jimba	0	4(50%)	0	2(25%)	2(25%)	8
Postclassic	0	3(43%)	3(43%)	1(14%)	0	7
All periods	3(8%)	16(40%)	8(20%)	10(25%)	3(8%)	40

TABLE 13

CARIES AND PREMORTEM TOOTH LOSS AT SEIBAL
(EVALUABLE YOUNG AND MIDDLE ADULTS ONLY)

Culture Period	Number of Teeth per Person					N
	0	1–4	5–8	9–16	17–32	
Preclassic	0	2(40%)	3(60%)	0	0	5
Late Classic	0	3(43%)	4(57%)	0	0	7
Postclassic	0	11(73%)	3(20%)	1(7%)	0	15
All periods	0	16(59%)	10(37%)	1(4%)	0	27

logical material in general. Only one previous occurrence in the Maya area seems to have been recorded. Interestingly, this case was recorded by Samuel George Morton (one of the founders of American physical anthropology) as he examined the female skeleton brought from Ticul, near Merida, Yucatan, by J. L. Stephens (one of the founders of Maya archaeology). Morton noted: "An interesting feature of this skeleton is the occurrence of a large spongy node on the upper and inner surface of the left tibia, on which it extends about two inches in length, one inch in breadth, and half an inch in thickness" (1842 : 203). This description is quite similar to that of an ossified hemorrhage found on an Altar specimen.

The possibility of vitamin C deficiency occurring in a setting where fruit and pepper and other sources abound does not at first seem reasonable, but the following comments on diet in recent Yucatan and the Peten suggest otherwise:

> For only a small part of each year is a variety of foods available for consumption. The tortilla made of corn is for many the only article of diet for considerable periods. That the diet of rural Yucatecans is not a balanced one is indicated by the prevalence of pellagra in the population. Furthermore, fruits and berries are not easily available at all times of the year. They are rather occasional delicacies, not constantly used articles of diet (Williams 1931 : 245).

> After five seasons in Yucatan, Morris Steggerda is confident that the Maya Indians eat little fruit as compared with white people in the northern United States. It is true that fresh fruits are available throughout the year, and in most yards belonging to the Indians some fruit is grown; yet they eat fruit sparingly (Benedict and Steggerda 1936 : 165).

> Years ago a high percentage of chicleros used to have scurvy and many died from it. Since 1931, antiscorbutic remedies have been sent to the camps and, consequently, the disease has become rare. It used to develop only in December, January, and February, i.e. toward the end of the season for gathering chicle when the men had been for perhaps six months continuously in the "bush." The diet there was beans, rice, and corncakes (Shattuck 1938 : 70).

Furthermore, vitamin C or ascorbic acid is very perishable and is easily reduced or destroyed by boiling or drying—the food preparation and storage techniques practiced in the Maya area.

2. *"Spongy or porotic hyperostosis cranii"* (*previously "osteoporosis symmetrica"*) is associated with lesions, primarily known from the skull, that involve hypertrophy or thickening of the diploe or cancellous tissue in combination with a sievelike atrophy or destruction of the outer table or cortex (Fig. 44). The interpretive and nomenclatural history of these lesions as found in various parts of the world has been discussed elsewhere (Hamperl and Weiss 1955; Moseley 1965; Angel 1967), but as long ago as 1930 Hooton noted what was then called "osteoporosis symmetrica" in 15 out of 19 subadult individuals and 9 out of 17 adults found in the Sacred Cenote at Chichen Itza (1930, 1940). Hooton referenced the condition to dietary deficiency, perhaps vitamin C, or to hemolytic anemia and then went on to foreshadow some of our present findings by adding: "Perhaps osteoporosis caused the downfall of the Mayan civilization. I make a present of this idea to Maya archaeologists, who are perennially questing for an explanation" (1940 : 275).

Spongy or porotic hyperostosis is also found in fairly high and continuing frequencies at Altar as is shown by Tables 14–16. The vesicular type of lesion that seems to represent the "active" condition is found only in young individuals, whereas swelling with smaller surface porosities is found in many older individuals and is postulated to be the

TABLE 14
SPONGY OR POROTIC HYPEROSTOSIS CRANII ("ACTIVE") AT ALTAR DE SACRIFICIOS (SUBADULTS ONLY)

Culture Period	?	0	+	N
Preclassic	6(75%)	0	2(25%)	8
Early Classic	0	1(50%)	1(50%)	2
Late Classic	8(100%)	0	0	8
Boca or Jimba	3(50%)	0	3(50%)	6
Postclassic	2(67%)	0	1(33%)	3
All periods	19(70%)	1(4%)	7(26%)	27

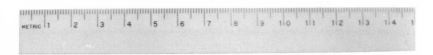

FIGURE 44. REAR VIEW OF THE FRAGMENTARY CRANIUM OF ALTAR DE SACRIFICIOS BURIAL NO. 37, Boca or Jimba Phase, probably about 10 years old, showing lesions of active "spongy or porotic hyperostosis cranii" of probable anemic origin.

TABLE 15
SPONGY OR POROTIC HYPEROSTOSIS CRANII
("HEALED") AT ALTAR DE SACRIFICIOS
(ADULTS ONLY)

Culture Period	?	o	+	N
Preclassic	8(62%)	2(15%)	3(23%)	13
Early Classic	8(89%)	1(11%)	0	9
Late Classic	9(53%)	0	8(47%)	17
Boca or Jimba	4(36%)	0	7(64%)	11
Postclassic	6(46%)	0	7(54%)	13
All periods	35(56%)	3(5%)	25(40%)	63

TABLE 16
SPONGY OR POROTIC HYPEROSTOSIS CRANII
("ACTIVE" AND "HEALED") AT ALTAR DE SACRIFICIOS
(SUBADULTS AND ADULTS)

Culture Period	?	o	+	N
Preclassic	14(67%)	2(10%)	5(24%)	21
Early Classic	8(73%)	2(18%)	1(9%)	11
Late Classic	17(68%)	0	8(32%)	25
Boca or Jimba	7(41%)	0	10(59%)	17
Postclassic	8(50%)	0	8(50%)	16
All periods	54(60%)	4(4%)	32(36%)	90

healed sequel to an earlier more active condition (Hooton 1940; Angel 1967). Recent studies have tended to emphasize the association of at least the "active" lesion with hereditary anemias such as thalassemia and sicklemia, but Moseley (1965) and Angel (1966), among others, have stressed the possibility of its association with other anemias as well.

The lesions seen in the Maya materials do not seem to have the extreme expansion of the diploe often associated with the hereditary anemias; and since there is no good evidence for pre-Columbian hereditary anemias in the Maya area, very likely the underlying cause involved iron deficiency anemia of nutritional and/or parasitic or other blood loss origin, including perhaps "scurvy." Such anemias are well known among present day inhabitants of the Maya area (Gann 1918; World

318

Health Organization 1967; Long 1969). Contemporary knowledge of iron deficiency anemia indicates that the immature period with its increased iron requirements was probably critical for all, with continuing critical times for pregnant and lactating females.

3. *Linear dental enamel hypoplasia* involves a malformation or wrinkling of the enamel prior to eruption. Aside from the nonlinear variety often hereditary in nature, linear enamel hypoplasia seems to be most frequently associated with developmental arrests caused by nutritional inadequacies, although other disease processes may also be involved. The lesions are quite frequent in both the Altar and Seibal adult samples (Tables 17 and 18) and also in the Lubaantun sample currently being studied. The location of the lesions when related to our present knowledge of dental calcification patterns indicates that most of the arrests occurred at about 3–4 years of age (Fig. 45). This age would coincide with the time when the critical period of weaning probably

TABLE 17

DENTAL ENAMEL HYPOPLASIA (LINEAR) AT ALTAR DE SACRIFICIOS (ADULTS ONLY)

Culture Period	?	0	+	N
Preclassic	3(23%)	2(15%)	8(62%)	13
Early Classic	4(44%)	0	5(56%)	9
Late Classic	8(47%)	1(6%)	8(47%)	17
Boca or Jimba	1(9%)	0	10(91%)	11
Postclassic	7(54%)	0	6(46%)	13
All periods	23(37%)	3(5%)	37(59%)	63

TABLE 18

DENTAL ENAMEL HYPOPLASIA (LINEAR) AT SEIBAL (ADULTS ONLY)

Culture Period	?	0	+	N
Preclassic	0	0	6(100%)	6
Late Classic	1(8%)	1(8%)	11(84%)	13
Postclassic	5(19%)	2(8%)	19(73%)	26
All periods	6(13%)	3(7%)	36(80%)	45

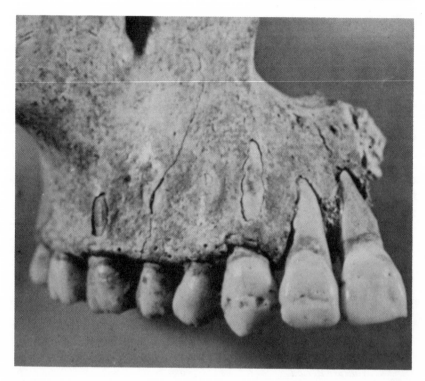

FIGURE 45. FRONT VIEW OF RIGHT MAXILLA AND TEETH OF ALTAR DE SACRIFICIOS BURIAL NO. 124, San Felix Phase, female, age ͻ0–24 years, showing linear hypoplasia or interrupted formation of the enamel of ᴉe permanent canine and incisors (also present on other upper and lower permanent teeth [not shown]). This sort of hypoplasia results from growth interruption due to malnutrition or other severe illness. The location of the hypoplasia in this individual suggests that the interruption occurred at about age 3–4 years (according to modern knowledge of calcification patterns). This would be about the age that weaning probably took place in ancient Altar. Similar hypoplastic lesions occur in the deciduous dentitions of modern Maya and are thought to be associated with infections during the first month of life (Sweeney, Cabrera, Urrutia, and Mata 1969).

took place among the ancient Maya. Such was the case at least at the time of contact, according to Landa (Tozzer 1941; see also D. B. Shimkin's comments on weanling diarrhea, chapter 13).

No comparative data on enamel hypoplasia are available for the ancient Maya as the condition does not seem to have been looked for, but it has been found in the deciduous dentitions of many modern Highland Maya children (Sweeney, Cabrera, Urrutia, and Mata 1969). The location and other circumstances led Sweeney and his associates to relate these lesions to infections during the first month of life. A quick review of the Altar deciduous dentitions shows the condition to be present in four individuals, absent in four, and not ascertainable in nineteen others.

Infectious Disease

Aside from the possibility that infectious disease might be implicated in some of the lesions listed under the previous category of nutritional disease, the major lesions likely to be associated with infectious disease are those involving bone inflammation of the sort generally categorized as osteitis with various subdivisions according to location and morphology.

This is not the time or place to become involved in the continuing arguments concerning the origin of syphilis (Cockburn 1963; Hudson 1965; Goff 1967; Brothwell 1970), but many of the osteitic lesions ("saber" tibia [Fig. 46] and cranial gumma [not shown]) found at Altar (Table 19) and also at Seibal are associated with both syphilis and

TABLE 19
OSTEITIS (ALL LOCATIONS AND VARIETIES) AT ALTAR DE SACRIFICIOS (ADULTS ONLY)

Culture Period	?	o	+	N
Preclassic	11(85%)	o	2(15%)	13
Early Classic	7(78%)	o	2(22%)	9
Late Classic	14(82%)	o	3(18%)	17
Boca or Jimba	7(64%)	o	4(36%)	11
Postclassic	12(92%)	o	1(8%)	13
All periods	51(81%)	o	12(19%)	63

yaws as seen today. The most definite statement on the subject comes from Goff, who states that his studies on two cranial specimens from Zaculeu "clearly point to the existence of syphilis in Guatemala, prior to contact with Europeans" (1953 : 319). Both syphilis and yaws do occur in the Maya area today (Shattuck 1933, 1938).

FIGURE 46. LEFT TIBIA OF ALTAR DE SACRIFICIOS BURIAL NO. 112, Veremos Phase, male, middle adult age, showing an osteitic swelling and curvature ("saber shin") that, together with anterior "buildup" revealed by roentgenography, is suggestive of syphilis or yaws.

SUMMARY AND DISCUSSION

The usual primary goal of a modern postmortem examination or autopsy is the determination of specific cause of death. Palaeopathologists rarely fulfill this goal, for ordinarily only when trauma or injury is involved and the weapon is still in place or has left distinctive marks on the bones can specific cause of death in ancient remains be determined with reasonable certainty. Fortunately, while it is sometimes useful for the archaeologist to know the cause of death (as in the case of the Maya, where battlefield death might relate to the decline of the Maya), at least equally important for the archaeologist is the knowledge of health status during life, for the latter information provides clues to the energy levels of the population.

In this chapter, I have presented a variety of information related to the health status of the ancient Maya primarily as seen in the skeletal remains from Altar de Sacrificios but also with miscellaneous insights from other sources. Instances of trauma, osteitis or bone inflammation of the sort associated with syphilis or yaws, and other pathologic conditions have been noted. While trauma and osteitis may have been involved in the decline of the Maya, the skeletal lesions indicating an apparently high and continuing incidence (at Altar at least) of

322

malnutrition and/or parasitic disorders and perhaps childhood infection are probably the most significant in relation to the functional ability of the ancient Maya. This group of lesions (listed and discussed in "Nutritional and Related Diseases," this chapter, pages 311–21) involve disorders that, while not always leading to death in childhood or occasionally in adulthood, do at least debilitate and impair normal function, often on a long-term basis.

Some potential implications of debilitating and chronic disease among the Maya were dramatically expressed by the physician-archaeologist, Gann, who in speaking of the recent Maya of southern Yucatan and northern British Honduras stated:

Indian men and women of all ages and classes, when attacked by any serious malady, are found to be lacking in vitality and stamina; they relinquish hope, and relax their grip on life very easily, seeming to hold it lightly and as not worth a fight to retain. An elderly man or woman will sometimes take to the hammock without apparent physical symptoms of disease beyond the anemia and splenitis from which nearly all suffer, and merely announce *lle in cimli*, "I am going to die." They refuse to eat, drink, or talk, wrap themselves in a sheet from head to foot, and finally do succumb in a very short time apparently from sheer lack of vitality and absence of desire to continue living (1918 : 36).

Although I have presented the Altar pathologic frequencies in terms of culture periods, I have not attempted to discern chronological trends as I believe the data to be inadequate at this time. The pathology is there, however, in apparently high and continuing frequency (and it must be remembered that only a relatively few diseases leave their "scars" on the skeleton). The present meaning of the findings at Altar (and a few other places), in relation to the decline of the Maya at Altar (and I suspect elsewhere), is that skeletal lesions indicate the presence of important health problems throughout the known past as well as in modern times; and a chronic precarious health status would be likely to magnify the impact of invasions or crop failures or any similar sudden negative occurrences, and thus could lead to the collapse of the Classic Maya.

It is true that my conclusions are based primarily on data from Altar de Sacrificios with an assist from just a few other sources. I suspect that my intensive reconstructions of the skeletal remains, followed by intensive examinations using recent advances in palaeopathology, have resulted in the recognition of pathologic conditions at Altar that might otherwise have been overlooked. The virtual absence of comparative data for other ancient Maya sites emphasizes the importance of the Altar findings while also limiting their application. Hopefully, others will be encouraged to conduct similar intensive studies on previously ignored remains from other sites in order to verify or disprove the applicability of the Altar data to the understanding of the ancient Maya as a whole.

NOTE

1. In addition to those individuals and institutions acknowledged within the text, I thank the following: For professional guidance, Drs. R. E. W. Adams, G. R. Willey, A. L. Smith, D. B. Shimkin, W. W. Howells, A. Damon, H. B. Haley, A. K. Freimanis, M. Garg, T. D. Stewart, D. M. Austin, and N. Hammond; for technical assistance, W. G. Mather III, J. M. Saul, T. S. Ellzey, C. A. Perkins, and D. M. Steffy; for financial assistance, The Medical College of Ohio at Toledo, The Milton Fund of the Harvard Medical School, The Pennsylvania State University, The Society of Sigma Xi, and The American Council of Learned Societies.

15

The Cultural Ecology of the Lowland Maya: A Reevaluation

WILLIAM T. SANDERS

Department of Anthropology
Pennsylvania State University

The major objective of this chapter is to update my earlier paper on Lowland Maya ecology (Sanders 1962, 1963) and to demonstrate the relevance of the ecological approach to the central question of this volume—the decline of Classic Maya civilization in the Southern Maya Lowlands.

In this chapter I will suggest a number of alternative reconstructions of Maya settlement, demographic, subsistence, and institutional patterns. Purely descriptive data have been intentionally suppressed to facilitate a more compact presentation focusing on issues rather than on attempts to present a body of information.

SETTLEMENT PATTERNS

Settlement pattern surveys have been conducted in a number of areas within the Lowland Maya region. These include surveys by Andrews in and around Dzibilchaltun in northern Yucatan (1965b); Sanders in Tabasco and Quintana Roo (1960, 1962, 1963); Willey et al. in the Belize Valley (1965); Willey et al. at Altar de Sacrificios (personal communication) and Seibal (personal communication) in the Peten; Pollock et al. (1962) at Mayapan in northern Yucatan; W. Coe (1967), Carr and Hazard (1961), and Haviland (1966a, 1968a, 1969) at Tikal in the northeastern Peten; and Bullard (1960, 1964) in the same area.

Most of these studies have involved intensive surveys of very small districts adjacent to major political centers, and the data have been extremely deficient in what we would call rural settlement patterns. Large-scale surveys comparable to recent surveys conducted in Central Mexico (Sanders 1965; Parsons 1968; Armillas, personal communication; Blanton 1970; Tscholl, personal communication), in highland Guatemala (Sanders and Michels 1969), and in the Valley of Oaxaca (Bernal 1965; Flannery et al. 1967) have not been conducted in the Maya area. Each of these surveys involved areas of several hundred square kilometers (varying from 200 to 700 sq. km.) and included all sites ranging from hamlets to major population centers. Willey's Belize Valley survey (Willey et al. 1965) was perhaps comparable to them; however, it involved a highly specialized ecological niche (the alluvial river terraces of the Belize Valley) atypical of much of the Maya Lowlands and included a total area of only 60 sq. km.

Bullard's northeastern Peten survey is perhaps the only Lowland Maya survey directly comparable to the kinds of large-scale surveys being conducted in the Mesoamerican highlands. The sampling method used by Bullard, however, is somewhat different from that used in Central Mexico. Essentially, Bullard surveyed a series of discontinuous linear strips along forest trails rather than a single large, continuous area. As a result, the relationships of settlement to the overall geography of the area are not clear.

On the basis of his survey and scattered data from other areas, Bullard concludes that the majority of the Maya, perhaps as many as 90 percent, resided in hamlet-size settlements. He estimates an average of from five to ten house groups per hamlet with each group consisting of one to three stone platforms placed around a court and presumably serving as the residence of an extended family. These houses are scattered over an area estimated at between four and nine hectares. The hamlets in some parts of the survey area are widely spaced and in other cases occur almost contiguously. With respect to terrain, they tend to occur primarily in upland positions, either strung out linearly along high ridges or widely spaced on separate hilltops and slopes. There is also a strong tendency for these clusters to occur near *bajos* or other water sources.

Considerable disagreement exists among Maya scholars about the nature of Maya centers and territorial levels of organization. Bullard, in his large area survey, defines two levels of centers—the minor ceremonial center and the major ceremonial center. Minor centers usually involved a single plaza complex with several public buildings, either temple pyramids or range-type structures. Stelae, ball courts, and sculptured ornamentation were absent in such centers. He also notes that minor centers occurred, on the average, associated with each 50 to 100 house groups or 10 to 15 hamlets, but that there was no apparent tendency of hamlets to cluster near the centers. The centers presumably served as foci of administrative and ceremonial activities for aggregates of hamlets. In Willey's Belize Valley survey, the *plazuela* mounds are presumably the counterpart of what Bullard calls minor ceremonial centers.

Above this level were major ceremonial centers which included a number of plaza complexes, connected by causeways and including ball courts and carved stelae as well as range-type structures and pyramid temples. The range-type structures were also considerably larger in size, with interior courtyards and much more complex plans than those in the minor ceremonial centers. Bullard estimates that such centers probably were supported by from ten to fifteen minor ceremonial centers. He estimates that the average size of territory served by a major center was 100 sq. km. of upland area suitable for agriculture. Adding patches of savanna, steep slopes, *bajos*, and other marginal or useless land, the average district size was probably closer to 250 sq. km. Bullard also states that at the major centers he saw no apparent clustering of population that could definitely be linked to the presence of the centers. In those cases where he noted an unusual concentration of hamlets near centers, the factor that stimulated the concentration was not so much the presence of the center as the presence of an unusually high percentage of good agricultural land. Where centers occurred in marginal positions with respect to agricultural productivity, the concentrations of housemounds were not present. Bullard's territorial levels and the types of sites related to them probably apply to much of the Maya Lowlands, but more surveys of the type he conducted are needed to establish this point.

I would disagree with his classification on one point, however; I believe that possibly, at least in Late Classic times, another territorial unit of even larger size and composed of several major centers emerged. The sustaining areas of a number of tributary states may have served macro-ceremonial centers. These would include truly large Maya centers such as Tikal, Copan, Palenque, Piedras Negras, Calakmul, Coba, Uxmal, Sayil, Kabah, Labna, Comalcalco, and possibly others as well. Tikal, for example, had several hundred public buildings, and the ceremonial center covered at least one square kilometer. The question is essentially whether the unusually large size of some Maya centers was owing to the fact that the immediate sustaining area, and, consequently, the supporting population, was larger than in other major centers, or whether the size was owing to the fact that such centers exacted labor tribute from conquered smaller centers in nearby areas. The settlement pattern at Tikal, as we shall demonstrate shortly, does suggest that it was a different kind of center, and this possibility in turn would suggest a different territorial base. The question is related to that of Maya Lowland sociopolitical organization as a whole, which we will reserve for later discussion.

DEMOGRAPHY

Over most of the Maya Lowlands, residences, as I have pointed out, consisted of buildings placed on stone platforms. The summit buildings usually possessed lime plaster floors. The walls varied in the amount of masonry as opposed to perishable materials used in construction. Roofs in the great majority of cases were thatched, although corbeled masonry roofs sometimes were used. These differences apparently related to rank distinctions within Maya society. Platforms rarely occurred singly, but usually in groups of two to four placed around a central courtyard. A major problem in estimating Maya population lies in calculating household size. The plaza groupings of platforms and the total floor space found in the roofed structures on the platforms suggest a larger residential group than the nuclear family. Spanish sixteenth-century documents on the Maya emphasize that multifamily residence was the rule. The censuses also indicate that the patrilocal extended family was the major family type. The same residential pattern is described by the Spaniards for Central Mexico. In the latter area, I have compiled a considerable amount of population data from the early and middle sixteenth century, and at that time the average nuclear family consisted of 3.3 individuals and the average extended family of 7.0 individuals (Sanders 1971). Perhaps Maya extended families were somewhat larger, but in terms of the average amount of roofed-over space, they could hardly have exceeded a population of from 8 to 10 persons.

A much more difficult problem in estimating Classic Maya population revolves around the question of contemporaneity of housemounds, as I pointed out in my earlier paper (Sanders 1962 : 96–99). The most convincing evidence of contemporaneity in any archaeological site is the integration of housing units in overall formal planning, since the planning would obviously make little sense if the units were not in use contemporarily. In densely nucleated sites, even without formal planning, most of the residences are likely to have been contemporary because the very factors that brought about this dense nucleation (defense, market dependence, and so on) would operate to place space at a premium. (A typical example is the modern city, where land values are extraordinarily high and where land is therefore always in use.) If this kind of architectural evidence is combined with short-phase chronological control, then the archaeologists can easily control for this factor. I might point out, however, that even in densely settled, planned communities in Central Mexico today (in the Teotihuacan Valley settlements, for example), from 5 percent to 20 percent of the houses are unoccupied at the time of particular censuses. This vacancy rate is the result of a variety of factors, the two major being migration or the dying out of family lines.

In the case of unplanned, dispersed settlement, the problem is much more acute, particularly in cases of a hamlet settlement pattern. The hamlet, on the basis of contemporary ethnographic accounts, tends to be abandoned and reoccupied in cycling patterns even where the population densities are relatively high. Where the densities are low, reoccupation of the same site may never occur. I have cited (Sanders 1962) specific evidences for such a pattern among the contemporary Maya in northern Yucatan and have suggested that the unusually high population densities calculated by archaeologists from the Lowland Maya archaeological surveys were probably the product of this kind of land use pattern.

More recently Haviland (1969) has challenged this suggestion on the basis of studies at Tikal. He accepts my criticism of the present Maya chronology as providing inadequate control for such a pattern, but he points out that excavations in housemounds have indicated several architectural rebuilding phases during a single ceramic phase, such rebuilding occurring approximately every 36 years. He interprets this as evidence of continuing use of the house with periodic rebuilding as structural features had to be repaired. In this rebuilding, parts of the older floors and walls were frequently reused. However, I think that this kind of evidence can be turned around and used as a strong argument in favor of my hypothesis and, in fact, the 36-year rebuilding average is very close to the hamlet abandonment cycle that I described for the Valladolid area in northern Yucatan today! His argument that in the Peten one could not abandon the house for any lengthy period of time (say 15 or 20 years) and still find the masonry in reusable condition because of the destruction from the growing forest may be true, but it has to be demonstrated and not simply asserted. In fact, if the version of Maya subsistence to be presented later is correct, much of the vegetation in the Peten consisted not of trees but of herbaceous plants and grass, and I doubt that a masonry house would be so totally destroyed after a 15- to 20-year period of abandonment that no portion of the walls or floors could be reused. Furthermore, my impression from archaeological excavations is that much of the floor and lower portions of the walls, even after a thousand years of abandonment, could be combined with new construction into a usable house. As a further ethnographic note, I might point out here that Sahlins (1962) describes a situation at Moala in the Fiji Islands where houses, as among the Maya, were built on platforms. House sites in this case were frequently abandoned and reoccupied, and lineages continued to hold title to the abandoned house platforms until reoccupation occurred.

My feeling today is that the pattern of cycling and reoccupation was probably common in the Maya Lowlands, particularly in the Preclassic and Early Classic periods, and even in Late Classic times in areas of relatively low population density and abundance of land. However, I suspect that in some portions of the Maya Lowlands, during Late Classic times when population density reached unusually high levels, there was a considerable reduction of mobility and that occupation did tend to become increasingly continuous. Haviland (1970), without elaborating, makes an interesting point in a new paper on Tikal, namely, that there is evidence of a lack of stability in the Early Classic housemounds in the peripheral areas of the settlement, but that the Late Classic houses closer to the center do give one the impression of considerably greater stability of residence.

Another major problem in making population estimates is that previously mentioned—the lack of large, continuous survey areas to eliminate the problem of skewing produced by geographic variation. We also urgently need good ecological surveys that break down the Maya Lowlands into smaller ecological zones that may have played an important role in the distribution of Maya population, and the whole matter of economic symbiosis among the Maya needs extensive reexamination.

I suspect that the population density of the Maya Lowlands during the Classic Period, particularly towards the end, was extremely variable with much higher densities in the Central Zone and an earlier achievement of a high density there; but in the absence of a series of areal surveys, this assertion is still only an educated guess.

What the studies in the Southern Maya Lowlands do show is a definite increase of population density from the Middle Preclassic to Late Classic times, then a catastrophic and rapid population decline during the Postclassic. At Tikal, for example, it is estimated that more than 90 percent of the houses were abandoned in Eznab times (Culbert, chapter 5). In other centers like Seibal and Altar, this abandonment was delayed for a century or two longer (Sabloff, chapter 7; Adams, chapter 8). The variability of this population decline, both in degree and in date, within the various portions of the Maya area is of critical importance to an understanding of the whole process of Maya adaptation to the tropical forest environment.

What the data do suggest, even allowing for the noncontemporaneity of house groups, is that the population density of the Maya Lowlands in Late Classic times was considerably higher than most earlier writers have thought and, most importantly, exceeded most estimates of the potential of the area to support populations with long-cycle swidden maize cultivation. I would suggest that the overall density of the 250,000 sq. km. area that made up the Maya Lowlands was probably not below 20 people per square kilometer and that the densities found in the core areas were probably well over 100 persons per square kilometer, probably closer to 200 in some small sectors of the core.

SUBSISTENCE PATTERNS

The question of Maya agriculture is part of the much broader problem of tropical forest agriculture generally, about which two widely differing points of view have emerged over the years. The differences lie essentially in what we might call the viability of the tropical forest biome as the habitat for cultivators.

Anthropologists have noted the ubiquitous occurrence in tropical forest areas of a system of cultivation called swidden in which the forest is cleared with hand tools, the resulting trash burned, and crops planted for brief periods of from one to three years. The land is then allowed to rest for extensive periods before recultivation. Differences have been noted in the ratio of the period of cultivation to the period of rest. The system as a whole has been viewed as an adaptation to two major problems of cultivation in tropical forest areas: low soil fertility and the great difficulty of removing grasses and herbaceous plants that invade recently cleared fields. The variations in the cycle have been tied in primarily to variations in soil fertility, but also to variations in the rapidity of the regrowth of the natural forest. Following this point of view, each variant in the system is seen as a relatively static adaptation to the particular local environment in which it is found.

In a very provocative book, Esther Boserup (1965) has turned the argument around. She starts with the basic premise that farmers will design a system of farming that yields the highest return per hour of work. Since less labor is lost in clearing forests than in weeding grasses and herbaceous plants, and since the yields on fresh lands are strikingly higher than those on lands that are used year after year for long periods of time, farmers definitely prefer extensive cultivation over intensive cultivation. The major factor tending to reduce the fallow period or to increase the period of cultivation is a shortage of land and, hence, a rise in population density. In this approach population density is considered the independent and the intensity of cultivation the dependent variable. Swidden cultivation, instead of being viewed as a primitive and static system, is viewed as a pioneer stage of occupation of new territory by subsistence farmers. As the population density rises, the availability of land is reduced; cycles are correspondingly reduced until, ultimately, permanent cropping appears. Boserup uses a particular set of terms to express the levels of intensity of land use, although the transition between levels is apparently a continuous, gradual process: forest fallowing, bush fallowing, grass fallowing, and permanent cropping. As intensification occurs, farmers shift their technology from digging sticks (forest and bush fallowing), to hoes (bush and grass fallowing), to plows (grass fallowing and permanent cultivation).

With respect to the applicability of this model to the Lowland Maya area, I have two major points to raise. First, although I agree that Boserup has made a major breakthrough in understanding agricultural evolution generally, and in the tropical forest environment in particular, the viability of her model has to be evaluated in terms of the capacity of native technology. In the first place, the Maya used stone and wooden hand tools for clearing the vegetation. These implements would place limits on their capacity to control weed growth. Even with metal hoes, weeding is a laborious task, and the lack of domestic animals meant that plows were not available. A further problem is that the lack of domestic animals meant that fertilizers for maintaining soil fertility for permanent cultivation were not available in great quantities. Boserup's model is drawn essentially from Southeast Asia where swidden farmers use iron tools and, furthermore, reside near wet-rice cultivators. As population pressure occurs among the swidden farmers, they can easily borrow techniques such as plowing, irrigation, and other techniques of rice paddy farming from the permanent cultivators located nearby. As Geertz (1968) points out, paddy farming does not rely on the fertility of the soil of the planted field, but rather on the nutrients in solution that come with the irrigation water. None of these options were available to the Lowland Maya.

One point should also be made about Boserup's basic premise that cultivators, where land is abundant, choose the most economic system in terms of yield per hours of labor. With steel cutting tools, clearing climax tropical forest is not a major problem, and forest fallowing is the most productive system. With stone tools, however, forest fallowing is probably less productive than bush fallowing because of the high labor requirement for clearing. A study in New Guinea conducted by

Townsend (1969) indicates that clearing high forest with a stone axe took 4.4 times the amount of time taken when steel cutting tools were used. An area 70 feet by 110 feet, including 96 trees, took 1,679 minutes to clear with stone tools; with steel machetes and axes the time needed to clear a comparable plot was 383 minutes.

Labor requirements for clearing grass-covered plots would also be considerably greater with neolithic tools. What I am suggesting here, therefore, is that neolithic cultivators had a much more circumscribed range of cycling systems than iron tool users and probably followed a bush-fallowing cycle whenever demographic conditions permitted. Only unusually strong pressures would have stimulated them into a reduction of cycle to a grass swidden system, and the pressure in favor of migration as against increasingly more intensive cultivation would have been heavy.

A more general criticism of Boserup's approach is that she tends to ignore the fact that there are striking variations in soil fertility in tropical forest areas and that not all soils are capable of sustained intensive cultivation, particularly in terms of native techniques of agriculture. With respect to the weed problem, although there has been much debate over the issue, the evidence from Africa and Indonesia very strongly supports the position that there is an overall succession from forest to grass when population densities reach certain levels in swidden agriculture. There are striking differences in the pace at which succession occurs. In areas with relatively light rainfall (100–1,500 mm.), and particularly in areas where such rainfall is sharply seasonal with a long dry season, succession occurs at a relatively rapid rate, even under conditions of relatively low population densities. In areas where abundant precipitation (for example, over 2,000 mm.) is well distributed throughout the year, such succession will occur only under conditions of unusually high density. In parts of southeastern Nigeria, for example, densities have reached figures well above 100 persons per square kilometer in some areas and succession has not yet occurred. Complicating the matter, however, is the fact that much of the area is in cultivated oil palm, which would tend to retard the expansion of grasslands since palm groves are, in a sense, artificial forests. Lundell (1937) has pointed out that soil variations may be important as well and suggests that the presence of a limestone-derived soil, typical of

334

most of the Maya Lowlands, would retard the process. The questions are, then, at what density level grass succession would occur in the various portions of the Maya Lowlands, whether these densities were achieved, and whether the Maya cultivators did then attempt to continue cultivation of grass-invaded areas and further intensify use of the land. If they did attempt this intensification, then a second major question concerns the fertility base levels of Lowland Maya soils and the capability of such soils to sustain permanent or very short cycle cropping without the addition of exotic nutrients. We have recently completed a study of cultivation practices in the Valley of Guatemala in the Guatemalan highlands in an area of unusually fertile soils. In the better soils of the valley floor the base level of fertilization (annual cropping without fertilization) is high enough to permit an annual maize crop of 500–600 kg. of grain per hectare, a yield that is still an economically viable return in terms of the amount of labor involved with cultivation with simple hand tools (in this case with iron hoes). Evidence indicates that the Peten soils do not measure up to this level, and I doubt that they can be permanently cropped over long periods of time without exotic nutrients.

Recently Simmons et al. (1959) published an overall survey of the soils of Guatemala with an elaborate classification of 181 varieties of soils. The purpose of the survey was to assess the agricultural potential of Guatemalan soils, and the classification was based on factors significant in terms of this objective. The attributes used included parent materials; fertility, including overall evaluation as well as specific measures of nutrients; susceptibility to erosion; soil texture; humidity retention qualities; and a statement as to the major problems of soil maintenance. For the Peten, Simmons defines 26 varieties of soil, suggesting that the area is not quite as homogeneous an environment as some writers, including the present author, had considered. It is still a relatively homogeneous area, however, when compared to the neighboring highlands. The Department of Quetzaltenango, for example, has 21 types of soil in a total area of 1,951 sq. km.; the Department of Guatemala, 26 varieties of soil in an area of 2,126 sq. km. as compared to the 26 varieties in an area of 33,854 sq. km. that comprise the Peten. It is very probable that a fair degree of variability in vegetation accompanies this variability of soil. Variability in both soil and vegetation is critical to our

335

understanding of the ecological processes of Maya settlement, and yet we know very little about the significance of the variability suggested in Simmons's study.

I have grouped the 26 varieties of soils for the Peten in terms of the two major criteria of significance in cultivation: susceptibility to erosion and overall fertility (see Table 20). With respect to the erosion factor, Simmons estimates that 22.56 percent of the soils are characterized by a very low susceptibility to erosion, 36.64 percent are rated as low, 7.29 percent as highly susceptible, and 33.83 percent as very highly susceptible. Based on what we know about erosional processes in humid areas, generally, and in humid tropical areas, particularly, the great amount of land—more than 40 percent—rated as highly to very highly susceptible is rather surprising. In a recent study of the soils of Tikal, Olson (1969) noted evidence of soil erosion and redeposition even under the present conditions of low population density and extensive practices of cultivation.

Of even greater interest is the fact that, of the soils rated as having a very low susceptibility to erosion (22.56 percent of the total) more than one-half of these soils (11.36 percent) are rated as low to very low in fertility, and 2.72 percent of only moderate fertility (soils of this lat-

TABLE 20
AGRICULTURAL POTENTIAL OF SOILS OF THE PETEN

Classification of Soils	Percentage	Special Problems
Very low susceptibility to erosion	22.56	
Low–very low fertility	11.36	Grass cover and heavy texture
Moderate fertility	2.72	Grass cover and heavy texture
High fertility	8.48	Heavy texture and drainage
Low susceptibility to erosion	36.64	
Low fertility	1.24	Grass cover and heavy texture
Moderate fertility	26.79	Heavy texture and drainage
High fertility	8.61	Heavy texture and drainage
High to very high susceptibility to erosion	41.12	
Low fertility	0.09	Drainage
Moderate fertility	3.89	Fertility maintenance
High to very high fertility	37.14	None

ter category, moreover, have a natural grass cover and would, therefore, present serious problems for neolithic cultivators). Furthermore, virtually all soils in the very low susceptibility category, including the remaining 8.48 percent rated as fertile, have dense, compact textures accompanied by serious drainage problems, and could have been cultivated only with a major labor investment.

Those soils classified as low erosional susceptibility (36.64 percent) are generally of better quality than those rated as very low with only 1.24 percent classified as having low fertility, while 26.79 percent are of moderate fertility and 8.61 percent are of high fertility. All of the soils of moderate to high fertility are *bajo* soils, characterized by dense, compact, sticky textures, and, frequently, poor drainage.

Of considerable interest is the fact that of the soils rated as highly or very highly susceptible to erosion (41.12 percent), 37.14 percent are classified as soils of high fertility. These are all soils with good friable texture and are easily cultivable in terms of primitive tools. They are found on well-drained slopes which, prior to cultivation, were covered with tropical forests.

I believe that these soil statistics contain the key to both the dramatic success and the equally dramatic failure of Maya agriculture. Particularly significant is the unusually high percentage of high quality soils (37.14 percent), and if we include the *bajo* soils of moderate to high fertility, the figure rises to 87.63 percent. The reason for the unusually high population density compared to other tropical lowland areas in Mesoamerica becomes evident in view of these figures. The fact that the highest quality soils include only 37.14 percent of the land has almost certainly had a powerful influence on the patterning of the colonization of the Peten and the ultimate distribution of its population. The very high susceptibility of these lands to erosion probably holds part of the key to the collapse. A major historical problem to be considered here is whether the Maya responded to these problems and resolved them as did the population in other portions of Mesoamerica. Archaeologically, there is no convincing evidence that they did, in fact, respond to the major problem of soil erosion. There is a striking contrast here with the Basin of Mexico, for example, where erosion is an even more serious problem and where the pre-Hispanic population responded to the problem very effectively by constructing extensive terrace systems involving earth, stone, and *tepetate* structures. The answer may lie in the difference between erosion rates in humid as opposed to arid environments and perhaps relates to the peasants' ability to conceptualize the problem. In the humid environment, erosion is a much slower process because of the faster rate of weed growth. It is therefore a less obvious phenomenon, and there is a serious question as to whether subsistence farmers respond to the problem. In environments with less rainfall and a slower regenerative rate of native vegetation, erosion is a very rapid, very destructive, and very obvious process; and steps to control it are taken almost immediately. In contemporary highland Guatemala, an area of heavy rainfall, erosion is a widespread phenomenon. In some areas attempts have been made to control this process by contour hoeing, but the interesting fact is that the areas, such as those around Quetzaltenango, where counteractive measures have been taken are areas of very dense population and lower rainfall than most of the Guatemalan Highlands. The areas of contour hoeing, then, seem to be comparable to erosion areas in Central Mexico. In many other parts of the Guatemalan Highlands little is done to counteract erosion. In the Valley of Guatemala, for example, erosion of both the sheet and gulley type is extensive and widespread and yet no attempts are being taken to control these processes. What I am suggesting here is that the Maya probably did not respond, and that the situation in the Peten, particularly by the end of the Late Classic Period, was very comparable to that in much of highland Guatemala today. Theoretically, one response to the situation of increasing erosion and consequent reduction of the amount of good agricultural land on the slopes would be the cultivation of the *bajo* areas. This cultivation would involve a considerably greater outlay of labor because of the heavy soils and drainage problems, but it is conceivable that the Maya attempted just that. To date, however, no one has presented any evidence that this was the case. At Tikal, the *bajo* soils nearest to the site are soils of very low fertility and probably would not be amenable to intensive cultivation, but at a distance of from 15 km. to 20 km. from the center of Tikal are *bajo* soils of high fertility which might have been brought under cultivation. Again archaeological data are lacking as to whether this was ever attempted.

Beyond the overall situation in the Peten, the Tikal data would suggest that major population clusters developed in small areas of unusually favorable circumstances in terms of the specific balance of the noted soil types. For example, Table 21 shows the distribution of the generalized soil types in an area of approximately 1,000 sq. km. around Tikal. In terms of spacing of Bullard's major ceremonial centers, this would be the maximal area that might have been directly controlled politically by the center. Within this area, 58.0 percent of the soils are of excellent quality.

TABLE 21
SOILS IN 1,000-SQ.-KM. AREA AROUND TIKAL

Soil Types	Percentage	Special Problems
Hilly terrain: Very high susceptibility to erosion, high fertility	58.0	None
Bajo terrain Very low susceptibility to erosion, high fertility	18.0	Drainage and heavy texture
Very low susceptibility to erosion, low fertility	24.0	Drainage and heavy texture

If Haviland is correct in his assessment that the 164-sq.-km. area surrounding the center of Tikal constitutes the immediate sustaining area of the site, and this assessment is supported by Olson's (1968) soil survey, an even higher percentage of the soils in this core area (86 percent) fall in the category marked by high fertility, good texture, good drainage, and high susceptibility to erosion.

Most reconstructions of Lowland Maya agriculture have assumed that the staple food was maize. In a recent paper, Bronson (1966) has suggested that the Maya may have depended as much, possibly even more, on such root crops as manioc and sweet potatoes. He points out that the caloric yield per hectare of root crops is considerably higher than that of maize and that the use of root crops, whatever the degree of intensity of cultivation, would considerably raise estimates of the demographic potential of the Maya Lowlands. He suggests that root crops can produce five to six times as much food per hectare as maize. In fact the caloric yield of a given weight of maize is at least two and one-half to three times that of the equivalent weight of manioc or sweet potatoes; thus the advantage is only about double. Even taking this yield into consideration, the use of root crops would have substantially raised the demographic potential of the Lowland Maya area. The major problem presented by a primarily root crop diet would be protein deficiencies. Root crops would have to be combined with some high-grade, protein-rich food. There is evidence from Conquest period documents that fish were imported regularly from coastal to inland communities (Roys 1943). A combination of root crops and seafoods would be an alternate ecological system and, in fact, would be very comparable to the Baganda nutritional complex found in Uganda today, where sweet potatoes, bananas, and lake fish are combined into a nutritional base capable of supporting densities of several hundred people per square kilometer. If such were the case among the Maya, then it must have involved a highly organized and efficient trade network between the coast and inland communities. We will return to this point later.

Puleston (1968) has recently presented another model for Maya subsistence patterns, at least for the northeastern Peten, that has even greater potential for population growth. Lundell (1937), in his study of the vegetation of the Peten, noticed the striking correlation of *ramón* trees with Maya settlements. Recent surveys by the Tikal Project have demonstrated an extraordinarily close relationship between the densities of *ramón* and house sites that indicates beyond any reasonable doubt that the Maya did plant groves of *ramón* trees near their houses. Puleston has pointed out that it is the nut rather than the fruit of the tree that is the major source of food and that such nuts could have been stored in great quantities in underground chambers called *chultun*s (Puleston 1971). Among the contemporary peasants living in the vicinity of Tikal, the *ramón* nut is still collected during years of crop failure, ground into flour, and made into tortillas. The yields per tree are considerable, and the nut is more nutritious than most cereals; the caloric yield per weight is equivalent to grains, but the protein content is as high as that found in beans. The major advantage of *ramón* as a staple crop lies in the fact that it is a permanent tree crop and a native plant, and is, therefore, perfectly adapted to the tropical forest conditions. Further, it requires virtually no labor for cultivation aside from that of harvesting, with the exception of the task of replacing aged, low-yielding trees. Each house group or cluster of house groups in Tikal was apparently nestled within a substantial orchard of *ramón*

340

trees, from which nuts could have been harvested easily and stored in *chultuns* located close to the house.

My major criticism of Puleston's argument is the extreme position he takes. He believes that most of the caloric intake of the Tikal Maya was derived from the *ramón* nut and that maize was of slight significance. However, nut-bearing trees are notoriously variable in their yields from year to year, and I doubt very much that the Maya would ever have depended entirely on such a resource. There is also such a thing as food preferences, and peasants have very definite preferences. *Ramón* nuts today are considered an emergency food and a poor substitute for maize, and maize was very probably the preferred food in Classic times. I suspect that the *ramón* nut was an important item in the diet, combined with maize and root crops, and presumably a great variety of secondary crops. The emphasis on *ramón* cultivation was apparently a northeastern Peten phenomenon and seems to have been lacking in the more peripheral areas. My suggestion of the higher density of population in the northeastern Peten is interesting in this connection.

In Table 22 I have presented a series of hypothetical models of the productivity levels of various subsistence systems, assuming that the Maya selected one crop as the staple. In fact, they probably had a system combining two or more patterns in Late Classic times.

MAYA SOCIOECONOMIC ORGANIZATION

A number of attempts have been made to delineate the institutional structure of the Classic Maya. Such reconstructions have been based primarily on the data from the period of the Spanish Conquest, plus the use of secondary support data from archaeological settlement patterns and contemporary Maya settlement patterns and socioeconomic organization. The most ambitious attempt has been that of Haviland (1968), who reconstructs an evolutionary history of social structure for the occupation of the area by hunters and gathers up to the Postclassic Period.

I will not attempt to summarize here the reconstructions of all aspects of Maya institutions but will focus attention on those characteris-

TABLE 22
COMPARISON OF SUBSISTENCE MODELS

1. Crop Yields (kg. per hectare)

| | Type of Cultivation | | | | | | | |
| | Forest Fallow (1:6); Yield per Hectare | | Bush Fallow (1:3); Yield per Hectare | | Grass Fallow (1:1); Yield per Hectare | | Permanent | |
Crop	Land Culti-vated	Total Agri. Land	Land Culti-vated	Total Agri. Land	Land Culti-vated	Total Agri. Land		
Maize	1,000	150	800	200	600	300	—	
Root crops[a]	2,500[a]	375	2,000[a]	500	1,500[a]	750	—	
Ramón	—	—	—	—	—	—	1,200	

[a] Corrected to equal caloric yield for grains.

2. Population Density Capacity (per km.²)

| | Forest Fallow | | | Bush Fallow | | | Grass Fallow | | | Permanent | | |
Crop	Yield per Ha. of Agr. Land (kg.)	Land Req. per Person (ha.)	Popul. Density (per km.²)	Yield per Ha. of Agr. Land (kg.)	Land Req. per Person (ha.)	Popul. Density (per km.²)	Yield per Ha. of Agr. Land (kg.)	Land Req. per Person (ha.)	Popul. Density (per km.²)	Yield per Ha. of Agr. Land (kg.)	Land Req. per Person (ha.)	Popul. Density (per km.²)
Maize	150	1.3	77	200	1.0	100	300	.65	154	—	—	—
Root crops	375	.53	189	500	.4	250	750	.27	370	—	—	—
Ramón	—	—	—	—	—	—	—	—	—	1,200	.17	588

3. Population Density (assuming 50% surplus for tax and trade)

Crop	Forest Fallow		Bush Fallow		Grass Fallow		Permanent	
	Dens. (sec. 2)	Recalc. Dens.	Dens. (sec. 2)	Recalc. Dens.	Dens. (sec. 2)	Recalc. Dens.	Dens. (sec. 2)	Recalc. Dens.
Maize	77	52	100	66	154	103	—	—
Root crops	189	126	250	166	370	246	—	—
Ramón	—	—	—	—	—	—	588	392

4. Population Density (assuming 40% of land cultivable)

Crop	Forest Fallow		Bush Fallow		Grass Fallow		Permanent	
	Dens. (sec. 3)	Recalc. Dens.	Dens. (sec. 3)	Recalc. Dens.	Dens. (sec. 3)	Recalc. Dens.	Dens. (sec. 3)	Recalc. Dens.
Maize	52	20.8	66	26.4	103	41.2	—	—
Root crops	126	50.4	186	74.4	246	98.4	—	—
Ramón	—	—	—	—	—	—	392	156.8

tics of Maya organization that led to the emergence, and possibly the collapse, of large, heterogeneous societies. More specifically, I will be concerned with the process of internal differentiation of Maya society by rank and economic specialization.

There has been considerable debate about the degree of development of ranking as a principle of social and political organization among the Lowland Maya and, consequently, the presence or absence of well-defined social classes on the one hand, and well-defined statelike political institutions on the other. Generally, the concern has been closely related to ideas about the Maya subsistence system and its capacity to support a class of non–food producers, along with the difficulty of maintaining a state with a relatively low population density and dispersed settlement pattern. These points are closely related to the idea that swidden agriculture in the Maya Lowlands was a static system with little capability of intensification.

It is true that much of the Maya population was dispersed in hamlets. The problem of integration of the outlying population must have been considerable, particularly during the early phase of Maya history when densities were low as well. Nevertheless, statelike political systems have flourished in swidden areas of Africa with densities as low as 10–20 people per square kilometer, and these densities would have been achieved in the Peten even with a long-cycle swidden system. The second position is that swidden agriculture does not require cooperation and organization above the level of the extended family and, therefore, does not have a positive effect on the emergence of large-scale political systems. We will return to this point later.

As to the archaeological evidence of a ranking principle in Maya social organization, a series of new studies, based on a careful examination of house types, burial furniture, and the deciphering of inscribed stelae that record historic events, are beginning to present a remarkably clear picture of the evolution of Maya society.

Late Classic house types at Tikal, particularly, show a striking range in quality and complexity that obviously relates to equally important distinctions in prestige of the householders (Haviland 1970). Houses at Tikal vary from small house platforms with pole-and-thatch summit structures to large complexes of platforms with masonry summit buildings. As Haviland points out, some of the larger structures even have smaller mounds with pole-and-thatch dwellings that look like attached servants', or at least clients', quarters associated with them.

Architectural complexes like the Palace at Palenque and the Central Acropolis at Tikal, in my opinion, are quite obviously residences. The plan, the quality of construction, and the carefully controlled access routes to these complexes and within them suggest that they are the residences of the top stratum of Maya society. Much of the Central Acropolis at Tikal has a monasterylike plan, but one internal architectural unit (Structure 5D-46) has a plan which suggests a royal residence. If it is the residence of a dynastic leader, the balance of the complex could have had dependent functions. The plan does differ, however, from, say, the royal palace at Knossos in its lack of storage areas for tax goods, craftsmen's quarters, and shops. This deficiency would indicate significantly different characteristics of the top position in the two political systems. The Maya leaders apparently did not have direct control over a large permanent royal household in the manner of Near Eastern rulers. In fact, the Central Acropolis could have served as the residence of the entire ruling lineage with Structure 5D-46 as the house of the lineage head. The architectural evidence of a ruling lineage and a kind of dynastic succession among the Late Classic Maya is strongly supported by Proskouriakoff's (1961) analysis of stelae at Piedras Negras.

Rank distinctions among the Maya are also reflected in burial customs, particularly in the variations of wealth of imported offerings. Apparently, differences in rank were even great enough to involve differential access to food; skeletal studies of the Late Classic Maya show definite nutritional deficiencies in burials from rural sites when compared to those in ceremonial centers. In fact, there is even evidence of stature repression among the lower class Maya in Late Classic times (see Haviland 1967; Willey et al. 1965; Saul, personal communication).

The architectural data, along with the data from the burials, seem to show a definite historical trend toward increasingly more significant differences within Maya society (Rathje 1970b). They also reflect increasing economic problems and a process of decreasing access of the ordinary Maya peasant to even basic goods. Burials tended to include more offerings, particularly of imported items, in the Early Classic Period, and adult male burials were found in rural settlements in much

345

lower frequencies in relationship to the total population. In Late Classic times, burials were generally poorer in goods, and a higher percentage of adult males were represented. The picture checks very neatly with data from ceremonial structures in Early Classic times, whereas all ages and both sexes were represented in the burials of the Late Classic Period. This picture suggests that the peasants in Early Classic times had greater access to elite goods than during the Late Classic and that a substantial number of the adult males from even small settlements were buried in the ceremonial centers in the Early Classic Period. In Late Classic times, the burial data would suggest much sharper cleavages in social class with a reduction of the peasant's ability to obtain elite goods and a tendency for burials, even of relatively high prestige individuals, to occur within the rural settlement.

One of the interesting supports for this reconstruction of an increasing tendency for strong social cleavages to evolve in Maya society is presented by the old Carnegie excavations of Structure A-V at Uaxactun (Smith 1950). In the earliest phase of its architectural history, the structure consisted of three small pyramid temples placed upon a low platform with completely open access. As each architectural phase of reconstruction was carried out, there was a tendency, first, for the unit to be increasingly tighter in its plan, with more controlled access, and second, for the function to shift from one of a public ceremonial unit to a private residential-ceremonial complex. In the final phase, Structure A-V could be described as a residential complex for an elite group with shrines in the interior. Some of the shrines were direct architectural survivors of the older temple pyramids characteristic of Phase One. The same pattern apparently is true of other Lowland Maya centers; that is, very few residential palaces were constructed during the Early Classic Period but great emphasis was placed on their construction during the Late Classic. The later palaces, furthermore, are much larger, with more complex floor plans than earlier counterparts.

Vogt (1961) has suggested a model for Classic Maya sociopolitical organization which can easily be applied to the Early Classic situation. His model is based on contemporary ethnographic data from the Maya of Zinacantan in the state of Chiapas, Mexico. The *municipio* of Zinacantan had a population in 1960 of 7,600 people. The central community of the *municipio* very closely approximates the orthodox concept of an Early Classic Maya ceremonial center, with a total permanent population of only 800. Even these 800 people do not live densely clustered around the public buildings but are widely dispersed in a small mountain valley. The balance of the population lives dispersed in the type of hamlet that we have described for the Classic Maya. The *Zinacantecos* have an elaborate religious ritual that is conducted by part-time laymen drawn from outlying hamlets rather than professional priests. There are approximately fifty-three positions in the religious hierarchy, called *cargos*, arranged hierarchically in four graded series. Men compete for offices to obtain prestige in the community, and the occupant is required to defray the expenses of the ceremony related to the specific *cargo* position. During the period of religious service, he resides at the ceremonial center. Individuals attempt to reach the top level by successively occupying positions in the various grades. By this means local farmers living in small settlements or hamlets are integrated into the larger society, and a high percentage of the total population (since the expenses of the ceremonies are defrayed in part by the *cargo* holder, but with considerable assistance from his ceremonial and actual kinsmen) has a sense of participation in the leadership of the religious system.

Vogt has suggested that this model might help to explain the apparent contradictions that we have previously noted about the nature of Early Classic Maya society. It offers an explanation as to how the relatively light, widely dispersed populations could have been integrated (without the need of coercion by an upper class) into a society large enough to carry out the construction of major Classic Maya ceremonial centers. The architectural characteristics of Early Classic Maya centers, along with the data from the burials, would strongly suggest a pattern like Vogt's *cargo* system for that period. I suggest, however, that there were also full-time priest-chiefs at the very top of the system living permanently at the center and supported by tribute contributions from the outlying populations, but that the strictly defined social classes and a tendency towards professionalization of ritual, a distinctive characteristic of the Late Classic Maya society, was probably absent.

Although extremely difficult to establish entirely on the basis of archaeological data, the remarkable persistence of unilineal kinship groups, both true and theoretical in level, up to the period of the Spanish Conquest suggests that these groups functioned throughout the history of Classic Maya society, adding a further dimension to the problem of integration of Maya society. (The inferential data presented by Haviland [1968] seem to support this idea also.) Particularly the large theoretical descent groups we call sibs must have functioned in this respect. I suspect also that either sibs, or the lineages within them, were ranked on a scale comparable to the kind of social ranking that Service (1962) refers to as the chiefdom. Presumably, the higher level, permanent statuses in Early Classic times were controlled by specific lineages. I also suggest that in Late Classic times, when a more truly bureaucratic, statelike structure evolved, these unilineal descent groups still had major functions in the larger political system. What I am suggesting is a situation comparable to that of the Baganda, where the overall picture certainly was of a fully evolved, statelike political system, but where members of the unilineal descent groups reserved the right to occupy certain status positions at court. Unilineal descent groups also probably functioned in the economic sphere as units of production and distribution.

There is increasing evidence from the funerary data from the Maya area that the burial ritual was extremely elaborate and that there perhaps was a focus on some kind of ancestor cult. As a matter of fact, a strong possibility exists that some of the temples found in Maya centers were dedicated not to high gods in the Central Mexican sense but rather to ancestral deities of descent lines. In other words, there was a great deal of persistence of kinlike organization in Maya social structure, even on the elite level, through the Late Classic Period when more bureaucratic, more truly political kinds of organizations seem to have appeared.

Concerning economic differentiation and symbiosis in the Classic Lowland Maya society, there have been many fundamental disagreements among the students of Maya culture (in some cases based on the same archaeological data). The argument revolves around the degree of craft specialization and the significance of organized trade in Maya economy—first on the elite level and second on the peasant level.

I think there is no question with respect to elite Maya technology that what we refer to as art was produced by full-time specialists. The disagreement concerns the system of production and the distribution of the more mundane goods used by the peasant household.

With respect to economic specialization generally, we might begin by agreeing that some specialization is characteristic of all societies. Very striking differences occur, however, in the quantitative significance of specialization which relates closely to the emergence of special institutions. A number of factors act as stimuli in the evolution of specialization of production in any society. A major stimulus is technological improvement in the efficiency of production. The craftsman must be able to produce enough goods cheaply enough so that his major customer, the peasant, can afford to pay for them in spite of the limitations of his production system. A potter with a potter's wheel can turn out many more pots than one using hand techniques in building a vessel and, therefore, can sell his product more cheaply. Thus even a swidden farmer with stone tools can pay for pottery with his crop surplus.

A second factor is ecological variability. In an environmentally complex area, natural resources are highly localized and even with a low population density tend to be jealously controlled by nearby communities. A system must be designed to permit the entire population access to such resources. Very frequently special resource areas also tend to be areas of much lower agricultural potential, acting as a further stimulus to groups residing in such niches to specialize in the extraction of the resource and to trade either the raw materials or finished products. In mountain valleys, for example, certain kinds of resources tend to occur on mountainsides where agricultural conditions are considerably poorer than in the alluvial plains of the valley floor. Even with primitive production techniques, groups living in marginal locations tend to become economically specialized. In most cases, however, the specialization would be part-time and associated with some subsistence cropping. When specialization of production increases, the stimulus for specialized institutions of distribution also rises, ultimately developing into markets and market towns.

The emergence of social class distinctions is another major stimulus to craft specialization, to long-distance trade, and to the development of special institutions to handle both trade in the raw materials and the production of the elite goods. This is because the upper class commands a greater share of the agricultural crop production which, in turn, underwrites the entire system in a preindustrial society. A high-ranking individual can afford to pay for unusually fine craft products, even considering the inefficient production techniques used by the craftsmen; and he can use the surplus production to finance the long-range trade expeditions necessary to secure the raw materials or the finished products. Among the Classic Maya, long-range trade seems to have been directly organized by the noble class rather than by a guild of middlemen like the Aztec Pochteca. We have little information on the organization of the elite craftsmen among the Maya, but presumably they were either directly attached to noble households or were organized as guilds of independent craftsmen, as among the Aztecs; we suspect that the former was the case and that the craftsmen were linked to particular high-ranking families through the kinship system.

A major process stimulating specialization in trade is increasing population density. As the density rises, agricultural production per hectare declines, land shortages appear, and an increasing stimulus toward nonagricultural activities to solve the economic pressure occurs. If areas of high population pressure are located within a relatively short distance of areas of low population pressure, then the stimulus toward increasing specialization is particularly strong, since a viable pattern of exchange of craft products from the high density area for agricultural surpluses from the low density areas can be worked out. In highland Guatemala today, this is precisely what has happened. Craft specialists are particularly common either in communities with low population densities located in areas with low agricultural potential or in areas with high agricultural potential but with very high population density. The system can work, however, only when such areas are located near regions of low population density and high agricultural potential, since surplus food production must underwrite the entire exchange system. As population densities rise, minor ecological variations become important and patterns of local specialization are encouraged, even in an area of relatively homogeneous environment. For example, one of the very common responses to increasing population density and land shortage is to specialize in certain agricultural crops whose production is closely tied to minor variations in soil and drainage conditions.

In a number of publications, I have stressed the difference between the ecological heterogeneity of highland Mesoamerica and the essential homogeneity of the Yucatan peninsula. In none of these publications have I ever stated that the Yucatan peninsula was an absolutely homogeneous environment—no environment ever is. Variations do occur in the thinness of soil, the quality of soil, the nearness to rivers and lake systems, the proximity to the coast, and the occurrence or at least the size of deposits of localized raw materials like pottery clay, flint, and hard-grained stone. Such variability, however, is far less than that in areas of equivalent size in the highlands where the ecological niches vary from sea level to 3,000 m. above sea level. Under conditions of increasing population, however, even minor distinctions increase in importance and, undoubtedly, acted as a major stimulus to developing patterns of local specialization and trade. Furthermore, as the Maya shifted in some of the more densely settled core areas to a pattern of grass swiddening and permanent orchard cropping, this shift must have produced shortages in a great variety of forest products that long-cycle swidden agriculture had tended to preserve. If, in areas of unusually dense population, the Maya indeed shifted to root crops as a staple food, this change would have required a development of interdependence with the coastal areas, a pattern of trade that Roys (1943) has described in northern Yucatan in Postclassic times.

In previous publications I have pointed out the rarity of references in the sixteenth-century Maya literature to local trade and specialization, in sharp contrast to the abundance of such references in the sixteenth-century documents for Central Mexico. Markets, for example, are referred to only in a few coastal localities, and in these cases they seem to be involved more with long-range trade, primarily in elite goods, than with local specialization. This absence undoubtedly relates to the considerably lower population density even in the well-settled areas of Yucatan, as contrasted to the Late Classic Period. On the basis of Roys's (1957) data, I (Sanders 1962, 1963) estimate population densities for the Conquest period of 10–34 persons per square kilometer, with a mode of between 15 and 25 persons per square kilometer. This density could have been supported with a forest or bush fallow system with maize as the staple food so that the stimulus for the development of local specialization and local exchanges in foods and other essential peasant goods was not very high. If our suggested figure for the central portions of the Lowland Maya area in Late Classic times is close to the mark, such a stimulus would have been considerably greater, and, as Culbert (chapter 5) pointed out, we do have evidence for such specialization at Tikal.

The most thorough analysis of Classic Maya trade in recent years is a study by Tourtellot and Sabloff (1972). They accept the Lowland Maya environment as a relatively homogeneous one with little stimulus for local specialization and exchange. Then they analyze excavated artifacts from a number of published Lowland Maya sites with respect to the possibilities of trade and specialization. They first classify trade into two types, long-range and local, then classify the raw materials or finished products used by the Maya into two categories, functional, that is, used primarily for sumptuary ceremonies related to religious and social activities, and useful, related to everyday subsistence and household needs. Thirty-two kinds of raw materials or artifacts were classified as derived from exotic resources, of which twenty were used exclusively for functional purposes, five only for useful artifacts (primarily dense-grained stone for grinding stones), and six for both (including obsidian for a variety of cutting tools). The list does not include trade in special craft goods that were manufactured from local materials but that, because of the skill required in their manufacture, were made in special centers and widely distributed (polychrome pottery, for example). The bulk of the exotic functional goods were found as artifacts in tombs or ceremonial caches in public buildings, and the authors believe that they were probably distributed as gift exchanges between royal lineages, possibly during life-crisis ceremonies such as those associated with birth, marriage, and death. Presumably, the ruler, in turn, redistributed some of these objects to the lower levels of Maya society through the pattern of kinship obligations.

The only substance that was both exotic and widely used as a useful artifact in the Maya Lowlands was, interestingly, obsidian. There is a considerable variability in its abundance within the area, with the northeastern Peten showing the highest concentration. Most of it seems to have come from the Chayal quarry located near Guatemala City. Recent work being conducted by me and Joseph Michels at Kaminaljuyu shows a heavy emphasis on obsidian mining and processing as one of the major craft activities on the site, as is evidenced by very extensive deposits of workshop debris. All of this takes on particular significance when compared to contemporary events in Central Mexico. Obsidian mining and artifact production was also one of the major activities at Teotihuacan (on a much greater scale) with a large number of specialized wards involved. In fact, as Spence (1966) points out, specialization by late Teotihuacan times reached the level at which wards specialized in the production of specific obsidian artifacts such as blades, points, or scrapers. These data are particularly interesting in connection with the conquest of Kaminaljuyu by *Teotihuacanos* in Middle Classic times and also in terms of the obvious evidence of Teotihuacan influence at Tikal in the northeastern Peten. Our reconstruction of these events is that the *Teotihuacanos* were trying to control the obsidian market in Mesoamerica as a whole by securing direct control of two major obsidian mines, the one at Pachuca and the other at Chayal. Tikal was probably a center of redistribution for obsidian over the Southern Maya Lowlands. The most likely institutional setting for such trade is that it was organized by *Teotihuacanos* living at Kaminaljuyu. There is evidence from Kaminaljuyu, furthermore, that this pattern of obsidian specialization actually began in Terminal Formative times (Verbena-Arenal). The *Teotihuacanos* simply took over and elaborated a well-established preexisting trade network.

With respect to artifact manufacture from local materials, Tourtellot and Sabloff (1972) postulated some intercommunity and intracommunity specialization, carried out primarily through the kinship network. In this connection, the lack of definite markets at Lowland Maya centers is a strongly supportive piece of evidence. W. Coe (1967) has suggested that structure 5E-32–36 at Tikal is a market, although direct supporting evidence is admittedly weak. If we accept this function for the structure and consider the enormous size of Tikal and its obvious political importance, it is an extraordinarily small market, only one-fortieth the size of the great market at Teotihuacan, defined by Millon (1967) from much better supporting data and is a convincing demonstration of the lack of significance of secular trade in the institutional structure at Tikal. Culbert's description (personal communication) of the pattern at Tikal where craftsmen's houses were dispersed throughout the settlement area rather than concentrated in wards as at Teotihuacan is further evidence for the wide institutional differences in local specialization in the two areas.

All of these data, it should be emphasized, are for the Late Classic Period, which according to our arguments should show a maximum intensity of trade, both internal and external. A paper by Rathje (1970a) challenges much of the above reconstruction of Maya economics. He points out that at least three useful artifacts or artifact raw materials —obsidian, igneous rock, and salt—were imported into the Central

Maya area. I think he exaggerates the significance of obsidian as a basic necessity among the Lowland Maya. Certainly it was used for a number of important household artifacts, and once trade networks were established the Maya depended heavily on these networks to obtain these materials, but generally obsidian was used for purposes to which local materials such as flint or chert could easily be adapted. These imported substances, following his point of view, not only would be classifiable as useful, but were critical materials necessary for the maintenance of the peasant life style. One of Rathje's major arguments in the same article is that this trade, since the sources of supply were located at considerably greater distances than is the case in the Mesoamerican highlands, required an unusually complex organization and carefully maintained trade routes. Because of these requirements, Rathje argues, a complex political and economic system evolved in the northeastern Peten. In rebuttal to this line of argument, I maintain that the obsidian trade was probably organized not by the rulers of Tikal or other Peten centers but by the Teotihuacan elite at Kaminaljuyu, at least during the Early and Middle Classic periods. Most igneous rock seems to have been imported from no farther away than a distance of 30–50 km. from neighboring areas of British Honduras, and I seriously doubt that it was necessary for the upper class to organize long-range trading expeditions to maintain a steady supply of this material. If these materials were brought from highland Guatemala, as seems to be one of Rathje's arguments, then I would agree that it would require a more highly organized institutional base.

URBANISM AMONG THE LOWLAND MAYA

One of the most persistent debates among Lowland Maya archaeologists is over the question of whether urbanism was characteristic of Lowland Maya centers. In recent years, this debate has centered particularly around the status of Tikal. In part—but only in part—the debate is based upon the definitional problem of what the term "urban" means. As I have pointed out (Sanders and Price 1968), instead of quarreling over definitions, the most useful approach is to deal with urbanism as an overall process characterized by the evolution of three internal processes: nucleation, population growth, and socioeconomic differentiation. These processes can be quantitatively measured and communities can be graded along a continuum of development of what we call urbanism. All of these processes are probably operative in any physical community, and there is a close functional relationship between the three—increasing size, for example, stimulates greater societal differentiation, which in turn leads to an increase in population density. But the feedback loops among these processes are extremely complex.

With respect to Tikal, my major criticism of the applicability of the term "city" to such a center is the low population density, which I feel is related in turn to a lesser degree of socioeconomic differentiation than what one usually thinks of as urban. I evaluated the pattern of population density and distribution (Sanders 1962, 1963) and concluded that approximately 2,200 structures in Carr and Hazard's (1961) 16 sq. km. survey area were house platforms. While there is an average density of 138 platforms over the 16 sq. km., the density actually varies from 16 to 524 platforms per square kilometer. There is a definite tendency toward a denser concentration of such structures within the central 8 sq. km. as opposed to the peripheral 8 sq. km. of the Carr-Hazard survey. I estimate a density of 190 platforms per square kilometer as opposed to 90 platforms in the two portions of the site.

In a very confusing article, Haviland (1969) presented new data on the settlement pattern of Tikal. A new survey was conducted to ascertain the total extent of Tikal and a series of four strips, each 500 m. wide, were surveyed to a distance of 12 km. from the Great Plaza in the four cardinal directions. Heavy concentrations of housemounds to the east and west extended as far as two very extensive *bajos* so that the limitation of the site in these directions was determined by natural topographic features. To the north and south, however, the density apparently dropped off very sharply at distances of 3.5 km. and 6.0 km. from the site center, respectively. At 4 km. to the north and 10 km. to the south, there were remains of earth and stone embankments that probably functioned as a combination boundary marker and defensive breastwork (Puleston and Callender 1967). The total area between the *bajos* and the walls was estimated by Haviland at 162.78 sq. km. He estimated that most of the population in Late Classic times resided in a 63.59 sq. km. central portion of this area, which he referred to as "Central Tikal." He noted that only in this central area was there evidence for Late Classic occupation of all or most of the structures, while the houses in the periphery seem to have been occupied primarily in Early Classic times and then for short periods, presumably the pattern that I originally suggested for Maya settlement.

Haviland then assumed an average population density of 600 people per square kilometer for the 64 sq. km. of Central Tikal and calculated the total population at 39,000, although no specific data on house platform density counts were presented to justify this figure. In the process, Haviland made assumptions that I cannot accept: (1) that there was absolute contemporaneity of occupation of all structures counted (which can never occur in any functioning community); (2) that each platform housed a nuclear family; and (3) that the nuclear families averaged 5.6 members (based on contemporary Maya patterns). The average nuclear family size of 5.6 is undoubtedly much too high, for the contemporary Maya are a people living during a period of major population growth and undoubtedly have a lower death rate than did the Late Classic Maya. Furthermore, there are numerous cases in Maya villages of expanded nuclear families or extended family households, so that the average cited involves a combination not only of nuclear families but of extended families as well. My data from the sixteenth century, as was pointed out earlier, suggest that a nuclear family in Central Mexico averaged only 3.3 persons and that extended families averaged about 7.0 persons. The use of either of these figures would considerably reduce Haviland's population estimates. A more important criticism of his paper, however, is the fact that he does not present comparative population density counts within the area of Tikal defined as Central Tikal. The overall picture of Tikal reported by others, as well as Haviland, is one of declining densities as one moves from the center. If this is true, the density of housemounds in the survey area outside of the 16 sq. km. area surveyed by Carr and Hazard (1961) could hardly have been greater than the 8 sq. km. peripheral portions of the Carr-Hazard survey. Taking the average densities for this portion of their survey, 90 house structures per square kilometer, and applying them to the remaining area of Central Tikal give the assessment of settlement pattern densities of Tikal presented in Table 23.

This assessment would seem to agree with the statements by Haviland in which he estimates a total of 1,430 structures (and this appar-

TABLE 23

PLATFORM DENSITIES AT TIKAL

Area	Density (platform per km.²)	Total Platforms
Central 8 km.²	190	1,520
The Middle 8 km.²	90	720
The Outer 48 km.²	90	4,320
Total		6,560

ently includes nonresidences as well) in the four radial strips, or an average of only 60 structures per square kilometer.

To obtain population figures from these housemound counts, we can either utilize a multiple of 3.3 times the number of platforms, assuming that each platform is the residence of a nuclear family, or we can assume that each group of platforms was the residence of an extended family and use the average of 7. The easiest technique to apply at this moment would be the assumption that each platform is the house of a nuclear family and to apply the 3.3 figure. If we do this, then the 64 sq. km. indicated by Haviland as Late Classic Central Tikal had a population of 21,548. If we assume that the cyclic shifting pattern does not apply to Central Tikal, we still have to make an allowance for some abandonment of houses at any given point in time. If we apply the average figures of 5 percent to 20 percent derived from nucleated settlements of Central Mexico, this figure reduces to between 17,238 and 20,047. To this figure we must add the elite population in the area near the site center, which I did not include in my original housemound counts. Keeping this in mind, I would estimate that the population in the central 64 sq. km. of Tikal was somewhere between 20,000 and 25,000 (313–391 persons per square kilometer), a figure substantially below Haviland's 39,000 estimate.

The most puzzling part of Haviland's paper is his estimate of the Late Classic population of the peripheral zone, an area of approximately 100 sq. km. He estimates a very respectable density of 100 persons per square kilometer, and yet states that much of this area was abandoned in Late Classic times and that most of the housemounds studied dated from the Early Classic Period. Assuming that he is correct, then the population for this area would be approximately 10,000 for the entire sustaining area, and 30,000–35,000 for all of Tikal. These figures yield an overall density of 200 persons per square kilometer.

With respect to the data previously presented, if we assume that 86 percent of the area defined by Haviland as the Tikal sustaining area was cultivable and subtract those areas completely covered by masonry or occupied by house sites, the result is a maximum of 130 sq. km. available for cultivation during the Late Classic Period. This result leads to an average density of 230–270 per square kilometer of cultivable land. An ecological model that would permit this density might be as follows: The central 64 sq. km., minus those areas used for residences and public buildings, were primarily given over to *ramón* orchards. This figure involves a maximum of no more than 40 sq. km. of land. The peripheral 100 sq. km., of which perhaps 80 sq. km. was cultivable land, was probably intensively used, certainly to the degree that it was a grass fallowing system and given over to root crops and maize with possibly a heavy focus on the former. This ecological system could support the population we have suggested for Tikal only if we assume that no food surpluses at all were produced, either for tiding the Maya over disaster or low-yield years or for export out of the area. It also assumes that no erosion took place from the intensive utilization, a conclusion which is undoubtedly incorrect.

The combination of *ramón* orchard cultivation plus a cycling of root crops and grains goes far toward explaining the Tikal settlement pattern. I am not arguing here that the practice of *ramón* orchard cultivation necessarily required that the population of Tikal should be concentrated within this central 64 sq. km. Theoretically, and in fact this would be the most economical arrangement, households could have been evenly distributed over the 64 sq. km. of the sustaining area with each house located next to a *ramón* orchard with its swidden fields located nearby. This kind of pattern is found among the Baganda today. Obviously, therefore, some other processes must be injected into the picture to explain the variations in settlement density at Tikal. What *ramón* orchard cultivation would do, however, is permit and make more viable a process of nucleation closer to the ceremonial center. I suspect that the stimuli for this nucleation at Tikal lies in the socioeconomic sphere with major stimuli being the needs for political integration and for defense against attack. A secondary factor would be the increasing degree of economic specialization among the Tikal Maya peasantry which stimulated close residence in order to facilitate the exchange of specialized goods. The fact, however, that this process of nucleation was never fully carried out is a strong argument that the latter function was not of major significance in the determination of the Tikal settlement pattern. As I have stated previously, there is an obvious and clear-cut relationship between settlement density and the dependency of the population upon the market system in urban centers. The more significant marketing becomes as an economic activity, the greater is the stimulation toward increasing nucleation. No known urban center with a fully evolved pattern of craft specialization has a density of less than 5,000 persons per square kilometer, and even the innermost 8 sq. km. of settlement at Tikal had a density, using our values, of only 1,000 persons per square kilometer.

CHANGING ECOSYSTEMS AND THE MAYA DECLINE

On the basis of the previous discussion, I have designed a hypothetical reconstruction of changing ecological systems among the Southern Lowland Maya that is presented in Figure 47. This figure shows a series of parallel processes that are closely interrelated. Subsistence patterns shift from a bush-fallowing, maize-based system to one of increasing diversification, to heavier yielding crops, to a dependence on imported foodstuffs, and finally to increasingly tighter control of land use and trade.

Paralleling this process are several closely related phenomena: rise of population density, decline of per capita income, increasing local specialization in crops, heavier reliance of the core area on the periphery for many basic materials, and more highly organized trade.

Territorial levels shift from tribal to two-level chiefdoms, to three-level chiefdoms, then to three-level and ultimately four-level states. The process is closely correlated with militarism, possibly involving a warrior class of Central Mexican type at the end. Correlated with these events is a shift from egalitarian to ranked to stratified society. At the same time that this last process is occurring, the older patterns of inte-

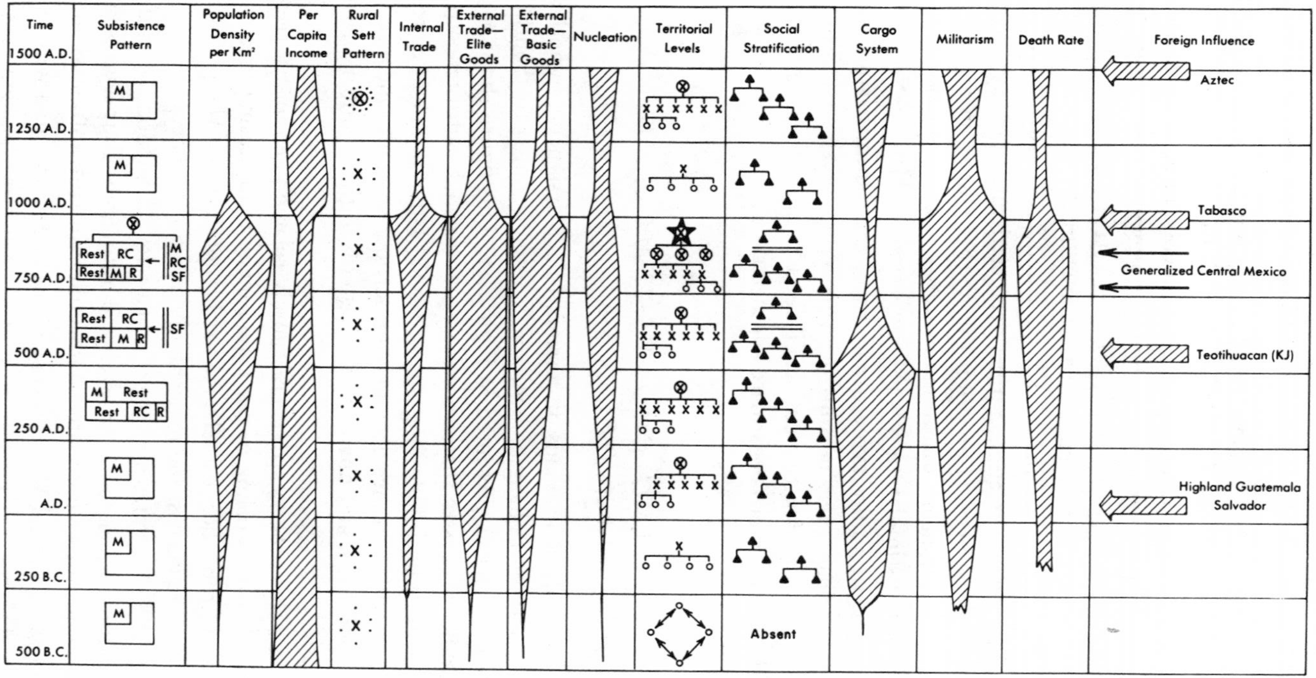

FIGURE 47. HISTORICAL PROCESSES IN THE EVOLUTION OF LOWLAND MAYA CIVILIZATION

gration, the *cargo* system and theoretical descent ties, are losing their strength as integrative mechanisms.

All of these events are correlated with increasing demands on the labor of the supporting peasantry in meeting their own caloric needs as well as those of the non-food-producing class, increasing problems of malnutrition, rise in death rates, and a reduction of per capita income.

In Figure 47 I have noted a series of events that reflect points in the Maya developmental sequence when foreign influences became important. Interestingly, these points seem to correlate with major changes in the ecosystem. Although outside contacts were undoubtedly important, I think that much of the evolution of Maya civilization can be best understood as an internal process. Diffusion may have stepped up the pace of change, but probably was not a basic cause. It should be emphasized that the model is generalized and the point at which changes occurred would vary from local area to local area.

Some of the ongoing processes noted in Figure 47 are not peculiar to the history of civilization in the Southern Maya Lowlands. The features that have intrigued scholars and produced the debates on the topic of the Southern Maya decline are the suddenness of the collapse and, more importantly, the fact that it was correlated with a massive population loss over an enormous area.

In the Teotihuacan Valley, the population declined from a peak of 140,000 to 30,000 during the one-hundred-year period following the collapse of Teotihuacan as a major center. The valley, however, measures only 600 sq. km., and the larger region within which it is located, the Basin of Mexico (8,000 sq. km.), did not suffer a comparable decline. In fact, recent surveys indicate that the basin as a whole may have had a somewhat larger population in the period succeeding the fall of Teotihuacan and a population several times larger by 1519.

In my previous paper, I discussed the pros and cons of various explanations of the collapse that have been offered over the years. Much of the variability in explanations was caused by the fact that the magnitude of population loss was not at all clear. Some writers, Thompson (1954), for example, argued that the Maya farmer did not abandon the area but simply stopped supporting the elite activities, that what occurred was a decline of civilization, but not of population. Virtually all recent archaeological studies in the Southern Lowlands agree that there was a catastrophic population loss. The date of the loss varies from the last one hundred years of the Classic Period to well within the Early Postclassic. Any explanation of the collapse, therefore, must deal with this population loss.

The key issue today is not so much the matter of population loss but rather whether it was the cause or the effect of the Maya decline. With respect to the first position, some scholars believe that a population loss on this scale must be the product of migration and/or disease caused primarily by the deterioration of the Maya environment for agriculture. In my earlier paper, I suggested a gradual process of grass conversion as the rising population density required increasingly shortened fallow cycles. This position assumes that the labor requirements in controlling grass growth were so great that they precluded a viable economic system, or at least required such a heavy investment in labor that the Maya farmers would not attempt it. As I pointed out previously, there is no question that grass succession occurs (see Hopkin's [1965] detailed discussion of the West African case in *Forest and Savanna*). In the absence of field studies involving the cultivation with stone tools of grass-invaded fields in the Maya Lowlands, this argument can still be supported. My position now is that grass swiddening probably is possible although enormously expensive, and that some Maya did, in fact, shift to a grass-fallowing system by Late Classic times.

Assuming that they did, then the question revolves around the long-range effects of several centuries of intensive cropping on the soils of the area. Again there are few data. Possible effects on the soil would be degradration of nutrients to a level so low that crops could not be produced at all and physical destruction of soil by erosion; however, the latter is not normally a problem in tropical forest areas under extensive cultivation. These processes are occurring in southeastern Nigeria today under demographic conditions similar to those I have suggested for the Late Classic Maya.

Either process (grass invasion or soil depletion) would result in a continuous reduction of agricultural land and caloric yield per capita, and an increasing dependence on the production of food in peripheral areas.

In the case of the savanna hypothesis, the recovery of the land would probably be a fairly rapid process since reseeding from the more lightly occupied peripheries would hasten the process. As Hopkins (1965) points out, however, once large areas are converted to grass, natural fires tend to retard this process. In the case of soil depletion, the retardation period would be considerably longer. Olson, based on his Tikal soil studies, suggests one thousand years as the requirement for restoration of these soils to their original fertility level. The slow Postclassic recovery is, therefore, supporting evidence for the soil depletion hypothesis.

The alternate hypothesis, that the underlying cause of the population decline was a series of political and economic events, has gained considerable ground in recent years. This argument assumes that the Lowland Maya elite had designed a complex internal and external trade network in both peasant and elite goods by Late Classic times and that symbiotic relationships among the Lowland Maya states and with surrounding areas had become of critical significance in the maintenance of Maya civilization. According to this hypothesis two sets of events occurred to upset the system. One was a series of military incursions into the southern part of the area (Altar de Sacrificios and Seibal) by Tabascans who cut off the trade between this area and the core and disrupted the trade network of the core itself by raids. The other sequence of events involved a shift of trade relationships by the periphery toward Central Mexico and the Gulf Coast, with the result that the trade network of the core dried up. As this happened, the population in the core area migrated to the peripheries.

In fact, these two explanations can be easily adapted to each other to give a much clearer picture of the Maya decline. The trade network, and consequently the military hypothesis, can have an explanatory value only if basic foods were involved. As I pointed out, none of the craft products derived from exotic sources were absolutely essential for the survival of the Maya peasant. The only product that would have presented survival problems was food. The elite do not need elite goods to maintain themselves as an elite, as some versions of the trade breakdown theory seem to suggest. As the deterioration of the core environment proceeded, the dependence on imported foodstuffs would rise. An important question in this respect is what the core area might have exported in exchange for foreign goods. Finished craft products were a possible export, but as peripheral centers acquired the skills to manufacture such products the demand would decline. As more land was brought under cultivation, there would be a corresponding decline of forest products, though some products derived from plants could have been obtained by cultivation. If peripheral areas shifted their trade ties elsewhere (one could relate this shift to the decline of productivity in the core area), the economic problems of the core would become increasingly acute.

Associated with these events would be an increasing distance between peasant and noble, an economic deterioration in the average peasant's lifestyle, and an increase of nutritionally based diseases.

One explanation of the mechanism of loss of population that has been offered is nutritional disease and elevated death rates. The population loss, from this point of view, is seen as an internal process. However, I don't believe this hypothesis is correct, since the effect would be a reduction of population to the point where a viable subsistence system would become reestablished and the process would start all over again—in other words, a cyclic pattern would emerge.

The only reasonable explanation for the loss is migration, stimulated by peasant dissatisfaction and permitted by the breakdown of the political system. But migration to where? If the population moved to the immediate Maya Lowland periphery the same problems created in the core area would rapidly be triggered again.

Although some population movement did occur into such areas, I believe that the major movement was into the adjacent highlands of Guatemala and Chiapas. On the basis of a few surveys by Richard Adams (unpublished paper) in the Cotzal district, Ledyard Smith (1955) in the Rio Negro Basin, and Robert Adams (1961) in Chiapas, there is evidence that the northern highlands were very lightly populated in Formative and Early Classic times, reached a respectable level of population density only in Late Classic times, and then became densely settled during the Postclassic. Although some of this growth may have been internal, there is a strong possibility that it was also the product of immigration from the Peten. This reconstruction checks rather well against Vogt's (1964b) assessment of the glotto-chronological evidence of Maya linguistic differentiation. For example, he states that Chorti (a predominantly highland language) separated from Chol (a lowland language and, according to some reconstructions, one of the major languages of the Southern Lowlands Classic Maya) between A.D. 700 and 900, that the Tzeltal moved into highland Chiapas from a lowland area between A.D. 500 and 750, and that the Pokomam split off from the Pokomchi around A.D. 900.

364

Cultural Ecology of the Lowland Maya

There is support for this reconstruction on the archaeological side, since some elements of Lowland Maya civilizations were introduced into the highlands in Late Classic times. Richard Adams objected to this hypothesis on the grounds that one would expect more evidence of such movements in the ceramics. I think it should be pointed out, however, that it was probably not a mass movement of hundreds of thousands of people but a gradual process of small group dispersion over a period of several hundred years, and furthermore involved movement into areas already settled. Conceivably, much of this movement was stimulated by the fact that the highlands were already well known to the Southern Lowlands Maya as a source of food surpluses through the postulated trade network.

16
The Peten Maya Decline Viewed
in the Perspective of State Formation

MALCOLM C. WEBB

Department of Anthropology and Geography
Louisiana State University, New Orleans

The cause or causes of the decline of Maya culture in the Peten and nearby areas at the end of the tenth century is a classic problem in anthropology. However, none of the many explanations suggested to date has received general assent, for reasons not difficult to understand. Briefly, the explanations may be grouped as follows: natural disaster; disease; environmental deterioration caused by overly intensive agriculture, which led to loss of soil fertility, excessive growth of grasses, or soil erosion; climatic change; revolt of the agricultural population; and invasion.[1]

As it happens, there is no evidence of large-scale climatic change, widespread natural catastrophe, or basic agricultural deterioration in the Peten. In addition, there is no indication that the population of the Peten as a whole was ever so great as to exceed the capacity of the agricultural cycle, although it may have been large enough to press heavily upon it—and indeed must have been in the areas immediately

367

around the larger centers (Cowgill 1962; Cowgill and Hutchinson 1963a, 1963b; Haviland 1970). In the same way, there is no real evidence for a peasant revolt, but a revolt would not represent a final explanation in any case since revolts do not just happen. They should be particularly unlikely in prestate or archaic societies, with their strong ties of kinship and tradition; therefore, a cause for such a revolt must be given in turn. This objection also applies to the disease hypothesis. In the absence of factors which introduce new plagues, one must specify some more basic set of changes which would lead to an abrupt decline in living standards or other deleterious shifts in the man-environment relationship. Finally, I note that while there apparently was a foreign invasion of the Usumacinta drainage associated with the spread of Fine Orange Wares from Tabasco and Campeche (Sabloff and Willey 1967; cf. Cowgill 1964), this invasion seems to have taken place after the decline had already begun. Here, too, one may ask why the invasion took place just then and why it is associated with a degree of decline nearly unique in the course of human culture. One would expect the conquerors, if not the survivors among the local population, to continue to make use of the area themselves if it were worth invading in the first place (Binford 1968; Erasmus 1968).

Although I believe that these objections, which could be developed in much greater detail (Cowgill 1964; Webb 1964; Willey 1964), are serious, indeed fatal, they do not represent the most basic flaw in previous explanations of the decline: that those explanations all appeal to factors which are essentially external to the long-term functioning of the culture in question, even those explanations which bring in local factors such as agricultural capacity. That is, they do not convincingly demonstrate how the decline could eventually be caused by the continued operation of the same processes which led to the initial development and florescence of the Peten Maya. Like many anthropologists, I believe that a culture ultimately is the mechanism by which a human group adjusts to a given environment, an environment which includes neighboring societies as well as such factors as soil, amount and distribution of rainfall, temperature range, topography, flora and fauna; and the culture itself is constantly changed and shaped by the process of adjustment. I also regard the range of possible responses open to a given society at a given level of energy use and organizational complexity as limited; so that, with care, one may use likely possibilities as a guide to cultural-historical reconstruction, always bearing in mind that the variety of responses possible is still very much a matter of investigation. Since the culture which continuously adjusts to the stresses and opportunities presented by the environment is itself the systemic product of previous culture-environment interaction, one would expect an essential continuity of development through time, as in biological evolution (cf. Huxley 1956; Childe 1963).

If this revised environmental determinism (which I have argued elsewhere is the distinctive feature of both "neoevolutionist" anthropology and of British prehistoric archaeology generally [Webb 1969] and which Harris [1966, 1968] has fruitfully applied under the term "cultural ecology") is true, then it should be possible to subsume the birth, persistence, and death of the Peten Classic pattern under one set of processes.[2] Indeed, since the Mesoamerican societies were in constant interaction, one would expect a theory to be satisfactory to the extent that it demonstrated the correlation of events in the Peten with Mesoamerican culture history generally. Even better would be a theory which fitted Mesoamerica as a whole into general rules of social development; Meggers (1954) attempted such an explanation, arguing that Maya high culture could only have evolved outside the Peten and then declined upon introduction into a tropical forest environment. And Willey's explanation (1964), in which the introduction of novel, more prestigeful religious and social-organizational concepts from more advanced areas of Mesoamerica was seen as causing the collapse of the Peten system of social control, was another such attempt.

But no explanation has determined successfully why the Peten Classic culture emerged when and where it did and collapsed when it did. Thus, Meggers's theory assumes an unrealistically low agricultural potential for tropical forest areas, too great a population density for the Maya Lowlands, and a history of continuous decline which is unsupported by archaeology, while Willey's theory gives too great a primacy to the action of aspects of culture which are more likely to be dependent variables. Although both are extremely useful in defining the problem, they are inadequate as stated. Because of these considerations, I have attempted to reverse the question, asking not why the Maya declined, but why they developed to the level they did and lasted so long (Webb 1964, 1968). This approach places emphasis upon a consideration of the manner in which civilizations evolve, the nature of the relationship between states, the antecedent social type from which they typically evolve (that is, chiefdoms), and the particular nature of the Peten environment.

STATES AND CHIEFDOMS

Two theories of state origins are especially prominent at this time. Carneiro (1961, 1970) has long argued that pristine states arise where a sharply segmented or constricted environment causes heavy population pressure on limited land and, hence, increasing warfare. This view is essentially shared by Fried (1967), while Dumond (1965) and Harner (1970) have suggested that the increased size and density of population lead to centralization and power concentration. Sahlins (1958, 1963), Service (1962), and Wolf (1959) have focused upon the importance of exchange between the environmentally diverse portions of a region for generating and concentrating wealth and power, thus causing chiefdoms to emerge from tribes and states to emerge from chiefdoms. Sanders (1957; Sanders and Price 1968) has applied both theories in combination to state origins in Mesoamerica, as has Gluckman (1968 : 174–76) for Africa south of the Sahara. I would agree in this application, although I see agricultural competition and war as more important for the generation of that differential wealth which Fried (1960, 1967), among others, regards as essential to pristine states and trade as more vital in the spread of states into secondary state areas as described (more or less) by Engels many years ago (Engels 1942; cf. Webb 1965, 1968). Again like Fried (1967), I suspect that only trade from an existing state is likely to be great enough to override tribal mechanisms for inhibiting stratification. Thus pristine or primary states are circumscription-conquest states, while secondary states tend to be caused by trade.

A rapid world survey suggests that we have six or perhaps seven primary state areas. These, along with the approximate times of their origins, are: Egypt (about 3100 B.C.), lower Mesopotamia (at the same time, or shortly before), the Indus Valley (before 2500 B.C.), the Yellow River basin of northern China (shortly after 2000 B.C.), highland Mesoamerica (between 100 B.C. and A.D. 800—it would appear that the region is marked by an unusually long transitional stage), and coastal Peru (about the time of Christ). Although it has been suggested that the Egyptian state represents a response to Mesopotamian influence (for example, Frankfort 1956), the cultural patterns of the two areas are distinct. Egypt's achievement of union over its entire river valley prior to unification in Mesopotamia and the consideration that Mesopotamia was not developed enough in this period to penetrate Egypt directly (in contrast with the diffusion of specific ideas or motifs) indicate an independent process in each area (Childe 1957, 1959). A recent reexamination of the Egyptian sequence, in fact, indicates that there is no artifactual evidence of cultural intrusion sufficiently great to warrant regarding developments there as anything other than native (Arkell and Ucko 1965).

I believe that the same points can be made in regard to the Indus Valley and northern China, despite the relatively undeveloped state of our knowledge in the former case and the relatively retarded date of developments in the latter (Piggott 1950; Clark and Piggott 1965 : 196–201; Wheeler 1966; Creel 1937a, 1937b; Cheng 1959, 1960; cf. Webb 1964). In the same way, although a case can perhaps still be made for the existence of a nuclear American diffusion sphere in the period between the birth of agriculture and the end of the Olmec or Chavin periods (for example, Willey 1955), I know of no major authority on either Mesoamerica or Peru who believes that any strong or continuous contact between the two areas occurred during their Protoclassic or Early Classic periods (for example, Wolf 1959; Willey 1962; Bennett and Bird 1960; Collier 1962; Lanning 1967). While it is possible to argue about the degree of independence of development in each of these six cases, I believe that one would be on safe ground in regarding them as the *most* primary among the early state areas of which we have knowledge.

All of the regions mentioned share one common feature: they are areas of extremely productive land surrounded by very dry zones. The situation in Egypt, Mesopotamia, and Pakistan at the present time is well known. However, I should perhaps mention that while Egypt was rather less arid in the neolithic stage, by the time the evolution of the state was well advanced, conditions there had begun to approach those of recent times so that land outside the valley was not able to support settled, high-level agriculture (Butzer 1964 : 438–60; Clark 1962). In the same way, it seems certain that at the relevant time both lower Mesopotamia and Pakistan were as dry as they are today, or nearly so (Butzer 1964 : 461–71; Raikes and Dyson 1961). It may possibly not be so well known that conditions of climate, soil, and topography combine to severely hinder intensive agriculture away from the river margins in the Yellow River basin (Stamp 1938 : 500–18; Cressey 1955). In early Shang times conditions were no better, and the great irrigation canals were not yet built (Von Wissmann et al. 1956; Chi 1936). Central highland Mexico south to the Isthmus of Tehuantepec is also rather dry and, in addition, suffers from severe rain shadow effects in the highland basins and stream valleys that were the aboriginal population centers (Walker n.d.; West and Augelli 1966). I imagine that no one would question the severity or long-continued nature of the aridity that characterizes the Peruvian coast (Lanning 1967 : 7–12, 41–65).

The great merit of the circumscription hypothesis is that it demonstrates a way in which the widespread process of intertribal warfare, ineffective as a mechanism of state formation for most tribal peoples since such societies lack the military organization necessary to prevent defeated groups from simply moving away, could, in the special circumstances of limited agricultural land, generate more advanced social systems. Carneiro (1970) noted that, while a great many portions of tropical Latin America which never developed states, or even chiefdoms, were theoretically able to support such systems under native conditions of subsistence, chiefdoms in fact appeared only in areas where good land was limited in extent and sharply bounded by markedly poorer land, and that such areas were marked by especially severe warfare as well. From this evidence he concluded that in these areas, as population inevitably grew to the point at which unused good land was becoming scarce, the necessary struggle for agricultural resources among neighboring, confined groups generated more complex and centralized tribal organization. Because no group could retreat without abandoning all hope of gaining the highly desirable territory, there would be a premium on staying put and fighting it out. This situation in turn would greatly increase the power of tribal rulers both by creating an obvious need for firm leadership and by enabling leaders to reward their followers by plunder from raided groups (who could not easily move out of range). Such intensified warfare would more likely be touched off by incursions into lightly settled buffer zones used for hunting or pasture than by invasions of the tribal heartland, but this would not alter the argument.

Carneiro then considered what might happen if *very* populous chiefdoms in *very* rich areas with very sharply constricted agricultural zones, such as river valleys or lake basins in arid regions, were to fight in this way. Applying this hypothesis to the primary state areas with their highly limited land, we expect chiefs to be able to escape controls on the alienation of group property and the individual accumulation of tribal wealth. The war chief, with the right to divide spoils, could take the surplus of defeated groups, who would be absolutely tied down by the environment and unable to resist. Because the land, while limited, was so highly productive, this loot would provide the chief with a source of wealth unparalleled in quantity and freedom from internal controls. Even after the customary distributions of loot had been made, enough would remain to enable him to overcome kin loyalties and gather a group of retainers, a war band, large enough to keep in check all other groups in the society. With his following he could enforce decisions, collect taxes, undertake public works, and mobilize the society for external defense—in a word, subvert the tribal constitution and establish the state (Carneiro 1970).

Moreover, this subversion could happen in gradual stages, with each new acquisition of power representing only a small departure from current practice. By the time the remnants of the old council of tribal elders finally sank into impotence before the rising power of the king (the situation seen in early historic Mesopotamia or among the Aztec, for example [Adams 1966 : 139–42]), the earlier time at which the king had been only a war leader holding his office temporarily and at the pleasure of the council would no longer be remembered. Over the same time span the emerging leadership group would have become so powerful and wealthy that they would seem quite different kinds of creatures than the common tribesmen, who even if their own condition had come to be as bad as that of defeated groups, also could not move out because of the environment (cf. Adams 1966 : 109–10; Fried 1967 : 153–54; Sanders and Price 1968 : 215–17). That the mechanism in question operated only in the large dryland river valleys and lake basins explains the otherwise puzzling fact that primary states arose only in such areas, and did arise in the majority of such areas into which agriculture was effectively introduced sufficiently early to allow a large population buildup before the entrance of secondary state factors (a saving clause put in to exclude the Colorado drainage and the Niger bend area).

But, were all of the primary state regions, in fact, characterized by war at the appropriate times? The answer seems to be that they were. Egypt's legendary history begins with a tale of conquest, and the archaeological record shows the process of territorial consolidation and associated social stratification matched by a shift in artistic productions from representations of quarrels between nomes to celebrations of victory by high chiefs already wearing the regalia associated with the historic pharaohs. Weapons and (apparently) fortifications appear at the appropriate points (Childe 1957). The same process took place in Mesopotamia with destruction levels, population displacements, weaponry, and representations of slaves and battles all appearing by the Uruk Period and culminating late in Early Dynastic times (Childe 1954 : 71–73, 88, 99–100; 1957). The historical record shows a process of replacement of theocratic and kin leaders by increasingly conquest-minded secular rulers (Adams 1966 : 139–41, 156–59). The documentary record from Shang China indicates possibly even greater emphasis on militarism than was the case in the areas just mentioned, while fortifications are a prominent feature of the immediately preceding Lungshan culture, one site of which shows evidence of having withstood a siege (Creel 1937a : 57–60, 141–57, 1937b : 179–82).

The remaining example of the certain Old World primary state areas, the Indus Valley, until recently appeared to be something of an exception to this rule, if only because so little evidence was available for the early stages of the Harappan culture. It is, therefore, interesting that more recent work in this area (at the site of Kot Diji near Khairpur, in the Harappan heartland) has uncovered evidence of a Harappan town immediately underlain by a strongly fortified neolithic village which was either evolving into the Harappan civilization or was under strong influence from it, and whose occupation was terminated by conquest (Bacon 1961 : 211–12; Wheeler 1966 : 30–33, 57–60).

Coastal Peru provides an especially good example of the process under discussion: possibly defensive hilltop platforms appear in the

Chavin horizon (Late Guanape Period), while forts and defensive walls become quite common in the later Preclassic periods (Willey 1953 : 92–101, 358–59, 395–96). The importance of warfare among the Classic Period Moche is indicated by the frequent representations of fighting, captivity, and torture in their art, while the south coastal Nazca placed a high value on trophy heads (Mason 1957 : 68–74, 82; Kidder II, Lumbreras, and Smith 1963; Lanning 1967 : 92–94, 106–11).

Since in the cases just discussed there does appear to be a coincidence of warfare areas of limited land with the rise of the primary states, it would appear appropriate to regard the process suggested by Carneiro as the chief factor in primary state formation. Growing mercantile wealth or the use of religious sanctions might play a role as well, for kings could easily have patronized merchants or used religious symbols, while priests may sometimes have assumed direction of the use of military force and become kings.

Turning to the question of secondary state formation, Engels maintained that large-scale trade within and between tribes would lead to the concentration of economic and hence of police powers in the hands of a small number of favorably placed, shrewd chiefs and kin elders who would then form a ruling merchant class. This contention is supported by events in many ancient and recent societies. Such trade would be particularly likely in areas in which separate microzones contained mutually complementary resources, as would be especially the case with river valleys and their surrounding regions. If such areas were also highly productive (as, again, might be the case in river valleys), the increasing wealth and the demand for technological improvement and occupational specialization might lead to the breakdown of kin controls and property sharing with a consequent growth of social stratification and of new, political forms of social control, as noted by Sahlins (1958), Wolf (1959), Sanders and Price (1968) and Fried (1967). I feel that customs such as compulsory sharing of goods and *cargo* systems, which compel persons of wealth to expend it for the common good, would render unlikely the formation of primary states through trade. And I have difficulties in conceiving how trade could become the monopoly of one portion of the population, except as merely one aspect of a generalized leadership status (cf. Sahlins

375

1960). However, I would agree that the trade mechanism is of great importance in the *spread* of state organization into new, secondary state areas.

The ethnographic and historical literature relating to the European penetration of North America, southern Africa, Guinea, and Polynesia contains perhaps two dozen fairly good examples of such state formation, while medieval sources dealing with the fringes of Arabic, European, or Chinese civilization would provide many more. But these cases are precisely those in which trade with an already functioning state has introduced surplus wealth in amounts far larger than any tribal society can begin to generate on its own. When this wealth provides an excess beyond what is needed by the leadership for customary redistributive activity, the redistributive channels clog up and overflow, as it were. The surplus has in these cases actually been observed to be used to hire war bands made up of individuals from defeated tribes, exiles, and other rootless men who are not bound by traditional ties to the society and can, therefore, be used in enforcing the will of the chief, as opposed to that of the tribe as a whole. This surplus of wealth may also be used to offer the common tribesmen rewards greater than those available in the traditional system so that force is supplemented by positive inducements to obedience to the chief.

It is the surplus of trade wealth which first enables the emerging king to support the army and bureaucracy necessary to collect the taxes needed if the army and bureaucracy are to be supported internally. Because of the importance of this wealth, tribal chieftains have frequently tended to keep a monopoly control over trade with more advanced groups (for example, Gluckman 1940, 1960; Webb 1965). The same concern is seen in the large role played by the government in commerce among archaic states generally (Polanyi 1966; Polanyi et al. 1957). It would even seem that in the absence of new, excess, external wealth "unneeded" in the traditional system, there is no conceivable way in which a state could begin at all, since without an army (or at least a band of reliable retainers) one cannot collect the taxes needed to support the army needed to collect the taxes, and so on.

Renfrew (1969, 1970) has recently objected to the view that the growth of complexity in late Neolithic and Bronze Age European societies, a growth which led ultimately to the emergence of the state, was caused by diffusion from the older Near Eastern centers of civilization, and prefers instead an explanation in terms of local intertribal and intratribal exchange. I would suggest, however, that his real quarrel is with the notion that the Europeans were led to more advanced technology and social controls by "stimulation" or teaching by members of more advanced cultures. I fully agree that the evolution in question is an internal one for each society undergoing the transformation. However, what the more developed, richer outsiders provide is not teaching, but the extra wealth that local leaders can put to their own use. One might well expect such growing cultures to innovate in many aspects of life and even to do so in some cases before their more advanced trading partners, as Childe (1950, 1958) noted for Europe, an area in which, as I have suggested elsewhere (Webb 1969), such developments were especially likely. Perhaps we do not expect this innovation to occur because in recent centuries the vast technological superiority of state societies over nonstates has generally resulted in the conquest of the latter early in the contact process. (Conquest itself does, of course, represent a clear-cut mechanism by which an existing state can extend state controls into new areas, which might later become independent. Even attempts at conquest might have the same effect by providing tribal peoples both with an obvious need for organization and also with the required wealth in the form of plunder.) My point is that granted the strong pressures against the alienation and concentration of surplus production in tribal societies and the consequent inhibition of economic specialization, preexisting states would be the only source of trade goods sufficient in quantity and quality to lead to state formation among tribal societies.

So much for states. What of chiefdoms? There appears to be general agreement that chiefdoms develop out of egalitarian tribes in situations in which the factors productive of states are only partially present, or present to an insufficient degree. Sahlins (1958, 1963), Service (1962), Sanders (1957), Sanders and Price (1968) and Gluckman (1968 : 174–76) have pointed out that chiefdoms are likely to emerge in areas capable of producing a surplus and in which a wide distribution of resources makes it advantageous to have a chief to serve as a central redistributive node. Although, as noted, I cannot agree that these factors alone could ever lead to the emergence of states, they are surely correlated with the occurrence of chiefdoms. While chiefdoms apparently do occur in situations in which it is physically possible for one family to personally reach all subsistence resources (Finney 1966), and while the sums actually redistributed—let alone retained by the chief—may be rather small (Lambert 1966), there should be an advantage in terms of efficiency. Carneiro (1961) argues that a degree of circumscription insufficient to produce states would result in chiefdoms, a view supported by Reichel-Dolmatoff's (1961) and Vayda's (1956, 1961) papers on tribal warfare. Fried (1967) suggests that population pressure could give rise to chiefdoms both by generating small-scale war and by leading to differential rights to land. I would guess that trade on a small scale with an existing state might effect this degree of consolidation and no more.

It is, then, upon these preliminary bases that true states have emerged. But if the factors discussed above were insufficient to produce an adequate amount of "extra" or "external" wealth, that is, wealth which came from outside the society through conquest or trade, progress beyond the chiefdom level would be impossible. Even though societies of this sort might indeed be able to do rather spectacular things and even if the roots of a bureaucracy were present in the chief's following of subchiefs, retainers, and, perhaps, part-time specialists, who form, as it were, the material cause of the state stretching back into the chiefdom and even to the simple tribe (Lowie 1960; Adams 1966 : 110), these systems would still be dependent upon free obedience and so lack a truly effective locus of sovereignty (Service 1962 : 159–60, 170–72).

It is precisely the ability to enforce absolutely the wishes of the rulers which even the largest, richest, and most successful chiefdom lacks. Although this power may grow by slow accumulation until the point is reached at which these commands will be unfailingly obeyed, the difference between chiefdom and state is one of kind and not of degree. The inability of the leadership to enforce unpleasant orders would prevent the collection of taxes or the provision of services which would give them that very ability. Kept relatively small in size and absolutely simple in organization, these societies could not develop those economic or social interdependencies that might suggest the value of truly governmental controls, as Gluckman (1968 : 190–98) has noted. This inadequacy means that the level of integration would constantly fluctuate owing to local circumstances such as inheritance of office, chiefly rivalries, or the extent to which various chiefs were able to manipulate the system. Indeed, Sahlins (1963) and also Epstein (1968) point out that the very act of gathering the goods required to act as chief puts enormous strains on the larger chiefdoms, since the accumulation process tends to divert too much of the chief's resources to the support of the chiefly apparatus and away from immediate general economic redistribution—the only means of securing the good will needed to accumulate the goods. Moreover, the power of the chief to innovate would also be severely limited since his position ultimately rests upon kin and customary ties (Webb 1965).

These considerations explain the two characteristic features of chiefdoms. The first feature is cyclical instability, the tendency of large chiefdoms to break apart into their component segments, then to reunite only to fall apart again (Service 1962 : 151–53; Gluckman 1968 : 168–70). It appears that any expansion of the system to the point of linking disparate groups, of undertaking novel tasks (or even traditional tasks in amounts exceeding customary levels), or of requiring innovative policy-making causes the system to snap. The second feature is that chiefdoms, especially those whose size and complexity approach the maximum for the type, inevitably are theocracies (cf. Service 1962 : 171; Schapera 1967 : 125; Fried 1967 : 137–41; Gluckman 1968 : 298–99; Turner 1966; Davenport 1964; Park 1966). I would suggest that this is the case for other reasons than just the strength of religious sanctions. Perhaps as important to the strength of chiefly theocracies is the fact that religious ceremonies, in contrast to the "selfish" needs of the rulers or even to public works, can be seen as of benefit to participants gathered from throughout the entire chiefdom. In addition, cult activities are likely to be strongly patterned and to reflect the established ways. Gods are not bound by time or space and "have been" from the beginning. Religion thus supports the society in the absence of political controls. Clearly, however, the strength of the cement which holds the system together depends basically upon the believability of the cult itself. Granting this, we would expect the most advanced of chiefdoms—those most like states in their ability to support the characteristic features of civilization—to be at once the most theocratic of societies and the most unstable and subject to total collapse. This point is, of course, directly relevant to the Classic Period

Maya of the Peten. But a full explanation of why this is so requires a brief reconstruction of the probable course of state evolution in Mesoamerica as a whole.

THE ECOLOGY OF STATE EVOLUTION IN MESOAMERICA

Any attempt to apply the points just made to Mesoamerica obviously must begin with an examination, however brief, of the environment, since it is upon this that all else depends. We have noted that the great highland lake basins and river valleys of Central Mexico were zones of rainfall stress. These were also areas of great potential fertility, provided water were available. Similar conditions prevailed in the region about Monte Alban. The highlands and Pacific coastal slope of Guatemala also were extremely fertile with relatively plentiful rainfall. The level surfaces found in all of these regions, in contrast to the rugged country which surrounded them, were also advantageous to digging-stick cultivators (cf. M. Coe 1963). Because of the richness and durability of the soils in these areas, which could be increased by irrigation waters or *chinampas*, quite a small plot could support a family and could be reused indefinitely (Sanders 1957; West and Augelli 1966). These areas were able to sustain large and dense populations but, with the partial exception of southern Guatemala, were sharply circumscribed. The surrounding regions—the better-watered portions of the lower highland *tierra templada* and the highland margin of the lowland, largely coastal *tierra caliente*—were less circumscribed in extent and, owing to more broken topography and to soils of less durable fertility, were unable to support such large and dense populations as could the first of the broad environmental types. More land was required per family and a one-to-one or two-to-one ratio of fallow-to-planting seasons was necessary to maintain fertility. In consequence, population concentrations could not be so great as in the first areas considered.

A third zone, also consisting of uncircumscribed regions—the humid sections of the *tierra caliente* proper—was even less able to support dense populations. Here the problems of soil depletion and grass growth associated with tropical forest farming in the absence of metal tools led to fallow-planting ratios as high as eight or twelve to one. In consequence, a rather widely dispersed settlement pattern was the most efficient. A partial exception to these limitations were the large river systems which crossed this zone, along whose banks constantly renewed deposits of alluvial soils encouraged much more dense populations. This riverbank subzone was, therefore, more similar to the *tierra templada* (Sanders 1953). On the other hand, the *tierra caliente* may have offered special advantages if, as Coe and Flannery (1964) have argued, this zone was marked by a close clustering of useful microenvironments, particularly along the coast.

In any event, we see that, as Palerm (1955) noted, Mesoamerica is characterized by three basic environmental types, each of which has differing possibilities both for the support of public works, which in ancient America were achieved through the mobilization of manpower in whatever concentration was naturally present, and for the development of the social controls needed to undertake these works.

Although our knowledge of Mesoamerican culture history is still seriously defective, it seems that the sequence of events occurred as we have predicted. After a long period of initial experimentation, extending back to perhaps 7000 B.C., essentially full reliance upon agriculture and village life was achieved by shortly after 2000 B.C. (MacNeish 1962, 1964a, 1964b). Apparently, the major steps toward this new way of life took place in the highlands owing to causes which I believe can be best understood in terms of evolving adjustments to the environment, but which lack of space prohibits discussing here. In any event, although agriculture had begun to diffuse through the New World by the latter part of this period, blending to some extent with independently developed traditions of cultivation in such areas as Peru (Rouse 1962; Collier 1962; Lanning 1967 : 50–75), on the basis of present evidence it appears that the tropical forest lowlands of Mesoamerica were only lightly settled until after 2000 B.C. (M. Coe 1963; Coe and Flannery 1964; Willey, Culbert, and Adams 1967; cf. Webb 1964).

While the highlands had a head start, the next major movement toward civilization—the rise of the Olmec and "Olmecoid" cultures —took place in the *tierra caliente* of Veracruz and Tabasco around 1200 B.C. It would now appear that this efflorescence grew naturally out of the prior base provided by the simple early farming peoples in the region as well as in Chiapas and the Guatemalan coast (M. Coe 1965a, 1967, 1968a; Coe, Diehl, and Stuiver 1967; Heizer, Drucker, and

Graham 1968). It is also possible that the earliest pottery-using cultures of the Valley of Mexico and nearby areas took shape under strong Olmec influence, although the precise relationship between the Olmec "intruders" and the Zacatenco culture remains uncertain (Piña Chan 1955b; Covarrubias 1957 : 13–44, 79–83; M. Coe 1965a; Tolstoy and Paradis 1970). There is no question that the Olmec were organized on a high chiefdom level and that they provided the principal stimulus for further developments throughout Mesoamerica (Coe 1968b : 98–110; Sanders and Price 1968 : 126–128). It would appear that the bases of the controls necessary to the Olmec system were the need for redistribution of the products of the various microenvironments (Coe and Flannery 1964), desire for assured access to limited areas of riverine land (Coe 1968a, 1968b : 105–10), and the wish to participate in more wide-ranging intertribal trade networks (Grove 1968; Coe 1968b : 92–98). Nevertheless, the unlikelihood of securing a monopoly control over local products, the ceremonial rather than practical nature of the long distance trade, and the consideration that forest land away from the rivers could be used in farming if need be all seem to have inhibited local developments beyond an urban formative or chiefdom level, though these were very splendid chiefdoms indeed. The next developments could only occur in the dry highland areas of truly limited land.

During the later half of the first millennium B.C., certain areas in the highlands which until then had lagged behind the "metropolitan" Olmec began to forge ahead. Always strongly influenced by the Olmec tradition, they nevertheless displayed an essential continuity with their local village-dwelling predecessors. The outstanding examples are the Valley of Mexico, in which Cuicuilco and Tlapacoya in the south flourished and then were gradually replaced by Tzacualli-phase Teotihuacan (Barba de Piña Chan 1956; West 1965; Dixon 1967; Parsons 1968), and the Valley of Oaxaca during the Monte Alban I and II periods (Flannery 1968; Paddock 1966a, 1966b : 91–120). Cholula and Kaminaljuyu probably should also be included here, though little recent data are available for the former and the latter appears to reach its Preclassic (Miraflores) peak rather late in this period—perhaps reflecting less intense land limitation. Although evidence is scanty, Kaminaljuyu appears to show the same broadly Olmec influence as the more northerly centers, but in more diffuse fashion (Shook 1951a; Proskouriakoff 1968).

This same period is marked by strong evidence of fairly well-developed, small-scale irrigation systems and by the orientation of sites toward these systems in the Valley of Mexico (Millon 1954, 1957; West 1965), Puebla (MacNeish 1964a; Woodbury 1966; Fowler 1969), and the region about Monte Alban (Flannery 1968; Neely 1967). The fact that the great Protoclassic and Classic efflorescence of these regions occurred in the locations with irrigation potential rather than throughout the much larger zones which their Middle and early Late Preclassic ancestors had dominated (Paddock 1966a; McBride 1969) suggests that this potential played a key role in their rise. I see no reason to believe that the irrigation systems in question had reached a size or degree of integration so great that a small group could control society by controlling the allocation of water in the manner suggested by Wittfogel (1959). Woodbury (1961) has demonstrated that peoples on the tribal level can maintain rather large canal systems, while Gray (1963 : 161–71) provides ethnographic data which indicate that, although direction of irrigation works may play a role in social control, this does not result in the concentration of wealth or power in a few hands (cf. Adams 1956, 1960). The importance of the Late Preclassic and Early Classic irrigation systems is that they indicate water stress, almost certain conflict over hydraulic works, and the inability of defeated groups to move away. In the same way, I have no doubt that trade in useful items formed another "resource" over which these early highland groups could struggle among themselves and that control of such trade was highly useful to the tribal leadership, in the manner suggested by Sanders (1957). What I am concerned with is the effect of these factors in the generation of coercive power.

Indeed, highland Mesoamerica may be something of an exception to our hypothesis of primary state formation, since the Late Preclassic and Early Classic periods (the "theocratic" stage) generally have been regarded as relatively peaceful. If this area was indeed peaceful, I would suggest that it was because of an unusually rich environment, one whose productive potential could be greatly expanded by rather small-scale public works. This led to dense populations able to undertake more ambitious projects than might be the case in less favored areas of the world, and at the same time delayed somewhat the effect of land limitation (until population reached its Postclassic peak). As a result tribal priests could, by religious sanctions, achieve rather more in the way of monumental works and other features of civilization and also maintain themselves longer against military leaders than was the norm. Intratribal social controls probably depended largely upon increasingly great differences in rank between traditionally defined and ascribed statuses, backed up by novel coercive powers which would, however, be most effective when applied for traditionally sanctioned ends. Early Classic conditions probably resembled Adams's (1966 : 34–36, 86–95) characterization of the fifteenth-century Mexica, although I believe he seriously underestimates the degree to which state controls had been achieved in *Postclassic* Mesoamerica as a whole, if not among that people in particular. In the perspective of world history Mesoamerica should actually be considered an area with an unusually extended and rich period of transition from tribal to state society. It is interesting to note that Steward (1955) classified the Meso-american Classic Period with those periods which marked the transition to civilization in the Old World, a view shared by Sanders and Price (1968 : 53–56, 118–34, 142–45; cf. Webb 1968).

What we really have is a retardation or delay in the expected process, not its absence. Representations of weapons and strife are by no means uncommon in Olmec and Late Preclassic contexts (Corvarrubias 1957 : Figs. 27, 28, 31; Piña Chan 1955a : 22–25, pl. 19, photos 15–19; Stirling 1943 : 18–19, 41, 50–51, 63, pls. 17, 18, 31, 34, 35, 50a, 51). The Terminal Preclassic shift to fewer, more nucleated settlements, often located on high ground in the Valley of Mexico, the area north of Cholula, and the region about Monte Alban, indicates defensive needs (West 1965; Snow 1969; Bernal 1958), while the occurrence of markedly empty zones separating densely settled areas during this period and the Early Classic strongly suggests concern with territoriality (Parsons 1968; Snow 1969). Projectile points in some quantity and possible destruction debris occur at the Protoclassic site of Tezoyuca, near Teotihuacan (West 1965), while the well-known glyphs at Monte Alban, which possibly symbolize conquest, date Monte Alban II in the same Protoclassic Period (Paddock 1966a). One may also note that the increasingly large ceremonial mounds of this epoch, often placed on high ground (Piña Chan 1955b : 64–66; Barba de Piña Chan 1956), could have served defensive ends as they did in the Postclassic Period (Palerm 1956). Moreover, while violence does not seem especially prominent during the Early Classic Period proper, the final collapse of the Classic pattern in Central Mexico was marked by considerable warfare (Covarrubias 1957; Wolf 1959; Adams 1966). Thus, although the crystallization of the full Classic theocratic pattern may have temporarily inhibited the growing violence, so that in a sense Mesoamerica does approach the ideal of statehood achieved by priestly sanctions—in the manner suggested, for example, by Childe (1954)—it could not prevent the final breakdown of these controls.

The highland Classic cultures were nevertheless very splendid achievements. By the Teotihuacan II and Monte Alban II–III *Transición* periods in the first century A.D., these sites had attained the attributes of civilization by any reasonable definition (Bernal 1966; Paddock 1966a). Teotihuacan, whose remarkably large size and population early in the Classic Period (Parsons 1968; Millon 1970) no doubt endowed it with exceptional expansive potential, apparently played the role of primary civilization and stimulated further developments toward statehood in other regions of Mesoamerica. Teotihuacan traits are prominent at the start of the Classic in both Cholula and Monte Alban (Noguera 1954 : 302–3; Bernal 1966; Paddock 1966a), although the typically primary state environment of these sites indicates that their evolution required little outside influence.

It would, on the other hand, seem reasonable that the widespread Early Classic contacts between Teotihuacan and such sites as Remojadas, Tajin, Cerro de las Mesas, Tres Zapotes (Upper), and generally throughout Veracruz (García Payón 1943, 1953; DuSolier 1945; Drucker 1943a, 1943b; Medellín Zenil 1955a, 1960) did have such an influence since this region is not a primary state environment. The apparent slope upward in time which characterized Teotihuacan influences as they moved from west to east, especially in the lowlands, remarked upon some time ago by Lathrap (1957), also fits this interpretation. The beginnings of Tajin, and the time of Teotihuacan influence there, are rather earlier than is often assumed, even if the site's maximal florescence is not (DuSolier 1945; Medellín Zenil 1960 : 180–91). The equivalent period at Cerro de las Mesas, on the other hand, seems rather later in the Early Classic (Drucker 1943a : 69–84). It is, of course, obvious that the highland penetration did not call these sites into existence for the first time—the area clearly could develop and support chiefdoms—nor did it lead to completely formed states at this time. The formation of states had to await the final emergence in the highlands during the Terminal Classic of more secular polities with their larger scale, long-distance trade in practical, as opposed to ceremonial, items. The Teotihuacan influence must, rather, have carried these lowland sites further in the direction of true states than they would have been likely to achieve on their own.

Turning to the southeast, however, it would seem that whatever kind of society existed at Kaminaljuyu before the Teotihuacan incursion, the influence of the latter must have been overwhelming, since during the Esperanza Period Teotihuacan transformed the site into a copy of itself (Kidder, Jennings, and Shook 1946 : 159–70, 218–32). In contrast, Teotihuacan influence in the peninsula of Yucatan seems rather diffuse, though undoubtedly present fairly early at the site of Acanceh, for example. In the Peten the rather prominent traces of Teotihuacan influence seem to be rather late, terminal fifth century at Tikal, the site for which data are most abundant (W. Coe 1965a).

Although the relatively late entrance of Teotihuacan influence into the Southern Maya Lowlands reflects the distance separating the two areas, developments in the Peten seem to have been delayed generally throughout this period in comparison with much of Mesoamerica. Defining the stage by the period indicators used for each area, the Classic begins perhaps 150 years later in the Peten than it does at Teotihuacan, Cholula, and Monte Alban, and perhaps somewhat later than it does in central and northern Veracruz. Even granting that this argument is a bit formal, clearly, despite the unexpectedly rich Preclassic remains recovered at Tikal in the last 15 years (W. Coe 1965a, 1965b, 1967), developments in the Peten during the later Preclassic do not match those at Kaminaljuyu (Shook and Kidder 1952), Santa Lucia Cotzumalhualpa (Parsons et al. 1963; Parsons 1966), Izapa (Parsons 1967), Salvador (Sharer 1968, 1969; Sharer and Gifford 1970), or northern Yucatan (Andrews 1962), nor those at Cuicuilco (Dixon 1967) and Monte Alban (Paddock 1966b : 111–26). The explanation of this slow initial development may be found in the environment of the Peten. Moreover, the distinctive features which the local geographic framework imposed upon the emerging Classic Maya culture provide the key to understanding the ultimate collapse of that culture.

SETTLEMENT PATTERNS AND SOCIAL CONTROLS AMONG THE PETEN MAYA

From the point of view of our problem the critical feature of the central Maya environment is its essential uniformity. While the area is by no means homogeneous, it does not possess either environmental boundaries sharp enough to generate land conflict or a distribution of resources essential to life sufficiently diverse to necessitate either extended trade or internal redistribution. Thus, whether one regards land circumscription with consequent warfare, the exchange of localized critical resources, or some combination of the two as the primary process involved, the Peten is an area peculiarly unsuited for the local generation of centralized political controls and the consequent formation of pristine states. This would appear to be so whether one stresses the region's agricultural homogeneity, as has M. Coe (1961), or the lack of zonal boundaries and of potential trade goods, as in the present case. Moreover, this lack of valuable trade goods and a location off the most natural routes of communication between northern Mesoamerica and the south would inhibit the spread into the region of forces to induce a secondary state.

It is not surprising that recent work indicates that a substantial population first moved into the Peten from the western, southern, and eastern margins (Willey, Culbert, and Adams 1967; Gifford 1968) and that the origins of Classicism were introduced into the area in Chicanel and later times from a (perhaps ultimately Olmecoid) Guatemalan and Salvadoran highland base (Willey and Gifford 1961; M. Coe 1963; Parsons 1967; Sharer 1968, 1969; Andrews 1969). Possible ties to highland Mexican primary state areas may exist by way of Chiapas and Oaxaca in the Chiapa de Corzo VI–VII and Monte Alban II periods (the "Q Complex"), although these links are rather vague (Shook 1951b; Covarrubias 1957 : 148–53; Lowe 1962; Paddock 1966b : 112–20).

Two important considerations are that to the end of the Early Classic Period population size within the Peten never became so great as to demand concentration and that the apparent subsistence base of the Maya, swidden agriculture, put a positive value on scattered settle-

387

ment. Despite these facts, there does appear to have been a considerable degree of nucleation of settlement around the principal ceremonial centers (Bullard 1960, 1964; Haviland 1965; Sanders 1962, 1963; Willey et al. 1965 : 7–18, 561–81). Although the concentration of activity and probably population in these centers undoubtedly served valuable ideological and social ends such as access to a prestigeful cult, status positions, exotic trade goods and luxury craft products, organization for communal work or protection, and opportunities for celebration and general sociability, no really vital survival needs were met. On the contrary, the centers were actually a poor fit for the environment. In other words, this nucleation was caused not by any environmental advantage but rather by the operation of belief systems and social prestige in conjunction with kin ties.

It is probable that the leaders of major kin groups were able to gather followers to provide the labor needed for programs of large-scale religious and building activity largely because of the pleasures which these activities themselves provided. The leadership would want to collect the population about them partly for convenience for the theocratic program and partly because the theocratic life style was subject to influences from the highlands where large population concentrations were part of the system. It should be emphasized that the populations associated with the centers, though much smaller than the highland cities, were almost certainly large enough that the work of construction and maintenance need not have been overly burdensome in comparison to the rewards offered—at least, as long as the priest-chiefs kept their demands to a reasonable level (Erasmus 1965; cf. Webb 1964).

The pattern of organization might well have consisted of linking small and junior kin groups and a few unattached individuals to wealthy, senior kin groups in a fashion similar to the ramage system common in Polynesia. Such a gathering of population about himself in typical chiefly fashion apparently was the device used by Don Pedro Paxbolon to reconstitute his much-diminished Acalan chiefdom in post-Conquest times (Scholes and Roys 1948). It is possible that some sort of *cargo* system [3] bound separate descent groups together in the manner suggested by Vogt (1961, 1964a). A Maya ceremonial city was then the creation of kinship mechanisms extended beyond their usual range of functioning by ritual rewards and sanctions (cf. M. Coe

1965b). As I have suggested elsewhere (Webb 1968), the Peten Maya represent one case—perhaps the only case—where theocratic civilization called into existence states (or rather quasi-states) rather than the reverse. One might doubt that such a development took place, or at least reached the heights it did in the Late Classic, had not the high theocratic state already evolved in areas more suitable for state formation (cf. Sanders and Price 1968).

This being so, there would be an element of instability at the very heart of the Maya ceremonial center. It did, indeed, provide important services, services which, in some cases such as labor organization or other mechanisms for increasing food supply, would become more important as population in the Peten reached its Late Classic peak. Yet at the same time, because it had not arisen to meet antecedent environmental factors, the cult center had no reason for existence except belief in the cult itself. It would, therefore, be subject to collapse if any set of circumstances caused a cessation of belief. In fact, those developments which would make the centers more socially necessary, such as population growth, would also increase the strain on the subsistence base and thereby render residence near and orientation to the centers ever more inconvenient. This burden would be increased if the rulers, acting as theocrats, met emerging crises by devoting more and more of the limited or even shrinking resources to cult ends, as the sudden spurt of stela erection and monument construction just before the collapse indicates was the case (cf. Morley 1946 : Figs. 1, 2).

Indications are that the Late Classic Peten Maya were reaching or (just) surpassing the upper limit of the possibilities of the chiefdom. There was an apparent shift at the end of the Early Classic toward greater status inequality, as indicated by differential grave wealth and location (Rathje 1970b) and by residence patterns (Smith 1950; Willey 1956; Bullard 1960; Haviland 1965) and an increasing emphasis on war, as indicated by the iconography. Still, the Maya clung to a basically theocratic orientation. Our discussion of similar societies indicates that this kind of system will remain stable only so far as "believability" is maintained by the success and generosity of the leadership, in short, by their ability to put on a good show generally in a ceremonial context. This showmanship typically involves extensive use and redistribution of prestige products.

A consideration of the prestige goods used at various periods in

Mesoamerican history, such as jade, pyrites, cinnabar, feathers, hides, shells, shark teeth, exotic rocks, polychrome pottery, and so forth (Blom 1932; Cardos de Méndez 1959; Thompson 1964), reveals that most are foreign to the Southern Maya Lowlands, while those which are found there typically occur in other areas, often on easier transportation routes. As Kidder (1950) remarked, the Peten seems to have had an unfavorable balance of trade. This imbalance would not have bothered the Maya greatly in the Preclassic and Early Classic periods, when long-distance trade was largely concerned with the importation of rarities valued for their ritual or magical properties. It would, however, become a problem when long-distance trade became reoriented toward the movement of large amounts of more secular luxury consumption goods and even of nonprestige items—such things as metals, honey, cacao, and salt. This kind of trade did exist at the time of the Spanish Conquest and represents a situation in which considerations of ease of transportation, accessibility, and relative cost were significant. In such circumstances, trade might be expected to bypass the Peten, which commanded neither monopoly resources nor efficient trade routes.

Tourtellot and Sabloff (1972) have demonstrated a high correlation between social prestige items and imports in Lowland Classic Maya sites which would support the hypothesis that the Maya were vulnerable to such a shift in trade. The greater ability of sites outside the Peten to benefit from foreign trade is also suggested by the fact that excavations at Chichen Itza and Mayapan produced as many shell objects and considerably more obsidian than did work at Uaxactun or Piedras Negras, despite the short time spans of the northern sites (Pollock et al. 1962; Kidder 1947; Coe 1959). While Tikal, on the other hand, seems to have exceeded Mayapan but not Chichen Itza in quantity of shells to a degree roughly proportionate to its longer occupation (Moholy-Nagy 1963), it was, of course, a much larger site (Pollock et al. 1962 : 211; Haviland 1965, 1966b, 1969). It would seem, then, that the growth of secondary states in the regions bordering the Peten would present an especially serious threat to the stability of Peten society because of the extremely precarious nature of its trade. The key question is, when might such a reworking of trade patterns have been achieved?

POSTCLASSIC TRADE PATTERNS
AND THE MAYA COLLAPSE

From the earlier discussion of state origins, we would expect a re-working of long-distance commercial networks to occur when more secular, militaristic, "Bronze Age" primary states with their demands for goods secured on advantageous terms through conquest or by trade with less developed areas had finally emerged fully in Central Mexico. In other words, the shift should have taken place by the Toltec hori-zon, which dominates Mesoamerica shortly after the Peten collapse. We would, moreover, expect this transformation to have begun well back in the Late Classic Period, with the late seventh century fall of Teotihuacan perhaps marking a major stage in the process. Further-more, there are data that support such a reconstruction. The Conquest period Mexica, as well as the peoples who ruled immediately before them, were much concerned to control a Gulf Coast–Yucatan trade route and directed war and diplomacy to this end (Kelly and Palerm 1952 : 14–24; Barlow 1949 : 51–53, 83). The generally similar pat-tern of the Toltec expansion suggests that a similar motivation existed earlier in the Postclassic.

It is, therefore, most interesting to note the emergence in the later Classic of a zone of extensive and persistent architectural, sculptural, and ceramic intercontact which linked together highland and Gulf Coast centers—at first Cholula alone, then both Cholula and Tula, Xochilcalco, Tajin, Remojadas, Cerro de las Mesas, Cerro Montoso, Tabasco, the Puuc sites, the lower Usumacinta (less clearly), and the central Grijalva valley—which then experienced maximal prosperity and its sole period of extensive outside contacts, and which had more diffuse connections with coastal Oaxaca, the Guatemalan High-lands, and lower Central America (Noguera 1945, 1954; Marquina 1951 : 116–29, 143–45, 1968; Acosta 1957; DuSolier 1945; Spinden 1933; García Payón 1943, 1950, 1951a, 1951b, 1953; Medellín Zenil 1960; Drucker 1943a; Berlin 1953, 1956; Brainerd 1958; Rands 1967a, 1967b; Barthel 1964; Sanders 1960; Sáenz 1963, 1968; Piña Chan 1964; Butler 1935; Vaillant 1927; Proskouriakoff 1951, 1953, 1963 : 44, 48, 52, 72; Robertson 1963 : 26, 30; Foncerrada de Molina 1962; Thompson

1952, 1966a; McVicker 1967; Morley 1935 : 137–40; Kubler 1962 : 71–79, 92–99, 138–58, 212–17; Brockington 1970; Seler 1904a, 1904b; Von Winning 1965; M. Coe 1962). It may also be of significance that this zone of intercontact was marked by fairly numerous resemblances linking neighboring areas, instead of the previous quite widespread but scattered diffusion of a smaller number of outstanding traits from a few centers. The result was a kind of overlapping chain, each major link of which—highlands to central Gulf Coast, central Gulf Coast to Tabasco-Campeche, Tabasco-Campeche to Puuc, Tabasco-Campeche to Chiapas-Guatemala—was analogous to the stages of the Conquest period trade network. I believe, therefore, that this represents the beginnings of the shift in long-distance trade from theocratic importation of highly exotic ritual and prestige goods toward movement of more secular luxury goods for elite consumption.

I must admit, however, that hard evidence for trade goods is scanty at the period in question, the late ninth and early tenth centuries A.D. On the other hand, much of the material traded in the Postclassic would leave little or no archaeological evidence, and for pottery, one item which would be preserved, we see that the later portion of the Classic was marked by a turning of ceramic ties away from the Peten toward more peripheral areas. While this time is usually seen as one of regional differentiation among the Maya, such links as do exist generally point to our postulated trade network (Willey, Culbert, and Adams 1967; Pendergast 1967a, 1967b, 1969b). For example, the early fine paste wares of Tabasco-Campeche foreshadow the later spread of the X (Silho) and Y (Altar) Fine Orange trade wares (Rands 1967a, 1967b). Along the Oaxacan coast, Brockington (1970) reports a widespread Late Classic ceramic style which, though manufactured locally, resembles Tabascan and Puuc types in such great detail as to indicate very strong contact with that area. The strong stylistic links in pottery, sculpture, and architecture among all the areas in question suggest the kind of extensive, long-term—and, at least occasionally, friendly—contacts which are most likely to have been owing to trading relationships.

The time of the presumed intercontact also fits very well into the regional culture history. It is becoming clear that the period of maximal prosperity at the great site of Cholula, the time of the largest expansion of the great pyramid, of the beginnings of the "Cholultecan" Ceramic Complex—whose point of origin may be nearby (Nicholson 1966; West 1965)—and of the tyranny of the historic Olmecs (Jiménez Moreno 1966), immediately postdates Teotihuacan and precedes Tula, as Jiménez Moreno has maintained for many years (1955, 1966; cf. Vaillant 1938; Noguera 1954; Acosta 1957; Webb 1964). I would assign the same Epiclassic date to the Puuc florescence, a view which returns to Brainerd's original temporal placement (Brainerd 1958; Covarrubias 1957 : 235–38). It also provides a possible compromise of those differences which have kept Andrews at odds with his colleagues on the issue of Maya chronology (for example, Andrews 1960) in that it allows rather less time than he desires to account for the extensive building projects of the Florescent stage, but explains this rapid growth in terms of a sudden burst of prosperity. The architectural sequence has always indicated such a placement (Ruz Lhuillier 1945; Foncerrada de Molina 1962).

Two of the major links on our chain thus rise to prominence together immediately after the collapse of Teotihuacan, at the same time as the Maya collapse and in the area which was shortly to become a route of Toltec expansion and later the scene of Mexica commercial expansion. The same period is marked by a shift of major activity in the Valley of Mexico to such sites as Azcapotzalco and Cerro Portezuelo in the southwest and south—both of which contain forms ancestral to "Toltec" ceramics—and to the area about the Patlachique range in the northeast, suggesting an orientation to Cholula and Xochicalco to the south and to the emerging Tula in the north (Tozzer 1921; Armillas 1950; Jacobs-Müller 1956–57; Cook de Leonard 1956–57; Hicks and Nicholson 1964; Parsons 1968). Xochilcalco's florescence at this time and its strong stylistic ties to both the Puuc and Cholula are well known (Marquina 1951 : 143–45; Noguera 1945, 1954). In the same way, architectural and ceramic resemblances link the final major expansion of Tajin at Tajin Chico with the Puuc and with Cholula's (apparent) period of maximal prosperity, while the Toltec-related "X" Fine Orange occurs only at the very end of the occupation (Marquina 1951 : 118–29; García Payón 1951a : 40–44, 1953). The presence of Cholultecan "Policroma Laca" and the absence of Plumbate, metals, and Fine Orange in Cerro de las Mesas Upper I support this placement of the Cholula-Tajin-Puuc horizon on a Postclassic, pre-Toltec time level (Drucker 1943a : 48–50, 82–87; Noguera 1954 : 138).

Although this horizon precedes the Toltec Period, the relative absence of religious architecture at Azcapotzalco, Cerro Portezuelo, and Tajin Chico, the symbols of sacrifice and death at Tajin and in the Puuc, the defensible nature of Xochicalco, and the legendary history of Cholultecan imperialism and tyranny all indicate that militaristic, secular, "true" state controls were becoming established (García Payón 1951a : 28–33, 42–43, 1957; Piña Chan 1964; Jiménez Moreno 1966). Recent radiocarbon dates from Lambityeco in Oaxaca (Paddock, Mogor, and Lind 1968) can be extended to both Tajin and the Puuc through the occurrence of the Greek key or greca motif in architecture (Sharp 1970; Seler 1904b; Jiménez Moreno 1966), thereby placing this network of interaction firmly in the late eighth and early ninth centuries A.D. This dating means that the replacement of the theocratic pattern by new ways of life had begun to take place—indeed, was well under way—in highland and Gulf Coastal Mexico more than one hundred years before the Peten collapse. This delayed effect can scarcely be attributed to any weakness of the impulses radiating from the north and west; it is becoming increasingly clear that the societies involved were among the most vital and expansive in Mesoamerican history (M. Coe 1963; Jiménez Moreno 1966; Paddock 1966b : 174, 200–11, 233–34; Thompson 1970).

A unitary explanation for all these events would be economical, to say the least. An explanation in terms of the gradual rise and expansion and then the rapid conquest and transformation of a trade network seems ideal. Readers of Acosta Saignes (1945), Chapman (1957), Cardos de Méndez (1959), Miles (1957), and Roys (1943) will be aware of the great importance of long-distance trade in later Postclassic Mexica and Maya society. This trade was carried on among the Mexica by a wealthy class or caste, the Pochteca, who were both protected and dominated by the rulers and by the chiefs themselves, for whom it was a vital source of power among the Maya. Legends and ritual trappings, in fact, imply that the Pochteca entered Central Mexico from the Gulf in pre-Aztec times precisely by way of Cholula (Acosta Saignes 1945). A large central Gulf element lies in the background of Mixteca-Puebla polychromes, the large unreported site of Cerro Montoso providing the link (Noguera 1954; Medellín Zenil 1960; Strebel 1885–89). Mixteca-Puebla culture is, of course, commonly regarded as largely ancestral to later Central Mexican societies (Covarrubias 1957 : 293–03, 318–31). The strong resemblances which I believe exist between Plumbate and the Gulf Coast "Ceramica Metalica" (Shepard 1948; Medellín Zenil 1955 : 44–49, 1960 : 124–30, 192, 198) would support the conclusion that the Gulf Coast played a key role in the formation of Postclassic commercial patterns, as does the role it very probably played in the transmission of fine paste ceramic traditions between south and north at this time. In addition, even more striking suggestions of continuity in trading practices extending back to the Epiclassic occur in the region of the presumed Gulf Coast trading network, particularly among the Maya of Yucatan and Tabasco, peoples whose resources of salt, cacao, and honey supported trade so extensive as to be a mainstay of their total economy and, very probably, the major function of the local elite (Roys 1957; Cardos de Méndez 1959; Tozzer 1941 : 94–98, 107).

The evidence for this continuity consists of artistic representations of items associated with merchants or wealth in the late documents, such as small roundish fans, staves, tumplines, tumplines worn as headdresses, packs, and bags. Some of these things taken singly need not indicate trading; bags represented a large quantity of anything and fans were carried by ambassadors as well as by Pochteca or other merchants. Yet the occurrence of several of the traits together should be fairly conclusive. An ambassador habitually sent by his society to gather wealth through ritualized exchange because of his high kin status or of his rank earned in war would fully satisfy our needs, for neither the Maya nor the Mexica completely differentiated these occupations (Chapman 1957; Cardos de Méndez 1959 : 59–65; de Zorita 1963 : 181–88, 279–84). Also of interest are representations of the Maya merchant god, god M or Ek Chuah. An extensive search reveals that these symbols all tend to cluster along our suggested Gulf-Usumacinta trade route and that by and large they run from the Terminal Classic down to the Conquest.

Starting with Tajin, we find three scenes of persons with fans or bags. Two of them, which to my knowledge have never before been published, are said to be from the Building of the Columns in Epiclassic and Puuc-related Tajin Chico (Spinden 1933; García Payón 1951b; Kubler 1962). Carved in low relief on flat, rectangular slabs, both are

395

badly cracked and seriously incomplete (Figs. 48 and 49). The less fragmentary, about 4 feet 8 inches high by 3 feet 8 inches wide, shows a standing, full-face, male figure holding what appears to be a long-handled, round fan in the right hand and a bag or pouch in the left. As noted, such pouches symbolized large quantity or wealth among the sixteenth-century Mexica; the feather hanging from the bottom of the pouch could be the sign for 400. I would judge that the resemblance of the design on the pouch to a Tlaloc face is probably coincidental (cf. Tozzer 1957 : Figs. 221, 225–30). The other figure, apparently also male, is preserved only from the chest up. This section (actually two pieces) measures 2 feet 6 inches high and roughly 2 feet 8 inches wide. Enough is left to show what is probably the string of a pouch in the left hand and possibly a short-handled fan in the right. The headdress,

FIGURE 48. EPICLASSIC RELIEF CARVING, APPARENTLY REPRE-SENTING *POCHTECA*, from Tajin Chico

FIGURE 49. EPICLASSIC RELIEF CARVING, APPARENTLY REPRE-
SENTING *POCHTECA*, from Tajin Chico

which is less damaged than in the larger example, contains as one element what may be a knotted rope. If so, this would be an interesting
resemblance to the tumpline used as a headband which formed a principal element in the headdress of god M in the codices (Thompson
1966*b*). The costumes of the figures—breechcloth, shirt, necklace,
wristlets, anklets, knee bands, elaborate headdresses, and so forth—
are late Mexican generally but most closely resemble those of the deities in the codices of the "Borgia" group (Thompson 1966b). As will
be seen, this is of more than merely chronological significance. Less
close resemblances can be found with early Mexican Period material at
Chichen Itza (Proskouriakoff 1951; Tozzer 1957). The third example at
Tajin appears on the side of the Lesser Ballcourt (Spinden 1933 : pl. 16)
and shows a man with staff and fan (which may in this case be a

397

shield) standing facing a man seated on a throne holding a pouch. Some sort of tail or feather appears to dangle from the bottom of the pouch. The ball court sculptures generally show strong ties to Yucatan and to Xochicalco.

Moving south, Cerro de Las Mesas has two figures with bags; one of these is sitting on a throne holding a fan and the other is standing with staff in hand. Both are said to be stylistically late (Stirling 1943 : 43, 48, Figs. 12*b*, 14*c*,). Stela D at Tres Zapotes shows a figure with bag and spear, and an enthroned figure with some sort of paddle or staff is reported at Santa Lucia Cotzumalhualpa (Stirling 1943 : 14–16, 43–53, Figs. 4, 8). Neither is well dated. The figure on Stela D, however, appears to be, if not bearded, at least of very prominent chin and has a long, turned-up nose, both features of god M (Thompson 1966b). If this rather doubtful identification were correct, it would make this perhaps the earliest known representation of this deity, since Covarrubias (1957 : 63) regards the monument as having Olmec traits.[4] In the Southern Maya Lowlands there are few sculptural representations of fans, at least of the small hand fans with which we are concerned. I know of only three—one possibility at Yaxchilan and two far to the east at Naranjo, and, of these, that at Yaxchilan may be early while the persons holding the Naranjo examples also carry spears (Proskouriakoff 1950; Morley 1938 II : 71–72, 138–40, III : 469; Maler 1903, 1908 : 86–89). Bags, on the other hand, are common; while some are early or eastern as at Tikal, Yaxha, or Naranjo, the majority are in the Usumacinta drainage and later than 9.14.0.0.0 (A.D. 710) (Proskouriakoff 1950; Maler 1911 : 73–75, 1901 : 50–56, 62–74, 1903; Morley 1938 I : 304, 342, II : 427–77, III : 73–76, 92–99, 194–96, 237–41; Blom and LaFarge 1926–27 II : 421–35). Many of these figures also carry spears, but war and trade were especially closely related in Mesoamerica. The famous Late Classic Bonampak murals show two individuals with small fans (Ruppert, Thompson, and Proskouriakoff 1955). Sculptured Stone 1 at Bonampak shows figures with possible tumpline headdresses offering goods to a person seated on a throne (Thompson 1954 : pl. 10*a*). This scene is stylistically dated to the end of the seventh century and may be slightly earlier (Proskouriakoff 1950 : 118, 1955).

Turning to the Yucatan Peninsula, I have found four representations of persons with fans (including one woman) among the Jaina-Jonuta figurines (Groth-Kimball 1961 : pls. 13, 26, 32; Aveleyra and Ekholm 1966). While these figurines covered a long time-span, the tradition runs back into the Classic. A Late Classic vase said to be from Jaina portrays a figure holding a spear and a shield. This individual is painted black, has large red lips, possibly has horseshoe designs about the eyes, and wears a rather doubtful tumpline headdress (Monti 1969 : 84, pl. 36). These are all attributes of god M, but a possibly better identification would be god L, the war god closely associated with god M. At Chichen Itza two old men with fans appear on a pillar of the Chacmool Temple below the Temple of the Warriors, and similar figures are shown on the Warriors' Colonnade and North Colonnade (Morris, Charlot, and Morris 1931 I : 253–56, 299 ff.). What may be fans are held by several figures on a gold disk from the Cenote of Sacrifice (Lothrop 1952 : 50–51), and figures with packs and staves appear in the murals of the Temple of the Warriors (Morley 1946 : pl. 90). These examples from Chichen Itza are later than our critical period, but merchants with staff and pack appear in a Florescent context on a sherd from the Cenote of Sacrifice (Poppy and Harrington 1968 : 24; Piña Chan 1968) and on the back of a slate mirror from the nearby town of Uayma (R. H. Thompson 1962). These mirrors were a major Veracruz export to the Maya area.

J. E. S. Thompson (1966b) has noted that representations of the sharp-nosed merchant god are especially common in the late Yucatecan Madrid Codex and in the Mexican codices, Borgia, Laud, and Fejervary-Mayer. Nicholson (1962, 1966) points out that a good case can be made for the Codex Borgia having been produced at Cholula itself, while Fejervary-Mayer can be located in or near Veracruz. God M also appears in stone, metal, or pottery at Mayapan, Chichen Itza, Champoton, and in the Alta Verapaz (at Nebaj and Chama, for example) and in murals at Santa Rita (Thompson 1957, 1966b; see also, Gann 1890 : 665–67, pls. 29–33; Shepard 1948 : 107, 154, Figs. 20*i*, *l*; Smith and Kidder 1951 : 44, 73–74, Figs. 79*a*, *b*, 80*a*, 89, 90). With very few exceptions, these examples are Middle or Late Postclassic.

However, god M may appear in the Late Classic at Palenque, and god L certainly does (Kelley 1965). Moreover, the most striking of all representations of merchants or Ek Chuah do occur toward the later part of the Classic Period. These are on the "Chama" vases of Verapaz. The famous Chama vase of Dieseldorff (1904) and Seler (1904c) shows a

399

blackened man with a fan, flint-tipped staff, jaguar skin cloak, long nose, lower lip extension, and possible tumpline headdress like god M of the codices (cf. Morley 1946 : pl. 88*a;* Tozzer 1957 : 223–29). Other figures on the vase carry fans and wear what I regard as the tumpline—on Verapaz examples it looks like one or two flower blossoms coming out on long thick stems from a knot on top of the head. The Ratinlinxul vase (Morley 1946 : pl. 88*b*) shows a merchant in a litter. No fans are shown on the Nebaj jar, but persons with tumpline headdresses are shown discussing a basket of goods (Joyce 1914 : pl. 24). Vases showing individuals with this headdress and bales of goods are reported for Zacualpa (Lothrop 1936 : 33–35, pl. 7) and Jecaro (Spinden 1957 : 140–41, Fig. 193). The Chama style is now securely dated by the occurrence of this pottery in a tomb at Altar de Sacrificios, where it occurs together with a vase associated with a ruler of Yaxchilan whose reign began in A.D. 752 (R. E. W. Adams, personal communication; Adams 1963; Willey and Smith 1969 : 26; Haviland 1971). A Late Classic vase at Tikal provides at least one example of possible tumpline headdresses worn by tribute bearers (W. Coe 1965 : 42–43), however; and doubtful examples of the tumpline headdress occur in the Full Classic Copador Ware of Copan (Longyear 1952 : Figs. 74*b*, 118*f*). Thus one should not, perhaps, exaggerate the extent to which traders had become specialized or the lead of the western border areas in trading.

Nevertheless, a trend does emerge. It would seem that, from the later part of the Classic Period on, the societies of central highland Mexico, the Gulf Coast, Yucatan, and highland Guatemala were marked by an increasing occupational differentiation of the role of merchant ambassador. Adding to this the undoubted existence of Gulf Coast and south highland long-distance trade networks at the time of the Conquest, the importance of trade in the social systems of all the societies concerned at that time (especially vital to the Maya ruling classes in Yucatan and Tabasco), and the great amount of Central Mexican influence which entered the Maya area during the Terminal Classic and Early Postclassic, it seems reasonable to conclude that secondary state-inducing influences were now strongly penetrating southern Mesoamerica. It was probably at this time that the shift from very long-distance trade of ceremonially precious items in small amounts to a trading network dealing largely in useful items took place. The result would be the relatively rapid transformation of those areas able to participate in these trading activities on a large scale—notably Yucatan with its extensive salt deposits and command of the sea routes (Scholes and Roys 1948; Chamberlain 1948; Roys 1957) and highland Guatemala with its mineral resources and situation near the great cacao area of Soconusco (Bergmann 1969)—into secondary states.

Now wealthy both from trade and from increasing political control over their own people, the rulers of these areas could expand their activities. No doubt this consisted, especially at first, of an expanded program of ceremonialism and redistribution in a fashion typical of chiefdoms, since all the Maya were somewhat peripheral to the process of state formation. Lacking adequate resources for trade, the leadership of the Peten centers could not keep up, and their attempts to do so by expanding their own programs on the basis of their internal resources along with whatever small portion of the expanding trade they could secure would simply overburden their population. Having less of the resources needed for state controls than their neighbors, they would be more subject to the collapse typical of chiefdoms. Since the same intercontact which brought the new trading orientation to the area also introduced the new Postclassic politico-religious ideology, the Peten centers would seem poor and old-fashioned in contrast (Thompson 1954; Willey 1964).

The populations artificially nucleated about these centers were certainly large enough to make movement away from the centers attractive in terms of basic subsistence (Haviland 1970), especially if by so doing the emigrants could more easily participate in new wealth and novel ideas. Withdrawal to new areas appears to be a common Maya reaction to crisis (Thompson 1971; cf. Webb 1964 : 392–95). Whatever weak development of state controls might have begun to emerge in response to Classic Period population growth throughout the Peten as a whole would still be inadequate to overcome the relative disadvantage of the region in terms of positive rewards. Centers unable to attract sufficient numbers to their ceremonial programs were probably severely weakened, and by losing their believability lost their reason for existence. The expected steady movement away from the Peten centers would precipitate further crises. Some of these emigrants undoubtedly settled nearby at first, but no longer practiced the full theocratic cult. Others probably moved, perhaps indirectly and in several stages, into the expanding border areas. However, the ultimate survival of any center would tend to be in inverse proportion to its retention of the old patterns.

Had the Peten Maya been left alone by their neighbors, their decline might not have been so rapid or total. Indeed, when I first formulated this hypothesis in the early 1960s, I supposed that the end of the Peten Classic came about through a long process of relative economic impoverishment, social decay, and gradual abandonment, a view which the archaeological data then permitted. But the actual relative rapidity of the collapse reflects the fact that the Maya of the Southern Lowlands seem *not* to have been left alone. At the time of the Conquest and, as we have seen, probably earlier, rivalry over trade was a major cause of war among the recently evolved Mesoamerican states. This rivalry was especially the case in Yucatan (Roys 1957, 1965). Moreover, it was perfectly reasonable.

The basic dependence of the prosperity and even existence of the local polities upon commerce is suggested by the fact that Tula's achievement of hegemony in the highlands—which surely included greater control of trade—was followed by the collapse of the Tajin-Puuc network. Then Tula's decline witnessed the rise of Mayapan, which fell in turn when the Aztec again gathered all political and commercial threads into one highland-based system. This alteration of power between areas provides further proof that in the Postclassic the highlands and the Maya for the first time formed one politico-economic order (Roys 1965).

The Peten centers probably commanded relatively little trade, but not too little to be of interest to the western and northern Maya. The invasion suggested by Sabloff and Willey (1967) was the result. If the basic structure of society and the bases of power in the Peten were undergoing the strains suggested above when this crisis struck, collapse would surely result. Any attempt to meet this challenge on the part of a leadership still dependent on tribal controls to mobilize resources would itself simply precipitate destructive intercity wars and internal revolts. Probably in many cases allegiance was simply transferred to the intruders, since the way of life they represented was similar enough to traditional patterns to be familiar while at the same time being obviously much more successful. The logic of social control in chiefdoms almost demands such an act. Since the changing basis of wealth and power rendered the Peten valueless to the successor states, recovery would be highly unlikely.

But the basic point remains. By the very nature of its environment, the Peten could not evolve the more secular Postclassic pattern of state organization on its own. Representing a developmental dead end, these ultimately maladaptive centers were uniquely subject to collapse under external pressure from the very societies which had earlier stimulated their development. The ultimate cause of this collapse was the inevitable evolution of true states elsewhere in Mesoamerica; the proximate cause was the resultant spread of the Postclassic pattern of secular trade and commercial war into the Maya area.[5] Thus the end of Peten Classic culture was contained in its very beginning: without the existence of more rapidly evolving societies located in more favorable areas, it is very doubtful that the Maya could have reached the level they finally did; yet these more advanced societies formed a nemesis which in time necessarily destroyed them.[6]

NOTES

1. No attempt will be made to cite here the original formulators of these hypotheses since they are dealt with elsewhere in this volume and are in any case well known to most students of the problem. They have been treated in considerable detail by Webb (1964) and more briefly by Morley (1946), G. Cowgill (1964), and Willey (1964), among others.

2. A review of the long debate concerning culture evolutionism would be inappropriate since the controversy will be familiar to most readers. The recent exchange between Heston (1971) and Harris (1971) may be of interest because it deals with the extent to which cultural ecology actually does come to grips with economic realities. Trigger (1971) raises similar questions and also denies the theoretical similarity between modern evolutionism and British prehistoric archaeology. See, too, Service (1968) and Harris (1969).

3. Participation in such a system might perhaps have to be limited to senior men within kin groups, since otherwise the population of available candidates might exceed the number of offices (Haviland 1966b; Vogt and Cancian 1970).

4. Another very early portrayal of this deity might be the stone mask described by Thompson (1965b)—if the mask does, indeed, represent the merchant god and is really an example of "Neo-Olmec" work.

5. The reconstruction suggested here resembles recent conclusions by Thompson (1966b, 1970 : 3–47, 124–38, 156–58). Thompson also argues that Maya society in the Terminal Classic witnessed so great an increase in emphasis on trading and merchants as to cause a considerable cultural reorientation and that this trade was centered roughly in the regions I have proposed. He does not, however, relate these events directly to the collapse of the Peten, supposing that

the new rulers and the old vanished together in the south, although the former survived until the Conquest by moving to the north. As noted, this suggestion ignores the close association of events throughout Mesoamerica in time and space and the differential survival of the old and new systems, both of which imply a single process at work. Also the scheme presented here does not commit itself to Thompson's identifications of ethnic groups for several centuries prior to the conquest, which seem rather daring.

6. A preliminary report, only recently made available to me, on the Cholula excavations (Marquina 1970) and the recently published survey of the ceramics of the Classic-Postclassic transition in Central Mexico (Dumond and Muller 1972) suggest that the reconstruction of the role of Cholula requires modification in that the site may have suffered some interruption of occupation at the very end of the Classic, the great pyramid having attained its largest size shortly prior to this event. Nevertheless, the fact that the earliest ceramics of the transition period occur in Puebla-Tlaxcala (as a development out of classic Teotihuacan roots) and do so during the ninth century (Dumond and Muller 1972) indicates that the area which was soon to be the Mixteca-Puebla heartland was becoming a key region at precisely the time of the Maya collapse. While I would not now argue that the Cholula site proper had its maximal prosperity at this time, the continuance of considerable building activity about the south side of the great pyramid into the Terminal Classic Period, along with the rapid recovery of the site, suggests that the general region maintained its dynamism throughout the period. The prominence of grecas and interlaced volutes in this Terminal Classic building activity indicates strong ties specifically with Tajin and the Mixtec region in the eighth century, much as we would expect.

17

Classic Maya Development and Denouement: A Research Design

WILLIAM L. RATHJE

Department of Anthropology
University of Arizona

The decline and fall of Lowland Classic Maya civilization has provided archaeologists with a wondrous mystery. The search for simple causes and effects in the last days of the Classic ceremonial centers has led to an understanding of the complexity of the collapse. By the time disintegration was imminent, invaders, overpopulation, agricultural failures, diminishing trade returns, disease, and "moral" decay were interrelated in a complicated exponential progression of disaster.

This volume presents several descriptions of the Lowland Classic Maya collapse. Each author has contributed, from his own perspective, to an outline of the important processes in the collapse and to proposals for future research. The perspective utilized in this chapter is dependent upon a specific assumption (presented below) and should be evaluated in light of chapter 18. This research design is presented to supplement the designs and hypotheses outlined in other chapters of this book.

Assumption Base

Classic Maya cultural organizations are systems of adaptation to eco-logical and sociopolitical environments. General systems theory pro-vides a set of concepts which are important in the analysis of cultural systems. To paraphrase Buckley (1968 : 491), an adaptive sociocultural system must manifest: (1) *irritability* vis-à-vis its environment such that it carries on a constant interchange with environmental events; (2) *va-riety* to act as a potential pool of adaptive variability to meet the prob-lem of mapping new behavior in a changeable environment; (3) *selec-tive* criteria against which the "variety pool" may be sorted into those variations that more closely map the environment; and (4) an arrange-ment for *preservation* of successful mappings.

One of the crucial nodes of adaptation is the "variety pool." The amount of potential variety in a system's pool (that is, the number of potentially viable alternatives) constrains the ability of a system to con-struct new "maps" in response to changes in the environment to which it has to adapt (Buckley 1968 : 491). For the purposes of this paper, the amount of variety in a system is equated with "adaptability." If there are few constraints upon variety, a system has the potential to success-fully modify its structure in response to environmental variation. If the constraints upon internal variety are severe, a system's potential to modify itself in response to change is low.

As the environment—cultural or ecological—changes, the con-tinued survival of the constituents of a cultural system may demand major revisions in the system's mappings. If such revisions are beyond the parameters of the system's variety pool, it will collapse. When ex-ternal constraints against the locally potential forms of variety remain severe, a new system may not develop and major depopulation will re-sult.

The lowland milieu into which the Maya moved in the Preclassic placed constraints upon variety in the specific types of dynamic inter-actions developed between segments of social systems and the environ-ment. Reconstructing the Classic Maya system's internal interaction structure as an adaptation to its environment provides a coherent perspective from which to discuss the system's variety pool, adaptation to change, and subsequent demise.

A Research Design

This study will focus upon the effect of basic resource, ecological, geographic, and demographic constraints upon variety within Lowland Classic Maya cultural systems through time. A model will be constructed of two types of Classic Maya cultural systems. Temporal and spatial differences in the internal lowland constraints upon variety within the systems will be derived from the model and briefly tested. The model will also be used to predict specific reactions of Classic Maya cultural systems to changes impinging from outside their immediate lowland environment. These predictions will be used to suggest an organization for one possible scheme of future research. Although the model does not present a complete and tested picture of the collapse, it does present the collapse as an integral part of the dynamic interaction through time between the Lowland Maya environment and adaptive cultural systems.

A Model of Variety and Constraints

All systems produce patterned variety. Constraints describe the interaction of the variables that produce patterned variety. The concepts of "variety" and "constraint," as outlined by Ashby (1968), can be utilized to describe models of Classic Maya cultural systems.

Variety, for the purposes of this paper, can simply be defined as the potential number of arrangements of distinct elements in a system. Thus, for each specific application of the concept of variety, the "elements" must be defined. Once variety is identified, the constraints upon that variety can be isolated. Constraints control variety. For example, the elements of variety can be defined as six men (A, B, C, D, E, F). One aspect of variety is the potential number of ways the six men can be placed in a single file (after Ashby 1968; Luebbermann, personal communication). With no constraints a variety of 720 orderings are possible (ABCDEF, BACDEF, CBADEF, DCBAEF, and so on). A moderate constraint would be applied if the men were ordered by eye color, blue (left) to brown (right). If A, B, and C have blue eyes and D, E, and F have brown eyes, there are still 36 possible orderings (ABC/DEF, ACB/DEF, ACB/DFE, and so on). The constraint of ordering the men by absolute height, tall to short, is severe and allows no variety in the way the men are placed in a file. "The intensity of the constraint is thus shown by the reduction it causes in the number of possible arrangements," that is, in variety (Ashby 1968 : 130).

The effect of some of the constraints upon Lowland Classic Maya cultural systems through time can be used to build models of these systems. Within complex cultural systems many sources of constraint, such as population size and technology, vary directly with changes in variety. However, fluctuating constraints alone do not determine the parameters of change. Some important constraints upon complex cultural systems, such as ecological variety and geographic position, often remain constant as others vary. By constructing a model of constant and variable constraints on specific Lowland Classic Maya cultural systems, variations in variety within and between systems can be derived.

THE CORE AREA–
BUFFER ZONE MODEL

It is important for purposes of this paper to divide large lowland areas in Mesoamerica into two parts (Fig. 50): (1) The outer Buffer Zone borders highland resource areas and/or contains or borders major bulk-transport systems (rivers and the Atlantic Ocean). The juxtaposition of tropical rain forest with several other ecozones creates general ecological variety throughout the Buffer Zone. (2) The inner Core Area is landlocked and sequestered from highland resources by the Buffer Zone. Tropical rain forest is the only major ecozone in the Core Area and general ecological variety is minimal. The Core Area and Buffer Zone impose different constraints upon complex cultural systems.

Constraints upon Lowland Classic Maya Systems

Some of the most critical constraints in any cultural system occur at the interface of environment and technology. Every household (the minimum production-consumption unit, that is, nuclear family, extended family, and so on) needs basic resources to efficiently exploit a given ecozone. Basic resources are defined as those which are present archaeologically, ethnohistorically, and ethnographically, in every household in a specific subsistence configuration—in this case the maize agriculture-silviculture complex. At least three resources were

408

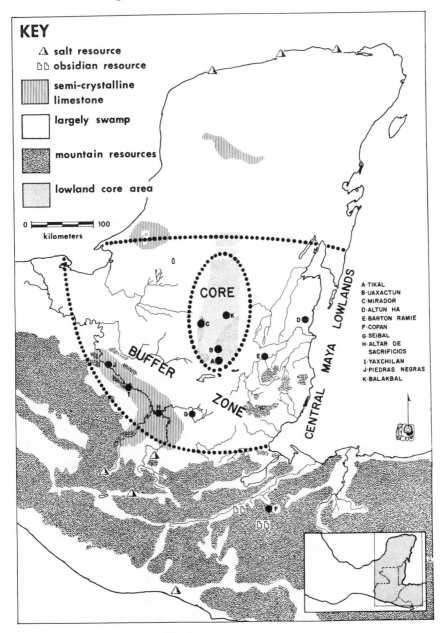

FIGURE 50. BASIC RESOURCES AND THE MAYA LOWLANDS

basic enough to the standard efficiency of slash-and-burn and/or silviculture subsistence patterns to be imported to all parts of the Maya Lowlands in all time periods: igneous or hard stone *metates* for grinding corn or *ramón* nuts, razor-sharp obsidian tools, and salt (Rathje 1971a : 57–67, 1971b for the rationale behind this statement; for a similar definition and use of "basic resources" see Fried 1967 : 52, 186–87, 191; Leone 1968 : 43, 126–28).

Most areas of highland Mesoamerica are not far from sources of these essentials. In the Southern Maya Lowlands (Fig. 50), however, sources are few and far between. Basic household tools and condiments were imported everywhere in the lowlands in quantity and over considerable distances (Rathje 1971a : 57–67). The lack of basic resources was a constant constraint (Constraint 1) on lowland cultural systems. Although Constraint 1 (basic resources) applied to the entire lowlands, its effect was not the same throughout. It was acted upon by other constant constraints that occurred differentially in the Southern Maya Lowlands.

Core Constant Constraints

In the Core Area, Constraint 1 (basic resources) interacted with two additional constraints upon the variety pool within the cultural systems. Constraint 2 upon Core Area systems is limited ecological variety. Constraint 3 is the Core Area's isolated geographic position (spatial distance from basic resources) and the total lack of bulk-transport systems. Constraint 1 (basic resources) required that nonlocal commodities be imported from the Buffer Zone and/or highland resource areas. Constraints 2 (ecological) and 3 (geographic) severely limited the potential variety of resource exchange interactions.

Constraint 3 (geographic) narrowed the variety of exchange interactions to long-distance trade carried out by complex resource procurement organizations. Long-distance trade was not merely an extension of the face-to-face exchanges common in highland market systems (Chapman 1957 : 115; Thompson 1964). In premule days the upper limit a single *cargador* could carry was 100 pounds, for example, two *metates* and six *manos*. The difficulties of consistently supplying large inland areas were considerable. The Core Area's geographic position, translated into transport of goods, time investments, and the dangers of long-distance travel selected against independent household procurement efforts. Because of Constraint 3 (geographic), the prerequisites of successful procurement of resources were capital accumulation and security and leadership organization far above that which a single household could muster (cf. Rathje 1971a, n.d.).

Traders need items with exchange potential. Since all Core Area resources were duplicated in the Buffer Zone, there was little potential for Core Area—Buffer Zone trade in natural resources. Highland markets for lowland products could be more easily supplied by Buffer Zone neighbors than by Core Area long-distance traders. Thus, there was little potential for exchange of Core Area natural resources for other basic commodities (Fig. 51). Constraint 2 (ecological) selected for the development of scarce "artificial" resources.

If complex organization was necessary to procure resources, then community ceremonial interaction and luxury paraphernalia were equally necessary to maintain local Core Area stratification and organization (cf. Flannery 1968 : 100; Fried 1967 : 32; Rappaport 1967 : 105–7; Binford 1962). The products and services that reinforced community integration and complex organizations were scarce artificial resources with exchange potential. Constraint 2 (ecological) selected for complex organizations and resource concentration that produced trade items through support of craft specialization (ceremonial paraphernalia—polychrome pottery, decorated textiles, carved wooden objects, featherwork, and so on) and esoteric knowledge production (calendrics, glyphic writing, stone carving, and so on). The production of such commodities for long-distance exchange was also beyond the capacity of individual households and reinforced the need for complex resource concentration and procurement systems.

For trade in basic resources to reach every household consistently, goods and authority extracted at the expense of every household had to be concentrated within a highly organized procurement system. Constraint 1 (basic resource), Constraint 2 (ecological), and Constraint 3 (geographic) selected for lowland developments in sociopolitical interaction and organization (cf. Sahlins 1958, 1963; Fried 1967). The Core Area ceremonial center provided the suprahousehold capital, organizational potential, and integration of scattered population for successful resource procurement and redistribution. The ceremonial center—sustaining area system was the minimal unit of autonomous

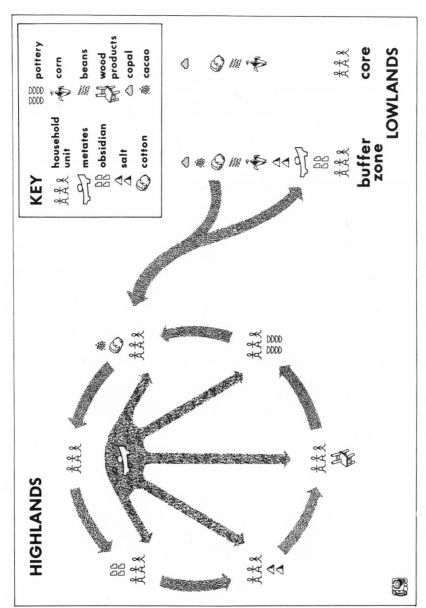

FIGURE 51. A MODEL OF EXCHANGE POTENTIAL BETWEEN HIGHLAND, BUFFER, AND CORE ZONES

economics (Leone 1968 : 127–28; for tests of this construct see Rathje 1971a, 1971b).

The Hypothesized Core Cultural System

From the constraints discussed above, a hypothesized Core Area cultural system can be described (Diagram 1). CH represents the minimum Core Area production-consumption unit—the individual household. CH_1 represents all of the subsistence households in the sustaining area of one ceremonial system. To move through the system, start at CH_1 when a harvest is collected. The arrows in the diagram stand for actions of processes.

Action Set 1 represents the consumption and storage of part of the harvest. This process provided the nutrition and the resources to be invested in gaining subsistence from the limited set of Core Area natural resources. In the Core Area, Constraint 2, the availability of the same limited range of ecological variety to all, placed constraints upon the amount of resulting variety in return on investments of labor and capital. Action Set 1 is the only basic viable investment opportunity for

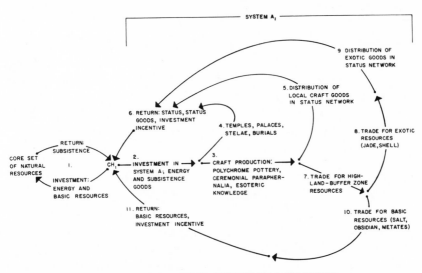

CH_1 = THE MINIMUM PRODUCTION-CONSUMPTION UNIT, i.e. THE HOUSEHOLD

DIAGRAM 1: CLASSIC MAYA CORE CEREMONIAL CENTER—INDIVIDUAL HOUSEHOLD SYSTEM household resources independent of the complex resource procurement organization, System A_1.

Trade as an extension of the lowland Core Area environment required that individual household resources be concentrated. Thus, a major part of the household harvest was invested in System A_1. Action Set 2 represents the process of resource concentration as households invested in the ceremonial center system's functions. The actions supported, especially craft production and other aspects of long-distance trade, required a constant influx of resources that had to be manipulated by a few individuals.

Action Set 3 represents craft production. Action Set 4 represents public conspicuous consumption (construction of stelae, temples, palaces, and so on). Action Set 5 stands for the local distribution of local craft items. These action sets provided the trappings indicative of a successful procurement organization. The vector of Action Sets 3, 4, and 5 culminated in lavish burials and other complex ritual potlatches which produced community integration and distribution of local craft items that *supported* status networks and filtered down as a strong positive feedback to the small investor. It is assumed in the system that the return (economic, social, political, and so on) on individual household investments was relatively proportional to the original investment. Action Set 6 represents strong ideological and sociological investment returns and investment incentives in the form of social status, status items, and ideological cohesion. Action Set 6 continually reactivated Action Set 2.

Some of the resources invested in System A_1 went directly into supporting bearers, merchants, trade routes, and trade factories. Those craft items that did not follow Action Set 5 followed Action Set 7 and were exchanged for highland and Buffer Zone resources. Two kinds of resources were procured—basic resources and exotic resources. The exotic items followed Action Set 9 to local redistribution in Action Set 6. The basic resources, for the most part, followed Action Set 11. These basic commodities (salt, obsidian, *metates*) formed the second part of the prerequisites to production and maintenance of CH_1. Action Set 11 also continually reactivated Action Set 2.

The efficient continued operation of the complex resource procurement organization (System A_1) required a *constant* influx of capital not subject to the inconstant fluctuations of immediate supply and demand (cf. Rappaport 1967 : 105–9). Continuous advance resource concentration was needed to support craft specialization, to feed and lead expeditions, and to maintain successful trading relations. During the early development of the system, the "open" environment mitigated against the efficient use of coercive force to obtain resource investment in advance of basic resource return from a scattered and potentially mobile population (Carneiro 1961, 1970; Webb 1964, this volume, chapter 16). Thus ceremonial centers were more than simply foci of collection and redistribution. Large, ornate temples, spacious plazas, stelae, flamboyant ceremonies and burials which consumed large quantities of exotic imports (such as jade, shell, obsidian, and hematite), and the local production and distribution of craft items (polychrome pots, decorated textiles, carved wooden objects) were the overt signs of a successful procurement organization. System A_1 integrated ideology and economics in a soft-sell approach that proved effective in bringing farm surplus to procurement organizations. The return on investment for household constituents was basic resources as well as status and a stake within the system. Investment in both Action Set 1 and Action Set 2 (System A_1) was essential to the survival of the local Core Area household.

Buffer Zone Constant Constraints

Constraints 2 (ecological) and 3 (geographic) are not severe in the Buffer Zone. The tropical rain forest in the Buffer Zone is broken by clusters of other ecozones (alluvial, riverine, ocean, and so on). The ecological variety provides rain forest products (such as cotton, *copal*, and dyes), cacao and other alluvial products, and marine shell and fish —all with high exchange potential in highland resource areas. The Buffer Zone abuts highland resource areas, trade routes, and the Atlantic Ocean, which at the time of the Conquest was a major means of bulk transportation (Thompson 1964, 1970). Several navigable river systems (the Usumacinta, Pasion, Chixoy, Hondo, Belize, New) run through the Buffer Zone. Thus the geographical position and ecological variety of the Buffer Zone placed relatively few constraints upon highland–Buffer Zone trade interactions. As a result, the effect of Constraint 1 (basic resources) upon Buffer Zone systems was rather limited.

The Hypothesized Buffer Zone System

Complex systems that did develop in the Buffer Zone (A₂) functioned somewhat like the Core Area's System A₁. However, BZH₁ (Buffer Zone households) had the potential of investing resources, independent of System A₂, in additional action sets created by ecological variety and access to the highlands (Diagram 2). The Core Area Action Set 1 was replaced by Buffer Zone Action Sets 1′, 1″, and 1‴. A limited range of natural resources were available to most Core Area households. In the Buffer Zone several ecological zones were within reach of most households. For example, at Altun Ha (Fig. 50), located one mile inland from the Belize coast, exploitation of ocean resources,

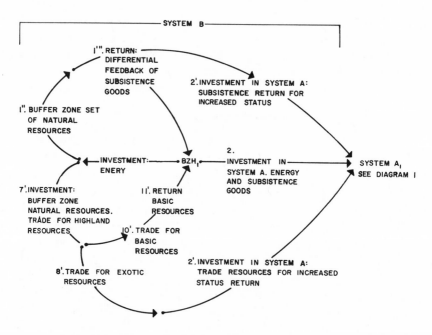

BZH₁ = THE MINIMUM PRODUCTION-CONSUMPTION UNIT, i.e. THE HOUSEHOLD

DIAGRAM 2: CLASSIC MAYA BUFFER ZONE CEREMONIAL CENTER —INDIVIDUAL HOUSEHOLD SYSTEM seafood and exotic items, of estuaries, and of slash-and-burn agriculture were all possible subsistence (Action Sets 1′, 1″, 1‴) activities (Pendergast 1967a : 100). A variety in avenues of investment created a potential for differential returns on investments.

Additional action sets also provided the Buffer Zone with the potential for independent procurement efforts. Owing to differential resource distribution, bulk-transport systems, and proximity to the highlands, the potential existed for households and small kin groups to independently collect local natural resources and exchange them for highland products (Fig. 51). Exchanges could have been made in the highlands or locally along Buffer Zone–highland trade routes. Action Sets 7′, 8′, and 11′ in System B are alternatives to the actions in System A_2. Thus, additional differential returns on investment were possible in the Buffer Zone independent of System A_2.

System A_2 in Buffer Zone systems functioned both as a social, political, and ceremonial interaction sphere and as a procurement organization. Households invested in System A_2 for social, political, and ceremonial returns as well as for ease of resource procurement. System B merely provided an alternative for obtaining a variety of investment returns independent of System A_2. It is assumed that in System B many returns were invested in Action Sets 2 and 2′ to obtain new status positions within the hierarchies of System A_2.

A TEST OF THE CORE AREA–BUFFER ZONE MODEL

The model this paper will use of Lowland Classic Maya social systems is made up of the hypothesized Core Area and Buffer Zone systems. A test of this model is essential to evaluate its utility for organizing future research.

Internal Variety within Core Area and Buffer Zone Systems

The parameters of *internal variety* within Core Area and Buffer Zone cultural systems can be predicted from the model, and the predictions can be tested. *Internal variety* within a cultural system, for present purposes, is defined as the number of different arrangements of specific households and small kin groups (the elements) possible within economic, social, religious, political, and other status hierarchies.

By definition internal variety and social mobility vary directly. If there is a high social mobility potential for household or small kin groups within status hierarchies, then a large number of arrangements of households within status hierarchies will be possible and will actually occur through time. In such a situation, the constraints upon internal variety are minimized. If social mobility potential for households or small kin groups is minimal, only a limited number of arrangements of households within status hierarchies will be possible and will actually occur through time. In this case the constraints upon internal variety are severe. Internal variety within a cultural system varies directly with the social mobility potential for households or small kin groups within status hierarchies.

Predictions of relative social mobility potential (internal variety) can be generated from the Core Area–Buffer Zone model and from a set of assumptions.

It is assumed that economic attributes, such as access to differentially distributed resources, will partially affect an individual's position in various status hierarchies. It is further assumed that variation through time in the distribution of resources among individuals will create variation through time in the specific economic attributes of individuals. If the economic attributes of individuals change, the position of those individuals within status hierarchies will be restructured. The result is increased social mobility potential (internal variety). Factors that affect variation in resource distributions will also affect social mobility potential.

Variable constraints, such as population size, affect the parameters of social mobility potential within Classic Maya systems. Over the 1,500 years from the beginning of the Preclassic to the end of the Late Classic there were many changes in the population profile of the Maya Lowlands. Although the nature of many of the demographic differences through time is unclear, there is evidence that Late Classic population levels exceeded Preclassic and Early Classic levels (Rathje 1971a : 145–52). In addition, there are few data to indicate major technological innovation that would have increased productivity from the Preclassic to the Late Classic. There have been several recent suggestions that through time craft production (Rathje 1971a, 1971b) and agriculture were intensified, including the increasing cultivation of the highly productive *ramón* trees (Puleston and Puleston 1971). However, many of those who make and support such suggestions also state that by the middle of the Late Classic (Tepeu 2), populations were placing severe stress upon the resources of even the most intensified systems (among others, Culbert, Sanders, Willey, Shimkin, this volume). It is therefore assumed that as population grew, production of resources did not increase at the same rate, especially during the Late Classic.

In addition, it is assumed that each individual in a population requires a minimum quantity of resources to survive. Differential distribution of resources, above this subsistence requirement, supports stratification and public projects that sustain community subsistence and integration. The constraints upon variation in resource distribution are a partial function of the total quantity of resources available and the number of people integrated by a given sociopolitical system.

If population increases but the production of resources does not increase proportionally, the percentage of resources needed for the minimum subsistence requirement of the population will increase. In addition, increased population will amplify the need for intensification of the integrative functions of sociopolitical systems. Proportional to population, however, there will be fewer resources available for differential distribution. As a result, the percentage, and perhaps the total quantity, of resources concentrated at critical nodes of the sociopolitical system will increase. Those individuals with access to these nodes will have access to differentially distributed resources. The availability of access to such resources at the subsistence household level will decrease.

Thus, if population increases without proportional resource increase, severe constraints will intensify resource concentration at the critical nodes of the sociopolitical system. The number of individuals who have access to differentially distributed resources will be restricted, and the number of individuals who can potentially change their economic attributes will decrease. Variation through time in the differential distribution of resources will be minimized. If change through time in the economic attributes of individuals is minimized, social mobility potential will also be minimized.

Hypothesis of Internal Parameter (1). Based on the above models one statement of the internal parameters of change within cultural systems reads: Other factors constant, as population increases without an equivalent increase in total resources, variety in resource distribution will decrease and social mobility potential (internal variety) will decrease. (A similar hypothesis phrased in terms of office recruitment mechanisms was proposed and briefly tested by Rathje [1970b].)

Test Implication (1). Given that Late Classic populations were larger than Preclassic or Early Classic populations and given the lack of major technological innovations, there should be less social mobility potential (internal variety) within Late Classic systems than within Preclassic and Early Classic systems.

From the Core Area–Buffer Zone model it can be deduced that constant constraints affected the parameters of social mobility potential (internal variety) within Classic Maya systems. Because of Constraint 3 (geographic), Core Area households could not independently procure basic commodities. Status hierarchies (which by definition involved differential access to resources) developed as a prerequisite of basic resource procurement. To obtain resources households were forced to invest heavily in highly stratified systems (System A_1) which concentrated resources in ways that constrained social mobility potential and reinforced the established order. Because of Constraint 2, a limited ecological range available to all, differential distribution of resources based upon differential investment in a variety of ecozones was minimized. In sum, the Core Area lacked ecological variety and variety in trade interactions. These factors constrained variation in resource distribution and social mobility potential through time.

In the Buffer Zone, ecological variety, spatial position, and bulk-transport systems allowed variety in subsistence investment and variety in trade interactions. Households had the potential of changing economic statuses outside of System A_2 and then using that change to transform social and political statuses within System A_2. Buffer Zone systems had more ecological and trade variety than Core Area systems. Through time, as a result, there were fewer constraints upon variation in resource distribution. Buffer Zone systems should have had more social mobility potential than Core Area systems.

Hypothesis of Internal Parameter (2). Based on the above models, a second statement of the internal parameters of variety within cultural systems reads: other factors constant, as ecological variety and potential trade interaction variety increase, social mobility potential (internal variety) will increase.

Test Implication (2). Given relatively similar fluctuations in variable constraints in the Core Area and Buffer Zone systems, there will be more social mobility potential (internal variety) within Buffer Zone systems than within Core Area systems.

A Material Culture–Social Mobility Model

The ability of the above model and assumptions to accurately predict the parameters of internal variety within Classic Maya cultural systems can be briefly tested using Classic Maya burials and a material culture–social mobility model (for a more detailed statement of the model see Rathje 1971a : 74–107).

A *social identity* is a culturally distinguished social position or category (Goodenough 1969; Keesing. 1967). Adult, male, priest, distributor of goods in Ceremony X, all are separate social identities. A *social persona* is the composite of several identities appropriate to a given social interaction (Goodenough 1969; Keesing 1967), such as: adult, male, chief priest of God Z, and distributor of goods in dealing with adult male worshippers at Ceremony X. These concepts can be used to build models of socially *mobile* and *nonmobile* systems.

The following mobile and nonmobile constructs do not exist in reality, but the sharp contrast between them is helpful in comparing differences in social mobility potential among real systems. In *nonmobile* systems social identities are not easily interchanged. The general status level of identities is consistent within social personae. For example, the nobles in highly stratified Western Chou China manipulated bronze urns in rites for their ancestors. These acts were not only based on elite kin and religious statuses, but also validated elite political authority and economic interactions. When a Chou noble manipulated a bronze vessel, his political, economic, religious, and kinship identities were all employed in an elite social persona (Cheng 1963: xxx; Reischauer and Fairbank 1960 : 51, 61).

In nonmobile systems with little internal variety, specific identities tend to cooccur in replicated sets. If Family A, in a nonmobile system, monopolizes political leadership positions, then each member of Family

A is either a political leader or a potential political leader (subject to age and sex restrictions, for example, adult male). There will be no potential or actual political leader who is not an adult male member of Family A. No potential or actual political leader will do anything that an adult male member of Family A does not do. In overt behavior the two identities directly covary. Nonelite social personae do not include elite social identities. No adult male member of Family B is either a political leader or a potential political leader. Thus, social identities in nonmobile societies tend to occur in mutually exclusive, consistently replicated sets.

In a *mobile* social system with a great deal of internal variety, which by definition means that individuals can potentially change their positions in a number of hierarchies; specific genealogical and other identities will not covary directly with one another. An adult male who has the general political identity of leader may be a member of Family A or Family B or Family C. As a result of a certain amount of independent assortment, the general status level of identities in individual social personae is not always consistent. For example, among the Basoga Bantu there are situations in which high-level political leaders hold low-level positions within kinship authority systems (Fallers 1965). The social identities that constitute social personae in a mobile system are changeable and often incongruous at any one time.

To apply the above model to past cultures, it must be translated into material culture terms. For efficient social interactions, the individuals involved must inform each other of their respective social identities (Goodenough 1969; Binford 1962, 1971). It is assumed that material culture symbols will vary in form and distribution characteristics in direct relation to the form and distribution characteristic of hierarchically ranked social identities. Variation in symbol distribution will be used in the following tests.

Symbol Distribution. In mobile systems with a great deal of internal variety material symbols will not directly covary in social persona clusters. In a system responsive to individual achievements, numerous symbols will be acquired and manipulated in small-scale increments. For example, specific family and political leadership identities and their symbols may sort relatively independently (Fig. 52–3, 52–2). In nonmobile systems with little internal variety, material symbols will significantly covary in sets. Symbols will be acquired and manipulated

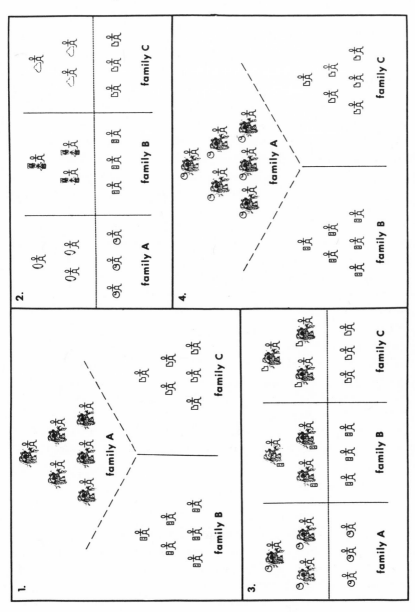

FIGURE 52. FOUR IDEALIZED IDENTITY ALLOCATION SYSTEMS AND ASSO-
CIATED SYMBOL DISTRIBUTIONS. The headdress represents leadership identity. The
three symbols in the top half of segment 2 each represent both a political leadership and a
specific family identity. The other symbols represent specific family identities.

in clusters. For example, specific family and political leader symbols will directly covary. Leadership symbols will be associated with the symbols of one family and not with the symbols of other families (Fig. 52–1, 52–4).

Social Mobility Potential. Two systems can be described as mobile or nonmobile by comparing the amount of independent assortment versus significant covariation of identity symbols in social personae (regardless of the symbols' subjective statuses). Such material culture–social mobility characterizations do not directly measure social mobility. They describe the potential for expressing social identity mobility within the material culture distributions of a system (Shimkin: personal communication). *This social mobility potential is assumed to be responsive to the actual amount of internal variety within a system.* This measure for comparing two cultural systems can only be applied within bounds. Symbol clusters studied must be shown to relate to relatively complete individual or family group social personae. Cluster proveniences, or "scenes," must be equivalent, and potential artifact inventories must be comparable in both systems.

Classic Maya Burials: Statistic 1 and Statistic 2. The artifacts in Classic Maya burials represent terminal social personae clusters and provide an array of data relevant to the material culture–social mobility model (Rathje 1971a : 108–15; cf. Binford 1971). The same kinds of artifacts and materials were generally available for inclusion in burials throughout the Maya Lowlands. The social mobility model was employed by creating individual symbol units. Fifty-eight variable categories were defined (Table 24). To make differences in burial goods meaningful, freaks of preservation were ignored. Only variables that could be definitely recorded present or absent for every interment were used. Each of the fifty-eight variables was given a numerical loading based on a subjective ordering. The number of occurrences of each variable in a burial was multiplied by that variable's loading. The results were summed to obtain Statistic 1 for each burial. Each Statistic 1 rating is, therefore, the product of the kind and quantity of all the variables present in a burial.

Since Statistic 1 is based on a subjective loading of variables, Statistic 2 was developed as an *independent* description of a burial's contents. For Statistic 2 each of the fifty-eight variables was given an objective numerical loading as a function of the rarity of its occurrence in a total

TABLE 24
CLASSIC MAYA BURIALS:
LOADINGS OF THE FIFTY-EIGHT VARIABLES

	Variable Category	Loading Statistic 1	Loading Statistic 2
01	Facial ornaments	58	0.32
02	Ceremonial paraphernalia	57	0.72
03	Pendants	56	0.58
04	Stingray spines	55	0.81
05	Unworked shell	54	0.46
06	Body ornamentation	53	0.10
07	Bead necklaces	52	0.24
08	Figurines	51	3.57
09	Tubes	50	2.63
10	Associated carving	49	0 09
11	Blades	48	0.22
12	Unidentified objects	47	2.56
13	Utilitarian objects	46	0.50
14	Seated humans	45	1.04
15	Standing humans	44	1.07
16	Head-only humans	43	1.14
17	Reclining humans	42	8.33
18	Real glyphs	41	0.12
19	Pseudo glyphs	40	0.96
20	Deities	39	2.17
21	Jaguars	38	2.43
22	Birds	37	1.53
23	Snakes	36	3.70
24	Deer	35	5.00
25	Doglike animals	34	4.00
26	Monkeys	33	6.66
27	Frogs	32	9.09
28	Aquatic animals	31	4.54
29	Fruits	30	7.69
30	Miscellaneous	29	1.29
31	Shell count	28	0.16
32	Type of shell count	27	0.34
33	Jade count	26	0.19
34	Other stone count	25	0.54
35	Type of other stone count	24	0.56
36	Obsidian count	23	0.68
37	Flint count	22	0.89
38	Bone count	21	0.40
39	Clay count	20	2.04
40	Pottery count	19	0.07

TABLE 24 (*Continued*)

Variable Category	Loading Statistic 1	Statistic 2
41 Polychrome pottery	18	0.26
42 Relief pottery	17	0.36
43 Filed teeth	16	0.25
44 Ceremonial pottery	15	2.43
45 Legged flat-bottom dishes	14	1.06
46 Vases	13	0.54
47 Deep bowls	12	0.13
48 Legged round-bottom bowls/dishes	11	2.70
49 Deep full bowls	10	1.13
50 Medium bowls	09	0.59
51 Shallow bowls/dishes	08	1.44
52 Shallow flat-bottom dishes	07	0.71
53 Incurving bowls	06	1.33
54 Restricted bowls	05	2.70
55 Miniature cups	04	1.56
56 Miniature jars	03	3.51
57 Ollas	02	1.06
58 Monochrome pottery	01	0.14

sample of 1,009 Classic Maya burials, that is, the fewer the occurrences, the higher the loading (Table 24). Statistic 2 was then obtained for each burial by the same procedure as Statistic 1.

A *social mobility potential profile* was obtained by plotting the statistics for a set (defined by date and provenience) of burials on logarithmic paper. The burials were ordered along the x axis on the basis of an ascending y (Statistic 1 or 2) value. Burials with no preserved grave goods were excluded. The burials were spaced to make the x-axis length of each set comparable. The plotted points were then connected to form a graph, or profile. The statistic values were normalized so that each graph was the same height and only differences in profile form were recorded. This operation made differences in the range and internal variation of social personae present in a given set of burials clear (Fig. 53).

It is assumed that in any status system the number of holders of specific identities generally decreases exponentially as the identities become more advantaged, that is, 1,000 household constituents, 100 priests, 10 chief priests, 1 high priest. In addition, it was obvious from the data that the burial statistic values (quantified material-culture so cial persona) increased exponentially. It is therefore assumed that if a profile forms a continuum of statuses in a consistently rising exponential slope, it reflects the relative independent sorting of social identities and social identity symbols in a system with a high social mobility potential (cf. Set 40, Figs. 54, 56). If the rising graph forms plateaus, it reflects the significant covariation of symbols in low social mobility potential identity clusters (cf. Set 47, Figs. 55, 56). Profiles were compared and rated as having a high or low social mobility potential (internal variety) by the following method.

Experiments were made in an attempt to evaluate objectively the relative social mobility potential (internal variety) represented in two burial sets and their graphs. The experimental burial sets were not used to test hypotheses or models. Set 40 clearly had a high social mobility potential (as defined in this chapter); Set 47 had a low social mobility potential (Figs. 54, 55). A fourth-power exponential curve between the end points of the graphs was found to best fit the mobile graph (40) and still deviate greatly from the nonmobile graph (47). The fourth-power exponential curve was assumed to represent a continuum of social personae, the profile of an ideal mobile social identity system that could be compared to every set to evaluate relative social mobility potential. An "ideal" profile was arbitrarily fitted to both the Statistic 1 and Statistic 2 profiles of each set. The differences between the observed ("real") and expected ("ideal") values of all the burials in a set were summed. The number of burials in a profile was divided into the sum to normalize the result and make it comparable to those from sets with different numbers of burials. The final statement, a Statistic 1 or Statistic 2 rating for a set, is the average deviation between a profile and an "ideal" mobile exponential continuum connecting its high and low points—the greater the deviation the less the social mobility potential. Thus, Set 40 (Statistic 1 rating 5.78; Statistic 2 rating 9.13) is more mobile—has more internal variety—than Set 47 (Statistic 1 rating 20.04; Statistic 2 rating 23.30) (Fig. 56).

The data used in the following tests are from a sample of 1,009 burials from thirteen Southern Maya Lowland sites (for the specific details of the sample see Rathje 1971a : Appendix C). Owing to small burial

MOBILITY POTENTIAL:
STATISTIC · I

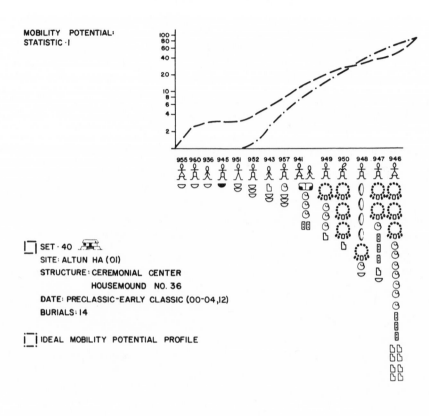

☐ SET · 40
   SITE: ALTUN HA (01)
   STRUCTURE: CEREMONIAL CENTER
              HOUSEMOUND NO. 36
   DATE: PRECLASSIC-EARLY CLASSIC (00-04,12)
   BURIALS: 14

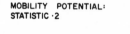 IDEAL MOBILITY POTENTIAL PROFILE

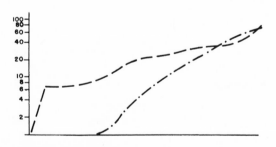

MOBILITY POTENTIAL:
STATISTIC · 2

FIGURE 53. THE IDEAL MOBILITY POTENTIAL PROFILE COMPARED
TO A REAL MOBILITY POTENTIAL PROFILE

428

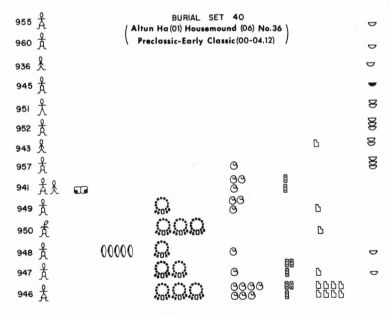

⬤	POLYCHROME POT
▽	MONOCHROME POT
◨	OBSIDIAN ARTIFACT
◼	FLINT ARTIFACT
△	ARTIFACT OF STONE OTHER THAN OBSIDIAN OR FLINT
(	CRYSTALLINE HEMATITE OR OTHER EXOTIC STONE ARTIFACT
⚬	JADE ARTIFACT
⊙	SHELL ARTIFACT
▤	BONE ARTIFACT
⬛	UTILITARIAN STONE ARTIFACT
▮	CLAY ARTIFACT
▱▱▱	FILED TEETH
⚓	ADOLESCENT 18
⚓	YOUNG ADULT 18-25
⚓	MATURE ADULT 26-50
⚓	OLD ADULT 50
⚓	FEMALE
⚓	MALE

BURIAL SET 40
(Altun Ha (01) Housemound (06) No. 36)
(Preclassic-Early Classic (00-04,12))

FIGURE 54. THE GRAVE GOODS IN BURIAL SET 40

429

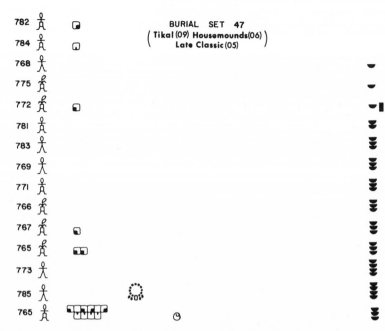

FIGURE 55. THE GRAVE GOODS IN BURIAL SET 47

set sizes and obvious sampling error, the social mobility potential ratings are only tentative indicators of social mobility potential. However, when these indicators consistently follow test implications, they can be considered a tentative confirmation of the model and hypotheses.

Statistic 1, Statistic 2, and Test Implication 1. Test Implication 1 stated that given Late Classic populations larger than Preclassic or Early Classic populations and given the lack of major technological innovations, there will be less internal variety, less social mobility potential, within Late Classic systems than within Preclassic and Early Classic systems. A high Statistic 1 or Statistic 2 rating indicates a low social mobility potential (internal variety). Preclassic and Early Classic sets should have lower Statistic 1 and Statistic 2 ratings than Late Classic sets.

For control purposes, the burials were separated on the basis of the location of interment in either housemounds or ceremonial structures (definitions of excavators were used with a few exceptions, cf. Rathje 1971a : Appendix E). Burials were then sorted into sets based on time

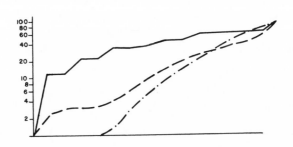

MOBILITY POTENTIAL:
STATISTIC·1

☐ SET · 40 🏛
  SITE: ALTUN HA (OI)
  STRUCTURE: CEREMONIAL CENTER
        HOUSEMOUND NO. 36
  DATE: PRECLASSIC-EARLY CLASSIC (OO-O4,12)
  BURIALS: 14

░ IDEAL MOBILITY POTENTIAL PROFILE

☐ SET · 47 🏛
  SITE: TIKAL (O9)
  STRUCTURE: CEREMONIAL CENTER HOUSEMOUNDS
  DATE: LATE CLASSIC (O5-IO)
  BURIALS: I5

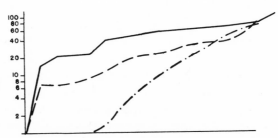

MOBILITY POTENTIAL:
STATISTIC·2

FIGURE 56. A COMPARISON BETWEEN MOBILITY POTENTIAL PRO-
FILES FROM BURIAL SETS 40 AND 47 AND THE IDEAL PROFILE

periods. Both ceremonial structure and housemound burials were separately placed in Preclassic, Early Classic, Tepeu 1, Tepeu 2, summary Preclassic–Early Classic, and summary Late Classic sets. A total of twelve sets were constructed (Table 25). Following Test Implication 1, sets of burials from time periods with the highest population levels will have a lower social mobility potential (higher Statistic 1 and Statistic 2 ratings), less internal variety, than other sets. This prediction can be tested in two ways.

The summary Late Classic sets (Set 72 [housemound] and 58 [ceremonial]) can be considered to have been the product of higher population levels than those which produced the burials in other sets (with the exception of Tepeu 2, Sets 3 and 8). Comparing the relative Statistic 1 and Statistic 2 ratings of Late Classic sets with the other sets, sixteen out of sixteen predictions are confirmed (Table 26).

As a further test, Tepeu 2 sets (Set 3 [housemound] and 8 [ceremonial]), from the demographic peak of the Late Classic, can be isolated and predicted to have less social mobility potential than any other sets. Comparing the Statistic 1 and Statistic 2 ratings of the Tepeu 2 sets with the ratings of the other sets, the prediction is confirmed eighteen out of twenty times (Table 27).

The probability of predicting correctly, by chance, which of two statistic ratings will be higher sixteen out of sixteen times or eighteen out of twenty times is less than .03. The predictive power of Hypothesis 1 is, thus, tentatively confirmed. To further test this model, temporally defined sets should be compared within separate sites where sample sizes permit (cf. Rathje 1971a : 152–79).

Statistic 1, Statistic 2, and Test Implication 2. Given relatively similar fluctuations in variable constraints in the Core Area and Buffer Zone systems, through time there will be more social mobility potential (internal variety) within Buffer Zone systems than within Core Area systems. Buffer Zone Statistic 1 and Statistic 2 ratings should be lower than Core Area ratings.

Burials were sorted by site and structure provenience into sets. Housemound structure burial sets from six sites were compared. Housemound sets were selected because the local household seemed to be the node at which the contraints upon social mobility were most obvious and clear-cut. In addition, the wide range of variation throughout the lowlands in ceremonial and palace structures makes the context of bur-

TABLE 25
CENTRAL LOWLAND MAYA MOBILITY POTENTIAL SETS

Burial Sets	Number of Burials	Date: Preclassic	Preclassic–Early Classic	Early Classic	Tepeu 1	Late Classic (except Tepeu 1)	Late Classic	Structure Type: Housemound Burials	Ceremonial Structure Burials	Site: Altar de Sacrificios	Ahun Ha	Baking Pot	Barton Ramie	Copan	Holmul	Mountain Cow	Pomona	Palenque	Piedras Negras	San Jose	Seibal	Tikal	Uaxactun	Mobility Potential Statistic 1	Mobility Potential Statistic 2
Set 301	(34)	X						X		X	X		X			X					X	X	X	8.71	9.01
Set 302	(52)			X				X		X	X		X			X						X	X	7.12	7.04
Set 1	(107)				X			X		X	X		X								X	X	X	7.21	7.23
Set 2	(80)					X		X		X	X		X								X	X	X	10.72	13.60
Set 3	(137)						X	X		X	X	X	X		X					X	X		X	13.58	11.50
Set 72	(301)	X								X	X	X			X	X				X	X		X	12.42	14.21
Set 303	(46)		X						X	X	X	X			X	X			X	X			X	13.99	12.21
Set 304	(55)			X					X	X	X	X		X	X		X		X	X			X	9.85	10.31
Set 6	(138)				X				X	X	X	X	X	X	X	X	X	X	X	X			X	14.02	11.97
Set 7	(34)					X			X		X	X	X	X		X		X	X	X		X	X	6.07	4.23
Set 8	(71)						X		X	X	X	X		X	X		X		X	X		X	X	15.68	14.43
Set 58	(125)						X		X	X	X	X		X		X			X	X			X	14.97	13.63

433

KEY TO TABLES 26, 27, and 29
    PCL = Preclassic (800 B.C.–A.D. 300)
    ECL = Early Classic (A.D. 300–600)
PCL/ECL = Preclassic/Early Classic (800 B.C.–A.D. 600)
    TEP 1 = Tepeu 1 (A.D. 600–700)
    TEP 2 = Tepeu 2, Late Classic except Tepeu 1 (A.D. 700–900)
    LCL = Late Classic (A.D. 600–900)

    UAX = Uaxactun (CORE)
    TIK = Tikal (CORE)
    B.R. = Barton Ramie (BUFFER ZONE)
    A.H. = Altun Ha (BUFFER ZONE)
    A.S. = Altar de Sacrificios (BUFFER ZONE)
    SEI = Seibal (BUFFER ZONE)

    H.M. = Housemound Burials
    C.S. = Ceremonial Structure Burials

    S_1 = Statistic 1 Rating
    S_2 = Statistic 2 Rating
    $>$ = is greater than, i.e. has LESS mobility potential
    $<$ = is less than, i.e. has MORE mobility potential
    $*$ = CORRECT Prediction
    $\dagger$ = INCORRECT Prediction

TABLE 26

POPULATION MOBILITY POTENTIAL PREDICTIONS BASED UPON LATE CLASSIC SETS

1.	LCL	H.M.	S_1	>	PCL/ECL	H.M.	S_1	*	12.42 > 7.21
2.	LCL	H.M.	S_2	>	PCL/ECL	H.M.	S_2	*	14.21 > 7.23
3.	LCL	H.M.	S_1	>	PCL	H.M.	S_1	*	12.42 > 8.71
4.	LCL	H.M.	S_2	>	PCL	H.M.	S_2	*	14.21 > 9.01
5.	LCL	H.M.	S_1	>	ECL	H.M.	S_1	*	12.42 > 7.12
6.	LCL	H.M.	S_2	>	ECL	H.M.	S_2	*	14.21 > 7.04
7.	LCL	H.M.	S_1	>	TEP 1	H.M.	S_1	*	12.42 > 10.72
8.	LCL	H.M.	S_2	>	TEP 1	H.M.	S_2	*	14.21 > 13.60
9.	LCL	C.S.	S_1	>	PCL/ECL	C.S.	S_1	*	14.97 > 14.02
10.	LCL	C.S.	S_2	>	PCL/ECL	C.S.	S_2	*	13.64 > 11.97
11.	LCL	C.S.	S_1	>	PCL	C.S.	S_1	*	14.97 > 13.99
12.	LCL	C.S.	S_2	>	PCL	C.S.	S_2	*	13.64 > 12.21
13.	LCL	C.S.	S_1	>	ECL	C.S.	S_1	*	14.97 > 9.85
14.	LCL	C.S.	S_2	>	ECL	C.S.	S_2	*	13.64 > 10.31
15.	LCL	C.S.	S_1	>	TEP 1	C.S.	S_1	*	14.97 > 6.67
16.	LCL	C.S.	S_2	>	TEP 1	C.S.	S_2	*	13.64 > 4.23

TABLE 27
POPULATION MOBILITY POTENTIAL PREDICTIONS
BASED UPON TEPEU 2 SETS

1. TEP 2 H.M.	S1 > PCL/ECL	H.M.	S1	*	13.58	>	7.21
2. TEP 2 H.M.	S2 > PCL/ECL	H.M.	S2	*	11.50	>	7.23
3. TEP 2 H.M.	S1 > PCL	H.M.	S1	*	13.58	>	8.71
4. TEP 2 H.M.	S2 > PCL	H.M.	S2	*	11.50	>	9.01
5. TEP 2 H.M.	S1 > ECL	H.M.	S1	*	13.58	>	7.12
6. TEP 2 H.M.	S2 > ECL	H.M.	S2	*	11.50	>	7.04
7. TEP 2 H.M.	S1 > TEP 1	H.M.	S1	*	13.58	>	10.72
8. TEP 2 H.M.	S2 > TEP 1	H.M.	S2	†	11.50	<	13.60
9. TEP 2 H.M.	S1 > LCL	H.M.	S1	*	13.58	>	12.42
10. TEP 2 H.M.	S2 > LCL	H.M.	S2	†	11.50	<	14.21
11. TEP 2 C.S.	S1 > PCL/ECL	C.S.	S1	*	15.68	>	14.02
12. TEP 2 C.S.	S2 > PCL/ECL	C.S.	S2	*	14.43	>	11.97
13. TEP 2 C.S.	S1 > PCL	C.S.	S1	*	15.68	>	13.99
14. TEP 2 C.S.	S2 > PCL	C.S.	S2	*	14.43	>	12.21
15. TEP 2 C.S.	S1 > ECL	C.S.	S1	*	15.68	>	9.85
16. TEP 2 C.S.	S2 > ECL	C.S.	S2	*	14.43	>	10.31
17. TEP 2 C.S.	S1 > TEP 1	C.S.	S1	*	15.68	>	6.67
18. TEP 2 C.S.	S2 > TEP 1	C.S.	S2	*	14.43	>	4.23
19. TEP 2 C.S.	S1 > LCL	C.S.	S1	*	15.68	>	14.97
20. TEP 2 C.S.	S2 > LCL	C.S.	S2	*	14.43	>	13.64

ials within them less comparable than the context of burials within simple housemounds (for examples using ceremonial and palace structure sets see Rathje 1971a : 251–68). Tikal and Uaxactun represent Core Area systems; Barton Ramie, Altun Ha, Altar de Sacrificios, and Seibal represent Buffer Zone systems.

Even though the numbers of burials are small, both statistic ratings consistently agree that each of the three Preclassic–Early Classic Buffer Zone housemound burial sets has more social mobility potential (lower Statistic 1 and Statistic 2 ratings) than the Preclassic–Early Clasic Core Area set (Table 28). The Statistic 1 ratings for the Late Classic sets totally confirm the test implication. Each of the four Late Classic Buffer Zone sets has more mobility potential than Tikal or Uaxactun, separately or combined. The Statistic 2 ratings also generally support Test Implication 2.

If the sets are compared by pairs within specific time periods by Statistic 1 and Statistic 2 separately, thirty specific predictions can be made. Twenty-nine out of the thirty are confirmed (Table 29). The

TABLE 28
CENTRAL LOWLAND MAYA HOUSEHOLD
MOBILITY POTENTIAL SETS

PRECLASSIC–EARLY CLASSIC HOUSEHOLD
MOBILITY POTENTIAL

		Statistic 1	Statistic 2
CORE:	Set 54 Uaxactun-Tikal (7) [a]	15.48 [b]	15.73 [b]
BUFFER ZONE:	Set 55 Barton Ramie (14)	6.36	8.54
	Set 12 Altun Ha (58)	7.32	8.57
	Set 143 Altar de Sacrificios (22)	6.15	6.58

LATE CLASSIC HOUSEHOLD MOBILITY POTENTIAL

		Statistic 1	Statistic 2
CORE:	Set 22 Uaxactun-Tikal (26)	18.05	12.55
	Set 47 Tikal (16)	20.04	23.30
	Set 166 Uaxactun (10)	14.80	10.80
BUFFER ZONE:	Set 56 Barton Ramie (50)	11.99	12.45
	Set 69 Altun Ha (111)	11.30	7.78
	Set 149 Altar de Sacrificios (37)	9.26	10.74
	Set 148 Seibal (19)	7.81	9.70

[a] This figure is the number of burials in each set. The burials that make up each set are listed in Rathje 1971a: Appendix G.
[b] A high Statistic rating indicates a small mobility potential, a low Statistic rating indicates a large mobility potential.

probability of guessing for each comparison which of the two sets will have the higher statistic is .50. The probability of predicting correctly by chance which of two statistics will be larger twenty-nine out of thirty times is less than .0001.

In the preceding tests, the model predicted internal variety with a fair degree of accuracy. Statistical ratings, however, may be the result of factors not considered by the model. To test the efficiency of the model's ability to predict ratings, it should be compared with predictions based upon other considerations.

Ratings might be a function of the number of sites represented in burial sets: the more sites, the more potential variation in symbol distribution. The two sets with burials from the most sites—Set 1 (housemound) and Set 58 (ceremonial)—would then have a higher mobility potential—lower Statistic 1 and Statistic 2 ratings—than the other

TABLE 29
CORE–BUFFER ZONE MOBILITY POTENTIAL
PREDICTIONS

1. PCL/ECL	UAX/TIK	S_1	>	PCL/ECL	B.R.	S_1	*	15.48 >	6.36
2. PCL/ECL	UAX/TIK	S_2	>	PCL/ECL	B.R.	S_2	*	15.73 >	8.54
3. PCL/ECL	UAX/TIK	S_1	>	PCL/ECL	A.H.	S_1	*	15.48 >	7.32
4. PCL/ECL	UAX/TIK	S_2	>	PCL/ECL	A.H.	S_2	*	15.73 >	8.57
5. PCL/ECL	UAX/TIK	S_1	>	PCL/ECL	A.S.	S_1	*	15.48 >	6.15
6. PCL/ECL	UAX/TIK	S_2	>	PCL/ECL	A.S.	S_2	*	15.73 >	6.58
7. LCL	UAX/TIK	S_1	>	LCL	B.R.	S_1	*	18.05 >	11.99
8. LCL	UAX/TIK	S_2	>	LCL	B.R.	S_2	*	12.55 >	12.45
9. LCL	UAX/TIK	S_1	>	LCL	A.H.	S_1	*	18.05 >	11.30
10. LCL	UAX/TIK	S_2	>	LCL	A.H.	S_2	*	12.55 >	7.78
11. LCL	UAX/TIK	S_1	>	LCL	A.S.	S_1	*	18.05 >	9.26
12. LCL	UAX/TIK	S_2	>	LCL	A.S.	S_2	*	12.55 >	10.74
13. LCL	UAX/TIK	S_1	>	LCL	SEI	S_1	*	18.05 >	7.81
14. LCL	UAX/TIK	S_2	>	LCL	SEI	S_2	*	12.55 >	9.70
15. LCL	TIK	S_1	>	LCL	B.R.	S_1	*	20.04 >	11.99
16. LCL	TIK	S_2	>	LCL	B.R.	S_2	*	23.30 >	12.45
17. LCL	TIK	S_1	>	LCL	A.H.	S_1	*	20.04 >	11.30
18. LCL	TIK	S_2	>	LCL	A.H.	S_2	*	23.30 >	7.78
19. LCL	TIK	S_1	>	LCL	A.S.	S_1	*	20.04 >	9.26
20. LCL	TIK	S_2	>	LCL	A.S.	S_2	*	23.30 >	10.74
21. LCL	TIK	S_1	>	LCL	SEI	S_1	*	20.04 >	7.81
22. LCL	TIK	S_2	>	LCL	SEI	S_2	*	23.30 >	9.70
23. LCL	UAX	S_1	>	LCL	B.R.	S_1	*	14.80 >	11.99
24. LCL	UAX	S_2	>	LCL	B.R.	S_2	†	10.80 <	12.45
25. LCL	UAX	S_1	>	LCL	A.H.	S_1	*	14.80 >	11.30
26. LCL	UAX	S_2	>	LCL	A.H.	S_2	*	10.80 >	7.78
27. LCL	UAX	S_1	>	LCL	A.S.	S_1	*	14.80 >	9.26
28. LCL	UAX	S_2	>	LCL	A.S.	S_2	*	10.80 >	10.74
29. LCL	UAX	S_1	>	LCL	SEI	S_1	*	14.80 >	7.81
30. LCL	UAX	S_2	>	LCL	SEI	S_2	*	10.80 >	9.70

ten sets used in Table 25. Comparing the relative Statistic 1 and Statistic 2 ratings of pairs of sets—housemound set with housemound set, ceremonial set with ceremonial set—only ten out of twenty predictions are confirmed.

Ratings might be a function of time. A 1,000-year period (the Preclassic) provides the potential for expressing a great deal more variation in symbol distribution in burials than a 300-year period (the Early

Classic). The two sets with the longest time span—Set 1 (house-mound) and Set 6 (ceremonial)—would then be predicted to have a higher mobility potential than the other sets in Table 25. Comparing the relative Statistic 1 and Statistic 2 ratings of pairs of sets, only twelve out of twenty predictions are correct.

The predictions generated from the model seem to be much more accurate than could be expected on the basis of chance alone or on the basis of other factors that might affect statistic ratings. In sum, tentative tests of the ability of the Core Area–Buffer Zone model to predict the parameters of internal variety, social mobility potential, within Classic Maya cultural systems seems confirmed. Before the constraints upon the parameters of variety within cultural systems can be accurately defined, many more tests must be conducted. For example, within the Test Implication 2 sets, population was not held constant. Each of the Core Area sites seems to have had a denser population than the Buffer Zone sites. Thus, until further tests can be made that hold population constant, the confirmation of Test Implication 2 may be only a further confirmation of Test Implication 1.

The Core Area–Buffer Zone model and the proposed constraints upon internal variety will surely be modified in the future. For now they present a clearly defined set of problems for further work. The most crucial of these problems seems to be: what effect did the lack of trade and of ecological and internal variety have upon the origin, development, and collapse of Core Area systems?

A CORE AREA–BUFFER ZONE RESEARCH DESIGN

The previous section has tentatively demonstrated that the Core Area–Buffer Zone model is a useful abstraction of Classic Maya cultural systems. This model, or any model, can be evaluated on the basis of its success in simulating or predicting the parameters of extant raw data. Most data necessary to test any comprehensive model are disjointed or uncollected. The following section uses the model to briefly outline the culture history of the Maya Lowlands from the Preclassic to the present day. The outline is not presented to assert the validity of the model introduced in this chapter. It is presented first to demonstrate that using a comprehensive model of cultures as adaptive systems enables us to see the collapse not as an idiosyncratic event but as an integral part of the dynamic interaction through time between the Lowland Maya environment and Maya cultural systems (see also Webb, chapter 16). Second, it is presented to illustrate the broadly based kinds of data organization and collection procedures that can be developed from any comprehensive model's problem focus. Such procedures are necessary to produce a data bank that can be used to evaluate competing comprehensive models. In addition, using the predictions of a comprehensive model to outline relevant data and future research allows the model to be evaluated, refined, or even discarded in conjunction with data organization and collection procedures. With such techniques, models can be efficiently refined as important research tools.

Hypothesis 1 (Core Development, Preclassic). From the model, it can be deduced that the Core Area environment placed severe constraints upon the variety within cultural systems that adapted to it. Constraints 1 (basic resources), 2 (ecological), and 3 (geographic) required that core cultural systems maintain complex organizations and ceremonial centers—System A_1—if population units were to be efficiently sustained. The constraints upon variety in Buffer Zone cultural systems were minimal. Population in the Buffer Zone could be efficiently sustained with or without a major emphasis upon complex organizations and ceremonial centers—System A_2 (for one test of Hypothesis 1 see Rathje 1971a, 1971b).

Test Implications and Future Research. Owing to the severe constraints on the variety of Core Area cultural systems, complex organizations and large ceremonial centers probably developed earlier in Core Area settlements than in Buffer Zone settlements, even though the Buffer Zone was almost surely populated earlier than the Core Area. To effectively test Hypothesis 1, effort must be expended to clearly define the earliest settlements in specific areas and to date the earliest ceremonial structures.

Another test implication of Hypothesis 1 states that early ceremonial structures should consume a greater proportion of community capital in the Core Area than in the Buffer Zone. Following Willey and Shimken (chapter 18), studies of capital investment in internal subsystems 1 and 2 (burials, building construction, and so on) should be made. Weight-volume estimates would provide a tentative measure of the capital invested by individual communities in ceremonial architecture. The effort involved in moving and carving building materials should also eventually be considered. The population levels at specific sites would have to be controlled in any estimate of relative capital expenditures.

Hypothesis 2 (Core Area–Buffer Zone Contact, Preclassic–Early Classic). Because of the Core Area basic resource constraint, Core Area cultural systems had to be efficient procurement systems. The Buffer Zone had all of the natural Core Area products, and the potential for Core Area–Buffer Zone trade in natural commodities was minimized. As long as the Buffer Zone systems did not develop large complex organizations, however, the Core Area did have artificial scarce commodities (craft items and esoteric knowledge) which were a product of, and a means to sustain, a complex organization. These items became the Core Area's trade capital. Craft products and esoteric knowledge were traded to the Buffer Zone and exchanged for Buffer Zone products (such as cacao and ocean shell), which were used in highland trade or exchanged directly for highland resources previously traded to the Buffer Zone.

Test Implications and Future Research. In the Buffer Zone, Core Area influence will take the form of wholesale importation of techniques and commodities utilized to sustain complex organization—cult ideology, cult technology, and manufactured cult paraphernalia from the Core Area. This importation will be associated in the Buffer Zone with little evidence, relative to the Core Area, of large, local complex organizations or ceremonial centers. A minimal quantity of Core Area material culture will be found in the highlands, but highland obsidian and highland and Buffer Zone *metates* will be found in quantity in the Core Area.

The distribution of the Core Area–derived stela cult in the Buffer Zone has been used in one test of Hypothesis 2 (Rathje 1971a : 46–52, 1971b), but more evidence is necessary. Studies of structure construction and stela and jade carving are potentially useful in defining trade and other types of interaction between sites. These studies, however, are by nature extremely subjective. Sayre, Chan, and Sabloff (1971) have done pioneering work in neutron activation to determine the source areas of pottery clay. Such techniques could be used to determine the quantity of ceramics that were imported from the Core Area to the Buffer Zone through time. On an intersite scale the work of

Rands (chapter 9) and Fry (1969) are excellent examples of this type of study.

Hypothesis 3 (Teotihuacan–Core Area Contact, Early Classic). There is evidence (following Sanders and Price 1968) that Teotihuacan representatives entered the Guatemalan Highlands in the fifth century A.D. and took over direct control of Kaminaljuyu and other highland basic resource areas. Control of the El Chayal obsidian source, just a few miles from Kaminaljuyu, made the Teotihuacan control of obsidian in Mesoamerica a virtual monopoly (Sanders, chapter 15). For this paper it will be assumed that Teotihuacan influence is found in areas where resources are concentrated (Parsons and Price 1971).

From this characterization of Teotihuacan practices and the model for the Maya Lowlands, the Early Classic highland-lowland trade relationship can be derived. It would have been a waste of effort for Teotihuacan to try to control all lowland trade once resources reached the lowlands (Parsons and Price 1971 : 186). Maintaining distribution and collection links to a scattered population does not fit Teotihuacan's economic profile. It follows from this characterization that Teotihuacan dealt in trade directly with the Core Area, since in the lowlands, Core Area systems had the most highly concentrated resources and trade potential.

The Core Area organizations probably functioned to collect and distribute resources over large areas in the lowlands. Thus Teotihuacan would have been involved only in the direct supply of the Core Area, where resources and demand were the most intensely concentrated, and Core Area agents would have handled distribution of highland resources in the Buffer Zone as well as in the Core Area.

Test Implications and Future Research. If the Core Area's System A_1 distributed both highland resources, obtained from Teotihuacan-controlled resource areas, and cult objects and ideology to the Buffer Zone, then Teotihuacan–Buffer Zone contacts (contacts between virtual neighbors in some areas) were minimal. In addition, if all resource collection, concentration, and redistribution were carried on by Core Area organizations, the Core Area probably became a magnet drawing excess population from the Buffer Zone to staff growing production and resource procurement organizations.

Adams (1969) has stated that most direct Teotihuacan influence in the lowlands occurs in the Core Area. The data upon which this conclusion rests must be carefully quantified. All Teotihuacan material culture in the Maya Lowlands should be identified as direct (made at Teotihuacan or Kaminaljuyu) or indirect (Maya copies). Quantities should be plotted by time on maps. Influences before A.D. 400, when Teotihuacan took over Kaminaljuyu, will be relatively random in the Maya Lowlands. Direct Teotihuacan influence in the Maya Lowlands after A.D. 400 will occur almost exclusively in the Core Area. Population figures should be studied in relation to the amount of Teotihuacan–Core Area interaction. As interaction increases Core Area population should increase relative to Buffer Zone population.

Hypothesis 4 (Buffer Zone Development, Tepeu 1). In the sixth century A.D., Teotihuacan influence in highland Guatemalan resource areas collapsed (Cheek 1971). The withdrawal of one-half of the highland-lowland procurement and distribution system created a vacuum in the control of highland resource trade. The model suggests that owing to geographic proximity of highland areas and ecological variety in trade items, there were few constraints upon variety in forms of Buffer Zone systems. In response to the power vacuum, Buffer Zone cultural systems would have developed sociopolitical complexity that could control and direct highland-lowland trade to the Core Area. Core Area products and specialists probably contributed to the early stages of the development of complex organizations in the Buffer Zone.

Test Implications and Future Research. Many small Buffer Zone centers should have increased dramatically in size and internal complexity as Teotihuacan influence faded from Kaminaljuyu and the Guatemalan Highlands. Testing this implication would entail accurate control of construction phases. Quantified estimates (cf. under Hypothesis 1) by phases of labor and capital investments in monumental construction relative to population would provide one measure ·of change in the complexity of organization and the ability to concentrate resources at specific sites. A measure of changes at specific sites in degree of social stratification, defined as "differential distribution of resources," could be developed from burial data.

Hypothesis 5 (Core Collapse, Tepeu 2). The Teotihuacan–Core Area partnership had been profitable because of differential distribution of resources and the ability of the Core Area to exchange its craft commodities in the Buffer Zone. As Buffer Zone centers developed and became capable of producing their own status items and cult ideology, the Buffer Zone–Core Area partnership became a competition. This had tragic results for all Lowland Classic Maya ceremonial center systems.

In lowland rain forest environments several constraints limit variety in Core Area systems. In addition to the constraints already mentioned, slash-and-burn agriculture (even where intensified through the use of silviculture) restricted variety (cf. Meggers 1954; Coe 1961; Sanders 1963; Sanders and Price 1968). It is assumed for this paper that land-use, fallow, and production patterns led to settlement patterns and production capacities which selected against the development of complex production-distribution techniques that depended upon massive population concentrations or professional military organizations.

Core Area systems had to trade for basic resources to survive. The only scarce resources that the lowland Core Area had to market for strategic resources were the products of superior sociopolitical organization. When the sociopolitical development of Buffer Zone and/or resource areas reached the same level of complex organization as the Core Area, Buffer Zone and/or resource area systems would replace Core Area imports with local products. The Core Area would lose its exportable commodities and have to compete for basic resources on an equal organizational level with Buffer Zone and/or resource area systems. Because of spatial advantages, Buffer Zone and highland systems would control strategic resource distribution.

Because of constraints upon variety, the Core Area would be unable either to reach a new level of organization, mercantile or military, or to develop new products that could protect its trade routes and markets from usurpation by well-organized competitors. The constraints upon variety in the Core Area required that Core Area systems (at least those which integrated and supported anything above a vestigial population) maintain effective resource procurement systems. However, the Core Area would find it hard to sustain complex procurement organizations without returns proportional to investments. When efficient procurement systems could not be sustained, Core Area systems would no longer have integrated and supported household constituents. Depopulation would result.

Test Implications and Future Research. One test implication suggests that once Buffer Zone systems attained complex organization (with the aid of Core Area exports and market potential) Buffer Zone importation of Core Area craft products decreased as local Buffer Zone production of craft items increased. At the same time Buffer Zone systems had probably begun to consume locally greatly increased quantities of available non–Core Area basic and exotic resources. Thus, for Core Area systems the competition for resources increased as the uniqueness and value of the items Core Area Classic Maya produced for exchange decreased.

The above prediction has been briefly tested (Rathje 1971a : 52–54, n. d.), but the test was largely based on subjective evaluations of raw data by excavators. To supplement this, neutron activation and additional studies as outlined under Hypothesis 2 will be needed to quantify changes in trade and other forms of interaction between Core Area and Buffer Zone sites. The differential distribution of imported items (shell, jade, obsidian, and so on) in the Maya Lowlands should be quantified. Preclassic, Early Classic, and Late Classic distributions in the Core Area and the Buffer Zone could then be compared. The bulk of such items should occur in the Core Area in the Preclassic and Early Classic. A marked shift to the Buffer Zone should occur in the Late Classic. Burials would be especially useful in providing data. Not only numbers of objects, but volume and weight must be considered to make measures meaningful.

To fully define the stresses upon the Core Area as the Buffer Zone developed, the model requires that the nature of the cultural systems in resource areas be considered. At the same time that Buffer Zone markets dried up and Buffer Zone systems began to monopolize resources, the Core Area may also have had competition for resources from highly organized Mexican and / or Mexican-Maya groups in resource areas on the periphery of the Maya Lowlands (see Webb, chapter 16, for a description of the development of these influences). The dispersion of Mexican warrior groups was disruptive to Classic Maya systems (Sabloff and Willey 1967), but competition for basic resources with Mexican-Maya trading groups may have had a much more devastating effect upon Classic Maya cultural systems. Mexican and / or Mexican-Maya groups may have developed new techniques that competed effectively against Classic Maya trade commodity production and distribution procedures.

If new complex organizations, above the parameters of complexity of the Core Area's variety pool, were competing to advantage with the

Core Area, new non–Core Area artifacts and artifact distributions should have appeared that would demonstrate the development of new production-distribution techniques. Both groups, Classic Maya and Mexican-Maya, must be shown to have been trading in the same market areas at the same time. Trade in the new production-distribution commodities in resource Buffer Zone areas should have increased as trade in Core Area commodities decreased.

The "invading" Mexican-Maya groups are associated with a characteristic Fine Orange pottery. The most obvious feature of this pottery is its uniformity in consistency of paste, shape, and design. Some types are moldmade. The design elements associated with nonmold Fine Orange pottery are simple (Sabloff 1970). Recent neutron activation studies have shown that the production of Fine Orange pottery probably occurred in only one area in Tabasco (Sayre, Chan, and Sabloff 1971; Sabloff, personal communication). One reasonable conclusion from these data is that most of the Fine Orange pottery was mass-produced by something approaching assembly-line techniques, accomplished by organizing large units of the population. Similar manufacturing techniques were employed in Northern Yucatan ceramic production at the beginning of the Postclassic Period (Smith 1971). This image contrasts markedly with that of the Classic Maya artisans who carefully painted intricate sets of figures on Tepeu pottery. The production techniques of Classic Maya potters must be compared with those of Fine Orange producers. Time estimates based on experimentation could be used to quantify and evaluate efficiency differences in production systems.

Fine Orange and other fine ware ceramics probably provide an outline of the bloodstream of a new trading system. Complex new manipulations of pottery manufacture and trading organizations seem to have been used in the distribution of the pottery (Webb 1964, this volume, chapter 16; Thompson 1970). The Tabasco manufacture location lent itself to easy distribution by sea, while Classic Maya traders of Core Area products were landlocked. Transport distances and ease of transport should be quantified. A contrast between land and water transport could be developed by estimating the poundage per canoe paddler and poundage per land porter that could be carried efficiently. Time-distance and carrier food consumption estimates should be made. The weight to volume ratio of Fine Orange and Classic Maya pottery should be added to measures of transport ease. Shapes of Fine Orange and Classic Maya pottery could be evaluated quantitatively in terms of utility for movement of solids and/or liquids and their stability and compactness when stacked. All of the above measures could be used to contrast the efficiency of Fine Orange and Classic Maya trade commodity distribution systems.

If the characterization of the Fine Orange traders as a complex and efficient production-distribution outfit is confirmed by the data collected in the future, it will be clear that the Classic Maya were faced with an effective competitor in Buffer Zone and resource areas using population concentrations and transport systems beyond the parameters of the constraints upon the Classic Maya Core Area. The most important aspect of the test implications to support the critical effect of the distributors of Fine Orange pottery upon Classic Maya cultural systems is evidence to indicate that they were competing at the same time and in the same markets. The fact that Fine Orange pottery appears in Maya sites only after A.D. 800 is emphasized in several papers (although possibly related earlier Fine Orange types appear in Maya sites as early as A.D. 600). This appearance would not be strange even if Fine Orange traders were competing with Maya traders by as early as A.D. 700 to A.D. 750. Classic Maya sites are precisely the places where Fine Orange pottery should make its latest appearance. In fact, the small amount of Fine Orange pottery that is found in the Maya Core Area would be expected if Core Area trading systems were being cut out of the main resource trading network. If this reconstruction of the importance of the Fine Orange traders is correct, Fine Orange pottery should be found in critical resource areas (Northern Yucatan) and nodes on trade routes (Cozumel, for example) by A.D. 700 or A.D. 750.

The preceding speculations suggest that Classic Maya procurement systems, especially in the Core Area, were finding increasingly strong competition from Buffer Zone and resource area trading systems. From earlier sections it can be asserted that Core Area systems were unable to draw upon a large pool of variety for responses. The decrease in the Classic Maya ability to compete for resources with Buffer Zone and resource area systems can be tested indirectly by viewing the Core Area procurement system as a whole (Diagrams 1 and 3). The first critical node in the system is the decision by local households about resource investment—whether it should go into Action Set 1 or Action Set 2.

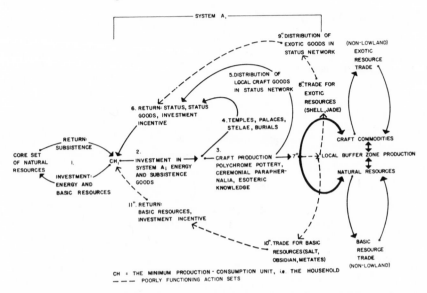

DIAGRAM 3: CLASSIC MAYA CORE SYSTEM—LATE CLASSIC

All of the other transformations (3–11) feed back to influence that decision toward Action Set 2. Four basic subsystems stimulate household investment incentive and the procurement of basic resources. They sustain local households and determine whether resources end up in 1 or 2. Two subsystems are completely internal to the system (Subsystem 1: 2→4→6→2; Subsystem 2: 2→3→5→6→2). Two depend upon success in adapting to the outside environment, that is, trade (Subsystem 3: 2→3→7→8→9→6→2; Subsystem 4: 2→3→7→10→11→2). Both Subsystems 3 and 4 include Action Set 7; they both depend upon long-distance trading success and are extremely vulnerable to changes in other competing systems. The whole of System A_1 procures basic resources most efficiently when investment in Subsystems 1 and 2 (conspicuous consumption) are minimized and investment in Subsystems 3 and 4 (trade) are maximized.

If success were being reduced, then basic resource input, agricultural production, and investment incentive would decline. The only way agricultural production could have been returned to its former level required reestablishment of trading success and basic resource inputs. Because of lack of incentive in basic resource return, and because of decreased productivity (Action Sets 1 and 11), investment incentive and ability to invest would have dropped. Therefore, the only way to reestablish trading success, given the constraints upon Core Area systems, would have been to increase household investment incentive drastically.

If the Core Area model is correct, then goods blocked at Action Set 7 (Diagram 3) would be fed back into the subsystems to increase investment incentive. Since two subsystems (3 and 4) that stimulated investment were failing, more goods would be pushed through the internal incentive subsystems (1 and 2) to insure increased household investment. Because population integration was breaking down, Subsystems 1 and 2 also had to be heavily utilized to reinforce control over constituent households. The system can be envisioned as a series of pluses, normally functioning channels, and minuses, poorly functioning channels that could no longer stimulate production or Action Set 2 investment. Thus, more goods would be forced into the plus channels (Subsystems 1 and 2) that were still functioning to make up for the minus channels. Because of a lack of variety in environmental resources and potential population distributions, the increased investment would continue to circulate within outmoded channels until production finally failed altogether.

One test implication of Hypothesis 5 states that as procurement of *metates*, obsidian, shell, and so on through trade became less successful, rich burials, temple construction, ceremonials, and local distribution of *local* products should increase (see Diagram 3). Both lack of trade success and increased conspicuous consumption should occur just before the system's collapse.

The Maya Lowland sample of 1,009 burials provides excellent data on the local distribution of commodities. In comparison to Preclassic, Early Classic, and Tepeu 1 burials, the percentage of Tepeu 2 burials which contained shell, jade, and obsidian decreased. The percentage of burials with locally produced pottery increased in Tepeu 2 over Preclassic, Early Classic, and Tepeu 1 percentages (see Table 30, Fig. 57). This increase is especially true of Core Area centers like Tikal where practically the only offering in Late Classic household burials was locally produced polychrome pottery (Haviland 1963). Many more potential studies, including weight and volume analyses, remain to be completed.

448

TABLE 30
DIFFERENTIAL DISTRIBUTION OF RESOURCES
IN BURIALS

	Percentage of Burials with Pots, Obsidian, Shell, Jade			
Date	*Pots*	*Obsidian*	*Shell*	*Jade*
Preclassic	51.9	5.8	24.0	23.1
Early Classic	51.6	14.7	23.2	22.1
Tepeu 1	56.7	20.5	22.2	18.2
Tepeu 2	65.4	3.8	14.1	15.4

	Number of Burials without/Number of Burials with Pots, Obsidian, Shell, Jade			
Date	*Pots*	*Obsidian*	*Shell*	*Jade*
Preclassic	50/54	98/6	79/25	80/24
Early Classic	46/49	81/14	73/22	74/21
Tepeu 1	78/98	140/36	137/39	144/32
Tepeu 2	27/51	75/3	67/11	66/12

For the test implications to be fully evaluated the number of *metates*, obsidian blades, and such must be shown to have decreased relative to population as the amount of temple construction, palace construction, wealthy burials, and local distribution of local status items increased. Individual site culture histories of the quantity and distribution of local and exotic resources will be necessary, as will detailed estimates of labor and capital, relative to population, invested in construction and interment activities.

Hypothesis 6 (Buffer Zone Collapse; Tepeu 2–3). A hypothesis explaining the collapse of the Core Area systems has been outlined, but the collapse of Buffer Zone systems is still unexplained. From the lack of constraints upon variety in Buffer Zone systems it can be assumed that the complex organizations that developed in the Buffer Zone were not all a direct response to local environmental constraints. This inference is supported by the lack of Buffer Zone development of complex procurement organizations or ceremonial centers through most of the Preclassic and Early Classic periods.

Once the Buffer Zone systems developed in complexity in the Late Classic, there were two basic problems in the total environment. First,

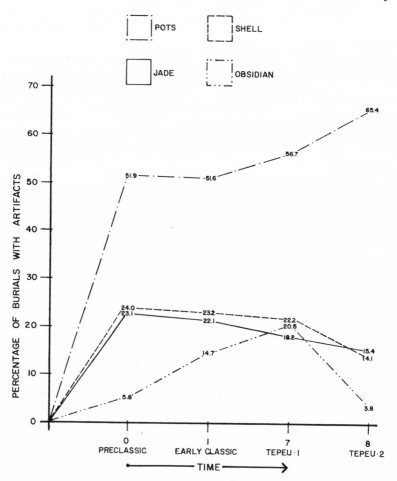

FIGURE 57. THE DISTRIBUTION OF POTTERY, SHELL, JADE, AND OBSIDIAN GRAVE GOODS THROUGH TIME

because there were too many Buffer Zone systems, competition for trade became important. Second, the Core Area no longer produced a scarce tradable resource to exchange for highland and scarce Buffer Zone resources. In addition, Buffer Zone systems also had to deal with competition from Mexican and Mexican-Maya groups. When the Core Area was no longer producing an exportable commodity, large Buffer Zone middleman trade centers were no longer functional. When the

450

Core Area collapsed many large Buffer Zone centers found they had overreached their carrying capacity.

Not all Buffer Zone centers fell at the same time. In some areas near the highlands or possessing valuable lowland resources like ocean shell and cacao, trade for basic resources could be maintained without complex organizations. In many populated Buffer Zone areas complex organization did not develop until the Late Classic. The main function of the complexity of many centers was to act as middleman between highland and Core Area traders. In these areas the complexity collapsed along with the Core Area systems. In other areas, especially those where complexity developed in the Early Classic, complex organizations functioned to some degree to procure basic resources for the local population. Such centers maintained complexity even after the Core Area collapsed.

The Buffer Zone centers with (1) the most advantageous trade position in relation to basic resources and (2) the largest number of locally available natural resources should cease to function earliest in the Buffer Zone. An inverse relation can be proposed: the earlier a Buffer Zone center developed, the longer it should last as a center after the fall of the Core Area.

Test Implications and Future Research. The early demise of Copan has long been a puzzle, especially since it is situated on a small alluvial plain far from Mexican influence. The local populace was located within easy distances of obsidian and hard stone resources, alluvial and rain forest soils, and riverine resources. The early abandonment of the site does fit a model of diminishing investment in trade beyond subsistence needs as complex organizations could not match input with equivalent returns. Several sites in Belize, and Palenque and Piedras Negras on the Usumacinta, ceased to function early. These sites were located near basic resources and near numerous environmental niches with tradable commodities.

Those Buffer Zone sites which lasted longest were situated farthest from basic resources. They were the sites where trade had the dual function of passing goods on to the Core Area and of supplying the local populace with basic resources. Altar de Sacrificios survived into the late Terminal Classic. Altar was one of the few import centers functioning in the Buffer Zone during the Early Classic. Seibal also survived as a large-scale Terminal Classic center. Both sites imported hard stone for *metates* and obsidian from the highlands; both were located in largely rain forest, riverine zones. Detailed studies of local ecological variety and resource trade potential should be compared with the latest stela dates and evidences of abandonment from Buffer Zone sites.

Hypothesis 7 (*Lack of Core Area Recovery*). In A.D. 800 almost 50,-000 people inhabited the 163 square kilometers of greater Tikal (Haviland 1969). In 1967 only 20,000 persons occupied the 36,000 square kilometers of the surrounding Peten (*Encyclopedia Britannica* 1967, vol. 8 : 302). One of the key factors in the mystery of the Maya collapse was the lack of recovery. It is known, for example, that small population units survived in the Core Area after the downfall. If disease, warfare, poor soil, atrophy, or other commonly espoused factors were the *only* causes of depopulation, this surviving population segment should have had time to gain back its health, peace, soil, and spirit, and to increase. In most areas it did not (Thompson 1967, 1970).

One possible explanation is based on the Core Area–Buffer Zone model. There are severe constraints on variety of sociopolitical development in rain forest environments, and especially in their Core Areas. The only scarce resources that lowland Core Areas have to market for strategic goods are the by-products of *superior* sociopolitical organization. Therefore, if Buffer Zone and resource areas are sociopolitically developed, the best a Core Area can do is compete with Buffer Zone and other resource areas for strategic goods on an equal organizational base. Because of transport advantages and the number of local resources scarce in other areas, the Buffer Zone and resource areas will obviously maintain control over strategic commodities.

Given Core Area constraints, systems to support large populations cannot develop in the Core Area if, at the time of settlement, competing Buffer Zone and resource areas are already developed to or beyond the organizational potential of the rain forest. As long as complex organizations and state level systems surround the Core Area, large populations and complex systems will not develop or be maintained (without substantial external support) in the Core Area.

Test Implications and Future Research. Because of the ethnohistoric record, it is possible to plot the population distributions for post-Conquest Southern Yucatan. Within the Buffer Zone, the lack of constraints upon variety in potential systems allowed populations integrated by complex (such as Chetumal and Itzamkanac) as well as simple systems (such as the Belize Valley and the Usumacinta drainage) to survive (Thompson 1967, 1970). The only area that can be confirmed by available data as largely uninhabited (relative to other reported regions) is the Core Area, the center of the northeast Peten (Fig. 51; Thompson 1951 : 390, 1967 : 29; Scholes and Roys 1948 : 463–64; Means 1917 : 124–29; Sanders 1962 : 110). This pattern of thin Postclassic population in the northeast Peten is also supported archaeologically (Bullard 1960, 1970b, this volume, chapter 11). The area is still largely vacant today (Maler 1911 : 150; Lundell 1937 : 4; Bullard 1970b : 357). Sanders sums it up well: "During the period from the 6th to the 10th century the Maya area was one of the most densely populated parts of Mesoamerica, and the demographic center was precisely in that part of the area which since that period has been extremely thinly settled" (1962 : 110). Quantification of the data supporting the above conclusions should be attempted.

Summary of Hypotheses. The Core Area–Buffer Zone model can be used to encapsulate lowland culture history. Constraints 1 (basic resources), 2 (ecological), and 3 (geographic) limited the variety of Core Area systems that could sustain population to those systems which were able to maintain a complex procurement organization. The lack of variety in tradable resources limited exports from the Core Area to the products of complex organization. Throughout the entire history of Core Area settlement, complex organizations were maintained.

In the Buffer Zone constraints upon variety of cultural systems and exports were less severe. During the Preclassic and Early Classic periods few complex systems developed. Owing to a power vacuum in the Late Classic, a number of large-scale organizations blossomed in the Buffer Zone. These systems began manufacturing the craft products of complex organization and destroyed the Core Area's trade potential.

Without this trade potential Core Area systems could not maintain procurement functions. Because of constraints on variety, the constituents of cultural systems without efficient trading networks could not be sustained, and large-scale depopulation resulted. In response to the weakening and collapse of the Core Area some Buffer Zone complex systems collapsed, others developed. In areas both with and without complex organizations some depopulation occurred; but at the time of the Conquest the Buffer Zone was still well inhabited.

As long as the Core Area was surrounded by complex organizations, the Core Area's only possible products (superior craft products and esoteric knowledge) were not valuable enough to maintain an efficient large-scale procurement system. Thus, the constraints upon variety in cultural systems in the Core Area kept the region depopulated. Only with large-scale outside support will Core Area systems be reestablished. A lack of variety in the Core Area was passed through adaptive cultural systems so that there was little variety in the successful Core Area systems that supported populations efficiently. Effective population support was extremely susceptible to changes in social, political, and ecological environments. Because of severe constraints upon variety in Core Area systems, large populations were only supported in the Core Area from 400 B.C. through A.D. 900. In the Buffer Zone, without such constraints, populations were supported from 800 B.C. through the present.

NOTE

1. This paper was made feasible by the expertise, patience, and encouragement of Gordon R. Willey, Demitri B. Shimkin, T. Patrick Culbert, David M. Pendergast, Richard G. Sanders, Jr., Lawrence Manire, and Henri A. Luebbermann, Jr. Unpublished burial data were furnished by A. Ledyard Smith, James B. Gifford, Gair Tourtellot, and David M. Pendergast. The statistics, testing procedures, and necessary computer programs were developed and implemented by Richard G. Sanders, Jr., and Lawrence Manire. Detailed constructive criticisms of various stages of the paper were furnished by Keith H. Basso, T. Patrick Culbert, Frederick Gorman, Henri A. Luebbermann, Jr., Jeremy and Paula Sabloff, Michael B. Schiffer, Demitri B. Shimkin, and Richard A. Thompson. Parts of this paper were developed through support from the Wenner-Gren Foundation for Anthropological Research, the Bowditch Exploration Fund, and the National Science Foundation.

PART IV

Concluding Assessment

18
The Maya Collapse:
A Summary View

GORDON R. WILLEY

Department of Anthropology
Harvard University

DEMITRI B. SHIMKIN

Center for Advanced Study
in the Behavioral Sciences

INTRODUCTION

The purpose of this chapter is to perform a synthesis of the opinion and argument presented and developed in the preceding chapters (see also Willey and Shimkin 1971a, 1971b). It will be organized along three axes: historical, analytical, and hypothetical. The findings of archaeology which bear upon the Maya collapse and the failure of recovery will first be presented in a chronological and descriptive-historical manner. Secondly, we will analyze the nature of ancient Classic Maya society and culture from the standpoints of their structural features and of their dynamic aspects. Thirdly, we will construct our hypothetical model of the processes involved in the Maya collapse. We will close by posing a series of new questions, generated by our inquiry, for future research.

We feel—and the other authors in this volume concur in this—that the problem of the Maya collapse, besides being of unusual culture-historical interest in its particulars, has a broader significance for archaeology and anthropology at large. What we have attempted in our discussions, essays, and this summary is to develop a social anthropology of the Maya, particularly of prehistoric culture change, from archaeological data. To whatever extent we have been successful, our findings should have a bearing on other questions of a similar nature.

A HISTORICAL SYNOPSIS OF CLASSIC MAYA CIVILIZATION AND THE COLLAPSE

Early Classic Period Antecedents

As has been related elsewhere in this volume, Maya civilization appeared in the Southern Lowlands in its developed form by the third century A.D. Its development was in situ, although influenced to a significant extent by stimuli from outside the Southern Lowlands. In the Early Classic Period (A.D. 250–550) the elements characterizing the elite aspects of this civilization spread throughout the Southern and Northern Lowlands. Although some population movements may have been involved in this spread, it seems most likely that the process chiefly involved the relatively rapid acculturation of a number of Maya-speaking communities that were already interrelated by a common Late Preclassic culture base.

During the Early Classic the Maya Lowlands maintained trade contacts with the major political and economic power of that time— Teotihuacan in Central Mexico. Tikal, especially, was a focus of such contacts and of Teotihuacan influences. In the sixth century A.D., with the waning of Teotihuacan power, these influences disappeared from Maya culture. For a brief period of from 40 to 60 years, the Classic Maya seem to have undergone a period of crisis, quite probably in the course of a readjustment of trade routes and patterns that had been occasioned by the weakening—and eventual death—of Teotihuacan; but beginning with the katun ending of 9.8.0.0.0 (A.D. 593),[1] Maya culture in the Southern Lowlands enjoyed a vigorous renewal in the Late Classic Period. Thus, it is quite likely that the decline of Teotihuacan opened the way for an era of Maya florescence. Conversely, the re-emergence of Central Mexican political and commercial hegemony, at the close of the Late Classic Period, hastened and intensified the Maya Lowland collapse.

The Late Classic Period Climax

While Maya Late Classic culture shows a clear continuity with Early Classic, there are differences in degree and in structure. For one thing, there are indications that Late Classic society was more sharply differentiated into elite and commoner strata than had been the case in Early Classic times. Multiroomed buildings or "palaces," presumably residences for the aristocracy, are more numerous in the Late Classic. Rathje (1970b; this volume, chapter 17) has noted Early Classic–to–Late Classic changes in the variables of age, sex, tomb or grave types, elaborateness of burial accouterments, nature of burial ornament symbolism, and the location of graves with reference to temple, palace, or ordinary domestic structures; and these changes point to a solidification of class lines and an increasing trend toward ascribed as opposed to achieved status. Another supporting line of evidence for this trend can be seen in the hieroglyphic inscriptions and associated sculptural representations. Early Classic inscriptions tended to be short, frequently little more than dedicatory dates; those of the Late Classic, insofar as they can be translated (Proskouriakoff 1963b, 1964; Kelley 1962), tell of royal lineages, ascensions to kingship, dynastic struggles, and intercity wars. In sum, our inferences from the evidence lead to a picture of a hereditary aristocracy steadily increasing its influence in the early part of the Late Classic Period.

As this process of an elite consolidation went on, the Maya Late Classic social order must have become more complex, with a related development of a class of bureaucrats and craft specialists. The clues to craft specialization, both in the nature of the products themselves and in the urban-type settlement findings, indicate that the presence of full-time artisans is a reasonable possibility. The institution of long-distance trade—both in luxury items and in more general produce—probably involved the services of a large staff of bureaucratic officials. Certainly, if Rathje's (chapter 17) and Webb's (chapter 16) theses are accepted, we must believe this increase to be the case. While we are still of the opinion that a redistributive system, controlled at the top by the aristocracy, was the basic form of Maya economics, such a system would have engaged the services of many persons; and such a system was probably undergoing expansion during the first 200 years or so of the Late Classic Period.

The proliferation of ceremonial centers during the Late Classic Period indicate trade and political expansion. New sites sprang up in numbers, especially along the western, southern, and eastern peripheries of the old Maya Lowland Peten "core." The sites of the Usumacinta drainage did not come into prominence as important centers until the Late Classic; in the south, sites such as Chinkultic and Comitan were found; and to the south and east the centers of southern British Honduras (Lubaantun, Pusilha), of the Motagua-Chamelecon (Copan, Quirigua), and of the Ulua periphery were being settled for the first time or rising to importance.

This political and commercial expansion of the Lowland Maya, as seen in the rise of many new sites, undoubtedly reflects population growth. From those regions where we have adequate settlement surveys, such as in the Belize Valley (Willey et al. 1965), at Tikal (Haviland 1965, 1969), and at Seibal (Tourtellot 1970), there are indications of an increase in the number of domestic quarters from Early Classic to Late Classic times which is most reasonably interpreted as an absolute increase in population numbers. Proportionately, however, the rate of this increase, in view of the already substantial Early Classic population, was not as great as that which occurred in the Maya Lowlands from Middle Preclassic to Late Preclassic times.

The Late Classic Period in the Southern Lowlands is subdivided chronologically. The earliest part of the period, from 9.8.0.0.0 (A.D. 593) to 9.13.0.0.0 (A.D. 692; see Rands, chapter 4 : Fig. 6), is most frequently referred to by the ceramic phase name and number, Tepeu 1. Pottery of Tepeu 1 shows definite linkages back to antecedent Early Classic (Tzakol) styles, but there are also a number of changes. The earlier basal-flange bowl disappears, and figure painting—with scenes of men, gods, and animals—becomes quite common in polychrome decoration. Tepeu 2, dating from 9.13.0.0.0 (A.D. 692) until 10.0.0.0.0 (A.D. 830), marks a climax in polychrome figure painting, especially in the production of handsome cylinder jars, often ornamented with hieroglyphic inscriptions, as well as with life or mythic scenes.

For most of the Southern Lowlands the climax of Maya Classic civilization occurred in Tepeu 2 times, and especially within the earlier part of that subperiod, or from 9.13.0.0.0 (A.D. 692) to 9.17.0.0.0 (A.D. 771). For example, more dedicatory monuments or stelae date from the 9.17.0.0.0 *katun* ending than from any other; and, considering all of the Southern Lowland ceremonial centers, it is probable that the sheer mass of architectural construction dating to this earlier part of Tepeu 2 was greater than for any other equivalent period of time in Maya history, before or since. There is, however, some regional and zonal variation in this tempo of cultural growth, and some centers appear to have begun to "boom" earlier than others. For instance, the greatest Late Classic building surge at Tikal may have been in Tepeu 1, rather than in Tepeu 2, times,[2] and the same seems to be true for Palenque (Rands, chapter 9) and Altar de Sacrificios (Adams, chapter 8). But, whatever the finer chronological subdivisions of events, there is no question but that Tepeu 1 and 2—or the centuries from approximately A.D. 600 to 800—saw the spectacular climax of Lowland Maya civilization in the south.

During this two centuries of climax, Maya civilization in the south was integrated at the elite level in a more impressive fashion than ever before. The various regions and centers were linked by a monumental art style in stone sculpture and by a variant of this style in the polychrome figure-painted pottery. The same mythic or god figures are represented in this art; and this, together with the same hieroglyphic and calendrical systems, often expressed from center to center in identical texts and in the same complex lunar count formulations, leaves little doubt of a shared religion, ritual, and history.[3]

However, some signs of regionalism in this culture of the elite are apparent. "Emblem" glyphs, which appear to be the heraldic insignia of the different centers (and/or their ruling families) suggest such feelings of regional identity; and portrayals of warfare, on wall paintings and in monumental carvings, in which Maya are obviously fighting other Maya, imply a degree of rivalry. Such regionalism or localism is further reinforced—but with implications for a commoner level of society—by differences in ordinary domestic ceramics between ceremonial centers. Very likely, there were rules and regulations in the elite tradition which attempted to restrain or control such rivalry, and the widespread popularity of the ball game in the Maya Lowlands in Late Classic times may have served the function of mitigating intercity strife. But, as we shall see later, it is highly probable that competition

461

between centers and regions was a definite dynamic factor in Maya
Late Classic life.

In the later part of the Tepeu 2 subperiod (after 9.17.0.0.0 or A.D.
771) and in the Tepeu 3 subperiod (10.0.0.0.0–10.3.0.0.0 or A.D.
830–889) Maya civilization in the Southern Lowlands descended rapidly from its Tepeu 1–Tepeu 2 climax and, eventually, collapsed
completely. In the light of the details presented in the accompanying
symposium papers, let us review the events of this decline and collapse.

The Collapse

In considering the events of the collapse as these are registered in the
archaeological record, we shall refer to the chronological charts presented by Rands in chapter 4 (Figs. 5–8).

The Western Data. Beginning on the left hand side of these charts
—at what represents the western edge of the Southern Maya
Lowlands—are the columns for Trinidad, Palenque, and Piedras Negras. The Trinidad column, which subsumes information from that site
and from Calatrava and Tierra Blanca, is known chiefly from ceramic
information. A Taxinchan Phase is contemporaneous with the later
part of Tepeu 1 and dated (although without benefit of directly associated Long Count dates) from 9.10.0.0.0 to 9.13.0.0.0 (A.D. 633–692).
(These are the mean or standard dates offered on Rands's chart, Fig.
5. For the possible range of "slippage" or error for these and other
dates discussed in this section see Rands's Fig. 6.) Taxinchan is Peten-
oriented in some of its polychrome ceramics; however, even at this
early date there are some temperless or fine paste wares in the complex.
At this point it should be noted that a fine paste tradition in pottery
making begins earlier in the Usumacinta sector than it does farther to
the east and that these earlier fine paste types are not the Terminal
Late Classic Balancan, Altar, and related Fine Orange and Fine Gray
types which help define the Tepeu 3 horizon.

The Naab Phase—9.13.0.0.0–9.19.0.0.0 (A.D. 692–810)—follows
the Taxinchan and marks a break away from Peten-oriented ceramic
traditions. Naab pottery is predominantly fine paste (of the earlier
fine paste styles); however, late in the phase some true Fine Gray
appears. Fine Orange does not make an appearance at either Trinidad or Tierra Blanca, but it is well represented on the Jonuta horizon

at Calatrava. In general, the cultural decline in which we are interested is not seen clearly in these sites in Terminal Late Classic times although, as Rands points out, the disappearance of the Taxinchan polychromes correlates with the fading out of Peten-like polychromes elsewhere in the Southern Lowlands. It is possible that the late Naab influx of Fine Gray may mark a cultural displacement, occurring just antecedent to the Jonuta horizon.

At Palenque the latest Long Count date is a 9.18.9.0.0 (A.D. 799) reading from an early fine paste vessel of the Balunte Phase. In Rands's opinion, the climax of the site's architecture occurred in the late Otolum–early Murcielagos phases, or between about 9.11.0.0.0 and 9.15.0.0.0 (A.D. 652–731), corresponding to late Tepeu 1 and early Tepeu 2. After that, building slacked off and then all elite activity ceased at the break between the early and late Balunte Phase. This cessation is dated on the chart at 9.19.0.0.0 (A.D. 810), although Rands is of the opinion that it may have occurred slightly earlier—at about A.D. 800. This effective abandonment, along with that at Piedras Negras, is one of the earliest which occurred at a major ceremonial center in the Southern Lowlands.

The latest date at Piedras Negras is 9.18.5.0.0 (A.D. 795); at Bonampak 9.18.10.0.0 (A.D. 800); at La Mar 9.18.15.0.0 (A.D. 805); at El Cayo 9.19.0.0.0 (A.D. 810); and at Yaxchilan, somewhere between 9.19.0.0.0 and 10.0.10.0.0 (A.D. 810–840).

At Piedras Negras the cessation of activities at the site came at just about the end of the Chalcahaaz Phase. Early fine paste wares are found in the succeeding Tamay Phase; however, in this case, the horizon-marking Altar Fine Oranges do not appear until post-Tamay times, or until about 10.3.0.0.0 (A.D. 889).

Thus, in the west we see the extreme northwestern sites, those of the Lower Usumacinta, being somewhat atypical in the brand of Classic Maya hierarchical culture which they display. This is especially true of the smaller centers (Calatrava, Trinidad, Tierra Blanca) in their lack of monuments and great art; and even Palenque virtually lacks stelae and is without such very Mayan traits as caches of eccentric flints and obsidians. We see the Peten-like polychrome pottery tradition being terminated early in the northwest. The elite collapse occurs at Palenque at about A.D. 800, that of Piedras Negras, farther up the Usumacinta, at just about the same time, and the other Upper Usumacinta sites follow rapidly. The appearance of some fine paste wares begins very early on the Lower Usumacinta sites, with the switch from polychromes to fine pastes constituting the changeover from Classic to Postclassic. These, however, are early fine paste wares, presumably the prototypes of the later Altar and Balancan Fine Gray and Fine Orange wares which constitute the ninth century A.D. Fine Orange–Fine Gray horizon.

The Altar de Sacrificios and Seibal Data. Altar de Sacrificios, at the confluence of the Pasion and Chixoy rivers, had a thriving stelae cult and was a center for fine Maya polychrome pottery in the Pasion Phase (9.9.0.0.0–9.17.0.0.0 or A.D. 613–771). Pasion is correlated with Tepeu 1 and the earlier half of Tepeu 2. After 9.17.0.0.0 there were no more dated monuments at the site, and the pottery of the Boca Phase (estimated at 9.17.0.0.0–10.4.0.0.0 or A.D. 771–909) dropped off in the quantity and quality of polychrome ceramics. The site was by no means abandoned, and some ceremonial construction continued after 9.17.0.0.0; but it is fair to say that there was a decline in the old-style elite activities.

Fine paste pottery first occurred in the site sequence in the Boca Phase, apparently coming in as trade and being used along with polychromes. However, this earlier fine paste ware was not the Fine Orange–Fine Gray horizon material, which appeared about 10.0.0.0.0 (A.D. 830), or halfway through the Boca Phase. Following 10.4.0.0.0 (A.D. 909), with the advent of the Jimba Phase, major construction at Altar ceased, and the site was occupied by groups whose total ceramic complex was in the Fine Orange–Fine Gray tradition (as opposed to the earlier Boca Phase occurrences of Fine Orange–Fine Gray as trade). Site abandonment is estimated at about 10.6.0.0.0 (A.D. 948).

Seibal, at the great bend of the Pasion River in the south-central Peten, flourished as a typical Peten-type Maya ceremonial center from about 9.12.0.0.0 (A.D. 672) until 9.18.0.0.0 (A.D. 790)—the Tepejilote Phase. Ceramics are affiliated with the northeastern Peten, and it may be that Seibal's Late Classic population actually came from the Tikal-Uaxactun region.

At some time between 9.18.0.0.0 (A.D. 790) and 10.0.0.0.0 (A.D. 830) Seibal was probably invaded by non–Classic Maya peoples. These newcomers may have been from Yucatan. Their leaders are portrayed on the stelae at the site, and the monuments showing this influence are some of the most impressive sculptures of Seibal, dating from the

10.1.0.0.0 (A.D. 849) *katun* ending. The persons depicted are garbed in a basic Maya Classic manner, though their countenances are quite non-Maya. Significantly, and quite at variance with other Southern Maya centers of the time, Seibal enjoyed its greatest boom of pyramid and platform building activity and monument dedication in these early decades of the ninth century, the beginning of the Bayal Phase, and the Fine Orange pottery of this phase is to be correlated with the Fine Orange horizon occurrence in the Boca Phase of the Altar de Sacrificios Sequence. Stelae dedication continued at Seibal until 10.3.0.0.0 (A.D. 889) or slightly later (Graham, chapter 10). The carvings on the 10.2.0.0.0 (A.D. 869) and 10.3.0.0.0 (A.D. 889) monuments include figures dressed in the Classic Maya style as well as others whose accouterments and general appearance are more like those seen in the carvings of western Yucatan and Campeche. Quite probably, these figures represent Maya, but they are not the Classic Maya of the Southern Lowland artistic tradition. Throughout the Bayal Phase, which may have lasted until about 10.5.0.0.0 (A.D. 928), Fine Orange–Fine Gray wares increase in occurrence, and there is a disappearance of polychromes. Seibal, and its nearby sustaining area, were abandoned after this phase.

In summary, we can say that typical Peten Maya Classic activities declined in these two Pasion River sites after about A.D. 771–790, with the decline setting in a little earlier at Altar de Sacrificios. Some construction continued at Altar for a time after that but stopped by A.D. 909, after which the site was occupied by foreigners, who probably came from the Gulf Coast. At Seibal, stelae and construction activities enjoyed a florescence after A.D. 771–790, but this florescence seems to have been under foreign tutelage. Seibal was no longer important after A.D. 889. Both Seibal and Altar were abandoned altogether about A.D. 928–948. In this Terminal Late Classic time both sites were influenced by fine paste wares, Altar earlier than Seibal; however, the inception of the Fine Orange–Fine Gray horizon pottery can be dated at about A.D. 830 at both sites.

The Tikal and Uaxactun Data. The great building period at Tikal, according to Culbert (chapter 5), was between 9.13.0.0.0 (A.D. 692) and 9.16.0.0.0 (A.D. 751). This 60 years marked the first half of the Imix Phase, corresponding to the first half of Tepeu 2 at Uaxactun. Building at Tikal continued for a time, with some big construction probably occurring as late as 9.19.0.0.0 (A.D. 810), but no building occurred after

10.0.0.0.0 (A.D. 830). The Eznab (corresponding to Tepeu 3) architecture at Tikal is extremely impoverished, and Culbert estimates that the population at Tikal in Eznab times (A.D. 830–909) was reduced by as much as 90 percent from its Imix Phase maximum. A probable Eznab monument is dated at 10.2.0.0.0 (A.D. 869).

At Uaxactun, in the Tepeu 3 Phase, there is a dated monument at 10.3.0.0.0 (A.D. 889). After this date there are no more Long Count stelae at either site. The Maya polychrome pottery tradition of the Imix and Tepeu 2 phases carried over, in reduced fashion, to Eznab and Tepeu 3; but both phases are also marked by Fine Orange–Fine Gray horizon types.

In brief, Tikal and Uaxactun show signs of decline in stelae construction by 9.19.0.0.0 (A.D. 810). Over the next 80 years this decline became ever more rapid, and by the close of the ninth century (A.D. 889–909) both sites were virtually abandoned, although a desultory and probably intermittent occupation of Tikal by Postclassic Period groups continued for some decades. Culbert emphasizes the point that the Tikal decline seems to have been under way before the first signs of fine paste wares and several decades before the first appearances of the Fine Orange horizon markers of the Altar and Balancan series.

The Belize Valley Data. In the Belize Valley the Early Spanish Lookout and Benque Viejo IIIB phases correspond in time to Tepeu 2 and show the last full vigor of polychrome styles. These polychrome styles, while recognizably linked to those of the Peten tradition, are divergent from those of Tikal and Uaxactun. In the Late Spanish Lookout and Benque Viejo IV phases, polychrome pottery disappeared. These phases are cross-dated with Tepeu 3 and Eznab and probably can be bracketed between 10.0.0.0.0 and 10.3.0.0.0 (A.D. 830–889), although it is possible that late Spanish Lookout lasted somewhat longer. Probably Benque Viejo, the major ceremonial center in the Belize Valley, was largely abandoned shortly after 10.0.0.0.0, for many of the buildings seem to have fallen into disuse and disrepair in the Benque Viejo IV Phase. In other words, signs indicate that hierarchical culture came to a close in the Belize Valley at about A.D. 830; however, the domestic occupation at Barton Ramie (the principal site from which Spanish Lookout is known) continued on with vigor for 60 years or more. There is no fine paste pottery in these Belize Valley sites, in either the late Spanish Lookout or the Benque Viejo IV phases—which is the time horizon on which it might be expected—or in any other.

The Maya Collapse: A Summary View

The New Town Phase, which follows Late Spanish Lookout at Barton Ramie, is represented by a much-reduced ceramic complex, and no ceremonial center components appear in the valley that can be attributed to this phase. The New Town Ceramic Complex, which has no fine paste wares, is a part of what Bullard (chapter 11) has designated as the Central Peten Postclassic Tradition.

Summary. On a factual and descriptive level, we can sum up by saying that marked cultural decline, as reflected by curtailment of ceremonial center activities and population loss, began on the northwestern and western frontier of the Southern Lowlands at some time between 9.18.0.0.0 and 9.19.0.0.0 (A.D. 790–810). Palenque and Piedras Negras collapsed at about this time, and the other Upper Usumacinta sites were effectively deserted very soon after. Altar de Sacrificios suffered a decline after 9.17.0.0.0 (A.D. 771), although populations continued to live there and to do some building until as late as 10.4.0.0.0 (A.D. 909). At Tikal, farther to the east and north, decay, marked by construction decline and population loss, was registered between 9.19.0.0.0 and 10.0.0.0.0 (A.D. 810–830), with virtually complete abandonment by A.D. 909. In the Belize Valley, at the very eastern edge of the Maya Lowlands, ceremonial center functions apparently stopped by 10.0.0.0.0 (A.D. 830) or shortly after; but here outlying domestic dwelling sites continued to be occupied until the middle or later part of the tenth century A.D.

On the same factual and descriptive level, we record the earliest appearances of fine paste wares in the northwest, their somewhat later occurrences as one moves east, and their absence in the extreme east in the Belize Valley. It should be pointed out that the earliest of these fine paste wares dates some two centuries before the appearance of Fine Orange and Fine Gray horizon-marker Altar and Balancan types. These later types effect a nearly horizontal time-band on the chart (Rands, chapter 4 : Fig. 8). Their first occurrence is at about 9.19.0.0.0 (A.D. 810) in the west, and they are slightly later in occurrence to the east, where they appear a little after the first signs of the collapse.

The Failure of Recovery

There was no recovery of Classic Maya civilization in the Southern Lowlands following its eclipse. It is true that the area was not entirely abandoned, and some Postclassic centers were established, especially in

467

those territories peripheral to the old Peten "core." Some of these centers were on the northwestern frontier, as at Potonchan and Izamkanac (Thompson 1967). This was Chontal Maya country, and the Chontal were strongly influenced by the Central Mexicans and their ruling families and intermarried with them (Thompson 1970). A few other Postclassic Maya centers were established elsewhere: on the eastern coast of the Yucatan Peninsula near Chetumal; in the southeast near the mouth of the Chamelcon River; and even in the old Southern Lowlands proper at Tayasal and Topoxte. Topoxte, which is better known archaeologically (Bullard 1970b), seems to be allied in its architectural styles to Yucatan rather than to be a continuation of the old local Classic traditions. Both its ceramics and those of Tayasal were of the new Central Peten Postclassic Tradition. Tayasal is assumed to have been a settlement of the Itza after their flight from northern Yucatan. According to Spanish accounts (Thompson 1967), Tayasal and the Lake Peten Itza were important politically and militarily, but on a small, local scale. They also controlled trade to some extent, but not to the degree attributed to former Classic centers.

There are some indications that reduced populations lived in or near the old centers and communities of the Classic Period after the collapse. This seems to have been the case at Tikal, Altar de Sacrificios, and Seibal—three Southern Lowland centers where extensive housemound surveys have been carried out. It is also true that there was a Postclassic dwelling site occupation at Barton Ramie, in the Belize Valley (Willey et al. 1965; Willey, this volume, chapter 6). Named the New Town Phase, this period of occupation appears to postdate the abandonment of the nearest major ceremonial center at Benque Viejo. We have been uncertain as to just how long this New Town Phase lasted, but Bullard's (chapter 11) definition of the Central Peten Postclassic tradition has helped in this regard. New Town pottery belongs to this tradition, and the great bulk of the pottery belongs to the earliest ceramic group within the tradition, the Augustine. The somewhat later, probably Middle Postclassic, pottery group of the tradition, the Paxcaman, is present at Barton Ramie but is restricted to a very few housemounds and probably is to be attributed to occasional later reoccupation of house sites by relatively small numbers of people.

The Maya Collapse: A Summary View

Problems and Speculations

We have recounted the archaeological facts that appear to bear directly on the Maya collapse and the failure of recovery. These facts bring to mind immediate questions. One of these is what the relationship was between the Terminal Late Classic appearance of fine paste horizon wares, Fine Orange and Fine Gray, and the collapse of the cities of the Southern Lowlands. Were these wares brought by an invading people from the west, and were these invaders the cause of the downfall? The answer would appear to be no. For instance, Culbert (chapter 5) points out that Tikal was already in decline before the horizon wares appeared at that site.

Are we then to conclude that the Fine Orange–Fine Gray pottery types are in no way a clue to the events of the collapse? Again, we would answer no. There can be little doubt that such wares developed in the Tabasco lowlands, in a region immediately adjacent to that of the Lower Usumacinta. It is in the Lower Usumacinta region that we have our first signs of the replacement of the Maya Classic ceramic traditions by the fine paste wares. In some sites this replacement was rather gradual, and there was no abandonment; but Palenque, the greatest of the old Maya ceremonial centers of the region, collapsed at this time, among the first of the Maya Classic centers to be deserted. These circumstances suggest that alien peoples, or at least peoples with a culture not typically that of the Classic Maya, were in some way involved with the Maya decline on the northwestern frontier of the Southern Lowlands.

The fact that deeper within the Southern Lowlands evidences of the decline precede appearances of the foreign fine paste pottery tradition could be interpreted variously. The conquest on the northwestern frontier might have frightened peoples within the Southern Lowland core into withdrawing to other regions, leaving their cities vacant. But the sequence of the collapse events in most sites does not appear to have been quite that rapid, and such a sudden flight seems improbable. More likely, a series of events occurred on the northernwestern frontier which transformed the local Maya cultures through conquest and acculturation. Old patterns of behavior and of sociopolitical and commercial control were changed. A traditional seat of power such as Palenque was abandoned. In effect, a former segment of the Maya Classic system was detached from the old body, and this segment was so situated geographically as to be able to destroy the trade routes and relationships on which the peoples of the central and northeastern Peten were dependent.

Such an interpretation follows Rathje's (chapter 17) argument that in the course of the evolution of a redundant resource zone, like the Peten, its core will eventually be shut off from areas of more diversified resources by the development of "buffer" zones which drain off or hold these resources so that they never reach the core. There is logic to the argument, but we also feel that in this case evidence suggests that the process was put in motion and hastened when the northwestern frontier or Lower Usumacinta "buffer" zone fell under the domination of the alien peoples of the Fine Orange and Fine Gray pottery.

Another major problem which arises from a consideration of the facts of the collapse is what happened to the people who lived in the Southern Lowlands and were so numerous at the Tepeu 2 climax of Maya civilization. It is, indeed, possible that many were lost, over the century of the decline and collapse, through the economic and social disruptions that ensued in the period of crisis. Intensified competition among cities, intercity fighting, crop loss and destruction, malnutrition, and disease—this chain of events, as Shimkin (chapter 13) has argued, could have reduced population greatly. Would it have been enough to result in the decimation implied by Culbert's 90 percent reduction estimates for Tikal?

Sanders (chapter 15) does not think so and favors migration out of the disaster area. Where, then, did they go? His suggestion of a movement into the northern Guatemala Highlands (the Alta and Baja Verapaz regions) is not supported by archaeology, according to Adams, who has worked in these regions in recent years. Could the movement have been to the north?

This last question raises a very old hypothesis about the Maya, one associated with the earlier writings of Morley and Spinden—that of the Maya "Old Empire" and "New Empire." According to this hypothesis, the "Old Empire" in the south (what we are calling the Classic Maya civilization of the Southern Lowlands) was abandoned at the end of the ninth century A.D., at which time the Maya moved north into the empty Yucatan Peninsula and built there the great cities of the

Puuc, Chenes, and Rio Bec cultures. This idea tended to be discredited when it was shown that there was a long history of cultural development in the Northern Lowlands from Preclassic times on; however, the fact that there was already some population in the north need not preclude later populations from moving in to join them. Andrews's (chapter 12) interpretation of Maya culture history is readily reconciled with this "New Empire" view or a modification of it. In brief, did the populations of the Southern Lowlands move north to take up residence around emerging new centers in the Rio Bec, Chenes, and Puuc regions in the ninth century A.D.? G. L. Cowgill suggested something like this a few years ago (Cowgill 1964), with the added speculation that they might have done so under foreign or non–Classic Maya direction.

This interpretation of a northern movement of Classic populations out of the Southern Lowlands at the end of the Late Classic Period leads us into the problem of the correlation of Southern Lowland and Northern Lowland sequences which we have not yet considered. At this point, it might be well for us to consider this correlation problem, for the whole matter is closely bound up with Andrews's (chapter 12) views of Maya culture history as seen from the north. The crux of the Northern and Southern Lowlands chronological alignment controversy is in the placement of what Andrews calls the Northern Lowland "Pure Florescent Period" (embracing the Puuc, Chenes, and Rio Bec developments) in relation to Southern Lowland Tepeu. Most of the archaeologists writing for this volume prefer to see the Northern Pure Florescent as being essentially coeval with Tepeu; Andrews, in opposition to this, maintains that it is largely post-Tepeu. Lack of sufficient Long Count dates in the northern sites has led archaeologists to seek a solution to the question through pottery associations and comparisons, but this solution has been made difficult by the divergences between southern and northern Late Classic ceramic traditions. As of now, the debate is still unresolved, and Rands (chapter 4 : Figs. 5–8) has not attempted to chart the Northern Lowland columns alongside those of the south; but the question is closely related to the formulation of any hypotheses about south-to-north migrations.

With the conventional chronological alignment of southern and northern sequences, the collapse of the Puuc–Chenes–Rio Bec sites would have been more or less synchronous with the Southern Lowland collapse. Toltec Chichen would then have been established after the northern cities had died. With the Andrews alignment, the Puuc–Chenes–Rio Bec florescence would have taken place after the abandonment of the southern cities, and Toltec Chichen would have been established as a conqueror's city in the context of a thriving Pure Florescent culture. It is, of course, possible that the truth and the proper alignment lie somewhere in between. That is, the northern Pure Florescent centers of Puuc–Chenes–Rio Bec affiliation could have had their start in the Tepeu 3 Period (10.0.0.0.0 to 10.3.0.0.0 or A.D. 830–889) as groups of southerners abandoned the old Classic leadership around sites like Tikal and moved north to cluster around the viable centers of Yucatan which, under a non–Classic Maya domination, were a part of new trading networks. This dating would mean that the whole Pure Florescent Period in the north was relatively brief, lasting between 100 and 200 years. At the close of this period the Puuc–Chenes–Rio Bec sites may then have been—or may not have been—in decline before the Toltec conquered Yucatan.[4]

All of the above must remain highly speculative—an attempt to account for the massive population losses in the south. There is, however, one line of supporting evidence. This comes from Seibal which, it will be recalled, displayed a quite different pattern of events during the time of the collapse than that of other southern centers. Seibal's heyday was in the Bayal Phase, especially from 10.0.0.0.0 to 10.2.0.0.0 (A.D. 830–869), or in the Tepeu 3 Period. The Seibal stelae of this time show definite ties to Yucatan (see Sabloff and Graham, chapters 7 and 10), and there are also Seibal-Yucatecan architectural resemblances (Andrews, chapter 12). It is suggested that non–Classic Maya invaders, perhaps peoples of Maya speech but acculturated to Mexicanized ways in the Gulf Coast or Yucatecan regions, assumed positions of leadership at Seibal in the ninth century A.D. and that under their tutelage that site had a brief remission of the illness that was affecting other southern centers at this time. In fact, Seibal even enjoyed a small florescence. This was short lived, however, and it may be that such a non–Classic Maya leadership withdrew to Yucatan or perished along with the site.

These problems are some of the most immediate and major posed by the data of the collapse, and we could detail variations on these, as well as on many others. Quite obviously, we do not have the data with which to answer these questions. Rather than pursuing this line of speculative inquiry further, it is more to our purpose at this time to construct a hypothetical model of the Maya collapse, a model which will accommodate the widest possible range of the data now available and which will also suggest new directions for research. Before we can do this, however, it is necessary to take another view of Classic Maya civilization. We have already presented it in historical synopsis. Let us now take an analytical view of its structure and its dynamic aspects.

AN ANALYTICAL CONSIDERATION OF LATE CLASSIC MAYA SOCIETY AND CULTURE

It is evident from the chapters in this volume that there has been much new fieldwork in Maya archaeology in the last 20 years, that many new findings have resulted from this work, and that new interpretations have grown out of these. One point which has emerged from the preceding chapters is the extent to which these new data and opinions have confirmed or changed our previously held conceptions of Maya culture. Maya civilization is colorful and spectacular; it has received a large share of attention relative to other pre-Columbian cultures; and it is fair to say that over the years a standard body of opinion has tacitly grown up among Maya scholars about certain features of the structure and organization of Classic Maya society. This shared opinion is apparent in the general and semipopular books on the Maya, and has tended to be accepted as a given in most of the considerations of the Maya downfall discussed by Adams and Sabloff (chapters 2 and 3). Although most of the authors had doubts about parts of these assumptions, we had continued to accept the basic framework. In retrospect, one of the most valuable aspects of this volume is that it has led us to examine the old image of Classic Maya civilization and to revise this image. For in discussing the collapse it has become apparent that we must be quite specific about the nature of the society that collapsed. Old assumptions had to be reconsidered; and in the process, the gaps and disjunctions among them became evident.

The old model of the Maya Classic civilization had two major weaknesses. First of all it lacked a convincing systemic structure. Its various segments were not interconnected in any necessary relationships, and it was difficult to understand the actions of one part of the system in terms of the other parts. For example, it was not easy to explain the actions of the commoner segment towards the elite in terms of the role the elite was considered to have played. Second, the application of explanatory principles, particularly those starting from natural environment and subsistence, frequently led to disjunctions with the actual data. A good example of these explanatory disjunctions is the difference between maximal population densities predicted on the basis of the subsistence system assumed to have been used and the higher population densities computed from settlement pattern studies at several sites.

But to examine these disjunctions more systematically, let us consider the features of the conventional and revised models of Classic Maya society and culture under a series of semiseparate but interdependent parts. We will first analyze the structural features or conditions of the society and, after this, the dynamic aspects of the interactions among these features and conditions.

Structural Features

Subsistence. The conventional model of Maya Lowland subsistence held that the subsistence system consisted of slash-and-burn agriculture with maize as the staple crop. This viewpoint was based upon analogy with presently used agricultural practices in the Maya Lowlands and in neighboring ecologically comparable areas. It was also based upon the apparent absence and presumed impracticability of such labor-intensive features as irrigation and terracing, both of which are crucial features of agriculture in the rain-poor Mesoamerican highlands. According to this conventional view, the primary constraints upon such a subsistence system were declining yield after the first year of cropping, the length of fallow time necessary, and the amount of land unusable for agriculture because of seasonal flooding or lack of sufficient soil.

But the high population density estimates which have been derived from settlement pattern studies in recent years have demanded a reevaluation of this traditional subsistence picture. Actually, this is not an altogether new line of argument. When Culbert (chapter 5) states that the settlement density for Tikal could not have been sustained by the ethnographically known model of slash-and-burn maize farming, one is reminded of Ricketson's similar pronouncement of more than 30 years ago (Ricketson and Ricketson 1937). Ricketson, too, conducted settlement pattern studies, in his case around the Uaxactun center, and this was an important factor in leading him to consider the possibility that the Classic Maya had practiced more intensive methods of cultivation. At the time, Ricketson's settlement and population figures were held in doubt, but as Adams, in his review of downfall hypotheses (chapter 2), observes, most Maya archaeologists today believe that Ricketson's estimates were much too low.

What are, or were, the possibilities for more intensive cultivation or more abundant subsistence resources in the Southern Maya Lowlands? As Shimkin (chapter 13) indicates, studies of the agricultural potential of these lowlands are still far from adequate, but the very facts of marked regional variability in soil potential and rainfall "give strong grounds" for attributing some variability of farming and food-getting techniques to the Maya. Sanders also notes that some of Peten soils are very much richer than others. Such regions or localities, through high crop yields, could have allowed for rapid population buildups, and this, in turn, could have provided an incentive for grass-swiddening, or the relatively short-term fallowing, cutting, and burning of fields that were allowed to return to grass and weeds but not to trees. This grass-swiddening requires enormous labor time, especially with the stone tools available to the ancient Maya; but Sanders is of the opinion that the Maya did shift to it, at least in some regions, in Late Classic times. This system is also destructive of the land if fertilizers are not added, through degradation of nutrients, erosion, or both. This hypothesis is, of course, closely related to Ricketson's hypothesis about the Maya collapse.

Another possibility for subsistence improvement in Maya Classic times was in crop diversification. Bronson (1966) has made the case that manioc and sweet potatoes were important dietary supplements to maize; and Puleston (1968) has established the importance of the breadnut tree even more convincingly. Although Sanders, in his present paper, is inclined to feel that Puleston has overestimated the breadnut resource, he admits its very probable importance at Tikal and goes on to say that the site density in the northeastern Peten region, which is *ramón* or breadnut tree country, may be related to this protein food supplement.

Finally, Culbert, Shimkin, and Sanders all mention the possibility that Maya food resources in the core of the Southern Lowlands may have been supplemented by imports of foodstuffs from neighboring areas. In this connection, fish, a high protein source, are especially mentioned (see also Lange 1971).

The conventional view of Maya subsistence is, thus, seriously challenged. Regional and local population densities, as these have been carefully derived from settlement studies, are clearly too large to have been supported by *milpas* or swidden maize farming alone. More intensive cultivation, possibly grass-swiddening as opposed to forest-swiddening, or possibly the utilization of swamp or *bajo* lands for farming, is suggested.[5] Considerable regional variation in subsistence potential is also suggested. Root crops and breadnut harvests are very likely supplementary food possibilities; and, finally, the importation of foodstuffs as a part of a trading network can no longer be completely disregarded.

Population Density. As noted, low population density is linked to the kind of subsistence practices that the old Maya were believed to have followed, and the conventional Classic Maya model was one of low population density.

Sanders, in commenting on settlement evidence, says:

> What the data do suggest, even allowing for the noncontemporaneity of house groups, is that the population density of the Maya Lowlands in Late Classic times was considerably higher than most earlier writers have thought and, most importantly, exceeded most estimates of the potential of the area to support populations with long-cycle swidden maize cultivation. I would suggest that the overall density of the 250,000 sq. km. area that made up the Maya Lowlands was probably not below 20 people per square kilometer and that the densities found in the core areas were probably well over 100 persons per square kilometer, probably closer to 200 in some small sectors of the core (chapter 15 : 331–32).

In commenting upon Sanders's position it should be noted that the 250,000 square kilometers of the lowlands at large includes those sections of poor farming lands, or lands impossible for farming, as well as the good farm lands. By "long-cycle swidden" Sanders is referring to forest-swidden, in contrast to short-cycle grass-swidden. "Core areas" and "core" refer, especially, to the great sites of the northeastern Peten

476

and also to some of the centers of the Usumacinta and Palenque zones. However, these figures do not refer to the very heavy concentrations in the inner zone of a site such as Tikal, which are estimated at much higher than 200 persons per square kilometer. In these observations it should be noted, also, that Sanders tends now (within the last 10 years) to be on the conservative side in these estimates. Although any population figures are, indeed, relative, and figures for Mesoamerican upland areas are substantially higher, the estimates given here indicate a surprisingly dense population for a lowland jungle terrain.

Sociopolitical Organization. Reasoning from the assumptions of low subsistence yield and low population density, the conventional model of the Maya Classic provided for little administrative organization in sociopolitical or economic matters. Since the long-cycle swidden agricultural system involved neither large-scale labor nor techniques unavailable to the family-level farming unit, it was assumed to be largely self-regulating on the commoner level. The one possible articulation of the commoners or peasantry with the elite stratum of the society was believed to have been in the guidance the former received from the latter concerning seasonal planting and harvesting, although even here there was some doubt about how esoteric such knowledge may have been. In general, the elite were considered to have led a life of their own that was of little concern or interest to the lower classes—a separatist view quite possibly prompted by the long research emphasis in Maya archaeology on such esoterica as astronomy and hieroglyphic writing. Of course, the lower classes maintained the elite and constructed the great ceremonial centers under their direction. This, it was believed, was motivated largely by fear of religious sanctions or by religious zeal. On the more strictly political scene, it was held that political units were small—city-states, in effect—each under the direction of a major ceremonial center. The relationships between such states were pictured as concerning only matters of interest to the elite classes, such as the exchange of calendrical information and trade in luxury goods.

Were the attitudes and functions of the Maya elite as introverted and as limited as this conventional model implies? It seems unlikely. Shimkin (chapter 13) has drawn an analogy between the Classic Maya and the small central Asian states of the first millennium A.D. These Asian states had social components of a hereditary aristocratic leader-

477

ship and a pious peasantry, and the loyalty of the peasantry to the aristocracy was maintained in large degree by religious feeling. Nevertheless, the management functions of the leadership were of key importance in the workings of the society. They allocated labor and resources; sponsored craft manufactures, graphic artistry, and elaborate ceremonialism; dispensed justice; and arranged for measures of social security.

Any serious considerations of the range, variety, and complexity of Classic Maya material remains in a great ceremonial center suggests that neither Maya agricultural labor nor labor for other purposes could have been "self-regulating." Labor demands and labor allocations would, inevitably, have been in conflict without careful and planned scheduling; and, in our opinion, labor demands would have been great. Allowances surely had to be made not only for land clearance and agricultural tasks but also for road and monument construction and maintenance and for crafts, food preparation, ceremonial activities, and the education of an intellectual and management class. Another very important management function must have been the maintenance of trade.

As to the nature of the Maya Lowland "state," and the relationships between such states, it now seems very likely that there were regional "capitals" exercising economic, religious, and political hegemony over other, lesser ceremonial centers. Culbert suggests the probability of such a role for Tikal. Copan, Palenque, and Yaxchilan are other possible "supersites" or "capitals." Such centers of power and prestige would have been key points in trading networks. The presence of the emblem glyph of Tikal at a number of lesser ceremonial centers hints at its "metropolitan" importance. That such hegemony had a dimension of military and political force and dynastic involvement receives support from Proskouriakoff's (1963b) analyses of the hieroglyphic texts, dates, and sculptures at Yaxchilan (see Graham, chapter 10).

The conclusion must be that we have tended to underrate the mundane, but highly important, functions of the Maya aristocracy. There were numerous and crucial articulations between the aristocracy and the farming commoners and, probably, between it and an emergent "middle class" of craftsmen and bureaucrats. At the same time, the degree to which such an aristocracy had the ability to enforce its dictates—Webb's criterion for separating the "chiefdom" from the "state"—is still a moot point. In attempting to refashion the model of the Maya elite as a separate and "other-wordly" group we should take care not to go too far in the opposite direction.

Religion. In the standard model, religious statuses were seen as the keys to prestige and power, and, as we have seen, religious sanction was conceived of as the true basis of the body politic. In comparison to other Mesoamerican societies, and especially those of the Postclassic Period, Maya Classic investment of labor and goods in religious activities was considered to be very high.

We feel that this appraisal still has considerable merit. Webb, in his accompanying paper, points out that the most advanced societies on the "chiefdom" level tended to be the most theocratic. In other words, the structure of the society had grown to a complexity that demanded sanctions; force could not be resorted to in the manner of the "state"; the result was an intensification of religious sanctions.

Without subscribing altogether to the chiefdom-state dichotomy and assigning the Classic Maya to one or the other, we think this reasoning may be applicable to the Maya religious and social order. Although a method for measuring the investment of labor and goods given to religious activities, as distinct from secular ones, has not been devised, we are of the impression that such investment in Classic Maya times was very high. Similarly, there can be little doubt that religious status was the key to prestige and power; at least, individuals who seemingly held positions of high status appear, always, closely associated with symbols and paraphernalia connected with religious contexts. The degree to which religious and secular persons, or religious and secular functions in the same person, can be separated in the Maya archaeological record is still undefined.

Militarism. The old view, consistent with the sacred rather than the secular power of the chiefdom (or the state), was that militarism was poorly developed among the Classic Maya.

This view is, indeed, "old," for archaeologists have been pointing out for some time that the "peaceful" and "pious" Maya engaged in their share of violence. Late Classic stelae representations of brutal treatment of prisoners or captives are quite common, and it is likely that these depict the military and political subjugation of one group by another. Battle scenes also occur in Maya art, as in the murals of Bonampak.

Still, there is little in Maya art, or elsewhere in the archaeological record, to indicate that there was anything resembling the professional military orders of Central Mexico, or that Maya governments, in either their internal or external policies, depended upon the services of "standing armies." [6]

Urbanism. It was formerly thought that Maya ceremonial centers were, indeed, just that—religious or politico-religious precincts with little or no domestic population. Such a view was in keeping with the image of the Maya elite as a segment of the Classic Maya society remote from the sustaining peasantry. It also conformed to the picture of a sacred, rather than a secular, leadership.

The intensive settlement studies in and around Tikal now leave little doubt that the "vacant town," or the pure ceremonial-center-without-resident-population, image does not apply there. In this volume both Culbert and Sanders refer to these studies (made by Haviland, Fry, and others) in considerable detail; and although there is some difference of opinion between the way Haviland (1969, 1970) and Sanders (chapter 15) estimate population densities from the "housemound" findings, there can be no denying that Tikal had urban dimensions. A core zone of approximately 63 sq. km., immediately surrounding the major constructions of the center, is densely dotted with small platform structures, many of which on excavation have proved to be housemounds or domestic sites. Haviland estimates a population of 39,000 persons for this 63-sq.-km. core, a density on the order of 600–700 persons per square kilometer. An outer periphery, surrounding the core zone and adding another 100 sq. km. to it, shows a thinner distribution of housemounds, but raises the figure from 39,000 to about 45,000 people for a greater Tikal. This greater Tikal was bordered on the east and west by natural *bajos* or swamps, but the strong possibility that the inhabitants of the site had a concept of some kind of "city limits" is seen in defining walls or earthworks at distances of 4.5 km. and 10 km. from the north and south of the center of the city, respectively.

Sanders's differences of opinion with Haviland arise principally from the lower figure of persons per family which he applies to the housemound settlements and housemound countings. He thinks that an overall greater Tikal maximum of from 20,000 to 25,000 persons would be more realistic. Although we appreciate the importance of the differences in these formulae for estimating population sizes from settlement data and sampling, we cannot, in the present context of discussion, become overly concerned in this debate. Even Sanders's halved figure is within the range of preindustrial urbanism and bespeaks urban functions of some sort, not an empty ceremonial precinct.

The matter of urban functions is, perhaps, even more important than sheer size, although the two undoubtedly are related. Certainly Haviland must be correct in arguing that not all of the inhabitants in the core zone of Tikal were food-producers. At least it is difficult to conceive of them as having been maize farmers, though many of them may have cultivated *ramón* or breadnut trees. Haviland also has some evidence for socioeconomic differentiation within the city zone in that some dwelling clusters appear to have housed families specializing in different crafts; and Tikal may also have had a marketplace. Nevertheless, these evidences of socioeconomic diversity within the city, which, in Sanders's opinion, are the key criteria of urban life (Sanders and Price 1968), are relatively weak in contrast to the evidence present in a huge urban agglomeration such as Teotihuacan in the Mexican central highlands. This difference, according to Sanders, correlates with the lesser population density of the Tikal city zone in contrast to that of Teotihuacan. While evidence at Tikal would indicate a density of 600–700 (or at most 1,000) persons per square kilometer, that at Teotihuacan indicates an estimated 5,000 persons.

In our opinion, the Classic Maya had made some important steps on the way to urban life. In their greatest center, Tikal, they enjoyed a form of urban life, although this form differed from what we know, and can reasonably infer, about a place like Teotihuacan. The extent to which the Tikal pattern can be extended to other Maya centers is unknown, although it seems probable that some other Classic Maya "supersites" or metropoli had population congestions in their immediate environs; however, other centers, of a somewhat lesser size and extent in their ceremonial constructions, seem to have lacked these congestions (Bullard 1960).

Trade and Markets. According to the old model, trade and markets were little developed among the Classic Maya. This lack of development was believed to be linked to the lack of ecological zoning within the lowland setting and, as a result, the lack of product diversity seen in the Mesoamerican highlands, where the trade-market institutions were highly developed. Some long-distance trade was admitted, involving regions outside the lowlands, but was seen as being devoted to low volume, luxury goods that were distributed largely to the elite.

How has this model been modified? A closer look at the archaeological data, especially the new data now coming in from recent excavations at Tikal, on the Rio Pasion, and elsewhere, shows more hard evidence for trade than was present, or at least appreciated, before. Obsidian was definitely imported into the Maya Lowlands as a raw material, being brought or traded from sources in the Guatemalan Highlands, and Central Mexico. The extent to which it was a luxury and a ritual item or, instead, a necessity is debated. Sanders (chapter 15) considers obsidian to be a luxury item, arguing that chert, which was available in the limestone beds of the lowlands, would have provided for all of the cutting tools necessary for life in the rain forests; Rathje (chapter 17) sees it as a necessity or near-necessity. We feel that while life in the Peten was possible without the fine-cutting-edge tools that obsidian provided, it would not have been possible to maintain the level of technico-artistic competence that characterized Maya civilization without these tools.

Salt was, indeed, a necessity. If it were obtained from sources in the Guatemalan Highlands a considerable trade organization would have been needed for its regular procurement; even if it came from the Yucatan coast or from deposits on the Salinas River, not far above Altar de Sacrificios, its transport into the central Peten would have involved substantial distances—too far, at least, for a day's walk or a day's canoe trip. Fish and shellfish, we know, were imported to the Peten from the coasts. Igneous rocks for *metates* could have been obtained from the Maya Mountains, a short journey, or from the Guatemalan Highlands, a relatively long journey. Other highland items were traded into the Maya Lowlands. Most of these, including jade, were luxury items. Items traded out of the lowlands included Maya polychrome pottery and, probably, textiles, cacao, and tropical feathers.

The significant change that we see in all this, in contrast to the old model about Maya trade, is that several commodities obtained in long-distance trade may have been more basic to Maya economy than what we usually think of under the heading of "luxuries." We think this view might be conceded even if there are some reservations about the Rathje hypothesis that long-distance trade was the underlying cause for the development of complex society and an elite class in the lowlands.

So far we have been talking about long-distance trade, and the produce of long-distance trade could have been distributed without marketplaces. As yet, we do not know if the Classic Maya had markets or not, although there is a tentative identification of one at Tikal (W. Coe 1967). It seems reasonable to assume the existence of such a mechanism for the exchange of local food produce, if for nothing else; however, there may have been food distribution arrangements without markets. Finally, it is also possible that food staples were brought into some parts of the Maya Lowlands from other regions, in the manner of long-distance trade. Culbert (chapter 5) has suggested the possibility for Tikal. It cannot be demonstrated as yet, but it is a possibility to be kept in mind.

Maya Isolationism. Isolationism is a condition rather than a structural feature. While the conventional model of Maya Lowland culture recognized the Early Classic Period influence of Teotihuacan, the Late Classic Maya were thought of as having been little influenced by, or having little influence upon, other Mesoamerican societies until the time of the collapse. In fact, some scholars looked upon the Terminal Late Classic Mexican or Mexicanoid influences as essentially incidental to the problem of the fall of Maya civilization.

This isolationist view can no longer be maintained. Although we do not yet fully understand the Teotihuacan–Classic Maya relationships, they must have been of considerable importance. After the recession of Teotihuacan influence, the Maya Lowland centers appear to have suffered a brief crisis, and when the lowland Late Classic culture resumes its stride it shows definite signs of change. Sanders (Sanders and Price 1968; Sanders, this volume, chapter 15) has argued that this Teotihuacan influence instituted the development of the state among the Lowland Maya; and Webb (chapter 16) would consider this the process whereby a "secondary state" (in which he would class the Maya) arose from contact with a "primary state"—with the principal vehicle of contact being trade.

As to later foreign Mexicanoid influences or impingements upon the Maya Lowlands, several chapters deal with the subject in detail. Webb and Rathje, convinced as they are of the importance of trade in the

483

growth and decline of Maya civilization, demand that the Maya be considered only in the larger context of Mesoamerica. Sabloff, Adams, Rands, and Graham all point to specifics of non-Mayan influences. And even those of the seminar group more "internally" oriented in their views of Maya culture history and the Maya collapse acknowledged the importance of wider Mesoamerican relationships in the discussions.

Dynamic Aspects

With these revisions of the structure and conditions of Maya society and culture in mind, we want now to analyze the dynamic aspects of the structure. In so doing we will be attempting to visualize the stresses and strains that must have existed within Maya civilization in its Late Classic climax period. In this analysis we feel that the most vital of these aspects were: (1) the roles of the elite class, (2) the widening social gulf between the elite and the commoners, (3) the competition between centers, (4) the agricultural problems, (5) the demographic pressures and disease burdens, and (6) the changing effects on the Maya polity of external trade.

The Role of the Eite. In the preceding section we have referred to the role of the elite in the sociopolitical structure and in religion, militarism, trade, and markets. Here we wish to focus on selected aspects contributing to the Maya climax and collapse. The multiplicity of the roles of the Maya elite, in contrast to the specialization of the elites in Mexico, is brought out by these several references to the Maya aristocracy in the above contexts. Such a multiplicity of roles was made possible by the prestige of aristocratic descent and the conduct of protracted training. Longevity contributed importantly to the effectiveness of the elite and validated their differential access to improved food, housing, clothing, and other resources. Given all these circumstances, whether or not polygamy was a practice, a member of the elite would have had more surviving offspring than a commoner. The expansion of the hereditary elite population was clearly a major force in the geographical expansion of Late Classic Maya civilization. Moreover, as long as resource margins were ample the growing elite would have harnessed these resources, and the commoners would have benefited as well. However, in the later phases of Maya Classic culture, and especially in the populous central regions, the role of the elite must have become increasingly exploitative as resource margins declined.

The Widening Social Gulf. Consistent with the above would have been a widening social distance between the Maya Classic elite and the commoners. Such is an inevitable accompaniment of the evolution of a ranked, and probably kin-based, society to a class structured one (see Rathje 1970b; this volume, chapter 17). Such a widening gulf need not have led to a "peasant revolt," as some earlier workers have hypothesized (Thompson 1966c), to have had deleterious effects on the Maya system. A growing upper class (Haviland 1966b), together with its various retainers and other members of an incipient "middle class," would have increased economic strains on the total society (Willey et al. 1965 : 580–81), particularly in conjunction with ecological-demographic stress factors. In some areas, it is quite possible that by the end of the Late Classic the numbers of commoners were being maintained only by recruitment and capture from other centers. Yet the upper class continued to grow, to expand its demands for luxury and funerary splendor, and to strive to compete with rival centers and aristocracies. This expansion required the allocation of considerable resources, including resources for the conduct of long-distance trade and the production of fine manufactures for export in such trade.

Competition Between Centers. There was undoubtedly considerable competition between ceremonial centers or cities in the Southern Lowlands. Overt signs of this competition are to be seen in pictures of captives, such as those on the wall paintings at Bonampak or in the numerous Late Classic stelae representations of crouching bound figures being stood upon by haughty and imperious conquerors. All such representations show both sides as clearly Maya in physical type; the prisoners are not foreigners in the sense of being non-Maya. The competition is to be seen more covertly in the magnificence of the ceremonial centers themselves. The centers represent great numbers of man-hours in both unskilled labor and skilled craftsmanship and, on the highest social level, of priestly-aristocratic scholarship.

As expounded by Rands, especially in the seminar sessions, the priestly leaders of these great centers, in their efforts to outdo each other, to draw more wealth and prestige to themselves, and to bring more worshippers and taxpayers into their particular orbits, must have diverted all possible labor and capital to their aggrandizement. New emerging centers and ruling lineages—and these, as we have noted, sprang up in numbers during the Late Classic Period—needed particularly to consolidate their statuses through ceremonial splendor. And this competition, too, involved more mundane and crucial matters such as foodstuffs, a point at which this stress relates to the previous ones. Add to all this the competition for trade, which Rathje and Webb propose as a dynamic element in Maya culture history and development, and we can see the situation brought to a fighting pitch.

Culbert (chapter 5), gives an imaginative insight into the plight of the great city of Tikal in such a sea of rivalry. The largest and strongest of all the Maya centers, it was also the most vulnerable in that its great size and prestige demanded the services of more adherents; and as these were lost to jealous rivals the effect could have been a rapid down-spiraling to extinction, not unlike what indeed did happen.

Agricultural Problems. We conceive of Maya agricultural problems as being of a four-fold nature. First, the expansion from the prime lands, which were probably occupied by the end of the Early Classic, if not before, was associated with increasing demands on agronomic knowledge and technique in the handling of the poorer soils, of areas subject to erosion, and of wet lands. In addition, the expansion of land clearance, for either permanent use or slash-and-burn agriculture, might have reduced the availability of forest resources and, especially, the supply of land game.[7] This process would have been accelerated in areas of high population density where potential fodder was gathered for fuel.

Second, the expansion of crop lands to marginal areas and the probable shortening of fallow periods, in zones of high population, promoted both weed and insect infestation and the probability of plant disease. It must be noted that, while the Maya apparently brought a variety of crops, such as breadnut trees, into cultivation, there is no evidence that they practiced plant selection to improve yields or resistance to disease. Maize, in particular, would have been subject to serious infestation in low-lying areas; cotton also is vulnerable to both disease and insect pests.

Third, the question of climatic variability in the Maya Lowlands and its effects on agricultural production is still unresolved; but quite certainly the different regions of the lowlands would have been susceptible in varying degrees to drought or to major damage from hurricanes.

Fourth and finally, the variations in population distribution and in agricultural production made increasingly necessary augmentation in the capacity and network of food storage and distribution. This, again, would have required investments of labor and materials and placed additional burdens on management.

These agricultural problems notwithstanding, there is no real evidence that Classic Maya farming ever reached the absolute limits of its productive capacity. What we are indicating, instead, is that as the expansion of Maya agriculture in the Late Classic became more costly and less reliable, the consequences of managerial mistakes or natural disasters would have become increasingly serious. In brief, there was no margin of safety.

Demographic Pressures and Disease Burdens. From the data at hand it would appear that there was essential continuity in Maya populations, with those of the Classic Period being the descendants of the earlier Preclassic colonists of the lowlands. The overall pattern of population growth is still uncertain, but indications point to a decline in growth rate through the Classic Period, largely because of increased mortality.[8] Nevertheless, the large population base, which had been assembled by the end of the Late Preclassic Period, permitted substantial absolute population increments so that Late Classic populations, as we have said elsewhere, were the largest of all.

Evidence for heavy disease burdens is most extensive in regard to malnutrition (Saul, chapter 14), which had massive effects on infant and maternal mortality. Deficiencies of animal proteins were most severe and had considerable effects on the work capacity of adults. In addition, urbanization and, especially, sedentary life in thatched structures provided environments suitable for insects, particularly the triatomid bugs, the carriers of Chagas' disease, which is both an acute illness and a source of chronic disability through endocarditis. Less certain is the possibility, particularly in the wake of land clearance or hurricanes, of epidemics of jungle yellow fever (Shimkin, chapter 13).

Disease exposures and malnutrition were highly differentiated, as far as we can judge, first, between old areas of intense colonization and the more marginal regions and, second, between commoners and the elite. The resulting differences in mortality surely led to differential population trends, both geographically and by social class. In consequence, population trends acted in four basic ways as dynamic cultural factors:

(1) population growth increased the demand on resources; (2) the growth of able-bodied manpower, a varying fraction of the population, was the foundation of economic expansion; (3) the differential growth and longevity of different social classes and regions brought about changes in the balance of power within the Maya Lowlands; (4) efforts to compensate for manpower shortages, and the shortages of wives, were increasingly important causes of warfare.

External Trade. There has been considerable interest in trade in recent Mesoamerican archaeological writings, including an article dealing specifically with Lowland Maya trade (Tourtellot and Sabloff 1972); and in our reappraisal of Maya civilization, we have just argued for its importance. Webb and Rathje (chapters 16 and 17) see it as the paramount institution in the rise and in the fall of Maya civilization. Rathje has argued that the demand for such items as obsidian and salt was the lever that started the Maya on their way toward the organization of a complex society, and Webb sees the choking off of trade into the core of the Southern Lowlands as the prime proximate cause of the collapse. If one accepts these hypotheses, one must concede to trade, and its stoppage, the key role in the Lowland Maya collapse. If trading entrepreneurs were able to elevate themselves to positions of power by the control and distribution of goods, and if this trade was instrumental in maintaining the positions of such an elite, it was a most integral part of the Maya system. It demanded time, wealth, and administrators or managerial personnel. It was both a great benefit and, at the same time, a point of great vulnerability for the system. For if trade routes were changed or disrupted the structure of the civilization would be bound to change.

Some authors in this volume, Sanders in particular, were disinclined to see trade, and especially trade in symbolic status items, as being this crucial to the maintenance of the system and of the elite who directed it. In his opinion, such an elite could have held their positions of leadership without the symbols of status. Others seem inclined to side with Webb and Rathje and see trade, with its prerogatives for the disbursement of goods to all levels of the society, as the real mechanism for keeping a Maya elite in power and for keeping the system going.

Trade, as a key mechanism in Maya society and as a potential stress factor for that society, leads us directly into the matter of potential external pressures upon the Maya Lowland Classic civilization. Foreign trade put Maya society into contact with the more dynamic and aggressive societies to the west and north. We have already mentioned these contacts with Teotihuacan in Early Classic times. Following the fall of Teotihuacan, Maya trade with Mexican or Mexican-influenced cultures continued, especially in the northwest along the Gulf of Mexico. It is uncertain just what Mexican civilizations were dominant on the political and trading scene at this time. Webb has suggested several as exercising important roles: Xochicalco, Tajin, Cholula. In general, better craft organization and, often, access to superior resources made these Mexican societies formidable competitors. Along the Gulf Coast and on the Lower Usumacinta, these societies were in a position to develop peripheral Maya peoples as allies, and it would appear that they did so. The representatives of these Mexican and Mexicanized groups were shrewd professional merchants, probably often backed up by military force, in the Mexican trading manner, and eager to profit from Maya wealth and disunity. Their presence, on the northwestern frontier of the Southern Maya Lowlands, did not bode well for the Classic Maya.

A MODEL OF THE COLLAPSE

With this historical and analytical preparation, we come now to our model of the collapse of Late Classic Maya civilization.

A *model* (and, admittedly, in some of the foregoing discussion we have used the term more loosely) is a precise statement of the characteristics and dynamics of a system. Its precision makes possible more exact and testable propositions. Through its mathematical properties, the model suggests, by analogy with other systems of the same type, certain predictions which can be further tested.

The model which we are here proposing is a qualitative and general one which will be compatible with the known facts and which will suggest leads for more complicated models and, particularly, for models which will be ultimately quantified. For example, our model is more general than, but nevertheless compatible with, the quite specific economic model that Rathje has proposed in chapter 17.

In briefest form, and in general terms, our model attributes to a special development of elite culture a primary role in the generation of the climax manifestations of Maya Lowland civilization. The success of the system produced growths of population and of competing centers which led to increasing rigidity in the system as it was subjected to internal stresses and external pressures. The system failed through inadequate recognition of these stresses and pressures and through inappropriate responses to them. The economic and demographic bases of the society were weakened; the consequences were the collapse of the system, the decimation of the population, and a retrogression to a simpler level of sociopolitical integration.

This model is not unique to Maya culture history. It is, in fact, an example of the general model of sociopolitical collapse proposed by Karl W. Deutsch (1969 : 28–30).

The model, as it can be detailed, comprises the following:

1. After the withdrawal of Teotihuacan influence (and power?) from the Maya Lowlands, the managerial functions of the Maya elite were intensified in two ways. First, they contributed to the growth of the Maya economy by promoting central place development, agriculture, manufacturing, and long-distance trade involving commodities for both general and elite consumption. Second, they intensified a system of economic motivation through the competitive splendor of ceremonialism and ceremonial centers.

2. At the beginning of the Late Classic Period the Maya elite approximated a corporate body which shared like training, mutual recognition of prestige, common beliefs, and systems of interregional cooperation which acted to control warfare and promote the geographical expansion of Lowland Maya civilization. All of these characteristics of the elite increasingly separated them from commoners.

3. Throughout the course of the Late Classic Period, the general growth of population, pressure on natural resources, and urbanization generated increasing competition between the elite leadership of the various regions. This competition engendered prestige-building activities to attract resources to the various regional centers. Concurrently, the pressure on resources decreased the productivity of labor, and increasing allocations to prestige-building activities were at the expense of the commoner population.

4. As a result, malnutrition and disease burdens increased among the commoner population and further decreased its work capacity.

This decrease, in turn, intensified elite pressures through the competitive exploitation of the commoners by the elite.

5. Despite these internal stresses, the Maya of the Late Classic Period apparently made no technological or social adaptive innovations which might have mitigated these difficulties. In fact, the Maya managerial elite persisted in traditional directions up to the point of collapse. A contributing factor in this failure was clearly the inadequacy of bureaucratic technology—the systems of information gathering, record keeping, decision making, and control —to cope with an increasingly complex and unstable social situation. It is also quite likely that the very nature of managerial recruitment in Maya Classic society—presumably restricted to a small aristocratic elite—further contributed to these problems.

6. Up to now, we have been considering the Maya Classic system from an internal point of view; however, the Maya were also a subsystem of a greater Mesoamerican system. During the Late Classic Period, Central Mexican peoples and cultures were impinging with increasing intensity on the western frontier of the Maya Lowlands. The full consequences of these impingements are not as yet understood. But it is clear that a minimal effect was the disruption of Maya trade patterns to the west. As we have already noted, this trade was a critical element in the maintenance of Maya Classic elite prestige and, possibly, important for the effective operation of commoner households.

7. As a result of these internal stresses and external pressures, the Classic Maya polity, a level of sociocultural integration encompassing the lowlands and maintaining a partly urbanized population of as many as five million people at its peak, was no longer viable.

8. Our analysis rules out a single "internal" or "external" phenomenon as the agent of the Classic Maya collapse. Rather, the coincidence of an array of disturbing factors—trade disruptions, social unrest, agricultural difficulties, disease—appears to have coalesced to administer a shock to the Maya polity, around 9.17.0.0.0 (A.D. 771) to 9.18.0.0.0 (A.D. 790), which exceeded the recuperative capacity of the Maya Lowland sociocultural system, especially its capacity of elite management. Despite some few partial continuities of the Maya elite tradition in the lowlands, no general recovery of the Late Classic Maya civilization took place.

Clearly, our model is incomplete. For example, and as we have related earlier, we do not know the degree to which populations of the Southern Maya Lowlands either died out or migrated. Quite possibly, a part of the old Classic populations of the south moved north where they contributed to the florescence of the Rio Bec, Chenes, and Puuc cities of the Northern Lowlands; but we have no proof of this migration, and indispensable to this question is the resolution of the alignment of southern and northern sequences. Also unclear are the factors which must have inhibited a Classic-type recovery in the south. It is our belief that difficulties in the accumulation of critical resources—manpower, skills, and materials—were engendered by the rise of competing Mexican states, but we cannot yet be sure.

Our model-building seeks economical and plausible synthesis of the known facts about the Classic Lowland Maya. On a more general level, and at the same time, we have suggested that the Maya collapse exemplifies phenomena recurrent in culture history. We have cited Karl Deutsch's general model, and we have elsewhere in this volume drawn attention to broad similarities between this history and that of the rise and fall of Angkor. We must caution, at this time, against the temptation to draw unwarranted conclusions evoking the traditions of Spengler and Toynbee. There are many unknowns in the Maya collapse. Why, for example, was the turbulence of the Late Classic Period not terminated by the emergence of a unified state? Why did the Maya pay so little attention to the improvements in labor productivity available within the known technology of their times in Mesoamerica? Questions such as these call for much tentativeness: we believe we are contributing to history, but we are uncertain of the degree to which we have illustrated evolutionary determinism.

RESEARCH DIRECTIONS
FOR THE FUTURE

In general, we believe that the model formulated above provides the best possible fit with the established and evaluated data that present knowledge permits. Our previous discussions have pointed out a number of research questions. At the same time, additional research appears worthwhile on the following questions related to and arising out of the study (see also Adams 1969).

1. How can presently collected data and future excavations be utilized and future research designed to provide firmer evidence directed toward understanding the Maya cultural collapse?
2. How can comparative historical and ethnographic data contribute to the search for better understanding of this collapse?
3. How can experimental archaeology and model construction best be utilized? What hazards need to be avoided with these techniques?
4. What light can analysis of the collapse of Maya Classic civilization throw upon the general (or "genetic") history of the Maya people as a whole? On the regional history of Central America and Southern Mexico? On the comparative understanding of cultural history in the wet and wet-dry tropics?

Let us examine these questions in more detail. Our model of the collapse itself suggests a good many ideas which need to be confirmed by better evidence: the implied contrasts between Early and Late Classic in expansion and solidification of the elite class, the exploitation of commoners by the elite, the extent of malnutrition, the kinds of disease, and so on. To determine with greater reliability and in greater detail the basic facts of what happened, where, and when, we need to employ the kinds of refined descriptive techniques that have been developed for pottery studies. For example, the breakdown of observations to directly reportable and measurable attributes seems particularly important in the development of comparability for settlement analyses and population estimates.

Specifically, we urge that space be reported as *covered*—with the amount given over to housemounds and monumental structures separately calculated (structures of determined use, sweat-baths, chapels, and so on, should be subdivided again)—and as *developed open space*—such as plazas, "ceremonial" causeways, and so on. The data so developed would not only eliminate intervening uncertainties about, say, unsupported and varying estimates of family size, but would also provide new analytical indices. For example, a settlement in which the ratio of housemound ground space, monumental covered space, and developed open space ran, say, 100, 20, and 300 would indicate profoundly different politico-economic properties from one with ratios of 100, 50, and 100, respectively. Obviously, the development of such indices would be a complex task. A topographic factor, among others, would have to be brought into this formula, and corresponding estimates of the volumes of building, by types—housemound, pyramid, and so on, would also be of great interest.

The broad outlines of architectural variability laid out by Pollock (1965) need to be supported by more fully plotted distributions and by refined analysis. In particular, the distribution and detailed variations of ball courts need fuller study. Water management—reservoirs, ditches, aqueducts, bridges—also merit special attention.

Within settlements and structures, the distribution of economic activities needs much better definition. Food preparation (*manos*), spinning (spindle whorls), tool manufacturing, pottery making, and other crafts need to be mapped to establish the presence of household, ward, or other patterns. Related to this type of study is the need to collect soil samples and cores, to observe vegetational clusterings, and to establish local hydrological conditions. In short, local environmental data closely related to settlements and activities are a needed prerequisite for meaningful ecological interpretations.

All of these observations have, of course, been made in particular investigations. The need is to establish comparable regional and temporal data. This can be done with good economy by utilizing the data from carefully studied localities as spatial models for the design of sampling schemes for new surveys.

Data of standardized nature, from pottery onwards, should be used to develop *indices of resemblance and difference* between localities and over time. Such indices could be used to examine, for example, the degree to which the links expressed by identical city glyphs denote corresponding similarities in other realms of culture. In general, routes and boundaries indicated by various sources need to be correlated as a basis for better understanding of socioeconomic and sociopolitical structures and spatial organizations. The time-space correlation of the distribution of exotic articles can also give important information on the relative significance, the rise and fall, of long-distance communication centers. In particular, the careful comparison of nearby sites, such as San Jose (Thompson 1939) and Benque Viejo (Thompson 1940), which seemingly show very different levels of involvement in long-range trade, should be fruitful.

Finally, the profound results of the dynastic interpretations of hieroglyphic texts may justify the search for indications of drought, famine, war or other, especially dated, events in these monuments.

The data obtained in these ways could be aggregated into structural models that would yield basic information on space-time continuities and breaks, the keys to politico-economic and historical interpretation. To tie these structural models more effectively into estimates of population dynamics, labor-force utilization, and inferences of stress will require further materials. These materials include especially the continued analyses of skeletal data; and the judicious use of comparative historical and ethnographic data, and of experimental archaeology. The end results would be the formulations of dynamic models of Maya culture and its history.

The utility of models or formally stated sets of compatible hypotheses has been discussed in this volume; Rathje (chapter 17) exemplifies this use of a very promising market model. Here it is important to stress the utility of models in locating data gaps and inconsistencies in some cases and in defining the more probable alternatives in others. Models force the researcher to define how a phenomenon is supposed to have taken place. Often, unfortunately, failures of imagination block the most plausible answers. An illustration is the question of manpower needs in monument building as stated by Erasmus (1968) and Heizer (1960). These authors accept a totally implausible span of continuous activity in order to hold labor-force needs to a minimum; the reverse views, that the sustaining area had many more people or that the building activity mobilized manpower from beyond the area, seem in fact to be demonstrated by the calculations of these authors.

Underlying model-building is the need to look at archaeological data in functional and operational terms. If we look at the plan of Central Tikal, for example, in W. R. Coe's book (1967), the great width and length of the causeways—35 m. to 50m., up to 2 km., respectively —must be related to the masses of users that might be visualized by its builders. Certainly, a procession of fewer than 5,000 persons on foot or in litters would look puny on the Maudslay or Mendez causeways. The plaza at the foot of the Temple of Inscriptions, some 17,000 sq. m. in area, would hold 15,000 to 25,000 spectators without difficulty. This level of design seems compatible with the 3,000 plotted structures and the 9 reservoirs located so far, and with an estimate of a minimal sustaining-area population of about 50,000.

In general, the most fruitful models to aid the better understanding of the Maya zenith and collapse might be the following:

1. A labor-force supply and demand accounting which would disclose a total population, a distribution of that population by age and sex, and an inventory of activities. Such a model would be useful in providing reasonable structural estimates, for example, that "ceremonial site" (in other words, central-place) populations did not exceed 10 percent of the total (Sanders, chapter 15). Our suggested model might also help in perceiving the possible effects of perturbing changes, such as hurricanes or the loss of able-bodied men through raids.

2. A much more difficult model would be that of capital investment, capital coefficients (that is, ratios between the costs of the investment measured, say, in manpower terms, and its incremental contribution to output), and capital durability. Underlying this model is the realization that investments in land (clearance, cultivation, tree-planting, and so on), water resources, manufacturing and storage facilities, "infrastructure" (sites for social interaction and social regulation), and manpower (particularly specialist education) had specific yields of an economic nature, and that these yields varied. Moreover, since the investments had varying durabilities (for example, the rate of weed infestation versus the life expectancies of priestly agronomists) and varying possibilities and consequences of deferral, choices would be available on a short-time basis (for example, more temple building versus more *ramón*-tree planting) that could have cumulative effects of a decisive nature. Finally, the interdependence of capital needs to be stressed— reducing some key component below a level of need would reduce the capacity of the entire system, provided compensatory inputs could not be gained from other areas. At the present time, no more than a very approximate capital model appears attainable. Yet even this approximation seems worth a research effort for the kinds of questions it might raise.

3. A different, much needed, type of model is that of the structure and dynamics of sociopolitical control. This model requires an examination and perhaps a differentiation of functional places: were the "ceremonial sites" at Tikal and Jaina similar? Or could the contrasts of Athens and Delos be useful analogies? How important were the local and regional integrations and controlled competitions developed through the ball games? Not only are the Olympic games and gymna-

The Maya Collapse: A Summary View

sia of Greece to be recalled, but also the passionate involvements in ball games of the towns in the southern United States (Natchez, and so on) need to be remembered (Swanton 1946).

4. Finally, rising out of the other models are those of the actual pathways, the reconstructed histories, of social downfall. In the Maya case, the evidence for mass invasions or other physical catastrophes is largely negative; the question as to whether or not a concatenation of smaller upsets is sufficient needs more formal testing than our volume has been able to undertake. Central to such a model of fragility is the idea of close-to-equilibrium conditions—high death rates and high birth rates, high agricultural bioproductivity and intense weed and disease problems, and (sociopolitically) the balancing options of "command" versus "market" economies and of "gardening" systems of low labor and high land productivity versus "*milpa*" systems of high labor and low level productivity.

The data requirements of these models are large and cannot be satisfied by direct archaeological materials alone. Consequently, a variety of comparative and experimental information must be used.

It is suggested that such data be used at two levels. The first is one of critical suggestions, wherein widespread sources can be used without too much reference to context. The second is that of controlled comparisons, wherein systems that appear analogous are matched after careful examination of their differences.

In all cases, the great importance of protohistorical and early historical information on the Maya area must be stressed. While these data reflect the changes imposed by Toltec and, in part, Spanish impact, and by some important changes in technology, especially the use of metals, their basic validity seems fundamental. While the data on the Yucatec clearly have first importance in this regard, it appears also that materials on the Cakchiquel and Quiche (Miles 1965) may have substantial relevance to the lowlands as well. In particular, the data on the kinship system (Miles 1965 : 280–82) appear to be most compatible and applicable. The contemporary ethnography of the Lacandon and the Tzotzil are of immense relevance, as is well known; however, it is important here to take more account of such factors as the inhibitions on centralization imposed by Ladino dominance. The problem is essentially one of reconstructing a "Great Tradition" from remnants found in "Little Traditions"; comparative studies (see Shimkin 1964) would indicate that the identification of apparent inconsistencies, for example, where a bridegroom is referred to ceremonially as "the leader of 1,000 men," may be especially important.

For other areas, the most fruitful comparisons would, we believe, include Polynesia (especially the Marquesas) for technology and economic organization; the Yoruba of Nigeria for sociopolitical organizations (especially the intercity kingly ties and the rural-urban interactions [Bascom 1969]); and Angkor, as previously mentioned (Shimkin, chapter 13), for the general model of peaking and collapse.

Experimental archaeology has advanced the understanding of tool types and provided important clues to past astronomical knowledge; it has been much less persuasive in its reconstructions of labor-force use and organization. At present, one of the most promising areas of such investigations would be the determination of the degree to which measures, volumes, and weights may have been standardized. The spans of such standardizations would give a fundamental guide to the corresponding spans of economic management, tribute collection, and commercial law. This standardization can often be of great persistence: the Greco-Roman storage jar continued as the basic Russian volumetric measure to 1917.

Assuming that additional fieldwork, including environmental studies and the model-building suggested, is undertaken and better knowledge of the Maya collapse is gained thereby, what would be the significance of these advances?

First we would gain a better understanding of the Maya people in *genetic* terms, that is, as a partial integration through time and space of languages, other cultural features, and biological populations. Such a genetic approach is inherent in all major taxonomies of culture—the "Romans," the "Arabs," the "Chinese,"—yet it is rarely defined. For the Maya, work on this problem is still at a pioneering level, despite the contributions made to it in the Vogt-Ruz study (Vogt and Ruz 1964), and in Juan Comas's critical assessment, *Características Físicas de la Familia Lingüística Maya* (1966).

The relations between linguistic history and other components of the climax cultural features of the Maya remain unclear. A careful phonological analysis and interpretation of the calendrical vocabularies (Satterthwaite 1965) is an immediate need. Our impression is that these words are relatively late secondary loans within the Maya stock. Their relation to the model of Maya differentiation would be likely to contribute heavily to the understanding of Classic culture; likewise, the better understanding of the breakdown of the "Intertribal Tzolkin" could well lead to important suggestions about the mechanics of the decline. Similar studies of the vocabularies of chieftainship, priesthood, and ballcourts drawn from the protohistoric and specialized ethnological literature also would have great promise.

In general, while the genetic model of the Maya is by no means a developed concept, it has substantial theoretical promise not only for general understanding but for the specific issues of the downfall problem.

The relation of the present study to the regional history of Middle America has already been raised, especially in a previous paper (Willey and Shimkin 1971a). We believe, however, that much more can be done. The coincidences of population growth and decline in the highlands as well as the lowlands of Guatemala present a research area. In addition, the degree of complementarity and exclusive competition between the great centers—Teotihuacan, Kaminaljuyu, Tikal, Dzibilchaltun; later, Tula, Chichen Itza, and Mayapan—needs, and would probably reward, more formal specification. Some kind of balance exists here between market and influence possibilities and the limits of resource generation for urban life which needs further specification. Finally, while we are concerned about the dangers entailed in a too enthusiastic evolutionary view in regard to social systems, we feel that a more extended look at specific technical and social inventions and their potential effects may be rewarding. We have in mind such questions as molds and other serial-production techniques in pottery, the acceptance of cacao as a general currency, or the introduction of large coastal canoes for trade.

A few words on the broadest levels of comparisons. An understanding of the comparative histories and cultures of humid tropical areas —in the Americas, West Africa, South Asia, and, above all, Southeast Asia—is of great importance in correcting the culture-historical bias of all anthropology toward temperate-lands foci. In addition, the significance of tropical flora and fauna as genetic pools for man's future use, combined with their vulnerability to destruction as population growth continues, add a dimension of pragmatism to the study of disasters such as the Maya and Angkor downfalls. Man-land relations in the tropics do have a very general relevance. That our findings to date indicate that these downfalls involved complicated interactions with sociopolitical events rather than simple environmental causation simply requires a broader definition, not a negation, of this work as a study of human ecology.

NOTES

1. Throughout we use the 11.16.0.0.0 or Goodman-Martínez-Thompson correlation of Mayan and Christian calendars.

2. Haviland (1971, personal communication) tends to see the building peak of Tikal in Tepeu 1; Culbert (chapter 5), in Tepeu 2. This difference of opinion is not, however, crucial to our thesis of a Late Classic climax.

3. An excellent example of this sharing of hierarchical culture is seen in a burial at Altar de Sacrificios where an apparent great lady of that site was buried with high mortuary rites, and her funeral was attended by dignitaries from other major Maya Lowland centers (Adams 1971 : 159–61).

4. The 12.9.0.0.0 or Spinden correlation of Mayan and Christian calendars would allow more chronological "room" for the Puuc-Chenes-Rio Bec development, and for this reason Andrews tended to favor it; however, the 11.16.0.0.0 correlation is preferred by all other authors in this volume, and it allows a seemingly adequate, if compressed, span of time.

5. Puleston and Puleston (1971) describe and illustrate riverine lowlands, along the Lower Usumacinta and Candelaria rivers at the northwestern margin of the Southern Maya Lowlands, where cultivation ridges are visible. These imply farming methods of a more intensive sort than the slash-and-burn system. According to the Pulestons' argument, such riverine lowlands, peripheral to the central Peten, were the locations of the first Maya Lowland settlements in the Preclassic, and the subsequent settlement of the heart of the Peten, distant from any such riverine lowlands, was made possible by an intensive use of the *ramón* nut.

6. David Webster, whose views were brought to our attention by R. E. W. Adams, would see militarism as definitely "institutionalized" by the time of the Late Classic Period in the lowlands. He bases this opinion on the evidences of ceremonial center fortifications of Early Classic date at the Rio Bec center of Becan, in Campeche, and upon inferences which can be made involving demographic pressures, competition between centers, and the growing importance of centers as the organizational means of controlling and protecting dispersed farming population. We cannot present his ideas in full here, but it is to be hoped that he will develop them in a future publication.

7. It may be that slash-and-burn clearance could actually increase some species of game (especially deer and brocket) by providing a greater variety of fodder, especially young growth. What is needed, with reference to this question and with reference to arguments that have been raised by the Pulestons (1971) about the importance of wild game in the Maya Late Classic, are studies on kinds and volumes of animal remains by regions and time periods.

The Maya Collapse: A Summary View

8. Unlike peoples of many early agricultural civilizations of the Old World, the Maya give no clear evidence of having been concerned with the promotion of human fertility ("fertility cults" and so on) in Classic times. The only Maya figurines that would appear to qualify as "fertility" fetishes would be those of the much earlier Middle Preclassic Period.

References

ACOSTA, JORGE R.

1957 "Interpretación de Algunas de Los Datos Obtenidos en Tula Relativos a la Época Tolteca," *Revista Mexicana de Estudios Antropológicos*, vol. 14, part 2, pp. 75–110.

1968 "Exploraciones en Palenque, 1968," *Boletín, Instituto Nacional de Antropología e Historia*, no. 34, pp. 1–8.

ACOSTA SAIGNES, MIGUEL

1945 *Los Pochteca, Acta Antropológica*, época I, vol. 1, no. 1 (Mexico, D. F.: Sociedad de Alumnos, Escuela Nacional de Antropología e Historia).

ADAMS, RICHARD E. W.

1963a "Seibal, Peten: Una Secuencia Cerámica Preliminar y un Nuevo Mapa," *Estudios de Cultura Maya*, vol. 3, pp. 85–96.

1963b "A Polychrome Vessel from Altar de Sacrificios," *Archaeology*, vol. 16, no. 2, pp. 90–92.

1964 "The Ceramic Sequence at Altar de Sacrificios and Its Implications," *XXXV Congreso Internacional de Americanistas*, vol. 1 (Mexico: the congress), pp. 371–78.

1965   "Uaxactun, Guatemala: A Reevaluation," unpublished manuscript, University of Minnesota.

1969   "Maya Archaeology 1958–1968, a Review," *Latin American Research Review*, vol. 4, no. 2, pp. 3–45.

1970   "Suggested Classic Period Occupational Specialization in the Southern Maya Lowlands," <u>Monographs and Papers in Maya Archaeology</u>, ed. by W. R. Bullard, *Papers of the Peabody Museum of American Archaeology and Ethnology, Harvard University*, vol. 61 (Cambridge: the museum), pp. 487–98.

1971   *The Ceramics of Altar de Sacrificios, Guatemala, Papers of the Peabody Museum of Archaeology and Ethnology, Harvard University*, vol. 63, no. 1 (Cambridge: the museum).

ADAMS, RICHARD E. W., AND AUBREY S. TRIK

1961   *Temple I (Str. 5D-1): Post-constructional Activities, Tikal Reports*, no. 7, *Museum Monographs, The University Museum, University of Pennsylvania* (Philadelphia: the museum).

ADAMS, ROBERT McC.

1956   "Some Hypotheses on the Development of Early Civilizations," *American Antiquity*, vol. 21, no. 3, pp. 227–32.

1960   "The Origin of Cities," *Scientific American*, vol. 203, no. 9, pp. 153–68.

1961   "Changing Patterns of Territorial Organization in the Central Highlands of Chiapas, Mexico," *American Antiquity*, vol. 26, no. 3, pp. 341–60.

1962   "Agriculture and Urban Life in Early Southwestern Iran," *Science*, vol. 136, no. 3511, pp. 109–22.

1966   *The Evolution of Urban Society* (Chicago: Aldine Publishing Company).

ALTSCHULER, MILTON

1958   "On the Environmental Limitations of Maya Cultural Development," *Southwestern Journal of Anthropology*, vol. 14, no. 2, pp. 189–98.

ANDERSON, A. HAMILTON

1958   "Recent Discoveries at Caracol Site, British Honduras," *International Congress of Americanists XXXII* (Copenhagen: the congress), pp. 494–99.

1959   "More discoveries at Caracol, British Honduras," *Actas del XXXIII Congreso Internacional de Americanistas*, vol. 2 (San Jose: the congress), pp. 211–18.

ANDREWS, E. WYLLYS, IV.

1942   "Yucatan: Architecture," *Carnegie Institution of Washington Year Book*, no. 41 (Washington, D.C.: the institution), pp. 257–63.

1943   *The Archaeology of Southwestern Campeche, Contributions to American Anthropology and History*, vol. 8, no. 40, *Carnegie Institution of Washington Publication*, no. 546 (Washington, D.C.: the institution).

1960   "Excavations at Dzibilchaltun: Northwestern Yucatan, Mexico," *Proceedings of the American Philosophical Society*, vol. 104, pp. 254–65.

1961   "Review of *Prehistoric Ceramics and Settlement Patterns in Quintana Roo, Mexico*," by Wm. T. Sanders, *American Antiquity*, vol. 27, no. 1, pp. 123–24.

References

1962   "Excavations at Dzibilchaltun, Yucatan, 1956–1962," *Estudios de Cultura Maya*, vol. 2, pp. 3–35.

1965a   "Archaeology and Prehistory in the Northern Lowlands: An Introduction," *Archaeology of Southern Mesoamerica, Handbook of Middle American Indians*, vol. 2, ed. by G. R. Willey (Austin: University of Texas Press), pp. 288–330.

1965b   "Dzibilchaltun Program," *Middle American Research Records*, vol. 4, *Middle American Research Institute, Tulane University, Publication*, no. 31 (New Orleans: the institute), pp. 23–67.

1965c   "Explorations in the Gruta de Chac, Yucatan, Mexico," *Middle American Research Records*, vol. 4, *Middle American Research Institute, Tulane University, Publication*, no. 31 (New Orleans: the institute), pp. 1–21.

1968   "Dzibilchaltun, a Northern Maya Metropolis," *Archaeology*, vol. 21, no. 1, pp. 36–47.

1970   *Balankanche, Throne of the Tiger Priest, Middle American Research Institute, Tulane University, Publication*, no. 32 (New Orleans: the institute).

ANDREWS, E. WYLLYS, V

1969   "Excavations at Quelepa, El Salvador," paper presented at the 68th Annual Meeting of the American Anthropological Association, New Orleans, La.

ANGEL, JOHN LAWRENCE

1966   "Porotic Hyperostosis, Anemias, Malarias, and Marshes in the Prehistoric Eastern Mediterranean," *Science*, vol. 153, no. 3737, pp. 760–63.

1967   "Porotic Hyperostosis or Osteoporosis Symmetrica," *Diseases in Antiquity*, ed. by D. R. Brothwell and A. T. Sandison (Springfield, Ill.: C. C. Thomas), pp. 378–89.

ARKELL, ANTHONY JOHN, AND PETER J. UCKO

1965   "Review of Predynastic Development in the Nile Valley," *Current Anthropology*, vol. 6, no. 2, pp. 145–66.

ARMILLAS, PEDRO

1950   "Teotihuacán, Tula y los Toltecas," *Runa*, vol. 3, pp. 37–70.

ARRIAGA, EDUARDO E.

1968   *New Life Tables for Latin American Populations in the Nineteenth and Twentieth Centuries, Population Monograph Series*, no. 3 (Berkeley: Institute for International Studies).

ARTHES, FEDERICO

1893   "Description of the Peten Department," *El Guatemalteco*, vol. XXIII, no. 16, May 31 (Guatemala City, Guatemala).

ASHBY, WILLIAM ROSS

1956   *An Introduction to Cybernetics* (New York: J. Wiley).

1968   "Variety, Constraint, and the Law of Requisite Variety," *Modern Systems Research for the Behavioral Scientist*, ed. by W. Buckley (Chicago: Aldine Publishing Co.), pp. 129–36.

AUSTIN, D. M.

1970   "Dental Microevolution in Two Ancient Maya Communities," unpublished master's thesis, Pennsylvania State University.

AVELEYRA ARROYO DE ANDA, LUIS, AND GORDON EKHOLM
1966 "Clay Sculpture from Jaina," *Natural History*, vol. 75, no. 4, pp. 40–47.

BACON, EDWARD
1961 *Digging for History* (New York: John Day Company).

BARBA DE PIÑA CHAN, BEATRIZ
1956 *Tlapacoya, un Sitio Preclásico de Transición* (Mexico, D.F.: Sociedad de Alumnos, Escuela Nacional de Antropología e Historia).

BARLOW, ROBERT H.
1949 *The Extent of the Empire of the Culhua Mexica, Ibero-American*, vol. 28 (Berkeley: University of California Press).

BARTHEL, THOMAS S.
1964 "Comentarios a las Inscripciones Clásicas Tardías de Chichén-Itzá," *Estudios de Cultura Maya*, vol. 4, pp. 223–44.

BARTLETT, HARLEY H.
1956 "Fire, Primitive Agriculture and Grazing in the Tropics," *Man's Role in Changing the Face of the Earth*, ed. by W. L. Thomas (Chicago: University of Chicago Press), pp. 692–720.

BASCOM, WILLIAM R.
1969 *The Yoruba of Southwestern Nigeria* (New York: Holt, Rinehart and Winston).

BEHAR, M.
1968 "Food and Nutrition of the Maya before the Conquest and at the Present Time," *Biomedical Challenges Presented by the American Indian, Pan American Health Organization Publication*, no. 165 (Washington, D.C.: the organization), pp. 114–19.

BELL, H. IDRIS
1957 *Cults and Creeds in Graeco-Roman Egypt* (Chicago: Argonaut House).

BENEDICT, FRANCIS G., AND MORRIS STEGGERDA
1937 *The Food of the Present-Day Maya Indians of the Yucatan, Contributions to American Anthropology and History*, vol. 3, no. 18, *Carnegie Institution of Washington Publication*, no. 456 (Washington, D.C.: the institution), pp. 155–88.

BENNETT, WENDELL C., AND JUNIUS BIRD
1960 *Andean Culture History* (New York: American Museum of Natural History).

BERGMAN, JOHN F.
1969 "The Distribution of Cacao Cultivation in Pre-Columbian America," *Annals of the Association of American Geographers*, vol. 59, no. 1, pp. 85–96.

BERLIN, HEINRICH
1953 *Archaeological Reconnaissance in Tabasco, Carnegie Institution of Washington, Current Reports*, vol. 1, no. 7 (Washington, D.C.: the institution).

1955a "Apuntes Sobre Vasijas de Flores, El Petén," *Antropología e Historia de Guatemala*, vol. 7, no. 1, pp. 15–17.

References

1955b "News from the Maya World," *Ethnos*, vol. 20, no. 4, pp. 201–09.

1956 *Late Pottery Horizons of Tabasco, Mexico, Contributions to American Anthropology and History*, vol. 12, no. 59, *Carnegie Institution of Washington Publication*, no. 606 (Washington, D.C.: the institution).

BERNAL, IGNACIO

1958 "Monte Alban and the Zapotecs," *Boletín de Estudios Oaxaqueños*, no. 1, pp. 1–9.

1965 "Archaeological Synthesis of Oaxaca," *Archaeology of Southern Mesoamerica, Handbook of Middle American Indians*, vol. 3, ed. by G. R. Willey (Austin: University of Texas Press), pp. 788–813.

1966 "Teotihuacán: Capital de Imperio?" *Revista Mexicana de Estudios Antropológicos*, vol. 20, pp. 95–110.

BINFORD, LEWIS R.

1962 "Archaeology as Anthropology," *American Antiquity*, vol. 28, no. 2, pp. 217–25.

1968 "Some Comments on Historical Versus Processual Archaeology," *Southwestern Journal of Anthropology*, vol. 24, no. 3, pp. 267–75.

1971 "Mortuary Practices: Their Study and Their Potential," *Approaches to the Social Dimensions of Mortuary Practices*, ed. by J. A. Brown, *Memoirs of the Society for American Archaeology*, no. 25 (Salt Lake City: the society), pp. 6–29.

BLACKISTON, A. H.

1911 "The remains at Quirigua," *Records of the Past*, vol. 10, no. 2, pp. 59–76.

BLANTON, RICHARD E.

1970 "Prehispanic Settlement Patterns of the Ixtapalapa Peninsula Region, Mexico," unpublished doctoral dissertation, University of Michigan.

BLOCK, M. R.

1963 "The Social Influence of Salt," *Scientific American*, vol. 209, no. 1, pp. 88–98.

BLOM, FRANS

1932 "Commerce, Trade and Monetary Units of the Maya," *Middle American Papers, Middle American Research Institute, Tulane University, Publication*, no. 4 (New Orleans: the institute), pp. 531–56.

BLOM, FRANS, AND OLIVER LA FARGE

1926 *Tribes and Temples, Middle American Research Institute, Tulane University, Publication*, no. 1 (New Orleans: the institute).

BORHEGYI, STEPHAN F.

1963 "Explorations in Lake Peten Itza, Guatemala," *Archaeology*, vol. 16, no. 1, pp. 14–24.

1965a "Archaeological Synthesis of the Guatemalan Highlands," *Archaeology of Southern Mesoamerica, Handbook of Middle American Indians*, vol. 2, ed. by G. R. Willey (Austin: University of Texas Press), pp. 3–58.

1965b "Settlement Patterns of the Guatemalan Highlands," *Archaeology of Southern Mesoamerica, Handbook of Middle American Indians*, vol. 2, ed. by G. R. Willey (Austin: University of Texas Press), pp. 59–75.

BOSERUP, ESTER

1965 *The Conditions of Agricultural Growth* (Chicago: Aldine Publishing Company).

BRAINERD, GEORGE W.

1958 *The Archaeological Ceramics of Yucatan, University of California Anthropological Records,* vol. 19 (Berkeley and Los Angeles: University of California Press).

BROCKINGTON, DONALD L.

1970 "Cultural Sequences on the Coast of Oaxaca, Mexico," paper presented at the 35th Annual Meeting of the Society for American Archaeology, Mexico City.

BRONSON, BENNET

1966 "Roots and the Subsistence of the Ancient Maya," *Southwestern Journal of Anthropology,* vol. 22, no. 3, pp. 251–79.

BROTHWELL, DON R.

1970 "The Real History of Syphilis," *Science Journal,* vol. 6, September, pp. 27–32.

BUCKLEY, WALTER

1968 "Society as a Complex Adaptive System," *Modern Systems Research for the Behavioral Scientist,* ed. by W. Buckley (Chicago: Aldine Publishing Co.), pp. 490–513.

BULLARD, WILLIAM R., JR.

X 1960 "Maya Settlement Pattern in Northeastern Peten, Guatemala," *American Antiquity,* vol. 25, no. 3, pp. 355–72.

1961 "Archaeological Investigations of the Maya Ruin of Topoxte," *American Philosophical Society, Year Book 1960* (Philadelphia: the society), pp. 551–54.

X 1964 "Settlement Patterns and Social Structures in the Southern Maya Lowlands during the Classic Period," *XXXV Congreso Internacional de Americanistas,* vol. 1 (Mexico: the congress), pp. 279–87.

1970a "The Status of Postclassic Archaeology in Peten, Guatemala," paper presented at the 35th Annual Meeting of the Society for American Archaeology, Mexico City.

1970b "Topoxte, A Postclassic Site in Peten, Guatemala," *Monographs and Papers in Maya Archaeology,* ed. by W. R. Bullard, *Papers of the Peabody Museum of American Archaeology and Ethnology, Harvard University,* vol. 61 (Cambridge: the museum), pp. 245–307.

BULLARD, WILLIAM R., AND MARY R. BULLARD

1965 *Late Classic Finds at Baking Pot, British Honduras, Occasional Papers of the Royal Ontario Museum, Art and Archaeology Division,* no. 8 (Toronto: University of Toronto Press).

BUTLER, MARY

1935 *Piedras Negras Pottery, Piedras Negras Preliminary Reports,* no. 4 (Philadelphia: University Museum).

BUTZER, KARL W.

1964 *Environment and Archaeology* (Chicago: Aldine Publishing Company).

508

References

CARDOS DE MÉNDEZ, AMALIA
1959   El Comercio de los Mayas Antiguos, Acta Antropológica, época 2, vol.
       2, no. 1 (Mexico, D. F.: Sociedad de Alumnos, Escuela Nacional de
       Antropología e Historia).

CARNAP, RUDOLF
1939   "Foundations of Logic and Mathematics," International Encyclopedia
       of Unified Science, vol. I, no. 3 (Chicago: University of Chicago Press),
       p. 71.

CARNEIRO, ROBERT L.
1961   "Slash and Burn Cultivation among the Kuikuru and its Implica-
       tions for Cultural Development in the Amazon Basin," The Evolu-
       tion of Horticultural Systems in Native South America: Causes and
       Consequences, ed. by J. Wilbert (Caracas: Sociedad de Ciencias Na-
       turales La Salle), pp. 47–68.
1970   "A Theory of the Origin of the State," Science, vol. 169, no. 3947,
       pp. 733–38.

CARR, ROBERT F., AND JAMES E. HAZARD
1961   Map of the Ruins of Tikal, El Peten, Guatemala, Tikal Reports, no. 11,
       Museum Monographs, The University Museum, University of Pennsyl-
       vania (Philadelphia: the museum).

CARRASCO, PEDRO
1964   "Family Structure of Sixteenth Century Tepoztlan," Process and Pat-
       tern in Culture, ed. by R. A. Manners (Chicago: Aldine Publishing
       Company), pp. 185–210.

CENTER FOR HUMAN ECOLOGY
1969   Introduction to Human Ecology, 2nd Ed. (Urbana: University of Illi-
       nois Press).

CHAMBERLAIN, ROBERT S.
1948   The Conquest and Colonization of Yucatan 1517–1550, Carnegie In-
       stitution of Washington Publication, no. 582 (Washington, D.C.: the
       institution).

CHAPMAN, ANNE M.
1957   "Port of Trade Enclaves in Aztec and Mayla Civilizations," Trade and
       Market in the Early Empires, ed. by K. Polanyi, C. Arensberg and H.
       Pearson (Glencoe: Free Press), pp. 114–53.

CHEEK, CHARLES D.
1971   "Excavations at the Palangana, Kaminaljuyu, Guatemala," unpublished
       doctoral dissertation, University of Arizona.

CHENG TE-K'UN
1959   Archaeology in China, Volume 1: Prehistoric China (Cambridge: W. Heffer).
1960   Archaeology in China, Volume 2: Shang China (Cambridge: W. Heffer).
1963   Archaeology in China, Volume 3: Chou China (Cambridge: W. Heffer).

CHERNIKOV, S. S.
1949   Drevnaya Metallurgiya i Gornoye delo Zapadnogo Altaya (The Ancient
       Metallurgy and Mining of the Western Altay) (Alma-Ata: Izd. Akademiyi
       nauk Kazakhskoy S.S.R.).

CHI, CH'AO-TING
1936   *Key Economic Areas in Chinese History* (London: George Allen and Unwin).

CHILDE, V. GORDON
1954   *What Happened in History* (Harmondsworth: Penguin Books).
1957   *New Light on the Most Ancient Past* (New York: Grove Press).
1959   "The Birth of Civilization," *Readings in Anthropology*, ed. by M. H. Fried, vol. 1 (New York: Thomas Y. Crowell Company), pp. 412–21.
1963   *Social Evolution* (Cleveland: Meridian Books).

CLARK, J. DESMOND
1962   "Africa South of the Sahara," *Courses Toward Urban Life*, ed. by R. J. Braidwood and G. R. Willey (Chicago: Aldine Publishing Company), pp. 1–33.

CLARK, JOHN G. D., AND STUART PIGGOTT
1965   *Prehistoric Societies* (New York: Alfred A. Knopf).

COCKBURN, AIDAN
1963   *The Evolution and Eradication of Infectious Diseases* (Baltimore: Johns Hopkins Press).

COE, MICHAEL D.
1961   "Social Typology and the Tropical Forest Civilizations," *Comparative Studies in Society and History*, vol. 4, no. 1, pp. 65–85.
1962   "Costa Rican Archaeology and Mesoamerica," *Southwestern Journal of Anthropology*, vol. 18, no. 2, pp. 170–83.
1963   "Cultural Development in Southeastern Mesoamerica," *Aboriginal Cultural Development in Latin America: An Interpretative Review*, ed. by B. J. Meggers and C. Evans, *Smithsonian Institution, Smithsonian Miscellaneous Collections*, vol. 146, no. 1 (Washington, D.C.: the institution), pp. 27–44.
1965a *The Jaguar's Children: Preclassic Central Mexico* (New York: The Museum of Primitive Art).
1965b "A Model of Ancient Community Structure in the Maya Lowlands," *Southwestern Journal of Anthropology*, vol. 21, no. 2, pp. 97–114.
1967   "La Segunda Temporada en Sán Lorenzo Tenochtitlán, Veracruz," *Boletín, Instituto Nacional de Antropología e Historia*, no. 27, pp. 1–10.
1968a *America's First Civilization* (New York: American Heritage).
1968b "San Lorenzo and the Olmec Civilization," *Dumbarton Oaks Conference on the Olmec*, ed. by E. P. Benson (Washington, D.C.: Dumbarton Oaks Research Library and Collection and Trustees for Harvard University), pp. 41–71.

COE, MICHAEL D., AND ELIZABETH P. BENSON
1966   *Three Maya Relief Panels at Dumbarton Oaks, Dumbarton Oaks Studies in Pre-Columbian Art and Archaeology*, no. 2 (Washington, D.C.: Dumbarton Oaks Research Library and Collection and Trustees for Harvard University).

COE, MICHAEL D., RICHARD A. DIEHL, AND MINZE STUIVER
1967   "Olmec Civilization, Veracruz, Mexico: Dating of the San Lorenzo Phase," *Science*, vol. 155, no. 3768, pp. 1399–1401.

References

COE, MICHAEL D., AND KENT V. FLANNERY
1964   "Microenvironments and Mesoamerican Pre-History," *Science*, vol. 143, no. 3607, pp. 650–54.

COE, WILLIAM R.
1957   "Environmental Limitations on Maya Culture: A Reexamination," *American Anthropologist*, vol. 59, no. 2, pp. 328–35.

1959   *Piedras Negras Archaeology: Artifacts, Caches and Burials, Museum Monographs, The University Museum, University of Pennsylvania* (Philadelphia: the museum).

1962   "A Summary of Excavation and Research at Tikal, Guatemala: ✗ 1956–61," *American Antiquity*, vol. 27, no. 4, pp. 479–507.

1963   "A Summary of Excavation and Research at Tikal, Guatemala," *Estudios de Cultura Maya*, vol. 3, pp. 41–64.

1965a   "Tikal: Ten Years of Study of a Maya Ruin in the Lowlands of Guate- ✗ mala," *Expedition*, vol. 8, no. 1, pp. 5–56.

1965b   "Tikal, Guatemala, and Emergent Maya Civilization," *Science*, vol. 147, no. 3664, pp. 1401–19.

1967   *Tikal: A Handbook of the Ancient Maya Ruins* (Philadelphia: University Museum).

COE, WILLIAM R., AND VIVIAN L. BROMAN
1958   *Excavations in the Stela 23 Group, Tikal Reports, no. 2, Museum Monographs, the University Museum, University of Pennsylvania* (Philadelphia: the museum).

COE, WILLIAM R., AND MICHAEL D. COE
1956   "Excavations at Nohoch Ek, British Honduras," *American Antiquity*, vol. 21, no. 4, pp. 370–82.

COE, WILLIAM R., EDWIN M. SHOOK, AND
LINTON SATTERTHWAITE
1961   *The Carved Wooden Lintels of Tikal, Tikal Reports, no. 6, Museum Monographs, the University Museum, University of Pennsylvania* (Philadelphia: the museum).

COLLIER, DONALD
1962   "The Central Andes," *Courses Toward Urban Life*, ed. by R. J. Braidwood and G. R. Willey (Chicago: Aldine Publishing Company), pp. 165–76.

COMAS, JUAN
1966   *Características Físicas de la Familia Lingüística Maya, Universidad Nacional Autónoma de México, Instituto de Investigaciones Históricas, Cuadernos: Serie Antropológica*, no. 20 (Mexico, D. F.: the university).

COOK, SCOTT
1970   "Price and Output Variability in a Peasant-Artisan Stoneworking Industry in Oaxaca, Mexico: An Analytical Essay in Economic Anthropology," *American Anthropologist*, vol. 72, no. 4, pp. 776–801.

COOK, ORATOR F.
1921   "Milpa Agriculture, A Primitive Tropical System," *Annual Report of the Smithsonian Institution, 1919* (Washington, D.C.: the institution), pp. 307–26.

COOK DE LEONARD, CARMEN
1956-7 "Algunas Antecedentes de la Cerámica Tolteca," *Revista Mexicana de Estudios Antropológicos*, vol. 14, part 2, pp. 37–43.

COOKE, C. WYTHE
1931 "Why the Mayan Cities of the Peten District, Guatemala, were Abandoned," *Journal of the Washington Academy of Sciences*, vol. 21, no. 13, pp. 283–87.

COTTIER, J. W.
1967 "Preliminary Archaeological Investigations at X-Kukican, Yucatan, Mexico," mimeographed, University of Alabama.

COVARRUBIAS, MIGUEL
X 1946 *Mexico South, The Ithmus of Tehuantepec* (New York: Alfred A. Knopf).
1957 *Indian Art of Mexico and Central America* (New York: Alfred A. Knopf).

COWGILL, GEORGE L.
1963 "Postclassic Period Culture in the Vicinity of Flores, Peten, Guatemala," unpublished doctoral dissertation, Harvard University.
1964 "The End of Classic Maya Culture: A Review of Recent Evidence," *Southwestern Journal of Anthropology*, vol. 20, no. 2, pp. 145–59.

COWGILL, URSULA M.
1961 "Soil Fertility and the Ancient Maya," *Transactions of the Connecticut Academy of Arts and Sciences*, vol. 42, pp. 1–56.
1962 "An Agricultural Study of the Southern Maya Lowlands," *American Anthropologist*, vol. 64, no. 2, pp. 273–86.
1971 "Some Comments on *Manihot* Subsistence and the Ancient Maya," *Southwestern Journal of Anthropology*, vol. 27, no. 1, pp. 51–63.

COWGILL, URSULA M., AND GEORGE E. HUTCHINSON
1963a "Ecological and Geochemical Archaeology in the Southern Maya Lowlands," *Southwestern Journal of Anthropology*, vol. 19, no. 3, pp. 267–86.
1963b *El Bajo de Santa Fé, Transactions of the American Philosophical Society*, vol. 53, Part 7 (Philadelphia: the society).
1963c "Sex-ratio in Childhood and the Depopulation of the Peten, Guatemala," *Human Biology*, vol. 35, no. 1, pp. 90–103.

CREEL, HERRLEE G.
1937a *The Birth of China* (New York: Reynal and Hitchcock).
1937b *Studies in Early Chinese Culture, First Series* (Baltimore: Waverly Press).

CRESSEY, GEORGE B.
1955 *Land of the 500 Million: A Geography of China* (New York: McGraw Hill Book Company).

CULBERT, T. PATRICK
1963 "Ceramic Research at Tikal, Guatemala," *Cerámica de Cultura Maya*, vol. 1, pp. 34–42.
1968 *The Ceramic Complex*, mimeographed, University of Arizona.
1969a "Irrigation and Natural Resource Control in Prehistoric Mesoamerica," paper presented at the 34th Annual Meeting of the Society for American Archaeology, Milwaukee, Wisconsin.

References

1969b "Review of *Mesoamerica*," W. T. Sanders and Barbara Price, *Science*, vol. 166, no. 3912, pp. 1497–98.

DAVENPORT, WILLIAM H.
1964 "Hawaiian Feudalism," *Expedition*, vol. 6, no. 2, pp. 14–27.

DEUTSCH, KARL
1969 *Nationalism and Its Alternatives* (New York: Alfred A. Knopf).

DIESELDORFF, ERWIN P.
1904 "A Pottery Base with Figure Painting, from a Grave in Chama," *Mexican and Central American Antiquities, Calendar Systems, and History, Bureau of American Ethnology Bulletin*, no. 28 (Washington, D.C.: U.S. Government Printing Office), pp. 639–64.
1933 *Kunst und Religion der Mayavölker*, vol. 3 (Berlin: J. Springer).

DIXON, KEITH A.
1967 "Progress Report on Excavations of Terminal Late Preclassic Ceremonial Architecture, Temexco, Valley of Mexico (summer 1965)," *Katunob*, vol. 6, pp. 30–69.

DRUCKER, PHILLIP
1943a *Ceramic Sequences at Tres Zapotes, Veracruz, Mexico, Bureau of American Ethnology Bulletin*, no. 141 (Washington, D.C.: U.S. Government Printing Office).
1943b *Ceramic Stratigraphy at Cerro do las Mesas, Veracruz, Mexico, Bureau of American Ethnology Bulletin*, no. 143 (Washington, D.C.: U.S. Government Printing Office).

DUMOND, DONALD E.
1961 "Swidden Agriculture and the Rise of Maya Civilization," *Southwestern Journal of Anthropology*, vol. 17, no. 4, pp. 301–16.
1965 "Population Growth and Culture Change," *Southwestern Journal of Anthropology*, vol. 21, no. 4, pp. 302–24.

DUMOND, DONALD E. AND FLORENCIA MULLER
1972 "Classic to Post Classic in Highland Central Mexico," *Science*, vol. 175, no. 4027, pp. 1208–15.

DU SOLIER, WILFRIDO
1945 "La Cerámica Arqueológica de El Tajín," *Anales del Museo Nacional de Arqueología, Historia y Etnografía*, época 5, no. 3, pp. 147–91.

EASBY, ELIZABETH K., AND JOHN F. SCOTT
1970 *Before Cortes: Sculpture of Middle America* (New York: Metropolitan Museum of Art).

ENGELS, FRIEDRICH
1942 *The Origin of the Family, Private Property and the State* (New York: International Publishers).

EPSTEIN, A. L.
1968 "Power, Politics and Leadership: Some Central African and Melanesian Contrasts," *Local-level Politics*, ed. by M. J. Swartz (Chicago: Aldine Publishing Company), pp. 53–68.

ERASMUS, CHARLES J.

1965 "Monument Building: Some Field Experiments," *Southwestern Journal of Anthropology*, vol. 21, no. 4, pp. 277–301.

X 1968 "Thoughts on Upward Collapse: An Essay on Explanation in Archaeology," *Southwestern Journal of Anthropology*, vol. 24, no. 2, pp. 170–94.

ESTRADA, EMILIO, AND CLIFFORD EVANS

1963 "Cultural Development in Ecuador," *Aboriginal Cultural Development in Latin America: An Interpretive Review*, ed. by B. J. Meggers and C. Evans, *Smithsonian Institution, Smithsonian Miscellaneous Collections*, vol. 146, no. 1 (Washington, D.C.: the institution), pp. 77–88.

FALLERS, LLOYD A.

1965 *Bantu Bureaucracy: A Century of Political Evolution among the Basoga of Uganda* (Chicago: University of Chicago Press).

FERREE, LISA

1967 "The Censers of Tikal, Guatemala: A Preliminary Sequence of the Major Shape-types," unpublished master's thesis, University of Pennsylvania.

FINNEY, BEN R.

1966 "Resource Distribution and Social Structure in Tahiti," *Ethnology*, vol. 5, no. 1, pp. 80–86.

FLANNERY, KENT V.

X 1968 "The Olmec and the Valley of Oaxaca: a Model of Inter-Regional Interaction in Formative Times," *Dumbarton Oaks Conference on the Olmec*, ed. by E. P. Benson (Washington, D.C.: Dumbarton Oaks Research Library and Collection and Trustees for Harvard University), pp. 119–30.

FLANNERY, KENT V., ANNE V. T. KIRKBY, MICHAEL J. KIRKBY, AND AUBREY W. WILLIAMS, JR.

1967 "Farming Systems and Political Growth in Ancient Oaxaca," *Science*, vol. 158, no. 3800, pp. 445–54.

FOLAN, WILLIAM J.

X 1969 "Dzibilchaltun, Yucatan, Mexico: Structures 384, 385, and 386: A Preliminary Interpretation," *American Antiquity*, vol. 34, no. 4, pp. 434–61.

FONCERRADA DE MOLINA, MARTA

1962 "La Arquitectura Puuc dentro de los Estilos de Yucatán," *Estudios de Cultura Maya*, vol. 2, pp. 225–38.

FOSTER, GEORGE M.

1960 *Culture and Conquest: America's Spanish Heritage, Viking Fund Publications in Anthropology*, no. 27 (New York: Wenner-Gren Foundation for Anthropological Research).

FOWLER, MELVIN L.

1969 "A Preclassic Water Distribution System in Amalucan, Mexico," *Archaeology*, vol. 22, no. 3, pp. 208–15.

FRANKFORT, HENRI

1956 *The Birth of Civilization in the Near East* (Garden City, N.Y.: Doubleday and Company).

FRIED, MORTON H.

1960 "On the Evolution of Social Stratification and the State," *Culture in His-*

References

tory: Essays in Honor of Paul Radin, ed. by S. Diamond (New York: Columbia University Press), pp. 713–31.

1967   *The Evolution of Political Society* (New York: Random House).

FRY, ROBERT E.

1969   "Ceramics and Settlement in the Periphery of Tikal, Guatemala," unpublished doctoral dissertation, University of Arizona.

1970   "Mesoamerican Trading Systems and the Maya Collapse," paper presented at the 35th Annual Meeting of the Society for American Archaeology, Mexico City.

FUENTE, BEÁTRIZ DE LA

1965   *La Escultura de Palenque* (Mexico, D.F.: Instituto de Investigaciones Estéticas, Universidad Nacional Autónoma de México).

GANN, THOMAS W. F.

1890   "Mounds in Northern Honduras," *Ninth Annual Report of the Bureau of American Ethnology, 1890* (Washington, D.C.: U.S. Government Printing Office), pp. 655–92.

1918   *The Maya Indians of Southern Yucatan and Northern British Honduras, Bureau of American Ethnology Bulletin,* no. 64 (Washington, D.C.: U.S. Government Printing Office).

1925   *Mystery Cities: Exploration and Adventure in Lubaantun* (London: Duckworth).

1930   "A Recently Discovered Maya City in the Southwest of British Honduras," *Proceedings of the XXIII International Congress of Americanists* (New York: the congress), pp. 188–92.

GARCÍA PAYÓN, JOSÉ

1943   *Interpretación Cultural de la Zona Arqueológica de El Tajín: Seguida de un Ensayo de una Bibliografía Antropológica del Totonacapan y Región sur del Estado de Veracruz* (Mexico, D. F.: Imprenta Universitaria).

1950   "Exploraciones in Xiuhtetelco, Puebla," *Uni-Ver,* vol. 2, pp. 397–426, 447–76.

1951a   *La Ciudad Arqueológica de Tajín, Contribución de la Universidad Veracruzana a la V Reunión de la Mesa Redonda de Antropología* (Jalapa: the university).

1951b   *Breves Apuntes Sobre la Arqueología de Chachalacas* (Jalapa: Universidad Veracruzana).

1953   "Que Es lo Tontonaco?" *Revista Mexicana de Estudios Antropológicos,* vol. 13, pp. 379–87.

1957   *El Tajín, Guia Oficial* (Mexico, D. F.: Instituto Nacional de Antropología e Historia).

GAYDUKEVICH, BORIS F.

1949   *Bosporskoye Tsarstvo (The Bosphorus Kingdom)* (Moscow: Izd. akademiyi nauk S.S.S.R.).

GEERTZ, CLIFFORD

1963   *Agricultural Involution: The Process of Ecological Change in Indonesia* (Berkeley: University of California Press).

GENOVÉS, SANTIAGO

1967   "Proportionality of the Long Bones and their Relation to Stature among

Mesoamericans," *American Journal of Physical Anthropology*, vol. 26, no. 1, pp. 69–79.

GIFFORD, JAMES C.

1968   "The Earliest and Other Intrusive Population Elements at Barton Ramie May Have Come from Central America," paper presented at the 67th Annual Meeting of the Americal Anthropological Association, Seattle, Washington.

GIRARD, RAFAEL

1959   "El Colapso Maya y los Nahuas," paper presented at the VIII Mesa Redonda of the Sociedad Mexicana de Antropología at San Cristóbal de las Casas, Chiapas, México.

GLUCKMAN, MAX

1940   "The Kingdom of the Zulu in South Africa," *African Political Systems*, ed. by M. Fortes, and E. E. Evans-Pritchard (London: Oxford University Press), pp. 25–55.

1960   "The Rise of a Zulu Empire," *Scientific American*, vol. 202, no. 4, pp. 157–68.

1968   *Politics, Law and Ritual in Tribal Society* (New York and Toronto: Mentor Books).

GOFF, CHARLES W.

1953a   "Anthropometry of a Mam-speaking Group of Indians from Guatemala," *The Ruins of Zaculeu*, R. B. Woodbury and A. S. Trik (Boston: United Fruit Company), pp. 288–94.

1953b   "New Evidence of Pre-Columbian Bone Syphilis in Guatemala," *The Ruins of Zaculeu*, R. B. Woodbury and A. S. Trik (Boston: United Fruit Company), pp. 312–19.

1967   "Syphilis," *Diseases in Antiquity*, ed. by D. R. Brothwell and A. T. Sandison (Springfield, Illinois: C. C. Thomas), pp. 279–94.

GONZÁLEZ-ÁNGULO, WILBERT, AND R. E. RYCKMAN

1967   "Epizootiology of *Trypanosoma cruzi* in Southwestern North America. Part IX: An Investigation to determine the incidence of *Trypanosoma cruzi* infections in *Triatominae* and man on the Yucatan Peninsula of Mexico," *Journal of Medical Entomology*, vol. 4, pp. 44–47.

GOODENOUGH, WARD H.

1969   "Rethinking 'Status' and 'Role': Toward a General Model of the Cultural Organization of Social Relationships," *Cognitive Anthropology*, ed. by S. A. Tyler (New York: Holt, Rinehart and Winston).

GORDON, GEORGE B.

1896   *Prehistoric Ruins of Copan, Honduras, Memoirs of the Peabody Museum of Archaeology and Ethnology, Harvard University*, vol. 1, no. 1 (Cambridge: the museum).

GOUROU, PIERRE

1958   *The Tropical World*, 2nd Edition (London: Longman, Green and Co.).

GRAHAM, IAN

1967   *Archaelogical Explorations in El Peten, Guatemala, Middle American Research Institute, Tulane University Publication*, no. 33 (New Orleans: the Institute).

References

GRAHAM, JOHN A.
1961 "Field Notes: Altar de Sacrificios, Seibal, Dos Pilas, Aguateca, Tamarindito, Amelia, Caribe, Aguascalientes, Pabellon," manuscript, University of California at Berkeley.
1963 "Epigraphic investigations at Altar de Sacrificios and Seibal," unpublished doctoral dissertation, Harvard University.
1971 "Non-Classic Inscriptions and Sculptures at Seibal," *Papers on Olmec and Maya Archaeology, Contributions of the University of California Archaeological Research Facility*, no. 13 (Berkeley: University of California Press), pp. 143–53.

GRAY, ROBERT F.
1963 *The Sonjo of Tanganyika: An Anthropological Study of an Irrigation-Based Society* (London: Oxford University Press).

GREENE ROBERTSON, MERLE
n. d. *Rubbings of Maya Monuments*, The California Arts Commission.

GROTH-KIMBALL, IRMGARD
1961 *Mayan Terracottas* (New York: A. Praeger).

GROVE, DAVID C.
1968 "The Pre-Classic Olmec in Central Mexico: Site Distribution and Inferences," *Dumbarton Oaks Conference on the Olmec*, ed. by E. P. Benson (Washington, D.C.: Dumbarton Oaks Research Library and Collection and Trustees for Harvard University), pp. 179–85.
1970 "The San Pablo Pantheon Mound: A Middle Preclassic Site in Morelos, Mexico," *American Antiquity*, vol. 35, no. 1, pp. 62–73.

GRUNING, E. L.
1930 "Report on the British Museum Expedition to British Honduras, 1930," *Journal of the Royal Anthropological Institute of Great Britain and Ireland*, vol. 60, pp. 477–83.

HALL, DANIEL G. E.
1968 *A History of South-east Asia*, 3rd Ed. (London: Macmillan).

HAMPERL, H., AND P. WEISS
1955 "Uber die Spongiose Hyperostose an Schadeln aus Alt-Peru," *Virchows Archiv*, no. 327, pp. 929–42.

HARNER, MICHAEL J.
1970 "Population Pressure and the Social Evolution of Agriculturists," *Southwestern Journal of Anthropology*, vol. 26, no. 1, pp. 67–86.

HARRIS, MARVIN
1966 "The Cultural Ecology of India's Sacred Cattle," *Current Anthropology*, vol. 7, no. 1, pp. 51–60.
1968 *The Rise of Anthropological Theory* (New York: Thomas Y. Crowell).
1969 "Monistic Determinism: Anti-Service," *Southwestern Journal of Anthropology*, vol. 25, no. 2, pp. 198–206.
1971 "CA Comment on A. Heston, An Approach to the Sacred Cow of India," *Current Anthropology*, vol. 12, no. 2, pp. 199–201.

HARRISON, PETER D.
1970 "Form and Function in a Maya 'Palace' Group," *Verhandlungen des*

XXXVIII Internationalen Amerikanistenkongresses, vol. 1 (Stuttgart, München: the congress), pp. 165–72.

HARVEY, H. R., AND ISABEL KELLY
1969   "The Totonac," *Ethnology, Handbook of Middle American Indians*, vol. 8, ed. by E. Z. Vogt (Austin: University of Texas Press), pp. 638–81.

HAVILAND, WILLIAM A.
1963   "Excavation of Small Structures in the Northeast Quadrant of Tikal, Guatemala," unpublished doctoral dissertation, University of Pennsylvania.
1965   "Prehistoric Settlement at Tikal," *Expedition*, vol. 7, no. 3, pp. 14–23.
1966a   "Maya Settlement Patterns: A Critical Review," *Archaeological Studies in Middle America, Middle American Research Institute, Tulane University, Publication*, no. 26 (New Orleans: the institute), pp. 21–47.
1966b   "Social Integration and the Classic Maya," *American Antiquity*, vol. 31, no. 5, pp. 625–31.
1967   "Stature at Tikal, Guatemala: Implications for Ancient Maya Demography and Social Organization," *American Antiquity*, vol. 32, no. 3, pp. 316–25.
1968   "Ancient Lowland Maya Social Organization," *Archaeological Studies in Middle America, Middle American Research Institute, Tulane University, Publication*, no. 26 (New Orleans: the institute), pp. 93–117.
1969   "A New Population Estimate for Tikal, Guatemala," *American Antiquity*, vol. 34, no. 4, pp. 429–33.
1970   "Tikal, Guatemala, and Mesoamerican Urbanism," *World Archaeology*, vol. 2, no. 2, pp. 186–97.
1971   "Entombment, Authority and Descent at Altar de Sacrificios, Guatemala," *American Antiquity*, vol. 36, no. 1, pp. 102–05.

HAVILAND, WILLIAM A., DENNIS E. PULESTON, ROBERT E. FRY, AND ERNESTINE GREEN
1968   "The Tikal Sustaining Area: Preliminary Report on the 1967 Season," mimeographed, The University of Vermont.

HEIZER, ROBERT F.
1960   "Agriculture and the Theocratic State in Lowland Southeastern Mexico," *American Antiquity*, vol. 26, no. 2, pp. 215–22.

HEIZER, ROBERT F., PHILLIP DRUCKER, AND JOHN A. GRAHAM
1968   "Investigaciones de 1967 y 1968 en La Venta," *Boletín, Instituto Nacional de Antropología e Historia*, no. 33, pp. 21–28.

HELM, JUNE
1962   "The Ecological Approach to Anthropology," *The American Journal of Sociology*, vol. 67, no. 6, pp. 630–39.

HERSKOVITZ, MELVILLE J.
1938   *Dahomey* (New York: J. J. Augustin).

HESTON, ALAN
1971   "An Approach to the Sacred Cow of Indian," *Current Anthropology*, vol. 12, no. 2, pp. 191–97.

HEWETT, EDGAR L.
1912   "Excavations at Quirigua," *Archaeological Institute of America Bulletin*, vol. 3, pp. 163–71.

References

HICKS, FREDERIC, AND HENRY B. NICHOLSON
1964   "The Transition from Classic to Postclassic at Cerro Portezuelo, Valley of Mexico," *XXXV Congreso Internacional de Americanistas*, vol. 1 (Mexico: the congress), pp. 493–505.

HIRSHBERG, RICHARD I., AND JOAN F. HIRSHBERG
1957   "Meggers' Law of Environmental Limitation on Culture," *American Anthropologist*, vol. 59, no. 5, pp. 890–91.

HOOTON, EARNEST A.
1930   *The Indians of Pecos Pueblo* (New Haven: Yale University Press).
1940   "Skeletons from the Cenote of Sacrifice at Chichen Itza," *The Maya and Their Neighbors* (New York: D. Appleton-Century), pp. 272–80.

HOPKINS, BRIAN
1965   *Forest and Savanna* (Ibadan and London: Heinemann).

HUDSON, E. H.
1965   "Treponematosis and Man's Evolution," *American Anthropologist*, vol. 67, no. 4, pp. 885–901.

HUNTINGTON, ELLSWORTH
1917   "Maya Civilization and Climatic Changes," *Proceedings of the Nineteenth International Congress of Americanists* (Washington, D.C.: the congress), pp. 150–64.

HUXLEY, JULIAN S.
1956   "Evolution, Cultural and Biological," *Current Anthropology, A Supplement to Anthropology Today*, ed. by W. L. Thomas, Jr. (Chicago: University of Chicago Press), pp. 3–23.

JACOBS-MÜLLER, E. FLORENCIA
1956-7 "Azcapotzalco: Estudio Tipológico de la Cerámica," *Revista Mexicana de Estudios Antropológicos*, vol. 14, no. 2, pp. 25–31.

JELIFFE, DERRICK B.
1968   *Infant Nutrition in the Subtropics and Tropics*, 2nd Edition, *World Health Organization, World Health Monographs*, no. 29 (Geneva: the organization).

JIMÉNEZ MORENO, WIGBERTO
1955   "Síntesis de la Historia Precolonial del Valle de México," *Revista Mexicana de Estudios Antropológicos*, vol. 14, no. 1, pp. 219–36.
1966   "Mesoamerica Before the Toltecs," *Ancient Oaxaca*, ed. by John Paddock (Stanford: Stanford University Press), pp. 1–82.

JOYCE, THOMAS A.
1914   *Mexican Archaeology* (London: Philip Lee Warner).
1926   "Report on Investigations at Lubaantun, British Honduras, in 1926," *Journal of the Royal Anthropological Institute of Great Britain and Ireland*, vol. 56, pp. 207–30.

KAPLAN, DAVID
1963   "Men, Monuments and Political Systems," *Southwestern Journal of Anthropology*, vol. 19, no. 4, pp. 397–410.

KEESING, ROGER M.
1967   "Toward an Ethnographic Theory of 'Roles'," manuscript, Harvard University.

KELLEY, DAVID H.

X 1962 "Glyphic Evidence for a Dynastic Sequence at Quirigua, Guatemala," *American Antiquity*, vol. 27, no. 3, pp. 323–35.

1965 "The Birth of the Gods at Palenque," *Estudios de Cultura Maya*, vol. 5, pp. 93–134.

KELLY, ISABEL, AND ÁNGEL PALERM

1952 *The Tajin Totonac, Part I: History, Subsistence, Shelter and Technology,* Smithsonian Institution, Institute of Social Anthropology Publication, no. 13 (Washington, D.C.: the institution).

KENDEIGH, S. CHARLES

1961 *Animal Ecology* (Englewood Cliffs, N.J.: Prentice-Hall).

KIDDER, ALFRED V.

1947 *The Artifacts of Uaxactun, Guatemala, Carnegie Institute of Washington Publication,* no. 576 (Washington, D.C.: the institution).

1950 "Introduction," *Uaxactun, Guatemala: Excavations of 1931–1937,* by A. Ledyard Smith, *Carnegie Institution of Washington Publication,* no. 588 (Washington, D.C.: the institution), pp. 1–12.

KIDDER, ALFRED V., JESSE D. JENNINGS, AND EDWIN M. SHOOK

1946 *Excavations at Kaminaljuyu, Guatemala, Carnegie Institution of Washington Publication,* no. 561 (Washington, D.C.: the institution).

KIDDER, ALFRED V., II, LUIS G. LUMBRERAS S., AND DAVID B. SMITH

1963 "Cultural Development in the Central Andes—Peru and Bolivia," *Aboriginal Cultural Development in Latin America: An Interpretive Review,* ed. by B. J. Meggers and C. Evans, Smithsonian Institution, Smithsonian Miscellaneous Collections, vol. 146, no. 1 (Washington, D.C.: the institution), pp. 89–101.

KÖBERLE, FRITZ

1968 "Chagas' Disease and Chagas' Syndromes: The Pathology of American *Trypanosomiasis,*" *Advances in Parasitology,* vol. 6, pp. 63–116.

KROEBER, ALFRED L.

1944 *Peruvian Archaeology in 1942, Viking Fund Publications in Anthropology,* no. 4 (New York: Wenner-Gren Foundation for Anthropological Research).

KUBLER, GEORGE

1962 *The Art and Architecture of Ancient America* (Baltimore: Penguin Books).

LAMBERT, BERNDT

1966 "The Economic Activities of a Gilbertese Chief," *Political Anthropology,* ed. by M. J. Swartz, V. W. Turner and A. Tuden (Chicago: Aldine Publishing Company), pp. 155–72.

LANGE, FREDERICK W.

1971 "Marine Resources: A Viable Subsistence Alternative for the Prehistoric Lowland Maya," *American Anthropologist,* vol. 73, no. 3, pp. 619–39.

LANNING, EDWARD P.

1967 *Peru Before the Incas* (Englewood Cliffs, N.J.: Prentice-Hall).

LATHRAP, DONALD W.

1957 "The Classic Stage in Mesoamerica," *Kroeber Anthropological Society Papers,* no. 17, pp. 38–74.

References

LAUGHLIN, ROBERT M.
1969a "The Tzotzil," *Ethnology, Handbook of Middle American Indians*, vol. 7, edited by E. Z. Vogt (Austin: University of Texas Press), pp. 152–94.
1969b "The Huastec," *Ethnology, Handbook of Middle American Indians*, vol. 7, ed. by E. Z. Vogt (Austin: University of Texas Press), pp. 298–311.

LEHMANN, HEINZ
1935 "Le Fonds Maya du Musée d'Ethnographie du Trocadéro de Paris," *Maya Research*, vol. 2, pp. 345–66.

LEONE, MARK P.
1968 "Economic Autonomy and Social Distance: Archaeological Evidences," unpublished doctoral dissertation, University of Arizona.

LIZARDI RAMOS, CÉSAR
1961 "Las Estelas 4 y 5 de Balancán-Morales, Tabasco," *Estudios de Cultura Maya*, vol. 1, pp. 107–30.
1963 "Inscripciones de Pomoná, Tabasco, México," *Estudios de Cultura Maya*, vol. 3, pp. 187–202.

LONG, E. C.
1969 *Final Report of the Medical Expedition to Peten, June 27–July 25, 1968* (Durham: Duke University School of Medicine).

LONGYEAR, JOHN M., III
1952 *Copan Ceramics, Carnegie Institution of Washington Publication*, no. 597 (Washington, D.C.: the institution).

LOTHROP, SAMUEL K.
1936 *Zacualpa: A Study of Ancient Quiche Artifacts, Carnegie Institution of Washington Publication*, no. 472 (Washington, D.C.: the institution).
1952 *Metals from the Cenote of Sacrifice, Chichen Itza, Yucatan, Memoirs of the Peabody Museum of Archaeology and Ethnology, Harvard University*, vol. 10, no. 2 (Cambridge: the museum).

LOWE, GARETH W.
1962 "Algunos Resultados de la Temporada 1961 en Chiapa de Corzo, Chiapas," *Estudios de Cultura Maya*, vol. 2, pp. 185–96.

LOWIE, ROBERT H.
1960 "Some Aspects of Political Organization Among the American Aborigines," *Lowie, Selected Papers in Anthropology*, ed. by C. Dubois (Berkeley and Los Angeles: University of California Press), pp. 262–90.

LUNDELL, CYRUS L.
1937 *The Vegetation of Peten, Carnegie Institution of Washington Publication*, no. 478 (Washington, D.C.: the institution).

MAC ARTHUR, ROBERT, AND JOSEPH CONNELL
1966 *The Biology of Population* (New York: John Wiley and Sons).

MACDONALD, GEORGE
1961 "Epidemiologic Models in Studies of Vector-borne Diseases," *Public Health Reports*, vol. 76, no. 9, pp. 753–64.

MACKIE, EUAN W.
1961 "New Light on the End of Classic Maya Culture at Benque Viejo, British Honduras," *American Antiquity*, vol. 27, no. 2, pp. 216–24.

References

MACNEISH, RICHARD S.

1954   An Early Archaeological Site near Panuco, Veracruz, Transactions of the American Philosophical Society, vol. 44, part 5 (Philadelphia: the society).

1964   "Ancient Mesoamerican Civilization," Science, vol. 143, no. 3606, pp. 531–37.

MAHOLY-NAGY, HATTULA

1963   "Shells and other Marine Material from Tikal," Estudios de Cultura Maya, vol. 3, pp. 65–83.

MALDE, HAROLD E.

1964   "Environment and Man in Arid America," Science, vol. 145, no. 3628, pp. 123–29.

MALER, TEOBERT

1901–3 Researches in the Central Portion of the Usumatsintla Valley: Report of Explorations for the Museum 1898–1900, Memoirs of the Peabody Museum of Archaeology and Ethnography, Harvard University, vol. 2 (Cambridge: the museum).

1908   Explorations of the Upper Usumatsintla and Adjacent Regions, Memoirs of the Peabody Museum of Archaeology and Ethnology, Harvard University, vol. 4, no. 1 (Cambridge: the museum).

1911   Explorations in the Department of Peten, Guatemala: Tikal, Memoirs of the Peabody Museum of American Archaeology and Ethnology, Harvard University, vol. 5, no. 1 (Cambridge: the museum).

MALINOWSKI, BRONISLAW

1935   Coral Gardens and Their Magic (London: George Allen and Unwin).

MARQUINA, IGNACIO

1951   Arquitectura Prehispánica, Memorias del Instituto Nacional de Antropología e Historia, vol. 1 (Mexico, D. F.: the institute).

1968   "Exploraciones en la Pirámide de Cholula," Boletín, Instituto Nacional de Antropología e Historia, no. 32, pp. 12–19.

1970   (ed.) Proyecto Cholula, Instituto Nacional de Antropología e Historia, Serie Investigaciones, no. 19 (Mexico, D. F.: the institute).

MATHENY, RAYMOND T.

1970   The Ceramics of Aguacatal, Campeche, Mexico, Papers of the New World Archaeological Foundation, Brigham Young University, no. 27 (Provo: the foundation).

MAUDSLAY, ALFRED P.

1889–1902 Archaeology, Biologia Centrali-Americana, 5 vols. (London: Porter and Dulau).

MC BRIDE, HAROLD W.

1969   "The Extent of the Chupicuaro Tradition," The Natalie Wood Collection of Precolumbian Ceramics from Chupicuaro, Guanajuato, Mexico, at UCLA, ed. by J. D. Friedman, Museum and Laboratories of Ethnic Arts and Technology, Los Angeles, Occasional Papers, no. 1 (Los Angeles: the museum), pp. 33–49.

MC BRYDE, F. WEBSTER

1945   Cultural and Historical Geography of Southwest Guatemala, Smithsonian Institution, Institute of Social Anthropology Publication, no. 4 (Washington, D.C.: the institution).

References

MC VICKER, DONALD
1967   "Prehistoric Trade in Central Chiapas, Mexico," paper presented at the 66th Annual Meeting of the American Anthropological Association, Washington, D.C.

MEANS, PHILIP A.
1917   *History of the Spanish Conquest of Yucatan and of the Itzas, Memoirs of the Peabody Museum of Archaeology and Ethnology, Harvard University*, vol. 7 (Cambridge: the museum).

MEDELLÍN ZENIL, ALFONSO
1955a   "Desarollo de la Cultura Prehispánica Central Veracruzana," *Anales del Instituto Nacional de Antropología e Historia*, vol. 7, no. 36, pp. 101–09.

1955b   *Exploraciones en la Isla de Sacrificios* (Jalapa: Gobierno del Estado de Veracruz, Dirección General de Educación, Departmento de Antropología).

1960   *Cerámicas del Totonacapán* (Jalapa: Universidad Veracruzana).

MEGGERS, BETTY J.
1954   "Environmental Limitation on the Development of Culture," *American Anthropologist*, vol. 56, no. 5, pp. 801–24.

MENDIZÁBAL, MIGUEL O.
1930   "Influencia de la Sal en la Distribución Geográfica de los Grupos Indígenas de México," *Proceedings of the 23rd International Congress of Americanists* (New York: the congress), pp. 93–100.

MERWIN, RAYMOND E., AND GEORGE C. VAILLANT
1932   *The Ruins of Holmul, Guatemala, Memoirs of the Peabody Museum of Archaeology and Ethnology, Harvard University*, vol. 3, no. 2 (Cambridge: the museum).

MICHELS, JOSEPH W.
1969   "Testing Stratigraphy and Artifact Reuse through Obsidian Hydration Dating," *American Antiquity*, vol. 34, no. 1, pp. 15–22.

MILES, SUZANNE W.
1957   *The Sixteenth Century Pokom-Maya, Transactions of the American Philosophical Society*, vol. 47, no. 4 (Philadelphia: the society).

1965   "Summary of Preconquest Ethnology of the Guatemala-Chiapas Highlands and Pacific Slopes," *Archaeology of Southern Mesoamerica, Handbook of Middle American Indians*, vol. 2, ed. by G. R. Willey (Austin: University of Texas Press), pp. 276–87.

MILLER, JAMES G.
1965   "Living Systems Cross-Level Hypotheses," *Behavioral Science*, vol. 10, no. 5, pp. 380–411.

MILLON, RENÉ F.
1954   "Irrigation at Teotihuacan," *American Antiquity*, vol. 20, no. 2, pp. 177–80.

1957   "Irrigation Systems in the Valley of Teotihuacan," *American Antiquity*, vol. 23, no. 2, pp. 160–66.

1967   "Teotihuacan," *Scientific American*, vol. 216, no. 6, pp. 38–48.

1970   "Teotihuacan: Completion of Map of Giant Ancient City in the Valley of Mexico," *Science*, vol. 170, no. 3962, pp. 1077–82.

References

MONTI, FRANCO
1969   *Precolumbian Terracottas* (London and New York: Paul Hamlyn).
MORLEY, SYLVANUS G.
1911   "Ancient Temples and Cities of the New World, Copan, Mother City of the Mayas," *Union Panamericana Bulletin*, vol. 32, no. 5, pp. 863–79.
X 1913   "Excavations at Quirigua, Guatemala," *The National Geographic Magazine*, vol. 24, no. 3, pp. 339–61.
1920   *The Inscriptions of Copan*, Carnegie Institution of Washington Publication, no. 219 (Washington, D.C.: the institution).
1935   *Guide Book to the Ruins of Quirigua*, Carnegie Institution of Washington Supplementary Publication, no. 16 (Washington, D.C.: the institution).
1938   *The Inscriptions of Peten*, Carnegie Institution of Washington Publication, no. 437 (Washington, D.C.: the institution).
1946   *The Ancient Maya* (Stanford: Stanford University Press).
MORLEY, SYLVANUS G., REVISED BY GEORGE W. BRAINERD
1956   *The Ancient Maya*, 3rd Edition (Stanford: Stanford University Press).
MORRIS, EARL H., JEAN CHARLOT, AND ANN AXTELL MORRIS
1931   *The Temple of the Warriors at Chichen Itza, Yucatan*, Carnegie Institution of Washington Publication, no. 406 (Washington, D.C.: the institution).
MORTON, SAMUEL G.
1842   "Verbal Communication on Portions of a Human Skeleton from Ruins of San Francisco, near Ticul, Yucatan," *Proceedings of the Academy of Natural Science*, vol. 1, no. 17, pp. 203–04.
MOSELEY, J. E.
1965   "The Paleopathological Riddle of 'Symmetrical Osteoporosis'," *American Journal of Roentgenology, Radium Therapy and Nuclear Medicine*, vol. 95, pp. 135–42.
NADER, LAURA
1969   "The Zapotec of Oaxaca," *Ethnology, Handbook of Middle American Indians*, vol. 7, ed. by E. Z. Vogt (Austin: University of Texas Press), pp. 329–59.
NAGEL, ERNEST, AND J. R. NEWMAN
1958   *Gödel's Proof*, 2nd Printing (New York: New York University Press).
NASH, JUNE
1964   "The Structuring of Social Relations: An Activity Analysis," *Estudios de Cultura Maya*, vol. 4, pp. 335–59.
NATIONAL RESEARCH COUNCIL
1962   *Tropical Health. A Report on a Study of Needs and Resources. National Academy of Sciences—National Research Council Publication*, no. 9961 (Washington, D.C.: U. S. Government Printing Office).
NEELY, JAMES A.
1967   "Organización Hidráulica y Sistemas de Irrigación Prehistóricos en el Valle de Oaxaca," *Boletín, Instituto Nacional de Antropología e Historia*, no. 27, pp. 15–17.
NICHOLSON, HENRY B.
1962   "The Mesoamerican Pictorial Manuscripts: Research, Past and Present,"

References

Akten des 34 Internationalen Amerikanistenkongresses, vol. 1 (Wien: the congress), pp. 199–215.

1966 "The Problem of the Provenience of the Members of the 'Codex Borgia Group'," *Summa Antropológica en Homenaje a Roberto J. Weitlaner*, ed. by A. Pompa y Pompa (Mexico, D. F.: Instituto Nacional de Antropología e Historia), pp. 145–58.

NOGUERA, EDUARDO

1945 "Exploraciones en Xochicalco," *Cuadernos Americanos*, año 4, no. 1, pp. 119–57.

1954 *La Cerámica Arqueológica de Cholula* (Mexico, D. F.: Editorial Guarania).

ODUM, EUGENE P.

1969 "The Strategy of Ecosystem Development," *Science*, vol. 164, no. 3877, pp. 262–69.

OLIVER DOUGLAS L.

1955 *A Solomon Island Society* (Cambridge: Harvard University Press).

OLSON, GERALD W.

1969 *Descriptions and Data on Soils of Tikal, El Peten, Guatemala, Agronomy Mimeograph, Department of Agronomy, Cornell University*, vol. 69, no. 2 (Ithaca: the department).

PADDOCK, JOHN

1966a "Monte Albán: Sede de Imperio?" *Revista de Estudios Antropológicos*, vol. 20, pp. 117–46.

1966b "Oaxaca in Ancient Mesoamerica," *Ancient Oaxaca*, ed. by J. Paddock (Stanford: Stanford University Press), pp. 83–242.

PADDOCK, JOHN, JOSEPH R. MOGOR, AND MICHAEL D. LIND

1968 "Lambityeco Tomb 2, A Preliminary Report," *Boletín de Estudios Oaxaqueños*, no. 25, pp. 1–24.

PALACIOS, ENRIQUE J.

1937 "Mas Gemas del Arte Maya in Palenque," *Anales del Museo Nacional de Arqueología, Historia y Etnografía*, epoca 5, vol. 2, pp. 193–225.

PALERM, ÁNGEL

1955 "The Agricultural Bases of Urban Civilization in Mesoamerica," *Irrigation Civilizations: A Comparative Study*, ed. by J. Steward (Washington, D.C.: Pan-American Union), pp. 28–42.

1956 "Notas Sobre las Construcciones Militarres y la Guerra en Mesoamerica," *Anales del Instituto Nacional de Antropología e Historia*, vol. 8, no. 37, pp. 123–34.

PALERM, ÁNGEL, AND ERIC R. WOLF

1957 "Ecological Potential and Cultural Development in Mesoamerica," *Pan American Union, Social Science Monographs*, vol. 3, pp. 1–38.

1961 *La Agricultura y el Desarrollo de la Civilización Mesoamérica, Revista Interamericana de Ciencias Sociales*, época 2, vol. 1, no. 2 (Washington, D.C.: Panamerican Union).

PARK, GEORGE K.

1966 "Kinga Priests: the Politics of Pestilence," *Political Anthropology*, ed. by M. J. Swartz, V. W. Turner and A. Tuden (Chicago: Aldine Publishing Company), pp. 229–37.

PARSONS, JEFFREY R.
1968   "Teotihuacan, Mexico, and Its Impact on Regional Demography," *Science*, vol. 162, no. 3856, pp. 872–77.

PARSONS, LEE A.
1966   "Primer Informe sobre las Investigaciones hechas en 'Las Illusiones' (Bilbao), Santa Lucía Cotzumalguapa, Guatemala," *Antropología e Historia de Guatemala*, vol. 18, no. 2, pp. 3–18.
1967   "An Early Maya Stela on the Pacific Coast of Guatemala," *Estudios de Cultura Maya*, vol. 6, pp. 171–98.
1969   *Bilbao, Guatemala, Vol. 2, Milwaukee Public Museum, Publications in Anthropology*, no. 12 (Milwaukee: the museum).

PARSONS, LEE A., STEPHAN F. DE BORHEGYI, PETER JENSEN, AND ROBERT RITZENTHALER
1963   "Excavaciones en Bilbao, Santa Lucía, Cotzumalgualpa, Guatemala: Informe Preliminar," *Antropología e Historia de Guatemala*, vol. 15, no. 1, pp. 3–13.

PARSONS, LEE A., AND BARBARA J. PRICE
✗ 1971   "Mesoamerican Trade and its Role in the Emergence of Civilization," *Observations on the Emergence of Civilization in Mesoamerica*, ed. by R. F. Heizer and J. A. Graham, *Contributions of the University of California Archaeological Research Facility*, no. 11 (Berkeley: the university), pp. 169–95.

PASO Y TRONCOSO, FRANCISCO DEL
1905   *Papeles de Neuva España* (Madrid: Sucesores de Rivadeneyra).

PAVLOVSKY, EVGENY N.
1966   *Natural Nidality of Transmissible Diseases: With Special Reference to the Landscape Epidemiology of Zooanthroponoses* (Urbana: University of Illinois Press).

PENDERGAST, DAVID M.
1967a   "Altun Há, Honduras Británica: Temporadas 1964 y 1965," *Estudios de Cultura Maya*, vol. 6, pp. 149–69.
1967b   "Occupación Post-Clásica en Altun Há, Honduras Británica," *Revista Mexicana de Estudios Antropológicos*, vol. 21, pp. 213–24.
1969a   "An Inscribed Jade Plaque from Altun Ha," *Archaeology*, vol. 22, no. 2, pp. 85–92.
✗ 1969b   *Altun Ha: A Guidebook to the Ancient Maya Ruins* (Belize: The Government of British Honduras).

PIGGOTT, STUART
1950   *Prehistoric India* (Harmondsworth: Penguin Books).

PIÑA, CHÁN, ROMÁN
1955a   *Chalcatzingo, Morelos, Informe de la Dirección de Monumentos Prehispánicos*, no. 4 (Mexico, D. F.: Instituto Nacional de Antropología e Historia).
1955b   *Las Culturas Preclásicas de la Cuenca de México* (Mexico, D. F.: Fondo de Cultura Económica).
1963   "Informe Preliminar sobre Mul-Chic Yucatán," *Anales del Instituto Nacional de Antropología e Historia*, vol. 15, no. 44, pp. 99–118.

526

References

1964 "Algunas Consideraciones Sobre las Pinturas de Mul-Chic, Yucatan, *Estudios de Cultura Maya*, vol. 4, pp. 63–78.

1968 "Exploración del Cenote de Chichén Itzá 1967–68," *Boletín, Instituto Nacional de Antropología e Historia*, no. 32, pp. 1–5.

PIÑA CHÁN, ROMÁN, AND CARLOS NAVARETTE

1967 *Archaeological Research in the Lower Grijalva River Region, Tabasco and Chiapas, Papers of the New World Archeological Foundation, Brigham Young University*, no. 22 (Provo: the foundation).

POLANYI, KARL

1966 *Dahomey and the Slave Trade, American Ethnological Society Monographs*, no. 42 (Seattle: University of Washington Press).

POLANYI, KARL, CONRAD M. ARENSBURG, AND HARRY W. PEARSON (eds.)

1957 *Trade and Market in the Early Empires* (Glencoe: Free Press).

POLLOCK, HARRY E. D.

1952 "Annual Report of the Director of the Department of Archaeology," *Carnegie Institution of Washington Year Book*, no. 51 (Washington, D.C.: the institution), pp. 235–43.

1965 "Architecture of the Maya Lowlands," *Archaeology of Southern Mesoamerica, Handbook of Middle American Indians*, vol. 2, ed. by G. R. Willey (Austin: University of Texas Press), pp. 378–440.

1968 "Brainerd y Ruppert en Xpuhil en 1949," *Estudios de Cultura Maya*, vol. 6, pp. 67–80.

1970 "Architectural Notes on Some Chenes Ruines," *Monographs and Papers in Maya Archaeology*, ed. by W. R. Bullard, *Papers of the Peabody Museum of American Archaeology and Ethnology, Harvard University*, vol. 61 (Cambridge: the museum), pp. 1–87.

POLLOCK, HARRY E., RALPH L. ROYS, TATIANA PROSKOURIAKOFF, AND A. LEDYARD SMITH

1962 *Mayapan, Yucatan, Mexico, Carnegie Institution of Washington Publication*, no. 619 (Washington, D.C.: the institution).

POPPY, JOHN, AND PHILLIP HARRINGTON

1968 "You Dive for Gold and Find Pieces of the Past," *Look*, vol. 32, no. 5, pp. 20–25.

PORTER, MURIEL N.

1953 *Tlatilco and the Preclassic Cultures of the New World, Viking Fund Publications in Anthropology*, no. 19 (New York: Wenner-Gren Foundation for Anthropological Research).

POZAS, RICARDO

1959 *Chamula: Un Pueblo Indio de los Altos de Chiapas, Memorias del Instituto Nacional Indigenista*, vol. 8 (Mexico, D. F.: the institute).

PROSKOURIAKOFF, TATIANA

1950 *A Study of Classic Maya Sculpture, Carnegie Institution of Washington Publication*, no. 593 (Washington, D.C.: the institution).

1951 "Some Non-Classic Traits in the Sculpture of Yucatan," *The Civilizations of Ancient America, Selected Papers of the XXIXth International Congress of Americanists* (Chicago: University of Chicago Press), pp. 108–18.

References

1953   "Scroll Patterns (Entrelaces) of Veracruz," *Revista Mexicana de Estudios Antropológicos*, vol. 13, nos. 2, 3, pp. 389–401.

✕ 1960   "Historical Implications of a Pattern of Dates at Piedras Negras, Guatemala," *American Antiquity*, vol. 25, no. 4, pp. 454–75.

1961   "The Lords of the Maya Realm," *Expedition*, vol. 4, no. 1, pp. 14–21.

1963a   *An Album of Maya Architecture* (Norman: University of Oklahoma Press).

✕ 1963b   "Historical Data in the Inscriptions of Yaxchilan, Part I," *Estudios de Cultura Maya*, vol. 3, pp. 149–66.

✕ 1964   "Historical Data in the Inscriptions of Yaxchilan, Part II," *Estudios de Cultura Maya*, vol. 4, pp. 177–201.

1968   "Olmec and Maya Art: Problems of Their Stylistic Relation," *Dumbarton Oaks Conference on the Olmec*, ed. by E. P. Benson (Washington, D.C.: Dumbarton Oaks Research Library and Collection and Trustees for Harvard University), pp. 119–30.

PROSKOURIAKOFF, TATIANA, AND J. ERIC S. THOMPSON

1947   *Maya Calendar Round Dates such as 9 Ahau 17 Mol, Notes on Middle American Archaeology and Ethnology, Carnegie Institution of Washington*, vol. 3, no. 79 (Washington, D.C.: the institution).

PUIGBÓ, J. J., J. R. NAVE RHODE, H. GARCIA BARRIOS, AND C. G. YÉPEZ

1968   "A 4-year Follow-up Study of a Rural Community with Endemic Chagas' Disease," *Bulletin of the World Health Organization*, vol. 39, no. 3, pp. 341–49.

PULESTON, DENNIS E.

1968   "New Data from Tikal on Classic Maya Subsistence," paper presented at the 33rd Annual Meeting of the Society for American Archaeology, Santa Fe, New Mexico.

1971   "An Experimental Approach to the Function of Maya Chultuns," *American Antiquity*, vol. 36, no. 3, pp. 322–35.

PULESTON, DENNIS, AND CALLENDER, DONALD W., JR.

1967   "Defensive Earthworks at Tikal," *Expedition*, vol. 9, no. 3, pp. 40–48.

PULESTON, DENNIS, AND OLGA S. PULESTON

1971   "An Ecological Approach to the Origins of Maya Civilization," *Archaeology*, vol. 24, no. 4, pp. 330–37.

RAIKES, ROBERT L., AND ROBERT H. DYSON, JR.

1961   "The Prehistoric Climate of Baluchistan and the Indus Valley," *American Anthropologist*, vol. 63, no. 2, pp. 265–81.

RANDS, ROBERT L.

1954   "Artistic Connections between the Chichen Itza Toltec and the Classic Maya," *American Antiquity*, vol. 19, no. 3, pp. 281–82.

1967a   "Cerámica de la Región de Palenque, México," *Estudios de Cultura Maya*, vol. 6, pp. 111–47.

1967b   "Ceramic Technology and Trade in the Palenque Region, Mexico," *American Historical Anthropology: Essays in Honor of Leslie Spier*, ed. by C. L. Riley and W. W. Taylor (Carbondale: Southern Illinois University Press), pp. 137–51.

1969a   "Relationship of Monumental Stone Sculpture of Copan with the Maya

References

Lowlands," *Verhandlungen des XXXVIII Internationalen Amerikanistenkongresses*, vol. 1 (Stuttgart, München: the congress), pp. 515–29.

1969b *Mayan Ecology and Trade: 1967–1968, Research Records of the University Museum, Southern Illinois University, Mesoamerican Studies*, no. 2 (Carbondale: the museum).

RANDS, ROBERT L., AND BARBARA C. RANDS

1957 "The Ceramic Position of Palenque, Chiapas," *American Antiquity*, vol. 23, no. 2, pp. 140–50.

RANDS, ROBERT L., AND ROBERT E. SMITH

1965 "Pottery of the Guatemalan Highlands," *Archaeology of Southern Mesoamerica, Handbook of Middle American Indians*, vol. 2, ed. by G. R. Willey (Austin: University of Texas Press), pp. 95–145.

RAPPAPORT, ROY A.

1967 *Pigs for the Ancestors: Ritual in the Ecology of a New Guinea People* (New Haven: Yale University Press).

RATHJE, WILLIAM L.

1970a "The Daily Grind," paper presented at the 35th Annual Meeting of the Society for American Archaeology, Mexico City.

1970b "Socio-political Implications of Lowland Maya Burials," *World Archaeology*, vol. 1, no. 3, pp. 359–74.

1971a "Lowland Classic Maya Socio-political Organization: Degree and Form in Time and Space," unpublished doctoral dissertation, Harvard University.

1971b "The Origin and Development of Lowland Classic Maya Civilization," *American Antiquity*, vol. 36, no. 3, pp. 275–85.

n. d. "Praise the Gods and Pass the Metates: An Hypothesis of the Development of Lowland Rainforest Civilizations in Mesoamerica," *Contemporary Archaeology*, ed. by M. P. Leone (Carbondale: Southern Illinois University Press).

REICHEL-DOLMATOFF, GERARDO

1961 "The Agricultural Basis of the Sub-Andean Chiefdoms of Colombia," *The Evolution of Horticultural Systems in Native South America: Causes and Consequences*, ed. by J. Wilbert (Caracas: Sociedad de Ciencias Naturales La Salle), pp. 83–100.

REINA, RUBEN E.

1967 "Milpas and Milperos: Implications for Prehistoric Times," *American Anthropologist*, vol. 69, no. 1, pp. 1–20.

REISCHAUER, EDWIN O., AND JOHN K. FAIRBANK

1960 *A History of East Asian Civilization* (Boston: Houghton Mifflin).

RENFREW, COLIN

1969 "Trade and Culture Process in European Prehistory," *Current Anthropology*, vol. 10, no. 2,3, pp. 151–69.

1970 "New Configurations in Old World Archaeology," *World Archaeology*, vol. 2, no. 2, pp. 199–211.

RICKETSON, OLIVER G., JR.

1931 *Excavations at Baking Pot, British Honduras, Contributions to American Anthropology and History*, vol. 1, no. 1, *Carnegie Institution of Washington Publication*, no. 403 (Washington, D.C.: the institution).

References

RICKETSON, OLIVER G., AND EDITH B. RICKETSON
1937   *Uaxactun, Guatemala, Group E 1926–1937*, Carnegie Institution of *Washington Publication*, no. 477 (Washington, D.C.: the institution).

ROBERTSON, DONALD
1963   *Pre-columbian Architecture* (New York: George Braziller).
1970   "The Tulum Murals: The International Style of the Late Post-Classic," *Verhandlungen des XXXVIII Internationalen Amerikanistenkongresses*, vol. 2 (Stuttgart, München: the congress), pp. 77–88.

ROUSE, IRVING
1962   "The Intermediate Area, Amazonia and the Caribbean Area," *Courses Toward Urban Life*, ed. by R. J. Braidwood and G. R. Willey (Chicago: Aldine Publishing Company), pp. 34–59.

ROWE, JOHN H.
1962   *Chavin Art, an Inquiry into its Form and Meaning* (New York: The Museum of Primitive Art and University Publishers).

ROYS, RALPH L.
1943   *The Indian Background of Colonial Yucatan*, Carnegie Institution of *Washington Publication*, no. 548 (Washington, D.C.: the institution).
1957   *The Political Geography of the Yucatan Maya*, Carnegie Institution of *Washington Publication*, no. 613 (Washington, D.C.: the institution).
1962   "Literary Sources for the History of Mayapan," *Mayapan, Yucatan, Mexico*, by H. E. D. Pollock *et al*, Carnegie Institution of Washington Publication, no. 619 (Washington, D.C.: the institution), pp. 27–86.
1965   "Lowland Maya Native Society at Spanish Contact," *Archaeology of Southern MesoAmerica, Handbook of Middle American Indians*, vol. 3, ed. by G. R. Willey (Austin: the University of Texas Press), pp. 659–78.
1967   *The Book of Chilam Balam of Chumayel*, New Edition (Norman: University of Oklahoma Press).

RUMNEY, GEORGE R.
1968   *Climatology and the World's Climates* (London: Macmillan).

RUPPERT, KARL, J. ERIC S. THOMPSON, AND TATIANA PROSKOURIAKOFF
1955   *Bonampak, Chiapas, Mexico*, Carnegie Institution of Washington Publication, no. 602 (Washington, D.C.: the institution).

RUZ LHUILLER, ALBERTO
1945   *Campeche en la Arqueología Maya, Acta Antropológica*, época 1, vol. 1, nos. 2 and 3 (Mexico, D. F.: Sociedad de Alumnos, Escuela Nacional de Antropología e Historia).
1952a   "Exploraciones en Palenque," *Proceedings of the Thirtieth International Congress of Americanists* (Cambridge: the congress), pp. 5–22.
1952b   "Investigaciones en Palenque," *Cuadernos Americanos*, vol. 11, no. 6, pp. 149–65.
1952c   "Exploraciones Arqueológicas en Palenque: 1949," *Anales del Instituto Nacional de Antropología e Historia*, vol. 4, no. 32, pp. 49–60.
1952d   "Exploraciones en Palenque: 1950," *Anales del Instituto Nacional de Antropología e Historia*, vol. 5, no. 33, pp. 25–45.
1952e   "Exploraciones en Palenque: 1951," *Anales del Instituto Nacional de Antropología e Historia*, vol. 5, no. 33, pp. 47–65.

530

References

1953 "Presencia Atlántica en Palenque," *Revista Mexicana de Estudios Antropológicos*, vol. 13, nos. 2, 3, pp. 455–62.

1954 "Exploraciones en Palenque: 1952," *Anales del Instituto Nacional de Antropología e Historia*, vol. 6, no. 34, pp. 79–110.

1955 "Exploraciones en Palenque: 1952," *Anales del Instituto Nacional de Antropología e Historia*, vol. 6, no. 34, pp. 79–106.

1958a "Exploraciones Arqueológicas en Palenque: 1953," *Anales del Instituto Nacional de Antropología e Historica*, vol. 10, no. 39, pp. 69–116.

1958b "Exploraciones Arqueológicas en Palenque: 1954," *Anales del Instituto Nacional de Antropología e Historia*, vol. 10, no. 39, pp. 117–84.

1958c "Exploraciones Arqueológicas en Palenque: 1955," *Anales del Instituto Nacional de Antropología e Historia*, vol. 10, no. 39, pp. 185–240.

1958d "Exploraciones Arqueológicas en Palenque: 1956," *Anales del Instituto Nacional de Antropología e Historia*, vol. 10, no. 39, pp. 241–99.

1969 *La Costa de Campeche en los Tiempos Prehispanicos, Instituto Nacional de Antropología e Historia, Serie Investigaciones*, no. 18 (Mexico, D. F.: the institute).

SABLOFF, JEREMY A.

1969 "The Classic Ceramics of Seibal, Peten, Guatemala," unpublished doctoral dissertation, Harvard University.

1970 "Type Descriptions of the Fine Paste Ceramics of the Bayal Boca Complex, Seibal, Peten, Guatemala," *Monographs and Papers in Maya Archaeology*, ed. by W. R. Bullard, *Papers of the Peabody Museum of American Archaeology and Ethnology, Harvard University*, vol. 61 (Cambridge: the museum), pp. 357–404.

1971a "The Collapse of Classic Maya Civilization," *The Patient Earth*, ed. by J. Harte and R. Socolow (New York: Holt, Rinehart and Winston), pp. 16–27.

1971b "Review of *Maya History and Religion*," by J. E. S. Thompson, *American Anthropologist*, vol. 73, no. 4, pp. 915–17.

SABLOFF, JEREMY A., AND GORDON R. WILLEY

1967 "The Collapse of Maya Civilization in the Southern Lowlands: A Consideration of History and Process," *Southwestern Journal of Anthropology*, vol. 23, no. 4, pp. 311–36.

SÁENZ, CÉSAR A.

1963 "Exploraciones en la Pirámide de las Serpientes Emplumadas, Xochicalco, Morelos," *Revista Mexicana de Estudios Antropológicos*, vol. 19, pp. 7–25.

1968 "Exploraciones y Restoraciones en Yucatán," *Boletín, Instituto Nacional de Antropología e Historia*, no. 31, pp. 17–23.

1969 "Exploraciones y Restauraciones en Uxmal, Yucatán," *Boletín, Instituto Nacional de Anthropología e Historia*, no. 36, pp. 5–13.

SAHLINS, MARSHALL D.

1958 *Social Stratification in Polynesia* (Seattle: University of Washington Press).

1962 *Moala: Culture and Nature on a Fijian Island* (Ann Arbor: University of Michigan Press).

1963 "Poor Man, Rich Man, Big Man, Chief: Political Types in Melanesia

References

and Polynesia," *Comparative Studies in Society and History*, vol. 5, no. 3, pp. 285–303.

SANDERS, WILLIAM T.

1953 "The Anthropogeography of Central Veracruz," *Revista Mexicana de Estudios Antropológicos*, vol. 13, nos. 2, 3, pp. 27–78.

1957 "Tierra y Agua (Soil and Water): A Study of the Ecological Factors in the Development of Mesoamerican Civilizations," unpublished doctoral dissertation, Harvard University.

1960 *Prehistoric Ceramics and Settlement Patterns in Quitana Roo, Mexico, Contributions to American Anthropology and History*, vol. 12, no. 60, Carnegie Institution of Washington Publication, no. 606 (Washington, D.C.: the institution).

1962 "Cultural Ecology of the Maya Lowlands, Part I," *Estudios de Cultura Maya*, vol. 2, pp. 79–121.

1963 "Cultural Ecology of the Maya Lowlands, Part II," *Estudios de Cultura Maya*, vol. 3, pp. 203–41.

1965 *Cultural Ecology of the Teotihuacan Valley* (University Park: Pennsylvania State University).

1971 *The Population of the Teotihuacan Valley, The Basin of Mexico and the Central Mexican Symbiotic Region in the 16th Century, The Pennsylvania State University Teotihuacan Valley Project, Final Report*, vol. 1 (University Park: Pennsylvania State University).

SANDERS, WILLIAM T., AND JOSEPH W. MICHELS

1969 *The Pennsylvania State University Kaminaljuyu Project—1968 Season, Part I—The Excavations, Pennsylvania State University, Department of Anthropology Occasional Papers in Anthropology*, no. 2 (University Park: the department).

SANDERS, WILLIAM T., AND BARBARA J. PRICE

1968 *Mesoamerica: The Evolution of a Civilization* (New York: Random House).

SATTERTHWAITE, LINTON

1936 "Notes on the work of the 4th and 5th University Museum Expeditions to Piedras Negras, Peten, Guatemala," *Maya Research*, vol. 3, pp. 74–91.

1943 *Introduction, Piedras Negras Archaeology: Architecture*, Part 1, no. 1 (Philadelphia: University Museum).

1943–54 *Piedras Negras Archaeology: Architecture*, 6 parts (Philadelphia: University Museum).

1951 "Reconnaissance in British Honduras," *University Museum Bulletin, University of Pennsylvania*, vol. 16, no. 1, pp. 21–37.

1956 "Maya Dates on Stelae in Tikal Enclosures," *University Museum Bulletin, University of Pennsylvania*, vol. 20, no. 4, pp. 24–40.

1958a *The Problem of Abnormal Stela Placements at Tikal and Elsewhere. Tikal Reports*, no. 3, *Museum Monographs, University Museum, University of Pennsylvania* (Philadelphia: the museum).

1958b *Five Newly Discovered Monuments at Tikal and New Data on Four Others, Tikal Reports*, no. 4, *Museum Monographs, University Museum, University of Pennsylvania* (Philadelphia: the museum).

1964 "Dates in a New Maya Hieroglyphic Text as Katun-Baktun Anniversaries," *Estudios de Cultura Maya*, vol. 4, pp. 203–22.

References

1965   "Calendrics of the Maya Lowlands," *Archaeology of Southern Mesoamerica, Handbook of Middle American Indians*, vol. 3, ed. by G. R. Willey (Austin: University of Texas Press), pp. 603–31.

SATTERTHWAITE, LINTON, AND WILLIAM R. COE
1968   "The Maya-Christian Calendrical Correlation and the Archeology of the Peten," *XXXVII Congreso Internacional de Americanistas*, vol. 3 (Buenos Aires: the congress), pp. 3–21.

SATTERTHWAITE, LINTON, AND ELIZABETH K. RALPH
1960   "New Radiocarbon Dates and the Maya Correlation Problem," *American Antiquity*, vol. 26, no. 2, pp. 165–84.

SAUER, CARL O.
1966   *The Early Spanish Main* (Berkeley and Los Angeles: University of California Press).

SAUL, FRANK P.
1967a   "Osteobiography of the Lowland Maya of Altar de Sacrificios, Guatemala," *American Journal of Physical Anthropology*, vol. 27, no. 2, p. 237 (abstract).
1967b   "Osteobiography and the Interpretation of Maya History," paper presented at the 66th Annual Meeting of the American Anthropological Association, Washington, D.C.
1968   "Toward a Biological Definition of the Maya," *Bulletins of the American Anthropological Association*, vol. 1, no. 3, pp. 123–24 (abstract).
n. d.   *The Human Skeletal Remains from Altar de Sacrificios, Guatemala, Papers of the Peabody Museum of American Archaeology and Ethnology, Harvard University* (Cambridge: the museum). In preparation.

SAUL, FRANK P., AND DONALD M. AUSTIN
1970   "Dental Characteristics of the Ancient Lowland Maya," *Bulletins of the American Anthropological Association*, vol. 3, no. 3, p. 100 (abstract).

SAYRE, EDWARD V., LUI-HEUNG CHAN, AND JEREMY A. SABLOFF
1971   "High-Resolution Gamma Ray Spectroscopic Analyses of Fine Orange Pottery," *Science and Archaeology*, ed. by R. H. Brill, pp. 165–81 (Cambridge and London: MIT Press).

SCHAPERA, ISAAC
1967   *Government and Politics in Tribal Societies* (New York: Schocken Books).

SCHOLES, FRANCE V., AND RALPH L. ROYS
1948   *The Maya Chontal Indians of Acalan-Tixchel, Carnegie Institution of Washington Publication*, no. 560 (Washington, D.C.: the institution).
1968   *The Maya Chontal Indians of Acalan-Tixchel*, 2nd Edition (Norman: University of Oklahoma Press).

SCRIMSHAW, NEVIN S., MOISÉS BÉHAR, MIGUEL A GUZMÁN, AND JOHN E. GORDON
1969   "Nutrition and Infection Field Study in Guatemalan Villages, 1959–1964," *Archives of Environmental Health*, vol. 18, no. 1, pp. 51–62.

SCRIMSHAW, NEVIN S., C. E. TAYLOR, AND JOHN E. GORDON
1968   *Interactions of Nutrition and Infection, World Health Organization, World Health Monographs*, no. 57 (Geneva: the organization).

References

SELER, EDWARD

1904a "Antiquities of Guatemala," *Mexican and Central American Antiquities, Calendar Systems and History*, ed. by C. P. Bowditch, *Bureau of American Ethnology Bulletin*, no. 28 (Washington, D.C.: U.S. Government Printing Office), pp. 75–121.

1904b "Wall Paintings of Mitla, a Mexican Picture Writing in Fresco," *Mexican and Central American Antiquities, Calendar Systems and History*, edited by C. P. Bowditch, *Bureau of American Ethnology Bulletin*, no. 28 (Washington, D.C.: U.S. Government Printing Office), pp. 243–324.

1904c "The Vase of Chama," *Mexican and Central American Antiquities, Calendar Systems and History*, ed. by C. P. Bowditch, *Bureau of American Ethnology Bulletin*, no. 28 (Washington, D.C.: U.S. Government Printing Office), pp. 651–64.

SERVICE, ELMAN R.

1962 *Primitive Social Organization* (New York: Random House).

1968 "The Prime-mover of Cultural Evolution," *Southwestern Journal of Anthropology*, vol. 24, no. 4, pp. 396–409.

SHANNON, CLAUDE E., AND W. WEAVER

1949 *The Mathematical Theory of Communication* (Urbana: University of Illinois Press).

SHARER, ROBERT J.

1968 "New Archaeological Research at Chalchuapa, El Salvador," paper presented at the 67th Annual Meeting of the American Anthropological Association, Seattle, Washington.

1969 "Archaeological Excavation at Chalchuapa, El Salvador: the 1969 Season," paper presented at the 68th Annual Meeting of the American Anthropological Association, New Orleans, Louisiana.

SHARER, ROBERT J., AND JAMES C. GIFFORD

1970 "Preclassic Ceramics from Chalchuapa, El Salvador, and Their Relationships with the Maya Lowlands," *American Antiquity*, vol. 35, no. 4, pp. 441–62.

SHARP, ROSEMARY

1970 "Early Architectural Grecas in the Valley of Oaxaca," *Boletín de Estudios Oaxaqueños*, no. 32, pp. 2–12.

SHATTUCK, GEORGE C.

1938 *A Medical Survey of the Republic of Guatemala, Carnegie Institution of Washington Publication*, no. 499 (Washington, D.C.: the institution).

SHATTUCK, GEORGE C., JOSEPH C. BEQUAERT, AND FRANCIS G. BENEDICT

1933 *The Peninsula of Yucatan: Medical, Biological and Sociological Studies, Carnegie Institution of Washington Publication*, no. 431 (Washington, D.C.: the institution).

SHEPARD, ANNA O.

1948 *Plumbate, a Mesoamerican Trade Ware, Carnegie Institution of Washington Publication*, no. 573 (Washington, D.C.: the institution).

SHIMKIN, DEMITRI B.

1955 "The Economy of a Trapping Center: The Case of Fort Yukon, Alaska," *Economic Development and Cultural Change*, vol. 3, no. 3, pp. 219–40.

References

1964 "National Forces and Ecological Adaptations in the Development of Russian Peasant Societies," *Process and Pattern in Culture*, ed. by R. A. Manners (Chicago: Aldine Publishing Co.), pp. 237–47.

1966 "Adaptive Strategies: A Basic Problem in Human Ecology," *Three Papers on Human Ecology, Mills College Assembly Series, 1965–1966* (Oakland, California: the college), pp. 37–52.

1967 "Pre-Islamic Central Asia," *Canadian Slavic Studies*, vol. 1, no. 4, pp. 618–39.

SHOOK, EDWIN M.
1951a "Guatemala," *Carnegie Institution of Washington, Year Book*, no. 50 (Washington, D.C.: the institution), pp. 240–41.

1951b "The Present Status of Research on the Preclassic Horizons in Guatemala," *The Civilizations of Ancient America: Selected Papers of the 29th International Congress of Americanists*, ed. by Sol Tax (Chicago: University of Chicago Press), pp. 93–100.

1958 "The Temple of the Red Stela," *Expedition*, vol. 1, no. 1, pp. 27–33.

SHOOK, EDWIN M., AND A. V. KIDDER
1952 *Mound E-III-3, Kaminaljuyu, Guatemala, Contributions to American Anthropology and History*, vol. 9, no. 53, *Carnegie Institution of Washington Publication*, no. 596 (Washington, D.C.: the institution).

SIMMONS, CHARLES S., JOSÉ MANUEL TARANO T., AND JOSÉ HUMBERTO PINTO Z.
1959 *Clasificación de Reconocimiento de los Suelos de la Republica de Guatemala* (Guatemala: Editorial del Ministerio de Educación Publica).

SISSON, EDWARD B.
1967 "Late Classic Socio-political Organization in the Southern Maya Lowlands," seminar paper, Peabody Museum, Harvard University.

1970 "Settlement Patterns and Land Use in the Northwestern Chontalpa, Tabasco, Mexico: A Progress Report," *Ceramica de Cultura Maya*, no. 6, pp. 41–54.

SMITH, A. LEDYARD
1937 *Structure A-XVIII, Uaxactun, Contributions to American Anthropology and History*, vol. 4, no. 20, *Carnegie Institution of Washington Publication*, no. 483 (Washington, D.C.: the institution).

1950 *Uaxactun, Guatemala: Excavations of 1931–1937, Carnegie Institution of Washington Publication*, no. 588 (Washington, D.C.: the institution).

1955 *Archaeological Reconnaissance in Central Guatemala, Carnegie Institution of Washington Publication*, no. 608 (Washington, D.C.: the institution).

1968 "Reconstruction at the Maya Ruins of Seibal," *Monumentum*, vol. 2, pp. 82–96.

n. d. *The Architecture, Burials and Caches of Seibal, Guatemala, Papers of the Peabody Museum of Archaeology and Ethnology, Harvard University* (Cambridge: the museum), in preparation.

SMITH, A. LEDYARD, AND ALFRED V. KIDDER
1951 *Excavations at Nebaj, Guatemala, Carnegie Institution of Washington Publication*, no. 594 (Washington, D.C.: the institution).

SMITH, A. LEDYARD, AND GORDON R. WILLEY
1966a "The Harvard Explorations at Seibal, Department of Peten, Guatemala:

the 1964 Season," *XXXVI Congreso Internacional de Americanistas*, vol. 1 (Sevilla: the congress), pp. 385–88.

1966b "Ceibal, 1965: Segundo Informe Preliminar," *Antropología e Historia de Guatemala*, vol. 18, no. 2, pp. 71–80.

1970 "Seibal, Guatemala in 1968: A Brief Summary of Archaeological Results," Verhandlungen des XXXVIII Internationalen Amerikanistenkongresses, vol. 1 (Stuttgart, München: the congress), pp. 151–58.

SMITH, ROBERT E.

1937 *A Study of Structure A-1 Complex at Uaxactun, Contributions to American Anthropology and History*, vol. 3, no. 19, *Carnegie Institution of Washington Publication*, no. 456 (Washington, D.C.: the institution).

1955 *Ceramic Sequence at Uaxactun, Guatemala, Middle American Research Institute, Tulane University Publication*, no. 20 (New Orleans: the institute).

1958 "The Place of Fine Orange Pottery in Mesoamerican Archaeology," *American Antiquity*, vol. 24, no. 2, pp. 151–60.

1971 *The Pottery of Mayapan, Papers of the Peabody Museum of Archaeology and Ethnology, Harvard University*, vol. 66 (Cambridge: the museum)

SMITH, ROBERT E., AND JAMES C. GIFFORD

1966 "Maya Ceramic Varieties, Types and Wares at Uaxactun: Supplement to 'Ceramic Sequence at Uaxactun'," *Middle American Research Reports*, vol. 4, *Middle American Research Institute, Tulane University Publication*, no. 28 (New Orleans: the institute), pp. 125–74.

SNOW, CHARLES E.

1948 *Indian Knoll Skeletons of Site Ch. 2, University of Kentucky Reports in Anthropology*, vol. 4, no. 3, part 2 (Lexington, Kentucky: the university).

SNOW, DEAN R.

1969 "Ceramic Sequence and Settlement Location in Pre-hispanic Tlaxcala," *American Antiquity*, vol. 34, no. 2, pp. 131–45.

SPENCE, MICHAEL W.

1966 "Los Talleres de Obsidiana de Teotihuacán," paper presented at the 11th Mesa Redonda of the Sociedad Mexicana de Antropología, Mexico City.

SPINDEN, ELLEN S.

1933 "The Place of Tajin in Totonac Archaeology," *American Anthropologist*, vol. 35, no. 2, pp. 225–70.

SPINDEN, HERBERT J.

1913 *A Study of Maya Art: Its Subject Matter and Historical Development, Memoirs of the Peabody Museum of Archaeology and Ethnology, Harvard University*, vol. 6 (Cambridge: the museum).

1916 "Portraiture in Central American Art," *Holmes Anniversary Volume*, ed. by F. W. Hodge (Washington: J. W. Bryan), pp. 434–50.

1928 *The Ancient Civilizations of Mexico and Central America, American Museum of Natural History, Handbook Series*, no. 3 (New York: the museum).

1957 *Maya Art and Civilization* (Indian Hills, Colorado: Falcon's Wing Press).

STAMP, L. DUDLEY

1938 *Asia: A Regional and Economic Geography* (New York: E. P. Dutton).

References

1955   *Africa, A Study in Tropical Development* (New York: John Wiley and Sons).

STEGGERDA, MORRIS
1932   *Anthropometry of Adult Maya Indians, Carnegie Institution of Washington Publication*, no. 434 (Washington, D.C.: the institution).
1941   *Maya Indians of Yucatan, Carnegie Institution of Washington Publication*, no. 531 (Washington, D.C.: the institution).

STEVENS, R. L.
1964   "The Soils of Middle America and Their Relation to Indian Peoples and Cultures," *Natural Environment and Early Civilizations, Handbook of Middle American Indians*, vol. 1, ed. by R. C. West (Austin: University of Texas Press), pp. 265–315.

STEWARD, JULIAN H.
1955   *Theory of Culture Change* (Urbana: University of Illinois Press).

STEWART, THOMAS D.
1953   "The Skeletal Remains from Zaculeu," *The Ruins of Zaculeu* by R. B. Woodbury and A. S. Trik (Boston: United Fruit Company), pp. 295–311.

STIRLING, MATHEW W.
1943   *Stone Monuments of Southern Mexico, Bureau of American Ethnology Bulletin*, no. 138 (Washington, D.C.: U. S. Government Printing Office).

STREBEL, HERMANN
1885–1889   *Alt-Mexiko; Archaologische Beitrage Zur Kulturgeschichte Seiner Bewohner* (Hamburg and Leipzig: Leopold Voss).

STROMSVIK, GUSTAV
1937   *Notes on the Metates from Calakmul, Campeche, and from the Mercado, Chichen Itza, Yucatan, Contributions to American Anthropology and History*, vol. 3, no. 16, *Carnegie Institution of Washington Publication*, no. 456 (Washington, D.C.: the institution).

SWANTON, JOHN R.
1946   *The Indians of the Southeastern United States, Bureau of American Ethnology Bulletin*, no. 137 (Washington, D.C.: U. S. Government Printing Office).

SWEENEY, EDWARD A., JORGE CABRERA, JUÁN URRUTIA, AND LEONARDO MATA
1969   "Factors Associated with Linear Hypoplasia of Human Deciduous Incisors," *Journal of Dental Research*, vol. 48, no. 6, pp. 1275–79.

TAMAYO, JORGE L. in collaboration with ROBERT C. WEST
1964   "The Hydrography of Middle America," *Natural Environment and Early Cultures, Handbook of Middle American Indians*, vol. 1, ed. by R. C. West (Austin: University of Texas Press), pp. 84–121.

THOMPSON, J. ERIC S.
1938   "Sixteenth and Seventeenth Century Reports on the Chol Mayas," *American Anthropologist*, vol. 40, no. 4, pp. 584–604.
1939   *Excavations at San Jose, British Honduras, Carnegie Institution of Washington Publication*, no. 506 (Washington, D.C.: the institution).

References

1940   *Late Ceramic Horizons at Benque Viejo, British Honduras, Contributions to American Anthropology and History*, vol. 7, no. 35, Carnegie Institution of Washington Publication, no. 528 (Washington, D.C.: the institution).

1951   "The Itza of Tayasal, Peten," *Homenaje al Doctor Alfonso Caso*, ed. by J. Comas et al (Mexico, D. F.: Imprenta Nueva), pp. 389–400.

1952   *The Introduction of the Puuc Style of Dating at Yaxchilan, Notes on Middle American Archaeology and Ethnology, Carnegie Institution of Washington*, vol. 4, no. 110 (Washington, D.C.: the institution).

1954   *The Rise and Fall of Maya Civilization* (Norman: University of Oklahoma Press).

1957   *Deities Portrayed on Censors at Mayapan, Carnegie Institution of Washington, Current Reports*, vol. 2, no. 40 (Washington, D.C.; the institution).

1962   *A Catalog of Maya Hieroglyphs* (Norman: University of Oklahoma Press).

1964   "Trade Relations Between the Maya Highlands and Lowlands," *Estudios de Cultura Maya*, vol. 4, pp. 13–49.

1965a   "Archaeological Synthesis of the Southern Maya Lowlands," *Archaeology of Southern Mesoamerica, Handbook of Middle American Indians*, vol. 2, ed. by G. R. Willey (Austin: University of Texas Press), pp. 331–59.

1965b   "A Copper Ornament and a Stone Mask from Middle America," *American Antiquity*, vol. 30, no. 3, pp. 343–45.

1966a   "Maya Hieroglyphs of the Bat as Metaphorgrams," *Man*, n.s., vol. 1, no. 2, pp. 176–84.

1966b   "Merchant Gods of Middle America," *Summa Anthropológica en Homenaje a Roberto J. Weitlaner*, ed. by A. Pompa y Pompa (Mexico, D. F.: Instituto Nacional de Antropología e Historia), pp. 159–72.

1966c   *The Rise and Fall of Maya Civilization*, 2nd Edition (Norman: University of Oklahoma Press).

1967   "The Maya Central Area at the Spanish Conquest and Later: A Problem in Demography," *Proceedings of the Royal Anthropological Institute of Great Britain and Ireland for 1966*, pp. 23–37.

1970   *Maya History and Religion* (Norman: University of Oklahoma Press).

1971   "Estimates of Maya Population: Deranging Factors," *American Antiquity*, vol. 36, no. 2, pp. 214–16.

THOMPSON, RAYMOND H.

1958   *Modern Yucatecan Maya Pottery Making, Memoirs of the Society for American Archaeology*, no. 15 (Salt Lake City: the society).

1962   "Un Espejo de Pirita con Respaldo Tallado de Uayma, Yucatán," *Estudios de Cultura Maya*, vol. 2, pp. 239–49.

TOLSTOY, PAUL, AND LOUISE I. PARADIS

1970   "Early and Middle Preclassic Culture in the Basin of Mexico," *Science*, vol. 167, no. 3917, pp. 344–51.

TORQUEMADA, JUAN DE

1964   *Monarchía Indiana*, 3rd Edition (Mexico, D. F.: Editorial Sálvador Chávez Hayhoe).

TOURTELLOT, GAIR

1970   "The Peripheries of Seibal: An Interim Report," *Monographs and Papers*

538

References

in *Maya Archaeology*, ed. by W. R. Bullard, *Papers of the Peabody Museum of American Archaeology and Ethnology, Harvard University*, vol. 61 (Cambridge: the museum), pp. 405–15.

n. d. "The Archaeology of Seibal, Peten, Guatemala: Peripheral Survey and Excavations," unpublished doctoral dissertation, Harvard University (in preparation).

TOURTELLOT, GAIR, AND JEREMY A. SABLOFF

1972 "Exchange Systems Among the Ancient Maya," *American Antiquity*, vol. 37, no. 1, pp. 126–35.

TOWNSEND, WILLIAM H.

1969 "Stone and Steel Tool Use in a New Guinea Society," *Ethnology*, vol. 8, no. 2, pp. 199–205.

TOZZER, ALFRED M.

1907 *A Comparative Study of the Mayas and the Lacandones* (New York: Macmillan).

1921 *Excavation of a Site at Santiago Ahuizotla, D. F., Mexico, Bureau of American Ethnology Bulletin*, no. 74 (Washington, D.C.: U. S. Government Printing Office).

1941 (editor) *Landa's Relación de las Cosas de Yucatan, Papers of the Peabody Museum of Archaeology and Ethnology, Harvard University*, vol. 18 (Cambridge: the museum).

1957 *Chichen Itza and Its Cenote of Sacrifice; A Comparative Study of Contemporaneous Maya and Toltec, Memoirs of the Peabody Museum of Archaeology and Ethnology, Harvard University*, vols. 11 and 12 (Cambridge: the museum).

TRIGGER, BRUCE

1971 "Archaeology and Ecology," *World Archaeology*, vol. 2, no. 3, pp. 321–36.

TROTTER, MILDRED, AND GOLDINE C. GLESER

1958 "A Reevaluation of estimation of stature based on measurements of stature taken during life and of long bones after death," *American Journal of Physical Anthropology*, vol. 16, no. 1, pp. 79–123.

TURNER, VICTOR W.

1966 "Ritual Aspects of Conflict Control of African Micro-Politics," *Political Anthropology*, ed. by M. J. Swartz, V. W. Turner and A. Tuden (Chicago: Aldine Publishing Company), pp. 239–46.

VAILLANT, GEORGE C.

1927 "The Chronological Significance of Maya Ceramics," doctoral dissertation, Harvard University (reprinted as *Archives of Archaeology, Microcard Publication*, no. 12, Madison: Society for American Archaeology and University of Wisconsin Press).

1938 "A Correlation of Archaeological and Historical Sequences in the Valley of Mexico," *American Anthropologist*, vol. 40, no. 4, pp. 535–73.

VAYDA, ANDREW P.

1956 "Maori Conquests in Relation to the New Zealand Environment," *Journal of the Polynesian Society*, vol. 65, no. 3, pp. 204–11.

1961 "Expansion and Warfare Among Swidden Agriculturalists," *American Anthropologist*, vol. 63, no. 2, pp. 346–58.

VERMEER, DONALD E.
1970 "Population Pressure and Crop Rotational Changes among the Tiv in Nigeria," *Annals of the Association of American Geographers*, vol. 60, no. 2, pp. 299–314.

VILLA ROJAS, ALFONSO
1945 *The Maya of East Central Quintana Roo, Carnegie Institution of Washington Publication*, no. 559 (Washington, D.C.: the institution).

VIVÓ ESCOTO, JORGE A.
1964 "Weather and Climate of Mexico and Central America," *Natural Environment and Early Cultures, Handbook of Middle American Indians*, vol. 1, ed. by R. C. West (Austin: University of Texas Press), pp. 187–215.

VOGT, EVON Z.
1961 "Some Aspects of Zinacantan Settlement Patterns and Ceremonial Organization," *Estudios de Cultura Maya*, vol. 1, pp. 131–45.

1964a "Ancient Maya and Contemporary Tzotzil Cosmology," *American Antiquity*, vol. 30, no. 2, pp. 192–95.

1964b "The Genetic Model and Maya Cultural Development," *Desarrollo Cultural de los Mayas*, ed. by E. Z. Vogt and A. Ruz (Mexico, D. F.: Universidad Autónoma de México), pp. 9–48.

1964c "Some Implications of Zinacantan Social Structure for the Study of the Ancient Maya," *Actas y Memorias del XXXV Congreso Internacional de Americanistas*, vol. 1 (Mexico, D. F.: the congress), pp. 307–19.

VOGT, EVON Z., AND FRANK CANCIAN
1970 "Social Integration and the Classic Maya: Some Problems in Haviland's Argument," *American Antiquity*, vol. 35, no. 1, pp. 101–02.

VOGT, EVON Z., AND ALBERTO RUZ (EDS.)
1964 *Desarrollo Cultural de los Mayas* (Mexico, D. F.: Universidad Autónoma de México).

VON NEUMANN, JOHN, AND OSCAR MORGENSTERN
1947 *Theory of Games and Economic Behavior*, 2nd Edition (Princeton: Princeton University Press).

VON WINNING, HASSO
1965 "Relief-Decorated Pottery from Central Veracruz, Mexico," *Ethnos*, vol. 30, pp. 105–35.

1968 *Pre-Columbian Art of Mexico and Central America* (New York: H.N. Abrams).

VON WISSMANN, HERMAN, H. POECH, G. SMOLLA, AND F. KUSSMAUL
1956 "On the Role of Nature and Man in Changing the Face of the Dry Belt of Asia," *Man's Role in Changing the Face of the Earth*, ed. by W. L. Thomas (Chicago: University of Chicago Press), pp. 278–303.

WAGNER, HELMUTH O.
1969 "Subsistence Potential and Population Density of the Maya on the Yucatan Peninsula and Causes for the Decline in Population in the Fifteenth Century," *Verhandlungen des XXXVIII Internationalen Amerikanistenkongresses*, vol. 1 (Stuttgart, Müchen: the congress), pp. 179–96.

References

WAGNER, PHILIP L.

1964 "Natural Vegetation of Middle America," *Natural Environment and Early Cultures, Handbook of Middle American Indians,* vol. 1, ed. by R. C. West (Austin: University of Texas Press), pp. 215–64.

WALES, HORACE G. Q.

1965 *Angkor and Rome. A Historical Comparison* (London: Bernard Quaritch).

WALKER, J.

n. d. "A Study of the Rainfall of Mexico," unpublished master's thesis, Louisiana State University.

WAUCHOPE, ROBERT

1934 *House Mounds of Uaxactun, Guatemala, Contributions to American Anthropology and History,* vol. 2, no. 7, *Carnegie Institution of Washington Publication,* no. 436 (Washington, D.C.: the institution).

WEBB, MALCOLM C.

1964 "The Post-Classic Decline of the Peten Maya: an Interpretation in the Light of a General Theory of State Society," unpublished doctoral dissertation, University of Michigan.

1965 "The Abolition of the Taboo System in Hawaii," *Journal of the Polynesian Society,* vol. 74, no. 1, pp. 21–39.

1968 "Carneiro's Hypothesis of Limited Land Resources and the Origins of the State: a Latin Americanist's Approach to an Old Problem," *South Eastern Latin Americanist,* vol. 12, no. 3, pp. 1–8.

1969 "The Role of Environment and of Environmental Determinism in Modern Cultural Evolutionism," *Human Mosaic,* vol. 3, pp. 97–111.

WEST, MICHAEL

1965 "Transition from Preclassic to Classic at Teotihuacan," *American Antiquity,* vol. 31, no. 2, pp. 193–202.

WEST, ROBERT C., AND JOHN P. AUGELLI

1966 *Middle America, Its Land and Peoples* (Englewood Cliffs, N.J.: Prentice-Hall).

WHEELER, MORTIMER

1966 *Civilizations of the Indus Valley and Beyond* (New York: McGraw-Hill).

WHITE, LYNN

1963 "What Accelerated Technological Progress in the Western Middle Ages?", *Scientific Change,* ed. by A. C. Crombie (New York: Basic Books), pp. 272–91.

WIESENFELD, STEPHEN L.

1969 "Sickle-cell Trait in Human Biological and Cultural Evolution," *Environment and Cultural Behavior,* ed. by A. P. Vayda (Garden City, N.Y.: Natural History Press), pp. 308–31.

WILLEY, GORDON R.

1953 *Prehistoric Settlement Patterns in the Viru Valley, Peru, Bureau of American Ethnology Bulletin,* no. 155 (Washington, D.C.: U. S. Government Printing Office).

1955 "The Interrelated Rise of the Native Cultures of Middle and South America," *New Interpretations of Aboriginal American History: 76th Anniversary of the Anthropological Society of Washington,* ed. by B. J. Meggers (Washington, D.C.: the society), pp. 23–45.

1956   "The Structure of Ancient Maya Society: Evidence from the Southern Lowlands," *American Anthropologist*, vol. 58, no. 5, pp. 777–82.

1959   "The Intermediate Area of Nuclear America: Its Prehistoric Relationships to Middle America and Peru," *Actas de XXXIII Congreso Internacional de Americanistas*, vol. 1 (San Jose, Costa Rica: the congress), pp. 184–94.

1962   "Mesoamerica," *Courses Toward Urban Life*, ed. by R. J. Braidwood and G. R. Willey (Chicago: Aldine Publishing Company), pp. 84–105.

1964   "An Archaeological Frame of Reference for Maya Culture History," *Desarrollo Cultural de los Mayas*, ed. by E. Vogt and A. Ruz (Mexico, D. F.: Universidad Nacional Autónoma de México), pp. 135–75.

1965   "Distribución Cronológica de Algunos Tipos de Artefactos en Altar de Sacrificios, Guatemala," *Estudios de Cultura Maya*, vol. 5, pp. 33–40.

1970   "The Real Xe Ceramics of Seibal, Peten, Guatemala," *Monographs and Papers in Maya Archaeology*, ed. by W. R. Bullard, *Papers of the Peabody Museum of American Archaeology and Ethnology, Harvard University*, vol. 61 (Cambridge: the museum), pp. 313–55.

1971   "Commentary on: The Emergence of Civilization in the Maya Lowlands," *Observations on the Emergence of Civilization in Mesoamerica*, ed. by R. F. Heizer and J. A. Graham, *Contributions of the University of California Archaeological Research Facility*, no. 11 (Berkeley: the university), pp. 97–111.

WILLEY, GORDON R., AND WILLIAM R. BULLARD, JR.

1965   "Prehistoric Settlement Patterns in the Maya Lowlands," *Archaeology of Southern Mesoamerica, Handbook of Middle American Indians*, vol. 2, ed. by G. R. Willey (Austin: University of Texas Press), pp. 360–77.

WILLEY, GORDON R., WILLIAM R. BULLARD, JR., JOHN B. GLASS, AND JAMES C. GIFFORD

1965   *Prehistoric Maya Settlements in the Belize Valley, Papers of the Peabody Museum of Archaeology and Ethnology, Harvard University*, vol. 54 (Cambridge: the museum).

WILLEY, GORDON R., T. PATRICK CULBERT, AND RICHARD E. W. ADAMS, EDS.

1967   "Maya Lowland Ceramics: A Report from the 1965 Guatemala City Conference," *American Antiquity*, vol. 32, no. 3, pp. 289–315.

WILLEY, GORDON R., AND JAMES C. GIFFORD

1961   "Pottery of the Holmul I Style from Barton Ramie, British Honduras," *Essays in Pre-Columbian Art and Archaeology*, ed. by S. K. Lothrop, et al (Cambridge: Harvard University Press), pp. 152–70.

WILLEY, GORDON R., AND DEMITRI B. SHIMKIN

1971a   "The Collapse of Classic Maya Civilization in the Southern Lowlands: A Symposium Summary Statement," *Southwestern Journal of Anthropology*, vol. 27, no. 1, pp. 1–18.

1971b   "Why did the Pre-Columbian Maya Civilization Collapse?", *Science*, vol. 173, no. 3997, pp. 656–58.

WILLEY, GORDON R., AND A. LEDYARD SMITH

1966   "Seibal 1966: Third Preliminary Report," mimeographed, Harvard University.

1967a   "A Temple at Seibal, Guatemala," *Archaeology*, vol. 20, no. 4, pp. 290–98.

References

1967b   "Seibal 1967: Fourth Preliminary Report," mimeographed, Harvard University.

1968   "Seibal," *Archaeologia*, no. 22, pp. 27–29.

1969   *The Ruins of Altar de Sacrificios, Department of Peten, Guatemala: An Introduction, Papers of the Peabody Museum of Archaeology and Ethnology, Harvard University*, vol. 62, no. 1 (Cambridge: the museum).

WILLEY, GORDON R., A. LEDYARD SMITH, GAIR TOURTELLOT, AND JEREMY A. SABLOFF

1968   "Seibal 1968: Fifth and Terminal Preliminary Report," mimeographed, Harvard University.

WILLIAMS, GEORGE D.

1931   *Maya-Spanish Crosses in Yucatan, Papers of the Peabody Museum of Archaeology and Ethnology, Harvard University*, vol. 13, no. 1 (Cambridge: the museum).

WILSON, IRA G., AND MARTHANN E. WILSON

1965   *Information, Computers and System Design* (New York: John Wiley and Sons).

WITTFOGEL, KARL A.

1959   "The Theory of Oriental Society," *Readings in Anthropology*, vol. 2, ed. by M. H. Fried (New York: T. Y. Crowell), pp. 94–113.

WOLF, ERIC R.

1959   *Sons of the Shaking Earth* (Chicago: University of Chicago Press).

1967   "Levels of Communal Relations," *Social Anthropology, Handbook of Middle American Indians*, vol. 6, ed. by M. Nash (Austin: University of Texas Press), pp. 299–316.

WOODBURY, RICHARD B.

1961   "A Reappraisal of Hohokam Irrigation," *American Anthropologist*, vol. 63, no. 3, pp. 550–60.

1965   "Artifacts of the Guatemalan Highlands," *Archaeology of Southern Mesoamerica, Handbook of Middle American Indians*, vol. 2, ed. by G. R. Willey (Austin: University of Texas Press), pp. 163–79.

1966   "Prehistoric Water Management Systems in the Tehuacan Valley, Mexico," *XXXVI Congreso Internacional de Americanistas*, vol. 1 (Sevilla: the congress), pp. 345–47.

WORLD HEALTH ORGANIZATION

1967   *World Health Statistics Annual*, 1964 : 1, *Vital Statistics and the Causes of Death* (Geneva: World Health Organization).

WYNNE-EDWARDS, V. C.

1965   "Self-regulating Systems in Populations of Animals," *Science*, vol. 147, no. 3665, pp. 1543–48.

ZUBROW, EZRA B. W.

1971   "Carrying Capacity and Dynamic Equilibrium in the Prehistoric Southwest," unpublished doctoral dissertation, University of Arizona.

ZURITA, ALONSO DE

1963   *Life and Labor in Ancient Mexico* (New Brunswick, N.J.: Rutgers University Press).

Index*

Abandonment, 17, 22, 34, 127–28, 131, 148, 150–51, 156, 176, 178, 184, 200, 231–32, 236, 260–61, 263, 331, 451, 463–67, 469–70, 472
Acalan, 213–14, 388
Acanceh, 244–45, 286
Aguacatal, 184
Aguateca, 163, 209
Ake, 244
Altar de Sacrificios, 8, 29, 31–33, 44–45, 48–50, 55, 57–60, 62, 66, 108–9, 114–16, 119–24, 129–31, 133–63, 176, 209, 233, 302–24, 326, 331, 363, 435, 451, 461, 464–65, 467–68, 482, 500
Altun Ha, 6, 223, 239, 416, 435
Angkor, 291–95, 298, 492, 498
Architecture, 31–32, 99, 110, 128, 143, 155, 170, 197, 236–37, 246–47, 250–53, 256, 288, 328, 344–46, 466, 472, 494
Art, representational, 82, 125–28, 140, 142–43, 146–47, 153, 160–63, 174, 185–87, 192–94, 196, 211–18, 235, 251, 395–400, 403, 464–65, 479, 485
Atasta, 181
Azcapotzalco, 393–94

Baking Pot, 6, 96–97, 102, 237, 239
Balancan-Morales, 162
Barton Ramie (Belize Valley), 6, 33, 44–46, 48, 52, 57, 59–60, 62, 88, 93–106, 222, 224, 229–30, 236–39, 297, 305, 326, 435, 466–68
Becan, 11, 33–34, 62, 143, 155, 251, 253, 255, 260, 500
Benque Viejo (Xunantunich), 6, 26, 94–98, 102, 104–5, 466, 468, 495
Bobal, 70

Bonampak, 147, 150–51, 166, 169, 171–74, 201, 203–4, 208–9, 398, 463, 479, 485
Burials, 62, 75–80, 100, 106, 138, 308, 345–46, 348, 421, 424–38, 448–49, 459, 500

Cahal Pech, 96
Calakmul, 6, 161, 328
Calatrava, 178, 180, 182, 192, 200, 204, 462–63
Calendrical correlation, 14–15, 44, 204, 247, 253, 258, 264–65
Calendrics, 22, 52–54, 158, 203, 207–10, 215–16, 498–99
Caracol, 6
Cargo system, 347, 361, 375, 388
Central Peten Postclassic Tradition, 44, 60, 62, 101–2, 104, 127, 222–35, 467–68
Ceramics, 10, 16, 31–32, 43, 45–62, 65, 73, 75–76, 80–90, 95–99, 101–2, 109–10, 112–27, 129–30, 133–63, 176–84, 187–202, 204, 222–35, 239, 248–51, 255–56, 392, 399–400, 404, 440, 445–46, 460, 462–70
Ceremonialism, 64, 68, 74–80, 89, 102, 231, 236–38, 260–61, 347, 379, 388–89, 401, 411, 414–15, 439, 442, 461, 479
Cerro de las Mesas, 385, 391, 398
Cerro Montoso, 391, 394
Cerro Portezuelo, 393–94
Cessation of ceremonial construction, 22, 34, 73–74, 102, 105, 110, 125, 140, 171, 184–85, 192, 254, 463–67
Cessation of stela carving, 17, 22, 31, 120, 123, 151, 209, 463–64, 466

* This is not a traditional index. Feeling that the major contributions of the book are theoretical rather than substantive, we have chosen to list topics rather than objects or names as the index entries.—The editor

Index

Index